EXPLORING POLITICAL IDEAS

The figure on the cover is an interpretation of Auguste Rodin's
The Thinker (above), an iconic bronze and marble sculpture that has
come to symbolize the human search for wisdom.

EXPLORING POLITICAL IDEAS

Concepts That Shape Our World

Stephen L. Schechter and Thomas S. Vontz

with contributions by Margaret Stimmann Branson

CQ PRESS

A Division of SAGE
Washington, D.C.

CQ Press
2300 N Street, NW, Suite 800
Washington, DC 20037

Phone: 202-729-1900; toll-free, 1-866-4CQ-PRESS (1-866-427-7737)

Web: www.cqpress.com

Funded by the United States Department of Education under the Cooperative Civic Education and Economic Education Exchange Program, Grant Number R304A020002 of the Elementary and Secondary Education Act as amended by the No Child Left Behind Act of 2001 of the United States Congress.

The contents of this book were developed under a grant from the United States Department of Education. However, those contents do not necessarily represent the policy of the Department of Education, and you should not assume endorsement by the Federal Government.

Cover and interior design: Silverander Communications
Composition: C&M Digitals (P) Ltd.
Image credits:
AP Images: 27, 32, 40, 73
The Bridgeman Art Library: 223 (right), 251
Copyright © 2006 David Monniaux. Used under the GNU Free Documentation License: ii
Corbis: 13, 14, 20 (all), 68, 70, 77, 93, 113, 124, 133, 157, 168 (right), 172, 195, 198, 199, 201, 212, 256, 270 (right), 275 (left and center), 296, 315, 341, 345, 365, 413
Getty Images: 130, 217, 270 (left), 275 (right), 281, 284, 299, 318, 416
The Granger Collection/New York: 6, 8, 25, 42, 60, 67, 84, 86, 90, 99, 132, 145, 149, 152, 154, 155, 168 (left), 179, 193, 205, 222 (both), 223 (left), 225, 235, 237, 243, 244, 247, 254, 264, 273, 316, 324, 334, 337, 339, 344, 357, 359, 367 (both), 369, 380, 381, 384, 386 (both), 392
Image courtesy of the *Harvard University Gazette*: 46
International Mapping Associates: 253, 358, 396
Library of Congress: 78, 115, 127, 202, 405, 408
Russell Cox/Russmo: 24

Printed and bound in Canada

14   13   12   11   10   1   2   3   4   5

Library of Congress Cataloging-in-Publication Data

Schechter, Stephen L.
Exploring political ideas : concepts that shape our world / Stephen L. Schechter and Thomas S. Vontz; with contributions by Margaret Stimmann Branson.
    p. cm.
Includes bibliographical references and index.
ISBN 978-0-87289-918-6 (alk. paper)
   1. Political science. I. Vontz, Thomas S. II. Branson, Margaret Stimmann. III. Title.
JA66.S34 2010
320—dc22

                                                                                          2009044995

ABOUT THE AUTHORS

 **STEPHEN L. SCHECHTER** is a professor of political science at Russell Sage College, the director of the Council for Citizenship Education, and the author of multiple books and articles, including *Roots of the Republic.* Schechter's areas of specialization include comparative federalism and constitutionalism.

 **THOMAS S. VONTZ** is associate professor of education and director of Kansas State University's Center for Social Studies Education. He specializes in civic education and is the author of articles and a book on comparative civic education.

 **MARGARET STIMMANN BRANSON** is associate director at the Center for Civic Education and has served as an assistant superintendent, associate professor, and adviser to the U.S. Department of Education and other governments concerning the advancement of civic education. The author of several books and articles, Branson has received numerous accolades for her work in cultivating civic education, including the Civic Education Leadership Award and the Global Educator of the Year award.

BRIEF CONTENTS

CONTENTS

UNIT 5 CLASSICAL MODELS OF REPUBLICAN GOVERNMENT

UNIT 8 REPUBLICANISM AND DEMOCRACY IN THE MODERN AGE 374

Aim at an exact Knowledge of the Nature, End, and Means of Government. Compare the different forms of it with each other and each of them with their Effects on the public and private Happiness.

—John Adams, 1759

INTRODUCTION

What Is the Purpose of This Book?

Ideas are powerful. They shape the world we see and how we see the world. Some ideas, like freedom and justice, inspire, liberate, and foster hope. Other ideas, like racism and sexism, discriminate, segregate, and enslave.

This book invites you to think about ideas, particularly about political ideas. Political ideas have far-reaching consequences and affect people daily. They can inspire good deeds or justify evil ones; they can inform or misguide an entire nation. But they do not act alone.

Political ideas require human beings to give them life and set them in motion. But human beings cannot always be relied on to have the best of motives or judgment. Nor do circumstances or people always follow those with the purest motives.

The fallibility of human beings and the dynamic circumstances in which they interact are two big reasons why societies create governments with powers and limits.

Politics is complex. In the ever-changing political landscape, it is often difficult to find the best course—as a citizen or as a leader. The exploration of the political world is also complex and requires the people who study it to piece together data from a wide array of sources. While politics offers the reward of a good society, the exploration of the political world offers its students a lifetime of understanding of that world and the roles they may play within that world.

This book asks you to join us in that exploration—to think seriously and critically about the uses and misuses of political ideas and the influence of these ideas on people and politics.

As you proceed, you will consider three important sets of questions that have engaged thoughtful men and women over time and across cultures. You are invited to explore those questions, compare the answers offered by different political thinkers, and consider their importance in your own life and the lives of others.

Each set of questions opens up a different world of knowledge and skills:

1. **EXPLORING THE WORLD OF IDEAS:** The first set of questions introduces you to the world of political ideas. These questions have engaged philosophers, statesmen, and citizens since ancient times. Although political ideas are often abstract and controversial, they are essential to the study of politics. What are the key political ideas that have shaped world history? How were those ideas shaped by the individuals who invented and modified them? What are the core characteristics of each? How do those characteristics vary across cultures and over time?

2. **ENGAGING THE WORLD OF POLITICS:** The second set of questions takes you to the practical world of politics. This is the world of political ideas in action—a rough-and-tumble world in which people disagree about the importance of particular ideas and how to put them into effect. Entering this world requires a leap of faith. Political leaders use ideas for a mix of principled and practical reasons. How, and how well, do political leaders and citizens balance competing ideas and interests? How well have they applied ideas to the political challenges of creating good government, resolving conflicts peacefully, establishing justice, and making wise policy decisions? When you engage the political world, you will seek answers to these essential questions and others.

3. **COMPARING POLITICS IN THE WORLD:** The third set of questions introduces the comparative method as a way of seeking answers to the first two sets of questions. Comparison is a powerful and time-honored method of political inquiry. Simply put, comparison searches out the similarities and differences among polities (that is, political societies). How do polities differ in their understanding and application of political ideas? How do different polities apply political ideas to create governments, resolve conflicts, establish justice, and make policy decisions? What are the most important differences among polities, and what do they share in common? What interpretations have scholars offered to explain these similarities and differences?

As you proceed, you will soon discover that these three worlds interconnect and complement one another. Studying political ideas comparatively is not new. In fact, until the dawn of the modern civics textbook, it was standard practice to (1) compare how and why (2) ancient and modern states (3) organized themselves politically (4) around important political ideas.

How Is This Book Organized?

There are eight units in the book, subdivided into eighteen chapters. In each chapter, there are features that offer in-depth analyses of key ideas, people, and events of the political

Figure I.1 Units of This Book

1	**Themes** of the book—the comparative study of political ideas and their application to the world of politics	**5**	**Classical Models of Republicanism**—republicanism in ancient Greece, Rome, and Israel
2	**Polity and Government**—philosophies, origins, characteristics, and purposes	**6**	**Early European and Non-European Republics**—comparing European and non-European republics
3	**Political Culture and Institutions**—meaning, importance, and types of political cultures; forms of government and their historical and present-day applications	**7**	**Republics in Medieval and Modern Times**—republicanism in Europe from the Middle Ages to early modern times
4	**Power and Its Limits**—relationship between power and authority, importance of legitimacy, constitutional ways of harnessing government power	**8**	**Revolution and Democracy**—British, American, and French revolutions; evolution of republicanism and democracy to the twenty-first century

world. Taken together, the chapters in this book explore about thirty important political ideas. (For a classification of these ideas, see Chapter 1.)

Unit 1 introduces the themes of the book. Its chapters orient the reader to the three worlds of political ideas, politics in action, and comparative analysis.

Units 2–4 include seven conceptual chapters (4–10). Each unit focuses on two interrelated sets of ideas: polity and government, political culture and political institutions, and power and its limits. The chapters in these units explore the historical origins and development of particular ideas and their applicability to politics over time and in diverse civilizations.

Units 5–8 contain eight historical chapters (11–18). Each chapter explores a variety of ideas as they relate to a particular period of world history. Chapters 11–14 explore political ideas in ancient Greece and Rome, biblical Israel, and early republican societies in Africa, Asia, and the Americas. Chapters 15 and 16 chronicle the development of political ideas in medieval, Renaissance, and Reformation Europe. Chapter 17 examines the republican revolutions in Great Britain, America, and France, while Chapter 18 explores the spread of democracy around the world from 1800 to the present.

In each of these historical contexts, we explore the organizing political ideas, how those ideas were confronted by the dominant interests in society and the ambitions of political leaders, and how those ideas informed political decisions, institutions, and laws.

How Did John Adams Use the Comparative Method?

The quotation at the beginning of this Introduction, taken from John Adams's diary, is a fitting epigraph for this book for two reasons. First, it is a good example of how a bold thinker like Adams thinks comparatively about a political idea in theory and in practice. Second, it shows you how this book analyzes the words and deeds of a political thinker like John Adams. What did Adams mean and what is the importance of his quotations?

That question can be answered in a number of ways. . .

Understanding Context. Interpreting Adams's quotation begins with an understanding of its *context*. Adams was only twenty-four years old when he wrote those words as a diary entry in 1759. He had just become a lawyer, and he wanted to earn a good reputation. So he made several promises to himself in his diary; this quotation is part of that pledge. He challenged himself to learn more about government. In surrounding entries, he also promised to resist earthly temptations—girls, guns, cards, music, tobacco, and laziness.[1]

Analyzing Text. A second way of analyzing the meaning of this passage is to look carefully at the *text*. On first reading, Adams clearly intends to learn more about the nature of government. He wants to study its ends and the means available to it, to compare different governments, and to analyze how different forms of government affect the public happiness of the people as a whole and the private happiness of its individual members. Figure I.2 outlines the plain language of the text.

Figure I.2 An Outline of Adams's Quotation

I.	The nature of government
	A. Ends
	B. Means (including forms)
II.	The effects of forms of government on happiness
	A. Public
	B. Private

On closer inspection, Adams poses a classic means-ends relationship between two important ideas—government (the means) and happiness (the end). In scientific terms, he is hypothesizing that reform (that is, changing the form of government) can have an effect on the happiness of its people.

Was young Adams interested in that means-ends relationship from a philosophical perspective or from a practical perspective? In other words, did he seek to study government or to reform it? His experience and determination as a young man suggest a passion for both.

Uncovering Sources. Adams's quotation provides clues to its sources, and the *sources* of text are a third important key to unlock the meaning of the text. The political thought of Adams, like others of his generation, was influenced by a number of sources. But Adams's single-minded reference to "happiness" as the end of government draws most directly on the republican thinkers of the Scottish Enlightenment and one of its brightest lights, Francis Hutcheson. In Hutcheson's *System of Philosophy*, one finds the first reference to the utilitarian criterion of justice—"the greatest happiness for the greatest numbers." This work may have influenced Adams, who wrote his 1759 diary entry on government and happiness only a few years later.

Looking for Consistency. A fourth way of analyzing the early words of thinkers like Adams is to look for *consistencies and inconsistencies* in their later words and deeds. In keeping with his pledge of 1759, Adams remained an avid student of comparative government and a tireless advocate for good government. Seventeen years later, in 1776, he put his commitments and skills to historic use—as an impassioned advocate of American independence in the Second Continental Congress. He called for a declaration of independence, served on its drafting committee, and argued eloquently for its adoption. He readily accepted Thomas Jefferson's addition of "the pursuit of happiness" as an unalienable right and purpose of government, which was consistent with his early thinking about good government.

Making Comparisons. A fifth way of analyzing Adams's quotation is by *comparing* his main points with other political thinkers of his day. Adams's main points are not unique for the day. They are representative of the republican thinking of the eighteenth century in Europe and America. Among such thinkers there was a keen interest in government, particularly as an instrument in human happiness. Compared with other republican thinkers of his day, young John was a moderate. He became more conservative later in life. Of particular interest today is Adams's note to compare governments. This is not the statement of an isolationist but of an inquisitive scientific mind eager to learn more by comparing governments. This is also quite typical of the thinking of his day. We live today in a global age, but it is not the first global age. It may be too bold to argue that global connections are an important element of every age. But global connections were certainly an important part of the eighteenth century and the enlightened thinking of that age.

Examining Implications. A final way of interpreting Adams's quotation is by looking at its *implications*. Adams could have looked to society and cultural values as the means of happiness. Instead, he finds those means in the institutions of government. He could have looked to any type of government, but he singles out republican government as the only source of good government. Adams could have defined happiness in economic terms—as property or prosperity. Instead, he looks to the moral meaning of happiness as virtuous decisions contributing to the well-being of the individual and society as a whole.

Analyzing Adams's quotation not only reveals important clues about how and why one should study government; it also illustrates the exploration of political ideas in this book. As you proceed, you will analyze historical contexts and documentary texts to examine a variety of significant political ideas. You will learn where those ideas took root, how they grew, and how they affect people's thoughts and actions. You will consider the relevance of political ideas to a wide range of political issues, events, and peoples. You also will consider why some ideas have proved to be more important or controversial than other ideas.

NOTE

1 L. H. Butterfield, Leonard C. Faber, and Wendell D. Garrett, eds., *Diary and Autobiography of John Adams, Volumes 1–4, Diary (1755–1804) and Autobiography (through 1780)* (Cambridge, Mass.: Belknap Press of Harvard University Press, 1961), Vol. 1: xxx.

ACKNOWLEDGMENTS

This book is the product of a five-year international exchange program for American and Russian civics teachers called Civics Mosaic. That program and this book were funded by the U.S. Department of Education.

We gratefully acknowledge the department's funding support. And we take this opportunity to express our personal thanks to Rita Foy Moss, our department program officer, who believed in this project and shared our commitment to the study of civics in comparative perspective.

This book has benefited from the collaboration of teachers, students, and scholars from around the world. Civitas, an international civic education network, provided an intellectual forum for this collaboration. Civitas and Mosaic conferences in the Americas, Eurasia, and the Middle East provided occasions to present draft chapters and to gain feedback from colleagues from every region of the world.

We gratefully acknowledge the support and encouragement of the Civitas coordinator, the Center for Civic Education, Calabasas, California, and its executive director, Charles N. Quigley. Special thanks to Robert Leming, director of the center's We the People Program, who saw the connections between American and comparative civics and helped strengthen them over the years.

We owe another debt to the Center for Civic Education; namely, Margaret Stimmann Branson, associate director at the center. Stephen Schechter and Margaret Branson conceived this book, and the center graciously allowed Margaret to work on it. Her contributions are substantial in the conceptual chapters of the book.

Our Mosaic partners have been a part of this project from its inception. They have reviewed manuscripts, organized teacher workshops, analyzed teacher reviews, and provided moral support. Special thanks to Shannon Lederer at the American Federation of Teachers and to our state partners, Barbara Graves, Charles County Public Schools, Maryland; Deborah Lesser, Justice Resource Center, New York City; Stephanie A. Schechter, Council for Citizenship Education; Marcie Taylor-Thoma, Maryland State Department of Education; and Charles S. White, Boston University.

Special thanks also to our Russian partners and dear colleagues of many years for their insights and suggestions on various chapters of the book: Evgeny Belyakov, Andrei Ioffe, Sergei Lossev, and Natalia Voskresenskaya of Civitas Russia. And to our new Eurasian partners who have brought a rich diversity of views to the project: Arman Argynov,

Kazakhstan; Maia Gogoladze and George Nozadze, Republic of Georgia; Narangerel Rinchin, Mongolia; Tigran Tovmasyan, Armenia; and Rumen Valchev, Bulgaria.

Mosaic teaching fellows reviewed earlier drafts of the book and field tested them in their classrooms. With gratitude we acknowledge below the teams of teacher reviewers, field testers, and their coordinators. We gratefully acknowledge the project's independent evaluator, Tina Goodwin-Segal of Measurement, Inc., who organized the classroom field test process.

Alaska Team: Debbie Benson, Jennifer Faris, Letitia Fickel, Brian Gornick, Todd Heuston, Randy Karns, Roger Miller, Christine Scott; Mary Bristol, Coordinator.

Illinois Team: Ryan Gabey, Daniel Hicks, Matthew Klix, Chris Mangun, Mary Vicars; Fred Drake and John Sullivan, Coordinators.

Indiana Team: Louis Camilotto, Brent Davenport, Glen D. Dillman, Dan Ronk, Scott J. Royer, Bruce Walter; Lynn Nelson and Anatoli Rapoport, Coordinators.

Kansas-Missouri Team: Don Barzowski, Jeff Brown, Matthew Christensen, Elizabeth Heide, Dana Hoffman; Decoursey C. Lucas, Coordinator.

Maryland Teams: Pamela Beaty, Kelly Caswell, John Childers, Karl Craton, Steve Frantzich, Michael Haldwald, Karen Hodges, Rosellen Houser, Mark Howell, Gary Lesko, Brenda Peterson, Phil Stephenson, Ann Taylor, Jack Tuttle, Patricia Wyman; Barbara Graves and Marcie Taylor-Thoma, Coordinators.

Massachusetts Teams: Amy-Jo Aronsen, Brian Daniels, Robert Davidson, Michael Dlott, Megan Gaudette, Paul Graseck, Stephen McKenna, June Murray, Joshua Otlin, Joseph Roche, Cheryl Spear, Paul Stanish, Gavin Thomas, Todd Wallingford; Mary McCarthy, Charles White, Deborah White, Coordinators.

New York Teams: Danielle Altadonna, Kathryn Botta-Raso, Susan Burke, Ilene Colbert, Fabian Garcia, Martina Grant, Carla Heckstall, Erin Lasky, Eugene Lees, Robert Naeher, Nina Rosen, Carrie Sanchez, David Smith, Catherine Snyder, Sean Walsh, Donald Walton; Deborah Lesser and Stephanie Schechter, Coordinators.

Ohio Teams: Jason Apgar, Kay Benton, Jeff Bunck, Timothy Cave, Timothy Dove, Leanne Gabriel, Donald Haddox, Gary Huss, Frank Lenz, Mark Smith, Thomas Sorosiak, Michelle Stasa, Adam Wagner; Nancy Patterson, Alexander Sidorkin, Doreen Uhas-Sauer, Coordinators.

We have benefited greatly over the years from conversations with academic colleagues. Special thanks to R. B. Bernstein, New York Law School; the late Kermit Hall, State University of New York at Albany; John Patrick, Indiana University; Natalya Voskresenkaya, Russian Academy of Education; and Charles White, Boston University.

We are indebted to a great team of reviewers and researchers. Jason Apgar, a teacher at Anthony Wayne High School in Whitehouse, Ohio, carefully reviewed final chapters from a classroom perspective and designed some of the graphic organizers for the book. Cory Jensen, as research associate of the Council for Citizenship Education, cite checked and reviewed early drafts of the manuscript with meticulous care. Brad Burenheide assisted in the research and writing of Web resources.

Many people reviewed this book, but there was one editor who worked directly with the authors on a daily basis: Lance Cooper. CQ Press invited Lance to serve as editor because of his unusual combination of skills as a textbook editor and a member of the illustrious editorial team of *Black's Law Dictionary*. Lance helped us transform a manuscript into a book. We are grateful indeed for his tireless attention to details large and small and to the wise counsel he offered along the way.

Every enterprise needs a person who is responsible for keeping everyone on task, on schedule, and on budget without sacrificing the quality of the product. We are fortunate indeed that Doug Goldenberg-Hart, Senior Acquisitions Editor at CQ Press, served that role for this project. We also gratefully acknowledge the support and assistance of Julie F. Nemer, who copy edited the manuscript; Andrew Boney and Anastazia Skolnitsky, CQ Press development editors; Lorna Notsch, CQ Press Senior Production Editor; and Andrea Pedolsky, Editorial Director of CQ Press's Reference Information Group.

Finally, writing this book would not have been possible without the generous support and encouragement of understanding spouses and families. Dawn, Gabrielle, Victoria, Madeline, and Alexander Vontz, and the Schechter family (Stephanie, Sarah, and Kelly) inspired us daily.

Everyone involved in this project believes in the ability of young people to grasp complex concepts and issues that someone takes the time to explain. Whenever we forgot this point or doubted ourselves, Stephanie Schechter was there to keep us on the straight and narrow. This book is dedicated to her.

EXPLORING POLITICAL IDEAS

EXPLORING POLITICAL IDEAS

This unit introduces you to the three major themes of this book. The first theme explores the world of political ideas and why they matter. The second theme engages the world of politics where those ideas are put into practice. The third theme connects you with the world of scholarship, where you learn how to use the comparative method in studying political ideas.

The first chapter guides your exploration into the world of political ideas. With this guide, you will define an *idea,* explain its importance and uses, distinguish political ideas from other ideas, recognize core political ideas, and discover how political ideas relate to four other political "I" words: individuals, institutions, interests,

and issues. In the end, you will learn how political ideas can inform wise political judgments by society's leaders and its citizenry.

The second chapter is a guide through the political world where ideas are put into practice. By following this guide, you will learn how and why people enter the world of politics, how politics can become an obstacle course, why some leaders get mired in the pursuit of power, and how others stay focused on the larger interests of the people they serve. Along the way, you will encounter diverse points of view about politics: as a dirty business, as a noble enterprise, as the barrel of

CHAPTER 1:

WHY DO POLITICAL IDEAS MATTER?

CHAPTER 2:

WHAT IS POLITICS?

CHAPTER 3:

WHY STUDY POLITICAL IDEAS COMPARATIVELY?

a gun, and as the art of peaceful persuasion. In the end, you will learn how to recognize the common characteristics of politics and why they matter.

The third chapter is a guide to the use of the comparative method.

Comparison is a powerful and time-honored method of inquiry. In Chapter 3, you will learn the uses and benefits of the comparative method as it is applied to the study of political ideas. You also will explore several important approaches to the comparative method and illustrations of each.

BIG IDEAS

- Political ideas are powerful and affect people's lives directly and daily.

- Political ideas help people to explore the political world and its individuals, issues, interests, and institutions. Together with ideas, these are the "five I's" of politics.

- Wise political judgments depend on the understanding and effective application of political ideas.

Purpose of This Chapter

Ideas organize thinking. Your abilities to understand, interpret, analyze, and evaluate all depend on ideas. Of all the varieties of ideas, political ideas are among the most important. Often without their even realizing it, people's lives are deeply influenced by political ideas. Political ideas shape people's thoughts about fundamental issues such as the meaning of life, liberty, and the pursuit of happiness. This chapter provides a bird's-eye view of the world of political ideas. You will explore the purposes that political ideas serve, their importance in daily life, and their profound effect on the history of the world. This chapter also connects political ideas with individuals, interests, issues, and institutions that make up the political world.

Terms to Know

aspirational ideas	institutions	normative ideas
democracy	instrumental ideas	political judgment
descriptive ideas	interests	
ideas	issues	

WHY DO IDEAS MATTER?

Several centuries ago an anonymous writer declared, "There is one thing stronger than all the armies in the world; and that is an idea whose time has come."[1] The nineteenth-century French novelist, poet, and playwright Victor Hugo agreed: "A stand can be made against invasion by an army; no stand can be made against invasion by an idea."[2]

But why are ideas so important? To begin with, human beings think. Thinking is one of the essential ways in which human beings

4

differ from other living creatures. In fact, the seventeenth-century French philosopher René Descartes built a large part of his philosophical system on one sentence: "I think, therefore I am."[3]

Ideas are the abstractions that help people make sense of the world around them. When people use ideas to think and make sense of the world, they conceptualize their experiences and thoughts. A *concept* is a general idea that is used to organize specific examples of something. The concept "tree" can be used to describe oaks, elms, maples, or pines.

Terms like time and space are examples of ideas that serve as concepts. They help people organize their lives in the world around them. For example, when several students agree to meet in the library, they need to share common understandings: of when to meet, where in the library to meet, and what they will do when they meet. Will they set a specific time and place? Will they all understand the specifics in the same way? If they decide to meet at 4:00 p.m., does that mean the same thing to all of them? When should they leave for the meeting? When should they arrive? How late can they be? Should they bring a snack? The ideas of punctuality and sociability may have different meanings for different students in the group.[4]

Just as people use ideas to organize their thinking about the physical world, people use political ideas to make sense of their political world. Political ideas shape how and why human beings choose to organize themselves. As one scholar explains:

> In order to make sense of the world we must impose meaning upon it, and this we do through the construction of concepts. . . . We build up our knowledge of the political world not simply by looking at it, but through developing and refining concepts, which will help us make sense of it. Concepts are, in other words, the building blocks of human knowledge.[5]

Ideas not only help to describe and explain the world; they also contain norms or values that help people to form judgments. In this way, ideas serve as a guide to help people distinguish what is good or bad.

Thus, there are at least two kinds of ideas: **descriptive ideas** and **normative ideas**. To distinguish between them, consider the questions that each answers. Descriptive ideas are concepts that help to answer questions that begin "what is" and "why." For example, constitutional government is an idea that can be used descriptively to identify and organize those governments that are empowered and limited by a constitution. In contrast, a normative idea is an ideal or value. Normative ideas help to answer questions that consider "what is best" and "what should be." The idea of constitutional government is used normatively when someone proclaims that all governments should be limited and empowered by a constitution. This position rests on the belief that government should be held accountable to a higher authority. It so happens that in this case there is a special word that encapsulates the normative belief in constitutional government: constitutionalism.

A close look at the world today reveals some powerful ideas whose time has come—ideas that ring true as descriptive, normative, or both. For example, the idea of **democracy,** that people have the right and responsibility of governing themselves and of choosing how best to govern themselves, now has worldwide appeal. Even in such former dictatorships as South

Another powerful idea "whose time has come" is that all human beings—because they are human beings—have rights that governments must respect and protect. The idea of human rights began to have worldwide appeal at the end of World War II. Revulsion against atrocities committed during that war, such as the Nazi German government's mass murder of Jews, homosexuals, Gypsies, and other groups, spurred the United Nations General Assembly to adopt the Universal Declaration of Human Rights. This document proclaims rights that belong to all human beings, regardless of gender, religion, race, or age.

Eleanor Roosevelt played an instrumental role in drafting the UN Declaration of Human Rights. Here she is holding a poster of the Declaration in 1949, the year after it was adopted by the United Nations.

Subsequently, many countries signed a number of covenants (or binding treaties) that implement the Universal Declaration. The countries that signed those covenants accepted solemn treaty obligations. The United Nations monitors compliance and can impose sanctions on countries that continue to violate human rights.

Africa, Ukraine, and Iraq people prefer democracy (see More About . . . The Rise of Human Rights after World War II). Democracy is an idea that is both descriptive and normative; it describes a form of government, but it also is a political principle.[6]

WHAT PURPOSES DO IDEAS SERVE?

Ideas serve different purposes. **Instrumental ideas** play an important part in achieving a desired end or in advancing a cause. **Aspirational ideas** represent ultimate goals toward which people aspire. An instrumental idea is a means to an end, while an aspirational idea is a desired end or goal.

Some examples from history illustrate how people have linked instrumental and aspirational ideas. In biblical times, the Prophet Isaiah foretold, "They [the nations of the world] shall beat their swords into plowshares, and their spears into pruning hooks: nation shall not lift up sword against nation, neither shall they learn war any more."[7] Isaiah here uses both types of ideas. The instrumental idea is the idea of disarmament or the destroying or recycling of weapons, turning swords and spears into tools that can be used for productive purposes. Isaiah does not present this idea as an end in itself, however, but as a means to a higher end. That goal or aspirational idea is peace among all the nations; disarmament is the means to that end.

Another example is the Bill of Rights. The original United States Constitution of 1787 lacked a bill or declaration of rights, and many Americans believed that omission was a serious flaw. They insisted that a bill of rights be added. Thomas Jefferson, the principal draftsman of the Declaration of Independence, who in 1787 was the American minister to France, joined in the debate. He wrote to his friend and ally James Madison, who ultimately proposed the Bill of Rights in the First Congress: "A bill of rights is what the people are entitled to against every government on earth, general or particular, & what no just government should refuse, or rest on inference."[8] Jefferson's aspirational idea, the value he extolled, was a just government that would both respect individual rights and be barred from violating those rights. His instrumental idea was the addition of a Bill of Rights to the new Constitution. The Bill of Rights, he believed, would be one means toward the end of a just government.

Not all aspirational ideas are used to achieve worthy or good goals. Mao Zedong, the leader of the Communist Revolution in China, taught his followers: "Every Communist must grasp the truth: Political power grows out of the barrel of a gun." Mao added, "that is why the Party must always control the army."[9] Mao's directive to his followers stands in opposition to the prophecy of Isaiah. Unlike Isaiah, Mao's instrumental idea is armament. His aspirational idea is not peace but political power.

Ideas like those advanced by Isaiah, Jefferson, and Mao are powerful forces in human history. They stir the human imagination, arouse the human soul, and illustrate that powerful ideas do not exist in a vacuum. They need *individuals* to put them into action. As the noted anthropologist Margaret Mead once said, "Never doubt that a small group of thoughtful, committed citizens can change the world; indeed, it's the only thing that ever has."[10]

HOW ARE IDEAS USED IN THE POLITICAL WORLD?

Every realm of intellectual activity is concerned with ideas, but not every realm seeks to understand ideas for the same reasons or use them for the same purposes. In their study of Western traditions, the intellectual historians Jacob Bronowski and Bruce Mazlish have identified three intellectual realms: the pursuit of truth, the pursuit of justice, and the pursuit of beauty.[11] Scientists, philosophers, and theologians use ideas in search of the truth. They differ in how they conduct their search; however, once they believe that they have found the truth, they seek its acceptance. The arts incorporate ideas in their search for beauty. One artist may choose to paint a scene using a natural or realistic style, while other artists may see the same scene in abstract or surreal form. Although artists hope their work will find favor, Bronowski and Mazlish maintain that artists neither seek nor require widespread acceptance of their work. By contrast, political ideas are used in the search for what is right—or what is just and fair—in a particular situation (see Political Ideas in Action: Why Is Justice a Political Ideal?). In the realm of politics, ideas seldom, if ever, establish an absolute truth; political thought cannot be verified by mathematical proof or scientific experiment.

People may disagree about which aspirational goals are most important or which instrumental ideas are most useful to achieve their goals. Since ancient times, for example, people have disagreed about whether it is more important to be free, to be safe, or to be equal. Julius Caesar described human nature as "universally imbued with a desire for liberty, and a hatred of servitude." Yet Sallust, a friend and ally of Caesar and one of Rome's greatest historians, disagreed. Sallust wrote in his *Histories,* "Only a few prefer liberty—the majority seek nothing more than fair masters."[12] Even when people realize that some form of balance among clashing or competing goals is best, they may hold very different, even contradictory conceptions of how that balance should be achieved.

Today, for example, public opinion polls, called "democracy barometers," ask people in various countries whether they understand and support democracy in their region of the world. As we might expect, a majority of people support the idea of democracy. However, they differ in how well they think democracy is doing, what problems it faces, and how frustrated or disappointed they are with their democracies.[13]

In short, political ideas can be controversial. They create **issues**, or legitimate differences of opinion among reasonable people. People have disagreed about political ideas since the first human community was formed—and with good reason. Political ideas provide the norms on which human societies are based and the rules by which those societies are governed. It is only natural that people should have differing ideas about which norms are most important and how to achieve them.

Politics arises partly out of these disagreements about how people choose to organize themselves. This book defines *politics* as a complex process by which people seek to settle their differences peacefully and reach a binding decision that resolves public issues.

HOW CAN POLITICAL IDEAS BE COMPARED?

The sweep of human history has generated a bewildering spectrum of political ideas. One dictionary of political thought has 1,500 entries for ideas, concepts, and influential thinkers. This book focuses on roughly thirty of the most powerful political ideas that have helped shape the world and its history.

Those political ideas are set out in Figure 1.1, which presents those ideas along a continuum from instrumental ideas (means) to aspirational ideas (ends). The group of ideas to the far right—including justice, liberty, and equality—are typically seen as ends not means. The ideas on the far left—politics, government, and public policy—are typically viewed as means to achieve ends. The ideas that fall in between are partly means and partly ends, that is, partly instrumental and partly aspirational.

The ideas in Figure 1.1 are among the forces that continue to drive the decisions that political leaders and citizens make, the changes that they seek, and the events that they

Figure 1.1 Political Ideas as Means and Ends

Instrumental ideas (means)					Aspirational ideas (ends)
Politics	Power	Governance	Religion	Democracy	Justice
Polity	Authority	Social contract	Ideology	Republicanism	Liberty
Government	Legitimacy		Political culture	Constitutionalism	Equality
Public policy	Citizenship			Rule of law	Rights
	Leadership			Economic development	Happiness
	Civil society			Social change	Peace
	Nation-state			Participation	Prosperity
	Globalization			Representation	Security
				Accountability	

influence. These ideas also help shape the political **institutions** that people create. Those institutions, such as legislatures and courts, become important instruments, or means, to achieve and sustain societal goals.

WHAT IS THE ROLE OF POLITICAL IDEAS IN THE WORLD OF POLITICS?

Ideas are a powerful motivating force in the world of politics. Being committed to a particular idea, such as making the world a safer place, or a set of ideas, such as conservatism or liberalism, is one of the main reasons why people decide to get involved in politics. After individuals become involved in politics, their commitment to particular ideas is an important reason determining how they vote, whom they ally themselves with, and what they oppose.

Ideas do not, however, exist in a vacuum. In the complex world of politics, individuals may disagree about the importance or meaning of ideas. Moreover, ideas are not the only source of disagreement. People also disagree because of their **interests**. Competing political interests often give rise to political issues. And people rely on institutions to resolve those differences.

Taken together, these five terms—ideas, individuals, interests, issues, and institutions—make up the dimensions of politics presented in this book. All begin with the letter I, which is a good way to remember them (see Table 1.1 and Figure 1.2). Here are some of the relationships between political ideas and the other four I's:

- *Individuals* in their capacity as political leaders and citizens need political ideas to organize, prioritize, and make sense of the political world. Conversely, individuals breathe life into ideas. For example, the idea that a new nation could be founded in modern times

Table 1.1 The Five I's of Politics

Dimension	Description
Individuals	People who function as political thinkers, leaders, and citizens
Ideas	The political concepts and ideals that are important to those individuals
Interests	The benefit or advantage that individuals get from a particular action
Issues	The differences of opinions and interests that can divide individuals
Institutions	The permanent structures individuals create to advance their ideas and interests

Figure 1.2 The Five I's in Action

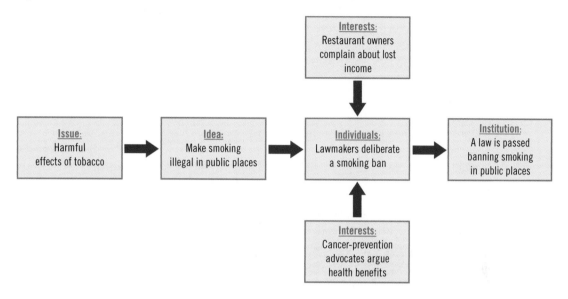

based on the ideals of a constitutional republic needed individuals to bring it to life. History has preserved a detailed record of the speeches and official actions of the delegates at the Federal Convention who wrote a new constitution for the United States. Far less is known about the many other individuals who gathered in taverns, store fronts, election stations, and state conventions to debate and decide whether to ratify or reject the new Constitution.[14]

- *Interests* join ideas as an important source of political motivation. In other words, interests and ideas help explain why individuals make political decisions. Interests are the personal or group benefits that people get from doing something or having something done for them. The framers of the U.S. Constitution in 1787 were guided by a mix of ideas and interests. They envisioned a new nation guided by republican ideals. At the same time, they were all too aware that the people of the United States had a wide range of interests that often clashed, and at least some of the delegates shared those interests and sought to defend them. They realized that the new nation had to both defend republican ideals and accommodate the clashes of interests that would result from bringing a large, diverse population under one government. This realization helped them to conceive and embrace a bold vision of a large, diverse federal republic that could regulate the clashes of interests and even possibly reconcile them. This book is written in the belief that most political decisions, whether to write a constitution or vote for a candidate, are guided by a mix of interests and ideas. In fact, this book goes a step further—we hold that rational political judgment requires individuals to calculate how a particular decision will affect their economic interests, their political interests, and the political ideals they hold dear.[15]

- *Issues* arise out of the differences people have over which ideas and interests matter most. For example, the proposed U.S. Constitution of 1787 raised several important issues when it was sent to the states for ratification. One of these issues was whether it was possible to create a republican form of government for a large, diverse nation. The American people soon divided into two camps. Anti-federalists opposed ratification in the belief that republics could survive only if they stayed small. They believed that power should continue to reside with the states. As small republics, the states would increase social homogeneity, lower the risk of political conflict, narrow the distance between citizens and their government, and reduce the economic gap between rich and poor. Federalists supported ratification in the belief that modern times called for large republics. They insisted that a strong federal republic would increase economic prosperity, control minority factions, and secure the vital interests of a new nation.

- *Institutions,* certainly political institutions, are designed by individuals who seek long-term ways to advance their interests and ideas in the political arena. Some institutions, such as a labor union or a chamber of commerce, represent only one set of interests and ideas; other institutions, such as a political party, may represent a variety of ideas and interests. Some institutions are governmental; others are nongovernmental. The political party, for example, transformed politics in the nineteenth century. The triumph of Jacksonian democracy in the late 1820s and early 1830s would not have been possible without Jackson's Democratic Party. That party registered voters, got them to the polls, redirected campaigns to address the voters' interests, ran candidates for the many new elected offices that opened up, and filled the new patronage jobs that came with a larger government closer to the people. People took more interest in politics, and voter turnout soared. In the presidential election of 1828, which elected Andrew Jackson, voter turnout rose to more than 50 percent of eligible voters—three times higher than in the 1824 election.[16]

WHAT IS THE RELATIONSHIP BETWEEN POLITICAL IDEAS AND STATECRAFT?

Statecraft is the art of leading a state or country. Like the captain of a ship, the good statesman (a term that includes men and women) must be prepared to steer "the ship of state" through all kinds of winds and waters—during times so calm that it is hard to make any progress, through troubled waters when mere survival becomes the goal, and in dense fog when it is easy to lose one's way.

What are the characteristics and qualities of a "good statesman"? Classical Greek thought distinguished three kinds of knowledge: theoretical knowledge of universal principles developed by scientists, technical knowledge of the skills needed for a particular craft like shoe making, and practical knowledge of how to apply values to make ethical or policy choices in a particular set of circumstances. The third type of knowledge is the knowledge on which wise political judgment rests.

For the eminent twentieth-century political thinker and historian of ideas Sir Isaiah Berlin, political judgment is the key to good statesmanship. **Political judgment** is the ability to make sound political decisions in a particular set of circumstances (see Bold Thinkers: Sir Isaiah Berlin). It requires the application of reasoning, practical experience, political ideas, and ethical values to a particular set of circumstances. But this is easier said than done in a situation where circumstances are rapidly changing, different people are whispering advice in your ear at the same time, and the choices seem unclear and surrounded by the fog of a rapidly brewing crisis.

For Berlin, statesmen are not "unpractical idealists, visionaries, Utopians."[17] Political judgment, according to Berlin, is "practical wisdom, practical reason, perhaps, a sense of what will 'work,' and what will not." As Berlin's essay "Political Judgement" illustrates, practical wisdom or judgment is the kind of knowledge that conductors have of their orchestras, not the knowledge that chemists have of the "contents of their test tubes."[18] In other words, it is the knowledge of what is best, right, or good in a particular circumstance.

BOLD THINKERS
Sir Isaiah Berlin

Sir Isaiah Berlin (1909–1997) was born in Riga, Latvia, and immigrated in 1921 to England where he became a much-admired historian and champion of ideas. He wrote many books but is best known as an essayist. In a single essay, he could leave the reader with a lasting impression of a powerful idea. In his famous essay "Two Concepts of Liberty" (1968), he distinguished negative and positive concepts of liberty. Berlin defined *negative liberty* as the freedom from outside interference in pursuing one's goals. It is the idea, Berlin wrote, that a person "should be left to do or be what he is able to do or be, without interference by other persons." Berlin defined *positive liberty* as the freedom to realize one's potential, "to be one's own master." At first, these two concepts may seem different ways of saying the same thing. Yet, as Berlin explained, they are "profoundly divergent and irreconcilable attitudes to the ends of life." The first is the liberal and pluralist idea of live and let live; the second gave rise to Marxism and other philosophies that promised to fulfill people's dreams—but at a price.

Isaiah Berlin, "Two Concepts of Liberty," in *Four Essays on Liberty* (New York: Oxford University Press, 1969), 122, 131.

At first glance, some people might think that statesmanship, as Berlin explained it, has little use for political ideas. That conclusion would be a mistake. Berlin likened the practical wisdom of statesmen to that of good doctors: "To know only the theory," Berlin admitted, "might not be enough to enable one to heal the sick"; however, Berlin continued, "to be ignorant of [theory] is fatal."[19] In other words, exercising sound political judgment, according to Berlin, blends practical experience with theoretical understanding and technical skill.

POLITICS IN ACTION
The Importance of Political Judgment

Wise political judgment is one of the most important expectations of citizenship. Citizens can and do influence their leaders and fellow citizens in a variety of important and effective ways. Voting, writing letters to political leaders, and taking part in political campaigns are a few of the formal avenues in which citizens exercise their political judgment. Citizens also influence public opinion through informal discussions with friends and family, in person or over the Internet. Public opinion has become an important force in democratic politics. In many countries, protest movements and demonstrations are another form of citizen participation. France and China are two historic examples of such countries.

Here is how a contemporary statesman, Fernando Henrique Cardoso, president of Brazil from 1995 to 2003, interprets Berlin's essay:

> *Updated knowledge, republican values, and a good deliberative process, important though they are, may not be enough to produce a successful statesman. The missing quality is what Isaiah Berlin identified as the capacity for good "political judgment." This entails not only the discernment to avoid the opposite risks of impractical idealism and uninspiring realism, but also the practical wisdom to grasp the character of a particular situation or moment in history and to seize the opportunities or confront the challenges that it presents.*[20]

A crowd gathers to celebrate Earth Day at the U.S. Capitol. Political rallies such as this one are one way to influence political opinion.

In representative democracies, where citizens elect their political leaders, the question of what makes a good statesman becomes doubly important. That question must be considered not only by leaders who aspire to be statesmen but also by citizens every time they enter the voting booth, read the newspaper, or watch a political debate. For these reasons, the citizenry needs to exercise sound political judgment (see Politics in Action: The Importance of Political Judgment). The question "What makes a good citizen?" prompts the broader questions that guide this book. Although this book is no substitute for the kinds of life experiences that help inform sound judgment, the political knowledge gained from this book will complement those experiences.

That knowledge includes a variety of examples of how real statesmen—such as Moses and Hammurabi, Pericles and Cicero, George Washington and Nelson Mandela, Franklin D. Roosevelt and Winston Churchill—behaved in real situations over time and around the world. How those actions compare is another vital dimension of this book. So, too, are comparisons between dictators such as Adolf Hitler and Joseph Stalin and between social leaders such as Mohandas K. Gandhi and Martin Luther King Jr.

An understanding of political ideas—their origins, development, and importance—informs wise political judgment and is one important key to a deeper understanding of the political world. The remaining chapters in this unit explore political ideas in the world of politics and use the power of comparison in that exploration.

REVIEWING AND USING THE CHAPTER

1. What do you think are the most important political ideas in the world today? Why?

2. What is the relationship between political ideas and (a) individuals, (b) interests, (c) issues, and (d) institutions? Illustrate your answer with one example for each relationship.

3. What informs wise political judgment? Provide specific examples.

EXTENSION ACTIVITY

The location of each idea on the means-ends continuum is not chiseled in stone. Take another look at the ideas on that continuum in Figure 1.1. Thinking of your own life as a citizen, or in preparing to become a citizen, what aspirational ideas, or goals, do you value most? What instrumental ideas, or means, might help you achieve them? What political ideas, if any, do you think are missing from Figure 1.1, and why should they be added?

WEB RESOURCES

Center for the Study of Great Ideas
www.thegreatideas.org

Founded by Mortimer J. Adler and Max Weismann, the Center for the Study of Great Ideas aims to make philosophy "everybody's business." Its Web site identifies 102 great ideas and offers an array of resources for the exploration of those ideas.

The Founders' Constitution
http://press-pubs.uchicago.edu/founders

A joint project of the University of Chicago and Liberty Fund, this Web site gathers documents on constitutional government written between the early 1600s and the 1830s. This is an excellent resource on sources of American constitutional ideas.

Henry Clay Center for Statesmanship
www.henryclaycs.org

Administered by the Henry Clay Memorial Foundation, this Web site "promotes the principles and practices of statesmanship and embodies Henry Clay's ideals of debate, diplomacy, communications and beneficial compromise." The center sponsors an annual student congress that focuses on developing the skills of statesmanship.

Internet Public Library
www.ipl.org/div/subject/browse/law00.00.00

This site has a section on "law, government, and political science" where users can find links to voluntary associations, special collections, and other resources devoted to particular ideas. The site was founded by the University of Michigan School of Information and is hosted by Drexel University's College of Information Science and Technology.

R. Freeman Butts
www.civiced.org/papers/morality/morality_ch4a.html

Known by many as the "Father of Civic Education," R. Freeman Butts left an extensive collection of writings from his years of research at Columbia's Teacher's College including this essay on twelve powerful ideas of civics.

Stanford Encyclopedia of Philosophy—Wisdom
http://plato.stanford.edu/entries/wisdom

Stanford University maintains a comprehensive electronic encyclopedia of philosophy that includes thousands of entries on ideas, philosophies, and philosophers. The entry here explains wisdom and judgment.

Universal Declaration of Human Rights (1948)
www.yale.edu/lawweb/avalon/un/unrights.htm

The Yale Law School's Avalon Project offers a wide range of historic and contemporary documents in law, history, and diplomacy. Documents are organized both by century and topic. Special features allow the user to compare texts and find documents mentioned in the searched document. The special collection "Project Diana" features documents on human rights such as the United Nation's Universal Declaration of Human Rights.

University College London Philosophy Study Guide: Political Philosophy
www.ucl.ac.uk/philosophy/LPSG/Political.htm

Although not a direct link to texts or sources, this study guide provides a large bibliography to begin exploration of political ideas, issues, and individuals.

NOTES

1 Anonymous, as quoted in Antony Jay, ed., *The Oxford Dictionary of Political Quotations* (New York: Oxford University Press, 1996), 13.

2 Victor Hugo, as quoted in ibid., 184.

3 René Descartes, *Principles of Philosophy* (1644), trans. John Veitch, available at www.classicallibrary.org/descartes/principles/01.htm, Pt. I, article VII.

4 See Edward T. Hall, "The Voices of Time," in *The Silent Language* (New York: Random House, 1990), 1–19.

5 Andrew Heywood, *Political Theory: An Introduction,* 2nd ed. (New York: St. Martin's Press, 1999), 3.

6 See John Dunn, *Democracy: A History* (New York: Atlantic Monthly Press, 2006).

7 Isaiah 2:4.

8 Thomas Jefferson to James Madison, December 20, 1787, quoted in R. B. Bernstein, *Thomas Jefferson* (New York: Oxford University Press, 2003), 72.

9 *Selected Works of Mao Tse-tung* [now, Mao Zedong] (Beijing: Foreign Languages Press, 1965), Vol. 2, 224.

10 Margaret Mead, see the Institute for Intercultural Studies Web site, www.interculturalstudies.org/faq.html#quote.

11 Jacob Bronowski and Bruce Mazlish, *The Western Intellectual Tradition* (New York: Harper & Brothers, 1960). As referenced in another useful source: Peter Watson, *Ideas: A History of Thought and Invention, from Fire to Freud* (New York: HarperCollins, 2005), 6.

12 Julius Caesar and Sallust, as quoted in Tom Holland, *Rubicon: The Last Years of the Roman Republic* (New York: Anchor Books, 2005), xxiv.

13 There are democracy barometers for Latin America, the Arab world, Africa, South Asia, East Asia, and Europe. The *Journal of Democracy* publishes the results. For a sampling, see International Institute for Democracy and Electoral Assistance Web site, www.idea.int/democracy/global-barometers.cfm.

14 On the Convention, see Max Farrand, ed., *The Records of the Federal Convention of 1787,* 4 vols. (New Haven: Yale University Press, 1911, 1937, 1966, 1987 [rev. supplementary vol. by James H. Hutson]). On the ratification controversy, see Merrill M. Jensen, John P. Kaminski, Gaspare J. Saladino, Richard Leffler, and Charles

Schoenleber, eds., *The Documentary History of the Ratification of the Constitution and the Bill of Rights, 1787–1791,* 19 vols. [to date] (Madison: State Historical Society of Wisconsin, 1976).

15 See Alan Gibson, *Interpreting the Founding* (Lawrence: University Press of Kansas, 2006); Alan Gibson, *Understanding the Founding* (Lawrence: University Press of Kansas, 2007).

16 Morton Keller, *America's Three Regimes: A New Political History* (Oxford: Oxford University Press, 2007), 71–80.

17 Isaiah Berlin, "Political Judgement," in *The Sense of Reality: Studies in Ideas and Their History,* ed. Henry Hardy (New York: Farrar, Straus and Giroux, 1996), 40.

18 Ibid., 47.

19 Ibid., 41.

20 Fernando Henrique Cardoso, "Scholarship and Statesmanship," *Journal of Democracy* 16, no. 2 (April 2005): 11.

BIG IDEAS

- Politics is the process by which people seek to settle their differences peacefully and reach binding decisions that resolve public issues.

- Politics is the responsibility of both political leaders and the citizen.

- People enter politics for a mix of reasons: to gain power, to serve their constituency, and to promote the common good.

- Politics reflects the best and worst tendencies of human nature.

Which Political Characteristics Remain Subjects of Debate?
   Why Does Politics Arise?
   Where Does Politics End?

Purpose of This Chapter

Politics has different meanings for different people. To some, politics is the exciting and dynamic subject of how human beings organize themselves in society. To others, politics means something negative, as when politicians "play politics" by avoiding an issue, posturing in the limelight, or using negative campaigning to attack their opponents. At its best and worst, politics is an essential theme of this book. Good ideas cannot be put into practice without it. So, roll up your sleeves and join us as we enter the rough and tumble world of politics.

Terms to Know

civil society arena	failed states	politics
constituency	idealist view of politics	realist view of politics
electoral arena	policy arena	

WHY DO PEOPLE PARTICIPATE IN POLITICS?

Politics happens when people disagree—sometimes strongly—about who should govern, what issues they should address, and how they should do so. In this book, we define **politics** as the complex

Figure 2.1 Political Arenas

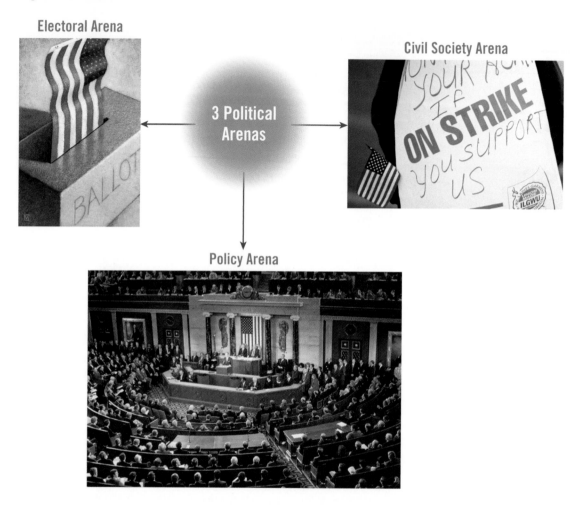

Electoral Arena

Civil Society Arena

3 Political Arenas

Policy Arena

process by which people seek to settle their differences peacefully and reach binding decisions that resolve public issues.[1]

Much of today's politics takes place in three arenas (see Figure 2.1):

• The **electoral arena** is the sphere where candidates campaign for citizens' votes and citizens decide who governs. Countries differ widely in their type of electoral system and the extent to which their elections are free, fair, and competitive. However, these differences do have identifiable patterns (a subject addressed in a later chapter).

• The **policy arena** is the area where the people's representatives must decide how to govern and why. Countries also differ widely in the principles governing their policymaking institutions, processes, and performance (these patterns are also discussed in later chapters).

- The **civil society arena** is the place where people are free to form nongovernmental associations. In Western and Western-style polities, those associations include interest groups such as trade unions and neighborhood associations, independent political parties, and a free press. In non-Western polities, interest groups are less common and influential than more natural associations such as families, clans, tribes, neighborhoods, and religious associations. Whether as organized interest groups or more natural human associations, these civil society organizations monitor and seek to influence government and politics (a subject also detailed in a later chapter).

What attracts some people and not others to the rough-and-tumble world of politics? People enter the business world to make money, the ministry to save souls, and medicine to heal the sick. But what is the allure of politics for those who practice or observe it?

One of the most important and common answers to this question is power—the ability to influence others, to make decisions affecting public life, and perhaps even to change the course of history. Lee Hamilton, a former member of the U.S. House of Representatives (D-Ind.) for thirty-four years who served with distinction as vice chair of the 9/11 Commission, explains:

> Over the years, I've met with a lot of high-school and college students, and there's one question they come up with time after time: What, they want to know, is politics really about?
>
> Having spent a good part of my life in the trenches, I long ago arrived at an answer that I thought reflected reality and was sufficiently cynical to make me believable. Politics, I would tell them, is about power: getting it, keeping it, and using it to advance one's agenda.[2]

The news media often fuel the cynical view that power is the main reason why people enter politics. The daily news abounds with stories of politicians who use their office to feed their personal egos. All too often, Lee Hamilton bemoans, "it's about enriching oneself. It's about winning elections or wielding power for its own sake."[3]

Such views are not new. Max Weber (1864–1920), an influential German thinker, and one of the founders of modern sociology, wrote that politics "offers first of all the sense of power"[4] (see More About . . . Max Weber and the Politician). And over two hundred years earlier, in the seventeenth century, Henry Carey, an English songwriter, composed a paean (a song of joyful praise) to his sovereign:

> God save our gracious king!
>
> Long live our noble king!
>
> God save the king!

MORE ABOUT . . .
Max Weber and the Politician

Max Weber (1864–1920), the father of modern sociology, exerted tremendous influence on other disciplines as well, including political science, history, and economics. In his popular and powerful lecture "Politics as a Vocation," Weber addressed the qualifications of a politician. According to Weber, good politicians must be passionate about the ends of government and their responsibilities but somewhat dispassionate about the governed. He emphasized three qualifications of politicians: (1) passion, namely "a passionate commitment to a realistic cause"; (2) a sense of responsibility toward that cause; and (3) judgment as "the ability to contemplate things as they are with inner calm and composure before allowing them to affect one's actions." Weber is perhaps best known for his use of typology as a form of scientific classification. In the field of politics, he developed typologies of different political types of leadership, power, and authority, to name a few.

Max Weber, "Politics as a Vocation," in *From Max Weber: Essays in Sociology,* trans. and ed. H. H. Gerth and C. Wright Mills (Oxford University Press, 1946), 115–116.

Then Carey added a second verse in which he scolded members of Parliament:

> *Confound their politics,*
>
> *Frustrate their knavish [mischievous] tricks.*

But politics is about more than getting and using power. As Lee Hamilton discovered, power is only one piece of the puzzle. Hamilton urges people to dig deeper into the motives of officeholders, namely, into the mix of personal and altruistic reasons that impel people to enter politics.

For most politicians, power is not an end in itself but a means to achieve other ends. It is an instrumental, not an aspirational, idea. Aside from gaining personal power, there are two common ends that politicians seek to advance by going into politics and pursuing power. The first is serving the interests of their **constituency**, the people they were elected or appointed to represent (see More About . . . Pork Barrel Politics). Most legislators see one of their roles as being a delegate serving the people and groups of their district. They do this by guiding constituents through the labyrinth of government. But they also try to serve their district as a whole by bringing in government funding, jobs, and other benefits (see Figure 2.2).

The second common end of politics is serving the general good of the people as a whole—not just one's constituents. Edmund Burke expressed this view of the representative as a

Figure 2.2 How Political Figures Use Power

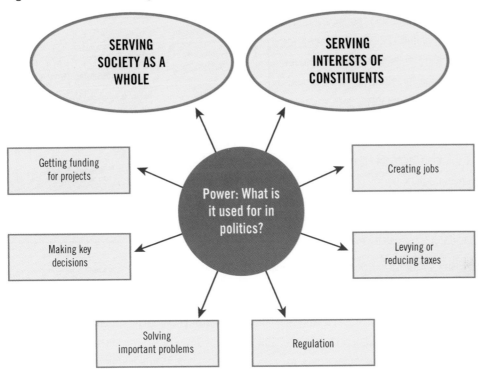

trustee who serves the common good of the people as a whole in a 1774 speech after he was elected to the British parliament:

> Parliament is not a Congress of Ambassadors from different and hostile interests; which interests each must maintain, as an Agent and Advocate, against other Agents and Advocates; but Parliament is a deliberative Assembly of one Nation, with one Interest, that of the whole; where not local Purposes, not local Prejudices ought to guide, but the general Good, resulting from the general Reason of the whole. You chuse a Member indeed; but when you have chosen him, he is not the Member of Bristol, but he is a Member of Parliament.[5]

In most constitutional governments, the general good of the people is invoked in the preamble to the country's constitution. The preamble to the U.S. Constitution, for example, includes justice, domestic tranquility, the common defense, the general welfare, and the blessings of liberty. However, as Lee Hamilton warns:

> If politics at heart is a means to an end—the end being an actual fix to a problem—then it is not just about the search for an answer, but about making that answer work. This

MORE ABOUT . . .

Pork Barrel Politics

In American politics, the expression "pork barrel politics" came into use after the Civil War as a term for the type of politics where politicians work to directly benefit their constituents in return for political support. In the days before refrigerators, pork was kept in a barrel. Politicians and journalists used the term to describe laws that allowed legislators to allocate special projects for their districts, like pork from a barrel. Some consider "pork barrel politics" to be a normal and acceptable way of distributing government resources to localities where it can do the most good; others consider it a necessary evil that greases the squeaky wheel. Still others see it as a wasteful and corrupt practice that favors some communities over others. In 1882, for example, President Chester Arthur vetoed the Rivers and Harbors Act and labeled it "pork barrel legislation"—a wasteful and extravagant expenditure of public money. Today, governments distribute funds for disaster relief, medical research, dams and reservoirs, ports and harbors, airports, highway exit ramps, and mass transit, to name only a few examples. Clearly, resources like these should not be distributed unfairly, wastefully, or without accountability.

means that the best politicians don't just dream up policy solutions regardless of context: They also think about how those solutions would work in the real world; they think about the forces that can help them and those that can block them; and perhaps above all, they think about how to build the broadest consensus possible behind their solutions, so they have a realistic chance of taking root and flourishing.[6]

At first glance, it may seem that these descriptions of politics and the motivations of politicians are in natural conflict with one another. However, Hamilton does not say that politicians are unable to dream and build solutions. Nor does Burke say that politicians must serve the common good and thereby reject their constituents' interests.

Many politicians try to balance the goal of addressing larger public problems while serving the specific interests of their constituents. This is no easy task, but the best statesmen try to do just that. Sometimes the needs and interests of the common good are in harmony with the specific interests of constituents, but at other times statesmen must consider the context of a specific issue and make a judgment that favors one side over the other.

Although people enter politics to acquire power and to achieve loftier goals, there is a third motive driving the other two. As Aristotle explained, it is ambition that drives people into politics—the desire to achieve something and be widely recognized (see Bold Thinkers: Aristotle).

For the ambitious, politics is truly a pinnacle of human achievement. Scottish novelist and statesman John Buchan (1875–1940) described it "as the crown of a career. . . . It is the worthiest ambition. Politics is still the greatest and most honorable adventure."[7] The writer Frederick Scott Oliver (1864–1934) agreed with Buchan: "With all the temptations and degradations that beset it, politics is still the noblest career any man can choose. . . . If the conscience of an honest man lays down stern rules, so also does the art of politics."

BOLD THINKERS

Aristotle

Man is a political animal.
—Aristotle, *Politics*

A Greek philosopher and student of Plato, Aristotle (c. 384–322 BCE) was one of the most important thinkers in the history of the world. He was the author of a

Roman marble bust of Aristotle, after a now lost Greek original.

number of books that continue to exert tremendous influence, including *Physics, Rhetoric, Ethics,* and *Politics.* In *Politics,* he explored the nature of the polity, human nature, the role of the citizen, forms of government, justice, the rule of law, the importance of civic virtue, and the advantages of mixed republican government. Aristotle's *Politics* became highly influential among European and Arabic thinkers after it was translated into Latin in the thirteenth century. This work remains the starting point for political thinkers and leaders today.

IS POLITICS FOR EVERYONE?

As a full-time occupation, political leadership is not for everyone. It is certainly not for the faint of heart, for those who shy away from confrontation, or for those who are unwilling to compromise. "Politics ain't beanbag," quipped the fictional character, Mr. Dooley.[8] Thomas Jefferson echoed this sentiment when he wrote, "Politics is such a torment that I would advise everyone I love not to mix with it."[9] A want ad for a full-time political leader might read something like the ad on page 26 and include the job requirements listed therein.

Politics is not just for leaders. After President Harry Truman completed his term in office, a reporter asked him how he felt leaving the highest office in the land. Truman responded, "I am not leaving the highest office. I am assuming the highest office, that of citizen." In world

POLITICAL LEADER NEEDED

Must be a people person. Must have a message and the will to succeed. Must be able to inspire and persuade others. Must like making speeches, reading the news, traveling, and eating out. Must be able to make difficult choices, strike balances, and live with compromise when necessary. Some experience helpful, but too much can be a liability.

history, the "office" of citizen is not a recent phenomenon. It has a long history in republican societies since ancient times. Except for early experiments in citizenship, notably in the ancient Greek polity of Athens, the citizen as a meaningful participant in politics is not much more than two centuries old. Being represented by elected officials does not mean that citizens should opt out of politics or rely entirely on their representatives to do their political work. President Dwight David Eisenhower—a peacemaker abroad, enforcer of racial desegregation at home, and counselor against the dangers of the military-industrial complex—believed that "Politics ought to be the part-time profession of every citizen."[10]

What did Eisenhower mean by that statement? He meant what he said—that politics is a full-time job for politicians but that all citizens should devote part of their time and responsibilities to keeping an eye on the politicians they've elected (see Figure 2.3). As the following words adorning the entrance to the Nebraska State Capitol proclaim:

THE SALVATION OF THE STATE IS
WATCHFULNESS IN THE CITIZEN.

Most citizens cannot devote all of their time to the responsibilities of citizenship. They must balance various responsibilities, to family, congregation, job, friends, neighbors, and, of course, to themselves. However, survey after survey shows that most people around the world believe that they should make time to exercise their civic responsibilities.[11]

Responsible citizens should keep up with the news, be prepared to make informed political choices, exercise the right to vote, abide by the law, and be good neighbors. Average citizens may not know enough to pass just laws in a legislature, but they know enough to make wise decisions about where they stand on particular issues and which candidates they support in elections. That is the citizens' part-time role in politics.

Philosophers approach the question "Is politics for everyone?" in another way. Most philosophers start with the premise that politics is part of human nature, a natural or inherent part of the human condition. That is the starting point for Aristotle.

Figure 2.3 How Citizens Can Get Involved in Political Concerns

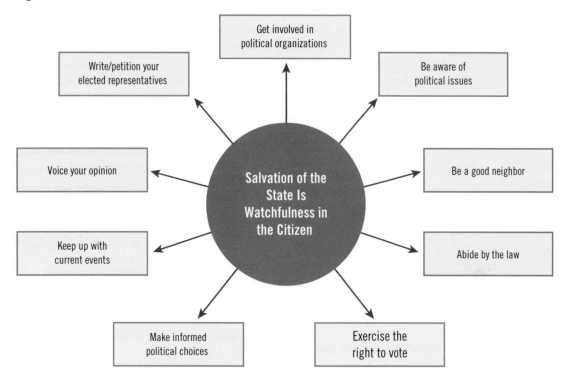

Get involved in political organizations

Write/petition your elected representatives

Be aware of political issues

Voice your opinion

Salvation of the State Is Watchfulness in the Citizen

Be a good neighbor

Keep up with current events

Abide by the law

Make informed political choices

Exercise the right to vote

Here is how Aristotle comes to this major point. First, Aristotle reasoned, human beings are not just social creatures; they also are sociable creatures. Human beings are not self-sufficient; they need one another for such basic wants as food, shelter, and protection. This is what makes them social creatures. Moreover, most human beings like to be with others. As modern psychology has discovered, people need to be recognized; they are fulfilled when they are recognized by others for their achievements, and they become hostile when they are not. And this is what makes human beings sociable as well as social. For these reasons, Aristotle continued, people form associations, beginning

Some teens, such as Eyck Freymann of New York, have created their own political blogs. Blogs allow people to offer opinions and learn about the political views of others.

with the family; and they develop a shared language to communicate. In these respects, Aristotle observed, human beings are not so different from other sociable creatures, such as bees.

The question then arises, how is humankind different from other creatures? Here is how Aristotle answered that question:

> It is thus clear that man is a political animal, in a higher degree than bees or other gregarious [sociable] animals. . . . It is the peculiarity of man, in comparison with other animals, that he alone possesses a perception of good and evil, of the just and the unjust, and other similar qualities; and it is association in these things which makes a family and a polis [the ancient city-state]. . . . The man who is isolated, who is unable to share in the benefits of political association, or has no need to share because he is already self-sufficient, is no part of the polis. . . . [12]

In short, for Aristotle, what makes humankind unique is also what makes us political. That distinctly human quality is ethical judgment, the ability to recognize good and evil, justice and injustice, and the like, in the public realm and in private life. That is the great gift that an informed and responsible citizenry brings to the enterprise of politics, and that is the philosopher's answer to why politics is indeed for everyone. It also helps to explain why the citizenry needs the polity and government and vice versa.

WHAT CAN BE INFERRED FROM POLITICS?

An *inference* is a conclusion drawn from propositions and facts. What inferences can be drawn from our discussion of the meaning of politics? What can be learned from studying politics? This chapter began with the definition of politics as a complex process by which people seek to settle their differences peacefully and reach a binding decision to resolve public issues. The remainder of this chapter takes a closer look at the characteristics of this definition and at the differing points of view surrounding some of them. Our definition contains five characteristics.

First, politics is a social activity; it is not a solitary pursuit. Politics requires human interaction, lasting human associations, a common language, and a common set of political ideals on which most people agree. Human beings seek the recognition that comes from those associations. If the more ambitious people do not achieve that social recognition peacefully in the world of politics, they may seek it elsewhere, for example, on the battlefield.

But there is something more. Politics requires a certain amount of public trust. For politics to work, people need to trust one another and the institutions that sustain a political life free of violence, disorder, and injustice.[13] The level of trust that is necessary to sustain and maintain a polity is a contested issue. The history of every inhabited continent, however, has shown that when a ruler or a government breaks the public trust on one too many occasions, only the most ruthless acts of repression can hold the people at bay.

Second, politics involves ethical considerations. People are not only social and sociable; they are ethical. They care about the difference between right and wrong, between justice and injustice. Therefore, some form of politics is needed in all human societies to decide—peacefully if possible—what is fair and just in those situations that require a collective response.

Third, politics typically arises from differences among people. A people must agree on certain political ideals; otherwise, public trust erodes. But people will not naturally agree on how to resolve all political issues. Out of these differences arise much of the rough-and-tumble of politics: the political competition for office, the political cross-pressures on office-holders (including the citizenry), and, on rarer occasions, the end of politics in civil war or other violent measures.

Some societies do not react well to such tensions. Their political cultures may value social harmony, or their political institutions may be too fragile to withstand constant tension. Other societies value political competition and see it as an engine of progress. In all societies, however, the peaceful accommodation of differences is what separates politics from war and other violent measures.

As the eminent British political scientist Sir Bernard Crick put it, politics is "that solution to the problem of order which chooses conciliation rather than violence and coercion."[14] Most people might prefer to avoid confrontation altogether. But those who enter politics must be prepared to air their differences and to debate the merits of their positions so that they can come to an agreeable compromise. That is why a compromised or conciliated response to a problem is called a "political solution."

Fourth, politics is decision making. A society is in trouble when its political institutions may be able to prevent violent disagreements but fail to solve problems. Politics requires collective decisions by people with the authority to make them. Political decisions often involve negotiations, which may include bargaining, compromising, and conciliating. Political decisions must be regarded as binding on the group, even if some people remain opposed.

Finally, the scope of political decisions extends to public matters, those things that affect the people organized politically as a public, either in whole or in part. The word *republic,* for example, comes from the Latin words *res publica,* meaning public things that matter to the people. Some public things are clear and universally accepted; all human societies, for example, regard defense against an external threat as a matter of public concern and public action. Other things are more difficult to distinguish as public or private; in Western societies, especially Anglo-American societies, for example, it has long been assumed that "a man's home is his castle," a private place beyond the reach of government. By contrast, some Eastern societies find privacy to be a foreign notion; the Chinese language, for example, has no word for "privacy."

WHICH POLITICAL CHARACTERISTICS REMAIN SUBJECTS OF DEBATE?

Some of the characteristics of politics are subjects of heated debate. Attempts to answer two fundamental questions illustrate these tensions: (1) Why does politics arise, and (2) where does politics end?

WHY DOES POLITICS ARISE?

Aristotle's response—man is by nature a sociable creature who wants to associate with others in order to create a good and just polity—is only one of the possible answers to the question of why does politics arise. A different view, expressed by the seventeenth-century English philosopher Thomas Hobbes, holds that man in a state of nature leads a life that is "solitary, poor, nasty, brutish, and short."[15] Both views see politics as an outgrowth of human nature and therefore as universal. However, these views begin with very different assumptions about human nature and what it means for politics.

The Hobbesian, or realist, view of politics sees politics as people pursuing power, usually for the purpose of dominating others. Harold Laswell, the noted American psychologist, captured this view in the title of a book he wrote on politics, *Politics: Who Gets What, When and How* (1936). This view may seem to represent a rather low expectation of politics. Realists argue that in a world where people try to dominate one another, it is prudent to protect one's self-interests against those of one's opponents.

In the history of philosophy, the Florentine diplomat, public servant, historian, and philosopher Niccolò Machiavelli (1469–1527) is credited with being the father of modern political realism. However, Machiavelli is much misunderstood. The standard view is that Machiavelli was evil, the kind of man who would cut your heart out without remorse if it served his own self-interest. But, in fact, Machiavelli prized *virtú,* or civic virtue, in leaders and citizens. Again and again, Machiavelli counseled the prince and the people that civic virtue means exercising wise judgment in advancing the general good of the republic over one's self-interest.

Machiavelli was, however, totally ruthless on one point. When the safety of the country is at stake, every citizen has the duty to set aside every scruple to save the country and its liberty. In this sense, realism is very much like civic patriotism—the good of the country comes first because a good country is the best way to secure the people's liberties and progress.[16] In other words, this particular end justifies *all* possible means.

The **realist view of politics** is particularly influential in the making of foreign policy in a world where aggression is still commonplace. There will always be those who look to win political battles by whatever means necessary, including violence. Vladimir Lenin (1870–1924) and Joseph Stalin (1879–1953) in the Soviet Union are good examples, as is Mao Zedong (1893–1976) in China, a man who (as you learn in Chapter 1) openly asserted that political power comes from "the barrel of a gun."

By contrast, the **idealist view of politics** sees a world in which the pursuit of power is replaced by the pursuit of justice and peace. The idealist envisions a world of peace, not power, in which people and polities exercise their goodwill by building a more just world peacefully and by mutual consent. The German philosopher Immanuel Kant (1724–1804) was one of the founders of modern political idealism. He envisioned a world of "perpetual peace" governed by an international federation of republics.[17]

In reality, most people in the world of politics are motivated by a mixture of realist and idealist goals. They seek to protect the interests of those who elected them, but they also seek to advance loftier ideals for the polity as a whole. As noted earlier, people who enter politics seek both power and loftier goals, in varying degrees but never purely for their own sake. It is ambition that drives people into politics, the desire to achieve something and be widely recognized for it. The question is how (and how well) different political leaders in history have combined idealism and realism to obtain their goals.

WHERE DOES POLITICS END?

Another difference of opinion over the meaning of politics occurs when people try to explain the end of politics. There are three major views on this question.

The first view holds that all political pursuits eventually lead to government because it is the only institution with the authority to resolve political differences and make political decisions. If you consult *Merriam-Webster's Collegiate Dictionary* (eleventh edition), the first definition of *politics* represents this position, defining politics as "the art or science of government" generally and "concerned with guiding and influencing governmental policy" and "winning and holding control over a government."

The second view is broader and more expansive. According to this view, politics is the means by which all social decisions are made and carried into effect in human social units and institutions. Politics, in this view, encompasses the totality of human relationships. *Merriam-Webster's* represents this view in one of its last definitions of *politics* as "the total complex of relations between people living in society." In this view, politics takes place not only in government but also in families, labor unions, schools, sports, religious groups, and other nongovernmental associations. This more expansive view sees politics everywhere and as the full-time responsibility of everyone. In this view, even the personal can become political.

The third view of politics is the realist view that politics begins where consensus ends. This is the view that conflict defines politics. Inherent differences divide human beings and the great end of politics is the peaceful resolution of conflict. *Merriam-Webster's* represents this view in its definition of *politics* as "political affairs or business; especially: competition between competing interest groups or individuals for power and leadership (as in government)."

The great danger in each of these views occurs when people come to believe passionately in the rightness of one view and succeed in imposing it on others. That is precisely the meaning of *factionalism,* a term that James Madison used in *The Federalist* No. 10 to refer to a majority or minority so consumed by passion and self-interest that it seeks to destroy any opposition and repress individual rights in the process.[18] Sadly, the full history of the twentieth century and the early years of this one demonstrates the horrible consequences of each of these three views taken to their unimaginable ends (see Figure 2.4).[19]

Authoritarianism has been the unhappy consequence of the first view—that only governments should govern—where power-seekers clothed in uniform, rags, or riches have gained control of government as an end in itself. Each year *Parade* magazine presents its "List of the World's 10 Worst Dictators." That list draws on reports by human rights organizations like Amnesty International, Freedom House, and Human Rights Watch. The list is a rogue's

Figure 2.4 The Ends of Politics

POINTS OF VIEW	View taken to extreme	Result
1. All political pursuits lead to government	→	1. **Authoritarianism** Examples: the regimes of Robert Mugabe (Zimbabwe) and Islam Karimov (Uzbekistan)
2. Politics is the means by which all social decisions are made	→	2. **Totalitarianism** Examples: Nazi Germany, Stalinist Russia
3. Politics begins where consensus ends	→	3. **Factionalism** Examples: former Yugoslavia, Rwanda

gallery of dictators who ruthlessly wield immense power while draining their country's economy. Included are various types of dictators in various regions of the world, for example, one-party African tyrants, former Soviet commissars in central Asia, Southeast Asian military generals, and Arab nationalist dictators.

Totalitarianism has been the sad result of the second view—that everything should be political. Examples of it were rarer than authoritarianism during the twentieth century, but its consequences were more devastating.

A North Korean soldier faces a South Korean soldier at the border between the two nations. Human rights organizations consistently identify the North Korean government as particularly repressive.

Factionalism is the great danger of the third view—that politics must involve conflict. This happens when the sources of conflict are magnified and when government and the people are no longer able to resolve those conflicts peacefully. This has taken various forms in the twentieth and twenty-first centuries: in the civil war between republicans and fascists in Spain, in the religious and ethnic acts of terrorism that have threatened to tear Iraq apart, and in the ethnic cleansing that reached genocidal proportions in Nazi Germany and other countries. This view is evident throughout the world today in the anarchy that plagues so many **failed states**, states that fail to satisfy the basic purposes of government such as protecting natural rights, promoting the common good, or providing order and security.

The great civic project of the current age lies in acquiring the political wisdom and exercising the moral judgment needed to restrain those excesses. Sadly, there is a long way to go. But if restraint is possible, perhaps the way will be paved for the nobler political ideas set forth in the Age of Sages over 2,000 years ago. Those ideas are the subject of the other units of this book.

REVIEWING AND USING THE CHAPTER

1. Do you consider yourself to be a political realist, a political idealist, or a mix of the two? Explain your answer.

2. Visit the Web site of the Fund for Peace (www.fundforpeace.org/web), where you will find a failed states index. Select a country on that index and assess why that country is on the list. What would you recommend be done to help turn that country's government from failure to success?

3. Consult recent public opinion polls and/or letters to the editor in local newspapers to assess the level of trust of politicians in your community. To what extent do people trust political actors in your community?

4. What is your view of politics? Do you agree with those who consider it a noble profession or with those who consider it shameful? Explain your answer.

EXTENSION ACTIVITIES

1. Conduct a survey in your school or class to determine the prevailing political attitudes of your peers. Do your classmates trust politicians? Do they believe government is responsive to their needs? How do you explain or interpret your findings?

2. Find and interpret three political cartoons depicting different views of politics. What view of politics is offered by each artist?

WEB RESOURCES

Daryl Cagle's MSNBC's Political Cartoon Web site

http://cagle.msnbc.com/politicalcartoons

Daryl Cagle, cartoonist for MSNBC, hosts a Web site of political cartoons and links to political cartoonists from around the world. The Web site and the cartoons are updated daily.

Fund for Peace

www.fundforpeace.org/web

A nonprofit research and educational organization, the Fund for Peace provides up-to-date reports on threats to peace throughout the world. The Web site contains country profiles, reports on current issues that threaten peace and security, and annual reports such as the *Failed States Index*.

In Defense of Politics, a lecture by Professor Steven Smith

http://oyc.yale.edu/political-science/introduction-to-political-philosophy/content/sessions/lecture 24.html

View Yale University Professor Steven Smith's lecture, "In Defense of Politics." Smith's lecture uses ideas from twentieth-century political scientists, novelists, and philosophers such as Sir Bernard Crick, E. M. Forster, and Carl Schmitt.

Lee Hamilton's Congressional Blog
http://centeroncongress.blogspot.com

Through his Center on Congress at Indiana University, former member of Congress Lee Hamilton writes biweekly on current issues of American politics and policy ranging from the role of Congress to the importance of civic engagement.

Machiavelli, Text of *The Discourses*
http://oll.libertyfund.org/?option=com_staticxt&staticfile=show.php%3Ftitle=775&chapter=76152&layout=html&Itemid=27

Read an excerpt from Machiavelli's *Discourses on Livy.* This excerpt comes from the Online Library of Liberty, a project of Liberty Fund, a private educational foundation.

This site gathers the full text of many classics of political thought.

Politics by Aristotle
http://classics.mit.edu/Aristotle/politics.html

Hosted by the Internet Classics Archive at the Massachusetts Institute of Technology, this site contains the entire text of Aristotle's *Politics*. The Web site also offers the full text of a variety of other classic works on political thought.

World Values Survey
www.worldvaluessurvey.org

This Web site reports the results of public opinion surveys conducted every five years since 1990 on cultural values and beliefs. Conducted by an internationally respected network of social scientists, the World Values Survey allows the user to compare public opinion in eighty countries on a wide range of social, political, and economic topics.

NOTES

1 Sir Bernard Crick, *In Defence of Politics* (Harmondswourth, UK, and New York: Penguin, 1983).

2 Lee Hamilton, "What Politics Should Be About," *Comments on Congress* (Bloomington, Ind.: Center on Congress at Indiana University, May 2007), 1.

3 Ibid.

4 Max Weber, "Politics as a Vocation," in *Princeton Readings in Political Thought: Essential Texts since Plato,* ed. Mitchell Cohen and Nicole Fermon (Princeton, N.J.: Princeton University Press, 1996), 499.

5 Edmund Burke, election speech, Nov. 3, 1774, quoted in Ross J. S. Hoffman and Paul Levack, eds., *Burke's Politics: Selected Writings and Speeches of Edmund Burke on Reform, Revolution, and Law* (New York: Alfred A. Knopf, 1949), 116.

6 Hamilton, "What Politics Should Be About," 2.

7 John Buchan also served in British Intelligence and wrote the spy novel *The Thirty-Nine Steps,* which Alfred Hitchcock made into a movie in 1935.

8 The brainchild of Chicago journalist Finley Peter Dunne (1867–1936), Mr. Dooley was a street-wise bartender who, as the saying goes, "spoke truth to power." He spoke for the unsophisticated but worldly-wise common man who understood the big-city politics of his day.

9 Thomas Jefferson, Letter to Martha Jefferson Randolph, 1800.

10 Dwight D. Eisenhower, Address Recorded for Republican Lincoln Day Dinners, January 28, 1954.

11 See, for example, the World Values Survey, available at www.worldvaluessurvey.org.

12 Aristotle, *Politics,* Book I, Chap. 2, trans. Ernest Barker (New York: Oxford University Press, 1995), 11.

13 Ted Honderich, ed., *The Oxford Companion to Philosophy,* new ed. (Oxford: Oxford University Press, 2005), 926. For more on the idea of trust, see Francis Fukuyama, *Trust: The Social Virtues and the Creation of Prosperity* (New York: Free Press, 1995).

14 Crick, *In Defence of Politics,* 123.

15 Thomas Hobbes, *Leviathan,* ed. Richard Tuck (Cambridge, UK: Cambridge University Press, 1996), 89.

16 See especially Niccolò Machiavelli, especially *The Discourses,* Book 3, Chap. XLI, titled "One's Country Must Be Defended with Glory or with Shame; It Must Be Defended Anyhow." For more, see Quentin Skinner (the dean of Machiavelli experts), *Machiavelli: A Very Short Introduction* (New York: Oxford University Press, 2000).

17 See Immanuel Kant, *Kant: Political Writings,* 2nd rev. ed., ed. H. S. Reiss (Cambridge, UK: Cambridge University Press, 1991).

18 Alexander Hamilton, James Madison, and John Jay, *The Federalist Papers,* ed. Clinton Rossiter (New York: New American Library, 1961).

19 For an eloquent statement of this view, written midway through the twentieth century but even more valid and persuasive today, see Isaiah Berlin, "Political Ideas in the Twentieth Century," in *Liberty,* ed. Henry Hardy (Oxford: Oxford University Press, 2002), chap. 1.

BIG IDEAS

- The comparative method is a powerful approach to the study of political ideas and politics.

- Comparativists must avoid the extremes of comparison: cultural relativism and ethnocentrism.

- Comparative research in political science uses within-country and between-country comparisons, as well as in-depth and broader comparisons.

- Comparative research focuses on the relationships among the five I's of political science.

Purpose of This Chapter

This chapter turns from the world of politics as an important subject to the use of comparison as a vehicle for understanding the political world. The comparative method is one of the most effective and time-honored ways of learning about political ideas and their application to the world of politics. Studying political ideas comparatively allows people to understand more fully the meaning, importance, and application of ideas in their own political systems and in others. The use of comparison highlights the similarities and differences of political ideas within a country or between two or more countries. Comparisons help people form a deeper understanding of the political world of ideas, individuals, interests, issues, and institutions.

Terms to Know

comparative method	ethnocentrism	state
comparative politics	government	unit of analysis
comparativists	nation	unit of observation
country selection	polity	
cultural relativism	research question	

WHAT IS THE COMPARATIVE METHOD?

Comparison is an effective and time-honored method of inquiry. In the scientific world, comparison is known as the comparative method. In a nutshell, the **comparative method** involves identifying and analyzing similarities and differences between two or more subjects.

In the classroom, comparison is frequently used to learn about an assigned topic such as election campaigns by comparing the platforms and styles of different candidates. In more elaborate research projects, the comparative method can be used to study the effects of one factor on another. For example, a researcher might investigate the effects of two or more anti-crime policies on the reduction of crime.

The comparative method is used in a wide variety of subjects, from biology to politics. According to nineteenth-century political philosopher John Stuart Mill (1806–1873), the two classic forms of reasoning (inductive reasoning and deductive reasoning) rely on the comparative method. The first, inductive reasoning, uses the comparative method to draw generalizations about politics by deriving or inducing a general principle from the examination and comparison of two or more particular cases. The second, deductive reasoning, uses the comparative method to work from a general idea or principle to the specific by testing general propositions in the real world and comparing the results.

Comparative politics is an important field of political science that relies heavily on the comparison method. Comparative politics seeks to identify and explain the essential similarities and differences among political systems across time and culture. In today's world of nation-states, comparative politics tends to focus on between-country comparisons. For example, students might compare British and French politics, political parties in Latin American countries, or democracy in post-communist countries. However, the comparative method also can be applied to the study of other types of political systems in world history—ancient republics, empires, medieval cities, and absolute monarchies, to name a few examples.

College courses in comparative politics emphasize the five I's of political science—ideas, interests, issues, individuals, and institutions—and how they operate in countries around the world. Some students who major in comparative politics may choose to specialize in the politics of a particular region of the world such as East Asia, the Middle East, sub-Saharan Africa, or Western Europe.

Other fields that use the comparative method include world history, comparative law, political philosophy, public policy, and international relations. This book draws from all of these fields to explore political ideas—their origins, historical development, and contemporary applications.

WHAT ARE THE USES AND DANGERS OF THE COMPARATIVE METHOD?

The comparative method is an essential part of political inquiry. Let's say you want to learn about a particular political system (in Mexico, for example) or a particular idea (such as democracy). How would you go about doing that? First, you might attempt to identify its important characteristics. At some point, you might study how it developed (that is, its history) and how it functions today. Sooner or later, however, comparison becomes necessary. Comparison is a bridge to deeper understanding that allows its users to place an idea in its

appropriate context, to view an idea from different perspectives, and to form generalizations from several unique examples.

One of the most basic uses of the comparative method is to identify similarities between
two or more political objects. From this use, researchers can derive two essentials of understanding: classification and commonalities. With which countries, for example, does Mexico
share the most political characteristics? What are those shared political characteristics? How
does the Mexican political system demonstrate those characteristics relative to other political
systems in that classification?

A second use of the comparative method is the identification of the differences between
two or more political objects. From this use, researchers derive two more essentials of political knowledge: uniqueness and variability. The American historian Louis Hartz posed an
interesting question: "How can we know the uniqueness of anything," he asked, "except by
contrasting it with what is not unique?"[1] This question leads to another set of questions: In
what ways does the object of investigation (the Mexican political system, for example) vary
from other similar political systems? What explains those variations?

A third use of the comparative method is to vary the point of view in studying a political
object. From this use, researchers gain perspective and a broader understanding of the subject
being studied. What, for example, does the Mexican political system look like if you study it
from the perspective of a citizen of the United States or of Mexico? What changes? What
remains the same?

A final use of the comparative method is in the process of generalization. To do this,
the comparative method must be used with other methods. To return to the previous
example, comparison obviously helps draw generalizations and conclusions about the
Mexican political system. But comparison also can help point toward generalizations and
conclusions about the larger category of Latin American democracies of which Mexico is
a part, about a common characteristic (such as strong presidential systems) of these countries, or about a political idea (such as democracy) and how it works in Latin American
political systems. To understand a complex political idea like democracy, it is essential to
see how it works, and fails to work, not only in one country but in similar and differing
situations.

According to R. Freeman Butts, considered by many to be the father of civic education in
the United States, Americans have much to learn from comparison: "We can learn much from
those who have long lived under tyranny and terrorism. They understand and appreciate the
value of freedom and civic community. They can learn much from our long experience with
a sturdy and stable democracy."[2] These uses of the comparative method are applied on a daily
basis—not only in classrooms but in research projects, in the news media, and in making
public policy.

The comparative method is widely used in the making of public policy. It would be
unwise, for example, to make a foreign policy decision without a comparative assessment of
how other countries are likely to respond to that policy. That holds true whether the policy
involves relations with a particular country or seeks to resolve a particular problem (for
example, nuclear proliferation, global warming, or terrorism).

POINTS OF VIEW

Should the U.S. Supreme Court Consider Foreign Law?

When the U.S. Supreme Court decides a question of constitutional law, it takes into account various factors. These factors include the language of the Constitution, its original meaning, and earlier court decisions or precedents set by American courts. Recently, the Court has added foreign court decisions and international conventions to its repertoire of factors. This comparative method has become a subject of lively debate among the justices of the Court.

In 2002, in *Atkins v. Virginia*, the Court cited the opinion of "the world community" when it concluded that "death is not a suitable punishment for a mentally retarded criminal." Three years later, in *Roper v. Simmons*, the Court ruled the death penalty unconstitutional for juvenile offenders. The Court's opinion noted with dismay that every country in the world except the United States and Somalia had ratified the United Nations Convention on the Rights of the Child, which prohibits the execution of juvenile offenders.

After the Supreme Court ruled, the Atkins v. Virginia *case continued in litigation for several years. In a Yorktown, Virginia, courtroom, Judge Prentis Smiley Jr. reads the definition of mental retardation to the jury in that case in 2005.*

Justices Stephen G. Breyer and Anthony M. Kennedy and former Justice Byron R. White have been among the most prominent advocates supporting the use of foreign law in decisions about U.S. constitutional issues. They claim that the justices should know about and even cite relevant foreign laws. They do not maintain that the Court should follow or rely on foreign law. The advocates of this position point to the use of foreign law in other fields of American law, such as copyright, contract, commerce, and family law. They also argue that American courts should consider the standards of Western and world civilization as well as those of our own culture.

Justices Antonin Scalia and Clarence Thomas are among those who strongly oppose even the consideration or mention of foreign law. Both believe that the Court should defer only to American policymakers, American precedents, and American public opinion. Both argue strenuously that using foreign law exceeds the bounds of the Court's judicial power and jurisdiction. They also maintain that foreign law is so different from American law that one simply has no bearing on the other.

Comparison is also important when you consider domestic policies, especially in a global age. For example, making a policy judgment about illegal immigration depends partly on comparing what pushes people out of one country and what pulls them into a new one. Even a seemingly local issue, such as how to dispose of a city's garbage, requires a comparative assessment of how other cities deal with the problem, how garbage is now hauled across city and state borders, and how garbage contributes to international problems of pollution. The comparative method has even become a legal issue. (See Points of View: Should the U.S. Supreme Court Consider Foreign Law?)

Finally, businesses increasingly rely on international sources of supply, demand, investment, and employment. In this global environment, legions of comparative specialists monitor the political environments where those firms conduct business. People who understand more about the complexities and nuances of the world in which they live are at a competitive advantage in seeking employment, in running for office, or in making sound judgments as citizens.

There are, however, two basic extremes to avoid in using the comparative method. The first is **ethnocentrism**, the tendency to see others through one's own subjective lens. Ethnocentrism has led some researchers to exaggerate the importance or rightness of their own values, to downplay or dismiss other peoples and cultures, and to study other peoples and cultures out of their context. The second, and opposite, tendency to avoid is **cultural relativism**. This is the tendency to excuse a moral wrong like slavery because most people of a particular culture or time period accept that moral wrong as morally right. The comparative approach must steer a careful and responsible course between those two extremes. That task is especially difficult when most countries in a particular time period accept an institution like slavery that later generations regard as unacceptable.

WHAT DO COMPARATIVISTS STUDY?

Economists compare economies and sociologists compare societies; political scientists compare polities. **Comparativists** in political science explore the similarities and differences between two or more polities. Comparativists use the term **polity** to refer to an organized society with a political system of governmental and nongovernmental institutions. They often use *polity* as a synonym of the term *state*, but we prefer the term polity.

Louis XIV (1643–1715) of France gave the term *state* an ominous tone when he supposedly proclaimed "I am the State." Over time, *state* has softened in meaning, and *polity* and *state* have become closer in meaning. Today, the standard definition of *state* comes from international law: a **state** is "an entity that has a defined territory and a permanent population, under the control of its own government, and that engages in, or has the capacity to engage in, formal relations with other such entities."[3] The term *state* focuses on governments in the political system; the term *polity* widens the focus to the political system as whole, including governments, citizens, and political organizations.

The many fleur-de-lis—the enduring symbol of France—on and around King Louis XIV (1638–1715) reflect his view that he personally was the state.

Government is that part of the state or polity with the authority to make and enforce rules binding on itself and other members of the polity. There are different forms of government, of which democracy and autocracy are two examples, and these forms of government are sometimes referred to as regimes. For example, we might say that North Korea has an autocratic form of government or that it is governed by an autocratic regime.

The term **nation** is a social, not a legal, term. Nation refers to a people with their own history and culture. Today, most polities are *nation-states*, distinct geographical territory governed by a distinct and sovereign form of government by people with a shared sense of national identity. Nearly two hundred such entities are members of the United Nations and the broader international system of which it is a part. Although these terms are discussed in detail throughout the book, two warnings should be noted here. First, we should not assume that a nation-state is a state composed of a single and complete people who define themselves as one nation. Politics is not so simple. There are states like the former Yugoslavia that were composed of many different nations or peoples, including Serbs, Croats, and Bosnians. There are states like India with many different official language groups, and states like Nigeria with various official tribal groups. In fact, most states are heterogeneous; that is, they are composed of various ethnic, religious, and linguistic groups. Japan is one of the few relatively homogeneous nation-states composed primarily of one people of the same ethnic group. There also are peoples, like the Palestinians, Kurds, and Basques, who consider themselves nations but do not have a state. Second, the nation-state is a relatively recent phenomenon. Today's world of nearly two hundred nation-states is an outgrowth of several factors, including the Treaty of Westphalia of 1648, which recognized the large territorial states of Europe (for example, England, France, and Spain); the rise of nationalism in the nineteenth century; and its identification in the twentieth century with a people's right of self-determination.

In earlier times, the world has been composed of other types of states. Some examples include:

- *City-states* (in Greek, *polis*) such as Athens, Sparta, and Rome, which were relatively small (usually fewer than 250,000 people, including citizens and slaves) but considered themselves complete worlds, even worshiping their own gods.

- *Tribal states* like the Igbo, which developed an early form of republic in what is now Nigeria.
- *Dynastic states* like the ancient Persian Empire, the Chinese Empire, and Tsarist Russia, which were governed by a successive line or dynasty of rulers who sought to expand their domain by conquering other lands and peoples.

HOW DO COMPARATIVISTS DECIDE WHAT TO COMPARE?

Comparativists must consider three important elements: (1) a topic or research question on which to focus their investigation, (2) the unit of analysis and observation that is appropriate to the question they pose, and (3) the countries that will generate the best data for their research question. Usually, those decisions reflect a mix of personal and professional considerations.

UNIT OF ANALYSIS AND UNIT OF OBSERVATION

Carefully selecting the appropriate **unit of analysis** is essential in comparative research. Researchers must be sure they are comparing similar units. To do otherwise runs the risk of breaking one of the cardinal rules of comparative research—"Thou shall not compare apples and oranges." In comparative political research, the unit of analysis is usually the national polity.

The unit of observation, however, may differ from the unit of analysis. The **unit of observation** describes the source of data. For example, in the 1990s Judith Torney-Purta and a team of researchers decided to study national differences in student attitudes toward citizenship and government. As part of their research, the researchers interviewed 90,000 adolescents in twenty-eight countries.[4] The team looked at questions such as: How do students define and understand the concept of citizenship, do male and female students develop different conceptions and roles of citizenship, do differences in the students' family economic and educational resources affect differences in student civic attitudes, how does civic education vary from one country to another, and how do various types of civic learning affect civic attitudes and performance? Researchers used the interviews to draw cross-national comparisons of student attitudes. In this way, researchers could compare student attitudes in one country with student attitudes in other countries. In this example, the unit of observation is the student and the unit of analysis is the country.

This book focuses on contemporary nation-states as the unit of analysis, with two important exceptions. First, the book examines earlier periods of world history when polities were city-states, dynastic states, or empires; and, second, the book occasionally shifts the unit of analysis from the nation-state as a sovereign and independent polity to the international system as an incomplete and imperfect polity. The constant focus of this book remains the polity, whether it be national, imperial, or international.

RESEARCH QUESTIONS AND TOPIC SELECTION

Many political research topics, comparative or otherwise, can be classified in terms of the five I's introduced earlier in this book (ideas, individuals, interests, issues, and institutions). Comparativists often formulate their **research question** by looking more closely at a relationship of some kind: between two institutions, between an institution and an idea, between important interests in the political world, or between some other combination of the five I's. There is no lack of possible research topics.

At different times in history, some comparative research topics have been more popular than others. John Adams was the first American to write a full-fledged study of comparative government.[5] The focus of his study was the constitutions of governments, and it was written at a time (in 1787–1788) when constitution-making was a subject of heated debate in the United States and Europe. Defending American constitutional principles, such as checks and balances, he compared nearly twenty-five modern republics (including many of the tiny Swiss republics), over fifteen ancient republics, and the thinking of twenty ancient and modern philosophers.

A half century later, during the presidency of Andrew Jackson, interest turned from the constitutions of republics to the conditions of democracy. In the early 1830s, the French government official and political thinker Alexis de Tocqueville traveled to the United States. Although he was only twenty-six, he quickly realized that something about democracy was different in the United States compared to democracy in his native France. Tocqueville spent nine months traveling around the United States, visiting its big cities and small towns, interviewing all sorts of people, and observing American life firsthand. On his return to France he settled down to years of writing about what he had experienced in less than one year in the United States. The result of his labors, titled *Democracy in America,* is a masterwork of political theory published in four volumes between 1835 and 1840.[6] As Tocqueville confesses, "in America, I saw more than America; I sought there the image of democracy itself . . . in order to learn what we have to fear or hope from its progress."[7] (See also More About . . . The Study of Democracy.)

COUNTRY SELECTION

A final consideration is the selection of the actual units for comparison. In most comparative political research, the unit of analysis is the national polity or country. But how many countries should be selected and which ones?

Country selection, much like selecting research questions or topics, depends partly on the topic selected and partly on personal preference. If the topic is "varieties of democracy," for example, the comparativist will select countries representing different types of democracy. The comparativist might be interested in comparing new and older democracies, Western and non-Western democracies, or parliamentary and presidential democracies. But there are many democracies in each category, so the comparativist may rely partly on personal preference in selecting countries within each category. Comparativists also may select countries that are easier to research because they have access to more information about a given country.

Since 1973, more than half of the world's nations have moved from authoritarian rule to democracy, at least in name if not in practice. Dozens of books and scores of journal articles are published each year on democracy. Centers and think tanks focus on democracy. As one example, the University of California at Irvine's Center for the Study of Democracy sponsors research, conferences, lectures, fellowships, and exchange programs. In 1990, inspired by the collapse of the Soviet Union, the National Endowment for Democracy, a nonprofit organization founded by the U.S. government, established the *Journal of Democracy*. The journal is published four times a year and includes as regular features (1) the Democracy Barometers, which provide public opinion surveys on democracy from various regions of the world; (2) the Freedom House Annual Survey on Freedom, which rates the extent to which countries promote and protect freedom; and (3) Election Watch, which reports recent election results from countries throughout the world.

HOW DO COMPARATIVISTS CONDUCT THEIR RESEARCH?

Although there are many ways to conduct comparative research, one of the first questions comparativists must answer is what kind of research their questions require. Some research questions require the in-depth analysis of two or three countries, while others require an approach that casts a wider net.

The in-depth approach allows the researcher to take a closer, deeper look at a few countries and compare their similarities and differences. Samuel Beer, for example, limited his research to two countries (see Bold Thinkers: Samuel Hutchinson Beer). There are several advantages to taking a closer look at fewer countries: it provides the researcher with an opportunity to look more closely at the rich historical and cultural context of the countries under investigation; it becomes possible to visit the countries and observe their politics; and that, in turn, allows the researcher to see more of the complexities and nuances of politics. Those who prefer this approach say that comparing the politics of different countries requires an understanding of their political culture, which is like peeling an onion. Each layer takes time to peel back, but each reveals a different facet of what the researcher is studying, which informs the analyses and enriches the interpretations.

Some research questions, however, require a broader net. This may require gathering large amounts of data (usually quantitative data) from many countries and then using statistical techniques to search for relationships. One example is the World Values Survey that asked wide-ranging questions about national attitudes around the world. From 1999 to 2002, researchers surveyed more than 200,000 people in eighty-one countries. Their results allowed other researchers to compare how people in these countries perceive life, family, work, politics, society, religion, morality, and national identity.[8]

BOLD THINKERS

Samuel Hutchinson Beer

Samuel Beer (1911–2009) turned ninety at the dawn of the twenty-first century. As a Rhodes Scholar (an honor reserved for those with superior athletic and academic ability), he traveled to Britain before the outbreak of World War II. He took that opportunity to travel throughout Europe, where he observed firsthand the rise of fascism and Britain's resistance to it. From that experience, he developed a lifelong interest in British politics.

Samuel Beer (second from left) makes a point during a celebration in his honor at Harvard University.

After World War II, Beer became a political science professor at Harvard. By the mid-1950s, he and many other American political scientists began to study interest groups and their influence on American government, especially on Congress. Beer decided to write a paper comparing the influence of interest groups in American and British politics.

Beer decided to find the center of post–World War II British power. After much research, often with members of Britain's "the old-boy network," he picked up the power trail. Finally, he found its center, not in Parliament but in the British civil service. Beer discovered that British civil servants made many of the important decisions affecting the country's economic interests. With that discovery, he wrote a brilliant paper in which he compared American and British interest-group pressures. Beer's paper got page-one billing in the *American Political Science Review.*

Beer revolutionized the way scholars approached British politics. He did so by refusing to heed conventional wisdom and by doggedly pursuing the power trail to unfamiliar places.

There are several advantages of the broader approach. This approach provides a bird's-eye view that lets researchers see the forest above the trees. Rich detail is sometimes clouded, but new perspectives are gained and new patterns emerge. The broader approach still allows researchers to take a closer look at particularly interesting results, but it is virtually impossible without country teams to study the historical and cultural context of the individual countries. Researchers can identify, collect, and classify particular cases by their similarities. Researchers also can search for patterns of behavior and for factors that explain why those patterns occur and how they change over time. With these results, researchers can begin to build a theory that explains the political behavior that is observed.

Many comparativists design their research to combine the best of both approaches. One strategy is to start by focusing on a few countries and then widen the angle of vision applied to each country. Another strategy starts with a large number of countries, which allows researchers to select a few case studies for a closer look. Both strategies are limited by time, money, and other resources.

Robert Putnam, professor of public policy at Harvard University, combined methods when he conducted intensive research of the political culture of Italy. Putnam and his colleagues did a within-country study, starting from a narrow base and broadening out; they compared Italy's fifteen newly created (in 1970) regional governments: which ones succeeded, how they succeeded, and why they succeeded. According to Putnam, Italy's regional experiment was perfect for a comparative study:

> Just as a botanist might study plant development by measuring the growth of genetically identical seeds sown in different plots, so a student of government performance might examine the fate of these new organizations, formally identical, in their diverse social and economic and cultural and political settings. Would the new organizations actually develop identically in soils as different as those around Seveso and Pietrapertosa?[9]

Putnam's strategy included a closer inspection of six of the fifteen regions of Italy. Researchers interviewed more than seven hundred leaders in these six regions. They then went to the local level in the six regions, where they interviewed hundreds of community leaders and conducted six specially commissioned national surveys and several dozen voter surveys. They also gathered data on institutional performance, street-level responsiveness to citizen inquiries, case studies, and observations from their visits to selected regions.[10] How long did it take to gather all this information? Roughly twenty years (from 1968 to 1989). This intensive comparative study allowed Putnam and his team to document and explain the relationship between the health and vitality of community life and the performance of democratic institutions.

An example of the opposite strategy (starting wide and narrowing in) is the International Association for the Evaluation of Educational Achievement's (IEA) study of civic education in twenty-eight countries. A research team in each country prepared a case study. These cases formed the basis of the larger study, which compares citizenship and education across countries. The case study process gave the researchers a sense of the rich historical and cultural context of the countries they studied.

The ancient Greek philosopher Aristotle's study of politics is probably the earliest recorded example of the comparative method. Certainly, he was among the first to pose and answer many of the essential questions that remain at the heart of political science today. Writing on scrolls of parchment while traveling by foot, animal, and ship, Aristotle and his students collected information on 158 Greek and non-Greek city-states, colonies, and empires. They then prepared in-depth case studies of the politics, culture, society, and economy of some of these examples. Unfortunately, the only document that remains of that research is a fragment of their case study on Athens. Nonetheless, Aristotle's early work helped to crystallize two enduring questions of government: Who rules, and who benefits from that rule?

Table 3.1 Aristotle's Typology of Government

	Rule by one	Rule by a few	Rule by the many
Healthy	Monarchy	Aristocracy	Democracy
Corrupt	Tyranny	Oligarchy	Anarchy

One of the many important results of their work is a typology, or classification of distinctive types of cases. Aristotle's typology distinguishes six forms of government based on who rules and who benefits. According to Aristotle, government can be ruled by the one (a single individual), the few (a small group), or the many (the citizenry as a whole). In each case, rulers can govern for the benefit of the entire polity or for their own selfish benefit. The six forms of government continue to provide the starting point for most studies of comparative government. Table 3.1 lists those six forms.

The importance of political ideas and the use of comparison are two important themes that run throughout this book.

REVIEWING AND USING THE CHAPTER

1. What do researchers of comparative politics study?

2. Identify a political issue that is important to you. Explain how comparison can be used to inform your judgment about that issue.

3. What are the basic types of comparative research and the advantages of each?

4. Explain how comparison can be used both as a research method and as a way of gaining perspective.

EXTENSION ACTIVITY

Using Aristotle's typology of government, classify the following countries and explain your classifications: United States, North Korea, Iran, Mexico, Nigeria, China, and Russia.

WEB RESOURCES

Alexis de Tocqueville's *Democracy in America*
http://xroads.virginia.edu/~HYPER/DETOC/home.html

Hosted by the University of Virginia, this Web site contains detailed notes and a virtual tour of Alexis de Tocqueville's exploration of the United States in 1831–1832—travels that inspired his classic, *Democracy in America*.

Comparative Politics
www.nd.edu/~apsacp/documents/Winter2007 APSANewsletterMarch8_3.pdf

Visit the Web site of the Comparative Politics Section of the American Political Science Association. The address given here takes the reader to a sample newsletter reporting news and views of comparativists in the field.

Ethnocentrism
www.iupui.edu/~anthkb/ethnocen.htm

Professor Ken Barger of Indiana University/Purdue University–Indianapolis offers a thorough analysis of ethnocentrism and its threats to comparative analyses.

International Association for the Evaluation of Educational Achievement
www.iea.nl

Since 1958, the International Association for the Evaluation of Educational Achievement (IEA) has conducted twenty-three cross-national research studies on educational achievement. The results of the 1994–2002 study on civic education can be obtained here.

The Internet Encyclopedia of Philosophy—John Stuart Mill
www.iep.utm.edu/m/milljs.htm

The Internet Encyclopedia of Philosophy is hosted by the University of Tennessee–Martin and contains an alphabetical index of ideas, issues, and individuals important in political theory. The address given here is the entry for John Stuart Mill.

Stanford Encyclopedia of Philosophy—Relativism
http://plato.stanford.edu/entries/relativism

The Stanford Encyclopedia of Philosophy Web site contains a database of searchable concepts important in political philosophy. The address given here leads to the entry on relativism in the Stanford Encyclopedia of Philosophy. "Relativism is not a single doctrine but a family of views whose common theme is that some central aspect of experience, thought, evaluation, or even reality is somehow relative to something else."

NOTES

1 As quoted in C. Vann Woodward, ed., *The Comparative Approach in American History* (New York: Oxford University Press, 1997), 13.

2 R. Freeman Butts, "Many Blueprints for Democracy," *Christian Science Monitor,* June 23, 1995, 18.

3 *Restatement (Third), Foreign Relations Law of the United States,* Section 201. See also Article 1 of the Montevideo Convention of 1933 on Rights and Duties of States.

4 Judith Torney-Purta, Rainer Lehmann, Hans Oswald, and Wolfram Schulz, *Citizenship and Education in Twenty-Eight Countries: Civic Knowledge and Engagement at Age Fourteen* (Amsterdam: International Association for the Evaluation of Educational Achievement, 2001).

5 John Adams, *A Defence of the Constitutions of the Government of the United States.* This work was originally published in three volumes in 1787–1788. It was reprinted in Charles Francis Adams, ed., *The Works of John Adams, Second President of the United States,* 10 vols. (Boston: Little, Brown and Company, 1850–1856).

6 On Tocqueville, see Hugh Brogan, *Alexis de Tocqueville: A Life* (New Haven, Conn.: Yale University Press, 2007); Larry Siedentop, *Tocqueville* (Oxford: Oxford University Press, 1994); Andre Jardin, *Tocqueville* (New York: Farrar Straus Giroux, 1988); George W. Pierson, *Tocqueville in America* (Baltimore, Md.: Johns Hopkins University Press, 1996); James T. Schleifer, *The Making of Tocqueville's "Democracy in America,"* 2nd ed. (Indianapolis, Ind.: Liberty Fund, 2000).

7 The leading translations of *Democracy in America* are by Arthur Goldhammer (New York: Library of America, 2004); Harvey C. Mansfield and Delia Winthrop (University of Chicago Press, 2000); George Lawrence (New York: Harper & Row, 1967); and Henry Reeve, revised by Francis Bowen and edited by Phillips Bradley (New York: Alfred A. Knopf, 1945).

8 Ronald Inglehart, Miguel Basáñez, Jaime Díez-Medrano, Loek Halman, and Ruund Luijkx, eds., *Human Beliefs and Values: A Cross-Cultural Sourcebook Based on the 1999–2002 Values Surveys* (Ann Arbor, Mich.: World Values Survey, Institute for Social Research, University of Michigan, 2004).

9 Robert D. Putnam, with Robert Leonardi and Raffaella Y. Nanetti, *Making Democracy Work* (Princeton, N.J.: Princeton University Press, 1993), 7.

10 Ibid., 13–14.

POLITY AND GOVERNMENT

In this unit, you will learn the ways that societies organize themselves into polities. A *polity* is an organized society with a political system that includes the governing institutions of society as well as the ideas, interests, and citizenry that those institutions represent. Most societies create polities that divide the responsibilities of governance among government, the family, markets, civic associations, and the individual. A fundamental goal of a polity is the protection of its people. But polities also protect freedom and promote a better life. How do different polities address these needs and interests? How does one judge whether a polity has addressed these needs and interests fairly? You will explore these issues in the first chapter of this unit.

Polities have always differed from one another in assigning the responsibilities of governance.

Government, however, is frequently the most powerful player in the mix. So the study of government is important, and it has spawned a lively discussion among political philosophers. Some philosophers have asked: Is government even necessary? Perhaps people can take on the responsibilities of governance themselves? Other philosophers dismiss these ideas, insisting that government is the *only* legitimate holder of power in a polity. But these are the extreme views. Most polities lie somewhere in between. The philosophies that these polities follow include republicanism, conservatism, and liberalism. As you will learn in the second chapter of this unit, these philosophies maintain that governments are necessary instruments to achieve specific practical and moral purposes.

CHAPTER 4
WHAT ARE THE PURPOSES OF GOVERNMENT AND THE POLITY?

BIG IDEAS

- All societies require some form of governance, but few societies rely solely on government for all of their governing needs.

- Most societies create polities that divide responsibilities of governance among government, the family, markets, civic associations, and the individual.

- Government is the governing institution with the authority to make and enforce binding decisions on society and its members.

- The historical development of polities and governments is a response to increasingly complex human needs.

- The purposes of polities and governments include (1) preserving life, (2) protecting freedom, and (3) promoting human betterment.

- Justice is the universal standard for judging how fairly governments carry out the purposes assigned to them.

Purpose of This Chapter

All societies need governance. As a society develops, it organizes itself into a polity to meet its governing needs. Those needs include not only self-preservation but protecting freedom and promoting a better life. Most polities divide responsibilities for meeting those needs among various institutions (for example, governments, families, markets, and civic associations), while reserving some degree of self-government to the individual. These responsibilities become the purposes of a polity's governmental and non-governmental institutions. Polities vary widely in how and how well they divide up those responsibilities. How do polities differ in the way they are governed? What are the purposes of government relative to other governing institutions in the polity? This chapter will help you to explore answers to these and other basic questions about the purposes of government and the polity.

Terms to Know

authority	justice	polity
balanced constitution	legal constitution	procedural justice
chiefdoms	legitimacy	socioeconomic constitution
clan	moral constitution	state
conciliar republics	norms	substantive justice
extended family	patriotism	tribe
governance	political power	

WHAT IS THE POLITY?

A **polity** is an organized society (such as a modern nation-state) with a political system that includes the governing institutions of society as well as the ideas, interests, and citizenry that those institutions represent. In common parlance, a person's polity is his or her country and the principles for which it stands. For example, the *American polity* refers to the country formally called the United States of America.

In ancient Greece and Rome, polities were cities (for example, Athens and Rome). (The origin of the word *polity* is the Greek *polis*, which means "city.") Each ancient city was a world unto itself. Today, the term *city-state* is used as a convenient reference for these polities. But ancient Athens or Rome was more than a city-state. For its citizens, the city was their country, their community, and their civilization. Citizens of Athens identified themselves as Athenians, much like citizens of the United States think of themselves as Americans.

Patriotism, from the Latin *patria,* means "love of country." Country, in this context, means more than a common territory and government. It refers to a polity in which the people identify themselves in terms of their attachments to their land, their culture, and their constitution.

According to the Greek philosopher Aristotle (384–322 BCE), the good polity is a partnership among citizens who share certain things in common. The most important thing that citizens share is a commitment to justice and the common good. The citizenry also shares a common civic culture, a government, and the rights and responsibilities of citizenship. In Aristotle's polity, citizens are brought up with a commitment to informed participation and cooperation in civic affairs. The model, if not the reality, of leadership is the statesman who exercises good judgment based on prudent and practical wisdom. In this sense, the good polity is also known as the republic or commonwealth.[1]

Under tyranny, the polity is replaced by the state and crushed or forced underground. The great Argentine thinker and statesman Domingo Sarmiento (1811–1888)

MORE ABOUT . . .

The Rosas Dictatorship

Domingo Sarmiento and José Mármol were members of the May Brotherhood, a movement of liberal writers and other intellectuals formed in opposition to Juan Manuel de Rosas, who ruled the Buenos Aires Province of Argentina from 1835 to 1852 as a brutal dictatorship. Rosas did not hesitate to use violence to destroy his opponents. He even had a secret society, the *Mazorca,* that spied on dissidents, assaulted them, or worse.

lived under the Rosas dictatorship (see More About . . . The Rosas Dictatorship). As he explained, under Rosas "the public good is a word without meaning, because there is no public."[2] Sarmiento recollected how people opposed to the tyrant Rosas held meetings or rallies, but the tyrant's spies and thugs broke up the gatherings and intimidated the participants. Rosas waged a reign of terror designed to instill fear in the citizenry, and it worked. As Sarmiento's compatriot José Mármol lamented, such tyranny is fueled by "our lack of cooperation in everything and for everything."[3] Sarmiento and Mármol wrote from firsthand experience as exiled dissidents of the Rosas dictatorship.

The polity is more than a legal state. When people form a polity because they seek an organized society governed by human laws. Significantly, the organized society they create is not simply a government surrounded by a legal state. It also includes a variety of nongovernmental institutions and rules that people create as acts of self-government and as checks on government.

Aristotle came up with a useful way of analyzing and comparing polities (see Bold Thinkers: Why Does Aristotle's Political Philosophy Matter?). According to Aristotle, every polity has a constitution. By *constitution* Aristotle did not mean a single written document. Instead he used *constitution* to describe the composition or makeup of the polity.

Aristotle believed that every polity has three constitutional dimensions: the socioeconomic constitution that includes the classes, communities, and other interests in society and the associations that represent them; the moral constitution that comprises the ethical standards, cultural norms, and political ideals of the polity; and the legal constitution that includes all of a society's laws and governmental institutions. As Table 4.1 illustrates, in today's terms, these three dimensions are similar to a polity's civil society (socioeconomic

Table 4.1 Dimensions of a Polity's Constitution

Aristotle's terms	Today's terms
Socioeconomic constitution	Civil society
Moral constitution	Political culture
Legal constitution	Form of government

dimension), political culture (moral constitution), and form of government (legal constitution).

The **socioeconomic constitution** of a polity includes those social and economic interests that seek to hold government office or influence its policies. Even in a simple agricultural society, these interests are complex. They might include large landowners, middle-class farmers who are self-sufficient, small farmers who border on bankruptcy, farm workers and other laborers, merchants, money lenders, and priests. As society grows, its interests become more specialized, diverse, and institutionalized.

For Aristotle and a long line of political philosophers to the present, the most worrisome political concern is that "the few" (the numerical minority) or "the many" (the numerical majority) may become corrupt, causing their leaders to lose sight of the common good. This concern has the potential to divide a country in a bitter civil war over rival economic and political interests. The main concern of Aristotle and other like-minded theorists is how to ensure a balance of inter-

BOLD THINKERS

Why Does Aristotle's Political Philosophy Matter?

- Aristotle's philosophy of politics is timeless. Some dimensions of Aristotle's political philosophy are peculiar to the ancient Greek world, but Aristotle had a rare gift for practical wisdom and sound judgment that applies today as much as it did in the past.

- Aristotle's political philosophy has been widely used by other philosophers and statesmen throughout history. In particular, it is the starting point for those who subscribe to the constitutionalist approach. Aristotle's principles of balance and moderation provide the baseline for those who seek to follow this approach.

- In general, we can learn from all political philosophers whose thinking brings significant added value to what we seek. As long as a philosopher's thinking lives, it makes little difference whether the philosopher is alive or dead.

ests and a shared commitment to the common good between "the few" and "the many." Such philosophers believe this can be accomplished by civic education and a form of government in which each interest is represented fairly and serves as a political check on the other.

This Aristotelian concern is still relevant today. Consider the 2008–2009 debate in the United States over the Bush bail-out plan vs. the Obama stimulus package (see Politics in Action: The Debate over Bail Outs and Stimulus Incentives).

The socioeconomic constitution is not only about divided interests but also about shared interests. Throughout history, individuals have formed nongovernmental associations as a way of governing their own affairs. These include a long list of secret societies, village and neighborhood associations, veteran organizations, spiritual organizations, mutual-aid societies, charitable organizations, landowner associations, and craft guilds. These organizations dispensed land, settled justice claims, maintained religious shrines, arranged marriages, assisted the needy, and, in these and other ways, provided for an orderly society.[4]

POLITICS IN ACTION
The Debate over Bail Outs and Stimulus Incentives

When major financial institutions began to fail in the summer of 2008, politicians quickly staked out their positions on what should be done. Republicans, who are usually opposed to big government spending programs, advocated a two-part targeted approach. They supported bailing out endangered financial institutions on Wall Street and federal spending for projects that would stimulate the economy. Democrats accused Republicans of bailing out "the few" without helping "the many." The Democrats advanced a stimulus package that included a variety of spending programs to stimulate the economy, assist the needy, and make sure that important elements of the Democratic majority got their fair share of the pie. Republicans accused Democrats of advocating a giveaway program that would do little to stimulate the economy. The Republican plan assumed that helping "the few" would trickle down to "the many"; the Democratic plan assumed that spreading the wealth would help all boats rise.

Until the twentieth century, nongovernmental organizations and local governments were the primary source of assistance to the needy (including widows, orphans, and the disabled). Craft guilds and professional associations trained apprentices, helped people find work, and set professional codes of conduct. Nongovernmental organizations also provided an institutional check against the abuse of government power; in European history, the most powerful check on the power of government came from the Church, the nobility, and local governments.

Shared interests also include the resistance to tyranny in the name of freedom. This is not just a recent phenomenon. The first recorded instance of rebellion and reform occurred over 4,000 years ago in the Mesopotamian city-state of Sumer (see Bold Thinkers: Urukagina, the First Reformer).

The **moral constitution** of a polity consists of the norms that define the good society, its moral purposes, and the roles of its citizens, leaders, and governments. **Norms** are shared beliefs reinforced by rules. They are the basic rules that children learn in their family, school, and friendship networks. Without a shared core of civic norms, people would have no common language to communicate, no expectations of how others might behave, and no standards for distinguishing justice from injustice. Most important, without shared norms there would be no basis for trusting one another. It would be like driving without traffic lights, stop signs, speed limits, and street signs.

Shared norms provide the rules that allow people of diverse interests to drive along the pathways of life without too many collisions. Shared norms also supply the moral virtues that help shape people's civic identity, their moral character, and their vision of the good society. Benjamin Franklin's "List of Moral Virtues" is one such example. Written in 1784, these virtues helped to define what it meant to be an American (see More About . . . Ben Franklin's "List of Moral Virtues"). Do they still?

The **legal constitution** of a polity, also known as its form of government, is the framework of a polity's governmental institutions and fundamental laws. Those laws include constitutions, bills of rights, legal codes, and important court decisions. A polity's form of government is much more than a bundle of institutions. The legal constitution establishes the government and its authority or right to govern, prescribes its first principles and purposes, sets its powers and limits of government, creates public offices and the relations among them, regulates the selection of officeholders, and recognizes certain rights and responsibilities of citizens. In all these ways, Aristotle pointed out, the form of government is a polity's answer to two burning questions: Who governs, and who benefits?

These three constitutional dimensions are interrelated. Aristotle believed that all polities should strive for a **balanced constitution** in which the polity's three constitutions—the socioeconomic, the moral, and the legal—are in balance like the legs of a three-legged stool. In particular, he expected the polity's legal constitution (or form of government) to represent fairly the major interests of the socioeconomic constitution and to uphold the norms of its moral constitution. Aristotle also believed that a balanced constitution could moderate the excesses of rival interests. Aristotle's principles of balance and moderation were certainly influenced by the culture and context of his times. Balance and moderation had profound importance in ancient civilizations that were held together by a belief in social harmony. But, in general terms, the principles of balance and moderation are timeless—they apply as much today as they did in Aristotle's day.

BOLD THINKERS
Urukagina, the First Reformer

Urukagina, the king of Lagash in Sumer, may have been the world's "first reformer," according to the Sumer scholar Samuel Noah Kramer. Urukagina became king around 2350 BCE after the people rebelled against the government in power. That government had become corrupt—it had seized religious property for personal gain, raised taxes to excessive levels, increased the number of tax collectors, doled out government wealth to the rich, and interfered in personal matters such as divorce. But what triggered the revolt was the onerous practice of enslaving those who could not pay their taxes. Urukagina instituted reforms that lowered taxes, freed debtors, returned illegally seized lands, protected property rights, fired many tax collectors, prohibited the use of taxes to enslave debtors, and reformed the courts that had legitimized the corrupt practices. Scribes used the term *amagi* to refer to his reforms. The term literally means "return to the mother." This may have symbolized that people were given their freedom or liberty to return home and reclaim their property.

Samuel Noah Kramer, *The Sumerians: Their History, Culture, and Character* (Chicago: University of Chicago Press, 1963), 79–83. See also Susan Wise Bauer, *The History of the Ancient World: From the Earliest Accounts to the Fall of Rome* (New York: W. W. Norton, 2007), 88–95; Liberty Fund, "Amagi Symbol: Liberty Fund's Logo," available at http://oll.libertyfund.org/?option=com_content&task=view&id=389&Itemid=250.

MORE ABOUT . . .

Benjamin Franklin's "List of Moral Virtues"

1. *Temperance.* Eat not to dullness; drink not to elevation.
2. *Silence.* Speak not but what may benefit others or yourself; avoid trifling conversation.
3. *Order.* Let all your things have their places; let each part of your business have its time.
4. *Resolution.* Resolve to perform what you ought; perform without fail what you resolve.
5. *Frugality.* Make no expense but to do good to others or yourself; i.e., waste nothing.
6. *Industry.* Lose no time; be always employ'd in something useful; cut off all unnecessary actions.
7. *Sincerity.* Use no hurtful deceit; think innocently and justly; and, if you speak, speak accordingly.
8. *Justice.* Wrong none by doing injuries, or omitting the benefits that are your duty.
9. *Moderation.* Avoid extreams; forbear resenting injuries so much as you think they deserve.
10. *Cleanliness.* Tolerate no uncleanliness in body, cloaths, or habitation.
11. *Tranquillity.* Be not disturbed at trifles, or at accidents common or unavoidable.

Benjamin Franklin (1706–1790), in a 1789 painting by Charles Willson Peale.

12. *Chastity.* Rarely use venery but for health or offspring, never to dulness, weakness, or the injury of your own or another's peace or reputation.
13. *Humility.* Imitate Jesus and Socrates.

Louis P. Masur, ed., *The Autobiography of Benjamin Franklin with Related Documents,* 2nd ed. (New York: St. Martin's Press, 2003), 95–96.

WHAT IS GOVERNMENT?

Government is the authoritative, but not the only, governing institution in the polity. The English philosopher Thomas Hobbes (1588–1679) distinguished between governmental laws, which he referred to as "Rules Authorized," and other types of rules. Those other rules include cultural norms, religious commandments, ethical standards, professional codes of conduct (such as the Hippocratic Oath that doctors take), and family pressure.

Government is the institution in society with the authority to make and enforce collective decisions that are binding on society and its members. There are two key elements in this definition: the authority to act and the power to coerce. Without authority, government is a gang of thugs; without coercive power, government is a toothless tiger.

Maintaining a balance among government's authority, power, and legitimacy is one of the most important challenges that all polities face. **Political power** is the ability of governments and their officeholders to govern. Political power also includes the ability of officeholders to influence one another and the ability of citizens to change the positions of those who govern. **Authority** is the legitimate right or power to govern. Throughout history, the sources of such political legitimacy have included divine right, constitutions, and the consent of the governed. **Legitimacy**, then, is the belief that government has the rightful power to govern.

POLITICAL IDEAS IN ACTION
The Supremacy Clause of the U.S. Constitution

This Constitution and the Laws of the United States which shall be made in Pursuance thereof; *and all Treaties made, or which shall be made,* under the Authority of *the United States, shall be the supreme Law of the Land; and the Judges in every State shall be bound thereby, any Thing in the Constitution or Laws of any State to the contrary notwithstanding.*

Emphasis added.

According to the influential German sociologist Max Weber (1864–1920), these three concepts are mutually reinforcing. Government can more easily sustain its authority to govern if it has both power and legitimacy. The level of power a government possesses is important. Governments need enough power to be effective but not so much that they abuse the governed. Weber asserted that governments would not be able to govern effectively until the state possessed "the *monopoly of the legitimate use of physical force* within a given territory." The state, in Weber's words, is "the sole source of the 'right' to use violence," and others may use it only if "the state permits it."[5]

Weber's point about the state control of force, however, is a subject of controversy, not an iron-clad rule. Consider today's issue of gun control. Most European states have stricter gun-control laws than the United States, although there are a few interesting variations. Switzerland still follows the republican principle of a citizen army in which every man is a soldier. Swiss males who receive military training are issued a firearm that they are expected to keep in their home. Liberal gun laws in the Czech Republic allow most people over eighteen to own a gun and to carry a concealed weapon. In the United States, the Supreme Court affirmed the right to own guns as an individual right in *District of Columbia v. Heller* (2008).

In the American debate over gun control, Weber's position would be viewed by many Americans not as one of the ground rules but as one side of the debate—namely, the authority of the state to regulate gun ownership. According to this position, the state has the power to control the means of violence so as to better keep the peace, enforce the law, and protect the people from those who would do them harm. The other side of the debate argues an individual rights position—namely, that every individual has a right to own a gun. This argument rests on one chilling question: Who will protect the people from the danger of government tyranny?

In constitutional societies, a government's authority is not absolute. Government is the authoritative governing institution only (1) on those matters where it has the authority to act and (2) where it acts in a manner that does not exceed that authority. This distinction is made clear in the supremacy clause of the U.S. Constitution (see Political Ideas in Action: The Supremacy Clause of the U.S. Constitution).

The U.S. Constitution is unconditionally the supreme law of the land. Federal laws become supreme law only if they are "made in Pursuance [of]" the Constitution. This means that federal law cannot grant authority that exceeds the constitutional powers of the federal government. It also means that federal laws cannot violate constitutional principles (such as due process) in their passage or enforcement.

The last part of the supremacy clause serves as a reminder that the question of federal supremacy is not an idle debate. It becomes real when a particular state law is challenged in court on the grounds that it conflicts with a particular federal law. In the event of such a challenge in a state court, the state court's judge or judges are bound by the same standards as federal judges.[6]

This may seem like splitting hairs, but governments gain their legitimacy on the basis of some higher law—some ultimate source of authority. In ancient China, for example, emperors were counseled to obey the "mandate of heaven" and part of that mandate was to listen to the people. In the United States, governments' powers are bound by their constitutional authority to act and the consent of the governed (see More About . . . Government Powers Defined).

WHY IS GOVERNANCE A CENTRAL FUNCTION OF SOCIETY?

Decision making is at the heart of governing. The verb to *govern* has ancient roots. It comes from the Latin verb *gubernare*, which means "to steer." **Governance** consists of three parts:

(1) the process and rules by which societies govern themselves, (2) the outcomes of the public decisions they make, and (3) the system of governing institutions.

The process part of this definition is concerned with the rules of the game—the constitutional rules, including due process, justice, and the rule of law that govern the decision-making process. In the process portion, the issues have to do with how polities make, enforce, and adapt cultural norms and government laws. Proceduralists (those who focus on the process of governance) are often concerned with the question of legitimacy: Does government abide by the cultural norms and constitutional rules that legitimate its actions?

The outcome part of the governance definition focuses on the public decisions made and goals achieved. Public decisions are decisions made by governing institutions that affect the polity as a whole or a significant part of it. Outcome issues have to do with governability: Do governments and other governing institutions make and effectively implement wise decisions?

The system part of governance is concerned with the responsibilities of nongovernmental and governmental institutions. As a system, governance raises the issue of balance: What are the governing responsibilities of the institutions that make up a polity's system of governance? Are those roles, powers, and responsibilities compatible with one another? Do they represent the socioeconomic, moral, and legal constitution of the polity? Have they been subverted by a government that is too powerful or too weak?

Governance, then, consists of the decision-making process, the rules governing that process, the public decisions made, and the overall system of governing institutions. These factors determine whether a polity succeeds or fails. That is why governing is a central function of society.

Jared Diamond, an award-winning geographer, physiologist, and evolutionary biologist, is among the most recent in a long line of scientists who have underscored the importance of decision making. Diamond traveled the globe in search of the reasons why some societies succeed and others fail, and compared societies from prehistoric times to the present.

Diamond's conclusion is reflected in the title of his book, *Collapse: How Societies Choose to Fail or Succeed.* According to Diamond, societies succeed or fail because of the choices they make. Having weaker neighbors increases the chances of success, as do a bountiful and well-managed environment and a bit of good luck. But time and again Diamond found that no amount of bounty or luck could rescue a society that was poorly governed—that made one too many bad decisions or failed to make decisions and adapt to new circumstances when needed.[7]

A well-governed society depends in the first instance on the extent to which its citizens can control their own behavior. History teaches that the government must also be able to control human behavior when it runs afoul of the law. Imagine a highway system during rush hour, when major highways are filled with cars, trucks, and buses hurtling toward their destination at speeds well in excess of 50 miles per hour. What keeps this scene from total chaos? Is it the speed limit that government sets, the police who enforce the speed limit, or the willingness of most drivers to drive responsibly? Clearly, the right answer is "all of the above."

POLITICS IN ACTION
Dictatorship or Destruction?

What happens when a dire situation arises that was not anticipated by existing law? The U.S. president has emergency powers that are derived from the U.S. Constitution and limited by Congress. But these powers are not to be treated lightly. Consider Thomas Jefferson's response to the use of emergency powers in his letter to John B. Colvin, written September 20, 1810:

The question you propose, whether circumstances do not sometimes occur, which make it a duty in officers of high trust, to assume authorities beyond the law, is easy of solution in principle, but sometimes embarrassing in practice. A strict observance of the written laws is doubtless one of the high duties of a good citizen, but it is not the highest. The laws of necessity, of self-preservation, of saving our country when in danger, are of higher obligation. To lose our country by a scrupulous adherence to written law, would be to lose the law itself, with life, liberty, property and all those who are enjoying them with us; thus absurdly sacrificing the end to the means.

Quoted in Philip B. Kurland and Ralph Lerner, eds., *The Founders' Constitution* (Chicago: University of Chicago Press, 1986), Vol. 4, article 2, section 3, doc. 8, available at http://press-pubs.uchicago.edu/founders/documents/a2_3s8.html.

Constitutionality and governability should not be either-or alternatives. The political question is how best to balance energetic government in the name of governability and efficiency, on one hand, with limited government in the name of constitutionality and freedom on the other. National emergencies can challenge that delicate balance (see Politics in Action: Dictatorship or Destruction?).

In an ideal world, governments should have the authority to govern, they should govern constitutionally, government leaders should make wise decisions, and adequate space should be provided for other governing institutions. In the real world, polities, like other human systems, have varying degrees of success. Some succeed, some fail, and others fall somewhere in between. Table 4.2 distinguishes four possibilities: (1) viable polities, in which governments have both the power and authority to govern; (2) weak polities, in which governments have the authority but not the power to govern, with no alternative governing institutions; (3) authoritarian states, in which governments have the power but not the authority to govern; and (4) failed states, in which governments and other governing institutions have lost both the ability and right to govern.

Table 4.2 Four Conditions of Governance around the World

	Governable societies	Ungovernable societies
Constitutional government	Viable polities	Weak polities
Illegitimate government	Authoritarian states	Failed states

HOW DO POLITIES AND THEIR GOVERNMENTS COME INTO EXISTENCE?

Early human society developed over tens of thousands of years. During much of that time, societies were organized on the basis of family ties. They grew from biological families to extended families to clans. Only recently, beginning around 13,000 years ago, did societies begin to self-consciously organize themselves as polities, first as tribes and then as states. To piece together why polities came into existence, we need to take a closer look at these four stages of societal development: the extended family, the clan, the tribe, and the state.[8]

An **extended family** is a biological outgrowth of the nuclear family and often includes grandparents, aunts, uncles, cousins, spouses of children, in-laws, nieces, and nephews. A **clan** consists of a number of extended families whose members are directly related to one another. Historically, the clan was formed by biological ties and bound together by kinship (family) ties. Family members joined forces because of the natural instinct for self-preservation and the natural affinity among blood relatives. The population of a clan grew to dozens of members. In even the largest clans, clan members knew one another and were direct blood relatives. Scholars believe that many clans made decisions through open community discussion and consensus, relying on the advice of elders. In some instances, a strong leader dominated the clan.

As clans grew in size, they formed tribes. A **tribe** is a society composed of multiple clans that are *not* blood relatives but that claim a common ancestry. In some instances, tribes were created by conquest, and conquered clans had little choice in the matter. In other instances, the definition of a *tribe* suggests a peaceful process in which clan leaders made a self-conscious decision to come together. Even if a single chief governed a clan, a decision of this magnitude required the approval of the clan elders and some kind of consent of the adult members of the clan. Without that approval process, the legitimacy of the leader's decisions would have been suspect.

The tribe was the first stage of human society that organized itself self-consciously as a polity. Peacefully created tribes organized themselves as a loose confederation of clans. People's primary identity and loyalty were to their clans. Elders met in clan councils, and those councils resolved most issues within the clan. Clan leaders also formed tribal councils consisting of elders and the strong men from different clans.

Initially, clan and tribal councils were unstructured institutions that met when necessary. Over time, these tribal and clan councils took on institutional form and a clearer division of responsibilities. In addition, other, more specialized councils and leaders emerged to oversee war, trade, worship, and building projects. In some tribes these leaders became ruling chiefs, while in other tribes the councils retained authority and delegated power to lesser chiefs to administer the council's decisions. But there was no conception as yet of different sets of governmental and nongovernmental institutions, nor of executive, legislative, or judicial branches. Councils were an integral part of the polity.

The process of tribal organization did not happen overnight, of course. It took thousands of years. In the Fertile Crescent area of Mesopotamia, for example, tribal societies first appeared around 11000 BCE. Villages arose 2,000 years later, around 9000 BCE, followed by plant and animal domestication 500–1,000 years later. It was not until roughly 5500 BCE that tribes in Mesopotamia organized themselves more formally as (1) centralized **chiefdoms** ruled by a chief with the advice of a council or (2) **conciliar republics** governed by a structured tribal council system.[9]

A **state**, as studies of societal development use the term, is a stage of development in which large organized tribes combined and reestablished themselves primarily on the basis of political and territorial ties, not kinship ties. Although tribes gradually developed some form of government, the state is usually the first stage of development in which rulers and citizenry established a formal and structured system of government composed of specialized institutions with enumerated purposes, powers, and limits. In Mesopotamia, this process, known as state formation, began around 3700 BCE.

The state-formation process took time; a complete system of government did not spring forth at once. State formation is easier to chronicle than the earlier stages of development because it usually coincided with the development of writing and with royal scribes who wrote down laws and records and carefully maintained them in a secure place. Part of this process was the codification of laws in which scribes were instructed to collect existing laws and record them as one code. The code of the Babylonian King Hammurabi, written around 1760 BCE, is one famous example (see More About . . . Hammurabi's Code).

State formation continued the process of specialization that began in the late tribal stage of chiefdoms and conciliar republics. According to Diamond and others, the formation of specialized institutions was a response to rapid increases in population size. States were formed out of tribes that had grown in population to 50,000 people or more.

As population size increased, so too did the people's collective needs for food, water, shelter, fuel, an orderly life, a sense of community, and human betterment. Some traditional institutions were no longer up to the task; new institutions arose to fill the gap. People with an entrepreneurial spirit began to trade goods within the polity and abroad. Craftsmen saw opportunities to fashion tools, build homes, and produce weapons.

Development also produced new challenges. As people began to specialize, their ability to trade goods and services also increased. Increased trade, however, created new issues. Who would set a uniform system of weights and measures so that merchants, producers, and consumers knew what they were selling or buying? And who would resolve conflicts over the fair value of traded goods and services?

As a society's population grew, the problems and dangers increased. In a polity of tens of thousands, people no longer knew everyone or claimed everyone as a relative. "For the first time in history," as Diamond explained, people had to learn "how to encounter strangers regularly without attempting to kill them."[10] Many disputes crossed clan and tribal boundaries, which meant there was no well-established way of dealing with them. Examples included thefts, insults, murders, stray animals, and the wandering eyes of young people from different tribes. Who would resolve these conflicts and on what basis?

MORE ABOUT . . .
Hammurabi's Code

Hammurabi, a Babylonian ruler during the nineteenth century BCE, was a diplomat and conqueror. He is perhaps best known today for the code of laws that bears his name. Hammurabi's Code consolidated many tribal traditions and laws into one set of laws. Its 282 entries represent the most famous attempt to collect and publish laws on a range of criminal and civil topics such as stealing, negligence, murder, marriage, slavery, and contracts.

Although the topics of Hammurabi's Code are similar to today's laws, key distinctions remain. For example, Hammurabi's code is based on the concept of retributive justice, or *lex taliones* (law of retaliation). That concept is contained in Articles 196 and 200:

If a man put out the eye of another man, his eye shall be put out.

If a man knock out the teeth of his equal, his teeth shall be knocked out.

Another important difference between this ancient code and modern laws is the reference in Article 200 to "his equal." Equal justice was not "for all" but for people within certain social strata. Hammurabi's Code distinguished between people based on social class, gender, and their status as slaves or freemen. In this social context, equal justice meant that all people in a particular stratum should be treated equally. Articles 205 and 209 declare:

If the slave of a freed man strike the body of a freed man, his ear shall be cut off.

Hammurabi's Code is carved on a black basalt pillar. On the top of the pillar, King Hammurabi stands in front of a seated divinity and raises his right hand in a gesture of devotion.

If a man strike a free-born woman so that she lose her unborn child, he shall pay ten shekels for her loss.

"Hammurabi's Code of Laws (c. 1780 BCE)," trans. L. W. King, *Internet Ancient History Sourcebook*, Fordham University, available at www .fordham.edu/halsall/ancient/hamcode.html.

MORE ABOUT . . .

The Stele and the Law

A stele (plural, stelae) is a column made of wood or stone that is inscribed with a message and often decorated with artwork. In ancient civilizations in Europe, Asia, and the Americas, stelae were a form of public announcement that served various purposes. They were most commonly used to commemorate an event, mark a funeral site, or post the ruler's laws and decrees. The famous Rosetta Stone is an ancient Egyptian stele. Its message is written in several languages; this gave archeologists and linguists a unique opportunity to decipher hieroglyphic writing. Hammurabi's Stele was made of a hard black stone that has survived the centuries.

This Mayan stele of a high priest still stands in the jungle at Quirigua National Park in Guatamala.

The stele represented an important development in the law. By publicizing the law, stelae held the ruler and the people accountable for their actions. Laws written on stelae strengthened the ruler. It was the ruler, not the people, who made the law, and it was the ruler's soldiers and bureaucrats who enforced the law.

Centralized chiefdoms and kingdoms seized the opportunity to strengthen government and their power. In early republican societies, these issues were resolved by a mix of institutions that included not only state institutions but merchant associations, craft guilds, and arbitrators from different clans. Whether royal or republican, the purposes of the polity and its governments increased, and this in turn expanded the role of governmental and nongovernmental institutions in society and in the daily lives of the people.

Somewhere in the transition from tribe to state, society changed from a land of family and neighbors to a land of strangers.[11] The basis of trust also had to quickly change. Government, laws, order, and justice could no longer rely on an informal system in which everyone knew whom to trust, what to expect, and who was in charge. This was one of the practical reasons why law and government became more formalized. A uniform system of written laws, enforced by police and decided by professional judges, was now essential in a large and complex society where most people no longer knew one another.

As part of this process of state formation, polities and their governments also instituted measures to redirect the people's identity and loyalty from their tribe to the state. State citizenship was formalized, military conscription was instituted, and, sooner rather than later, government put in place a system of taxation enforced by the infamous tax collector. The state also instituted the census to track people for the purposes of taxation and military service. Kings carved their decrees into *stelae* (stone or wooden columns) that were posted around the country so that all could see the new laws (see More About . . . The Stele and the Law).

WHAT ARE THE PURPOSES OF POLITIES AND GOVERNMENTS?

People create polities and governments to satisfy three sets of human needs: the preservation of life, the protection of freedom, and human betterment. These three sets of needs correspond roughly to "life, liberty, and the pursuit of happiness," famously proclaimed in the U.S. Declaration of Independence. They also correspond to declarations dating back thousands of years.

These needs are universal human instincts, and the purposes of polities and governments are derived from these needs. So, too, is one measure of the legitimacy of government policies. People expect government to help meet the generally accepted needs of society within the limits that are imposed on government. Illegitimate governments—ones that use coercion or force as the basis of their power—serve the interests of those in power at the expense of others in society. Of course, countries differ in their expectations of government for various reasons, including cultural preferences and prohibitions. Cultures emphasizing community, for example, value freedom differently than cultures centered on the individual.

Aristotle was the first political philosopher to present these three human needs and connect them to the purposes of polities and governments. These connections, however, are not limited to the world of political philosophy. Recently, neuroscientists have distinguished similar human instincts, which they call the survival instinct, the social instinct, and the acquisitive and moral instincts for human betterment.[12]

The remainder of this section explores this relationship between these human needs and the purposes of polities and governments. Table 4.3 provides an outline of those purposes. To apply this list to a particular country, researchers might begin by consulting the preamble of that country's constitution or code (see Comparing Governments: Comparing Purposes

Table 4.3 Purposes of Polities and Governments

A. Preserve life
  1. Ensure basic subsistence
  2. Provide for the common defense
  3. Ensure domestic tranquility and public safety

B. Protect freedom
  1. Secure political freedom
  2. Protect property

C. Promote human betterment
  1. Advance material improvement
  2. Promote ethical and spiritual improvement

COMPARING GOVERNMENTS

Comparing Purposes of Government

Declarations of independence create polities; constitutions frame their governments. Both can provide important clues about the purposes of a particular government. The search for these clues often begins with the opening paragraphs, or preamble, of a country's declaration or constitution.

Preambles can be flowery, but this does not mean they are false. Beneath the hyperbole, we can often find important clues about the history and culture of a country and about the purposes of its government. Declarations of independence and constitutions are often colored by the context in which they were written.

For example, Japan's Constitution of 1946, written under the supervision of the Allied countries, stressed peace. Japan's constitution instructed its new representative government to "secure for ourselves and our posterity the fruits of peaceful cooperation with all nations and the blessings of liberty all over this land, and resolved that never again shall we be visited with the horrors of war through the action of government." Germany's Basic Law of 1949, written in a similar context, expresses a similar commitment, specifically "to serve world peace as an equal partner in a united Europe."

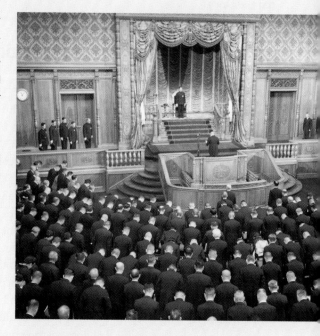

A general view of the Chamber of Peers at the Diet Building (the legislature) in Tokyo, during the ceremony at which Emperor Hirohito (higher dais) promulgated the 1946 constitution of Japan. On the lower dais, Prime Minister Shigeru Yoshida has turned to face the emperor, whose message set forth an organic law proclaiming the sovereignty of the people and renouncing forever the maintenance of armed force in Japan.

of Government). The categories in Table 4.3 correspond with the Preamble of the U.S. Constitution, but the ideas are of broader application. The earliest example is in the prologue of the Code of King Lipit-Ishtar (c. 1860 BCE), which provides that the king was called by the gods Anu and Enlil to rule the land "in order to establish justice in the land, to banish complaints, to turn back enmity and rebellion by force of arms, and to bring well-being to the Sumerians and Akkadians."[13]

PRESERVE LIFE

ENSURE BASIC SUBSISTENCE. *Subsistence needs* are the minimal requirements needed to sustain human life. These requirements include an adequate and sustained supply of food, water, air, shelter, and fuel.

Throughout history, most polities have relied primarily on households and markets to meet the basic necessities of human life. Before economies diversified, households produced their own food, found water, built shelters, and maintained their own fires. As societies grew and economies became more complex, some households continued to farm while others supplied more specialized services, becoming carpenters, miners, soldiers, merchants, and the like.

Markets made it possible to exchange private goods, and cooperative associations often arose to pool common resources. Examples of cooperative projects included irrigation projects, pasture management, mining, and forest harvesting. Governments played a role by building and maintaining large public works projects (such as irrigation projects) and public facilities (such as roads, food storage warehouses, and water reservoirs). Where powerful kings ruled, they often took the initiative and imposed forced labor on the people to build massive public works in the name of the state.

PROVIDE FOR THE COMMON DEFENSE. Polities need to be prepared to defend themselves against external threats.

Tribal polities tended to rely on militias for defense. These were citizen armies organized by clans and called into service when danger threatened. As part of the state-formation process, monarchies and empires turned to standing armies of professional full-time soldiers who remained mobilized for action. Many republics continued to rely on the citizen soldier long after they became states.

Today, war remains a reality. Its forms vary from conventional warfare to international terrorism and the ever-present danger that either can escalate to the use of weapons of mass destruction. Between 1945 and 2003, an estimated 25–30 million people worldwide died due to war-related violence, famine, or disease.[14]

Beyond war, other external threats call for national and international defense. These dangers include the international drug trade, nuclear proliferation, conventional arms sales, human trafficking, the spread of infectious diseases, and toxic spills. To be sure, governments around the world must be ever vigilant and prepared to combat such threats effectively. But so too must the individual—as a responsible consumer, employee, owner, and investor.

ENSURE DOMESTIC TRANQUILITY AND PUBLIC SAFETY. In most societies, the most immediate and visible purpose of government is the maintenance of an orderly and peaceful society. No human need has generated more cultural norms and government laws.

People need a sense of certainty and security in their lives. They need to know that their actions and the actions of others have predictable social and legal consequences. Since ancient times, laws and norms have served this purpose by regulating the type of behavior expected in an orderly society of law-abiding citizens.

To establish an orderly society, polities have relied on four types of laws: (1) criminal laws that set punishments for crimes against individuals (for example, murder), property (for example, theft), and the polity (for example, treason); (2) civil laws that establish property ownership and set responsibilities for compensating damages to someone's property; (3) contract laws that govern human relationships (in business, loans, marriage, divorce,

MORE ABOUT . . .

Juvenile Violence in Latin America

According to a World Health Organization study, the group most targeted for violence in the world today is the youth of Latin America. Youth ages ten to nineteen are the victims of nearly one out of every three homicides in Latin America. Many of these homicides are a result of gang-related acts of youth violence against other youth.[1] Youth gangs run rampant in countries such as El Salvador, Guatemala, Brazil, and Honduras. Governments in these countries have attempted to control these organizations through the use of the military. But using military force for police protection carries its own risks; for example, detention procedures used by military forces have resulted in numerous human rights violations.

One of the most infamous examples of police abuse in Latin America is known as the Candelaria Massacre (1993) in Rio de Janeiro, Brazil. Scores of street children, many involved in the illegal drug trade or prostitution, gathered daily at Candelaria, a Roman Catholic Church that provided food, education, and ministry to as many children as possible. On the night of July 23, 1993, a group of men shot into a crowd of seventy children—many in makeshift beds—who had gathered outside the church. Eight children (ages eleven to twenty) died and several others were wounded. Three military police officers were charged in the killings, but only one was convicted. According to one study, of the sixty-two survivors of the massacre, as many as thirty-nine have since died as a result of their life on the streets. One survivor, Sandro Do Nascimento, hijacked a bus in a botched robbery attempt in 2000, which became one of Brazil's most notorious crimes and the subject of the documentary *Bus 174*.

---

1. Paulo Sérgio Pinheiro, "Youth, Violence, and Democracy," *Current History* 106 (February 2007): 64.

---

inheritance, and so on); and (4) legal procedures for resolving disputes. Ancient codes began consolidating these types of laws over 4,000 years ago. Among the earliest examples are Hammurabi's Code and the Hebrew Bible. They each contain hundreds of laws regulating human relationships that were most likely to erupt in conflict, endanger life and property, threaten the public order, or violate God's law (see More About . . . Hammurabi's Code, page 67).

The earliest form of enforcement fell to tribal judges who decided cases and enforced their decisions. They also were responsible for the general maintenance of law and order. When states were created, they established courts and a law enforcement bureaucracy that included police and tax collectors.

Still, not all polities succeed. Today, many countries are beset by persistent civil disorder and violence that eludes control. Such was the case for decades in Colombia, which was overwhelmed by some of the world's highest rates of homicide, kidnapping, extortion, and drug trafficking committed by left-wing guerilla forces, right-wing paramilitary forces, and drug cartels. Elsewhere in Latin America, juvenile gang-related violence is out of control (see More About . . . Juvenile Violence in Latin America). Other countries have witnessed a complete breakdown of the state and society. Somalia, for example, degenerated in the 1990s into anarchy amid ongoing battles between Islamist militias and warlords.

POLITICS IN ACTION
Political Protests in China

The largest and fastest-growing protests in the world today are in China. Over a ten-year period, the official number of protests, riots, and demonstrations—officially recorded as "mass incidents" by Chinese authorities—increased from 10,000 in 1994 to 74,000 in 2004. Some say the actual figures are twice this. It is not uncommon for over 100,000 people to turn out for protests. Reasons for protests include factory workers objecting to poor working conditions, peasants opposing the seizure of land for development, and apartment dwellers protesting rent hikes.[1]

Family members of a man who neighbors said was killed by authorities grieve on the streets of Dongzhou village near Shanwei, Guangdong province, Monday, December 12, 2005. The man was killed at a protest where villagers were protesting the seizure of land for construction of a power plant.

An important arena of organized protest in China is the university. In many developing countries, the university is one of the best places to organize meetings. Young people, especially high school and university students, often serve on the front lines of social movements and protests throughout the world. In addition to providing a natural meeting place, universities provide resources to spread the word, such as copy machines, fax machines, and Internet access.

The Internet has opened another avenue of political protest in China. However, the Chinese government has retaliated. It has blocked access to Web sites with certain keywords and to information that the government considers subversive. The government requires service providers such as Yahoo to pledge to abide by state regulations. These powerful filters and regulations limit the use of the Internet by Chinese protesters.

---

1. Gordon G. Chang, "China in Revolt," *Commentary* (December 2006): 32.

PROTECT FREEDOM

SECURE POLITICAL FREEDOM. Freedom, like order, is a human instinct that can be traced back thousands of years. The earliest record of political revolution in the name of freedom dates to the reign of Urukagina over 4,350 years ago (see Bold Thinkers: Urukagina, the First Reformer, page 59). This is not the only ancient example. The ancient Spartans, Athenians, and Israelites all overthrew tyrannical rulers and selected new leaders to reform the laws.

Moreover, in all these cases, revolution was not meant to establish freedom as a new idea but to restore it as an old tradition. Less successful politically, but no less apparent, is the ancient tradition of revolution and protest in China. Today, China has the largest and fastest-growing incidence of protest in the world (see Politics in Action: Political Protests in China).

Until the modern era, freedom was understood primarily in collective terms, not as an individual right. The individual belonged by birth to an assigned category or class of people (for example, the general citizenry, the priestly class, nobility, or slaves). Each class had a particular status in the larger community and a role in maintaining an orderly society. The duties of a particular class flowed from its status and role in society. From those duties flowed the rights and privileges of its members.

How then did government protect freedom? First and foremost, government organized the common defense whenever the polity and its freedom were threatened by foreign invasion. Second, the law legitimized and enforced the equalities and inequalities of the society. The law recognized the special rights of each class and the inequalities between classes. At the same time, the law made sure that all individuals within a class received equal legal treatment. Grounds for revolution existed if the government suppressed the existing rights of one class over those of another, favored a particular class at the expense of the existing rights of other classes, or decided cases unfairly within a class by favoring those who paid bribes over others in the same class.

PROTECT PROPERTY. Private property is as old as recorded history. In fact, the earliest artifacts discovered in ancient Mesopotamian societies were clay stamps that people used to identify their property. The protection of private property was one of the first purposes of government. This purpose is most evident in the laws that criminalized property theft and the wanton destruction of private property.

The overwhelming majority of laws in Hammurabi's Code and other ancient codes dealt with crimes against property and civil claims for property damage. Hammurabi's Code protected private gardens, orchards, crops, fences, livestock, homes, and boat rentals, among other kinds of property. Hammurabi's Code also included laws that punished those who failed to live up to the obligations of maintaining their property, such as planting in season and keeping their dams in good condition. Other laws excused late payments on loans because of an act of nature, such as bad weather that destroyed a harvest.[15]

PROMOTE HUMAN BETTERMENT

Human betterment includes the material and spiritual advancement of the polity and its people. The English philosopher Adam Smith (1723–1790) described this as the "great purpose of human life which we call bettering our condition."[16]

The idea of human betterment has a venerable and varied history. Nearly 4,000 years ago, King Lipit-Ishtar promised to "bring well-being" to his people. The ancient Greeks believed that the purpose of the polity was not only to ensure life but to advance "the good life" of the citizenry and the common good of the polity. In 1776, the U.S. Declaration of Independence proclaimed "the pursuit of happiness" as a right that government is instituted to secure. A decade later, the Preamble of the U.S. Constitution listed among government's purposes the promotion of "the general welfare."

Early Christian societies divided the responsibilities of church and state, insisting that the state should stick to the material world and leave spiritual advancement to the church. Fatalistic societies believe that human life is predetermined and governments can do little to change destiny. But common to all societies is the idea that a better life must have meaning for both society as a whole and its members. Individualistic societies point to the cumulative benefits of individual achievements. Community-oriented societies believe individuals should benefit from the common good. Most societies also accepted the idea that human betterment had two dimensions: material advancement and ethical or spiritual improvement. In most societies, these two dimensions were seen as complementary, not competitive.

ADVANCE MATERIAL IMPROVEMENT. As polities grew and diversified, acquiring property became a way to escape mere subsistence. Successful farmers acquired more land so they could increase their harvest beyond subsistence levels and use their crop surplus to purchase more property. Merchants traded surplus resources for scarce resources, thereby satisfying public needs and increasing their wealth.

Even in the ancient world, centralized states took an active role in economic development. The Mesopotamian kingdom of Sumer is a well-documented example. The king's scribes laid the groundwork for a common market. They developed a uniform system of weights and measures, and they played an important role in the development of a written language. They also notarized (certified) property ownership and agreements.

The Sumerian kings instituted a system of taxation that was used for both good and ill. Kings used their tax revenues to increase the state bureaucracy, enlarge the army, and help the poor. The revenues were also used to construct and repair state buildings, temples and shrines, irrigation projects, and roads.

The state established a "storage redistributive" system, where the king's scribes and accountants recorded everyone's harvest so that a portion could be stored and reallocated in times of hardship and famine.[17] Another portion of the surplus was given to merchants, who traded the crops in foreign markets for needed resources such as wood and stone. The king's scribes and accountants used the uniform standards of weights and measures to assess everyone's harvest and the writing system to keep records in case of later disputes. The government established a similar arrangement for irrigation and the distribution of surplus water.[18]

In less centralized societies, such as ancient Athens, government had a far narrower economic purpose. There was no large government bureaucracy. Taxing the citizenry was considered inappropriate except in emergencies; instead, revenues were collected by taxing colonies. On the spending side, wealthy nobility, not the government, financed much of the city's public works. Wealthy patrons paid for the construction of public buildings such as temples and grain storehouses; they also paid for public theatre, sculpture, and even naval ships.

PROMOTE ETHICAL AND SPIRITUAL IMPROVEMENT. In addition to self-preservation and material enrichment, polities also are created for moral purposes. Some societies define a better life primarily in terms of the liberty of individuals to pursue their own interests; others cast human betterment in terms of civic virtue and the obligation of individuals to contribute in some way to the advancement of society. Still others define a better life in spiritual terms as prescribed by divine law and interpreted by clerics.

How societies define a "good life" has implications for the purposes of their government and the polity. In theocratic societies, for example, divine law defines the state, prescribes the purposes of government, and serves as the basis of all civil and criminal laws.

The civil constitution of the Kingdom of Saudi Arabia, for example, proclaims in Article I that "the Kingdom of Saudi Arabia is a sovereign Arab Islamic state with Islam as its religion; God's Book and the Sunnah [teachings] of His Prophet, God's prayers and peace be upon him, are its constitution. . . ." The Saudi government derives its powers from the Koran and uses those powers to strengthen the family, maintain Arab and Islamic values, provide public education that instills the Islamic faith, collect an alms tax for the needy, protect Islam, implement its laws, order the people to do right and shun evil, construct and maintain holy places, protect those who come for pilgrimage, protect human rights in accord with Islamic law, and maintain the armed forces for the defense of the Islamic religion and its holy places (Articles 7–30).

WHY IS JUSTICE A UNIVERSAL STANDARD?

Philosophers generally agree that justice is the ultimate standard to which all government decisions must be held accountable. For Confucius, justice was righteousness and therefore of the highest importance. Aristotle saw justice as "the [moral] good in the sphere of politics." The Islamic Koran teaches that being just brings one closer to piety. Reverend Martin Luther King Jr. (1929–1968) defined justice as moral rightness. James Madison put it succinctly in *The Federalist* No. 51: "Justice is the end of government. It is the end of civil society."[19]

Aristotle explained the connection between moral rightness and justice. He believed that human beings have an instinctive ability to make moral judgments. This moral instinct enables people to distinguish the difference between right and wrong and, in the political world, to distinguish justice from injustice. This moral instinct, Aristotle emphasized, sets the standard of good government. Government should make just decisions and act justly in carrying out those decisions.

The source of justice is moral law, not human law. Justice stands above human law. For this reason, governments cannot create justice because it already exists. It is the responsibility of good government to establish justice and live by it. As Reverend King explained, "A just law is a man-made code that squares with the moral law or the law of God. An unjust law is a code that is out of harmony with the moral law. . . . Any law that uplifts human personality is just. Any law that degrades human personality is unfair." Segregation laws, explained King, are

BOLD THINKERS

Letter from a Birmingham Jail, 1963

In spring 1963, Reverend Martin Luther King Jr. went to Birmingham, Alabama, to support a civil rights demonstration organized by Reverend Fred Shuttlesworth. Dr. King was arrested and jailed. From his jail cell, he wrote his "Letter from a Birmingham Jail." In this eloquent and moving letter, King explains the differences between justice and injustice, shows why segregation laws are unjust, defends civil disobedience and nonviolent direct action as necessary, chastises his fellow clergymen and white moderates who accuse him of extremism, and distinguishes his campaign of extremism in the name of love and justice from the extremism of the Black Muslim campaign of hate and power. Throughout his letter, King roots the claims of the civil rights movement in the Christian tradition of natural law.

In this 1967 photograph, Martin Luther King Jr. sits in a jail cell at the Jefferson County Courthouse in Birmingham, Alabama.

inherently unjust because "segregation distorts the soul."[20] It is unjust to treat equals unequally (see Bold Thinkers: Letter from a Birmingham Jail, 1963).

Justice is the idea that people who are in like situations should be assigned something of fair value and treated fairly in the process. In this definition, fairness is governed by two principles. The first is a special principle of equality called commensurateness—two or more people in like situations should receive similar things (rewards or punishments). For example, students taking the same examination in the same class should be graded similarly for similar work. The second principle is moderation, also known as "the golden mean"—the value or severity of the thing assigned should be reasonably related to the action committed. That is, no one should receive too much more or less than he or she deserves. For example, failing a classroom examination is not sufficient cause for flogging.

Justice is one of those ideas that seems reasonable in theory but raises thorny issues in practice. On what basis should similarities be assigned under the law? When does killing another human being become murder? Should similar sentences be handed down for all murders? If not, what circumstances should be considered mitigating? Who should be eligible for government assistance? How should assistance be assigned to dissimilar needs (for example, of the disabled, widows, and dependent children)? Who should decide who gets what, when, and why?

The definition of *justice* and the issues raised point toward two basic types of justice: substantive justice and procedural justice.[21] **Substantive justice** is the idea that people in like situations should be assigned similar things. To treat two unequal things as equal or to treat two equal things as unequal is, according to Aristotle, inherently unjust.[22]

Yet every law discriminates. Consider a law requiring all people younger than sixteen years old to wear a helmet when riding a bicycle. Why is the age limit fixed at sixteen, not fifteen or seventeen? Why set an age limit at all? Why only bicycles—what about monocycles or tricycles? If this helmet law were on trial, what criteria would be used to decide whether it is an unjust law?

Lady Justice.

Unjust laws are arbitrary. They discriminate capriciously, not on the basis of reason. Another criterion of unjust laws is the abuse of power. As Reverend King explained, a law is unjust when it favors those in power and discriminates against those out of power.[23]

Procedural justice is the idea that people should be treated fairly in the administration of laws. Fair treatment means that the law must be enforced consistently based on reasonable rules that have been made public. Moreover, no one is above these rules. Just laws should be carried out in a manner that is not arbitrary or capricious. As Reverend King put it,

"*Sometimes a law is just on its face and unjust in its application. For instance, I have been arrested on a charge of parading without a permit. Now, there is nothing wrong in having an ordinance which requires a permit for a parade. But such an ordinance becomes unjust when it is used to maintain segregation and to deny citizens the First-Amendment privilege of peaceful assembly and protest.*"[24]

Finally, disputes involving the law must be decided fairly. Since ancient times, the image of Lady Justice has symbolized this principle of procedural justice. She is shown with three weapons to combat injustice. In one hand, she holds the scales of justice, which allow her to deliberate or weigh arguments fairly. In her other hand, she holds a double-edge sword, which represents the power of the law to cut both ways and for whichever side is in the right. She also wears a blindfold, which keeps her from being influenced by one side or another by the color of their money or the color of their skin.

Lady Justice is also a reminder that justice is not automatic. Standards, principles, and rules are not self-executing. They are applied by lawmakers and judges to particular situations. This requires good judgment, which in turn requires practical wisdom. Some cultures tolerate judicial discretion more than others. But there would be no need for judges in a world where rules were so detailed that any judicial deviation was unacceptable.

REVIEWING AND USING THE CHAPTER

1. Aristotle's method of comparing and analyzing polities remains relevant today. Provide specific examples of the socioeconomic, moral, and legal constitutions in the United States today.

2. What is the relationship among power, authority, and legitimacy? What happens when a government is missing one of these elements?

3. What is the difference between governing and government?

4. How did governments develop? In what ways are the original purposes of government similar to the purposes of government today? In what ways are they different?

5. At times, the purposes of government identified in this chapter are in conflict with one another. Identify and describe a current issue that illustrates this conflict. In your judgment, how should this conflict be resolved?

6. What is justice, and how is it used by philosophers to judge and evaluate the performance of government?

EXTENSION ACTIVITY

What are the purposes of government listed in your state constitution? Where in that document are they to be found? Compare these purposes with those expressed in the constitution of another state or country.

WEB RESOURCES

Cato on Campus
www.catooncampus.org

Created by the Cato Institute, one of the leading public policy research foundations, Cato on Campus is an online student resource that provides videos, audios, and publications from leading scholars about the purposes of government and their relationship to current issues as well as links to compelling resources on the Internet.

Stanford Encyclopedia of Philosophy: Entry on Aristotle
http://plato.stanford.edu/entries/aristotle-politics

From one of the leading philosophy-oriented Web sites, this entry on Aristotle provides a clear, concise overview of

Aristotle's contributions to political philosophy, a glossary of Aristotelian terms, and a bibliography.

This Nation
www.thisnation.com

Focusing on the creation, purposes, and institutions of American government, This Nation offers easy access to an array of historical documents and online texts, updated political headlines of the day, and free access to its own American government textbook.

NOTES

1 Donald S. Lutz has written extensively on these similarities in *Principles of Constitutional Design* (Cambridge: Cambridge University Press, 2006), 200–208.

2 Domingo Faustino Sarmiento, *Facundo: Civilization and Barbarism,* trans. Kathleen Ross (Berkeley: University of California Press, 2002; originally published in 1845), 75.

3 Quoted in John A. Crow, *The Epic of Latin America,* 4th ed. (Berkeley: University of California Press, 1992), 586.

4 For an overview, see Steven Muhlberger, "Democracy's Place in World History," *Journal of World History* 4, no. 1 (1993): 23–45.

5 Max Weber, "Politics as a Vocation," in *From Max Weber: Essays in Sociology,* ed. H. H. Gerth and C. Wright Mills (New York: Oxford University Press, 1946), 78.

6 Donald P. Kommers, "Supremacy Clause," and Burns H. Weston, "Treaty Power," in *Encyclopedia of the American Constitution,* ed. Leonard W. Levy with Kenneth L. Karst and Dennis J. Mahoney (New York: Macmillan, 1986), Vol. 4, 1910–1911.

7 Jared Diamond, *Collapse: How Societies Choose to Fail or Succeed* (New York: Penguin Books, 2005).

8 This review draws on a summary of earlier studies of societal development in Jared Diamond, *Guns, Germs, and Steel: The Fates of Human Society* (New York: W. W. Norton, 1997), Chap. 14. Those earlier studies include Morton H. Fried, *The Evolution of Political Society: An Essay in Anthropology* (New York: Random House, 1967); Elman Rogers Service, *Origins of the State and Civilization: The Process of Cultural Evolution*; S. E. Finer, *The History of Government, Vol. 1: Ancient Monarchies and Empires* (New York: Oxford University Press, 1997). Diamond's study does not include conciliar republics.

9 Diamond, *Guns, Germs, and Steel,* 271, 273, 362–363.

10 Ibid., 273.

11 Ibid.

12 For a review of current research in the neurosciences, see Michael S. Gazzaniga, *Human: The Science behind What Makes Us Unique* (New York: HarperCollins, 2008). In psychology, the classic remains Abraham Maslow,

"A Theory of Human Motivation," *Psychological Review* 50 (1943), 370–376, available at Classics in the History of Psychology, http://psychclassics.yorku.ca/Maslow/motivation.htm.

13 In Samuel Noah Kramer, *The Sumerians: Their History, Culture, and Character* (Chicago: University of Chicago Press, 1963), 336. For this and other Sumerian texts, see the appendices in Kramer.

14 Jacob Bercovitch and Judith Fretter, *Regional Guide to International Conflict and Management from 1945 to 2003* (Washington, D.C.: CQ Press, 2004), 4.

15 "Hammurabi's Code of Laws (c. 1780 BCE)," trans. L. W. King, *Internet Ancient History Sourcebook,* Fordham University, available at www.fordham.edu/halsall/ancient/hamcode.html.

16 Adam Smith, *The Theory of Moral Sentiments,* ed. D. D. Raphael and A. L. Macfie (Indianapolis, Ind.: Liberty Fund, 1982; originally published in 1759), 50.

17 S. E. Finer, *The History of Government from the Earliest Times* (Oxford: Oxford University Press, 1999), Vol. 1, 100.

18 For more on the role of government in the Sumerian economy, see Kramer, *Sumerians,* Chap. 3.

19 Confucius, *Analects,* Book 17, available at http://classics.mit.edu/Confucius/analects.4.4.html; Aristotle, *Politics,* ed. and trans. Ernest Barker (New York: Oxford University Press, 1968), 129; Koran 5:8; Martin Luther King Jr., "Letter from a Birmingham Jail," April 16, 1963, available at King Papers Project, Martin Luther King Jr. Research and Education Institute, www.kingpapers.org; Alexander Hamilton, James Madison, and John Jay, *The Federalist Papers,* ed. Clinton Rossiter (New York: New American Library, 1961), 324.

20 King, "Letter from a Birmingham Jail."

21 For more on these types of justice, see Center for Civic Education, *Elements of Democracy* (Calabasas, Calif.: Center for Civic Education, 2007), 62–72.

22 Aristotle, *Politics,* 129.

23 King, "Letter from a Birmingham Jail."

24 Ibid.

CHAPTER 5

WHY DO PHILOSOPHERS DISAGREE ABOUT THE NEED FOR GOVERNMENT?

BIG IDEAS

- Many political philosophies begin by imagining life in a state of nature, a life without government.

- Political philosophers disagree about what life would be like in the absence of government.

- Political theorists come to different conclusions about the necessity of government, their visions of the good society, and how much they trust human beings or governments.

- The two extremes of political thought are occupied by anarchists, who envision a world without government, and statists, who envision a world dominated by government.

- Constitutionalist philosophies, including conservatism, republicanism, and liberalism, recognize the need for freedom and government, but they differ on the mix.

Purpose of This Chapter

Every society needs to be governed. But does every society need a government? Today, there are approximately two hundred sovereign states in the world. In addition, there are tens of thousands of local and regional governments. Most people take the existence of government for granted, but political philosophers long have raised challenging questions about the necessity of government. What would life be like without government? Would human beings seek to control or cooperate with one another? The answers to these questions reveal much about where philosophers put their trust and what they value. Do they value freedom and trust human beings to use it wisely? Or do they distrust human nature and seek the order that a strong government can bring? Is the good society a product of consent by the people or coercion by the government? This chapter begins with the extreme positions of anarchism and statism and then turns to three philosophies in the middle: conservatism, republicanism, and liberalism.

Terms to Know

absolutism	Daoism	natural rights theory
anarchism	democratic statism	negative rights
autonomy	divine right theory	positive rights
classical liberalism	human nature	representative democracy
classical republic	legalism	republicanism
classical republicanism	liberalism	social contract theory
Confucianism	libertarianism	sovereignty
conservatism	modern republic	state of nature
constitutionalist philosophies	natural law	statism

WHAT WOULD LIFE BE LIKE WITHOUT GOVERNMENT?

According to the twentieth-century political philosopher Leo Strauss (1899–1973), "the theme of political philosophy is mankind's great objectives, freedom and government or empire—objectives which are capable of lifting all men beyond their poor selves."[1] These objectives shape the philosopher's search for answers to the questions, what is the good society and how should it be organized? Through the ages, political philosophers have debated three possible answers to these questions: freedom without government, government without freedom, or some combination of freedom and government.

Political philosophers often begin their inquiry by asking, what is human nature? Without the answer to this question, it is difficult to understand what human beings want from society, what society can deliver, and what combination of freedom and government will best serve their needs.

Political philosophers use a variety of techniques to understand human nature. One of these techniques poses the question, what would life be like without government? To answer that question, philosophers imagine a **state of nature**, a world in which government does not exist and no one has the authority to rule. One common image of a state of nature is a prehistoric world in which a group of primitive people lives off the land as food gatherers and hunters. Another is a deserted island where the survivors of a shipwreck have been marooned. Yet a third image is a heavily populated society that has been ravaged by war and lawlessness.

A state of nature does not have to be a physically natural setting (such as a jungle, a forest or a deserted island). Nor is it necessarily set in primeval times before human beings entered society. Rather, it is a metaphor—a symbolic representation—for a world without human laws or governments in which human beings must rely on human nature and the laws of nature.

Human nature refers to the innate character traits of human beings. These are the traits that people are born with, as distinct from other traits that are learned or influenced by culture. Political philosophers have long been interested in both the social and moral traits of human beings. Today, neuroscientists have joined this inquiry, and later in this chapter, we compare some of their theories with political philosophy.

Natural law refers to the laws of nature or God that are universal, precede human law, and provide the standards (such as justice) against which human law (called positive law) is measured. Throughout the ages, the most widely recognized natural law has been the Golden Rule—do unto others as you would have them do unto you.

As one might expect, philosophers differ widely in their conclusions about human nature. Some philosophers see people in a state of nature as inherently good—people seek to cooperate with others and they exercise freedom with self-restraint. At the other extreme, some philosophers view human beings in a state of nature as inherently domineering and untrustworthy. In the middle are philosophers with a variety of views grounded in the belief that most people begin with good intentions that eventually are corrupted by self-interest and the quest for more power.

More than 2,500 years ago in China, three major schools of philosophy—Confucianism, Daoism, and legalism—pondered this question of human nature.

Confucianism is the ethical philosophy developed by Confucius (551–479 BCE) at a time of social discord when many self-proclaimed philosophers traveled from court to court advocating their views. Confucius was deeply troubled by what he saw as false philosophies. He had a mixed view of human nature, seeing both good and evil in the world. For Confucius, the ultimate purpose of society was social harmony; therefore, the goal of all human relationships, including the political relationship between the ruler and the people, also was harmony. To achieve harmony, he advanced five moral values: humanity and courtesy, followed by uprightness (that is, honesty), moral wisdom, and faithfulness. A harmonious society depends first and foremost on the people's sense of humanity (*ren*). The governing principle of humanity is the Confucian golden rule of compassion toward others: do unto others as you wish to be treated by them. Courtesy (*li*) is the idea that individuals should follow traditional rules of behavior (etiquette) in carrying out their obligations to others. Harmony comes from relationships in which everyone knows their obligations. *Li* is "the virtue which erects a dam against social chaos and the law of the jungle."[2]

Daoism (also spelled Taoism) was developed by the semi-mythical figure Laozi (Lao Tzu) around the time of Confucius. Daoism is preoccupied less with human relations than with human beings in the natural world. In this setting, "the secret for man is simply to abandon self-effort and ease himself into the rhythm of the universe, the cycle of the seasons, and the inevitable progression of day and night, life and death."[3] Daoists use the image of yin and yang to represent this world of contrasts.

Daoist yin/yang symbol.

Confucianism and Daoism both imagine a mythical golden age. In this idyllic age, people were free, innocent, and equal. However, Confucius saw this idyllic age as impermanent. He believed that sooner or later human beings would endanger themselves without some form of government. Daoists, in contrast, believe that people were at their best in a state of nature.

Legalism was set out by Lord Shang as the moral justification for his military actions to consolidate China in the mid-300s BCE. He did not reject the goal of a harmonious society, but he was more immediately interested in unifying society under one unified system of law and order—his system. Legalism is based on a belief in humanity's undisciplined character and in the need to control people by laws, not virtues. Legalists reject the idea of a prior golden age altogether. Legalists liken human nature to an unbridled wild horse. They argue that human beings are incapable of doing good deeds without strong government and strong laws; like wild horses, human beings need reins and whips.[4] Those laws must set clear standards of reward and punishment, and the ruler must hold everyone accountable to those laws.[5]

These three ancient Chinese philosophies represent the three basic views of human nature: the positive view of Daoism that some critics see as overly optimistic or idealistic; the darker negative view of legalism that critics see as pessimistic or cynical; and the mixed view of Confucianism that Daoists see as too pragmatic and legalists see as too soft. These three views of human nature—the positive, negative, and mixed—are not limited to ancient Chinese philosophy. They recur throughout history and across cultures.

In ancient Athens, for example, philosophy began with Socrates (469–399 BCE), who was born shortly after Confucius died. Much of what we know about Socrates comes from his disciple Plato (429–347 BCE). Plato had a decidedly low opinion of humankind. In his famous "allegory of the cave," Plato portrays the state of nature as a cave in which human beings watch their shadows dance along the walls and believe that the cave is reality. The one brave soul who ventures out of the cave discovers a brighter world within his reach. But when he returns with the good news, his companions refuse to believe that there is any reality but the confines of their little world.

Plato's student Aristotle (384–322 BCE) accepted the natural flaws and virtues of human beings. For Aristotle, human beings possess two qualities that distinguish them from other creatures. First, human beings are social by nature—they form society because they want to interact with others and to feel that they belong to something larger than themselves. Second, human beings are born with moral instincts—they have an innate sense of the difference between right and wrong. Both these points, by the way, have been supported by twenty-first-century theories of neuroscience and evolutionary biology.

Zeno of Citium on the island of Cyrus (344–262 BCE) journeyed to Athens, where he taught a philosophy later named stoicism. (Stoicism was named after the white porch, *stoa poikile*, under which Zeno taught.) Zeno argued that human reason was part of the natural reason of the universe. Similar in many ways to Daoism, stoicism was based on the egalitarian belief that all human beings are equally capable of attaining salvation by learning how to control their emotions and exercise the reason needed to place themselves in harmony with nature.

The debate over human nature was given modern form by two seventeenth-century English philosophers, Thomas Hobbes and John Locke.

Thomas Hobbes (1588–1679) lived at the time of the English Civil War (1642–1649). That war pitted the royal army of King Charles I against the forces loyal to Parliament in a fierce struggle for control of England. Hobbes feared that England was sinking into a state of nature—the absence of government and civil society. Hobbes was a royalist, supporting the king's cause. After the royalist defeat, Hobbes went into exile; he believed that order could be restored only by restoring the monarchy.

For Hobbes, the natural instinct of humans is self-preservation. The strong seek to dominate others, while the weak seek to check the strong by confederation and deceit. Hobbes saw human beings in a state of nature as being in a perpetual state of war until a strong ruler prevails. Hobbes created an imaginary state of nature in his book *Leviathan* to show what happens when rebellion breaks down the reciprocal relationship between the king and his subjects. Here, in part, is what Hobbes told his readers to expect in a state of nature.

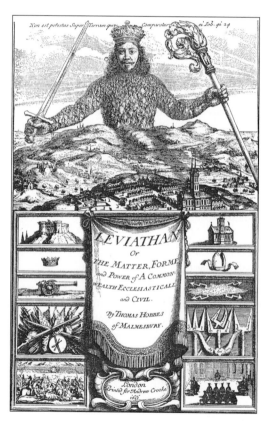

This illustration is from the frontispiece of Thomas Hobbes's 1651 edition of Leviathan. *It depicts Leviathan as the gigantic sovereign ruler who stands over and governs his domain—the state. He wears the crown of sovereignty, brandishes a sword as the symbol of power, and clutches a scepter as the symbol of authority. Attached to him, and holding on for dear life, are the people. On either side of the banner title there are symbols of the modern state.*

> *In [a state of nature] there is no place for Industry; because the fruit thereof is uncertain: and consequently no Culture of the Earth, no Navigation, nor use of the commodities that may be imported by Sea; no instruments of moving and removing of such things as require much force; no Knowledge of the face of Earth; no account of Time; no Arts, no Letters, no Society; and which is worst of all, continuall feare, and danger of violent death; and the life of man, solitary, poore, nasty, brutish and short.*[6]

John Locke (1632–1704), another prominent English philosopher, was only nineteen when Hobbes wrote *Leviathan*. Like Hobbes, Locke lived through the English Civil War; however, he drew different conclusions from that experience. Locke believed that the laws of nature included natural rights. Among the most important of these natural laws, Locke maintained, is the prohibition against harming others. He argued that human beings in a state of nature would use reason to discover natural law and that they would feel bound by those laws and the rights of others.

John Locke's State of Nature

In Locke's state of nature, individuals are both free and equal. Locke rejected the idea of a natural hierarchy, believing instead that everyone is equal before God. Because God created humans as equals, they should live in peace, cooperate, and not seek to control one another. Freedom has limits, however, and does not include a license to do whatever an individual wants.

Locke was also a pragmatist. He believed that the laws of nature apply fully to everyone, but he also realized that everyone would not follow those laws. He, therefore, agreed with Hobbes on one major point—some form of government is necessary. As Locke explained,

"Men, being as has been said, by nature all free, equal and independent, no one can put another out of his estate and subjected to the political power of another without his own consent, which is done by agreeing with other men, to join and unite into a community for their comfortable, safe and peaceable living. . . . When any number of men has so consented to make one community or government, they are thereby presently incorporated, and make one body politic; wherein the majority have a right to act and conclude the rest."[7]

IS GOVERNMENT NECESSARY, AND IS IT DESIRABLE?

The philosophical answer to the question of whether government is a necessity depends partly on how philosophers view human nature. As you might suspect, idealists (such as Daoists, who trust human nature) find no urgent need for government to come to the rescue. Pessimists (such as Chinese legalists, who distrust human nature) are far more likely to embrace the urgency of government.

The answer to the question of whether government is desirable depends on how philosophers view government's nature. By definition, government is an institution with the authority to make binding decisions and the power to enforce them. But is it the nature of governments to respect the source of their authority (that is, a higher law of some kind) and limit their actions accordingly? Or is power likely to corrupt those who hold it?

At one extreme of the answers to these questions is the philosophy of anarchism. Daoists and other anarchists see government as inherently corrupt and utterly contemptible. Anarchism categorically rejects the need for government. Libertarians are not much more trusting in government. They are opposed to all government regulation, but they accept the need for a minimal state to achieve certain purposes.

At the other extreme is the broad philosophical tent of statism, which includes philosophers of various persuasions who trust government and place great stock in it. Some statist philosophers believe that the state can bring out the best in people. Others, like Hobbes, see the state as the only way to control the worst in people. Many ancient societies deified the state and believed that the ruler was a god or descended from the gods. In early modern times, absolutists believed that kings ruled by divine right.

Table 5.1 Trust in Human Nature and Government

Main category	Philosophy	Thinkers	Trust in human nature/ government	Primary institutions	Scope of government
Statism	Absolutist statism	Shang Hobbes	None/high	Government control	Authoritarian
	Democratic statism	Rousseau	High/high	General will	Wide ranging
Constitutionalist philosophies	Conservatism	Confucius Burke	Low/medium	Moral virtue and cultural norms	Paternal
	Classical republicanism	Aristotle	Medium/medium	Civic virtue and balanced constitution	Integral
	Modern republicanism	Madison	Medium/medium	Constitutionalism and power balance	Limited
	Classical liberalism	Locke A. Smith	High/medium	Civil society and markets	Limited
	Twentieth-century liberalism	Wilson	Medium/medium	Public-private partnerships	Widening
	Libertarianism	Hayek	High/very low	Markets	Minimal
Anarchism	Anarchism	Lao Tzu Godwin	High/none	Voluntary associations	None

Most political philosophies lie somewhere between these two extremes of anarchism and statism. These philosophies include republicanism, conservatism, and liberalism. None of these rejects or deifies government. Instead, they all maintain that governments are necessary instruments to achieve specific practical and moral purposes. Depending on where they stand, these philosophies see government as either a necessary good or a necessary evil. In either case, they see government as an institution that must be empowered and limited by legitimate rules that are accepted by society. For this reason, we classify these philosophies as "constitutionalist."

Constitutionalist philosophies accept the necessity or utility of government. Generally speaking, they also accept human beings and governments as an imperfect mix of good and bad tendencies. Confucius, Aristotle, and Locke are examples of constitutionalists. They differ in many ways, but they agree that some government is necessary. They also agree about the need to limit government powers by constitutional and cultural means.

Table 5.1 provides a review of anarchism, statism, and the constitutionalist philosophies (conservatism, republicanism, and liberalism) in the middle. The table compares these philosophies in terms of their trust in human nature and government, what they see as the primary institution in society, and how they view the scope of government in society. The remainder of this chapter explores these five philosophies.

WHY DO ANARCHISTS REJECT GOVERNMENT?

Anarchism (from the Greek word meaning "without a ruler") is the theory that government is intrinsically corrupt and should be abolished. Anarchists believe that government is both unnecessary and undesirable. As Table 5.1 indicates, anarchists have a high level of trust in human nature but no trust in government. Hence, they reject the need for government. Anarchists believe that government is unnecessary because human societies can govern themselves by relying on the voluntary cooperation of their members. Anarchists prize human freedom, and they believe that the coercive power of government will endanger that freedom unless it is abolished. For the anarchist, the purpose of the good society is human fulfillment achieved through human cooperation.

Anarchists believe that most individuals are capable of exercising self-restraint. They also recognize that some human beings will engage in antisocial behavior. But they argue that the absence of government does not mean the absence of social control over individual behavior. They contend that peer pressure, public opinion, and fear of a bad reputation will control the worst tendencies of human behavior.

As a philosophy, anarchism can be found in many societies; it dates as far back as Chinese Daoism in the fourth century BCE. Like others who focus on an idyllic past, Daoists claimed that human beings could re-create a perfect world in the present without the assistance of government. Anarchists have been a part of almost every society, even societies in which most people expect strong government. One example is the Mu`tazilites, who lived in the eighth century CE in Islamic Basra and Baghdad, in what is today Iraq. They maintained that "believers could manage without any imam [community leader] at all."[8]

The British philosopher and novelist William Godwin (1756–1836) was a founder of modern European anarchism. In his *Enquiry Concerning Political Justice* (1793), Godwin argued that, as individuals come to recognize that the interests that bind them are stronger than the interests that divide them, they will spontaneously come into social harmony. When disagreements do occur, people will resolve their disputes through rational debate and discussion. Thus, the coercive arm of government is unnecessary. Government, Godwin and his followers contended, is not a safeguard against disorder and conflict; rather, government is the cause of disorder and conflict. Because government, in their judgment, is the tool of the powerful and propertied classes, it imposes rule from above that represses freedom, breeds resentment, and promotes inequality.

Another influential anarchist writer was the Russian prince Peter Kropotkin (1842–1921). Born into wealth and nobility, he served as a page to the tsar. Over time, however, the corruption and tyranny that, in his view, pervaded the tsarist court repelled him. A distinguished career as an army explorer and geographer did not cure his revulsion of government authority. He joined one anarchist group after another, first in Russia and then in France. He argued

San Francisco Chronicle.

VOL. LXXIV.   SAN FRANCISCO, CAL., SATURDAY, SEPTEMBER 7, 1901—SIXTEEN PAGES.   NO. 84.

PRESIDENT M'KINLEY SHOT BY AN ANARCHIST AT BUFFALO FAIR.

Two Bullets Fired by the Assassin, but Only One Penetrates the Body—Surgeons Hopeful of Recovery—An Attempt Made to Lynch the Cowardly Murderer.

Front page of the San Francisco Chronicle *of September 7, 1901, reporting the assassination of President William McKinley, in Buffalo, New York, the previous day.*

that, were it not for the corruptions imposed by governments, humans would develop bonds of instinctive solidarity that would make government unnecessary. To prove his assertions, Kropotkin pointed to evidence of cooperation within the animal kingdom. All animal species profit through mutual aid. Many animals, for example, cooperate in raising young, finding food, or seeking shelter. Therefore, if human beings (who also are members of the animal kingdom) would cooperate, they too would reap benefits. He wrote, "No more laws! No more judges! Liberty, equality and practical human sympathy are the only effective barriers we can oppose to the anti-social interests of certain among us."9

In 1876, Russian anarchists formed a secret society called Land and Liberty that advocated a revolutionary uprising to overthrow the government and replace it with self-governing economic communes. In 1879, a violent wing of this society, known as People's Freedom, embarked on a campaign of political assassinations that claimed the life of Tsar Alexander II in 1881. The Russian writer Fyodor Dostoevsky (1821–1881) based his novel *The Possessed* on this radical anarchist movement. According to James H. Billington, a professor of Russian history, Dostoevsky's novel anticipated the rise of modern political terrorism.[10]

In the last quarter of the nineteenth century, the anarchist movement spread from Europe to the United States with the wave of immigration from central and Eastern Europe. Although most American anarchists were peaceful, some were committed to the "propaganda of the deed"—a slogan used to justify anarchist violence. This violent fringe posed a genuine threat.

On May 4, 1886, when police attempted to break up a peaceful anarchist rally in Chicago's Haymarket Square, someone threw a bomb at the policemen, killing one and wounding others. A group of anarchists was arrested. Four were found guilty and hanged. Fifteen years later, a self-proclaimed anarchist named Leon Czolgosz (pronounced chol-gosh) assassinated President William McKinley at the Pan American Exhibition in Buffalo, New York. During the same period, there was a wave of anarchist bombings and assassinations of national leaders across Europe—in Russia, France, Spain, Italy, Greece, and Germany. Most anarchists remained committed to nonviolent change, but their public image was irreparably blackened by the actions of a few. American newspaper cartoons depicted anarchists as foreign-born, bearded, bomb-throwing maniacs.

After World War I, anarchism lost much of its original meaning as a belief in the cooperative spirit of humankind. By the 1960s, the word *anarchy* had come to mean a state of lawless confusion. Many who called themselves anarchists in the 1960s and 1970s were terrorists who used violence to undermine the social order. Examples included radical left-wing urban guerilla groups such as the Bader Meinhof Gang in West Germany.

WHY IS STATISM THE ANTITHESIS OF ANARCHISM?

Statism is the belief in the state as the framework of all political life. Some statist philosophers go so far as to compare the framework of the state to the mother's womb because it gives life to and nurtures the human being. In statist philosophies, government is the embodiment of the state, not a reflection of human nature.

Statism is the antithesis of anarchism. For the statist, human beings are naturally corruptible and not to be trusted; government is both necessary and desirable (see Table 5.1). The state is the ultimate source of authority, and government is the central, if not sole, governing institution in society. For statists, the purpose of the state is to provide a well-ordered society in which people are protected from one another and from foreign invasion. In exchange, the citizen is obligated to obey the law without question.

Statists advocate one strong and highly centralized government with no intermediate political institutions between it and the people. That means no political parties, no interest groups or voluntary associations, no media, and no local or regional governments—except those that are controlled by the central government.

Throughout history, statism has provided the theoretical justification for the creation of the centralized state. Chinese legalism is an early example of a statist philosophy. In the mid-300s BCE, Lord Shang used legalism to justify the often ruthless policies he used to build the small state of Qin into a political dynasty that eventually became the basis of unified China. Lord

Shang lived during the Warring States Period of Chinese history (roughly 475–220 BCE), when warlords were fighting one another for control of small states that they could consolidate into large empires. In the name of order and unity, he brought all the armed forces under his command, reduced the power of other noblemen who were his competitors, took their lands, and then gave those lands to his soldiers in exchange for their loyalty to him and the state.

In the modern era, statist philosophies have taken various forms. Two historically important examples are absolutism in defense of absolute monarchy and democratic statism adopted by the French Revolution.

ABSOLUTISM

Absolutism is the belief that the state should be ruled by one person, an absolute monarch who has absolute power over his or her subjects. Historically, absolutism was the first modern expression of statism. Two variations of absolutism developed in seventeenth-century Europe: divine right theory and Hobbes's social contract theory. These differed primarily on the source of the monarch's authority.

In France, Jacques-Bénigne Boussuet (1627–1704) became the most influential advocate of **divine right theory**. According to this theory, the monarch derived his or her right to rule from God. Boussuet was a bishop and a member of the royal court as tutor to King Louis XIV's son. He compared Louis's rule to King Solomon's in biblical Israel. Although the French king could not be deposed by any earthly body, the king was subject to God's laws. Therefore, the king had divine responsibilities and limits as well as divine rights.

The English philosopher Thomas Hobbes advanced a secular theory—social contract theory—as the basis of the king's authority. According to **social contract theory,** the king derives his authority from the people, not God. However, Hobbes also made it quite clear that the people could not withdraw their consent; once in power, the king and his heirs held complete **sovereignty** (supreme authority) over the state.[11]

Why would the people agree to such a one-sided contract? Recall that Hobbes believed that life in a state of nature without a social contract would be nasty and brutish. Guided by their passions, human beings naturally would seek self-preservation, and the stronger would seek to dominate the weaker. Hobbes argued that human beings eventually would realize their predicament and contract with one another to create a more secure world. In that social contract, the people must agree to give up their political power to a monarchy that protects them from their own worst instincts. Hobbes's monarchy is a highly centralized state. The monarch must have absolute power to prevent any slide back toward a state of nature. Furthermore, succession from one absolute monarch to the next must be based on heredity. For Hobbes, good government had to be powerful enough to protect social peace and good order against all challenges. And this meant the restoration of absolute monarchy.

Hobbes also recognized the dangers of such a system; occasionally it would produce a bad monarch. Nevertheless, he believed that this was far less dangerous than democracy in which the people (who could not be trusted in the first place) are given the keys to the kingdom: "In a democracy, where each man bears some part of the sovereignty, the number of those capable of enriching and serving themselves at the expense of the public interest is at a maximum."[12] Candidates will only fuel the flames of factionalism and civil war by competing with one another for political patronage to dole out to supporters.

DEMOCRATIC STATISM

Democratic statism is the belief that the will of the people can be realized only by a strong state that rules with complete authority in the name of the people. For people who are naturally suspicious of the state, this belief is a contradiction in terms. How can democracy, based on the idea of the consent of the governed, exist in a country where the state is the absolute source of authority?

The late-eighteenth-century Geneva-born philosopher Jean-Jacques Rousseau (1712–1778) answered this question. Rousseau based his philosophy on a unique and radical premise—neither human nature nor the state is the source of corruption and domination; the culprit is society. According to Rousseau, humans are naturally good because humans are naturally solitary and self-sufficient. When human beings

Portrait of Jean Jacques Rousseau by Maurice Quentin de la Tour.

enter society, they come to need one another but not to love one another. This, according to Rousseau, intensifies individual self-interest, forces individuals to ally themselves with others, and fragments the general will.

To overcome these dangers, Rousseau proposed a model of three parts.

- Small agrarian republics. Rousseau envisioned small agrarian republics with a strong sense of community and virtue. In these republics, there would be "relative equality and homogeneity of the population, an agrarian economic base, public education that cultivates virtue and patriotism more than talents, strict republican morals, patriotic public festivals, a civil religion, and censorship of the arts and sciences."[13] Such republics could become oppressive totalitarian states and crush the individual spirit. To prevent this possibility, Rousseau turned to the idea of the general will.

- The general will. Rousseau proposed to shift sovereignty from the state to the general will of the citizenry. Rousseau then proposed a popular assembly to express the general will of the people. Every citizen would become a member of the assembly and be entitled to vote. Rousseau proposed a number of ways to streamline and consolidate this cumbersome legislative body, including a draftsman responsible for writing most of the laws. He also designed reforms for a new educational system that would create introspective, compassionate, and virtuous citizens.

- The centralized state. Rousseau stood firm in his belief that nothing should stand between the general will of the people and the elected bodies of a powerful state. For Rousseau, the state was the ultimate voice, shield, and sword of the people. Therefore, intermediate institutions (such as interest groups, political parties, and regional or provincial governments) between the people and the state were unnecessary. Rousseau also viewed such institutions as undesirable because he believed they would divide the people.

Rousseau's philosophy provided a basis for the French model of the unitary democratic state. The French model is attractive to those peoples and leaders around the world who are accustomed to hierarchy, the promises of an activist government, and the freedom they believe democracy will bring.

WHAT IDEAS DO CONSTITUTIONALIST PHILOSOPHIES SHARE?

Most political philosophies lie somewhere between the two extremes of anarchism and statism. Unlike anarchism, these philosophies accept the necessity of government as an authoritative institution; unlike statism, they accept the necessity of external controls on government. We classify these philosophies as constitutionalist. Constitutionalist philosophies accept the necessity of government and focus on government's constitutional purposes, powers, and limits.

This book focuses on three of these constitutionalist philosophies: conservatism, republicanism, and liberalism. The differences among these philosophies are a matter of emphasis or degree. Therefore, let's first compare their similarities; in the next section, we take a closer look at the distinguishing features of each.

Constitutionalist philosophies—conservatism, republicanism, and liberalism—are similar in the following ways.

- Constitutionalist philosophies are guided by the principles of moderation and balance. In the classic debates of politics—such as freedom versus government, consent versus coercion, the individual versus the community—constitutionalists disagree, often vehemently, but these disagreements are a matter of emphasis. Classical liberal philosophy, for example, emphasizes the individual but not to the exclusion of community concerns. Classical republican philosophy is oriented toward the common good but not to the exclusion of individual freedoms.

- All three constitutionalist philosophies see human nature as a mix of virtues and vices. Human beings, according to constitutionalist theories, are neither angels nor demons. As the American statesman James Madison (1751–1836) observed, "there is a degree of depravity in mankind which requires a certain degree of circumspection and distrust, [but] there are other qualities in human nature which justify a certain portion of esteem and confidence."[14]

- Constitutionalist philosophies trust human beings—but only to a point. Conservative philosophies, for example, distinguish sharply between human nature and human development; they believe human beings are born in sin but redeemable. Classical liberal and republican philosophies, by contrast, are more confident about human nature.

- Constitutionalist philosophies view government as a reflection of human nature. Government, in other words, is no more or less trustworthy than the people. In this respect, constitutionalists differ from anarchists, who see government as a threat to human nature, and statists, who see government as a necessary constraint on human nature. Madison famously put the constitutionalist position as follows:

  "But what is government itself but the greatest of all reflections on human nature? If men were angels, no government would be necessary. If angels were to govern men, neither external nor internal controls on government would be necessary. In framing a government which is to be administered by men over men, the great difficulty lies in this: you must first enable the government to control the governed; and in the next place, oblige it to control itself."[15]

- Constitutionalist philosophies place great importance on the polity. This view is in stark contrast to statists—even democratic ones—who are opposed to political or civic associations between the citizen and government. Anarchists see the polity and its rich associative life as a desirable alternative to government, whereas constitutionalists see it as a way of complementing, civilizing, and checking government.

- Constitutionalist philosophies look to a mix of controls within the polity. Some constitutionalist philosophies focus on the need for legal limits on human behavior, while others focus on the importance of cultural limits that individuals learn in family and school. Still others look to the competition among rival political interests as a way of keeping each interest in check. These differences, however, are a matter of emphasis. All constitutionalists recognize the importance of government laws, cultural norms, and competing political interests in checking the excesses of citizens and governments.

- Constitutionalist philosophies see the good society as a balance of freedom *and* government, not a choice between freedom *or* government. However, these philosophies differ in the way they understand freedom. Conservative and republican philosophers emphasize the good of the community; hence, they define individual freedom in terms of the individual's larger responsibilities to the community. Classical liberal philosophers emphasize the individual's autonomy or freedom of choice; hence, they define the good of the community in terms of individual preferences.

HOW DO CONSTITUTIONALIST PHILOSOPHIES DIFFER?

Conservatism, republicanism, and liberalism are types of constitutionalist philosophies, but at the same time, each is a relatively separate and distinct philosophy with its own history and system of ideas. And those differences matter. The philosophical differences between twentieth-century liberals and conservatives in American politics are very real; they affect public opinion, policy preferences, and voting behavior.

Conservatism rests on the belief in an orderly and harmonious society that seeks to preserve the status quo (the existing order). Conservatism began thousands of years ago before the dawn of philosophy in traditionalistic societies that viewed change as a threat to existing institutions, interests, and values. Conservatism is also based on the belief that divine law is the ultimate source of authority.

As a philosophical orientation, conservatism begins with a relatively low level of trust in human nature—humans are born in sin but capable of redemption. Conservatives seek a harmonious society, and they look to moral virtue reinforced by cultural norms as the principal source of social order. Government plays a secondary role and cannot always be trusted to do the right thing (see Table 5.1).

At first glance, conservatism looks a lot like statism. One important difference between them is that philosophical conservatives seek limited government and value civilization, not the state, as the mainstay of society. Cultural norms and moral values are not only the source of social harmony; they are a check on governmental power; the ultimate source of authority is divine.

Confucianism, for example, relies on cultural norms and moral virtue not only as guidance for the people but as a check on the ruler. In Confucian thought, cultural norms such as *ren* and *li* are the glue that holds society together. Good rulers are expected to set an example of moral virtue by observing those norms. Rulers lose their legitimacy when they defy their heavenly mandate, refuse to listen to the people, and abuse their power. The role of government varies, but its image is often paternalistic—setting an example of behavior, enforcing rules, and promoting cultural education.

Edmund Burke (1729–1797) is the father of modern conservative philosophy in the West. An English statesman and member of Parliament, Burke was a practical political philosopher. In his famous work *Reflections on the Revolution in France* (1790), he denounced what he called the metaphysics of the French Revolution, in which revolutionaries used abstract principles to rouse mobs to kill aristocrats. He believed that laws and governments should reflect the manners (inherited traditions) and historical circumstances of a people. He favored the British constitutional system in which monarchy was checked by constitutional limits, by the people's belief in limited government, and by a Parliament of gentlemen who understood and represented the best interests of the country as a whole. He saw these gentlemen as members of a natural aristocracy that included not only noblemen but commoners of achievement and learning.

Burke supported equal rights for Irish Catholics, the gradual abolition of slavery, and relief for insolvent debtors. But he was suspicious of democratic rule. At a time when most reformers fought to make Parliament more representative of the people, Burke sought to make Parliament more responsible as a check on the monarchy.[16]

Burke's conservatism was neither right-wing nor reactionary. He never advanced his ideas in the service of absolute monarchs, unfettered markets, or the domination of one race over another. In the nineteenth century, conservative philosophy provided an intellectual foundation for moderate Conservative Party leaders in Britain such as Prime Minister Benjamin Disraeli.

In the twentieth century, the American political thinker Russell Kirk (1918–1994) inspired the revival of Burkean conservatism. Kirk's role is acknowledged by leading American conservatives such as Ronald Reagan (1911–2004) and public intellectual William F. Buckley (1925–2008), who founded the conservative magazine *National Review*. Kirk was a political theorist whose most influential work was *The Conservative Mind* (1953), a history of conservative philosophy from Edmund Burke to George Santayana. His list of conservative principles helped lay the intellectual foundations for the post–World War II conservative movement (see Bold Thinkers: Russell Kirk's Ten Conservative Principles, 1993). Kirk found kinship with classical liberalism, but was opposed to libertarianism and neoconservatism.

Republicanism comes from the Latin words *res* and *publica,* meaning public things or the public's things. Republicanism is the theory that the good society is a republic in which the citizenry share certain things— the most important being a commitment to the common good of the polity as a whole. Republican philosophies include the following "public things."

BOLD THINKERS

Russell Kirk's Ten Conservative Principles, 1993

1. Belief in an enduring moral order.
2. Adherence to custom, convention, and continuity.
3. Belief in the principle of prescription that relies on longstanding precedent and precept.
4. Guidance by the principle of prudence.
5. Attentiveness to the principle of variety respecting a healthy diversity of society.
6. Chastened by the principle of imperfectability and avoidance of utopian visions of perfection as dangerous.
7. Persuaded by the idea that freedom and property are closely linked.
8. Uphold the voluntary community and oppose involuntary collectivism.
9. Recognize the need for prudent restraints upon power and upon human passions.
10. Understand that permanence and change must be recognized and reconciled in a vigorous society.

Adapted from Russell Kirk, *The Politics of Prudence* (Wilmington, Del.: ISI Books, 1993), Russell Kirk Center for Cultural Renewal, available at www.kirkcenter.org/kirk/thought.html.

1. The republic or polity as a common territory (that is, one's country), a way of life, and the highest form of political association.
2. Citizenship, not simply as a person's legal status, but also as the source of one's civic identity as a free citizen.
3. Government as an integral part of the polity and subject to the consent of the citizenry and the rule of law.
4. Civic virtue, defined as the good citizen's responsibility to act in accord with the common good of the community.
5. Education that instills a sense of civic virtue and the ability to exercise it.[17]

Much of republican theory comes down to a basic exchange of freedom for responsibility. Citizens are entitled to government by consent. This rests on the belief that "one should not be subject to laws to which one has not directly or indirectly consented."[18] In exchange, free citizens are expected to act responsibly (virtuously) in the name of the common good.

In republican theory, the common good means that the best interests of the polity take precedence over the special interests of the individual, "the few," or even the majority. Even in democratic republics such as the United States, the common good is not whatever the majority deems it to be. Republics must have a moral purpose, and their citizens must have a moral compass. At a minimum, this means that justice must be upheld, even if that means overturning an unjust law passed by a majority of the citizenry or their representatives.

Today, especially in Western societies, terms such as *civic virtue* and *the common good* make some people nervous. These terms do indeed raise difficult questions. Who will decide what is virtuous and what is good? On what basis? What are the limits to the community's pressure to conform? Will dissent be tolerated? How will individual liberties be protected?

But republicanism dates back to a world in which such questions were not nearly so vexing. Republicanism, like conservatism, originated at a time when people were evolving from tribal societies to polities and from rural to urban lifestyles. As societies became more specialized, it fell on philosophers, prophets, and priests to adapt long-held traditions to organized political life. Strong community attachments and norms of virtuous behavior had been a matter of survival. These attachments and norms were needed not only as a defense against powerful neighbors but also as protection against disease, famine, unsafe foods, and angry gods.

Classical republicanism arose in the transition from tribe to polity wherever a people sought freedom and government. Greek polities (for example, Athens and Sparta) and the Roman Republic are the most famous classical republics in the West. But ancient republics also existed in biblical Israel, northern India, and West Africa. From today's perspective, we find these republics to be smaller, more homogeneous, and more community-centered than most modern republics. All citizens belonged to the polity, but usually no more than 10 percent of the population were citizens.[19] At the time, republican citizens and their philosophers looked on their world as being far freer than their monarchic and imperial neighbors.

Nothing symbolized republican pride more for the Greeks than their military prowess against the larger forces of the Persian Empire. The Greek historian Herodotus (c. 484–425 BCE) singled out the political system in which "everyone [has] a voice in the political process." He found the advantages of such a system to be wide ranging, but he singled out the military advantage—when the Athenians were ruled by tyrants they were no better than their neighbors, but they became "vastly superior" after they got rid of tyranny. This, concluded Herodotus, shows that soldiers underperform for masters and fight best when they are free and "want to achieve something for themselves."[20] Rome was much the same. When the Italian Renaissance philosopher Nicolò Machiavelli (1469–1527) looked back with admiration to the classical republicanism of ancient Rome, he was most impressed with the civic virtue of its citizens and the valor of its citizen army.

Until the mid-nineteenth century, most free societies were republics, not democracies, and their guiding philosophy was republicanism. The honor roll of republican philosophers includes many of the greatest political philosophers of Western civilization: Aristotle, Cicero, Machiavelli, Locke, Montesquieu, Hume, Rousseau, and Kant. Since the mid-nineteenth century, democracy has become increasingly popular around the world. But it has not replaced republics; rather, democracy has transformed republics. As a result, today people speak of democratic republics or representative democracies. There are various reasons for this development, but the rise of liberalism is among the most important.

Liberalism comes from the same root word as *liberty* and centers on the freedom of the individual in society. Liberal philosophers are interested in the full range of individual freedom, from freedom of thought and expression to freedom of association and other forms of civil and political action. Underlying all these freedoms is **autonomy**—the freedom of individual choice and action. The idea of individual autonomy envisions a society in which the individual is free to make decisions affecting his or her own life, as long as these decisions do not violate the rights of others.

Before the twentieth century, liberal philosophers focused primarily on individual freedom in terms of **negative rights**, that is, rights that protect the individual *from* government encroachment. Examples of these rights include free speech, freedom of association, and the right to legal counsel. The U.S. Bill of Rights contains a core list of such negative rights. Written in the late eighteenth century, it contains only negative rights. Many twentieth-century constitutions protect **positive rights**, rights based on the belief that people are entitled *to* certain things provided by government, such as affordable housing, a decent job, and adequate health care.

Modern liberalism had several phases, including early liberalism in the seventeenth century, Enlightenment liberalism in the eighteenth century, classical liberalism in the nineteenth century, and contemporary liberalism in the twentieth century. In the late seventeenth century, the English philosopher John Locke and other early liberal thinkers advanced **natural rights theory** based on the powerful idea that certain individual rights are inherent, universal, and derived from natural law, not the

TWO
TREATISES
OF
Government:
In the former,
The *false Principles*, and *Foundation*
OF
Sir *ROBERT FILMER*,
And his FOLLOWERS,
ARE
Detected and Overthrown.
The latter is an
ESSAY
CONCERNING THE
True Original, Extent, and End
OF
Civil Government.

LONDON,
Printed for *Awnsham Churchill*, at the *Black*
Swan in *Ave-Mary-Lane*, by *Amen-*
Corner, 1690.

Title page of the first edition of John Locke's Two Treatises of Government, *in which the author argued that certain rights derive from natural law, not government.*

government. In his *Two Treatises of Government* (1690), Locke identified these natural rights as life, liberty, and property. He argued further that (1) government should be a republic established by consent of the governed to protect these rights; (2) the supreme agency of republican government should be a parliament whose members represent the people, not the king; and (3) the people should have the natural right to reform or abolish governments that violate these rights.

In the second half of the eighteenth century, the Western world experienced a burst of liberal thinking characterized by reason, open-mindedness, and curiosity. Thinkers questioned what had been taken for granted in society, religion, politics, and economics. This period is called the Age of Enlightenment because this way of thinking illuminated areas held in darkness and uncertainty by tradition and dogma. As part of this development, liberalism was applied to social, economic, and political worlds.

Social liberal thought argued for freedom of thought, a questioning attitude toward religious dogma, and a belief in human progress. Economic liberal ideas were set out in the influential *Wealth of Nations,* published in 1776. Its author, English philosopher Adam Smith (1723–1790), argued for free markets and free trade in which producers were allowed to compete with one another in providing consumers with the best products at the best prices. Free of government control, markets would regulate themselves, meet a diversity of interests, and thereby promote the good of society. Smith believed that producers would be governed initially by their own self-interest but that they would discover that making a profit depended on producing what consumers needed and at a reasonable price.

In the political world, Enlightenment thinkers adopted liberal natural rights theory and republican models of government. Liberal republicanism was the early result. In the United States, the drafters of the Declaration of Independence based that document on the Lockean theory of natural rights. Eleven years later, the framers of the U.S. Constitution of 1787 turned to the establishment of a republican government grounded in the Declaration's principles. By contrast, the French Revolution sought to implement Rousseau's theory of natural rights and democratic statism.

In the early nineteenth century, the Enlightenment marriage of liberalism and republicanism occasionally proved incompatible. Republican attachments to the common good sometimes conflicted with the new liberal preferences for individual freedoms. Conflicts arose over the use of property, the interpretation of contracts, and the formulation of public policy. On other occasions, liberals and republicans reconciled their differences; this was the case in the writing of the American Declaration of Independence, the U.S. Constitution of 1787, and the U.S. Bill of Rights.

In the middle of the nineteenth century, **classical liberalism** sought a new reconciliation of the liberal-republican marriage. Among the leaders of this intellectual movement were the English philosopher John Stuart Mill (1806–1873) and U.S. President Abraham Lincoln. First, both sought to combine the best of Locke and Smith. Liberals envisioned a world in which all individuals were free to rise through their own efforts in a market-oriented society. Liberals favored free trade and opposed economic policies that protected the privileged few. However, they were not averse to government support of economic development to do "for a community of people, whatever they need to have done, but can not do, *at all,* or can not, *so well do,* for themselves—in their separate, and individual capacities."[21]

Second, classical liberalism also championed the idea of **representative democracy**, a new form of government in which the people are sovereign and govern through their elected representatives. Behind this new form of government were two modern ideas: electoral representation, by which citizens elect their representatives, and open citizenship, which allows noncitizens to gain citizenship and the right to vote. Over time, these ideas transformed the definition of a republic. A **modern republic** is a representative form of government in which the people elect their representatives. By contrast, a **classical republic** was based on the direct participation of the citizenry, not representation; and the citizenry was a relatively small percentage of the population.

In the twentieth century, a new generation of liberals grew increasingly concerned about the social and economic consequences of industrialization and urbanization. They pointed to the rise of economic monopolies that restricted competition, the plight of cities, unsafe working conditions, and the impoverishment of the working poor. This new generation grew critical of free markets as unfettered markets. They advocated a stronger role of government to regulate market excesses and the corrupting influence of special interests, relieve the plight of the disadvantaged, enfranchise women, and reform itself.

The first national statesmen of this new generation were U.S. President Woodrow Wilson (who held office from 1912 to 1920) and British Prime Minister David Lloyd George (who held office from 1916 to 1922). Both statesmen remained committed to the liberal creed of liberty, but they argued that substantial state intervention was necessary to achieve that goal. Wilson and Lloyd George maintained that new problems required new responses. As they saw it, classical liberals had opposed state intervention in the mid-nineteenth century because the state was feathering the nest of powerful landowners and other members of the old economic elite. According to Wilson and Lloyd George, the situation had changed completely in the twentieth century—now the new economic elite was benefiting from the lack of state intervention. They proposed using the power of the state to regulate the excesses of the industrialists and other members of the new economic elite who had benefited unfairly from the laissez-faire (hands-off) attitudes of the past.[22]

Wilson's and Lloyd George's proposals were adopted into law during their administrations. The Great Depression (which began in the late 1920s) provided President Franklin D. Roosevelt (who held office from 1932 to 1945) with the impetus to expand the role of government in society and the economy even further.

These events fueled a great debate that has raged ever since. On one side of the debate, classical liberals and conservatives argue that twentieth-century liberals, beginning with Wilson and Lloyd George, opened the door to state intervention that has squelched—not saved—liberty. In response, twentieth-century liberals maintain that desperate times call for desperate measures. Modern liberalism, they argue, simply adopted new methods of protecting old values.

In American politics, these developments have reversed the political labels, creating confusion along the way. Today, the term *liberal* connotes a person who advocates not only tolerance of differences and individual rights but also the permanent and active role of government in regulation, relief, and rights enforcement. In response, conservatives, who call for cutting back government, do so in the name of classical liberalism.

Libertarians argue the same point more directly. **Libertarianism** arose as a reaction against the transformation of liberalism in the twentieth century. Libertarians advocated a return to Adam Smith's ideas of free and unregulated markets. They also believed in the Lockean idea that a people would organize themselves into voluntary associations to meet those collective needs that markets could not address. For libertarian thinkers, those needs ranged widely from managing common resources (such as irrigation) to assisting the poor. Libertarian thinkers include the economists Friedrich Hayek (1899–1992) and Milton Friedman (1912–2006), who argued for a return to classical liberalism and free-market capitalism; and the philosopher Robert Nozick (1938–2002), who advocated a minimal state in which markets and associations perform all the polity's governing needs except for foreign policy and national defense.

REVIEWING AND USING THE CHAPTER

1. On balance, would you say that human nature is basically good and deserving of trust or basically bad and deserving of distrust? Why? What historical and contemporary evidence can you cite in support of your position?

2. What are the major differences between anarchism and statism?

3. Which ideas do the constitutionalist philosophies of conservatism, republicanism, and liberalism share and on which ideas do they differ? Provide specific examples to support your answer.

4. Which parts of the U.S. Constitution emphasize liberalism and which parts emphasize republicanism? Cite specific examples and explain your reasoning.

5. The U.S. Constitution was founded on a complex mixture of liberal and republican ideas. For example, the Constitution stresses both minority rights and majority rule, both liberty and order, and both individual rights and the common good. In your view, are the inherent tensions caused by this mixture a good thing or something that should be changed?

6. Do you agree or disagree with James Madison that "government is the greatest of all reflections on human nature"? Why or why not?

EXTENSION ACTIVITY

Does a state of nature (or life without government) exist anywhere in your community today? Use specific examples to support your answer.

WEB RESOURCES

International World History Project
http://history-world.org

Founded and run by current and former university professors, this Web site features a collection of history-related essays, maps, historical documents, educational videos, speeches, and music for over 330 historical topics and contains more than 2,000 pages.

New World Encyclopedia: Entry on Political Philosophy
www.newworldencyclopedia.org/entry/Political_ philosophy

This entry provides an excellent and brief treatment of the origins and development of political philosophy as a discipline

as well as a brief annotated list of influential political philosophers.

Project Gutenberg
www.promo.net/pg/index.html

This is one of the oldest and most comprehensive collections of e-books available at no cost on the Internet.

University of Michigan Documents Center
www.lib.umich.edu/govdocs/pstheory.html

This Web site contains an annotated list of Web resources as well as Library of Congress Subject Headings for political theory.

NOTES

1 Leo Strauss, "What Is Political Philosophy," in *Princeton Readings in Political Thought: Essential Texts since Plato,* ed. Mitchell Cohen and Nicole Ferman (Princeton, N.J.: Princeton University Press, 1996), 642–643.

2 W. Scott Morton and Charlton M. Lewis, *China: Its History and Culture,* 4th ed. (New York: McGraw-Hill, 2005), 38.

3 Ibid.

4 Ibid. See also Dennis Bloodworth and Ching Ping Bloodworth, *The Chinese Machiavelli: 3,000 Years of Chinese Statecraft* (New Brunswick, N.J.: Transaction, 2005).

5 Morton and Lewis, *China,* 43–44.

6 Thomas Hobbes, *Leviathan,* ed. C. B. MacPherson (Harmondsworth, UK: Penguin, 1968), 186. A fine, brief, general treatment of Hobbes is Richard Tuck, *Hobbes: A Very Short Introduction* (Oxford: Oxford University Press, 2002).

7 John Locke, *The Second Treatise on Civil Government* (Buffalo, N.Y.: Prometheus Books, 1986), 54–55. A fine brief treatment is *John Dunn, Locke: A Very Short Introduction* (Oxford: Oxford University Press, 2003).

8 Patricia Crone, *God's Rule: Government and Islam, Six Centuries of Medieval Islamic Political Thought* (New York: Columbia University Press, 2004), 66.

9 Peter Kropotkin, *Law and Authority: An Anarchist Essay* (London: International Publishing, 1886), 23.

10 James H. Billington, "Dostoevsky's Prophetic Novel: 'The Possessed' Foresaw Political Terrorism on the Eve of Its Birth," *Wall Street Journal,* January 28, 2006, 12.

11 For a comparison of Boussuet's and Hobbes's political philosophies, see Donald S. Lutz, *Principles of Constitutional Design* (New York: Cambridge University Press, 2006), Chap. 2.

12 Quoted in Laurence Berns, "Thomas Hobbes," in *History of Political Philosophy,* 3rd ed., ed. Leo Strauss and Joseph Cropsey (Chicago: University of Chicago Press, 1987), 410.

13 Arthur M. Melzer, "Jean-Jacques Rousseau," in *The Encyclopedia of Democracy,* ed. Seymour Martin Lipset (Washington, D.C.: Congressional Quarterly Inc., 1995), Vol. 3, 1089.

14 James Madison, "*The Federalist* No. 55," in *The Federalist Papers,* by Alexander Hamilton, James Madison, and John Jay, ed. Clinton Rossiter (New York: New American Library, 1961), 346.

15 James Madison, "*The Federalist* No. 51," in *The Federalist Papers,* by Alexander Hamilton, James Madison, and John Jay, ed. Clinton Rossiter (New York: New American Library, 1961), 322.

16 Harvey Mansfield Jr., "Edmund Burke," in *History of Political Philosophy,* 3rd ed., ed. Leo Strauss and Joseph Cropsey (Chicago: University of Chicago Press, 1987), 687–709. See also R. R. Palmer, Joel Colton, and Lloyd Kramer, *A History of the Modern World,* 10th ed. (Boston: McGraw-Hill, 2007), 334–335, 371.

17 Donald S. Lutz, *Principles of Constitutional Design* (New York: Cambridge University Press, 2006), 200–202.

18 Ibid., 23.

19 Aristotle, *The Politics,* rev. ed., ed. Trevor J. Saunders, trans. T. A. Sinclair (Baltimore, Md.: Penguin, 1981), 1337.

20 Herodotus, *The Histories,* trans. Robin Waterfield (Oxford: Oxford University Press, 1998), Book 5, section 78, 332.

21 Quoted in Richard Carwardine, *Lincoln: A Life of Purpose and Power* (New York: Vintage Books, 2006; originally published 2003), 14. Emphasis in original.

22 For a comparison of Wilson and Lloyd George, see Patricia Lee Sykes, *Presidents and Prime Ministers: Conviction Politics in the Anglo-American Tradition* (Lawrence: University Press of Kansas, 2000), Chap. 4.

POLITICAL CULTURE AND INSTITUTIONS

Political culture and institutions are among the most important factors shaping political behavior. For centuries, political thinkers have studied the relationships among political culture, institutions, and behavior.

Culture is the mental map that helps to orient people as they interact with the world. In this unit you will learn about a particular aspect of culture—political culture. Political culture includes the shared and learned beliefs that people have about their polity; their civic identity; and the role of citizens, government, and other institutions in the polity. A polity's political culture helps shape political beliefs, identity, behavior, and institutions in the polity. There are four types of political culture: individualistic, republican, statist, and traditionalist. Each type contains a unique set of expectations about the roles of government and the citizen in the polity. The ways political cultures combine in a polity can help explain the politics of that polity and the importance of democracy in it. In this unit, you will explore how political culture affects diverse polities.

As with political culture, a country's form of government is also significant. You will explore how a country's form of government relates to its dominant interests

CHAPTER 6:

HOW DOES POLITICAL
CULTURE INFORM
CITIZENSHIP AND
GOVERNMENT?

CHAPTER 7:

WHAT FORMS DO
GOVERNMENTS TAKE?

and values, its political institutions, and government performance. Forms of government also represent the political choices made by the people of a polity. Two choices are particularly important. First, who should govern? That is, which interests should be represented by which institutions and with what powers? Second, who should benefit? That is, by which institution or combination of institutions will government carry out its responsibilities and which interests will thereby benefit? Constitution-makers and reformers have grappled with these questions for thousands of years. In the second chapter of this unit, you will learn how the answers to these questions have affected polities around the world.

CHAPTER 6
HOW DOES POLITICAL CULTURE INFORM CITIZENSHIP AND GOVERNMENT?

BIG IDEAS

- Culture and human nature are two great factors that shape human thought and action, but they are not all powerful.

- Political culture shapes people's beliefs about the world of politics and their roles within that world.

- Types of political cultures include individualistic, republican, statist, and traditionalist cultures.

- Each type of political culture offers a different view of government and the roles of citizens.

- Democracy is not the special preserve of one political culture; different types of political cultures can support democratic systems.

- Although many polities emphasize one type of political culture, in practice most are mixtures of two or more political cultures.

Purpose of This Chapter

Political culture matters. It helps shape political beliefs, identity, behavior, and institutions in the polity. At the same time, political leaders and citizens use political institutions and public policy to reshape political culture. Political culture is a two-way street. From Plato to the present, political thinkers have studied the relationships among political culture, institutions, and behavior. Political scientists and anthropologists have identified four types of political culture: individualistic, republican, statist, and traditionalist. Each type contains a unique set of expectations about the roles of government and the citizen in the polity. Most polities consist of two or more political cultures. The ways political cultures combine in a particular polity can help explain the politics of that polity and the importance of democracy in it.

Terms to Know

acculturation	cynical individualism	secularism
citizen	human nature	social capital
citizenship	individualistic political cultures	statist political cultures
civic efficacy	personality	traditionalist political cultures
civic identity	political culture	
culture	republican political culture	

WHAT IS THE RELATIONSHIP BETWEEN HUMAN NATURE AND CULTURE?

Human nature and culture are two great forces that shape human thought and action. The Dutch organizational anthropologist Geert Hofstede (1928–) likened human nature to the operating system of the human mind and culture to the software of the mind.[1]

For more than forty years, Hofstede led an international team of IBM scientists, who studied the complex relationships between culture and organization. IBM was motivated to learn more about the role and influence of culture because, as a multinational corporation, its success depended on understanding more about the cultures of the people who made up their company.

Hofstede defined **human nature** as those universal and inherited traits that all people have in common.[2] In Chapter 4, we identify four universal human instincts based on the latest research of neuroscientists:

- The survival instinct of self-preservation
- The pack instinct of human beings as social creatures
- The acquisitive instinct that leads human beings to acquire property
- The moral instinct that enables people to distinguish right from wrong[3]

Human nature also includes the ability to reason and express universal feelings of anger, love, joy, and sadness.

Hofstede defined **culture** as patterns of thinking, feeling, and acting that are shared and learned by members of a group or society.[4] For Hofstede, culture is the way of life of a group of people, including not only their beliefs but also culturally acquired emotions, practices, institutions, symbols, and language.

More narrowly defined, culture is the mental map that helps to orient people as they interact with the world. Culture is acquired, not innate; it is learned from society, not inherited from nature. Although all human beings have universal and inherited instincts, the members of one culture learn to express those instincts differently than those of another culture.

Culture matters. Culture is an important source of our identity, beliefs, and values. Culture shapes who we are and how we see the world. Culture also establishes norms of behavior and the language and symbols by which members of a society communicate with one another.

But culture is not all powerful. Most countries do not have a single monolithic culture that dominates all spheres of life. A country may have a general culture with subcultures divided along regional, religious, or ideological lines. In Latin America, for example, the Roman Catholic Church and various socialist and communist parties have vied for people's attachments for decades.

Nor is culture chiseled in stone. People adapt their culture to new conditions, institutions shape and limit behavior, and powerful change agents (such as conquerors and tyrants) impose their own cultural values on subdued people.

Cultural influences are often subtle and difficult to discern from the influences of human nature. Is the love of freedom, for example, universal to human nature or peculiar to some cultures and not others?

Personality also affects culture and expressions of it. Each individual's personality is unique. **Personality**, according to Hofstede, is a person's unique mental programming. It is partly inherited and partly learned through interactions with others.[5] An individual's personality, for example, influences the groups he or she joins, the friends he or she makes, the candidates he or she votes for, and his or her particular feelings about values such as freedom and order (see Table 6.1).

Acculturation is the process by which a person is brought up in a culture, acquires the beliefs of that culture, and becomes a member of that culture. Acculturation plays a necessary role in preserving a society's culture and adapting that society to change. Acculturation is part of the larger process of socialization by which people become a part of society.

Examples of acculturation institutions include the family, the school, and religion. More specialized institutions vary depending on the dominant influences of a particular culture, such as religion, class, caste, and political party. In Latin America, for example, the Church has socializing institutions (neighborhoods, schools, camps, newspapers, and so on) as do the leading leftist parties.

Table 6.1 Three Sources of Human Beliefs and Identity

Universal	Specific to a group	Specific to an individual
Human nature	Culture	Personality
Inherited	Learned	Inherited and learned

Source: Adapted from Geert Hofstede and Gert Jan Hofstede, *Cultures and Organizations: Software of the Mind*, 2nd ed. (New York: McGraw-Hill, 2005), 4–5.

WHAT IS POLITICAL CULTURE?

Political culture is the mental map that orients people in their political world. As a subset of general culture, political culture includes the shared and learned beliefs that people have about their polity, their civic identity, and the role of government and other institutions in the polity.[6] According to Gabriel Almond and Sidney Verba, two pioneering scholars in the field of political culture, there are five important dimensions of political culture:

1. A sense of national identity
2. Attitudes toward oneself as a participant in political life
3. Attitudes toward one's fellow citizens
4. Attitudes and expectations regarding governmental output and performance
5. Attitudes toward and knowledge about the political process of decision making[7]

According to Almond and G. Bingham Powell, these five attitudes and expectations can be compressed into three levels. At the system level, do the people trust the political system? At the process level, do people approve of the processes by which decisions are made and their roles in those processes? At the policy level, do citizens agree with the policy goals of government?[8]

Since the dawn of political philosophy, political thinkers have recognized the importance of shared political beliefs as the bedrock of every polity. These beliefs provide a basis on which to build a polity's **social capital**, the levels of trust, networks of communication, and feelings of mutual cooperation needed to hold a polity together through thick and thin.[9] All polities require a minimal level of trust—individuals' trust in one another and in society's governing institutions. Where mistrust prevails, people pursue their own self-interests, hold other people suspect, and ignore the consequences of their actions for the common good.

Political culture is the glue that holds these beliefs together, but it is not impervious to change. Political culture shapes the roles of citizens and institutions, but citizens and institutions can reshape political culture. Political culture is a two-way street. In fact, the remaining chapters of this book document numerous instances in which political leaders and an active citizenry influenced cultural and political change.

A familiar example is the American cultural transitions in the decades after the Revolutionary War. The first change transformed a deferential colonial culture into an independent republican culture. Then, in the Age of Jackson, Democrats infused a national republican culture with liberal and democratic elements. These changes did not just happen. Radical, conservative, and moderate republicans and new liberals debated one another in state constitutional conventions, legislatures, courtrooms, town meetings, and election campaigns. They argued over the shape of the new union, the admission of new states, and the orientation of federal and state policies, laws, and institutions.

Cultural overtones colored these debates. State policy debates in the late 1770s and 1780s concerning the confiscation of Loyalist property and the reform of inheritance laws were also about dissolving a deferential culture. (See More About . . . Americanizing

MORE ABOUT . . .
Americanizing Inheritance Laws

Before the American Revolution, the colonies naturally followed British legal traditions. But in the wake of the conflict, the states began to depart from some aspects of British law to better conform to the political culture of the new nation. For centuries, large landed estates in England had been preserved by two legal concepts: entailment and primogeniture. Entailment prevented a landowner from, at his death, leaving his land to anyone other than his direct heirs. Primogeniture is the right of the first-born son to inherit all of his ancestor's lands. Together, these legal restrictions kept large landed estates intact generation after generation. They left younger sons of the aristocracy landless, leading many to choose careers in the military or the church. Other younger sons sailed to British colonies to seek their fortunes.

The status of entailment and primogeniture as protectors of a landed aristocracy made the concepts offensive to many leaders of the newly formed republic. Thomas Jefferson, for example, successfully led an effort to abolish entailment and primogeniture in Virginia. (Laws relating to inheritance were generally handled at the state, rather than the federal, level.) Jefferson and other leaders believed that the diffusion of land ownership aligned well with the values of the new republic.

Inheritance Laws.) The state constitutional debates of the 1820s, which included disputes about property requirements for voting and holding office, reflected the intense cultural debate sparked by efforts to democratize American culture.[10]

Americans understood that institutions and laws (of property confiscation, inheritance, and suffrage requirements) could serve as vehicles of cultural change. In the practical unfolding of politics, the influence of political culture on political institutions and the influence of institutions on political culture tends to blend and blur. The results depend not only on the political strength of opposing sides but on the resilience of existing political cultures. Understandably, those results varied from state to state. Differences also varied from country to country. (See Politics in Action: The Meiji Restoration.)

Throughout history, political thinkers realized that political beliefs varied not only from one polity to another but also within one polity. They also were aware that those beliefs shaped political institutions, and the reverse. In *The Republic,* the classical Greek philosopher Plato observed that "Governments vary as the dispositions of men vary."[11]

Aristotle developed a political philosophy in which political culture played an important role. Recall that according to Aristotle every polity has a constitutional makeup consisting of three dimensions: an ethical dimension prescribing the beliefs people hold dear, a socio-economic dimension that reflects the division of wealth and interests in society, and a legal dimension consisting of the laws and governing institutions of society. Political culture is roughly equivalent to Aristotle's pattern of political beliefs in his moral constitution (see Chapter 4).

Aristotle, however, used the term *ethical constitution* for a reason. Aristotle, like other political thinkers of his day, distinguished two sources of political culture: ethics (from the Greek *ethos*) and ethnicity (from the Greek *ethnos*). Aristotle's use of ethics referred to moral philosophy and

POLITICS IN ACTION
The Meiji Restoration

In 1853, a fleet of American warships led by Commodore Matthew Perry arrived in Japan. The visit surprised Japanese officials, who had kept the nation isolated from the West for more than two centuries. Perry brought a letter from the president asking for the opening of foreign relations between the two nations. The United States was one of a number of Western powers that wanted Japan to open up to trade with the West.

Japanese leaders eventually agreed to trade with the United States. But in an effort to resist domination by the West (something China had long suffered), Japanese leaders decided to modernize and to strengthen their national government. As a symbol of the new era, the Japanese emperor was restored to power in 1868. He called his reign the Meiji, or "enlightened rule."

For the next twenty years, Japan undertook a thorough study of Western political systems. In 1890, Japan adopted a constitution modeled on that of Imperial Germany. The constitution balanced power between the executive and the national legislature. Executive power lay in the hands of a prime minister and his cabinet of ministers (the emperor was essentially a figurehead). Members of the upper house of the legislature were appointed, while voters chose members of the lower house.

The Meiji Restoration profoundly changed Japanese culture. Before the restoration, Japan had functioned essentially as a feudal society. The new government fundamentally altered the traditional economic system by taking vast tracts of land away from the aristocracy and making it available to the peasants as private property. The government also accelerated industrialization. To resist Western military power, Japan modernized and increased the size of its military. By the turn of the twentieth century, Japan had emerged as an imperial power with a political culture that was dramatically different from what it had been just forty-seven years before.

Japan Defeats the Chinese Fleet Near Phungtao *by Kobayashi Kiyochika. When Japan and China went to war over control of Korea in 1894, Japan's modern navy was instrumental in China's defeat.*

the idea that a polity should stand for principles grounded in philosophy. By ethnicity, Aristotle meant the long-standing clan and tribal ties of common ancestry, language, homeland, and traditions that predated the dawn of philosophy. Aristotle saw ethnicity as an insufficient base on which to build a polity. Ethnicity might have sufficed during the tribal stage of Greek history, but the rise of cities as polities demanded a more intellectual and civilized source of political culture. Aristotle developed ethics, political philosophy, and rhetoric partly as an antidote to the cultural ties of ethnicity that competed with the newer loyalties of citizenship to the polity.

Ancient Rome faced a different variation of the conflict between tribal cultures and a newly fashioned civic identity. Rome expanded by conquering or allying itself with an ever-increasing variety of tribes or federations of tribes that the Romans called "nations." These conquered peoples and allies continued to identify with their tribe or nation. Eventually, Rome extended a diluted version of citizenship to these tribes and nations in the hopes of showing them that the benefits of Roman citizenship outweighed allegiance to outmoded tribal cultures.

These examples from ancient Greece and Rome are powerful reminders that political culture is not simply a neutral subject of academic study. It also has served as a policy instrument in the political formation of polities and the development of a responsible citizenry within polities.

WHAT IS THE RELATIONSHIP AMONG POLITICAL CULTURE, IDENTITY, AND CITIZENSHIP?

People are social creatures; they need to be with others, to belong to a larger community, and to identify with that larger community. Political culture is a source not only of political beliefs but of civic identity.

Civic identity refers to the identity that people derive from membership in a larger political community.[12] Civic identity can be supplied in various ways—by being part of a group, a class, a nation, or a faith. But, according to most political philosophers, civic identity can be fulfilled only by participation in the polity, the highest form of human association.

Citizenship is membership in the polity. Civic identity is defined as one's legal status as a citizen. According to the *Stanford Encyclopedia of Philosophy,* a **citizen** is "a member of a political community who enjoys the rights and assumes the duties of membership."[13] In the United States, for example, the political rights reserved to citizens are the rights to vote, hold elected office, and serve on a jury.

Independent states grant citizenship on the basis of one or more of three criteria:

- Citizenship by birth is based on jus solis ("the right of soil"), by which a child born in the territory of a country is a citizen of that country.
- Citizenship by descent is based on jus sanguinis ("the right of blood"), by which a child inherits citizenship of his or her parents.
- Citizenship by naturalization is acquired on the basis of adherence to common principles by individuals who must pass certain tests (for example, length of residence, language proficiency, and civic knowledge). In some countries, a person can become a naturalized citizen when he or she marries a citizen of that country.[14]

MORE ABOUT . . .

Conditions of U.S. Citizenship by Naturalization

- Eighteen years of age or older
- Resided in the United States for at least five years as a lawful permanent resident (three years if married to a U.S. citizen)
- Speak, read, and write English
- Good moral character
- Familiarity with the history and culture of the United States
- Attachment to the principles of the U.S. Constitution
- Renounce former citizenship

A 1919 poster extolling the benefits of American citizenship.

U.S. Office of Personnel Management, Investigations Service, "Citizenship Laws of the World," Washington, D.C., (March 2001), 10, available at www.opm.gov/EXTRA/INVESTIGATE/is-01.pdf.

Germany, for example, has relied historically on citizenship by descent. Only ethnic Germans could be German citizens. In 2000, Germany expanded its citizenship to include citizenship by birth if one parent has lived in Germany for eight years.[15]

The United States, by comparison, recognizes all three sources of citizenship. Citizenship is open to children born in a U.S. territory regardless of their parents' citizenship; children born outside the United States to one or both parents who are U.S. citizens, as long as the citizen parent resided in the United States prior to the child's birth; and foreign citizens who meet specified conditions of naturalization.[16] (See More About . . . Conditions of U.S. Citizenship by Naturalization.)

The three bases for citizenship—birth, descent, and naturalization—are modern expressions of ethnos and ethos as sources of political culture and citizenship. Their differences are part of history. Citizenship by birth first took hold in revolutionary France and America. It was inspired by a republican political culture that proclaimed a free land to which all were welcome. Practically, it also was an incentive to immigration and frontier settlement by young families throughout the Americas, where people were in short supply.

Citizenship by descent was adopted by Germany in the nineteenth century for a different set of reasons. In the early 1800s, Germany was a national vision fractured into more than three hundred states without a shared political culture. The movement for national unification in Germany built a nation of German-speaking people before it created a unified state. Citizenship by blood was an essential instrument of state unification.

Citizenship by naturalization rejects the automatic birthright approach of birth and descent. Instead, it provides an opportunity for adults who are willing to learn. Naturalization fits the political culture of an achievement-oriented society and a republic with an ethos—a way of life and set of principles—that can be learned. In this sense, it shares one important similarity with citizenship by birth—both carry the hope that a free republic will inspire a republican citizenry.

The French philosophers Montesquieu and de Tocqueville have much to offer on the subject of culture, identity, and citizenship. On this subject, they are modern equivalents of Aristotle. Charles-Louis de Secondat, Baron de La Brède et de Montesquieu (1689–1755), an influential Enlightenment thinker, is most often mentioned in textbooks because of his theory of separation of powers, which strongly influenced the American founders. But in that theory he also contributed significantly to the study of political culture. Montesquieu began his major work, *The Spirit of the Laws* (1748) with this assertion—that the principal challenge facing the modern state is the need to reconcile freedom and coercion.[17] Like Aristotle, Montesquieu searched for constitutional solutions to this challenge, comparing historical and contemporary republics and monarchies in terms of how well they responded to this challenge.

Like Aristotle, Montesquieu was particularly impressed by republics that balanced freedom and coercion by constitutionally legitimizing each as a check on the other. He singled out England as a model, identifying several factors that explained why it succeeded where other polities had failed. Among the most important factors were England's temperate climate, its commercial development, and its political culture. The key to England's political culture is contained in the title of Montesquieu's book. That is, England was not only a nation of laws but also of people who shared "the spirit of the laws." The English expected government to be ruled by the law, not the reverse.

The French Liberal philosopher Alexis de Tocqueville (1805–1859) shared Montesquieu's commitment to constitutional government and culture. Like other Europeans, de Tocqueville wondered why democracy seemed to be working in the United States and not in France. In the early 1830s, de Tocqueville had the opportunity to visit the United States to study its prison system. Andrew Jackson had just been reelected president in 1832, and the spirit of democracy was in the air. As de Tocqueville traveled the United States, he became intrigued by the *morés* ("customs") of American political culture and found in American political culture an explanation for the success of American democracy. In his classic work, *Democracy in America* (1835, 1840), de Tocqueville offered this explanation:

> *The customs of the people may be considered as one of the great general causes to which the maintenance of a democratic republic in the United States is attributable. I here use the word <u>customs</u> [to refer] . . . not only to manners properly so called—that is to what might be termed <u>the habits of the heart</u>—but to the various notions and opinions current among men and to the mass of those ideas which constitute their <u>character of mind</u>. I comprise under this term [custom or morés], therefore, the whole moral and intellectual condition of a people.*[18]

De Tocqueville viewed cultural customs as a combination of two elements: (1) moral "habits of the heart" that include manners and what we term values and (2) the intellectual "character of mind" that includes attitudes or opinions. The term *beliefs,* as we use it, includes both moral and intellectual elements.

What were these customs of American democracy? Among the most important for de Tocqueville was the Americans' enthusiasm for joining together to solve their public problems. He was amazed by this simple habit and its effects. Joining together in civic associations gave Americans valuable experience and skills in self-government.

This practice also gave Americans a powerful sense of civic pride and civic efficacy. **Civic efficacy** refers to the belief that people, both individually and collectively, can make a difference in their community, state, or nation. The goal might be a community project with tangible results, such as building a park. Or it might be changing national government policy and thereby ensuring that your voice will be heard by the government. Whatever the goal, successful participation is very important for Tocqueville. Successful participation increases the participants' trust in one another and in government. Successful participation also reduces alienation and the political distance between citizens and their government. Further, a successful participation process builds self-esteem, practical experience, and the feeling that you can make a difference. Even if your goals were not achieved, did the system work the way it was designed to work? Was your voice heard?

American political culture and civil society provided a fertile seedbed for democracy in the nineteenth century. But what about countries with different political cultures? And what about the United States today?

HOW DO POLITICAL CULTURES DIFFER?

In the late 1950s, two American political scientists, Gabriel A. Almond and Sidney Verba, helped launch the comparative study of political culture. They used the survey research techniques of questionnaires and interviews to study the relationship between political attitudes and democracy in five countries (Britain, Germany, Italy, Mexico, and the United States). They published their findings in an influential book, *The Civic Cultures.*[19] Like de Tocqueville, Almond and Verba were concerned with how and why democracy thrived in some countries and not in others.

Almond and Powell identified a pattern of democratic culture, which they called civic culture, that had characteristics similar to those found by de Tocqueville. As summarized by one of their colleagues, Lucian W. Pye, that pattern included "a high level of political awareness, a strong sense of competence, and considerable skill in cooperation, combined with rational participation in civic and political life."[20]

Almond and Verba found a strong relationship between this pattern of culture and democratic stability in Britain and the United States. In these two countries, they found a citizenry of active and informed participants. Elsewhere they found a citizenry of (1) subjects, who passively obeyed the law, and (2) parochials, who were largely unaware of politics or simply ignored it.

Beginning in the 1970s, Robert Putnam applied some of Almond and Powell's research to an intensive study of political culture. He too was interested in explaining why democracy worked in some places and not others. In 1970, the centralized Italian government created and empowered fifteen new regional governments. Each regional government had a similar institutional framework, similar enough for Putnam to focus on one thing that varied among regions—the political culture. Putnam wanted to find out which regional governments succeeded, how they succeeded, and why. He and his colleagues gathered data on institutional performance as well as on the attitudes of citizens and leaders.

Putnam found that democratic success depended in part on a democratic or civic culture.[21] However, he received considerable criticism for this finding. Was the American-style model of civic culture, critics asked, the only type of democratic culture?

American political scientist Daniel J. Elazar was another pioneer in the study of political culture. But, unlike others, he was not content with explaining democracy. He wanted to explain the politics of both democracies and nondemocracies. Elazar's method consisted of travel, observation, interviewing knowledgeable people, and collecting material for later review. He traversed most of the continents numerous times, inhibited only by polio, which he had contracted as a young man while traveling the Middle East.

Elazar first tested his theory of political culture in a comparative study of ten medium-size cities located in five American prairie and plains states: Illinois, Iowa, Minnesota, Wisconsin, and Colorado. His findings were published in 1970.[22] He then widened his research to a comparative study of nation-states. His international research uncovered four central features of society: traditions, the community, the individual, and the state. According to Elazar, all four features are present in every society, but each forms the basis of a different political culture. As a result, most societies are a mix of competing political cultures. Traditional political cultures are organized around ethnos and the institutions of family and tribe. Civic or republican political cultures are motivated by a strong sense of civil community and the advancement of the common good. Individualistic political cultures prize the freedom and integrity of the individual, and statist political cultures define the state as the central framework of society.[23]

Elazar found that each political culture could sustain democracy but in different ways. Democratization depended on the interaction of different political cultures in the same country. Elazar cautioned against trying to match a particular country with a particular political culture—although many countries emphasize one type, most are a blend of two or more.

Meanwhile, on the other side of the Atlantic, the British anthropologist Mary Douglas published a book in 1970 in which she developed a cultural typology similar to Elazar's.[24] Elazar and Douglas arrived at similar conclusions, published in the same year; but they arrived at their conclusions from different directions. Elazar began by identifying his four core values of society. Together, these values are present in all societies; separately, each is the organizing element of a different political culture. Douglas began by identifying two dimensions common to all societies. She referred to these dimensions as the group and the grid.[25]

The group dimension of society charts the importance of the group in people's lives. At one end of the group dimension are cultures in which people's lives are dominated by one or more strong groups that shape people's beliefs and behavior. This type of culture is similar to Elazar's traditional culture, in which people are tied by traditional kinship networks to their

Table 6.2 Four Types of Political Cultures

		Social inequality	
		Low	High
Group strength	High	Republican	Traditionalist
	Low	Individualistic	Statist

tribe. Douglas's group-based culture is also similar to a republican culture in which people are pressured to conform for the good of the community. At the other end of the group dimension, Douglas found societies with weaker group ties in which people behaved as free agents.[26] This type of culture is similar to Elazar's individualistic culture.

The grid dimension measures the relative power of inequality (that is, status differences) and regulation in society. At one end of this dimension, Douglas found hierarchical societies in which people are treated as unequal and constrained by their status in society and the regulatory power of the state. This type of culture is similar to Elazar's statist culture. At the other end of the grid dimension are more egalitarian societies in which citizens are treated as equals (at least under the law) and the state is held in check by various counterweights.[27] This type of culture is similar to Elazar's republican culture.[28] Table 6.2 shows how the dimensions of group strength and social inequality (grid) intersect and form four types of political culture.

- Republican political cultures (unlike individualistic cultures) have a high level of group strength with a strong sense of community. Like individualistic cultures, they have a strong sense of equality and tend to rely on community pressure, not government regulation, to keep people moving toward the common good.
- Individualistic political cultures have low group strength and a low level of inequality and governmental regulation.
- Traditionalist political cultures have a high level of social inequality, but they rely on group pressure more than on government regulation to maintain the status quo.
- Statist political cultures have high social inequality sustained by a strong government that suppresses all groups but state-sponsored organizations.

Each political culture has a preferred role for government, social organizations, and the citizen in society.

HOW DO POLITICAL CULTURES INFORM THE ROLES OF CITIZENS AND GOVERNMENTS IN SOCIETY?

Political culture orients people in their expectations about the roles of government and the citizen. People acquire these expectations as part of their upbringing in school, family, and other settings. But various factors intervene in the process, including personality differences,

differences among family attitudes, and the media's portrayal of politics in action. These factors can produce wide variations within a political culture by lowering or raising an individual's expectations. Some people become true believers, others become cynics, and most fall somewhere in the middle.

Another important set of factors influencing cultural expectations is the relationship between political culture and other belief systems. These systems include ethics, philosophy, religion, and ideology. Generally, cultural expectations are more strongly held and deeply ingrained when they are legitimized and reinforced by one or more additional belief systems. Each of these belief systems, however, interacts with political culture in a different way.

Political philosophy can enlighten the expectations of political culture by strengthening the knowledge base of those expectations. There is a philosophical equivalent for each of the Elazar-Douglas political culture types. For example, there is a strong correlation between the beliefs of individualistic political culture and the principles of liberal political philosophy. Also, obvious correlations exist between republican political culture and republican philosophy and between statist political culture and statist philosophy. Finally, there is a strong theoretical relationship between traditionalist political culture and conservative political philosophy.

Ethics and religion can inspire cultural expectations by providing a sense of moral purpose. In ancient Greece and Rome, for example, republicanism was a way of life, a set of cultural expectations, and an ethical code of human behavior. Before the common era, each city in the Greek and Roman world had its gods. Their religion, however, did not provide specific rules of behavior; for that, the Greeks and Romans relied on ethical codes. In contrast, republicanism reinforced very detailed commandments from God in biblical Israel.[29]

An ideology is a set of ideas designed to move large numbers of people from belief to action. In its modern form, the rise of political ideology occurred in the nineteenth century along with the rise of democracy. As more people gained literacy and the right to vote, there was a rush to translate philosophies into ideologies that had widespread popular appeal and carried a call to action. The nineteenth century also saw the rise of mass political parties. In Europe, most of these parties had an ideological platform; examples include Conservative, Liberal, and Socialist parties. Since the middle of the nineteenth century, political ideologies and mass political parties have sought to deepen and widen their popular appeal. Table 6.3 summarizes the roles of the citizen and government for each of Elazar-Douglas's political cultures.

Table 6.3 Roles of Government and the Citizen

Political culture	Source of authority	Political value	Role of government	Role of the citizen
Individualistic	People	Liberty	Protect individual rights	Free agent
Statist	State	Security	Provide law and order	Duty-bound subject
Republican	Community	Solidarity	Promote common good	Engaged participant
Traditionalist	Providence	Continuity	Prescribe behavior	Faithful servant

INDIVIDUALISTIC POLITICAL CULTURES

In **individualistic political cultures**, people see the polity as a political marketplace of public and private goods. The core political value is individual liberty.

In the political marketplace, the citizen is a rights-bearing individual, a free agent who has the right to make choices unrestrained by group loyalties or pressures. As free agents, citizens are expected to make rational choices on the basis of self-interest as long as they do not harm anyone in the process. The danger of this political culture is excessive individualism, in which rational self-interest turns into selfishness and a loss of compassion for other people. According to de Tocqueville, self-interest becomes enlightened when people learn that supporting the community is ultimately in their best self-interest.

The scope and power of government are limited in individualistic cultures. Individualistic cultures tend to emphasize three roles of government: protecting individual rights; creating a level playing field so all individuals have access to equal opportunities; and, where necessary, arbitrating among competing interests. The role of the law in individualistic cultures follows Thomas Hobbes's advice that the law should provide a hedgerow that keeps people moving along in the pursuit of their interests without colliding with one another.

STATIST POLITICAL CULTURES

In individualistic cultures, government serves the individual; in statist cultures, the reverse is true—people are raised to believe that the individual should serve the interests of government and other institutions of the state. **Statist political cultures** legitimize the primacy of the state as the framework of public life. Government is legitimized as the primary (and often sole) institution of the state. In statist cultures, government often winds up controlling many institutions such as political parties, the media, and even interest groups such as youth clubs.

Statist political cultures are based on the assumption that people seek the protection of a strong state for self-preservation and an orderly life. Security and order are the core political values of statist political cultures. Loss of freedom, however, is often the price that statist regimes exact.

The primary role of government is to provide the polity with a well-maintained system of law and order. Government carries out that role by tightly enforcing a code of detailed regulations that narrow the bounds of human freedom.

The primary role of the citizen is that of the duty-bound subject. Citizens are expected to respect authority, obey the law, and otherwise demonstrate their allegiance to the state. In the statist culture, governance is provided by rigid government bureaucracies and state-controlled organizations. The model is command and control, not voluntary compliance. The good citizen is a loyal subject and is otherwise passive in political participation.

REPUBLICAN POLITICAL CULTURE

Republican political culture arose in ancient republics as a defense against monarchy. The office of citizen was seen as the highest office in the land. Being a good republican citizen was a rejection of the idea that citizens were merely loyal subjects.

In republics, the source of political authority is the political community as a whole—the polity. The core political value is community solidarity and the advancement of the common good. The good citizen is fully engaged as an active participant in the life of the community. Good citizens also possess civic virtue that comes from putting the good of the community above their self-interests. The danger of republicanism occurs when community pressure is used to stifle a diversity of opinions and political dissent.

In the ancient republics, civic virtue was demonstrated primarily by courage on the battlefield. The Greek historian Polybius lived in Rome, where he observed republican life firsthand. In his *Histories,* Polybius (c. 203–120 BCE) described what it meant to be a good Roman citizen: "The good Roman is to be brave; he is to husband his resources, not flaunt them before his fellow citizen in need. . . . He is to be honest as Scipio was honest, taking absolutely nothing from Carthage, although he was not particularly well off. And he is to be responsible and active."[30]

In modern times, republican political cultures still value these virtues of citizenship. However, in most republics, a more peaceful world that offers widespread economic opportunity has allowed a shift in priorities from military service to civic participation.

The role of government in republican cultures is limited by several cultural beliefs. These include antimonarchism, the emphasis on community over the state, the reliance on civic organizations over government bureaucracy, and the belief that no one is above the law.

Republican cultures tend to be egalitarian societies in which people prefer to believe that no citizen is better than another. Historically, however, many republics had closed egalitarian societies in which only a small percentage of the population qualified as fully empowered citizens. Ancient Athens and Rome relied heavily on slavery—a practice accepted by most of its citizens. The American republic did not abolish slavery until 1865, although many spoke out against the practice and all the northern states had passed abolition or emancipation laws by 1804.

TRADITIONALIST POLITICAL CULTURE

All political cultures have traditions. **Traditionalist political cultures**, however, rely on ethno-religious sources of political beliefs, civic identity, and political leadership. Ethnic sources are organized around kinship networks of family, clan, tribe, and nation. Religious sources are based on the belief in divine providence as the source of political authority.

Traditionalist political cultures value continuity, but those cultures that survive modernization and other political changes rely on some measure of flexibility in interpreting past traditions and providence. To balance continuity and change, most traditionalist political cultures rely on oral traditions and unwritten customs. Leaders do not like to write things down. In practice, this gives elders, priests, political bosses, patrons, and other community leaders greater flexibility in selectively remembering and liberally interpreting long-held traditions. (See Table 6.4.)

There are two important roles of government in traditionalist cultures: to preserve the status quo and to prescribe behavior by bringing it into conformance with long-held traditions and divine providence. The role of the good citizen is that of the faithful servant guided by piety and respect for authority.

Table 6.4 Characteristics of Strong Traditionalist Political Cultures

1. A deferential attitude to traditional authority figures
2. A hierarchical society with various levels of inequality in status, wealth, and power
3. Expectations of social conformity, intolerance of diversity, suspicion of outsiders
4. An emphasis on consensus over confrontation
5. The use of private deals to reach agreement
6. A fatalistic resignation to providence or fate
7. A feeling of powerlessness to effect change
8. An acceptance of the political status quo

HOW DO NATIONAL POLITICAL CULTURES COMPARE?

Political culture is a powerful concept in explaining why polities, their citizens, and their governments behave as they do. The Elazar-Douglas typology is a useful tool in such studies. To make the most of this tool, it is best to assume that polities with more than one political culture are the rule, not the exception.[31] To illustrate this point, we turn to several examples.

CAN A STATIST COUNTRY BE DEMOCRATIC?

"No other nation in the world has as dense and passionate a relationship with the State as does France," according to French political scientist Lawrence Meniere.[32] The French love their state, yet they remain deeply suspicious of it.

Statism in France dates back to the age of kings, but it was Napoleon Bonaparte (1769–1821) who turned the ideas of the French Revolution into a system of democratic statism. Bonaparte mobilized an army of citizen recruits, created a national civil service with a broad base of citizen employees, consolidated French laws into a unified code applicable to all, and increased the number of local elected officials.

Despite their misgivings about government, the French rely on the state for an extensive system of social protection. Over the years, French governments have enacted one of the most extensive cradle-to-grave welfare programs of any country in the world.[33] It includes free health care, free university education, five weeks of paid vacation annually, low-cost day care, and generous old-age pensions. Checks are sent monthly to families with more than one child, a measure aimed at slowing the declining birthrate. To administer its many government programs, France relies on a large, top-heavy, and multilayered bureaucracy. Consider this: the day-to-day work of the state is now carried on by more than 2.5 million administrators—one for every twenty-two French citizens.[34]

The most important check on government in France is a strong tradition of individualism—France is not a nation of joiners. Interest groups are small, labor unions are weak, and church attendance is not as strong as in America. When government goes too far, the French people have taken to the streets in mass protests that have brought down

POLITICS IN ACTION

Mass Protests in France

During the last two centuries, the French have used mass protests to bring down unpopular governments. But the French also march in the streets when they want to bring about the repeal of specific governmental policies. Protests organized to accomplish this are viewed as a time-honored part of French political culture. Politicians who ignore such protests do so at their peril.

In early 2006, French Prime Minister Dominique de Villepin authored a law designed to create more jobs and to decrease unemployment. The law would do so by providing employers more flexibility in laying off workers under the age of twenty-six. Supporters of the law argued that the highly regulated nature of France's labor market discouraged the hiring of new workers, contributing to higher unemployment.

The law's detractors saw it as a serious threat to France's social safety net. As opposition to the law quickly developed, mass protests erupted across France. On March 28, for example, an estimated 2.5 million people marched through the streets of French cities to protest the law.

The protests proved effective—the law was set aside on April 11. Before the law was enacted, Dominique de Villepin had been seen by many as his party's leading candidate for the presidency of France in 2007. As the protests continued, however, de Villepin's popularity plummeted. He was eclipsed by his rival Nicolas Sarkozy, who, not long after, won the presidency.

Thousands of people march in Paris during a demonstration against the 2006 employment law.

Secularism is also deeply rooted in French cultural beliefs. According to the World Values Survey of 2000, only 11 percent of French surveyed considered religion important in their lives and only 12 percent attend religious services. Over 80 percent believed that religious leaders should not influence voters or the government. Only one other country in the survey (Indonesia) expressed a higher level of distrust of religious leaders.

Secularism remains the dominant mood in France today. It is fueled by the rise of religious self-identity and antisecularism among many young French Muslims. For French secularists, the headscarf worn by Muslim women symbolizes the oppressiveness of religion that Enlightenment thinkers warned against. In 2004, the French National Parliament passed a controversial law that banned the display of conspicuous religious symbols in public schools. These include Muslim headscarves, large Christian crosses, and Jewish skullcaps. While American courts would overturn such a law as an unconstitutional infringement of the right to religious expression, the French constitutional court did not choose to do so. The French civic creed respects freedom of religion as a sacred right but not in all public places.

monarchies and republics alike. France is now in its fifth republic, and most of those republics were founded in revolution. (See Politics in Action: Mass Protests in France.)

Individualism has forced France to democratize the state. Consider this: France has 1 elected local official for every 110 voters. Compare this to the ratio in Britain of 1 elected official for every 1,800 voters.[35]

France, of course, is a republic, and the French look back with pride to the French Revolution of 1789 and their model of republicanism. For the French, statism and individualism are two key elements in this model. That model is grounded in the philosophy of Jean-Jacques Rousseau (1712–1778), who believed that there should be nothing between the state and the general will of the people (see Chapter 5 for more on Rousseau's republicanism). This view was later challenged by de Tocqueville, who was impressed with the American model of republicanism and argued for strong voluntary associations and local communities as the seedbeds of democracy.

Among the four political cultures, the French have been least inclined toward traditionalism. Antitraditionalism was one of the hallmarks of the French Enlightenment and the French Revolution. Their proponents saw traditional institutions such as the Church and the nobility as the largest landholders, the most powerful intermediate institutions between government and the people, and the strongest defenders of feudal loyalties and Catholic beliefs. The Enlightenment and the French Revolution were committed to **secularism**, the belief in the complete separation of church and state. Voltaire and other French Enlightenment thinkers saw religion as a threat to a world of reason and rights. The French Revolution popularized this sentiment and the new republic seized Church property and forced priests to swear allegiance to the republic. (See More About . . . French Secularism.)

Historically, French law and public opinion have frowned on the open display of religious identity in public, especially in public schools. In 1905, French law established the separation of church and state, and the current French Constitution declared France to be a "secular, democratic" republic (Article I, 1958). Secularism remains the dominant mood in France today.

HOW DID RUSSIAN STATISM MARGINALIZE OTHER CULTURES?

Like China and France, Russia has a strong statist culture. Evidence of the other three political cultures can be found throughout Russian history. But, unlike China and France, there is no second political culture that is strong enough to check statism. Historically, Russia has marginalized the influence of republicanism, traditionalism, and individualism. How did Russian statism become so strong? Why are the other three cultures so weak?

MORE ABOUT . . .

Russia: From Principalities to Empire

Until the second half of the fifteenth century, there was no single Russian state but a variety of principalities. The Kiev principality claimed status as the first center of Russia. Later, power shifted to the principality of Moscow. Novgorod was a rival commercial power, but it never laid claim to Russian leadership. There were other principalities as well in the lands that the tsars, beginning with Ivan the Great in the 1470s, consolidated into the Russian state. Ivan the Terrible redefined the Russian state as an empire in the mid-sixteenth century.

Russians often explain their statism in geographical and historical terms. Russia has fought for centuries to protect itself against strong neighbors—especially the Mongols in the east and Turkic peoples (also called Tartars) in the south. As a result, Russians place a high value on national security and domestic order.

The Mongols captured Moscow in 1238 and Kiev in 1240. (See More About . . . Russia: From Principalities to Empire.) They ruled Russian lands until 1480, turning Russian princes into their vassals. Two hundred fifty years of Asian rule had a powerful impact on Russian history and culture. Russians became a mixed people of Slavic and Mongol parentage. Russia was cut off from Europe at just the time when European civilization was breaking out of its medieval shell. Cut off from the West, Russia fought alone to free itself from Mongol rule.

In 1453, about thirty years before expelling the Mongols, Russia suffered a major setback. The Ottoman Turks conquered Constantinople, the center of Eastern Christianity to which the Russian Church belonged. This isolated Russia even more. Thereafter, the Russian Orthodox Church saw itself as the defender of traditional Christian faith against nonbelievers in the east and the Reformation in the west. Russia saw itself as the Third Rome and a Eurasian power between Europe and Asia.

Meanwhile, another story was unfolding in the west. The city of Novgorod became an independent city in 1014, and for nearly 125 years, Novgorod was ruled as an aristocracy by

MORE ABOUT . . .

Guilt by Association

The tsarist Russian criminal code accepted the principle that a criminal's family members were guilty by association. Like other countries that used this principle, degrees of association were assigned to particular crimes. The more serious the crime, the more generations of family members had to pay, often with their life or exile. Political crimes such as dissent and treason were among the highest of crimes. Hence, it is not surprising that the entire families of Novgorod's political leaders were deported along with the leaders. Soviet Russia expanded the principle exponentially, round-

In this image from the mid-1880s, a group of exiles and convicted persons is being loaded onto a barge bound for a Siberian prison.

ing up families of political prisoners and killing them or sending them to prison or labor camps. The political reason is the classic paranoia of tyranny—destroy everyone who may bear a grudge and may one day rise up against you; and then destroy their associates, just in case.

local nobility. In 1136, Novgorod became a republic governed by its citizenry. For almost 350 years, Novgorod flourished as a commercial republic, similar to Venice in what is today northeastern Italy.

In the fifteenth century, Moscow was a rival principality still under Mongol rule. Prince Ivan the Great (1440–1505) of Moscow changed all that. He declared himself Grand Prince of all Russia, and then in 1478 he conquered Novgorod. Two years later, Moscow freed itself from Mongol rule. Novgorod seized the moment and rebelled against Moscow. Ivan responded by deporting Novgorod's wealthy merchant families and nobility to Moscow and elsewhere in Russia. (See More About . . . Guilt by Association.)

In 1547, Ivan the Terrible converted Russia into an empire and installed himself as Russia's first tsar (also spelled czar; the title is derived from the Latin *caesar*). The vision of Eurasia had become reality, and Russia now saw itself as the center of a third great civilization between Europe and Asia.

In old Russia, the crown, Church, and aristocracy were closely allied. They controlled the state, and the state controlled the rest of society. But there also was an important difference between the interests of the tsars and the interests of the nobility and Church. The tsars had statist ambitions, but the nobility and the Church wanted to preserve their local control over the villages in which most Russians lived as peasants, serfs, and vassals of the local nobility.

Peter the Great (1672–1725) centralized the relationship between tsars and nobility when he abolished the Council of Boyars (upper nobility) that had provided a check on the tsar's power. Thereafter, the tsars subdued the nobility and the Church and became the dominant influence in society. As one scholar points out, "All the classes of the nation, from top to bottom, except the slaves, were bound to the service of the state."[36] The conquest of Novgorod and the abolition of the boyar's council were also culturally significant events.

When the state conquered Novgorod, it also marginalized republicanism. Other republican possibilities, however, emerged later in Russian history. All of Russia's great revolutions had a republican element: the Decembrist Revolt of 1825, the anarchist movement of the late nineteenth century, the liberal revolution of 1905, and the brief republican leadership of Alexander Kerensky in the February Revolution of 1917 before Vladimir Lenin seized power eight months later in the October Revolution. But the tsars squelched the first three revolutions, and Lenin's Bolsheviks eventually destroyed the last.

POLITICS IN ACTION
Samizdat

Samizdat is a Russian word meaning "self-publish." Books such as *Nomenklatura* were outlawed in the Soviet Union. To avoid discovery, the author of an outlawed book would prepare a typed or handwritten copy of the book. This would then be circulated underground by people who often made handwritten copies and secretly distributed them in bits and pieces to readers, who would then pass on their copy to another reader after they finished reading it.

Traditionalism in Russia had a similar fate. After Peter the Great, the nobility and the Russian Orthodox Church lost their political power. Nevertheless, the Church came to play a supporting role in the development of the tsarist state. Statism and tsarist authority needed the legitimacy that traditionalism and the Church supplied. This was in contrast to the later communist state, which rejected traditionalism. Communist leaders redefined traditionalistic institutions, including the Church, as enemies of the state. The first wave of communist oppression destroyed them without mercy.

Soviet rule (1917–1991) imposed a system of complete state domination by coercion. Under Soviet rule, the citizenry became submissive—taking the initiative became risky; waiting for state direction was safer. In the workplace, this had disastrous effects. As one scholar explained, workers dependent on the state displayed "acts of work avoidance rather than self-discipline and productivity. [There was] a general disdain for work in all state-managed economic sectors, a specific disinclination to risk personal initiatives."[37]

The gradual decline of the Soviet state began during 1964–1982, when Leonid Brezhnev was the leader of the Communist Party and, hence, the state. In 1970, Soviet dissident Michael Voslensky wrote a book titled *Nomenklatura: The Soviet Ruling Class.* (See Politics in Action: *Samizdat.*) The book revealed and condemned the hidden world of the Soviet elite who controlled the top administrative positions. People holding these positions enjoyed many benefits, including special well-stocked stores where they shopped. Ordinary people

MORE ABOUT . . .
The Myth of Russian Collectivism

Soviet communist ideology emphasizes the group over the individual, the community over the group, and the state over the community. Soviet leaders instituted a wide range of policies and institutions to reinforce their ideology. One of the most disastrous was the collective farm, in which the workers owned the farm and its bounty but the farm was actually run by party functionaries, after they had killed the original owners or sent them to gulags (labor internment camps). Another example is the com-munity apartment, in which families had their own bedroom and living room but shared the kitchen and bathroom facilities. Less well known is the school policy that the same group of students should remain together with the same teacher from one grade to the next to build a sense of group solidarity.

Care must be taken in drawing cultural conclusions from these ideological examples. Russians do have a stronger group orientation than Americans. Russian culture disparages individualism, both positive and cynical, even though the latter form is widespread. But Russians do not have a collectivist mentality.

---

had a hard life that included daily annoyances such as standing in long lines for food. Their finding out that the *nomenklatura* had their own well-stocked stores was the straw that broke the camel's back.

One result of this was the emergence of a cynical form of individualism. Many people lost faith in the system and a government led by officials who served only their own interests. **Cynical individualism** is the attitude that everyone, including government officials, is out for him- or herself in a dog-eat-dog world. People who hold this view teach their children two lessons of life: your family comes first, and trust no one else. (See More About . . . The Myth of Russian Collectivism.)

In the years following the collapse of the Soviet Union, Russia has built a postcommunist state, economy, and way of life. Observers disagree in their assessment of Russia's present form of government. Some describe it as a hybrid democracy that is partly free and partly not. Others prefer the term *soft authoritarianism* because freedom is dwindling but the state is not yet repressive. The next chapter takes a closer look at Russia's form of government today.

But what is the current status of Russian political culture? The relative importance of the four political cultures in Russia has not changed significantly in the postcommunist state. Statism remains the dominant political culture in Russia. After decades of communist oppression and the economic instabilities of the 1990s, most Russians want a normal life. Many Russians distrust the state, but they still look to it as the first responder to their economic needs, the primary provider of national security and domestic order, and the only way to reclaim Russia's place in the world.

Russians expect a strong and highly centralized state. They see it as part of the solution, not part of the problem, as many Americans do. Russians prefer to wait for a single centralized policy, while Americans still prefer community control in their schools, police, and various other matters. (See Comparing Governments: Where Do Americans and Russians Bury Their Leaders?)

COMPARING GOVERNMENTS

Where Do Americans and Russians Bury Their Leaders?

Most American presidents are laid to rest in their hometown because the local community is so important to American culture and democracy. Woodrow Wilson is the only president buried in Washington, D.C. The only American president buried in New York City is Ulysses Grant, and that is because he and his wife settled there after his unsuccessful bid for a third presidential term. William Howard Taft (as a secretary of war) and John F. Kennedy (as a naval commander wounded in combat) are the only presidents laid to rest in Arlington National Cemetery.

By contrast, Moscow's Kremlin (or walled citadel) is the home of the Russian state and most of its tsars and Soviet commissars. That is where they lived, died, and are buried. Most tsars who were not buried there were laid to rest in the Peter and Paul Cathedral in St. Petersburg when that city was Russia's capital. In Soviet times, Lenin was entombed for public display in the middle of Red Square inside the Kremlin. Joseph Stalin was entombed beside him for eight years, but in 1961 he was removed by a vote of the Communist Party Congress after an old communist woman rose and told of a vision she had had in which Lenin told her that it was unpleasant to be next to Stalin.

Other esteemed Soviet leaders and heroes (including the American communist John Reed) are buried in a section of the Kremlin Wall that overlooks Red Square. Less hallowed communist ground, but still prestigious, is Novodevichy, Russia's national

The funeral procession of former Russian president Boris Yeltsin approaches the historic Novodevichy Cemetery for burial in Moscow. Russia bade farewell to Yeltsin in April 2007.

cemetery located outside Moscow. This is where Boris Yeltsin, the first of Russia's postcommunist presidents to die, is buried.

Traditionalism remains strong in Russian village life. The Church and other traditional institutions have been making a slow comeback after decades of communist suppression, although most Russians are atheists as a result of three generations of communist indoctrination.

Cynical individualism remains a powerful negative force. Corruption has become a serious problem at all levels. Many official decisions can be influenced by bribing the appropriate officials—from resolving traffic violations to getting accepted into the university. In June 2009, for example, the Swedish furniture chain Ikea suspended future investments in Russia because of bribes it was forced to pay.

Republicanism is still the weakest political culture in Russia. Republican political parties and candidates have been marginalized, and republican instincts of self-government are still weak. When Vladimir Putin was president, the Russian government passed a law allowing apartment residents to form improvement associations to maintain their building and grounds. Yet most residents are accustomed to state-run apartments, so they see maintenance as a state responsibility and lack the civic skills and interest needed to create their own improvement association to assume these responsibilities.

Russians often take these values with them when they emigrate to a new homeland. In the 1970s, a Russian family moved to Israel seeking religious freedom. They were settled in Beersheba, where they lived in a small house. One day, their house caught fire and their belongings were destroyed. Their neighbors wanted to help, so they brought furniture to the family. However, the Russian family's father called a televised press conference and called on his neighbors to take back their furniture. Why? According to the father, it was the government's responsibility to take care of them, not the job of their neighbors.

Most Russians prefer national security, domestic order, and economic stability over democracy. Based on surveys conducted in 1999–2002 by the World Values Project, Russians were consistently among the most distrustful of democracy. According to the World Values survey, a large majority of Russians surveyed believed that in democracies (1) "the economic system runs badly," (2) the political system is "indecisive and [has] too much quibbling," and (3) the political system is "not good at maintaining order." Equally large majorities of Americans in the United States disagreed with those three statements.[38]

Russian political culture creates a paradox. Russian citizens continue to be estranged from the state at the same time that they continue to look to it for direction. Fifty-six percent of Russians surveyed believed that authority should be given more respect; however, an unusually large majority (92 percent) thought that the individual should be given more respect.[39]

WHAT ARE CHINA'S TWO POLITICAL CULTURES?

The renowned China specialist Lucian W. Pye (1921–2008) wrote an important book on China's political cultures titled *The Mandarin and the Cadre*. In his book, Pye distinguished these two political cultures.

The mandarin culture is a blend of traditionalist and statist political cultures. It is, according to Pye, "an elitist high Confucian culture that glorified the established authority of the better educated."[40] As you learned in Chapter 5, the ideal Confucian polity is a hierarchical system, like a pyramid of different levels, in which people have differing obligations based on their status in society. The relationship between ruler and subject is like the relationship

Mao Zedong reviewing the Army of the Great Proletarian Cultural Revolution on Tiananmen Square in Beijing, China, 1967.

between father and son. Social harmony is achieved when people know their place, accept *ren* (compassion to others), and follow the traditional rules of social behavior (*li*) for their status. In this world, the obligation of the ordinary citizen is respect for and loyalty to their leaders. The obligation of the ruler is to serve as the "pole-star" of a harmonious society. To do this, the ruler must have integrity and thereby earn the respect and loyalty of the people.

In contrast, the cadre culture is a revolutionary republican political culture. It is, according to Pye, "a passionate, populist heterodox [that is, anti-orthodox] culture that glorified the rebel and trusted magical formulas to transform economic and social reality."[41] Cadre culture draws on Taoist and Buddhist mysticism. As you learned in Chapter 5, Taoism has an anarchist philosophy that idealizes human nature, believes in egalitarian values, and distrusts the state. The cadre culture incorporates these values and adds a revolutionary fervor that seeks to unite the peasantry around a mystical vision that is anti-intellectual, antimandarin, and antistate.

The Yellow Turbans of the Han period, the Taiping Rebellion of the nineteenth century, and Mao Zedong's Cultural Revolution are historical examples of the mass peasant uprisings inspired by messianic leaders who appealed to the cadre political culture. Mao (1893–1976) clearly presented himself as the cadre leader, from the simple uniforms he wore to the ideological passion of his speeches and the mass brutality he directed against entire classes on his enemies' list. Yet he was an expert on Chinese political history, and behind the scenes he brought a Machiavellian pragmatism to his decision making. His successors, beginning with Deng Xiaoping, however, have put pragmatism at the forefront of their policies, and to that extent, they are more representative of the mandarin culture.

Conspicuously absent from the political realm in China is the individualistic political culture. This is not accidental. As different as the mandarin and cadre cultures are, they both stress the harmony of social order and emphasize the community over the individual. Chinese political culture seems to push the individualist out of the polity, but today at least, more space has opened up in the economy for the entrepreneurial spirit.

CAN TRADITIONALIST SOCIETIES BE DEMOCRATIC?

Many traditionalist societies have republican pasts. In India, for example, great republics flourished about the same time as the Roman Republic. In Africa, many tribes, such as the Igbo, proudly called themselves free and governed themselves without resorting to kings or emperors. These republican moments from the past resonate today. People take pride in their republican past and learn from it. They can say, "We did this before, and we can do it again." In fact, many countries that are democratic today can look back to some moment in their past when they were a free republic. (See Comparing Governments: Why Is Botswana a Stable Democracy?)

Hernando de Soto, the Peruvian economist, provides a powerful example of the continuing relevance of republican traditions at the community level in traditionalist societies. He has devoted his life to studying and advocating for the poor who live in shantytowns around the world. He estimates their number to be more than 4 billion.[42]

Dharavi is a district of central Mumbai, India, and is Asia's second largest slum with a population of more than 1 million people.

De Soto found that most of these shantytown communities are forced to operate outside the formal legal system of their country because that system does not let them operate inside it. Many shantytown residents have applied to the government for title to their land, for building permits, for licenses to operate commercial vehicles, or for registration to expand their businesses. But red tape and the demand for bribes prevent these residents from obtaining legal documentation. So they buy their land, build their homes, drive their taxis, start up small businesses, and improve their property outside the legal system.

Shantytown residents live in an extra-legal world where democratic and constitutional history seems light years removed. Yet they have the will to govern themselves by legal means. So they improvise. They form social contracts. They create their own legally binding arrangements for the purchase, sale, use, saving, and investment of their meager property and capital. Just as important, they create their own self-governing institutions. They form agricultural cooperatives, housing associations, small-business organizations, water districts, and sanitation committees. Collectively, these organizations are known as mutual-aid societies.

In most countries, mutual-aid or self-help societies have existed for centuries. These organizations often provide the historical evidence of a democratic past at the village level—in countries such as China and Egypt that were empires in their own right or even part of larger European conquered republics that became empires. These traditions are democratic too, and those who use them to create a lawful, prosperous, and self-governing society consider themselves democrats.

HOW DOES POLITICAL CULTURE EXPLAIN AMERICAN POLITICS?

Most nations are a mix of political cultures. The United States is the birthplace of modern individualism, but it is also a nation of joiners. Can one nation be home to both loners and joiners?

COMPARING GOVERNMENTS

Why Is Botswana a Stable Democracy?

Botswana is one of the few countries in Africa with a stable democracy and a relatively prosperous national economy. Located in southern Africa, Botswana is a small country with an old tradition of republican political culture. Prior to British colonial rule, the people of what is now Botswana, like many African peoples, had a conciliar (council-based) republic. In Botswana, the governing institution was called the *kgotla*—a council of elders that held public forums where people could bring their disputes and discuss them openly.

When the British came to Botswana, they found little of value to them in the country, so few British settled there. (Little did anyone realize that this small country was sitting on large deposits of diamonds and other minerals.) In 1895, the British organized Botswana as the Bechuanaland Protectorate, placed it under the British colonial office in South Africa, established its administrative office in Mafeking outside Botswana, and periodically sent colonial officers to the protectorate to check up on local affairs.

Botswana also has a traditionalistic culture with a history of strong chiefs of the Tswana tribe. The egalitarian values of republicanism and the hierarchical values of traditionalism can come into conflict, but they also can reinforce one another when the country is endangered. For seventy years, the Tswana chiefs drew on political and diplomatic means to block most British efforts to intrude more deeply into their country's affairs. As a result, Botswana retained many of its local republican traditions and institutions, including its council of elders.

After independence, Botswana adapted its republican institutions to the requirements of a modern independent state. Its parliament is bicameral, with a popularly elected house and a House of Chiefs similar to the British House of Lords. The House of Chiefs ensures that proposed legislation does not violate historical traditions. Botswana also retained its local councils of elders who hold weekly public forums where people can bring matters for public discussion and resolution. If there were recipes for successful democracy, Botswana would have its fair share of ingredients: a relatively small and homogeneous population, a rich yet varied natural resource base, a prosperous economy with a broad middle class, an egalitarian political culture, traditional representative institutions, strong leadership traditions when needed, and a long history of successful leadership.

Compared to other countries, the United States projects an image of individualism. Many of its television, music, and movie heroes are loners—almost antiheroes—who refuse to join the pack. Individual rights are enshrined in the Declaration of Independence and the Bill of Rights. Citizens can pursue their own interests as long as no one else's rights are denied. The historic role of government is to create a level playing field, protect individual rights, and, where necessary, arbitrate among competing interests.

At the same time, America has a deep strain of republicanism in its history. Republican values of egalitarianism, civic engagement, and a belief in the common good were part of the Puritan experience of the seventeenth century, the Yankee migration westward, many of the social movements of the nineteenth century, and the Progressive movement of the twentieth century. Today, you can still find evidence of this moralistic orientation in many of the northern states, from Minnesota to the upper plains states to Oregon, Washington, and northern California. And in the campaign platforms and speeches of many American politicians.

Traditionalism also remains strong in America. Historically, its origins can be traced back to the plantation and hacienda systems of the American South. Another source of traditionalism is ethnic city neighborhoods that were settled by immigrants from the American South, Europe, Asia, Latin America, and the Caribbean. These immigrants brought their traditions with them and passed these traditions down to their children and grandchildren. Today, the strongest indicator of traditionalism in America is religious affiliation, especially among people who identify themselves as fundamentalist or orthodox.

Historically, Americans categorically rejected statism, the fourth political culture. But you can certainly find strains of the other three cultures throughout American history and today. The question is: How do they relate in the practical unfolding of politics? This question raises other questions that readers might consider in their own research:

- How did unifying presidents, such as Franklin D. Roosevelt, Ronald Reagan, and perhaps Barack Obama, appeal to all three American cultures? To answer this question, carefully read some of their most famous campaign speeches.
- What evidence of all three political cultures can you find in American civil society?
- Will politics in the digital age be able to attract all three political cultures? How and how well?

In the practical unfolding of politics, the relationship between political culture and political institutions is a two-way street. Political culture influences the shape of political institutions, but political leaders and citizens have long used political institutions as a vehicle to reform political culture. The next chapter turns to the importance of political institutions and the forms of government that organize those institutions.

REVIEWING AND USING THE CHAPTER

1. What are the differences among human nature, personality, and culture? In what way are all three important influences on human behavior?

2. On a scale of 1 (lowest) to 7 (highest), rate American political culture in terms of the question posed for each of Almond and Powell's three levels of political culture—system, process, and policy. Support your ratings with specific examples.

3. Using Tables 6.2 and 6.3, which political culture or mix of political cultures best describes your state? Support your answer with specific examples.

4. Individualists claim that the best way to achieve the common good is for each person to work for his or her self-interest. Through enlightened self-interest, the thought goes, people will come to understand that it is in their self-interest to cooperate with others to achieve common interests and address common issues. Do you agree or disagree with this view? Why?

5. Why is it that civic republican political cultures so rare today, but traditional cultures abound? Provide specific examples to support your ideas.

EXTENSION ACTIVITY

Some scholars argue that culture makes almost all the difference in a society. Using what you have learned in this chapter, compare the major differences in the political and personal lives of the individual in each of the four political cultures described.

WEB RESOURCES

Institute for the Advanced Studies in Culture
www.virginia.edu/iasc

Hosted by an interdisciplinary research center at the University of Virginia, this site offers free access to the institute's biannual journal, *Culture,* as well as archives of audio and video resources on trends and issues in political culture from leading scholars such as Samuel Huntington, Theda Skocpol, and Robert Kaplan.

Jerusalem Center for Public Affairs
www.jcpa.org/djeindex.htm

The center hosts the Daniel Elazar Online Library that provides free and full access to dozens of Elazar's papers on political culture.

University of California Berkeley e-Scholarship Repository
http://repositories.cdlib.org/csls/fwp

This link provides access to the working papers of fellows at the University of California Berkeley's Center for the Study of Law and Society. The scholarly papers address current issues in American political culture.

World Values Survey
www.worldvaluessurvey.org

The World Values Survey is an ongoing worldwide study of cultural values and their influence on social and political life. Social scientists have conducted national surveys in ninety-seven societies. To date, there have been five waves of surveys from 1981 to 2007.

NOTES

1 Geert Hofstede and Gert Jan Hofstede, *Cultures and Organizations: Software of the Mind,* 2nd ed. (New York: McGraw-Hill, 2005).

2 Ibid., 4.

3 See Michael S. Gazzaniga, *Human: The Science behind What Makes Us Unique* (New York: HarperCollins, 2008).

4 Hofstede and Hofstede, *Cultures and Organizations,* 3–4.

5 Ibid., 5.

6 This definition of *political culture* draws on the work of Aaron Wildavsky in Michael Thompson, Richard Ellis, and Aaron Wildavsky, *Cultural Theory* (Boulder, Colo.: Westview Press, 1990), 216.

7 Gabriel A. Almond and Sidney Verba, eds., *Civic Culture Revisited* (Newbury Park, N.J.: Sage, 1989), 27.

8 Gabriel A. Almond, G. Bingham Powell, Russell J. Dalton, and Kaare Strøm, *Comparative Politics Today: A World View,* 9th ed. (New York: Pearson Longman, 2008), 43.

9 On the importance of trust and social capital, see Francis Fukuyama, *Trust: The Social Virtues and the Creation of Prosperity* (New York: Free Press Paperbacks/Simon & Schuster, 1996); Robert D. Putnam, with Robert Leonardi and Raffaella Y. Nanetti, *Making Democracy Work* (Princeton, N.J.: Princeton University Press, 1993).

10 For two interesting uses of the political culture approach to early American history, see Joanne B. Freeman, *Affairs of Honor: National Politics in the New Republic* (New Haven, Conn.: Yale University Press, 2001); G. Edward White, *The Marshall Court and Cultural Change, 1815–1835,* abridged ed. (New York: Oxford University Press, 1991).

11 Plato, *The Works of Plato,* Vol. 1, trans. B. Jowett (New York: Dial Press, 1956), 445.

12 For a moving personal memoir on civic identity, see Natan Sharansky, *Defending Identity: Its Indispensible Role in Protecting Democracy* (New York: Public Affairs, 2008).

13 *Stanford Encyclopedia of Philosophy,* available at http://plato.stanford.edu/entries/citizenship.

14 U.S. Office of Personnel Management, Investigations Service, "Citizenship Laws of the World," Washington, D.C., March 2001, 5, available at www.opm.gov/EXTRA/ INVESTIGATE/is-01.pdf. This useful resource provides country-by-country summaries of citizenship requirements, loss of citizenship, and dual citizenship.

15 Ibid., 83.

16 Ibid., 10.

17 Baron de Montesquieu, *The Spirit of the Laws,* trans. Thomas Nugent (New York: Hafner Press/Macmillan, 1949), xxxi.

18 Alexis de Tocqueville, *Democracy in America* (New York: Alfred A. Knopf, 1945), 299.

19 Gabriel A. Almond and Sidney Verba, *The Civic Cultures: Political Attitudes and Democracy in Five Nations* (Princeton, N.J.: Princeton University Press, 1963).

20 Lucian W. Pye, "Political Culture," in *The Encyclopedia of Democracy,* ed. Seymour Martin Lipset (Washington, D.C.: Congressional Quarterly, 1995), Vol. 3: 966.

21 Putnam, Leonardi, and Nanetti, *Making Democracy Work.*

22 Daniel J. Elazar, *Cities of the Prairie: The Metropolitan Frontier and American Politics* (New York: Basic Books, 1970).

23 Daniel J. Elazar, *Covenant and Constitutionalism* (New Brunswick, N.J.: Transaction Press, 1998), 255–259.

24 Mary Douglas, *Natural Symbols: Explorations of Cosmology* (London: Barrie & Rockliff, 1970). Dame Mary Douglas has summarized her work in "A History of Group and Grid Cultural Theory," University of Toronto, 2006, available at www.chass.utoronto.ca/epc/srb/cyber/douglas1.pdf.

25 Douglas's culture theory was applied to the field of politics by the American political scientist Aaron Wildavsky and others in Thompson, Ellis, and Wildavsky, *Cultural Theory.*

26 Douglas, "History of Group," 2–4.

27 Ibid.

28 Ibid.

29 Martin Goodman, *Rome and Jerusalem: The Clash of Ancient Civilizations* (New York: Alfred A. Knopf, 2007), 268–269. This book is a wide-ranging comparison of these two civilizations by a British specialist in both Roman studies and Jewish studies.

30 Polybius, *The Histories,* quoted in Peter Reisenberg, *Citizenship in the Western Tradition* (Chapel Hill: University of North Carolina Press, 1992), 69.

31 Aaron Wildavsky in Thompson, Ellis, and Wildavsky, *Cultural Theory,* 215–216.

32 Lawrence Meniere, ed., *Bilan de la France 1981–1993* (Paris: Hachette, 1993), 12.

33 Mark Kesselman and Joel Krieger, "France," in *Introduction to Comparative Politics,* ed. Mark Kesselman and William A. Joseph, Brief Edition (Boston: Houghton Mifflin, 2009), 116.

34 Ibid., 111.

35 Jonathan Fenby, *On the Brink: The Trouble with France* (London: Time Warner Books, 1999), 286.

36 George Vernadsky, *The Moguls and New Russia* (New Haven, Conn.: Yale University Press, 1953), 337, quoted in Yale Richmond, *From Nyet to Da,* 3rd ed. (Yarmouth, Maine: Intercultural Press, 2003), 72.

37 Victor Zaslavsky, "From Redistribution to Marketization: Social and Attitudinal Change in Post Soviet Russia," in *The New Russia: Troubled Transformation,* ed. Gail W. Lapidus (Boulder, Colo.: Westview Press, 1994), 125.

38 Ronald Inglehart, Miguel Basáñez, Jaime Díez-Medrano, Loek Halman, and Ruund Luijkx, eds., *Human Beliefs and Values: A Cross-Cultural Sourcebook,* based on the 1999–2002 Values Survey conducted by the World Values Survey, Institute of Social Research, University of Michigan (Mexico City: Siglo Veintiuno Editores, 2004), Tables E120, E121, E122.

39 Ibid., Tables E017, E018, E120.

40 Lucian W. Pye, *The Mandarin and the Cadre: China's Political Cultures* (Ann Arbor, Mich.: University of Michigan Press, 1988), 39.

41 Ibid., 39.

42 Commission on Legal Empowerment of the Poor, *Making the Law Work for Everyone,* Vol. 1 (New York: Commission on Legal Empowerment of the Poor and the United Nations Development Programme, 2008), 19.

BIG IDEAS

- A society's form of government represents the dominant political interests in society, embodies society's political values, frames power relationships within government and between government and society, and serves as a blueprint for government performance.

- Aristotle developed a typology of forms of government based on two essential questions: Who governs and who benefits?

- Aristotle's typology identified six forms of government: three forms of constitutional government (monarchy, aristocracy, and democracy) and three forms of authoritarian government (despotism, oligarchy, and majority tyranny).

- Aristotle's typology provides important clues about the structures of government: how they work, why they are important, and the dangers they pose.

Purpose of This Chapter

A country's form of government matters. Studying a country's form of government provides important clues about its dominant interests and values, about the power of and relationships between its political institutions, and about how to evaluate a government's performance. Forms of government also represent hard-fought political choices by real people. Two choices are particularly important, choices that Aristotle discussed centuries ago. First, who should govern? That is, which interests should be represented by which institutions and with what powers? Second, who should benefit? That is, by which institution or combination of institutions will government carry out its responsibilities, and which interests will benefit? Constitution-makers and reformers have grappled with these questions for thousands of years. Many have relied on Aristotle's ideas as their guide.

Terms to Know

aristocracy	form of government	monarchy
collective responsibility	guilt by association	oligarchy
constitutionalization	hybrid democracies	one-party states
constitutional monarchy	idiocy	personal dictatorships
demagoguery	illiberal democracies	plutocracy
democracy	junta	pseudo-democracies
despotism	majority tyranny	state-controlled dictatorships
direct democracy	military dictatorships	typology
empire	mixed republic	

WHY DOES FORM MATTER?

Recall that the Greek philosopher Aristotle believed that every polity has a constitution or makeup consisting of three dimensions: a socioeconomic constitution composed of the majority and minority interests in society, a moral constitution expressing the cultural values of society, and a legal constitution comprising the governmental institutions and law of the polity. The previous chapter focuses on Aristotle's moral constitution, known today as political culture. This chapter turns to Aristotle's legal constitution, known today as form of government.

For Aristotle, the political importance of forms of government boiled down to two essential questions: Who governs, and who benefits? "Who governs?" focuses on representation of interests and institutional power, that is, on which interests should be represented by which institutions and with what powers. "Who benefits?" shifts attention from representation to performance; it focuses on which institution or combination of institutions government will use to carry out its responsibilities, and which interests will benefit.

Form of government refers to the framework of governmental institutions and laws in a polity. A polity's form of government is important for several reasons. Form of government is (1) an institutional expression of the dominant political values of a society, (2) an institutional representation of the dominant political interests in society, (3) an institutional map of power relationships within government and between government and society, (4) an institutional blueprint of government performance, and (5) an institutional consequence of hard choices made by real people. Let us take these one by one.

AN INSTITUTIONAL EXPRESSION OF THE DOMINANT POLITICAL VALUES IN SOCIETY

As a general rule, a form of government should fit the political culture and history of its people. Most people are naturally inclined to follow this rule. A people's cultural values shape the roles they expect government to serve. In individualistic political cultures, for example, the primary role of government is to protect rights, while in traditionalist cultures government is expected to prescribe behavior and maintain the status quo (see Chapter 6). People establish government and empower its institutions as a way of carrying out the roles they expect of government.

Matching a country's form of government with its culture and history, however, is easier said than done. As explained in the previous chapter, most countries have a mix of political cultures. Many of the former British colonies in Africa, for example, have four layers of political culture influenced by people who settled, colonized, and traded in the region. These layers include traditional tribal culture, Islamic culture, British culture, and the new statist values imposed by postindependence states controlled by one dominant political party. Today, the governments of these countries represent a mix of these four traditions. The national courts must find ways to accommodate customary tribal law, Islamic Shari'a law, British common law, and the statist laws of the one-party state. A new biography of Francis Nyalali, Tanzania's former chief justice who served 1976–1999, richly illustrates the challenges of reconciling conflicts among these diverse value systems.[1]

AN INSTITUTIONAL REPRESENTATION OF THE DOMINANT POLITICAL INTERESTS IN SOCIETY

As a general rule, government should represent a balance of majority and minority interests in society. Aristotle called for a balanced constitution and a mixed form of republican government as a way of achieving this ideal. By representing the interests of the many and the few, Aristotle believed that the interests of one could serve as a check on the others. In this way, government would be more likely to resist tyranny, more inclusive, more evenly balanced, and hence more moderate in its policies. But here, too, history has seen many exceptions to the rule.

People may not have the chance to create a balanced constitution. All too often, would-be tyrants seize power in those fateful moments when events turn their way. Generals are often in the best position to seize power. Julius Caesar in ancient Rome and Napoleon Bonaparte in Revolutionary France are among the most famous examples. But in the twentieth century, people outside the military have also been successful in seizing power. Vladimir Lenin of Russia, Benito Mussolini of Italy, and Adolph Hitler of Germany manipulated their way into power using political cunning and surprise with only minimal military experience or support.

Another exception is the failure to design a lasting balance that satisfies all interests. The leaders of various political interests may come together with the best of intentions, but fail to reach an agreement and turn in exasperation to the dominant interest at the time. Or the balance they create may result in constant bickering. Such situations create political instability and frequent changes in the form of government or the parties in power. For example, France bounced back and forth several times between republican government and monarchy in the nineteenth century.

The form a government takes cannot satisfy every demand or resolve every conflict. Disagreement is a natural and often healthy part of politics. However, a constitution should set the generally accepted rules and institutions by which future conflicts can be resolved peacefully.[2]

AN INSTITUTIONAL MAP OF POWER RELATIONSHIPS

The form of government is "a power map."[3] Today, written constitutions establish forms of government, frame their institutions, and assign powers and limits to those institutions. In fact, constitutions probably devote more pages to these tasks than to any other.

As a power map, constitutions make clear where specific powers are located as well as the most frequently traveled relationships between power holders. Those relationships are of three types: (1) relations among the legislative, executive, and judicial branches within government; (2) relations between national, local, and possibly regional governments within one polity; and (3) relationships among government, individuals, and nongovernmental institutions.

Mapping political power can seem like a bewildering mass of technical details. However, these details matter. A constitution not only creates the institutions that represent political interests; it also assigns real powers to those institutions.

The relationship between representation and power became apparent in the opening days of the federal convention that met in Philadelphia in 1787 to amend the Articles of Confederation. The first conflict at the Philadelphia convention erupted between the large (more populous) states and the small states. Both saw Congress as the most powerful federal institution. As a result, both sides wanted as much congressional representation as possible so they could control as much legislative power as possible. The states with large populations wanted congressional representation based on population size. In their plan, they proposed a bicameral (two-house) legislature with representation in both houses apportioned on the basis of population size. The larger the state, the more representatives it would have. The small states countered with a plan for a unicameral (one-house) legislature with representation assigned equally to each state. The famous compromise that was reached provided for a bicameral legislature in which representation in the lower house of the legislature was based on population and representation in the upper house was assigned equally among the states (two seats per state).

AN INSTITUTIONAL BLUEPRINT OF GOVERNMENT PERFORMANCE

In the final analysis, forms of government are judged not only by how well they represent society's interests but by how well a government carries out its responsibilities. Among other things, governments are expected to protect human life, preserve liberty, help better the human condition, and administer justice. A country's form of government not only provides the avenues by which government can achieve these purposes; it also helps to shape the effectiveness of the government.

There are two basic views on the relationship between a government's form and its performance. Alexander Pope (1688–1744), one of the greatest eighteenth-century English poets and satirists, eloquently expressed one view in his poem, *An Essay on Man*:

> *For forms of government let fools contest,*
> *Whate're is best administer'd is best.*[4]

Pope's couplet captures the popular sentiment that forms of government are dull distractions. The important point for Pope was not how government is structured but how well it performs.

The American founding fathers, focused as they were on framing constitutional governments, disagreed with Pope's sentiment. For them, identifying the best form of government was a fundamental goal of the new science of politics. John Adams spoke for his fellow constitution-makers in defending the importance of form: "Nothing is more certain from the history of governments, and the nature of man, than that some forms of government are better fitted for being well administered than others."[5]

Form shapes performance. But Adams made a good point—performance also shapes the form that you select. For example, some car chassis are designed for high-speed performance, while others emphasize endurance over rough terrain. Some cell phones are better for multitasking, while others offer wider reception or a longer battery life. The great challenge facing those who design a government is deciding what they want from the institutions they create and what those forms and institutions can reasonably deliver.[6]

AN INSTITUTIONAL CONSEQUENCE OF HARD CHOICES

A form of government is not just a bundle of institutions—it represents a bundle of choices made by real people. Forms of government do not suddenly appear, nor do they mysteriously evolve over time.

Consider the establishment of America's new federal form of government in 1787–1788. Fifty-five delegates from twelve states attended the federal convention that drafted a new U.S. Constitution in 1787. Nineteen hundred delegates attended fourteen state conventions (North Carolina held two conventions) that voted on whether to ratify the new Constitution.[7] Virtually all those delegates to the state conventions were elected. Joining in that process were all those delegates who ran and lost, the campaigners who supported the winners and losers, the pamphleteers who wrote stirring commentaries such as *The Federalist* advocating or opposing the new Constitution, and, of course, the eligible voters who cast their ballot in state convention elections. Each of these individuals is part of the collective biography of the birth of the American Constitution and the revolutionary form of republican government it created. Each provision of that document was debated, not once but hundreds of times—in town halls, street corners, voting places, taverns, churches, families, and state conventions—before it was ordained and established by the people.

The writing and ratification of the Constitution was only part of the story and, technically, the second part of the story. The first part includes the variety of choices made by all those who created the first state constitutions and the Articles of Confederation. Those choices were an important first step of trial and error not only in constitution-making but also in the formation of a constitutional people.

Imagine the constitutional choices that have been made since 1788 to keep the American republic. James Madison wrestled with his conscience, and the electorate, before deciding to take the lead in drafting a Bill of Rights. And Aaron Burr created a furor when he decided to run for president against Thomas Jefferson, after running with him as his vice presidential candidate—all because of a loophole in the Constitution (subsequently settled by the Twelfth Amendment in 1804). And many brave souls fought for the abolition of slavery, women's suffrage, and so many other constitutional changes in the form of American government.

WHY IS CHOOSING A FORM OF GOVERNMENT SO IMPORTANT? THE CASE OF PENNSYLVANIA'S FIRST GOVERNMENT

In the early months of 1776, while American political leaders were still debating whether to separate from England, they faced another issue. If they were to declare their independence, how would they govern themselves?

Thomas Paine (1737–1809) was among the first to answer this question. In January 1776, he published a pamphlet, *Common Sense,* in which he argued for independence and presented a plan for the new American state governments. Paine's model was simple—each state would have a government built around a large one-house legislature. Legislators would serve one-year terms. Paine advocated brief terms for two reasons: (1) short legislative terms would keep the legislators close to the people, and (2) more people could run for office. Further, Paine knew and approved of the old English political maxim, "When annual elections end, tyranny begins." In Paine's plan, there would be no upper house, no independent executive, and no independent judiciary.

Many of Paine's readers found his proposals too extreme, too radical, and too democratic for a new republic. They preferred a more moderate republic in which the majority was checked in the name of minority rights. A group of delegates to the Continental Congress asked John Adams to come up with a more moderate plan for the colonies, and Adams obliged in the pamphlet *Thoughts on Government* (1776).

In his pamphlet, Adams laid out an alternative model of republican government. He advocated the principle of separation of powers, supplemented by a system of checks and balances. He proposed three separate branches of government: a bicameral legislature, a popularly elected executive, and an independent judiciary. Each branch would be able to check the others, and each branch would serve a different constituency that would balance the others.

Despite their differences, Paine and Adams agreed on a number of points. They both wanted independence and a republican government. Both understood republican government as a form of government based on the consent of the citizenry and the rule of law. Both agreed that republican governments achieved consent by representation, not direct participation, of the people. Both understood that the form of republican government should reflect the principle government.

Paine and Adams disagreed, however, about which republican principles should be emphasized and, therefore, which form the republican government should take. Paine emphasized the principles of popular consent, majority rule, and liberty. From this starting point, he proposed a simple form of republican government that concentrated all the people's power of representation in one legislative assembly. Paine's plan did not provide for a balance of representation in different bodies, there were no checks by one body over another, and government was limited in the scope and intensity of its power. Paine believed that the people would check themselves and that any external check on them would be undemocratic.

By contrast, Adams emphasized the principles of

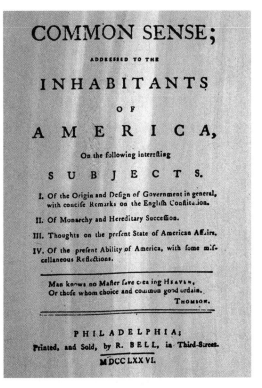

Title page of Thomas Paine's 1776 pamphlet Common Sense, *which sold hundreds of thousands of copies in the colonies and convinced many to support America's independence from Britain.*

rule of law, protection of minority rights, and civic virtue. Under his plan, the lower house of a bicameral legislature represented the great body of people and was therefore responsive to public pressure; the upper legislative house represented the elite and therefore provided for more deliberation in the legislative process (Adams argued that every society had some sort of aristocracy). Power in both the lower and upper houses needed to be checked and balanced, one against the other. The judiciary served as a guardian of the law, and executive administration allowed for an energetic government.

Immediately after America declared its independence, Pennsylvania leaders gathered in a convention to write their new state's first constitution. The convention adopted Paine's model with few alterations. Adopted in September 1776, the new constitution reflected the strong political and philosophical position of its authors, who favored unchecked liberty and democracy. Pennsylvania was not the first state to adopt a constitution, but its first constitution was regarded as the most radical and democratic.

The constitution provided for a one-house legislature, called an assembly, with six representatives from each of twelve counties elected for a one-year term. Paine, a Pennsylvania resident, served as the clerk of that assembly. Without a second house, the state government may have been more responsive to public pressure, but there was less chance for deliberation and debate. Equal representation by county meant that the lightly populated western counties enjoyed a disproportionate amount of representation. The one-year term increased the number of people who had a chance to serve while reducing the possibility of there being long-term officeholders who might try to monopolize power. However, the brief terms also reduced the stability and the continuity of the legislature and produced some very hasty legislation.

The state constitution vested the executive power in a plural executive—not one governor but a council composed of one representative from each county and the city of Philadelphia. The executives were elected for three-year terms. Plural executives had been common in earlier republics, but some constitutional thinkers were beginning to recognize that unity and duration were two preconditions for sound executive administration. Although Pennsylvania's plural executive failed to satisfy the first condition, its three-year terms satisfied the second.

The third branch was the Council of Censors. The council consisted of two representatives from each county and one from Philadelphia, each elected for a term of seven years. The council had the power to monitor the legislature and executive, to determine whether legislative or executive actions violated the constitution, and to censure or rebuke them for such violations. The censors were elected by and accountable to the people. Although the censors could claim to be the guardians of the people, they did not serve as a check on the majority. This system may seem odd today, but it was quite common in ancient and medieval republics.

With all three branches elected on the basis of equal county representation, the voters of the western parts of the state dominated all three branches of government by a two-to-one margin. To make sure of their margin, the state legislators quickly passed test laws that required voters and elected officials to swear an oath to uphold the constitution. Quakers and Mennonites, who lived mainly in the eastern counties, believed such oaths were a violation of their conscience and faith; thus, the test laws disenfranchised these two groups.

The Pennsylvania Constitution favored the western region over the eastern region, agricultural interests over commercial interests, rural values over urban values, and unlimited democracy over checks and balances. The resulting imbalance affected public policy. The new state legislature rushed through laws that fixed prices, regulated mercantile practices, and confiscated property not only of loyalists but also of past colonial leaders, including the Penn family. As Louis Hartz found in his path-breaking study of Pennsylvania, "economic control and political democracy became sister principles of the Radical position."[8]

The Pennsylvania experience illustrates the importance of the form of government. When the leaders of only one interest group or ideology design the form of government, they are more likely to create institutions in which they hold the power and derive the benefits.

Pennsylvania's first state government failed on four counts: (1) the entire government was unjust because it favored one interest group—the farmers in the western counties—over other interest groups in the state; (2) the one-house legislature did not provide for the patience and deliberation that good lawmaking requires and so fueled rash policies; (3) the plural executive did not provide the unity that good administration requires; and (4) the Council of Censors, although intended as a guardian of the people, failed to counter the tyranny of the majority. In sum, Pennsylvania's first constitution failed to balance not only the various political interests of the state but also the policymaking and administrative needs of a new state government. Pennsylvania's radical experiment in government began to unravel after its first decade. In 1790, it was replaced by a more moderate form of government.

HOW DO FORMS OF GOVERNMENT DIFFER?

More than 2,000 years ago, Aristotle identified six forms of government by constructing a **typology**, a systematic classification of the significant types of a larger category of objects. Aristotle's typology is still widely used today as a basis for comparing governments. It classifies types of government on the basis of Aristotle's two questions: Who governs, and who benefits? Note that "Who governs?" is an empirical question that allows the researcher to locate authority; "Who benefits?" is a moral question that allows the researcher to evaluate how well authority is exercised.

Aristotle used the first question (Who governs?) to identify three types of government: rule by the one, the few, and the many. He then turned to the second question (Who benefits?) and identified two possible answers: those who govern or the polity they serve. Constitutional government (good government) relies on the principles of limited government, rule of law, and consent of the citizenry, even if tacit, to advance the common good of the polity. Authoritarian government (bad government) uses absolute power and arbitrary decisions to benefit the rulers and their supporters. Table 7.1 presents Aristotle's famous typology with his six forms of government. According to Aristotle, each form of constitutional government represents a particular class in society and a set of political strengths that class brings to governance.[9]

- **Monarchy** is constitutional rule by the one in which power is limited by the law and the ruler's policies are expected to benefit the polity as a whole. In traditional monarchies ruled by kings and queens, the interests of the one represent the royal family, the court, and the crown. The strengths of rule by one are unity of command, coherence of policy, and speed. Because it is clear who rules, monarchy also brings accountability to governance.[10]

Table 7.1 Aristotle's Typology of Government

	Rule by one	Rule by few	Rule by many
Good government	Monarchy	Aristocracy	Democracy
Bad government	Despotism	Oligarchy	Majority tyranny

- **Despotism** is authoritarian rule by the one. It can be considered a corrupt form of monarchy. Under despots or tyrants, power is absolute and policies are self-serving.

- **Aristocracy** is constitutional rule by the few, such as a hereditary class of nobles, who accept the limits of the law and consent of the citizenry. In some countries, the nobility included the highest barons and the lowliest knights. Their number might equal 10–15 percent of a society's population. Included among the wealthy few were those who had the time, resources, and inclination to pursue knowledge, wisdom, and virtue. As a result, they often excelled at statesmanship based on moderation and deliberation.[11]

- **Oligarchy** is the authoritarian rule by the few. It can be considered a corrupt form of aristocracy in which the very few, usually the wealthy few, dominate all spheres of society. Aristotle found that the wealthy were attracted to government, and he believed that democracy could be mixed with oligarchy to control the excesses of each.

- **Democracy** is constitutional rule by the numerical many (that is, majority rule) in which the majority respects minority rights and the rule of law. Democracy represents the majority of the population and brings together those of the middle and lower classes. Aristotle believed that the many were less easily deceived and corrupted than the few. He also had faith in the practical wisdom of the people and praised their strength and courage under fire.[12]

- **Majority tyranny** is authoritarian rule by the many. It can be considered a corrupt form of democracy and is characterized by a majority that suppresses the law and the rights of individuals and minorities.

Aristotle presented his six categories as ideal types; they are distinct in theory, but blend together and blur in reality. Aristotle believed that the best form of government is a mixed republic with elements of monarchy, aristocracy, and democracy. Hybrid governments that illustrate the gray area between good and bad governments are common. Some governments are a relatively stable hybrid of good and bad elements. Others become corrupted by power and degenerate from constitutionalism to authoritarianism.

WHAT ARE THE VARIATIONS AND DANGERS OF MONARCHY?

Monarchy is one of the oldest forms of rule, in which power is embodied in a single individual called a king, queen, emperor, sultan, emir, or other title of preeminence. In a hereditary system, the crown passes from the reigning monarch to a designated heir, usually the oldest surviving child. During Aristotle's time, most governments in the world were monarchies or despots. Aristotle expected monarchs to accept limits on their power and serve the common good of the polity.

Constitutional monarchy in its modern form exists when the ruler is constrained by legal limits and meaningful political checks. Those checks are given institutional form in a representative assembly. In a genuine constitutional monarchy, the constitution is not mere parchment; the people know what it means, they believe in it, and most political interests agree to abide by it. The people, in sum, are a constitutional people who are raised in a constitutional culture.

In England, the road to constitutional monarchy began when King John (1167–1216) was forced by a coalition of barons, bishops, and community leaders to sign the Magna Carta in 1215. The Magna Carta was not a complete constitution, but it did establish the rule of law and individual and group-based privileges and liberties as limits on the power of the monarch. Several decades later, leaving nothing to chance, the English judge Henry of Bracton collected and codified the laws of England in a series of volumes titled *On the Laws and Customs of England*. In that magisterial work, Bracton provided one of the most famous and influential explanations of the rule of law and its relationship to the monarch: "For his is called *rex* [monarch or king] not from reigning

King John signed the Magna Carta at Runnymede, June 15, 1215. John later declared the document invalid on the grounds that he had been forced to sign it. This plunged England into a civil war that lasted until his death in 1216.

but from ruling well, since he is a king as long as he rules well but a tyrant when he oppresses by violent domination the people entrusted to his care. Let him, therefore, temper his power by law, which is the bridle of power, that he may live according to the laws . . . and acknowledge himself bound by the laws. Nothing is more fitting for a sovereign than to live by the laws, nor is there any greater sovereignty than to govern according to law, and he ought properly to yield to the law what the law has bestowed upon him, for the law makes him king."[13]

The English monarchy in the seventeenth century was one early European example of constitutional monarchy. However, it was not until the nineteenth century that most European monarchies transitioned to the modern form of constitutional government. This process, known as **constitutionalization**, entailed writing constitutions that placed limits on the power of the ruler. As part of that process, nineteenth-century monarchs allowed a written constitution, a bill of rights, and some type of representative assembly to be established. Some rulers, like Tsar Alexander II of Russia, genuinely sought to constitutionalize and liberalize their governments. Others, like Chancellor Otto von Bismarck of Germany, allowed such reforms as a way of pacifying troublemakers.[14]

During the twentieth century, most monarchies and empires were destroyed or simply collapsed from old age. Still, at the beginning of the twenty-first century there were more than forty-three monarchies, thirty-six of which were constitutional. Nearly half (sixteen) were in British Commonwealth countries and shared the same monarch and head of state, Queen Elizabeth II.[15]

In most of today's constitutional monarchies, the monarch is the head of state and performs primarily symbolic and ceremonial functions while policymaking powers usually reside with an elected legislative body. Still, the monarch can provide the people and their government with a sense of stability, memory, tradition, and good counsel. On occasion, the monarch can even play an influential political role. In 1981, for example, King Juan Carlos I of Spain successfully prevented a military coup and preserved his country's democratic constitutional monarchy, largely because he was a respected yet neutral arbiter.[16]

DESPOTISM

Despotism (also known as tyranny or dictatorship) takes the form of absolute, unaccountable, and arbitrary rule by one ruler. In ancient times, Greek tyrants and Roman dictators generally were of a different stripe than those today. In those polities, the tyrant might be brought to power by the ruling body to stop a foreign invasion or quell a domestic insurrection. After the crisis had passed, the ancient tyrant was expected to retire. Some did, for example, the Roman Lucius Cornelius Sulla,[17] but many did not.

Elsewhere in the ancient world, the tyrant was more likely to seize power, much like the tyrants of today. In ancient times, the tyrant often ruled more by manipulation and deception than by repression. The reason for this was more a matter of capacity than will. Ancient tyrants had networks of spies, but those spies lacked the modern-day conveniences of electronic surveillance and motorized transport.

Nonetheless, some ancient empires developed effective ways to control the population. Gao Mingxuan, professor of Chinese criminal law, identified two forms of control instituted by Emperor Shang Yang around 350 BCE: collective responsibility and guilt by association. The practice of **collective responsibility** required people to live in units of several households in which everyone was responsible for spying on his or her neighbors. **Guilt by association** held all members of the unit accountable for one another's actions. This meant that an entire unit could be killed for a serious crime committed by one of its members. Eventually this practice was extended to the army and government officials.[18]

Whatever combination of manipulation or physical force tyrants use, tyranny is based on fear, not freedom. This distinction is an all-important difference between republics and tyrannies.

Sadly, the twentieth and twenty-first centuries have witnessed many types of authoritarian regimes.[19] The list of despots ranges widely from one-party bosses to military strong men. At one level, they are all the same in their thirst for and abuse of power. However, they differ in their institutional base, how they wield power, and the cause they claim to advance. Some of the most widespread twentieth and twenty-first century patterns are listed here; they are explored further in later chapters.

- **Military dictatorships** are usually led by a high-ranking military officer who gains and holds power by force, drawing on the military organization or the branch of the armed services that he continues to command. In Latin America, for example, there is a long history of military strong men (*caudillos*) who drew on regional or even national armies in the name of order. Among the first was Juan Manuel de Rosas (1793–1877) of Argentina, who demanded "power without limits" and believed that "the ideal of good government," was "paternal autocracy."[20]

- **One-party states** are led by a party boss whose power base is the dominant party of the country. The government is staffed by party loyalists, the party's candidates win all or most seats in the legislature, and the party boss is the president. Communist states are an extreme version of this, in which the party is the leading force in society, sometimes led by a strong boss and other times by a coalition. One-party states also have been common in post-colonial African states. During the last half of the twentieth century, many newly independent African states elected as their first president the leader of their anticolonial national independence movement. Often, these leaders refashioned the independence movement into a political party and retained power over both the party and government for decades. Among the last of these powerful rulers is Robert Mugabe of Zimbabwe. He rose to power as a party leader in the early 1960s. He was first elected president in 1987 and has continued in power for more than twenty years through fraudulent elections, intimidation of the opposition, and corruption.

- **Personal dictatorships** are led by a tyrant who fashions a personal power base that remains his to command. While most dictators rule by relying on both personal power and an institutional base, the personal despot builds a base of power sustained by his private army of thugs. The Caribbean and Central America provide some of the most notorious examples of the twentieth century. One of the most infamous was François Duvalier, known as "Papa Doc," who controlled Haiti from 1957 to 1971 with his Tontons Macoutes (or bogeymen), who enforced his policies by terror.

- **State-controlled dictatorships** are led by a presidential dictator who draws his power from his office and the governmental machinery at his command. Several examples of this can be found in the former Soviet republics of Central Asia. When the Soviet Union collapsed, these republics became independent. In a few instances, the president of the Soviet republic was reinstated as the president of the newly independent country. In other instances, the president came from the ranks of the party faithful in the Soviet party, legislature, or government. Some, like Islam Karimov of Uzbekistan, swiftly consolidated power and ruled in a dictatorial manner; others became semi-authoritarian leaders. But most relied primarily on the state, not the party or the military, as their base of power.

HYBRID MONARCHIES

Hybrid monarchies have a mix of constitutional and authoritarian features. One example of this is the checkmated king who would love to rule absolutely but is surrounded by powerful knights who prevent him from doing so; King John (1166–1216) of England is a famous

Cyrus's Charter of Freedom was discovered in 1878. It is a 22.5 centimeters–long cylinder made of baked clay and inscribed in cuneiform.

example. A. A. Milne (1882–1956), author of *Winnie-the-Pooh,* wrote a poem that begins, "King John was not a good man."[21] Treacherous, ruthless, inept in military affairs, and despised by many of his subjects, King John is best remembered for signing the Magna Carta, England's Great Charter of Rights, in 1215 at Runnymede. But he did not do it willingly. As discussed previously, he was forced to sign the charter by a group of English barons, bishops, and city officials. And as soon as his challengers disbanded, King John reneged on the deal, causing a civil war. It took many more years of struggle before the Magna Carta was fully enforced.

Although opposition may provide limits on a monarchy, it may also make effective rule impossible. One example of limited but ineffective rule was the elective monarchy of the Polish-Lithuanian Commonwealth, in which hundreds of nobles met to elect the king and approve his decisions. But because unanimity was required, any noble could veto a decision. Eventually, a weakened Poland was carved up by its neighbors.

Another type of hybrid monarchy is headed by an enlightened or benevolent despot. One of the earliest examples is Cyrus the Great, who became king of Persia in 559 BCE. (See More About . . . Cyrus the Great and His Charter of Freedom.) He created the Persian Empire by conquering massive territories over the next twenty-nine years until he was killed in 530 BCE. Cyrus established his empire by conquest, and he ruled as the "king of kings." However, historians characterize Cyrus as a wise and benevolent emperor because he chose not to crush his opponents and conquered peoples.

There are two problems with benevolent despots: they can become less benevolent when things don't go their way, and it is impossible to ensure the benevolence of their successors. Herodotus, the Greek historian known as "the father of history," had this to say about Cyrus and two of his successors (his son Cambyses, who succeeded him, and Darius, who succeeded Cambyses): "Because [Darius] established the tribute system [forcing provinces to pay him annually], the Persians describe Darius as a retailer (since he put a price on everything), Cambyses as a master (since he was cruel and restrictive), and Cyrus as a father (since he was kind and everything he set up was for their good)."[22] (See Bold Thinkers: Herodotus.)

Sometimes the limits placed on an absolute ruler are religious. In theory, some absolute monarchs of seventeenth-century Europe saw their divine right to rule as a divine responsibility. Louis XIV of France believed in a divine right theory, in which the monarch is God's representative on earth and therefore responsible to God for his or her actions. According to this theory, "Royal power . . . was absolute but not arbitrary; not arbitrary because it must be reasonable and just, like the will of God which it reflected; absolute in that it was free from dictation by . . . subordinate elements within the country."[23]

MORE ABOUT . . .

Cyrus the Great and His Charter of Freedom

Cyrus the Great (c. 580–529 BCE) was an enlightened emperor. He allowed conquered peoples to keep their local religious beliefs and allowed local rulers to retain limited powers—as long as they didn't cross him. Cyrus appointed a provincial administrator, known as a *satrap*, to make sure that local rulers did not exceed their allotted powers. When Cyrus conquered Babylon in 539 BCE, he freed the Hebrews from captivity so that they might return to their homeland.

Cyrus proclaimed the Charter of Freedom in spring 539 BCE at his coronation as the ruler of Babylon. In that charter, Cyrus promoted his own benevolence while granting certain freedoms. He described how he offered relief to the people of Babylon, returned sacred objects captured by the Babylonians to their rightful temples across the Persian Empire, granted freedom of religion, and swore never to take people's property without compensation. He also promised not to use forced labor without payment. Some say this charter was the first charter of human rights, but other charters preceded it in Mesopotamia. In addition, its conception of rights differs from modern notions. Unlike modern conceptions in which a person's rights come from God or from being human, in Mesopotamia rights came from the emperor; and what the emperor gave, he could take away.

Today, most forms of rule by the one are a hybrid of constitutional and authoritarian features. Free elections are held, but the elections are rarely competitive and often rigged. Some rulers are very popular with a large majority of the voters. Some pledge to maintain law and order at a time of unrest, while others appeal to the poor with promises of land or a job. Most rule with a strong hand inside a velvet glove. Some were members of a previous authoritarian regime who became president and moved their country toward some measure of democracy. In other instances, they moved in the reverse direction; in other words, they won the election in a fragile or weak democracy and gradually became more authoritarian, although not completely.

HOW ARE EMPIRES RULED?

An **empire** is a large multiethnic political entity that is usually created by conquest or colonization and controlled from a single center by an emperor and his or her administration.[24] Many modern nation-states, such as France, Spain, Iran, China, and Russia, were once empires.

Most empires had a monarchic form of government. The emperor might be more or less enlightened or more or less tyrannical; the ancient world saw various types of imperial rule. One of the oldest empires was the Assyrian Empire (first established around 2000 BCE), centered in Mesopotamia. This empire was built by conquest and maintained by tyranny, and it became one of the most powerful and brutal states in the ancient world. As previously discussed, Cyrus also built the Persian Empire by conquest, but unlike the Assyrian

BOLD THINKERS

Herodotus

Herodotus (c. 484–425 BCE), considered to be "the father of history," was a contemporary of Aristotle, who is remembered as "the father of political science." Neither was born in Greece, although both settled there. Herodotus was born in Halicarnassus, located in Asia Minor (and now the port city of Bodrum in southwestern Turkey). Herodotus traveled widely, and thanks to his insatiable curiosity, he collected much firsthand information along the way. He traveled north to the Black Sea, east to Mesopotamia (now Iraq), south to Egypt, west to Athens, and beyond to Sicily. His masterwork is titled *The Histories*. It is a study of the Persian Wars, but this subject provided a starting point for wonderful narratives about Persia, Greece, and various other places in his world. *The Histories* is praised for the accuracy of its stories, the elegant simplicity of its writing, the power of its interpretations, and the critical eye that it cast on the rumors and myths of the day.

Herodotus reading his history before an assembly of Greeks.

emperors, he ruled by allowing some measure of local control. He sent representatives, known as *satraps* (governors), to supervise the conquered territories, but they normally allowed each territory to keep its local form of rule and religion.

But not all empires were monarchies. The Athenian Empire, for example, had a democratic and confederal form of government. Initially, the city of Athens sent colonists to different islands to settle and create colonies that became trading partners with Athens. As time progressed, Athens brought those colonies together into a loose confederation called the Delian League. Each colony contributed revenues to a common treasury that was located outside Athens. During the height of its democracy, Athens sought to expand its control over the league. It may seem paradoxical that a democracy had imperial ambitions, but Athens needed revenue for its war against the Greek city-state of Sparta. So, in one bold move, the

Athenian leader Pericles moved the league's treasury to Athens, transforming the league into a loose empire. Hence, it became an early example of an empire ruled not by a monarchy but by a democracy.

WHAT IS THE DIFFERENCE BETWEEN ARISTOCRACY AND OLIGARCHY?

Aristocracy is rule by the few limited by the rule of law and the tacit consent of the citizenry. In theory, this select few has the wisdom, experience, and virtue to know what is best for society. Historically, most aristocracies have been based on heredity. The first-born male (not necessarily the wisest member of the family) was often entrusted with representing the family in government.

In Aristotle's day, all Greek cities and Rome had an aristocratic class composed of the oldest, wealthiest, and most respected families. Class played an important role in Greek and Roman government. In fact, at some points in its history, ancient Athens was governed as a *timocracy,* where citizens were divided into four or five classes (each with specific rights) based on the amount of property they held.

In European city-states during the late Middle Ages and the early modern era, the most influential families governed aristocratic republics. In most cities, those families were hereditary members of the nobility. Aristocratic rule was often unstable and beset by rivalries between powerful families; Shakespeare dramatized such rivalries in his play *Romeo and Juliet.* A notable exception was Venice, known as the Most Serene Republic. The Venetian Republic was long-lasting, stable, peaceful, and prosperous.

Aristocratic republics are rare today. Malaysia's constitution has an aristocratic element. According to it, the presidency rotates every five years among nine hereditary sultans who head the Malay states and constitute a constitution-bound aristocracy. After its independence in 1957, Malaysia was governed by constitutionally minded leaders. But this changed in 1981 when Mahathir Mohamad became prime minister. His policies and politics strongly favored Malays over non-Malays (mainly Chinese and Indians). He repressed opposition with an iron hand. Observers thought that constitutionality

A fifteenth-century woodcut depicting the construction of a ship in Venice. Venice's long-lasting political stability allowed for the development of a thriving trade-based economy.

MORE ABOUT . . .
Michels's Iron Law of Oligarchy

Mere mention of *oligarchy* in a room of social scientists will cause someone to bring up Robert Michels's (1876–1936) iron law of oligarchy, the theory that all organizations, even democratic ones, eventually develop into oligarchies. Michels was a German sociologist who studied nongovernmental organizations, especially political parties and trade unions. He found that as organizations grow in complexity and size, they eventually require bureaucracies that elevate a few organizers to positions of great power at the expense of other members.

Critics argue that not all organizations are bureaucratic and that not all bureaucratic organizations are oligarchic. Organizations can remain democratic by the constant recruitment of new members; regular elections of officeholders; healthy competition with other organizations; and transparency or openness, which makes it difficult for a few officials to make backroom deals. Michels's law, however, may be even more relevant today. The increased importance of large organizations in modern life creates the possibility for a few people to dominate because they understand complex institutional arrangements and can ensure no one else does.

would be restored after he stepped aside in 2003. But, as of 2009, that has not been the case.[25] So, Malaysia was partly aristocratic in 1957–1981, but is not so now.

In theory, an aristocracy is composed of "the best and brightest"—individuals of wisdom, experience, and virtue. In reality, Aristotle found that the primary factor determining membership in an aristocracy is wealth not wisdom. This blurs the line between aristocracy and oligarchy (see More About . . . Michels's Iron Law of Oligarchy).

OLIGARCHIES

Oligarchy is unchecked and arbitrary rule by the few—a small group of people who focus on their own interests rather than on the common good. One form of oligarchy is **plutocracy**, rule by the wealthiest members of society or their representatives. In Aristotle's day, this was common in Greek cities. But so, too, were aristocratic and democratic forms, both alone and in combination. Toward the end of the Roman Republic, oligarchy proved to be the primary force in government.[26]

In the years following the breakup of the Soviet Union, a small group of businessmen, known as oligarchs, joined forces with corrupt government officials and wielded massive economic and political power in Russia. They rose to power immediately after the collapse of the Soviet economy when government was in chaos. As soon as major state-owned companies were privatized, the oligarchs bought them; they did so at dirt-cheap prices by bribing the corrupt government officials. At their height, the oligarchs dominated much of the national economy by virtue of their control over financial institutions, oil, natural gas, and metals such as steel and aluminum. Their climb to economic power coincided with Boris Yeltsin's election as the first president of the post-Soviet Russian Federation.

President Yeltsin and the oligarchs developed a cozy relationship during the 1990s. Yeltsin eased government regulations and licensing for the oligarchs, and the oligarchs contributed heavily to Yeltsin's reelection campaign in 1996. During Yeltsin's second term, his family and the oligarchs joined forces. They were called *Semya* (The Family), and their wealth grew. In 1999, Yeltsin resigned amid accusations of corruption. He appointed Vladimir Putin to replace him. When Putin assumed office, he granted Yeltsin and his family immunity from all prosecution.

In the 2000 elections, Putin won his first election bid by a wide margin, and during his first term, he moved swiftly to consolidate government power. He also initiated steps to reform the government and to improve the economy. Almost from the beginning, he sent out clear signals that he intended to bring the oligarchs under control. The public, in turn, signaled its overwhelming support. Most Russians perceived the oligarchs as greedy and corrupt robber barons. Before the end of his first year in office, Putin's popularity had soared to an 80 percent approval rating.

In October 2003, before the 2004 presidential elections, government officials arrested Mikhail Khodorkovsky, Russia's richest businessman and the president of the oil company Yukos. He was charged with fraud and tax evasion. Before his arrest, Khodorkovsky had openly challenged Putin. He had criticized the government's ineffectiveness in fighting corruption and had made large

Former Yukos oil company chief Mikhail Khodorkovsky sitting behind bars in a Moscow court in the summer of 2004. Jailed on charges of fraud and tax evasion, Khodorkovsky was later convicted and given an eight-year prison sentence.

campaign contributions to Putin's communist and liberal opponents. He was becoming a politician. The government argued in response that Khodorkovsky was actually bribing members of the Duma (Russia's congress) so they would not close tax loopholes.

As soon as Putin was reelected to a second term, the government promptly tried and convicted Khodorkovsky. Critics of the Kremlin (Russia's center of executive power) consider the trial a farce; supporters believe that Khodorkovsky violated the law and should be punished as an example (see Points of View: Putin and the Oligarchs). He was sentenced to nine years in prison, which was later reduced to eight years. Putin then turned on the other members of the oligarchy. The Kremlin deposed the oligarchs one by one, taking control of their companies and assigning their top positions to trusted members of the Kremlin's inner circle.

Another type of oligarchy is a military **junta**, a group of military officers that seizes governmental power. Military juntas often seize power during times of political crisis or chaos. The junta claims it will restore law and order and then return the government to the politicians. In this way, it attracts the support of large parts of the population that want to see order restored. In some countries, such as modern-day Thailand, a pattern has developed in which military leaders assume power in times of crisis or when they feel the current government has ventured beyond acceptable bounds, rule for a limited time, and then withdraw to

POINTS OF VIEW

Putin and the Oligarchs

Vladimir Putin's actions raise two familiar questions about power: Who holds it, and who benefits from it? Putin's supporters, including most Russians, say that Putin has restored the balance of power in Russia, consolidated governmental power, strengthened the economy, restored the people's pride in themselves and their government, and restored Russia's rightful place in the world. Putin's critics, including many in the West, charge that these accomplishments have come at too high a price. They argue that the Kremlin has replaced a private oligarchy with a Kremlin-based oligarchy, awarded billion-dollar company jobs to Putin's friends, created a state monopoly of key industries, gained control of the nation's television networks, suppressed opposition, and denied civil rights. Critics also charge that the upsurge in the Russian economy since 1999 was due less to governmental policy than to worldwide increases in oil and natural gas prices.

make way for elections. There are no firm guarantees, however, that the junta will withdraw in a timely manner.

HYBRID ARISTOCRACIES

A hybrid aristocracy has both constitutional and authoritarian features. The United Arab Emirates is one example of a hybrid aristocracy. It is a constitutional federation of seven emirates. Each emirate is ruled by an emir who is the reigning monarch in his own emirate and a member of the Supreme Council for the federation. In this sense, the federation is an aristocracy governed by emirs (princes). The Supreme Council appoints the president, who appoints the prime minister, who appoints his cabinet.[27] Inside their emirates, the emirs still rule as absolute monarchs.

In recent years, the federation and its emirates have instituted some modern constitutional and economic reforms. However, some emirs are more enlightened than others, and significant human rights violations persist. Some emirates restrict the rights of human rights organizations, journalists, women, and foreign workers (who make up about 90 percent of the private-sector workforce).[28]

WHAT ARE THE VARIATIONS AND DANGERS OF DEMOCRACY?

As noted in earlier chapters, *democracy* (from the Greek word *dēmokratia*) means "rule by the people." The people have the final say in who governs and who benefits. For the ancient Greeks, "the people" did not include the entire population. "The people," the numerical majority or the many, included all citizens except the aristocracy or oligarchy (the few) and the royal family (the one).

The ancient Greeks practiced a form of democracy known as **direct democracy**, in which all male citizens participate directly in government. (In ancient Greece, the male citizenry was only 10 percent of the total population.) Citizens were selected randomly to serve in large assemblies. The thinking was that all citizens were equally able to serve. Citizens who lost interest in civic participation and shunned their public duties were called the **idiocy** by the Greeks. (In ancient Greek, the word *idiot* meant a private person; today, the meaning has shifted to mean a foolish or stupid person.)

Direct democracy proved short-lived. It had a shining moment in Athens but was often divisive and unstable. In its place, Aristotle and others proposed the **mixed republic**—a constitutional government that combines elements of monarchy, aristocracy, and democracy. Its purpose is to represent all three interests in the polity in ways that maximize their strengths and minimize their dangers. By representing the interests of the many and the few, Aristotle believed that the interests of each would serve as a check on the other. The mixed republic has been the most widely adopted form of free government in world history. One of the earliest references to a mixed republic is in the Book of Exodus of the Hebrew Bible, which describes the form of government that Moses established around 1300 BCE at Mount Sinai. Since Aristotle's day, mixed republics have existed on every inhabited continent. Republics flourished in Western Europe, northern Russia, Israel, West Africa, northern India, the Melanesian Islands, and northeastern America. (Units 5–8 explore the history of this protean form of government.)

In the nineteenth century, representative democracy emerged as a constitutional form of democratic republic in which citizens elect members of the legislature (and the executive, in presidential systems), who represent them in the government. In the middle of the nineteenth century, liberal thinkers championed this form of government as a way of accommodating widespread popular interest in democracy and controlling the dangers of democracy. Those thinkers included the French philosopher Alexis de Tocqueville, the English philosopher John Stuart Mill, and the American statesman Abraham Lincoln. They pointed to the American model that took hold after Andrew Jackson was elected president in 1828. Elsewhere, however, distrust of liberal democracy, by both the left and right, forestalled the adoption of representative democracy until well into the twentieth century. Today, representative democracy with a constitutional government is the dominant form of democratic government throughout the world.

In the 1950s, American political scientist Robert Dahl developed a list of eight criteria distinguishing democracies in fact from democracies in name only.[29] Recently, Larry Diamond, co-editor of the *Journal of Democracy,* has organized Dahl's list into four sets of criteria of democracy.[30]

- Citizens must have the right to vote in free, fair, and competitive elections.
- Citizens must have the freedom to express their political views and to form parties and other political associations—even if they oppose the government in power.
- Citizens must have free access to all points of view.
- The government must be held responsive to the majority that elected its representatives.

MAJORITY TYRANNIES

Demagoguery is a form of leadership practiced by popular leaders called demagogues, who appeal to the people's baser motives. The demagogue's goal is to stay in power by stirring up the people's nationalistic emotions; turning the people against the wealthy few (his rivals); and winning the people's favor by spending large amounts of public money on visible public works projects, from bridges to schools. Such public projects fuel people's sense of pride, and they provide people with jobs and benefits, so at first it looks like the demagogue is serving the interests of polity as a whole. Inevitably, however, the public projects become a carrot-and-stick that demagogues use to reward their supporters and punish their opponents by denying them the benefits. So, in actuality, they are spending the money in their own interests. For example, in 2009 it was a well-known secret that Iran's President Mahmoud Ahmadinejad won reelection partly because he invested public funds in those rural areas where he found the greatest source of his political support.

The corrupt or authoritarian form of democracy is majority tyranny. Aristotle believed that most of the people (the many) are sensible, just, and compassionate. However, given the right timing, demagogues can build up a dedicated minority faction that catches the majority by surprise. If that faction seizes power, it can then use the coercive power of the state to force the majority into submission.

Pseudo-democracies are governments that are democracies in name only. A pseudo-democracy may have a constitution, and that constitution may have all the right words in it, but the government does not abide by it or the rule of law. Instead, the government acts arbitrarily in ways that are adverse to the rights of citizens and the common good of the polity. In short, a pseudo-democracy has a democratic constitution on paper and an authoritarian government in reality. Some scholars distinguish between constitutional governments based on the rule *of* law, in which no one is above the law, and authoritarian governments based on rule *by* laws, which those governments make to keep themselves in power.

HYBRID DEMOCRACIES

Hybrid democracies, or **illiberal democracies**, are governments that are partly democratic and partly authoritarian. Most illiberal democracies have constitutions that claim to protect individual rights, but these protections are often inconsistently applied or conveniently ignored. In illiberal democracies, there are regularly scheduled elections, but the government attempts to control the outcomes. Even though the government does not completely ban or rig elections, it may use its power to control the independent media, suppress the opposition, and silence human rights organizations.

Governments can exist for some time in this intermediate or hybrid form between democracy and authoritarianism. But they straddle a slippery slope and can easily slide into authoritarianism. Vladimir Putin's Russia and Hugo Chavez's Venezuela are early-twenty-first-century examples of illiberal democracies.

MEASURING DEMOCRACY

How do we measure how democratic a government is? We have already examined Dahl's four criteria. In addition, each year for the past thirty years, Freedom House has classified countries in terms of three levels of freedom (a measure of democracy): "free," "partly free," and

Table 7.2 Freedom House Ranking of Freedom around the World in 2008

Regions	Free	Partly free	Not free	Total
Americas	25 (13.0)	9 (4.6)	1 (0.5)	35 (18.1)
Western Europe	24 (12.4)	1 (0.5)	0 (0.0)	25 (12.9)
Asia and the Pacific	16 (8.3)	13 (6.7)	10 (5.2)	39 (20.2)
Central and Eastern Europe	13 (6.7)	8 (4.1)	7 (3.6)	28 (14.4)
Sub-Saharan Africa	11 (5.7)	23 (11.9)	14 (7.3)	48 (24.9)
Middle East and North Africa	1 (0.5)	6 (3.1)	11 (5.7)	18 (9.3)
Total	90 (46.6)	60 (30.9)	43 (22.3)	193 (100.0)

Source: Freedom House, *Freedom in the World: Annual Global Survey, 2008*, available at www.freedomhouse.org/template.cfm?page=395.

Note: Each cell contains the number of countries followed in parentheses by that number as a percentage of the total of 193 countries. Percentages may not total 100% due to rounding.

"not free." Their indicators include free and fair elections, open political competition, civil liberties, an independent civil society, and a media free of government interference. The regional results of Freedom House's 2008 survey can be found in Table 7.2.

As shown in the table, most "free" countries are located in the Americas and Western Europe. About one-third of the world's "free" countries are in the Asian-Pacific and Central-Eastern European regions; these regions now have more "free" than "not free" countries. The larger "free" countries in Asia include India (the world's largest democracy), Indonesia (the largest Muslim country), Japan (the most economically developed Asian country), Taiwan and South Korea, and Mongolia (the only postcommunist Asian country listed as "free").

Sub-Saharan Africa still has fewer "free" than "not free" countries, but the gap is shrinking. Botswana is one of the oldest and most stable African democracies. Other countries listed as "free" are Benin, Lesotho, Mali, Senegal, and, of course, South Africa (Africa's largest democracy).

The region of the world with the fewest "free" countries remains the Middle East and North Africa, where only one of the eleven countries is "free"—Israel. Still, the number of countries listed as "partly free" has increased to six.

Micro-states (countries with a population of less than 1 million people) are among the most democratic and freest countries of the world. Nearly one out of every four countries in the world falls into this category, and they are located in every region of the world. Many are islands in the Caribbean and Pacific.

REVIEWING AND USING THE CHAPTER

1. Why is Aristotle's typology of government still a powerful tool of comparative government?

2. What is the corrupt form of democracy? Identify and describe three examples of the corrupt form of democracy.

3. Contrast an absolute and a constitutional monarchy. What historical and contemporary examples can you cite of these two forms of monarchy?

4. What is the difference between an aristocracy and an oligarchy?

5. Evaluate the claim that rule by an aristocracy can be justified because it is composed of the best members of society who will rule for the public good.

6. Reexamine the major forms of government presented in this chapter. Under which form would you prefer to live? Why?

EXTENSION ACTIVITY

Using the authoritarian (military dictatorship, military junta, one-party state, personal dictatorship, state-controlled dictatorship, and so on) and hybrid regimes presented in this chapter, classify the contemporary governments in the following countries: Cuba, Iraq, North Korea, Pakistan, Venezuela. Be sure to support your classifications with examples.

WEB RESOURCES

American Studies at the University of Virginia
http://xroads.virginia.edu/~hyper/detoc/toc_indx
.html

This Web site contains the text of Alexis de Tocqueville's *Democracy in America*. Among other issues, de Tocqueville discusses American culture and democracy as a form of government in the United States.

Internet Classics Archive
http://classics.mit.edu/Aristotle/politics.html

This Web site contains the complete English translation of Aristotle's *Politics*. See Book V for Aristotle's discussion of forms of government.

WordIQ
www.wordiq.com/definition/List_of_forms_of_
government—List_by_autonomy_of_regions

WordIQ is a searchable reference tool that synthesizes information from a diverse array of dictionary, encyclopedia, thesaurus, and other valuable references. The address given here provides a comprehensive list of real and imagined forms of government. Users can click on each form to find a more complete description as well as historical and contemporary examples.

NOTES

1 Jennifer A. Widner, *Building the Rule of Law: Francis Nyalali and the Road to Judicial Independence in Africa* (New York: W. W. Norton, 2001).

2 For a similar view, see Donald S. Lutz, *Principles of Constitutional Design* (New York: Cambridge University Press, 2006), 208.

3 Ivo D. Duchacek, *Power Maps: Comparative Politics of Constitutions* (Santa Barbara, Calif.: ABC-Clio, 1973).

4 Alexander Pope, *Essay on Man, A PSU [Pennsylvania State University] Electronic Classics Series, Epistle III, "Of the Nature and State of Man with Respect to Society,"* 28, available at www2.hn.psu.edu/faculty/jmanis/a%7Epope/onman.pdf.

5 John Adams, "Thoughts on Government," reprinted in *Roots of the Republic: American Founding Documents Interpreted,* ed. Stephen L. Schechter, Richard B. Bernstein, and Donald S. Lutz (Madison, Wisc.: Madison House, 1990), 129.

6 Martin Diamond, "The Ends of Federalism," in *The Federal Polity,* ed. Daniel J. Elazar (New Brunswick, N.J.: Transaction Books, 1974), 129.

7 "A Chronology of Constitutional Events during the America Revolutionary Era, 1777–1792," in *The Reluctant Pillar: New York and the Adoption of the Federal Constitution,* ed. Stephen L. Schechter (Albany: New York State Commission on the Bicentennial of the United States Constitution, 1987), 236–239.

8 Louis Hartz, *Economic Policy and Democratic Thought: Pennsylvania, 1776–1860* (Chicago: Quadrangle Books, 1968; originally published by Harvard University Press, 1948), 8.

9 The following classification of classes and characteristics draws on Lutz, *Principles of Constitutional Design,* 195–198.

10 Ibid., 198.

11 Ibid., 197.

12 Ibid., 198.

13 Henry of Bracton, *On the Laws and Customs of England,* Vol. 3 (Cambridge, Mass.: Harvard University Press, 1968), 305–306, quoted in a brief yet thorough review of the rule of law by Brian Z. Tamanaha, *On the Rule of Law: History, Politics, Theory* (Cambridge, UK: Cambridge University Press, 2004), 26.

14 For a comparison of Alexander II, Bismarck, and Abraham Lincoln, see Michael Knox Beran, *Forge of Empires: 1861–1871, Three Revolutionary Statesmen and the World They Made* (New York: Free Press, 2007).

15 Joel Krieger, ed., *The Oxford Companion to Politics of the World,* 2nd ed. (New York: Oxford University Press, 2001), 173.

16 Ibid.

17 See Arthur Keaveney, *Sulla: The Last Republican* (London: Routledge, 2005).

18 Quoted in Xinran, *China Witness: Voices from a Silent Generation* (New York: Pantheon Books, 2008), 1–2.

19 Most studies on nondemocratic government focus on authoritarianism and its various types. Classic studies include Carl Friedrich and Zbigniew Brzezinski, *Totalitarian Dictatorship and Autocracy* (New York: Praeger, 1965); Juan Linz, *Totalitarian and Authoritarian Regimes* (Boulder, Colo.: Lynne Rienner, 2000, originally 1975). A more general introduction is Paul Brooker, *Non-Democratic Regimes: Theory, Government and Politics* (New York: St. Martin's Press, 2000).

20 Quoted in Joseph Lynch, *Argentine Dictator: Juan Manuel de Rosas, 1829–1852* (Oxford: Oxford University Press, 1981), 75.

21 A. A. Milne, "King John's Christmas," *Now We Are Six* (New York: Dutton Children's Books, 1988; originally 1927), 4.

22 Herodotus, *The Histories,* trans. Robin Waterfield (Oxford: Oxford University Press, 1998), Bk. III: 89, 208.

23 R. R. Palmer, Joel Colton, and Lloyd Kramer, *A History of the Modern World,* 10th ed. (Boston: McGraw Hill, 2007), 174–175.

24 See Stephen Howe, *Empire: A Very Short Introduction* (New York: Oxford University Press, 2002), 30.

25 Thomas B. Pepinsky, "Malaysia: Turnover without Change," *Journal of Democracy* 18, no. 1 (January 2007): 113–127.

26 S. E. Finer, *History of Government,* Vol. 1 (Oxford: Oxford University Press, 1999), Chaps. 7–8.

27 Arthur S. Banks, Thomas C. Muller, and William R. Overstreet, eds., *Political Handbook of the World, 2007* (Washington, D.C.: CQ Press, 2007), 1292.

28 *World Report, 2007* (New York: Human Rights Watch, 2007), 524–525.

29 Robert Dahl, *Polyarchy: Participation and Opposition* (New Haven, Conn.: Yale University Press, 1971).

30 Larry Diamond, "Thinking about Hybrid Regimes," *Journal of Democracy* 13, no. 2 (2002): 21.

POWER AND ITS LIMITS

What makes a particular government good? What makes another bad? Before you can answer these questions for any given polity, you will need to understand the concept of power. In politics, power is the ability to get what you want. People seek to acquire power to accomplish different and often competing goals. Those individuals and institutions holding the most power are usually the most successful at shaping governmental policies. An understanding of political power is essential in evaluating how—and how well—a particular government functions. The first chapter in this unit takes a closer look at the sources of power and its uses.

Since ancient times, polities have struggled with the best way to control power. A government needs enough power to accomplish legitimate purposes but not so much that it can easily abuse or exceed its proper authority. In the second chapter of this unit, you will learn how polities use constitutions to both dispense and curtail the powers available to government. This idea, known as constitutionalism, goes hand in hand with another concept—the rule of law. This idea rests on the principle that the governors and governed abide by just laws that apply equally to everyone. As you will see, creating a polity governed by a lasting legitimate constitution and a healthy respect for the rule of law is not easy. But it is an achievable goal—and one certainly worth pursuing.

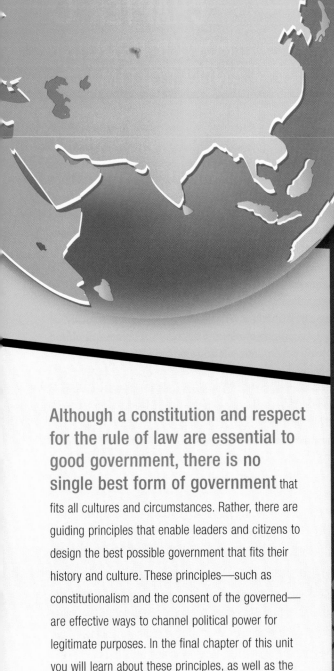

Although a constitution and respect for the rule of law are essential to good government, there is no single best form of government that fits all cultures and circumstances. Rather, there are guiding principles that enable leaders and citizens to design the best possible government that fits their history and culture. These principles—such as constitutionalism and the consent of the governed—are effective ways to channel political power for legitimate purposes. In the final chapter of this unit you will learn about these principles, as well as the characteristics of bad government and the forms that government can take.

CHAPTER 8

WHY DOES POLITICAL POWER REQUIRE AUTHORITY AND LEGITIMACY?

BIG IDEAS

- Power in the political system is the ability to achieve political goals.

- Power is closely related to two other important ideas: authority and legitimacy.

- The sources of authority include a Supreme Being, birth or heredity, extraordinary ability, consent of the governed, and constitutionalism.

- The political world comprises both legitimate and illegitimate governments.

- Political scientists assess the legitimacy of particular governments by looking at the procedures they follow and the outcomes they achieve.

- There are three moralities of power: the morality of official duty, the morality of aspiration, and the morality of constitutional norms.

Purpose of This Chapter

Political power is important in any discussion of politics. Simply put, power is the ability to get what you seek from the world of politics. The world of politics is filled with people who seek to acquire power to accomplish different and often competing goals. Power becomes a high-stakes game when players contend over public policy issues and seek to gain control of the reins of government power. Power is closely connected to two other core ideas: authority and legitimacy. What are the sources of authority and legitimacy? What are the legitimate instruments and uses of power? How (and how well) do authority and legitimacy constrain those who seek and wield governmental power? This chapter takes a closer look at the idea of power and seeks answers to these questions and others.

Terms to Know

authority	dynasty	popular sovereignty
charisma	illegitimate governments	power
constitutionalism	legitimacy	
divine right	legitimate governments	

WHAT IS POWER?

People enter politics for different reasons. Some seek public office, while others seek to influence those in office. The world of politics is filled with people seeking diverse goals and interests. In the political world, people of like interests form alliances and compete with their opponents to get what they want. To achieve their goals, opposing sides practice persuasion, manipulation, and, in some instances, coercion. In the process, goals and alliances sometimes shift in response to changing circumstances.

Simply put, power in a political system is the ability to achieve political goals. In the ever-changing world of politics, power becomes elusive. Acquiring the ability to succeed is a necessary element of success, but it is not a guarantee. One reason is basic—power does not exist in a vacuum; it involves relationships, and those relationships are constantly changing.

Because of these complexities, the German sociologist Max Weber (1864–1920) defined *power* in relational terms as "the probability that one actor within a social relationship will be in a position to carry out his own will despite resistance."[1] The noted twentieth-century philosopher Bertrand Russell put it succinctly: power is "the production of *intended* effects."[2]

Power in the political system is complex for another reason—politics is different from other social relationships. In the political world, people are competing over public goals that affect the polity as a whole or a significant part of it. The stakes are high and often affect everyone.

Countries often set ground rules for the use of power in their constitutions and other laws. They also create governments with the authority to enforce those ground rules and to make collective decisions that are binding on society and its members. In most polities, governments hold a near-monopoly over the legitimate use of physical force to enforce the law.

One great danger in the power game is that one faction will seize the reins of government and use coercion to achieve its own interests and suppress the interests of others. At the other end of the spectrum, there is the danger that a constitutional government will have too little power to enforce the law, preserve order, and protect national security.

As a result, assigning powers to government is always a delicate balance. Governments need enough power to govern properly but not so much that they can abuse the governed. In mature constitutional polities such as the United States, the rules of the game are written in a constitution. In newly created or badly divided constitutional polities, however, the players might find it difficult to agree on the ground rules. Some people might even decide to ignore the rules. In polities ruled by authoritarian governments, such as North Korea, the players must follow or resist rules that have been rigged in favor of the rulers. There also are failed states, in which the government has lost control, the rule of law has broken down, and anarchy prevails.

WHY DOES A GOVERNMENT'S POWER DEPEND ON ITS AUTHORITY AND LEGITIMACY?

In *The Social Contract* (1762), the French philosopher Jean Jacques Rousseau devoted a chapter to "The Right of the Strongest." He opened that chapter with this famous statement: "The strongest man is never strong enough to be always master, unless he transforms strength into right, and obedience into duty."[3]

Rousseau's opening statement is widely quoted out of context. Read alone, it seems like Rousseau endorsed the sentiment. But he did not. In fact, he spent the rest of the chapter refuting it. Might, argued Rousseau, never makes right. Either the strongest become rightful leaders by rightful means, or they keep their swords and bully people into accepting their illegitimate right to rule. In the first instance, the strong renounce the use of physical force unless it is for a just cause. In the second, they renounce the legitimate right to rule in favor of coercion. "Let us then admit," Rousseau concluded, "that force does not make right, and that we are obliged to obey only legitimate powers."[4]

Advocates of nonviolent resistance have long maintained that tyranny feeds on the obedience of the people and eventually withers away when the people refuse to obey. As true as that is, standing up to tyranny is not an easy thing to do. It requires bravery, to be sure, or perhaps defiance is a better way to put it. To succeed, it also requires planning, organization, leadership, and timing, and it may take decades or even centuries to succeed. Nonetheless, the refusal to obey (also known as civil disobedience and nonviolent resistance) is a special kind of power (see Politics in Action: Nonviolent Resistance in the Twentieth Century).

I want world sympathy in this battle of Right against Might.
Gandhi MKGandhi
5ᵗ.4.'30

"I WANT WORLD SYMPATHY IN THIS BATTLE OF RIGHT AGAINST MIGHT".

GANDHI'S MESSAGE ON APRIL 5, 1930, A DAY BEFORE HE BROKE THE SALT LAW. HE WAS ARRESTED ON MAY 4, AND WAS STILL IN PRISON WHEN THE FIRST ROUND TABLE CONFERENCE WAS HELD IN JANUARY, 1931.

In March 1930, Mohandas Gandhi led a march to a coastal village in India, picked up a small amount of naturally occurring salt from the ground, and boiled it in seawater. In doing so, Gandhi violated a British law that forbade the production of salt by anyone other than the British government. He was soon arrested for this offense. The day before, Gandhi wrote the message pictured here: "I want world sympathy in this battle of right against might." Gandhi's actions captured the world's attention and inspired people across India to begin making salt. Today, a large bronze monument in Delhi, pictured above right, memorializes Gandhi's Salt March.

POLITICS IN ACTION
Nonviolent Resistance in the Twentieth Century

In 1999, Peter Ackerman (1946–), chairman of the board of Freedom House, co-authored the book *A Force More Powerful* with Jack Duvall to accompany a television documentary of the same name. The book chronicles the history of nonviolent resistance movements in the twentieth century. The book includes the following episodes:

- In 1905, the Orthodox priest Georgii Gapon led a peaceful march of 150,000 workers in St. Petersburg, Russia, that began a nationwide movement that resulted in Russia's first popularly elected national parliament.
- In 1930–1931, Mohandas Gandhi drew on Henry David Thoreau's principles of civil disobedience to organize Indians to start making their own salt and stop paying salt taxes as the first step in India's struggle for independence from British rule.
- In 1944, under German occupation, the Danish Christian king dared to wear the yellow armband required of all Jews. He was joined by other Danish citizens, who refused to help the German war machine and brought it to a grinding halt.
- Also in 1944, in El Salvador students, doctors, and others organized a civic strike against the rule of a military dictator, whom they surrounded and peacefully forced into exile.
- In the early 1950s, the American civil rights movement led by Dr. Martin Luther King Jr. and others, drawing on the principles of Gandhi, began a lengthy campaign of nonviolent resistance that eventually ended the system of racial discrimination in the American South.
- In the early 1970s, Polish workers challenged communist tyranny in the port city of Gdansk and won the right to organize. They formed Solidarity, which led the struggle for freedom in Poland.
- In 1986, in the Philippines Corazon Aquino, the widow of a slain opposition leader, rallied hundreds of thousands of supporters in the streets and brought down the dictatorship of Ferdinand Marcos.
- On November 9, 1989, the East German government finally allowed its citizens to visit West Germany. East Berliners proceeded to the infamous Wall that had separated East and West Berlin since 1961, and in joyous celebration and quiet courage they climbed it and dropped to the other side, where they reunited with their loved ones.
- During the remainder of 1989 and 1990, the fall of the Berlin Wall became an inspiration to others in Soviet-controlled countries, which peacefully declared their independence from Soviet rule.
- In 1990, a national coalition opposed to apartheid in South Africa managed to secure the release of Nelson Mandela, who four years later joined with President F. W. de Klerk to bring an end to apartheid.
- In 1999–2000 (at century's end), a student-led resistance movement in Serbia used nonviolent resistance to topple President Slobodan Milošević, the last remaining dictator in Europe.

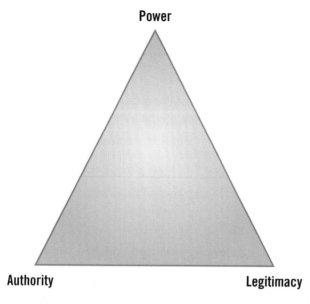

Power

Authority

Legitimacy

Figure 8.1 Power, Authority, and Legitimacy

In 2005, Freedom House researchers analyzed sixty-seven countries that became democracies between 1973 and 2002. They asked the question: What factors account for the successful transition from authoritarian to democratic government? For Freedom House, *successful* meant not only toppling a dictator but replacing the dictatorship with a democracy that lasted.[5]

Freedom House found that civic resistance was a key factor in fifty of the sixty-seven countries studied (70 percent). In other words, most democratic opposition movements used some form of resistance (or pushed back on illegitimate government) as a key strategy. Moreover, most of these fifty countries have remained free (thirty-two) or partly free (fourteen).

Looking more closely, Freedom House discovered two specific characteristics of successful transitions. First, the means of resistance was nonviolent, including tactics such as demonstrations, strikes, boycotts, and sit-ins. In fact, resistance movements using violence were most likely to create new governments that slid back from free to partly or not free after they were in power. Second, the resisters formed a broad-based yet cohesive popular coalition of interests. Some of these coalitions involved a segment of power holders (some members of the dictatorship in power); others did not.[6] These heroic examples show that "people power" is not a fiction. It has meaning, and it works. Used correctly, it can stand up to (and defeat) tyranny and lead to lasting democracy.

These examples and Rousseau's analysis also suggest several broad conclusions about the relationships of power to authority and legitimacy:

• Power, authority, and legitimacy are separate, yet interrelated concepts. Each has its own meaning, yet each depends for its success on the other two. (Figure 8.1 illustrates this relationship.)

• **Power** in the political system is the ability to achieve political goals. This ability requires appropriate resources (human, financial, and material), institutions, leaders, and policies. Sooner or later, however, these tangible elements of power evaporate without the authority to sustain them.

• **Authority** is the rightful or moral claim of government to exercise the powers granted to it.

• **Legitimacy** is the popularly accepted belief that government has the rightful or moral claim to govern. In other words, legitimacy is the acknowledged right to govern.

Sooner or later, using organized and sustained acts of resistance, people can dissolve the moral power of governments that have forfeited their right to govern. Gathering and managing appropriate resources, creating and exercising institutions that work, attracting good leaders, and making wise decisions all depend on the people's acceptance of the government they are asked to obey.[7]

- Government is the institution in society with the authority to make and enforce binding decisions affecting society. A government's authority is not absolute. Authority comes from a particular source (for example, God or the people). That source prescribes the scope of government's powers and the manner in which it can act. And authority must be legitimate in the eyes of the people. (See Politics in Action: Rights and Power.)

POLITICS IN ACTION
Rights and Power

People normally think of rights as guaranteed protections or entitlements that belong to individuals, not governments. People have rights; governments have power. But the phrase "right to govern" uses the word *right* in a different way. It is not an entitlement. It means that government has a morally defensible or justifiable claim to govern.

WHAT ARE THE SOURCES OF AUTHORITY?

Max Weber's typology of sources of authority is a natural place to begin. Writing in the early twentieth century, Weber, a German sociologist, identified three sources of authority: traditional authority, based on divine right and heredity; charismatic authority, held by a leader of extraordinary abilities; and legal-rational authority, based on the law and bureaucracy of the modern state.[8]

Some, however, criticize Weber's list. Traditional societies, some contend, are not the only societies that draw on divine right and heredity. And, as modern states evolved, they have turned to constitutions, not bureaucracy, as a source of authority. Finally, Weber excluded popular sovereignty from his list.

To address these concerns, we have modified Weber's list. Table 8.1 lists five major sources of authority, along with the principle associated with each source. Evidence of these sources can be found throughout history and across cultures. The first four sources may occur by themselves or in combination with other sources. The fifth source, constitutions, is a cross-cutting source; it usually accompanies one or more of the other four and does not exist independently.

SUPREME BEING

Divine right is the principle that the authority to govern comes from God or a Supreme Being. The ruler governs by God's will and is answerable only to God. Sometimes, especially

Table 8.1 Sources and Principles of Authority

Source	Principle
Supreme Being	Divine right
Birth	Right of inheritance
Extraordinary abilities	Merit
Consent of the governed	Popular sovereignty
Constitution	Constitutionalism

in ancient cultures, divine right was accompanied by the additional claim that the ruler was a god or descended from a god.

Divine right is often accompanied by two additional claims: the absolutist claim that the ruler is all-powerful and the legitimist belief that divine right is inherited and should be a basis of royal succession.

Czar Nicholas II was forced to shovel snow after he and his family were captured by communists in 1917.

An early example of divine right dates back to the Hebrew Bible. As the Bible recounts, the tribes of Israel were losing a war with the Philistines because tribal leaders were unable to unite. They asked the prophet Samuel to find a king who could unite them. Samuel was instructed by God to find Saul and anoint him as the first king (see Chapter 12).

In China, the emperor claimed his authority to rule from a "mandate of heaven." That mandate came with conditions, including the heavenly instruction that emperors listen to the people.

In medieval Europe, the idea of divine right erupted in disputes between popes and emperors over ultimate authority. Both agreed that political power ultimately came from God, who alone had the right to determine life and death. What they did not agree on was the route of that authority. The Church contended that it came through the Church and its ministers; the secular rulers contended that authority came directly from God to the monarch, whether elected or hereditary.

In Russia, the Romanov dynasty was established in 1613 under Mikhail Romanov and his son, Alexei Mikhailovich. They based their right to rule on the assertion that the tsar was the embodiment of God on Earth. Therefore, the tsar's will should be unrestrained by laws, the aristocracy, or the bureaucracy. The tsar should rule the country according to his own sense of duty and right.

Communists murdered Nicholas II, the last Romanov ruler, and his family in 1918 during the Russian Revolution. During his reign, Tsar Nicholas clung fervently to the idea of a divine right to rule as set down by his ancestors. Nicholas often justified his policies by saying that they "had come to him" from God. According to one of Nicholas's ministers, the tsar believed "that people do not influence events, that God directs everything, and that the Tsar, as God's anointed, should not take advice from anyone but follow only his divine inspiration."[9]

During the three hundred years that the Romanovs ruled Russia, they encouraged a belief in the tsar as a father figure. Just as God was seen as a kindly, wise, and just father in heaven, so too was the tsar, his embodiment on Earth. The ordinary peasant thought of the tsar not just as a king but as a god. As a father figure, the tsar was often portrayed in folk tales as the Tsar Batiushka (Father Tsar). The tsar was believed to know all the peasants personally and by name. Interestingly, the peasant tradition of sending direct appeals to the Good Father Tsar continued well into the communist era, when Russian men and women sent personal appeals to Lenin, Stalin, and Khrushchev.[10]

BIRTH OR HEREDITY

Throughout history, monarchs and aristocrats have claimed political authority as a right of birth. Based on this right, rule is inherited as a birthright. Usually, the inheritance of the right to rule is transferred within the royal family from the first-born ruler of one generation to the first-born successor, or heir-apparent, of the next generation. A royal family with an inherited line of succession is known as a **dynasty.** Some dynasties link birthright with divine right.

In a system of dynastic rule, everyone knows who should be chosen to succeed the previous ruler as long as the previous ruler has borne a child who meets the necessary qualifications of succession. In some dynastic systems, the heir-apparent must be the first-born male of the reigning ruler. In all dynastic systems, the heir-apparent must live long enough to inherit the throne.

In China, for example, the Zhou family founded a dynasty in 1027 BCE that lasted for eight hundred years, the longest in Chinese history. The Zhou dynasty based inherited authority on their mandate of heaven. Each succeeding dynasty in China claimed political authority on the basis of the inherited rights provided by their mandate of heaven.[11]

Various circumstances can intervene to create a crisis of authority. What if the ruler has no heirs? What if the ruler dies when the heir is an infant? What if the first-born are twins? What if the heir-apparent is assassinated? What if there are rivals for the throne who are from other branches of the royal family?

EXTRAORDINARY ABILITY

Many political thinkers have argued that ability, not birth, should be the source of political authority. The Chinese philosopher Confucius (551–479 BCE) counseled the Zhou dynasty against using birth as a criterion of political authority. He argued that the wisest and most virtuous of the emperor's male heirs ought to be chosen to rule.

The ancient Greek philosopher Plato (427–347 BCE) maintained that only those who know what is good are fit to rule or to exercise political authority. In *The Republic,* Plato used the Allegory of the Cave to illustrate his theory of knowledge. In Plato's allegory, a group of people are chained from birth within a cave. All they can see is the wall in front of them, on which flickering shadows appear. To those imprisoned in the cave, the shadows are reality, even though they are nothing more than reflections.

Plato argued that our world is like this cave. Humans are hobbled by their ignorance of the true nature of reality. To see the world as it really is, people must struggle out of the cave and into the sunlight. At first, the sunlight will be dazzling and blinding. The select few who are able to ascend from the "cave" of ignorance achieve true knowledge and thus should be entrusted with political authority. They constitute an aristocracy of merit because they are the ablest people of all backgrounds and both sexes. Today, some political observers use the phrase "the best and the brightest" to refer to such an aristocracy. Plato maintained that the polity should be governed by philosopher-kings selected from this aristocracy of merit.

The Hebrew Bible tells a different story of royal selection on the basis of ability. The story centers around the shepherd boy David, who killed the Philistine champion Goliath. God instructed the aging prophet Samuel to anoint David to succeed Saul after Saul grew despondent and consumed by his jealousy of David. David was then blessed with the charismatic authority to rule. According to this theory, God anoints a ruler who is blessed with **charisma**, the special ability to lead and inspire others, no matter who his family is.

But relying only on the best to rule raises an important question: Who will succeed the current ruler if there are no other succession rules in place? To overcome this problem, according to Weber, the ruler must provide for the "routinization of charisma."[12] This means that the ruler must establish a system of selection and succession that lasts and becomes routine over time.

CONSENT OF THE GOVERNED

Since ancient times, political philosophers have argued that rulers must heed the will of the people whether the ruler is popularly elected or claims divine right. In this broad sense, popular consent is part of the authority of all rulers. Less widespread in history is the democratic idea that political authority comes from the consent of the governed and the principle of **popular sovereignty.** According to this principle, the citizenry, not God or a king, is the source of political authority.

Republics and democracies rely on the principle of popular sovereignty to select their leaders. In the democracy of ancient Athens, all male citizens were expected to participate directly in the government. Citizens were selected randomly for participation in the belief that all citizens were equal in their ability to serve. In today's representative democracies, citizens elect officials to represent them. As a check against majority tyranny, however, most democratic constitutions provide elected officials with the power to appoint other officials who are more independent of popular pressure. Many countries, including the United States, subscribe to the idea of an independent judiciary and provide for the appointment of judges.

CONSTITUTIONALISM

Constitutionalism is the principle that government should be created, empowered, and limited by a constitution. This principle legitimizes all sources of authority. Whether the authority of government relies on a Supreme Being, birth, ability, or consent of the governed, its continued legitimacy also must rely on some kind of constitution. Legitimate government is constitutional government. This principle is introduced in the next section and developed more fully in the next chapter.

WHAT ARE THE CONDITIONS OF LEGITIMATE GOVERNMENT?

Political legitimacy is the popularly accepted belief that government has the moral power to govern. This requires that the people must be able to judge the moral fitness of their government. Four conditions are necessary if this is to happen: (1) the polity must have a political culture that includes shared norms of legitimate government; (2) there must be some kind of constitution that provides cultural norms with legal clarity and teeth; (3) the people must have the civic skills (including moral judgment) to recognize illegitimate government when they see it; and (4) where illegitimate government exists, the people must find the political will to resist it and the power to succeed in resisting.

Every polity has some form of constitutional system (what Aristotle called a *constitution*, broadly defined). That system includes the cultural norms, laws, and governing institutions that make up the polity. Today, most polities have a written and legally binding constitution as part of their constitutional system. For federal systems such as the United States, the constitutional system contains many constitutions and constitution-like documents. (See More About . . . The American Constitutional System.)

A constitutional system provides the principles, purposes, powers, and limits of

MORE ABOUT . . .
The American Constitutional System

The American constitutional system runs wide and deep. Its constitutional and constitution-like documents include the U.S. Declaration of Independence; the U.S. Constitution and its amendments; the fifty state constitutions; the founding charters of the District of Columbia and noncontiguous American territories and commonwealths; the constitution-like charters (for example, home-rule charters) of local governments; and all the statutes, treaties, and court decisions of constitutional import.

legitimate government. **Legitimate governments** are constitutional governments: they are created constitutionally, their officeholders are selected constitutionally, and those office-holders carry out their responsibilities within the limits and by the rules established in the constitution. **Illegitimate governments** also have constitutions, but these constitutions are ignored by the rulers or they are written to justify the actions of rulers who have seized power unlawfully or wield power arbitrarily.

Constitutional norms vary depending on the history, culture, and form of government of a polity. Constitutional norms of monarchies and republics differ as do the norms of particular monarchies. In the seventeenth and eighteenth centuries, Americans selectively borrowed British constitutional norms. Various rights in the U.S. Bill of Rights owe their origins to British rights, but they have been modified to fit American republican culture and law. Today, both countries cherish free speech, yet their courts interpret that right differently.

Norms differ from country to country, and they can be compared. There are three levels that political scientists use in comparing norms of legitimacy:

- The system level, which has to do with the legitimacy of the polity as a whole and whether its principles and institutions are just.
- The process or procedural level, which focuses on *how* well the government follows the constitutional procedures for making and enforcing the law.
- The outcome or performance level, which looks at *what* the government achieves in terms of the constitutional purposes of government and the expectations of the citizenry.[13]

SYSTEM LEGITIMACY

The system level refers to a people's belief in the legitimacy of the polity itself. It includes not only governmental actions but the entire political system of values and interests on which government is based. A serious crisis of legitimacy exists when a wide range of people have lost faith in their political system.

France in the late eighteenth century is a historical example of such a crisis, and the French Revolution of 1789 was the response. The French political philosopher Alexis de Tocqueville (1805–1859) was born into a noble family devastated by the revolution. De Tocqueville wrote a powerful analysis of the causes and consequences of the revolution, entitled *The Old Regime and the French Revolution*. His study was published in 1848—the same year that Karl Marx published his *Manifesto of the Communist Party* and that another revolution began in France and swept across Europe.

De Tocqueville analyzed the political order (the Old Regime) that had been destroyed by the 1789 revolution. He found two stages in the history of that regime. In the earlier stage, the Church and the nobility owned most of the land and enjoyed a wide range of rights and privileges. They were the most visible landlords and charged the peasantry high rents on land and high interest on debts. In return, the nobles were expected to protect the people and administer justice in their domain.

In the second stage, kings gradually centralized power in the name of the state. They did not succeed completely, but the state did take over many of the law-and-order functions previously carried out by the nobility—and many of the taxes to pay for those services. Kings bought the loyalty of Church and nobility by allowing them to keep their rights and privileges. The nobility, for example, got most of the government jobs and subsidies, which angered the middle class.

Despite the centralization of power, the Church and nobility still retained considerable land. As landlords, they continued to exact rents, interest payments, and forced labor for local building projects, which angered the peasantry. Increasingly, the state replaced the nobility as the primary protector and service provider in society. Because the state provided more services, the privileges enjoyed by Church and nobility seemed increasingly unfair.

Economic life was difficult and injustice weighed heavily on the system. Injustice united the peasants, middle class, and urban workers. It fueled a rising belief in the illegitimacy of the system, and it helped opposition leaders organize the peasants and workers in a revolution that spread rapidly across the cities and countryside of France.

"The object of the Revolution," said de Tocqueville, "was not merely to change an old form of government but to abolish the entire social structure of pre-revolutionary France."[14] As a result, he continued, the revolution "was obliged to declare war simultaneously on all established powers, to destroy all recognized privileges, to make short work of all traditions, and to institute new ways of life, new conventions." Thus, de Tocqueville concluded, one of the first acts of the revolution was to build on the people's sense of the illegitimacy of the existing order and "rid men's minds of all those notions which had ensured their obedience to authority under the old regime." The French Revolution became a model emulated by modern revolutionaries who sought to destroy the existing system and replace it with a new order.

PROCEDURAL LEGITIMACY

The procedural level shifts the focus of attention from the polity to the government. Procedural legitimacy is the expectation that government will act in a constitutional manner. The emphasis is on constitutional rules that prescribe how government acts.

Most governments, for example, have the constitutional power to build and maintain public roads, schools, and other projects in the public interest. But how may they do that and within what limits? If part of a planned public highway is on private property, should government have the power to take that property for public purposes? What procedures must government follow? Is government obligated to compensate the owner for the property taken? What is a fair basis for compensation? Does the property owner have the right to challenge the government's decision in a court of law?

Proceduralists are constitutionalists; they are willing to tolerate a certain amount of government inefficiency and inadequate public services as long as government acts constitutionally. Proceduralists carefully monitor two sets of processes: how government power is acquired, and how it is used.

In acquiring power, the government should follow legitimate and predictable constitutional procedures for the selection and succession (replacement) of government officials. Peaceful succession is often the first test of legitimacy in a newly created system of government. In world history, heredity became the first choice of kings not simply because they wanted to keep the crown in their family. They also believed that a clear line of inheritance would reduce in-fighting over the succession. Charismatic leaders need to institutionalize the succession to ensure that what they have established continues after their death.

In newly formed democracies, selection is based on free, fair, and open elections that are regularly scheduled. Peaceful succession also requires opportunities for competition in which opposition candidates can win elections. The first president must be willing to step aside and let others have a chance to lead, as George Washington did, for example. Or if they remain, they must do so only on the basis of free and fair reelections that are not rigged.

Some observers believe that the most important test of a new democracy is the first contested election when a sitting president or party loses reelection. In the U.S. election of 1800, for example, Federalist President John Adams lost a bitterly contested race against Republican Thomas Jefferson. The Federalists had occupied the presidency since 1789. Still, when the time came to leave office Adams did not block the peaceful succession of power.

As of the early twenty-first century, seventy countries hold free, fair, and competitive elections. This is more than at any other time in history, yet it is only 35–40 percent of all countries.[15] In fully free countries, incumbents have a natural advantage (see More About . . . The Power of the Incumbent); nevertheless, opposition candidates are free to challenge incumbents and to win on a level playing field. There are few if any legal barriers placed in the opponent's path.

In contrast, many partially free democracies and soft authoritarian systems have regular elections with some meaning, but the party in power makes it very difficult for opposition candidates to win. For example, the government party may pass laws making it difficult for opponents to register and freely campaign, or the elections may be disrupted and election results may be intentionally miscounted.

At the other end of the spectrum, in hard authoritarian systems opposition parties face an untenable situation. As the London-based weekly magazine the *Economist* observed, "All power tends to be concentrated in one person, the president. The government fixes the election; the opposition boycotts it or rejects the result;

MORE ABOUT . . .
The Power of the Incumbent

An incumbent is a person who currently holds public office. Even in a liberal democratic system, incumbents have an advantage over their challengers. Incumbents have an insider's knowledge of government and policy, ready access to information, visibility in the media, use of free resources (such as the telephone, Internet, and mail), and contacts in the government. Incumbents also can sponsor bills favorable to their constituency, and they have an easier time raising campaign funds from donors who prefer the known over the unknown candidate. In the United States, for example, most incumbents win contests for reelection most of the time. On the other hand, there are those times when the voters decide to "vote the rascals out." So, the power of the incumbent is not assured.

the government ignores the opposition. The problem is that tyrants have learned how to control the voting. Boundaries, the media, the economy and the voters' roll are all manipulated. Opponents are squashed."[16] In such situations, ending authoritarian rule by peaceful means can take decades. In American history, for example, the southern states imposed a system of racial domination after the Civil War and Reconstruction. That system disenfranchised black voters and made it virtually impossible for black candidates to get elected. A century passed before the civil rights movement secured the passage and enforcement of federal voting rights legislation to break up this system of disenfranchisement.

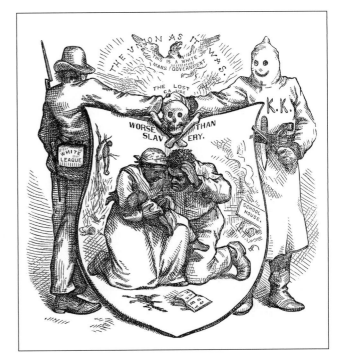

The title of this 1874 Harper's Weekly *political cartoon, "Worse Than Slavery," expresses the dismay that many Americans felt at the resurgence of states' rights during Reconstruction.*

Proceduralists face a different challenge when anti-democratic factions initially seek power. Should free societies ban such factions from the electoral process? Interestingly, political studies support the conclusion that most people do not freely vote for candidates who represent an extremist faction. Most people prefer the center when threatened by violent extremes. The danger is that political leaders and their base of supporters tend to polarize politics in troubled times, thereby reducing the number of viable centrist candidates.[17]

In a recent comparative study of fascism, Robert Paxton found that "even the [German] Nazi Party, by far the most successful electorally of all fascist parties, never exceeded 37 percent [of the vote] in a free election" before they gained control. And, in the election of March 1933, when Hitler was already chancellor and the Nazi Party controlled the state, the party barely got 44 percent of the vote, less than half, despite voter intimidation by storm troopers.[18]

The research by Paxton and others on twentieth-century Europe and Latin America suggests that most people are reluctant to trade their freedom for promises of a better life under authoritarian rule. Yet history shows that proceduralists often have been unprepared to resist the seizure of power by political manipulation and superior military force. Historically, this has been especially evident in Latin American and Southeast Asian countries, where the military periodically claims the right to restore order in unstable times. The twentieth century also provides numerous examples of organized fascist or communist factions in economically depressed societies, with strong paramilitary wings that promise material improvement and renewed national pride.

PERFORMANCE LEGITIMACY

Performance legitimacy is the expectation that government will deliver tangible results that advance the constitutional purposes of government. In Chapter 4, we present three sets of constitutional purposes of government: the preservation of life, the protection of freedom, and human betterment. Ideally, these three purposes go hand in hand—protecting freedom fosters human betterment, and preserving a safe and orderly society imposes limits on human freedom without endangering freedom.

Advancing all three purposes involves a delicate balance that may need to shift in response to changing circumstances or extraordinary conditions. Extraordinary situations such as war, economic depression, or a public health crisis may require unusual or even emergency measures. In such situations, the normal expectations of procedural and performance legitimacy may conflict.[19]

Countries living under the emergency conditions of endemic warfare and severe economic depression for a sustained time are particularly vulnerable to authoritarian rulers who promise to rescue them from their plight. In such situations, the lack of procedural safeguards may be tolerated by the people as long as the government provides an orderly society in which people can continue to earn a living and receive state services.

Authoritarian governments are trapped in their own delicate balance. To stay in power, they must provide enough services and security to justify their existence, but if they restore a "normal life," people will wonder why authoritarianism is still needed. People in such countries yearn for a normal life; yet a return to normalcy is not in the government's interest, so it must figure out a way to make life secure yet difficult. As long as people must face bureaucratic obstacles to keep up with life's basic demands, some authoritarian rulers believe the people will have little time or energy to resist.

The question is how best to balance the needs of procedural and performance legitimacy. On one hand, government must observe the procedural safeguards of limited government in the name of freedom and constitutionalism. On the other hand, government must have the legitimate authority and power required of energetic government in the name of effectiveness and governability.

The World Bank Institute has developed six governance indicators that provide one way to measure how well countries balance procedural and performance legitimacy. According to the World Bank, "governance consists of the traditions and institutions by which authority in a country is exercised."[20]

1. Voice and accountability (VA). This measures perceptions of the extent to which a country's citizens are able to participate in selecting their government and the extent to which they have freedom of expression, freedom of association, and a free media.
2. Political stability and absence of violence (PV). This measures perceptions of the likelihood that the government will be destabilized or overthrown by unconstitutional or violent means, including politically motivated violence and terrorism.
3. Government effectiveness (GE). This measures perceptions of the quality of public services, the quality of the civil service and the degree of its independence from

political pressures, the quality of policy formulation and implementation, and the credibility of the government's commitment to such policies.

4. Regulatory quality (RQ). This measures perceptions of the ability of the government to formulate and implement sound policies and regulations that permit and promote private-sector development.

5. Rule of law (RL). This measures perceptions of the extent to which agents have confidence in and abide by the rules of society and, in particular, the quality of contract enforcement, property rights, the police, and the courts, as well as the likelihood of crime and violence.

6. Control of corruption (CC). This measures perceptions of the extent to which public power is exercised for private gain, including both petty and grand forms of corruption, as well as "capture" of the state by elites and private interests.[21]

The first two indicators—voice and accountability and political stability and absence of violence—refer to the freedom and perceived ability of the citizenry to participate in politics and government in a peaceful and stable environment. The third and fourth indicators—government effectiveness and regulatory quality—point to the perceived ability and authority of the government needed to make and implement sound public policies that favor free markets and free trade without imposing excessive regulations. The fifth and sixth indicators—the rule of law and control of corruption—focus on the perceived ability of government and the people to maintain a system of fair and predictable rules of law as the basis of social relationships, economic dealings, and the use of public power for the public good.

WHAT ARE THE TWO MORALITIES OF POWER?

As noted earlier, political legitimacy is the popularly accepted belief that government has the moral power to govern. But what is the moral basis of power? Throughout history, diverse cultures have relied on two contending moralities of power: the morality of duty and the morality of aspiration.

THE MORALITY OF DUTY

According to the morality of duty, the first political obligation of leaders and citizens is to preserve the state. Advocates of this morality argue that without a strong state, government cannot achieve its purposes. To preserve life, assure freedom, and better human conditions, government must first protect its own survival and that of the state. Therefore, in a world of nation-states, the first criterion of public policy must be what today is known as the "national interest." This means that the interests of the nation-state come first in the making of public policy.

Advocates of this morality are often referred to as realists. One of the most influential realists in world history has been the Italian Renaissance philosopher Niccolò Machiavelli

(1469–1527). According to Machiavelli, "a prince, and especially a new prince, cannot observe all those things for which men are held good, since he is often under a necessity, to maintain his state." The prince, Machiavelli continued, should not "depart from good, when possible, but know how to enter into evil, when forced by necessity."[22] Realists are not averse to using peaceful persuasion to achieve their goals; however, realists such as Machiavelli counsel that rulers must also be prepared to use coercion and deception.

Machiavelli advocated the subtle use of power. He preferred the ethical use of persuasion, but for Machiavelli the end justified all means necessary—including force and deception—to preserve the state. Above all, the ruler must remain flexible in the face of ever-changing circumstances. As Machiavelli put it, the ruler must be prepared to act "against faith, against charity, against religion. And so he needs to have a spirit disposed to change as the winds of fortune and variations of things command him."[23]

The seventeenth-century English philosopher Thomas Hobbes is another influential realist. Hobbes viewed power as a dominant-subordinate relationship. In this relationship, power is viewed as the ability to exercise control over others. The exercise of power, he believed, was the general inclination of all human beings. Hobbes believed that the strong seek to dominate the weak. The weak, in turn, seek to deceive and join forces to overcome the strong. Living together in peace is not an option—not until one ruler controls everyone in the state.

The state for Hobbes will "live in the condition of perpetual war, and upon the confines of battle, with [its] frontiers armed, and cannons planted against [its] neighbors."[24] For Hobbes, the surest measure of a state's power was its military strength to make war, its access to economic wealth to pay for war, and the loyalty of the people who are recruited to fight.

THE MORALITY OF ASPIRATION

According to the morality of aspiration, the preservation of the state is not enough. The state must function as a polity and stand for something more than its mere survival. Therefore, the use of power must be held to a higher standard.

Advocates of this morality are often referred to as idealists. Among the most influential idealists in modern times is the American civil rights leader, Reverend Martin Luther King Jr., who explained power this way: "Power, properly understood, is the ability to achieve purpose. It is the strength required to bring about social, political, and economic changes. In this sense power is not only desirable but necessary in order to implement the demands of love and justice."[25]

Idealists tend to see power as a cooperative relationship *with* others, not a dominant relationship *over* others. For example, the English philosopher John Locke (1632–1704) disagreed with Hobbes. Locke believed that human beings were capable of forming communities by a social contract in which they voluntarily joined together as co-equals on the basis of reason and tolerance toward others.

For Hannah Arendt, power is "the human ability not just to act but to act in concert."[26] Arendt escaped Nazi Germany and migrated to the United States, where she became an eminent political thinker. Like John Locke, she believed that people do not live in a perpetual state of war or subordination; rather, they live amid perpetual opportunities to join together in peaceful cooperation. For Arendt, "Binding and promising, combining and covenanting are the means by which power is kept in existence."[27] Like Alexis de Tocqueville and other European visitors to America, she was fascinated by the American instinct for creating constitutions and voluntary associations to solve common problems.

Idealists recognize the need for legitimate coercion to enforce the law. Idealists accept that, for example, highway safety requires that speed limits be set and enforced, speeders be stopped and fined, and repeat offenders be punished. However, unlike realists, they presume that most citizens are self-regulating and therefore capable of controlling their own behavior without state intervention.

In the world of politics, statesmen face a moral dilemma. Should they follow their personal conscience or their official duty? Sometimes the two moralities are both good for the country and do not conflict, so it is possible to accomplish both. But when the two conflict, the statesman must try to find a way to reconcile them.

MORE ABOUT . . .
Abraham Lincoln's Stated Policy on Slavery and the Union

As to the policy I "seem to be pursuing" as you say, I have not meant to leave anyone in doubt. I would save the Union. I would save it the shortest way under the Constitution. . . . If I could save the Union without freeing any slave I would do it, and if I could save it by freeing all the slaves I would do it; and if I could save it by freeing some and leaving others alone I would also do that. . . . I have here stated my purpose according to my view of official duty; and I intend no modification of my oft-expressed personal wish that all men everywhere could be free.

Abraham Lincoln, letter to Horace Greeley (August 22, 1862), in *The Collected Works of Abraham Lincoln*, ed. Roy P. Bassler (New Brunswick, N.J.: Rutgers University Press, 1953), Vol. 5, 388–399.

As president of the United States, Abraham Lincoln faced this dilemma on the question of slavery. Personally, Lincoln abhorred slavery. His personal aspiration on the matter was no secret. However, as president, his official duty was to preserve the Union. On August 19, 1862, Horace Greeley, editor of the *New-York Tribune* and an abolitionist, asked the president why he did not fight more vigorously for the abolition of slavery. At the time, Lincoln was indeed planning to issue the first Emancipation Proclamation by executive order, but he did not think that it would be prudent to use this occasion to announce that strategy. Instead, he chose to reaffirm his official duty, perhaps to allay suspicions that he would risk the Union on the slave issue. Therefore, Lincoln's carefully worded response of August 22 was not completely candid. (See More About . . . Abraham Lincoln's Stated Policy on Slavery and the Union.) Exactly one month later, on September 22, he issued the first Emancipation Proclamation. But his letter is not a lie. Was it deceptive? Was it prudent? Was it the best decision at the time?

WHAT IS THE CONSTITUTIONALIST VIEW OF POWER?

As the Lincoln example suggests, the realist and idealist positions are not the only positions on morality. Statesmen and citizens often try to reconcile their official duty and personal aspirations by seeking a middle position.

The constitutionalist view is a well-traveled middle ground between the extremes of realism and idealism. Unlike the realist, constitutionalists do not see human beings as obsessed with power. For the constitutionalist, power, as the English statesman Lord Acton put it, *tends* to corrupt, but it does not necessarily corrupt unless it becomes absolute.

Andrew Hamilton (not Alexander) ably expressed the constitutionalist position. A New York lawyer in colonial times, Hamilton represented John Peter Zenger. In 1735, the colonial government of New York tried Zenger for libel because he had described the governor's actions as arbitrary and tyrannical. In Zenger's defense, Hamilton spoke eloquently on the subject of the government's power: "Power may be justly compar'd to a great River. . . . [W]hile kept within its due Bounds, [it] is both Beautiful and Useful; but when it overflows, its Banks, it is then too impetuous to be stemm'd, it bears down all before it, and brings Destruction and Desolation wherever it comes."[28]

The constitutionalist seeks to keep power "within its due bounds"—both the power of the government and the people. In a representative democracy, the power of the people is channeled into the power to vote and the power of association. Their representatives have the power to pass laws that regulate human behavior, but that power is limited by the constitution and the people's belief in it.

There are several constitutional strategies for keeping government power within its due bounds. These include familiar concepts such as the separation of powers, limited government, and federalism. These are taken up in the next chapter. The important point here is that constitutionalists view constitutionalism as the ultimate source of governmental power and of its limits.

REVIEWING AND USING THE CHAPTER

1. Why is political power important in any discussion of politics?

2. How are power, authority, and legitimacy related? Provide examples to illustrate your points.

3. What are the most common sources of authority in the political world today?

4. What distinguishes legitimate government from illegitimate government? How do governments establish their legitimacy? Provide examples to support your response.

5. Compare and contrast the morality of duty and the morality of aspiration. How are they alike, and how are they different?

6. How does the constitutionalist view of power differ from the realist or idealist view?

EXTENSION ACTIVITY

Some American presidents have been more successful than others in achieving their goals. Select a president and one political goal he set for his administration. Who were the major opponents of that goal? Explain how well he overcame opposition and achieved his goal. In your explanation, be sure to include at least three factors explaining his level of achievement.

WEB RESOURCES

Perspectives on Politics: Power and Political Institutions

http://politicalscience.stanford.edu/downloads/
moe-Power%20and%20Political%20Institutions.pdf

Written by Terry M. Moe, the William Bennett Munro Professor of Political Science at Stanford University and a senior fellow at the Hoover Institution, this excellent article examines the structures of power in political institutions. The article originally appeared in the June 2005 issue of *Perspectives on Politics*.

Polity IV Project: Political Regime Characteristics and Transitions, 1800–2008

www.systemicpeace.org/polity/polity4.htm

Maintained and updated by political scientists from George Mason University, Colorado State University, and the University of Maryland, this site provides comparative data on the authority characteristics of nations throughout the world, including the "State Fragility Index 2008."

Stanford Encyclopedia of Philosophy: Authority

http://plato.stanford.edu/entries/authority

This encyclopedia entry distinguishes between authority and power, legitimate and illegitimate uses of political power, and the various sources of political authority and their relationship to political theory.

Who Rules America?

http://sociology.ucsc.edu/whorulesamerica/
index.html

Maintained by G. William Domhoff, a research professor at the University of California, Santa Cruz, this Web site provides a sociological perspective on the study of power in the United States. Here you will find a variety of resources to help analyze power at the national and local levels, including theories of power and analyses of social change in the United States.

NOTES

1 H. Gerth and C. Wright Mills, eds., *From Max Weber: Essays in Sociology* (London: Routledge and Kegan Paul), quoted in Stephen D. Tansey, *Politics: The Basics* (London: Routledge, 1995), 5.

2 Bertrand Russell, *Power: A New Social Analysis* (London: Allen and Unwin, 1938/1975), 25. Emphasis added.

3 Jean Jacques Rousseau, *The Social Contract,* trans. G. D. H. Cole, Book I, Chap. 3, para. 1, available at www.constitution.org/jjr/socon_01.htm#003.

4 Ibid., para. 4.

5 Adrian Karatnycky and Peter Ackerman, *How Freedom Is Won: From Civic Resistance to Durable Democracy* (Washington, D.C.: Freedom House, 2005).

6 Ibid., 6–9.

7 Max Weber drew the distinction between *authority* as the right to rule and *legitimacy* as the acknowledged right to rule in *Theory of Social and Economic Organization,* trans. A. M. Henderson and Talcott Parsons (New York: The Free Press, 1947), 382. It has been used by Reinhard Bendix, *Kings or People: Power and the Mandate to Rule* (Berkeley, Calif.: University of California Press, 1978), 17; Carl J. Friedrich, *Man and His Government: An Empirical Theory of Politics* (New York: McGraw-Hill, 1963), 246; Seymour Martin Lipset, *Political Man* (New York: Doubleday, 1960), 77.

8 Weber, *Theory of Social and Economic Organization,* 324–329 for an overview.

9 Count Sergei Witte, quoted in Orlando Figes, *A People's Tragedy: A History of the Russian Revolution* (New York: Viking, 1996), 8.

10 Ibid., 10–11.

11 W. Scott Morton and Charlton M. Lewis, *China: Its History and Culture,* 4th ed. (New York: McGraw Hill, 2005), 22–25.

12 Weber, *Theory of Social and Economic Organization,* 363.

13 This distinction draws on Gabriel A. Almond, G. Bingham Powell Jr., Russell J. Dalton, and Kaare Ström, *Comparative Politics Today: A World View,* 9th ed. (New York: Pearson Longman, 2008), 43–48.

14 All quotations in this paragraph are from Alexis de Tocqueville, *The Old Regime and the French Revolution,* quoted in Jack A. Goldstone, ed., *Revolutions: Theoretical,*

Comparative, and Historical Studies, 3rd ed. (Belmont, Calif.: Thomson Wadsworth, 2003), 32.

15 Larry Diamond, "Elections without Democracy: Thinking about Hybrid Regimes," *Journal of Democracy,* 13, no. 2 (April 2002): 26.

16 "Polls to Nowhere," *Economist,* November 23, 1996, 20–21.

17 For a review of this literature, see Nancy Bermeo, *Ordinary People in Extraordinary Times: The Citizenry and the Breakdown of Democracy* (Princeton, N.J.: Princeton University Press, 2003). This book is also worth reading on its own merits.

18 Robert O. Paxton, *The Anatomy of Fascism* (New York: Vintage Books, Random House, 2005), 16, 96.

19 The distinction between *procedural legitimacy* and *performance legitimacy* was drawn by the American political scientist Samuel P. Huntington in *Political Order in Changing Societies* (New Haven, Conn.: Yale University Press, 1968).

20 World Bank, http://info.worldbank.org/governance/wgi2007.

21 Ibid.

22 Niccolò Machiavelli, *The Prince,* trans. Harvey C. Mansfield, 2nd ed. (Chicago: University of Chicago Press, 1998), 70.

23 Ibid.

24 Thomas Hobbes, *Leviathan,* quoted in Elisabeth Young-Bruehl, *Why Arendt Matters* (New Haven, Conn.: Yale University Press, 2006), 93–94; for a general discussion of Arendt's views on power, see 84–96.

25 Martin Luther King Jr., *Where Do We Go from Here: Chaos or Community* (1967), quoted in Robert L. Maddex, *The Illustrated Dictionary of Constitutional Concepts* (Washington D.C.: Congressional Quarterly, 1996), 223.

26 Hannah Arendt, *On Violence* (New York: Harcourt, Brace & World, 1970), 44.

27 Hannah Arendt, *On Revolution* (New York: Viking Press, 1963), 174.

28 Andrew Hamilton, "Argument in Zenger Trial (1735)," in *The Oxford Dictionary of American Legal Quotations,* ed. Fred R. Shapiro (New York: Oxford University Press, 1993), 406.

CHAPTER 9

HOW CAN CONSTITUTIONALISM HARNESS POWER?

BIG IDEAS

- Constitutionalism is the principle that governments are created, empowered, and limited by constitutions.

- Constitutions vary considerably in how and how well they establish constitutional governments, but there are patterns in these variations.

- Constitutionalism and the rule of law are interrelated principles that depend on one another.

- Constitutions limit government, but those limits are only as strong as the people's belief in them and the institutional safeguards that protect the people from tyranny.

Purpose of This Chapter

This chapter is about the law as a limit on power. It takes its theme from John Locke's famous and incontrovertible rule: "Wherever Law ends, Tyranny begins."[1] In this chapter, we investigate a persistent challenge that all polities face—how to establish a government with sufficient power to accomplish its legitimate purposes yet so structured and controlled that it cannot easily abuse or exceed its authority. Constitutionalism is the belief that polities should seek solutions to this challenge through constitutions. The rule of law rests on the related principle that the governors and governed abide by just laws that apply equally to everyone. Virtually all governments acknowledge these principles, but they do not always abide by them. How are constitutions and the rule of law built to last? What factors account for their success? This chapter seeks answers to these and other important questions about providing and controlling political power.

Terms to Know

autonomy	countervailing power	rule of law
balance of powers	federalism	separation of powers
check of powers	fundamentality	unicameral legislatures
constitution	negative rights	unwritten constitution
constitutionalism	parliamentary supremacy	
constitutional supremacy	positive rights	

WHAT IS CONSTITUTIONALISM?

All governments have some kind of constitution, but that does not make them constitutional governments. Constitutional governments abide by the constitutional limits imposed on them. Constitutions existed in Nazi Germany and in the former Soviet Union, but these governments ignored their constitutional limits, suppressed human rights, and ruled by force and intimidation. Constitutionalism was not practiced, and the rule of law was not followed.

In a recent comparative study of fascism, Robert Paxton described the utter contempt that fascist rulers had for the law. His description applies to all dictatorships, whether fascist, communist, or simply a government of thugs without an ideology.

> In fascist states, individual rights had no autonomous existence. The State of Law . . . vanished, along with the principles of due process by which citizens were guaranteed equitable treatment by courts and state agencies. . . . . A fascist regime could imprison, despoil, and even kill its inhabitants at will and without limitation. All else pales before that radical transformation in the relation of citizens to public power.[2]

Today, for example, the constitution of communist North Korea lists freedom of speech, the press, assembly, association, and demonstration as fundamental rights of its citizens. However, these provisions do not stop the government from suppressing those rights, often violently. In "soft" dictatorships, governments may provide people with some legal recourse, but they become selective about which people have legal recourse and under what circumstances.

Constitutionalism is the principle that governments should be created, empowered, and limited by constitutions. Constitutionalism also legitimizes government—it provides government with a rightful claim of legitimacy. Whether the authority of government relies on a Supreme Being, royal birth, ability, or the consent of the governed, its continued legitimacy must rely on some kind of constitution. Constitutionalism rests on three basic points:

- Legitimate governments are constitutional governments.
- Constitutional governments are limited governments.
- Limited governments abide by their constitutions.

However, constitutionalism raises some important questions. What is a constitution? How can constitutions both provide and limit power? How can constitutions be constructed to respond to current needs and remain durable enough to stay the course over time? What factors support constitutional government?

WHAT IS A CONSTITUTION?

Today, **constitution** refers to the fundamental law or laws that establish, frame, empower, and limit governments and prescribe the relationships between those governments and the people. Historically, this use of the term gained currency after the adoption of the U.S. Constitution of 1787, which became a model for many modern constitutions.

Before the eighteenth century, the term *constitution* had a different meaning. In ancient and medieval times, a constitution referred to the complete composition or makeup of a polity, including its cultural values, political interests, laws, and governing institutions. Aristotle used *constitution* in this sense and distinguished three dimensions of a polity's constitution: moral, socioeconomic, and legal (see Chapter 4). Aristotle's legal constitution is somewhere between the modern meaning and the classical meaning of *constitution*. In today's terms, Aristotle's legal constitution refers to a polity's form of government or constitutional system, including its fundamental laws and governmental institutions. This chapter emphasizes modern constitutions. Later chapters look back to earlier usages of the term.

Every constitution is unique, but all share one important characteristic—**fundamentality**. This means that constitutions set the essential ground rules of the political system. Polities must decide where authority resides, how governments are organized, for what purposes, and with what powers and limits. Polities must also establish the ground rules governing the relationships between the government and the people. This requires setting out the rights, responsibilities, and roles of the people. All these decisions are formalized in a polity's constitution.

HOW DO CONSTITUTIONS VARY?

Constitutions are considered fundamental law, yet countries differ widely in what they consider fundamental. As a result, constitutions come in all shapes and sizes.[3]

Some constitutions are brief, general, long lasting, and infrequently amended. For example, the U.S. Constitution is only 8,000 words in length. It has remained in use without interruption for more than two centuries, and it has been amended only twenty-seven times. Other constitutions are long, highly detailed, and frequently amended or replaced altogether. For example, India's constitution, adopted in 1950, is the longest in the world. Its text is 251 pages long and has 395 articles. France has had eleven different constitutions since 1791.

Most U.S. state constitutions are considerably longer and more detailed than the U.S. Constitution. In fact, the state constitutions are frequently criticized for being too long.

However, federal and state constitutions have different traditions. The U.S. Constitution focuses on fundamental ideas that are timeless, while many state constitutions respond to what each new generation considers fundamental. The two approaches complement one another. People frequently look to their state constitutions as agents of change because the U.S. Constitution is so difficult to amend.

Consider the New York State Constitution. At nearly one hundred pages with twenty articles, it is one of the longest and most frequently amended state constitutions. The first nine articles include a bill of rights, the framework for both state and local governments, and two articles on state and local finance. Subsequent articles leave the comfortable world of government structure and individual rights for the world of substantive public policy—a dimension absent from the federal constitution except for the nation's brief experiment in prohibiting the manufacture, sale, and transportation of intoxicating beverages (the Eighteenth Amendment).

New York's constitution lays out the fundamentals in policy areas such as education, environmental conservation, canals, social welfare, and housing. Constitutional provisions range in fundamentality from the creation of the country's first "forever wild" public park to the regulation of the width of ski trails in that park. (See Politics in Action: America's First Forever Wild Public Park.)

Some countries, such as Great Britain and Israel, do not have their constitution in a single document. They rely on what commentators refer to as an **unwritten constitution**—a series of documents, such as laws, judicial rulings, and proclamations, supplemented by unwritten rules, practices, and traditions known generally as "custom and usage." Because all these elements are not contained in a single document, these nations are said to have unwritten constitutions.

Great Britain is the classic example of a nation with a constitution that consists of a series of documents, including acts of Parliament, judicial interpretations, conventions, and customs. The British Constitution has been described as "a tapestry, deftly woven and embellished over time."[4] Among the most famous of the documents that make up the British Constitution are the Magna Carta (1215) and the Declaration of Rights (1689). The latter document was subsequently passed as a statute and became known as the English Bill of Rights.

When New Zealand became independent, it modeled its political system on that of its mother country, Great Britain. New Zealand did not adopt one constitutional document. Instead, New Zealand recognized certain treaties made with its indigenous people, the Maori, and various pieces of legislation as part of its constitution.

Although Israel has an unwritten constitution, it does have laws and rules that form the foundation of government and that outline the rights of the individual. Some of these rules are found in the nine basic laws enacted by its Knesset (or parliament), while others are defined in a series of Supreme Court decisions.[5] Israelis did attempt to write a formal constitution in February 1949. An assembly was convened for that purpose, but after two days of meetings, it adjourned. The religious and secular factions could not agree. Since then, Israel has adopted enactments of basic laws whenever Israelis could reach consensus on those laws. Many in Israel continue to advocate the writing of a constitution.[6]

POLITICS IN ACTION
America's First Forever Wild Public Park

North of Albany, New York, lies a lush forested wilderness known as the Adirondacks. It has stirred the imagination of poets and painters for three centuries. It also stirred the spirit of entrepreneurs. Lumbering depleted its pine trees, the tanning industry nearly destroyed its hemlocks, and the paper industry sought its spruce and fir. A movement began in the 1850s to keep "the forest forever," as the naturalist S. H. Hammond put it, under "the protecting aegis of the [New York state] constitution."

Concern for the park was not only for its natural beauty. Depleting the land of its trees hastened topsoil erosion and led to increased flooding. In 1892, the state legislature passed a law creating the Adirondack Park, but loopholes allowed state park commissioners to sell off land for lumbering. S. H. Hammond's dream was realized in 1894 when the state constitutional convention added a constitutional provision making the park "forever wild." A majority of the state's voters approved the provision (the first in the nation) later that year.

In the twentieth century, a new industry sought entry into the park—outdoor recreation. City-bound dwellers wanted to enjoy the great outdoors. The beautiful Adirondack lakes and mountains beckoned hikers, campers, boaters, and skiers. Environmentalists clashed, but a compromise for carefully managed multiuse parklands was reached. The state constitution was the only place that all sides agreed their compromise would be safe, so, over time, the constitution's conservation article was amended. In theory, the level of detail in those amendments is not the stuff of which constitutions are made. Specific numbers of miles were set aside in the constitution for a state highway and ski trails; and acreage was exchanged for a garbage dump, airport runway, village, historic buildings, cemetery, and better land management by the International Paper Company. Perhaps those details should have been set in ordinary legislation, but then again, they would have been much easier to change as the winds of political interests shifted.

Quotations are from the Adirondack Park Agency's official Web site, www.apa.state.ny.us/about_park/history.htm.

WHAT ARE THE PATTERNS IN CONSTITUTIONS AND CONSTITUTION-MAKING?

Constitutions vary in size, coverage, and stability; however, there are patterns that help explain some of these differences. The American political scientist Daniel J. Elazar identified five constitutional traditions.[7]

- *The constitution as a framework document.* According to this model, a constitution should provide a broad framework that lays out the structure, purposes, powers, and limits of government and the rights of citizens and others in the polity. All constitutions must provide such a framework, but this tradition limits constitutions to this task. As a result, constitutions following this tradition are brief, generally worded, and need amending only when a piece of the framework is broken or unresponsive to major changes in society. The U.S. Constitution is the model of this tradition.

- *The constitution as a code.* A code is a collection of all laws relating to a particular subject or field of the law. Codes can be highly detailed and long. To people raised in a constitution-as-framework tradition, codes and constitutions seem opposites, but in countries where all laws are codified and the constitution is law, it is quite natural to codify it too. Constitutions as codes are typically long, detailed, and rigid. This model is followed by Germany and other continental European countries.

- *The constitution as a revolutionary manifesto.* This tradition was developed by communist states that use their constitutions to justify the destruction of the old regime, the disenfranchisement of the elites from the old regime, the complete reconstruction of the polity along revolutionary lines, and the establishment of the Communist Party as the vanguard of the working class and the leading force in society. A current model of this tradition is the 1992 constitution of Vietnam.

- *The constitution as a political ideal.* This tradition was used by Latin American countries beginning in the nineteenth century to establish governments with high political ideals that nonetheless reflected current political realities. This type of constitution anticipates periodic revolutions or coups that change the government in power but not the ideals. This tradition is a blend of American and French traditions, so the constitution may be brief and lofty, but may be periodically replaced when new governments gain power. The new constitutions typically contain the same set of lofty ideals as the previous constitution.

- *The constitution as a series of traditions.* This model refers to countries such as the United Kingdom, New Zealand, and Israel that have an "unwritten constitution" that accumulates written constitutional documents and unwritten customs over time, but, for one reason or another, does not collect them into a single document.

Thus, constitutions vary partly because they rely on different constitutional traditions, but why do those differing traditions exist in the first place? One answer to this question is cultural, but another is political.

Constitution-making is "a pre-eminently political act."[8] Constitutions are formal documents, but that makes them no less real or political. Constitution-making is an extraordinary process, and that process is a political one. As the Adirondack Park example (Politics in Action: America's First Forever Wild Public Park) illustrates, constitutions are a kind of safety zone in politics. Players use this zone to protect their most fundamental concerns from the daily tussle of ordinary politics. But this does not eliminate politics. It merely substitutes one form of politics (constitutional politics) for another (ordinary politics).

Political thinkers disagree over how constitutional politics should be played and how constitutions should be made. Some political thinkers believe that constitution-making should

George Washington presiding at the Constitutional Convention in 1787.

be removed from party politics and held in a special convention composed of specially selected delegates. The advocates of conventions also may be opposed to those in power; in this case, the advocates see the convention route as a friendlier alternative to the legislative route. Other political thinkers believe that constitutions should be drafted in the legislature by a committee of regularly elected legislators who are experienced in lawmaking and more accountable to the people. Legislative advocates see convention advocates as trying to make an end run around the normal political process, party leaders, and the legislature.

Today, both convention and legislative advocates accept the need for a two-step constitution-making process. In the first stage, the constitution is written by a convention or legislative committee. In the second phase, in democracies, the constitution must be submitted for public discussion and ratification by the people or their elected representatives.

When the framers of the U.S. Constitution met in a convention behind closed doors, they sought to remove themselves from the pressures of political life but not from politics itself. The framers were statesmen, but they were also politicians. In fact, the convention opened with a major political issue. Some of the framers from large states came to the convention with a blueprint for a stronger national union (known as the Virginia Plan). But they quickly realized the need for a political compromise when the framers from small states introduced the New Jersey Plan. The art of compromise came gradually, but both sides found agreement in the Connecticut Plan—a form of government built on a compromise that gave both sides some of what they wanted.[9]

Describing constitution-making as a political act does not mean that it is accidental or random. The American political theorist Donald S. Lutz studied constitutional design as a political process in many countries. He found eight general principles that can serve as guidelines for designing constitutions that work. (See Politics in Action: Principles of Constitutional Design.)

POLITICS IN ACTION
Principles of Constitutional Design

1. Match the government to the people, their history, and political culture.
2. Seek the best possible constitution under the circumstances because the perfect constitution is not possible.
3. Understand and face the political realities of the political system, especially who has political power and how willing they are to share it constitutionally.
4. A critical problem of constitutional design is how to distribute power—among legislative, executive, and judicial institutions in one government and between national and local or regional governments in the new constitutional system.
5. The idea of a constitution is to marry power and justice. As important as power is, the ultimate end of government is the administration of justice.
6. Governments make decisions, and constitutions should enable the decision-making process.
7. Constitutions should be grounded in the political knowledge about how government officials behave in one institutional system or another. (For example, how do executives behave if they are elected by the people as opposed to being appointed by the legislature?)
8. Constitution-makers must anticipate the need for future constitutional change and provide some means for amending or replacing their constitution.

Donald S. Lutz, *Principles of Constitutional Design* (Cambridge, UK: Cambridge University Press, 2006), 218–220.

WHAT ARE THE MAJOR PURPOSES OF CONSTITUTIONS?

Well-designed constitutions must accomplish a variety of tasks. We have consolidated these tasks under three broad purposes of constitutions: to establish government, to frame government, and to define the relationships between government and the people (see Table 9.1).

ESTABLISH GOVERNMENT AND LAY OUT ITS PURPOSES

Establishing government involves four interrelated tasks. Constitutions create governments, define polities, fix governments' authority, and set forth their principles and purposes.

First, constitutions create governments, or to be more precise, constitutions legitimate the creation of governments. The Preamble of the U.S. Constitution of 1787 proudly proclaims that "We the People . . . do ordain and establish this Constitution for the United States of America."

Table 9.1 Purposes of Constitutions

I.   Establish government
   A.   Create government
   B.   Define the polity or state
   C.   Recognize the source of government's authority
   D.   Set forth government's principles and purposes

II. Frame government
   A.   Outline structure of government and its principal institutions
   B.   Assign powers to those institutions
   C.   Set limits to the powers of institutions
   D.   Establish the supreme law of the land
   E.   Provide modes of constitutional change

III. Delineate relationships between the government and the individual
   A.   Guarantee rights of citizens and other individuals and groups
   B.   [Optional] Assign responsibilities to citizens
   C.   [Optional] Assign roles to nongovernmental institutions

Second, constitutions define the polity or state. For example, the U.S. Constitution unpretentiously defines the American polity as "a more perfect Union" with a republican form of government (Preamble and Article IV, sec. 4). Article 20 of the German Basic Law of 1990 recognizes the Federal Republic of Germany as "a democratic and social federal state." And Article 1 of the French Constitution of 1958 declares that "France is an indivisible, secular, democratic and social Republic."

Third, constitutions affirm the source of the government's authority and perhaps the authority of the polity or state. Today, the most frequently mentioned source is the people and the consent of the governed. For example, Brazil's Constitution of 1988 provides, "All power emanates from the people, who exercise it by means of elected representatives or directly, as provided by this constitution" (Article 1). But there are exceptions. Article 4 of the Iranian Constitution of 1979 provides that all laws (including the constitution) "must be based on Islamic criteria"; provision is also made for a Council of Guardians to review all national legislation "to ensure conformity with Islamic law."

Visitors attend the citizens festival for the 60th anniversary of the Federal Republic of Germany in Berlin, Germany, May 23, 2009. The German constitution was put into effect on May 23, 1949.

The constitutions of federal systems may distinguish the federal government's source of authority from how the federal government or polity is established. Article 1 of Brazil's Constitution of 1988, for example, cites the authority of the people, but it also states that the Federative Republic of Brazil is "formed by the indissoluble union" of the states, municipalities, and federal district.

Finally, as part of establishing government, a constitution sets forth the principles and purposes of the government. Such statements are often declaratory (not legally binding) and placed in the preamble of the constitution or in a separate declaration. In the American constitutional system, the Declaration of Independence announces the principles of government, while the Preamble of the U.S. Constitution sets forth the authority and purposes of the federal government and the constitutional system as a whole.

The purposes that are set out normally include some combination of the following: preservation of life, protection of freedom, human betterment, and the administration of justice (see Chapter 4 for a review). Comparing preambles is one way to ascertain the similarities and differences among constitutions. Security, freedom, rights, well-being, welfare, and justice are among the most frequently cited ideals. But there are many distinctive purposes of government. Most Islamic constitutions, for example, commit their governments to the spiritual advancement of the people. Written after World War II, Germany's Basic Law of 1949 and Japan's Constitution of 1947 mandate that their governments search for world peace, implicitly as atonement for their aggressions in that war. South Africa's Constitution of 1997 recognizes the past injustices of apartheid and its Preamble looks to the constitution "to heal the divisions of the past." Nigeria's Constitution of 1999 does not explicitly recognize that country's deep-seated ethnoreligious divisions, but its Preamble does resolve that the people will "live in unity and harmony" as one nation. Preambles can afford to be noble because they are not legally binding; yet noble sentiments can stick in the minds of future generations.

FRAME GOVERNMENT AND ASSIGN ITS POWERS AND LIMITS

Constitutions provide the framework for government. To do this, they must outline the structure of government and then assign powers, set limits, and specify the supreme law.

Today, the basic structure of most governments begins with three types of institutions: legislative, executive, and judicial institutions. Constitutions create those institutions, organize their offices, provide for how people are selected for those offices, and set out the procedures that officers must follow in carrying out their responsibilities. To create a legislature, for example, constitution-makers must decide whether that body will have two houses (bicameral) or one (unicameral) and whether to organize each house into committees or leave that task to the legislature. Constitution-makers also must decide the number of legislators in each house, the ratio of legislators to constituents, how those legislators are selected, their qualifications for holding office, the length of their term of office, and whether there should be a limit on the number of terms that a legislator can serve.

Even these basic decisions have political implications. On one side are those who want a popular, responsive, and representative legislature composed of average citizens who simply carry out what the people demand. On the other side are those who prefer a more cautious, deliberative body composed of experienced legislators who heed their conscience as well as public opinion.

Unicameral legislatures, one-house legislatures composed of many members with small legislative districts of fewer constituents, are thought to be highly responsive and representative. Since 1934, Nebraska has maintained a nonpartisan unicameral legislature. Although a sparsely populated state, the Nebraska legislature has forty-nine senators who are limited to two 4-year terms. A host of smaller countries maintain unicameral legislatures, including Armenia, Bulgaria, Croatia, Denmark, Finland, Hungary, Israel, and Sweden.

To allow more people to serve, many unicameral legislatures require short terms (two years) and term limits (a maximum of two terms). One pitfall of this model is that legislators often have limited experience, a limited memory of past legislative actions, and greater exposure to community pressure. Add another house, decrease the number of members, increase the population size of their districts, increase the length of office, and remove term limits, and you move legislatures toward the cautious and deliberative model. Many countries prefer a compromise solution, with a lower, more responsive house and an upper, more deliberative house.

Constitutions also must assign powers to specific institutions. In this process, three related issues arise: What principles guide the assignment of powers, what limits are placed on those powers, and what is the supreme law of the land? The American model relies on five principles to accomplish these tasks: separation of powers, checks, balances, federalism, and constitutional supremacy.

Separation of powers creates three independent branches of government and assigns distinct powers to each branch. Using the principle of separation of powers, many constitutions create three independent branches of government: a popularly elected legislature, a separately elected chief executive, and an independent judiciary of appointed or elected judges. The constitution then assigns the primary responsibilities of lawmaking to the legislature, law implementation to the executive, and law adjudication (judging) to the judiciary. In Table 9.2, these assignments appear in cells 1, 5, and 9, marked with a "✓."

The second principle, **check of powers**, assigns additional powers to one branch that limit the power of another branch. Using the principles of separation of powers and checks, each

Table 9.2 The American Model of Separation of Powers

	Lawmaking	Law implementation	Law adjudication
Legislature	1 ✓	2 Budget approval	3 Budget approval
Executive	4 Veto bills	5 ✓	6 Appoint judges
Judiciary	7 Judicial review	8 Judicial review	9 ✓

branch is assigned additional powers that limit the other two branches. In the U.S. Constitution, for example, the legislature must pass the budget that both the executive and judiciary need to carry out their responsibilities. The executive can control the legislature by vetoing bills; and the executive may try to control the judiciary by using its power to appoint judges (subject to the approval of the Senate). The judiciary, in turn, has the power of judicial review, which means that courts can review the actions of both the legislature and executive to determine whether those actions are constitutional.

In truth, these checks are only partially successful as independent control mechanisms. The threat of checks is designed to push the three branches to work together and turn to the checks as a last resort. But politics can intervene. If the legislature is controlled by one political party and the president leads a rival party, they may be unable or unwilling to agree on controversial issues. In this case, both branches may go into conflict mode and check one another to the point where no one can accomplish anything of significance.

In 1987, the garbage barge Mobro, *owned by an entrepreneur named Lowell Harrelson, departed New York for North Carolina. The garbage was to be buried there so that it could produce methane gas, which Harrelson hoped to sell. But when North Carolina officials learned that the enormous barge had docked, they ordered it to leave. The barge then wandered down the coast as far south as Belize, unable to find a port willing to accept responsibility for disposing of the 3,000 tons of waste aboard. After more than 100 days at sea, the barge returned to New York, where it was finally decided that the waste would be transported elsewhere for incineration. In 1992, the Supreme Court ruled that the Commerce Clause prevented state governments from refusing to allow waste management companies from moving garbage across state lines.*

Balance of powers means that the checks and constituencies of the three branches of government should be in balance. When people refer to the system of checks and balances, they mean that each branch has an equal check or control on the others. The framers of the constitution also wanted to balance constituencies. For example, the House of Representatives is designed to represent local constituencies, the Senate represents state constituencies, the president represents a national constituency accumulated on a state-by-state basis through the Electoral College, and the federal judiciary represents the law.

Federalism divides power between two sets of constitutional governments: federal and constituent. The federal government is responsible for matters concerning the country as a whole. The constituent governments (called states, provinces, länder, cantons, or regions) are responsible for matters affecting interests within their jurisdiction. Federalism is a way of dealing with scale and diversity in very large countries such as the United States, Brazil, Russia, and India. It is also a way of responding to diversity in small plural societies such as Switzerland and Malaysia.

Federal systems vary considerably in the way they allocate power and balance federal-constituent powers. For example, Germany is highly centralized; the federal government makes most policies and the länder administer those policies. In contrast, Switzerland is highly decentralized, with significant powers residing with cantons and communities.

In the United States, there are hardly any powers that are the sole reserve of either the federal government or the states.[10] The federal government is responsible for making official U.S. foreign policy, but many states are involved in foreign trade, investment, immigration, and tourism. Local governments are responsible for garbage collection, but many local governments now send their garbage across state lines, a practice that falls within the regulatory power of the federal government. Education was primarily a local matter, but now it is truly intergovernmental, as are many policy areas from health care to national defense.

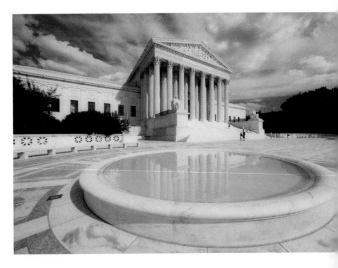

Unlike the British judicial system, the American system includes courts with the authority to judge the constitutionality of the actions of the legislative branch of government.

Constitutional supremacy means that the constitution is the supreme law of the polity and that it trumps all other laws. In the American constitutional system, this means that the U.S. Constitution is the "supreme law of the land" along with only those federal laws passed in pursuance of the Constitution (see Chapter 4 for more on this subject).

As a comparison, the British model rests on the principle of parliamentary supremacy. As the term suggests, **parliamentary supremacy** is the idea that the laws of Parliament, not the constitution, are the supreme law of the land.

A parliament is a legislative body. Most parliaments are either unicameral or bicameral with a weak upper house. Members of the lower house are popularly elected (sometimes members of the upper house are also). Unlike the American presidential system, the executive or head of government (called a prime minister, PM) is not separately elected by the people to "form a government" (that is, appoint a cabinet). The PM is the leader of the majority party, is elected as a member of Parliament (MP) along with other MPs, and is selected by Parliament to form a government. To do this, the PM forms a cabinet from members of his or her party. In this way, there is little possibility of a divided government in which one party controls one branch and another party controls another. The majority party is given a full chance to govern.

Historically, English courts had no power of judicial review (that is, the power to review and declare an act of Parliament void). Judicial review would have violated the principle of parliamentary supremacy. As a check on the abuse of power, Parliament has the power to issue a vote of no confidence in its government, in which case the government must resign. Alternatively, the PM or the cabinet can dissolve the Parliament. And, of course, the voters can switch their allegiance to another party in the next election.

DELINEATE THE RELATIONSHIPS BETWEEN THE GOVERNMENT AND THE PEOPLE

Constitutions define the fundamental relationships between governments and the people. These relationships have to do with the rights, roles, and responsibilities of individuals and institutions in society. Taken together, these rights, roles, and responsibilities serve as reference points that can be used to hold governments accountable for their actions.

Throughout much of history, constitutions have prescribed the roles and responsibilities of the individual in the polity. Those roles have varied because of inequalities in society. Even republics distinguished among full citizens, slaves, and a long list of partially free people in between. The leadership frequently included classes or orders of nobility and priests.

In such societies, responsibilities were assigned based on an individual's role or position in life. Rights were implied in responsibilities. The ancient commandment "Thou shall not steal," for example, explicitly states a responsibility, but it also implies a right—stealing is a wrong partly because it denies someone the right to be secure in his or her property.

Islamic law remains an example. Thus, in constitutions that follow Islamic law, rights flow from duties. As the American human rights expert Jack Donnelly explains, the right to be free flows from the duty not to enslave unjustly, the right to freedom of expression comes from the duty to speak the truth, and the economic right to subsistence stems from the duty to help the needy.[11]

Modern philosophy has reversed this flow. Today, constitutions guarantee fundamental rights; in most cases, the responsibilities are implied. Virtually all national constitutions have a list of rights, but it is much harder to find explicit statements of the roles and responsibilities of individuals and institutions.

Interestingly, most of the constitutions that explicitly prescribe individual responsibilities are in Asian societies. For example, Part 4A of the Indian Constitution, "Fundamental Duties," lists ten duties of every citizen: abide by the constitution, defend the country, render national services when called upon, preserve India's composite culture, protect the environment, safeguard property, abjure violence, develop humanism and a scientific temper, and strive toward excellence so that the nation rises. Chapter 3 of Japan's Constitution, "Rights and Duties of the People," holds the people partly responsible for the maintenance of their rights. Article 12 of that chapter provides that the rights listed "shall be maintained by the constant endeavor of the people, who shall refrain from any abuse of these freedoms and rights and shall always be responsible for utilizing them for the public welfare." Article 17 of Mongolia's Constitution on Citizen's Duties lists various civic duties and one "sacred duty"— "for every citizen to work, protect his or her health, bring up and educate his or her children and to protect nature and the environment."

Switzerland's Constitution may be the only Western constitution that mentions responsibility, and the contrast with Asian constitutions is striking. According to Article 6, "All persons are responsible for themselves."

Most modern constitutions do not explicitly single out the roles of nongovernmental institutions. There are two exceptions. Communist constitutions guarantee the role of the Communist Party as the vanguard of the working class and the leading force in society. Also, constitutions legitimize traditional institutions in societies seeking to reclaim a role for those institutions. For example, after decades of apartheid, South Africa's Constitution of 1997 seeks to strengthen the role of traditional leaders (tribal chiefs and elders) and customary tribal law. Chapter 12 recognizes "the role of traditional leadership," requires courts to "apply [tribal] customary law when that law is applicable," and allows national legislation to provide "a role for traditional leaders at the local level" and to establish houses and a council of traditional leaders.

Modern constitutions guarantee fundamental rights. However, constitutional guarantees do not work unless the government abides by and enforces those rights. Most constitutional rights are formulated as a relationship between the rights-holder and the government. As a result, these rights vary depending on four elements of that relationship:

President Nelson Mandela celebrates onstage with a choir in 1996 after the signing of South Africa's new nonracial constitution.

the nature of the rights-holder, the nature of the right itself, the nature of government's involvement, and the possibility of an intermediate institution (such as the press, a jury, or a voluntary association) between the government and the rights-holder.[12]

THE RIGHTS-HOLDER. There are three possible levels of rights-holders: the individual or person, a specific group or category of people, and the collective body known as "the people."

The U.S. Bill of Rights, for example, contains twenty-eight rights provisions spread over ten amendments. Most of these provisions are individual rights belonging to individuals. There are no group rights, but there are six references to the collective "people." The collective rights of the people are a safeguard against the arbitrary actions of the government. These rights include the First Amendment freedoms of assembly and petition, the Second Amendment right to bear arms (recently recognized by the Supreme Court as an individual as well as collective right), the Fourth Amendment right of the people to be secure in their person and property, the implied Seventh Amendment right of the people to trial by jury, and the residual rights and powers reserved to the people in the Ninth and Tenth Amendments.

American constitutional rights are not cast strictly in terms of group rights. However, the clear intent of the Nineteenth Amendment is to grant voting rights to all women. And, although group-based constitutional rights are not commonplace outside the United States, they do exist. The constitutions of Australia, Canada, and Malaysia, for example, grant rights to indigenous peoples. Also, the Canadian Charter of Rights and Freedoms of 1982 recognizes the bilingual character of Canada. Section 23, for example, provides that English or French speakers in a province where they are in the minority have the right "to have their children receive their primary and secondary school instruction in that language in that province."

Crowd braking parade up at 9th St. Mch 3 1913   16
TAYLOR-WASH. D.C

The women's suffrage movement in the United States battled for years with a determined and entrenched opposition. On March 3, 1913, a large procession marched in Washington, D.C. Even though the marchers had obtained the proper permits to march, the police did little to protect them from hostile crowds. More than two hundred marchers were injured because of the police department's failure to control the crowd. Order was restored when Secretary of War Henry L. Stimson ordered federal troops to protect the marchers. News of the assault of the procession helped galvanize support for women's suffrage.

THE RIGHT. In Chapter 5 we introduced two types of rights. **Negative rights** protect the individual from government encroachment; negative rights include freedom of expression, freedom of association, the rights of the accused, and the political rights of citizens (for example, to vote and hold office). **Positive rights** provide the people with entitlements to tangible benefits; positive rights include the rights to affordable housing, a decent job, adequate health care, and a clean environment.

Negative rights are worded in a way that is designed to prevent the government from denying rights. Usually the negative role of government is designed to protect procedural rights. Presented in the negative form, a rights provision might read, "Government shall not deny a person's right to X." Another wording might read, "No person shall be denied the right X." Positive rights obligate the government to provide rights. Typically, a positive role of government relates to substantive rights.

GOVERNMENT'S ROLE. Rights relationships cast the role of government in different ways. Government can be the violator or protector of negative rights and the benefactor or withholder of positive rights. Although constitutions are usually the source of fundamental rights, government is the provider of many other rights that are granted in legislation. In societies with a constitutional government, people look to government as the protector of their rights. However, government becomes a rights violator when it places an unreasonable limit on a right, unjustly denies that right to a particular group, or turns the other way when the police become lax in rights enforcement.

Underlying the idea of individual rights is **autonomy**, the freedom of individual choice and action. The idea of individual autonomy envisions a society in which individuals are free to make decisions affecting their own lives, as long as those decisions do not violate the rights of others (see Chapter 5).

INTERMEDIATE INSTITUTIONS. Sometimes, the rights relationship includes an implicit reference to an intermediate institution that organizes rights-holders and checks government excess. The U.S. Bill of Rights, for example, suggests six intermediate institutions.

- The First Amendment recognizes religious freedom, freedom of the press, and freedom of association. Religious freedom suggests the role of religious institutions in the advancement of civic as well as spiritual life. Freedom of the press implies the dual role of a free press in providing the people with a source of information and an outlet for their views. Freedom of association enables the formation of all sorts of voluntary associations, from charitable organizations to interest groups and labor unions.

- The Second Amendment recognizes the role of the militia as a citizen force under state control as a potential defense against an overreaching national professional army.

- The Seventh Amendment provides for the right of trial by jury, but whose right is this? The Sixth Amendment already provides for jury trials as a defendant's right. The Seventh Amendment provides the citizenry with the right to serve on juries as a way of keeping a watchful eye on the third branch of government.

- The Tenth Amendment recognizes the states as a repository of powers that might otherwise be taken by the federal government. In practice, the Tenth Amendment has not been an effective way to prevent the expansion of the federal government, but it has worked on occasion as a protection against onerous federal intrusion into core concerns of state and local governments.

WHAT IS THE RELATIONSHIP BETWEEN CONSTITUTIONALISM AND RULE OF LAW?

Constitutionalism and the rule of law are interrelated principles. In theory and practice, these two principles are mutually reinforcing. In fact, it is difficult to imagine a polity that relies on one of these principles without the other.[13]

The **rule of law** is the idea that no one is above the law and that the law applies equally to everyone. This concept has been expressed in several ways, including a form of government in which the law rules, a government of laws and not of men, and a society in which no one is above the law.

These simple phrases point to a complex truth that rests on two conditions. The rule of law is based on the idea that the law is supreme and just (1) because it applies to everyone and (2) therefore everyone abides by it. Today, it is assumed that the law applies *equally* to everyone. However, before the modern era, the law applied to everyone based on his or her status in life; hence, the rule of law meant that only people of the same status were treated equally. Even in early republics, there was only a small class of full citizens to whom all rights applied. Today, this practice would be unacceptable.

In Western societies, the rule of law is widely accepted as the first principle of a free society. At the Tenth Economic Summit, held in London in 1984, the leaders of seven major industrialized nations issued a joint Declaration of Democratic Values. Listed first was the rule of law: "We believe in a rule of law which respects and protects without fear or favor the rights and liberties of every citizen and provides the setting in which the human spirit can develop in freedom and diversity."[14]

There are, however, always rulers who hold the rule of law in contempt. As Getúlio Vargas, former president of Brazil, once put it, "For my friends, everything; for my enemies, the law."[15] In time, Vargas and his corrupt friends were driven from office because of their contempt for the rule of law.

Vargas and other tyrants follow a different principle—rule *by* law. As Chinese law professor Li Shuguang observed, "Chinese leaders want rule by law, not rule of law." Li explained the difference: "under the rule of law, the law is preeminent and can serve as a check against the abuse of power. Under rule by law, the law can serve as a mere tool for a government that suppresses in a legalistic fashion."[16]

Thus, the rule of law is meant to apply to every government official from presidents and kings to minor bureaucrats and traffic police officers. As John Locke famously put it, "Wherever Law ends, Tyranny begins. . . . Exceeding the Bounds of Authority is no more a Right in a Great, than a petty Officer; no more justifiable in a King, than a Constable."[17]

WHAT ARE THE CRITERIA OF THE RULE OF LAW?

According to the American legal and political historian James McClellan, the rule of law means that laws are "general, known, certain, and . . . applied equally."[18]

- *Laws must be general.* They cannot be ad hoc instructions or single out particular individuals or groups unless there is a rational and constitutional basis for such discrimination.

- *Laws must be made known and well publicized.* In this way, the law is accessible to everyone and government can be held accountable to the law. Ancient rulers carved the law into wooden or stone columns (called stelae) and placed those columns around the country so that the people knew when a new law had been adopted. (See Chapter 4 for more on stelae and the law.)

- *Certainty is at the heart of the law.* People need to know that the law reduces some of the great uncertainties of life. For example, what will happen if someone injures me or I injure someone? People need to know that government will enforce the law with predictability. This also means that laws must be consistent and stable.

- *The law today must apply to everyone equally.* This means that governments must be prepared to enforce the law equally. Government must not make or enforce laws in a manner that is arbitrary, capricious, or discriminatory. Moreover, government officials must be held accountable for their actions.[19]

Unfortunately, in many parts of the world, the rule of law is a dream, not a reality. As discussed in Chapter 6, the United Nations recently sponsored a report on legal empowerment of the poor, chaired by Madeleine K. Albright, former U.S. secretary of state, and Hernando de Soto, Peruvian economist. Their research found that 4 billion people living in shanty-towns are "excluded from the rule of law."[20]

Governments around the world have long struggled with corruption. In this 1894 political cartoon, a bribe paid to a New York police officer is equated with corporate contributions to senators.

Bribery is a serious challenge to the rule of law, according to the "Global Corruption Barometer Report for 2009."[21] According to the report, people around the world felt particularly frustrated by street-level bribery. In places where local police officers are underpaid, some officers routinely stop cars for minor inspection or traffic violations and then insinuate that they will forget about the violation if the driver pays them off with a small bribe. One out of every ten people surveyed said they had been involved in such a situation at least once in the last year.[22] In the corruption report, people also complained about corporate bribery, in which corporations bribe legislators and civil servants to make policies and issue regulations in the corporation's interest.

Happily, according to the corruption report, perceived judicial corruption has decreased. Opinion surveys reveal that judges are the least distrusted government official.

A third challenge to the rule of law is the unevenness and inequality of law enforcement. In many countries, there are two legal systems: one for the rich and another for the poor because they are easier to shake down for small bribes, cannot afford legal counsel, or simply accept their fate.

A fourth challenge to the rule of law is the high caseload in some court systems. In India, for example, according to one estimate it takes an average of twenty years to resolve a civil lawsuit.[23] This erodes people's faith in the rule of law because justice is neither sure nor swift. Given this problem, it is encouraging that the people polled in the corruption report still saw the judiciary as the least corrupt institution surveyed.

A fifth challenge to the rule of law is the abuse of power by those who hold the reins of power. There are still authoritarian regimes in which national leaders use their office to serve themselves and their friends, and then use the law to punish their enemies.

DO CONSTITUTIONS MATTER?

The British political scientist S. E. Finer began his book *Comparing Governments* with an introduction "On Whether Constitutions Matter." According to Finer, the answer to this question depends on whether the constitution is fiction or nonfiction.[24]

Finer found three answers to his question. Constitutions matter least in countries where they are works of fiction written by tyrants to justify their rule; that is, the people governing ignore the rule of law. Constitutions matter most in countries where they are works of nonfiction; these are countries where the governors and the governed alike abide by the constitution and the rule of law. Finally, there are countries in the middle, where constitutions and the rule of law are a mix of fiction and nonfiction; some of their constitutional provisions are purely decorative (window dressing), while others provide real limits on real power. According to Finer, most constitutions occupy this middle ground between the two extremes. Many if not most of their provisions are obeyed most of the time; they are reasonable, realistic, and honored.

How do most countries hold their ground in the middle where constitutionalism has real meaning and constitutions actually harness government power? Three factors are of particular importance: culture, constitutions, and countervailing powers. Aristotle was the first in a long line of political thinkers to underscore the interrelated importance of these three factors. As you recall, he referred to these factors as the ethical constitution (political culture), legal constitution (form of government and laws), and socioeconomic constitution (competing political interests) of the polity.

The importance of a constitutional culture is clear. Constitutions and the rule of law are merely words on paper unless a people and their leaders value constitutionalism, have some experience in making constitutions, and are willing to abide by the rule of law and the constitutions they have a hand in making.

U.S. federal judge Learned Hand forcefully made the cultural argument on May 21, 1944, at a gathering in Central Park, New York, celebrating "I am an American Day" at the height of World War II.

> What do we mean when we say that first of all we seek liberty? I often wonder whether we do not rest our hopes too much upon constitutions, upon laws and upon courts. These are false hopes; believe me, these are false hopes. Liberty lies in the hearts of men and women; when it dies there, no constitution, no law, no court can even do much to help it.[25]

Judge Hand argued persuasively that constitutions are only as strong as the constitutional will of the people and their belief in the power of constitutionalism as a safeguard of liberty.

But the reverse is equally true—people need constitutions. Constitutions and the rule of law provide the ground rules for and boundaries of government power and individual rights. Culture can support a constitution, but it cannot replace it. Without a constitution, people of goodwill have no commonly accepted blueprint to guide their actions and they have no legal means to harness ambitious rulers. And, as with other things in life, a well-designed constitution is better than a poorly designed one.

Finer suggests that the relationship between a constitution and its people is a two-way street. A constitution influences people, and people influence their constitution.

Constitutions and a constitutional culture are essential, but they are not sufficient. Sooner or later, ambitious leaders will attempt to gather the forces they need to assert their will over the will of the people and their constitution. "Ambition," as James Madison put it, "must be made to counteract ambition."[26]

Madison was a realist. He realized that the people and their leaders were human beings, not angels. He believed that in a world of ordinary mortals government must control its own excesses and those of the people. Madison was also a constitutionalist and a republican. He believed that the primary control on government should be a dependence on the people and the law. But Madison, ever the realist, also understood that such controls were not enough to protect liberty from ambition.

Countervailing power rests on the Madisonian idea that ambition must check ambition. In practice, it requires a double system of checks and balances. First, there must be a system within the government in which separate institutions have sufficient powers to check one another from the abuse of power. For example, today, as the power of government grows, parliamentary systems are also increasingly recognizing the importance of judicial review by an independent judiciary. This trend over the past fifteen years has begun to challenge the very idea of parliamentary supremacy in all matters. Second, there must be strong institutions or a vigilant people outside the government with the political power to serve as a counter-weight to government power and to control the abuse of government power. Examples of such nongovernmental counterweights are the nobility, religious institutions, commercial elites, local communities, an opposition party or coalition, and the people empowered as an electorate.[27]

"This policy," concluded Madison, "of supplying, by opposite and rival interests, the defect of better motives, might be traced through the whole system of human affairs, private as well as public."[28] We trace the historical origins and development of this system, in theory and practice, in later chapters of this book.

REVIEWING AND USING THE CHAPTER

1. How do you distinguish between a constitutional government and a government that has a constitution?

2. Analyze the constitution of your state. How does it address the purposes of constitutions outlined in this chapter?

3. Compare the advantages and disadvantages of written constitutions with those of unwritten constitutions.

4. Analyze the U.S. Constitution. How does it provide for limited government?

5. How can and how should the people act as "watchdogs" so that they constitute an effective check on the powers of government?

6. Do constitutions matter? Compare your answer to those of S. E. Finer and Judge Learned Hand.

EXTENSION ACTIVITY

Compare the goals announced in the constitutions of the United States, Nigeria, and Mexico. How are they alike? What are their major differences?

WEB RESOURCES

Comparative Constitutions Project
www.comparativeconstitutionsproject.org

This project collects data on the characteristics of written constitutions for most countries since 1789. The project sponsors a Web site, Constitutionmaking.org, that features reports on the prevalence of various constitutional provisions as well as sample clauses and a forum reporting recent news on constitutional design. The site also contains a searchable database of selected constitutional texts.

United States Government Printing Office's Analyses and Interpretation of the U.S. Constitution
www.gpoaccess.gov/constitution/browse2002 .html#2004

This Web site provides full access to a series of detailed government documents on the U.S. Constitution. The documents provide a thorough discussion of the history and

interpretation of specific parts of the Constitution as well as general commentaries.

University of Chicago's Researching Constitutional Law on the Internet
www2.1ib.uchicago.edu/~llou/conlaw.html

Maintained by the D'Angelo Law Library, this site provides an annotated list of links to dozens of excellent Web resources. The resources emphasize the study of the U.S. Constitution, state constitutions, and other constitutions throughout the world.

University of Richmond's Constitution Finder
http://confinder.richmond.edu

This database offers the constitutions, charters, amendments, and other related documents of countries throughout the world.

NOTES

1 John Locke, *The Second Treatise on Civil Government,* ed. Peter Laslett (Cambridge, UK: Cambridge University Press, 1988), Chap. 18, 418.

2 Robert O. Paxton, *The Anatomy of Fascism* (New York: Vintage Books, Random House, 2005), 142.

3 This section draws on the work of S. E. Finer, Vernon Bogdanor, and Bernard Rudden, *Comparing Constitutions* (Oxford, UK: Oxford University Press, 1995); Robert L. Maddex, *Constitutions of the World,* 3rd ed. (Washington, D.C.: CQ Press, 2007).

4 Maddex, *Constitutions of the World,* 369.

5 Susan Hattis Rolef, ed., *Political Dictionary of the State of Israel* (New York: Macmillan, 1987), 69–71.

6 Ibid., 70.

7 Daniel J. Elazar, "Constitution-Making: The Pre-eminently Political Act," in *Redesigning the State: The Politics of Constitutional Change,* ed. Keith G. Banting and Richard Simeon (Toronto: University of Toronto Press, 1985), 233–238.

8 Ibid., 232.

9 For a comparative study of politics of the U.S. Constitutional Convention and other episodes in world history, see William H. Riker, *The Art of Political Manipulation* (New Haven, Conn.: Yale University Press, 1986).

10 Daniel J. Elazar made this point in *American Federalism: A View from the States* (New York: Thomas Y. Crowell, 1966).

11 Jack Donnelly, *Universal Human Rights in Theory & Practice,* 2nd ed. (Ithaca, N.Y.: Cornell University Press, 2003), 72–73.

12 This formulation of rights is not unusual, but it has come to be attributed to Akhil Reed Amar, American constitutional law professor, *The Bill of Rights: Creation and Reconstruction* (New Haven, Conn.: Yale University Press, 1998).

13 This section draws on various studies, including Brian Z. Tamanaha, *On the Rule of Law: History, Politics, and Theory* (Cambridge, UK: Cambridge University Press, 2004).

14 U.S. Department of State, *Bulletin* no. 2089 (August 1984), 1–2.

15 Quoted in Frances Hagopian, "The Too-Low but Rising Quality of Democracy in Brazil and Chile," paper delivered at the Workshop on the Quality of Democracy, Institute for International Studies on Democracy and Rule of Law, Stanford University, October 2003, 8.

16 Quoted in Steven Mufson, "Chinese Movement Seeks Rule of Law to Keep Government in Check," *Washington Post,* March 5, 1995, A25.

17 Locke, *Second Treatise on Civil Government,* 418.

18 James McClellan, *Liberty, Order and Justice: An Introduction to the Constitutional Principles of American Government,* 3rd ed. (Indianapolis, Ind.: Liberty Fund, 2000), 350.

19 These criteria also correspond to lists compiled by Lon Fuller, Ignacio Sánchez-Cuenca, and Stephen Holmes in *Democracy and the Rule of Law,* ed. José Maríá Maravall and Adam Przeworski (Cambridge, UK: Cambridge University Press, 2003), 39, 68, 69.

20 Commission on Legal Empowerment of the Poor, *Making the Law Work for Everyone* (New York: Commission on Legal Empowerment of the Poor and the United Nations Development Programme, 2008), Vol. 1:1.

21 Transparency International, "Global Corruption Barometer Report for 2009," available at www.transparency.org/policy_research/surveys_indices/gcb/2009.

22 Ibid., 3.

23 Javleen Singh, "Law Long Arm, Late Embraces," quoted in Sumit Ganguly, "The Quality of Democracy: India and Bangladesh," paper delivered at the Workshop on the Quality of Democracy, Institute for International Studies on Democracy and Rule of Law, Stanford University, October 11, 2003, 6.

24 In literature, fiction is a work of imagination that is not designed to represent actual happenings; nonfiction is the honest attempt to represent reality as it is.

25 Learned Hand, text of the speech is available at "Liberty's Last Champion," National Association of Criminal Defense Attorneys, NACDL E-News, www.nacdl.org/public.nsf/ENews/2002e67?opendocument.

26 James Madison, *"The Federalist* No. 51," in *The Federalist Papers,* by Alexander Hamilton, James Madison, and John Jay, ed. Clinton Rossiter (New York: New American Library, 1961), 322.

27 For a history of constitutionalism and institutional checks, see Scott Gordon, *Controlling the State: Constitutionalism from Ancient Athens to Today* (Cambridge, Mass.: Harvard University Press, 1999).

28 Madison, *"The Federalist* No. 51," 322.

CHAPTER 10

WHAT ARE THE CRITERIA OF GOOD AND CHARACTERISTICS OF BAD GOVERNMENT?

BIG IDEAS

- The key to good government is balance and moderation.

- The criteria for good government include (1) representation, (2) the consent of the governed, (3) rule of law, (4) equal justice, and (5) the common good.

- Examples of good government include republican forms of constitutional government.

- The characteristics of bad government include (1) unaccountability, (2) arbitrary rule and the abuse of power for personal benefit, (3) absolute and unchecked rule, and (4) the use of repression to eliminate opposition and dissent.

- Authoritarian and totalitarian governments are types of bad government.

Purpose of This Chapter

Why Is Balance the Key to Good Government?

What Are the Criteria of Good Government?

    Representative Government Based on the Principle of Balance

    Free Government Based on the Consent of the Governed

    Limited Government Based on the Rule of Law

    Just Government Based on the Principle of Equal Justice

    A Citizenry and Leaders Who Are Guided by the Common Good

What Are the Norms of Good Citizenship?

What Are the Characteristics of Bad Government?

How Did Hannah Arendt Distinguish Totalitarianism and Authoritarianism?

What Forms Can Corruption Take?

Purpose of This Chapter

In this chapter, we review the core concepts introduced in the previous chapters in a search for the criteria of good government and characteristics of bad government. In this search, we rely on the thinking of a long line of political thinkers, which we identified as constitutionalists in Chapter 5. Constitutionalists do not seek the single best form of government that fits all cultures and circumstances. Rather, they seek the guiding principles or criteria that enable leaders and citizens to make the best possible decisions under the circumstances that fit their polity's history and culture. First among these criteria are balance and moderation of deeply held values and principles. Other criteria include the consent of the governed and representation, constitutionalism and the rule of law, and justice and the common good. Constitutionalists also provide specific examples of the characteristics of bad government. These include (1) unaccountability, (2) arbitrary rule and the abuse of power for personal benefit, (3) absolute rule with no checks or limits on the ruler, and (4) the use of repression to eliminate opposition and dissent. In this chapter, you will learn that, although no government is perfect, clear criteria exist to judge and evaluate a government and its performance.

Terms to Know

authoritarian government	consent by direct participation	gulag
balanced polity	consent by virtual representation	mixed republican government
citizenship norms	consent of the governed	republican government
common good	corruption in government	totalitarian government
consent by actual representation	doctrine of the golden mean	totalitarianism

WHY IS BALANCE THE KEY TO GOOD GOVERNMENT?

For centuries, philosophers have espoused balance and moderation in all things. In the late 500s BCE, the Chinese philosopher Confucius devised the doctrine of the golden mean to explain the principles of balance and moderation. About 150 years later, the Greek philosopher Aristotle independently developed this doctrine and applied it to politics and government.

The **doctrine of the golden mean** seeks the best possible middle path between two extremes. In the Western world, one of the origins of this doctrine is the ancient Greek myth of the artist Daedalus and his son Icarus. Daedalus and his son were imprisoned by King Minos of Crete to keep them from revealing the secret of the great labyrinth that Daedalus had built for the king's protection. To escape, Daedalus built a set of wings for himself and for his son. As they prepared to fly away Daedalus told his son to steer a middle course between the sun and the sea. Daedalus warned Icarus that flying too close to the sun would melt the wax holding his wings together while flying too close to the sea would make his wings too wet to fly. Icarus ignored his father's advice, flew too close to the sun, lost his wings, and tumbled to his death in the sea.

The golden mean is especially important in the world of politics in which people's lives and fortunes may hang in the balance while decisionmakers seek to resolve disagreements peacefully. Aristotle was the first in a long line of political philosophers who advocated the principles of political balance and moderation; for example, constitutionalists accept the necessity of government but insist that government must have constitutional limits.

Chapter 5 compares three major constitutionalist philosophies: republicanism, conservatism, and liberalism. These philosophies disagree on where the golden mean lies. For example, republicanism emphasizes the common good, while liberalism places more emphasis on individual freedom. But these are differences of degree, not kind, when compared to anarchists,

The Norse, who settled in Greenland in the Middle Ages, relied on traditional European farming techniques—the raising of crops and breeding of animals such as cattle and sheep. As Christianity gained hold in Norse society, churches such as the 13th-century one pictured here began to appear. Over time, the soil—already thin in such a far northern climate—became less fertile as it was trampled by the settlers' cattle and sheep. People and animals began to starve. As Jared Diamond details in Collapse, *the Norse civilization in Greenland collapsed as the people refused to adapt to Inuit techniques for surviving in the harsh climate. Archaeologists have found evidence that the people ate their farm animals down to the hooves before departing or dying.*

who completely reject government, and statists, who advocate the need for tight government control over individual behavior. In the enduring debates about political principles— freedom and government, power and authority, majority rule and minority rights, consent and coercion, liberty and order, the individual and the community—constitutionalists seek to balance the extremes rather than choosing one extreme over the other. Yet constitutionalists accept that when they apply important principles to political issues, they may have to emphasize one principle over another.

Based on the previous nine chapters, we can identify four ways in which constitutionalists seek balance and moderation. First, constitutionalists emphasize the importance of human judgment, but they do not trust human judgment entirely. Second, constitutionalists are proceduralists who see the need for constitutional safeguards in the decision-making process. Third, constitutionalists are political moderates and centrists in the policy outcomes they seek and in the ways they try to reconcile political interests. Fourth, constitutionalists are proponents of republican forms of constitutional government. They advocate the rule of law, the consent of the governed, and a balance of power in the design of constitutions and governments.

Constitutionalists emphasize the importance of human judgment. Evolutionary biologist Jared Diamond underscored the importance of human judgment in the title of his book, *Collapse: How Societies Choose to Fail or Succeed*.[1] According to Diamond, societies succeed or fail because of the choices they make. True, having weaker neighbors increases the chances of success—as does a bountiful and well-managed environment, and a bit of good luck. But time and again, Diamond found that no amount of bounty or luck could rescue a society that made one too many bad decisions or failed to make decisions and adapt to new circumstances when needed.

As explained in Chapter 1, human judgment is essential in making wise decisions. According to Fernando Henrique Cardoso, noted scholar and former president of Brazil, political judgment "entails not only the discernment to avoid the opposite risks of impractical idealism and uninspiring realism, but also the practical wisdom to grasp the character of a particular situation or moment in history and to seize the opportunities or confront the challenges that it presents."[2] Steering a middle course is important for Cardoso. He understands the importance of ideals and interests, but not to the exclusion of one another. Pursuing abstract and impractical ideals is like steering too close to the sun, but sinking too deeply into the real world and simply satisfying people's self-interests with no larger vision is like veering too close to the sea. Decision makers need to find the best possible combination of ideals and interests under the circumstances and within the culture of the polity they serve. They must, in other words, exercise practical wisdom.

According to Cardoso, practical wisdom is the ultimate job requirement of political leaders and citizens alike. Practical wisdom, sometimes called practical reasoning, is knowing what is best, right, or good given a particular set of circumstances. For Cardoso, practical wisdom in politics is the ability to recognize impending opportunities and dangers, to make the best possible decision under the circumstances, and to convince others to agree.

On this point, Cardoso agreed with the conclusion of the English philosopher Isaiah Berlin, who wrote a path-breaking essay about political judgment. In that essay, Berlin defined *political judgment* as "practical wisdom, practical reason, perhaps, a sense of what will 'work,' and what will not."[3] Political judgment, Berlin explained, is the kind of knowledge that conductors have of their orchestras, not the knowledge that chemists have of the "contents of their test tubes."[4]

Constitutionalists such as Cardoso and Berlin recognize the importance of ideas, experience, and the use of reason in decision making. They believe that decision makers—leaders and citizens alike—should be principled. But they caution against would-be tyrants who use ideologies based on abstract ideas as a cover for their desire for power.

Constitutionalists also insist on constitutional safeguards. Although they advocate practical reasoning and trust that human beings are capable of wise political decisions, they also realize that human beings are capable of corruption and poor decisions. Constitutionalists see human judgment as fallible and corruptible. Like James Madison, constitutionalists believe that "there is a degree of depravity in mankind which requires a certain degree of circumspection and distrust, [but] there are other qualities in human nature which justify a certain portion of esteem and confidence."[5]

Constitutionalists recognize that the power of government will attract ambitious individuals who seek power for its own sake, who abuse the authority of their office, or who are simply not up to the challenges of governing wisely. Therefore, they advocate a constitutional government in which the exercise of power is prescribed by constitutional procedures, checks, and limits. For this reason, constitutionalists are also proceduralists. They realize that government needs sufficient power to govern, but, as explained in Chapter 8, constitutionalists also expect government to be limited.

As discussed in Chapter 9, constitutionalists look to constitutionalism and the rule of law to establish the procedures for and limits of government. But they also look to two sets of auxiliary precautions: the cultural norms of a people who hold government accountable to the constitution and the rule of law, and the countervailing powers both in the government and in the larger polity that are prepared to push back against the unconstitutional exercise of power by a single interest, institution, or individual.

Constitutionalists are also politicians. As defined in Chapter 2, politics typically arises from disagreements among people. The peaceful accommodation of disagreement is what separates politics from war and other violent measures. According to the twentieth-century political philosopher Leo Strauss, the cardinal issue and fundamental source of political disagreement "is mankind's great objectives, freedom and government or empire—objectives which are capable of lifting all men beyond their poor selves."[6]

These objectives shape the philosopher's search for answers to the question, what is the good society and how should it be organized? Through the ages, political philosophers have debated three possible answers: freedom without government, government without freedom, and some balance of freedom and government. Chapter 5 explores the philosophies associated with these three answers. Recall that anarchists argue that human beings are entitled to freedom without government, while statists counter that human beings are ready only for government without freedom.

Constitutionalists occupy the middle ground between anarchists and statists. Constitutionalists recognize the need for government as an authoritative institution and the necessity of controlling government by constitutional means. Constitutionalist philosophies see the good society as a balance of freedom *and* government, not a choice between freedom *or* government.

But finding the right balance of freedom and government is an ongoing process, not a single decision. Every public policy issue—from setting speed limits to combating terrorism—raises questions of how to balance the rights of the individual in the name of freedom and government regulation in the interest of public safety and other public goods. By and large, constitutionalists seek a centrist position on most policy issues.

Constitutionalists seek the best possible combination of government involvement and free choice under the circumstances. But circumstances change, as do the preferences of the citizenry and their leaders. This is what makes politics so interesting and challenging in free societies.

Constitutionalists are proponents of republican forms of constitutional government. By and large, constitutionalists do not seek the single best form of government that fits all cultures and circumstances. Rather, they seek guiding principles or criteria that enable decision makers to design the best possible government under the circumstances and for a particular people.

WHAT ARE THE CRITERIA OF GOOD GOVERNMENT?

Leo Strauss distinguished between philosophies based on some combination of freedom and government and those based on empire. Since ancient times, most people in the world have been forced to live under empires. However, every period of world history is also colored by the existence of free and well-governed societies. Most of these societies adopted some form of republican government. And, regardless of where or when they existed, they prided themselves on being republican in their culture, their way of life, and their government.

Republican government is a broad category of government that is based on two essential principles: the consent of the governed and the rule of law. As explained in Chapter 7, republican government can come in various forms, including ancient conciliar (council-based) republics, mixed republics, aristocratic republics, and democratic republics. The chapters in Units 5–8 take a closer look at the history of republics from ancient times to the twentieth century. From this history and the principles of constitutionalist philosophy, we have identified five criteria of good government:

- Representative government based on the principle of balance
- Free government based on the consent of the governed
- Limited government based on the rule of law
- Just government based on the principle of equal justice
- A citizenry and leaders who are guided by the common good

REPRESENTATIVE GOVERNMENT BASED ON THE PRINCIPLE OF BALANCE

Recall from Chapter 4 that Aristotle believed that every polity (political system) has a constitution composed of three dimensions: the legal constitution, including all of a society's laws and governmental institutions; the social and economic constitution, including the various classes and communities in society; and the moral constitution, comprising ethical standards and political ideals. Aristotle advocated a **balanced polity**, in which all three constitutions were kept in balance like the legs of a three-legged stool. In particular, he expected the polity's legal constitution (or form of government) to represent the major interests in society and to uphold society's core cultural norms.

In addition, Aristotle advocated **mixed republican government** as the best form of government to represent the interests of both the aristocracy and the general citizenry. The ancient Romans used the idea of a mixed republic to form a government with four types of institutions: (1) an executive that relied on the strength of one or two leaders for unity and speed of administration, (2) a senate that drew on the deliberative skills of the wealthy few, (3) a popular assembly that represented the voice of the citizenry as a whole, and (4) juries to decide conflicts between two parties and crimes against the state.

The ancient Greeks and Romans believed that a balanced constitution and mixed republican government provided for moderation in government policies. Representing the interests of the aristocracy served as a check on excessive policies favoring the majority (such as over-taxing the rich) and brought deliberation and prudence into the making of public policy. Representing the interests of the majority served as a check on the excessive policies of the few (such as harsh penalties for late loan payments) and introduced common sense and honesty into the policymaking process. Interestingly, the principles of a balanced polity and mixed government arose not only in republics that were familiar with Aristotle's writings but also independently in the early republics in Asia and Africa that had never heard of Aristotle.

One great innovation in representative government was the American constitutional system, which provided for a written constitution that combined separation of powers, checks and balances, an independent judiciary, and federalism. A second innovation was the idea of representative democracy developed by American and European liberal thinkers in the nineteenth century.

FREE GOVERNMENT BASED ON THE CONSENT OF THE GOVERNED

Consent of the governed is the idea that "one should not be subject to laws to which one has not directly or indirectly consented."[7] Throughout history, republican societies have defined themselves as free polities of free citizens, not the subjects of royal sovereigns. They defined their republics as communities and ways of life in which free citizens lived and participated in their government.

Republican societies recognized that consent requires a citizenry with a political culture that values freedom and rule of law. For the ancient Greeks and Romans, for example, citizenship was a badge of distinction, and it required direct participation in legislative assemblies, on juries, and as soldiers in the army. Greek armies, like those of the Roman Republic, were renowned for the valor of their citizen-soldiers.

Consent of the governed is a familiar phrase, but it is not entirely accurate. More appropriate is the term *consent of the citizenry*. Today, there is a significant overlap in the meanings of these two phrases. In most countries, most of the governed are citizens and most citizens of voting age have the right to vote.

Until the late nineteenth century, however, most republics limited citizenship to a relatively small percentage of the population. Except for the United States, the percentage of politically empowered citizens was less than 15 percent of the total population in most republics from ancient Athens and Rome to the twentieth century. Many of these republics, including the United States, had large slave populations and denied women the right to vote and hold office. In some republics, citizenship was an inherited right limited to citizen families, and immigrants were prevented from becoming citizens.

The changes in the size of the citizenry in the late nineteenth century reflect broader changes in the nature of consent and representation. Consent has evolved from direct participation to virtual representation to actual representation.

Consent by direct participation is the ancient republican idea that all eligible citizens are called on to serve in their city's government. In ancient republics, citizens were obligated to serve in legislative assemblies and on juries. In this way, they gave or withheld their consent on all matters of law and public policy. All male citizens also were expected to serve in the military.

Consent by virtual representation was a system of representation introduced by medieval European republics.[8] Medieval societies were organized into classes and "orders." Three orders had full political rights: the nobility, the Church, and some towns and cities. The political rights of these three orders included membership in a common council or parliament. Strictly speaking, legislative members did not represent their order but, rather, their own conscience, making decisions they thought were best for society as a whole. Within this system, the people's consent was generally passive and tacit. Popular elections were unusual; when they occurred, the electorate was very small (typically less than 10 percent of the population).

At the time of the American Revolution, the British parliament was still an institution of virtual representation. Its seats were filled largely by inheritance and appointment. Power brokers emerged who were able to "buy" their seats in crafty political maneuvering. Voting was restricted to freeholders and landowners; as a result, the British electorate was no more than 2 percent of the total population. This process created "rotten boroughs," where only a handful of inhabitants received far more than their fair share of representatives. The size of the British electorate did not rise much above 15 percent of the population until 1918 when Parliament passed a law granting universal suffrage to adult male citizens (age twenty-one) and female citizens (age thirty).

In 1832 the British parliament passed a law designed to eliminate many rotten boroughs. In this cartoon from that year, a politician mourns the passing of the law.

(See More About . . . Representation in the British Parliament.) In some medieval republics, noncitizens were able to take their complaints to court. But their ultimate power was in their force of numbers, in their power to protest, resist, and in some cases rebel. Such acts were not everyday occurrences, but they were more frequent than you might assume.

Virtual representation was an elitist system. Most of the people had few political powers. Nonetheless, the group of powerholders, although small in number by today's standards, was a far larger group than the alternatives—monarchy and empire.

Consent by actual representation is the dominant system that exists today in representative democracies. In this system, the citizenry elect representatives who serve on their behalf. Today, we take this system for granted, but its requirements are complex. For electoral consent and representation to work, (1) the voting citizenry must be a sizable portion of the total population; (2) the citizenry must then elect a smaller group of representatives who retain the trust of the people; (3) the elections must be held on a regular basis prescribed by law; (4) the elections must be free, fair, and competitive; (5) elected representatives must have the power to make binding decisions; (6) the representatives must be accountable to the larger group of citizens by reelection; (7) all these elements must be authorized by a constitution; and (8) this system must be supported by the citizenry.

Modern representation brought about a profound change in the nature of republics and citizenship. For centuries, political thinkers believed that republics had to be small so that citizens could participate directly in public affairs. Citizenship, they believed, had deeper meaning: citizens had a stronger sense of patriotism and virtue when direct participation was required. Replacing direct participation with actual representation has allowed modern democratic republics to (1) expand in territory and population and (2) widen the electorate as a percentage of the total population. Today, in most countries of the world, most people are citizens and most adult citizens are entitled to vote.

LIMITED GOVERNMENT BASED ON THE RULE OF LAW

Aristotle borrowed the criterion of rule of law from Plato. However, the idea was not unique to Plato. Limited government by the rule of law was a value shared by most Greeks, and it was expanded and clarified by the Romans. The Greek poet Pindar wrote, "Law is the king of all."[9] Imagine Pindar's words reversed—the king is law. Without the limits of the rule of law, the ruler's powers can become absolute, his or her decisions arbitrary, and his or her actions unaccountable.

As it originally developed, the phrase *rule of law* had two meanings: (1) no one is above the law and (2) the law applies to all citizens. Both meanings were seen as a way to support the idea of consent in checking arbitrary and absolute rule. In this way, the rule of law seeks to resolve the age-old conflict among the freedom of the individual, the restraining influence of the law, and the coercive power of government. The citizenry exercises and protects its freedom through the law.

Over time, the term *constitutionalism* came to stand for the idea that there are legal limits to the power of government and that those legal limits trump the abuse of government power. (See Politics in Action: The Origins of Constitutionalism in England.) For more on constitutionalism and the rule of law, see Chapter 9.

POLITICS IN ACTION
The Origins of Constitutionalism in England

In 1215, King John of England was in a difficult situation. He needed additional funding and soldiers, but he realized that taxes were already too high. His barons and other leaders in England sensed that it was a time to make a play for more power. With the urging of the archbishop of Canterbury, they demanded recognition of their rights. Desperate for the barons' financial and military backing, King John signed the Magna Carta. Containing sixty-three provisions, the Magna Carta marked the beginning of constitutionalism in England.

JUST GOVERNMENT BASED ON THE PRINCIPLE OF EQUAL JUSTICE

As explained in Chapter 4, justice is one of the most important purposes of government. Justice and the rule of law are twin ideas. The rule of law is important not only as a limit on government's powers; it is also a necessary standard of equal treatment by which government allocates resources fairly and enforces the law equally. Athens and Rome endured as republics partly because they understood this dual function of the law. Cicero (106–43 BCE), Rome's greatest advocate of the law, explained, "It may thus be clear that in the very definition of the term 'law' there inheres the idea and principle of choosing what is just and true."[10]

Both justice and the rule of law carry the expectation of equality, that is, that people will be treated equally under the law. What has changed over the centuries is the scope of *equality*. In ancient and medieval societies, people were organized into classes, each with its own legal privileges, immunities, and liberties. In these societies, legal equality meant that people within the *same class* were entitled to equal justice and equal treatment under the law. Today, equal justice means "justice for all." All people, regardless of their economic class, race, or religious beliefs, are entitled to the same standards of justice and protection under the law.

In practice, equal justice today is administered primarily within the modern nation-state. But, increasingly, jurists point to the emergence of universal principles and precedents in international law that allow the courts of one country or an international tribunal to resolve disputes between parties of different countries and to try, convict, and sentence individuals who have violated laws against humanity.

A CITIZENRY AND LEADERS WHO ARE GUIDED BY THE COMMON GOOD

Philosophers generally agree that, at a minimum, the **common good** is based on the interests of the polity as a whole, not on the self-interests of the ruler or the interests of one part of society over another. But mere mention of the common good is enough to raise suspicions among those who prize liberty—and not without reason. On the one hand, republics need a citizenry and leaders with a moral compass, but, on the other, moralizers, who seek to impose their own brand of morality on others, can be dangerous.

Philosophers generally divide into two camps based on their view of the common good. In one camp are the proceduralists who believe that the common good lies not in lofty ideals of a better society but in the faithful adherence to the rule of law and consent of the governed. In the second camp are those who believe that government has an additional purpose (in addition to rule of law and consent of the governed), a moral purpose to help better society and the lives of its people.

Each of the four political cultures introduced in Chapter 6 has its own conception of the common good. In traditionalist cultures, the common good is understood as the maintenance of long-established traditions. In republican cultures, the wellspring of the common good is the civic virtue of a citizenry. As President John F. Kennedy eloquently put it, "ask not what your country can do for you—ask what you can do for your country."[11] In statist cultures, the common good is defined by the state, which, in democratic states such as France, is based on the general will of the people. Finally, in individualistic cultures, the common good is seen in proceduralist terms as the accumulation of individuals' efforts to advance their own interests, mindful of others and free of government intervention.

WHAT ARE THE NORMS OF GOOD CITIZENSHIP?

All criteria of good government rely for their success on the citizen's sense of civic responsibility. **Citizenship norms** are the political values of civic responsibility held by the people of a particular polity. How can they best be measured and understood? Political scientists have developed surveys that help uncover the norms that dominate different democracies. In 2005, for example, the Center for Democracy and Civil Society at Georgetown University carried out in-person interviews with 1,001 respondents in the United States about their political values. The survey listed a series of citizenship norms such as voting, volunteering, monitoring government, and reporting crimes.

Similar surveys have been conducted in Europe and the United States since 2005. Based on the responses to these surveys, the political scientist Russell Dalton and his colleagues have identified four categories of citizenship norms. These are participation, autonomy, social order, and solidarity (see Table 10.1).[12] One aspect of *participation* is voting, which is a fundamental element of any democracy, but participation also extends beyond voting to active involvement in groups and society as a whole. *Autonomy* addresses the citizen's role in being sufficiently informed about the government to participate effectively. *Social order* refers to the acceptance of state authority as part of citizenship, and *solidarity* speaks to the concept of social citizenship—a concern for others within the definition of citizenship.

These four categories of norms are related to the citizen roles in Daniel Elazar's four types of political cultures: republican, individualistic, statist, and traditionalist. All democracies require political participation. But the norms of a fully participatory society are very similar to the values of a republican political culture. Notice that the norms in this category include not only voting but joining associations and taking an active role in politics. Autonomy is more clearly related to the individualistic culture; the emphasis is on the self-sufficiency of the individual: keeping well informed, making independent decisions, and exercising consumer responsibility. The norms of social order are similar to the values of statism; the emphasis is on obedience, service, and duty to the state. And solidarity norms seem to be a blend of republican and traditionalist cultures. The emphasis is on helping others; however, the inclusion of people around the world who may be strangers but are part of humanity is new to the twentieth and twenty-first centuries.

WHAT ARE THE CHARACTERISTICS OF BAD GOVERNMENT?

Bad government begins when rulers pursue their own interests instead of the common good and become otherwise indifferent to the common good. According to Aristotle, every form of good government contains the seeds of bad government. As explained in Chapter 7, rule by the one is most susceptible to tyranny because so much depends on the honor, wisdom, and temperance of successive generations of kings. Rule by the few similarly relies on the good qualities of leaders who are subject to few checks. All too frequently, "the few" are those who wield the power of wealth or the sword. And rule by the many is susceptible to majority tyranny unless the majority is checked by auxiliary precautions. There are four essential characteristics of bad government:

- *Unaccountability of power,* which means that the ruler is not answerable for his or her actions. This violates the principle of consent of the governed.

Table 10.1 Categories of Citizenship Norms

Categories	Norms
Participation	Vote in elections
	Be active in voluntary organizations
	Be active in politics
	Choose products for political, ethical, or environmental reasons
Autonomy	Try to understand the reasoning of people with different opinions
	Form his or her opinion, independently of others
	Keep watch on the actions of government
Social order	Serve on a jury if called
	Always obey laws and regulations
	Be willing to serve in the military when the country is at war
	Report a crime that he or she may have witnessed
	Never try to evade taxes
Solidarity	Support people in your own country who are worse off than yourself
	Help people in the rest of the world who are worse off than yourself

Source: Russell Dalton, "Citizenship Norms and Political Participation in America: The Good News Is . . . the Bad News is Wrong," Occasional Paper Series, Center for Democracy and Civil Society, Washington, D.C., October 2006, 3.

- *Arbitrary use of power,* which means that the ruler makes decisions on the basis of his or her personal whims. This violates the rule of law.
- *Absolute power,* which means that the ruler's power is unlimited. This violates the idea of limited power, to be sure; but it also violates the principle of political balance.
- *Repressive power,* which means that the ruler uses violence to stamp out opposition and dissent. This violates the idea of enlightened rule (for the public good).

These characteristics of bad government and the criteria of good government are captured in a work of art completed 650 years ago. (See Special Focus: How Does Art Portray Good Government and Bad Government?)

HOW DID HANNAH ARENDT DISTINGUISH TOTALITARIANISM AND AUTHORITARIANISM?

Authoritarian government is the term principally used by scholars as a collective reference to most forms of bad government. **Authoritarian government** occurs when a single person, a minority faction, or a majority faction seizes the reins of governmental power and rules in an arbitrary manner.

HOW DOES ART PORTRAY GOOD GOVERNMENT AND BAD GOVERNMENT?

In Siena, Italy, not far from Florence, there is a beautiful medieval city hall. In that hall is a room where the city council met when Siena was one of many independent republics in medieval Europe. On three walls of the council room, more than 650 years ago, Ambrogio Lorenzetti (1290–1348) painted a series of frescoes (paintings on plaster) titled *Allegory of Good and Bad Government*. Lorenzetti, an early Renaissance painter of Siena, took two years to complete this impressive series of frescoes (1338–1340). When complete, the length of his series measured approximately 83 feet!

Allegory is an amazing work of fine art, a detailed, well-executed, panoramic mural that captures both a realistic style and the human imagination. *Allegory* is also a carefully designed work of civic art.

At the time, Siena was a city-state that included a city surrounded by countryside where crops, timber, and other natural resources were harvested. On paper, the government was a republic in which all the people had a stake. At the time, however, the

Scene 2: Effects of good government in the city.

city was governed by an oligarchy—a group of a few men who represented the dominant economic interests of the city.

Allegory is divided into four main scenes: good government and its virtues, good government and its effects on the people, bad government and its vices, and bad government and its effects on the people. The city government commissioned the fresco as a statement of civic pride, but Lorenzetti's fresco was also a warning—the first scene the visitor sees is bad government.

The ruler of good government is portrayed on a throne in the center of Scene 1 as the Common Good of Siena. Dressed in the city's colors of black and white, the ruler is an elder kingly figure. He holds a scepter of authority and the city's shield for protection. The mythical children who founded Siena play at the ruler's feet, where they are protected by a creature. Six female figures overhead represent the virtues of good

Scene 1: Good government.

government: Peace (reclining), Fortitude, and Prudence on one side, and Magnanimity, Temperance, and Justice on the other. This scene also shows a larger figure of Justice, who balances her scales; the scales are held up by Wisdom. In one scale, an angel administers distributive justice; in the other, an angel administers corrective justice. There is a procession of the nine council members with other civilians and soldiers tied by a cord from the ruler to the final symbol of good government—Concordance.

Another part of the fresco (Scene 2) depicts scenes of the effects of good government on the people. In the city, there is much productive and joyous activity—of workmen beautifying the city, merchants engaged in trade, maidens dancing, and so on. Over the city gates, there is a symbol of Security. Beyond the gates lies the countryside with scenes of the people productively engaged in farming, hunting, fishing, and so on.

The ruler of bad government (Scene 3) is portrayed very differently. At the center, Tyranny is shown enthroned as a demon, neither male nor

Scene 4: Effects of bad government seen in the demolition of a house.

Scene 3: Bad government.

female, bloated by corruption, with fangs, horns, a richly embroidered cloak, and gold cup. A goat (symbolizing Lust) is at its feet. Below is Justice bound; her scales are broken and scattered. Overhead are the vices of Avarice, Pride, and Vainglory. Tyranny is flanked by six more vices: Cruelty, Treason, and Fraud on one side, and Frenzy, Divisiveness, and War on the other.

In the scenes of the effect of bad government on the people (Scene 4) the viewer quickly finds the horrors of bad government. In the city, fire and rubble are everywhere, there is disorder, and soldiers are shown running amok committing acts of violence. No one is working except for one lone workman who is making weapons. The scenes in the countryside are equally stark—death and destruction are everywhere, with no trees bearing fruit and no farmers working the land.

Totalitarian government is an extreme form of authoritarian government in which the government exerts total control over all aspects of society and the lives of people under its control. **Totalitarianism** is the belief that the state should exert total control over *all* aspects of human life. Hence, the "total" of totalitarian government is twofold: complete control and the completeness of the things controlled.

Totalitarianism usually begins with a utopian vision of a perfect world advanced by a ruthless leader surrounded by a small cadre of loyal supporters. Among the most infamous examples of the twentieth and twenty-first centuries are Lenin's Bolshevik Russia, Mussolini's Fascist Italy, Hitler's Nazi Germany, Mao's Communist China, and Osama bin Laden's global Islamism. Scholars continue to debate the extent to which these "visionaries" sought complete control to achieve their philosophical vision or the reverse.

In philosophy, there is also a benevolent form of totalitarianism. This variant envisions a utopian world guided toward perfection by the state. One example of such a utopian view is Plato's vision of the ideal state ruled by a wise philosopher-king. In practice, such a world has yet to be created. George Orwell had Hitler and Stalin in mind, not Plato, when he wrote *1984*. "If you want a picture of the future of humanity," wrote Orwell, "imagine a boot stamping on a human face—forever."[13]

This nightmarish vision squares with the conclusions of Hannah Arendt (1906–1975), who wrote extensively on totalitarianism and authoritarianism in the twentieth century. (See More About . . . The Shaping of Hannah Arendt's Intellectual Work.) Arendt understood exactly why benevolent totalitarianism is impossible. As she explained, totalitarianism requires an utter and complete reign of terror that first must be used to prepare the way for total control. Before a people can be totally controlled, they must *have* nothing and they must *be* nothing. Terror obliterates the fabric of society and the dignity of the individual. The concentration camp was the instrument of Nazi terror. In Soviet Russia, it was the **gulag**, or slave labor camp, which systematically dehumanized those who entered its world. In these and other examples, rulers sought to reduce prisoners into uncomplaining creatures, jailers into mindless bureaucrats, and the citizenry into a mass of soulless human beings who walk with blank stares for fear of being next.[14]

Arendt used the common onion to illustrate totalitarianism. At its center sits the leader, who rules outward from the safety of the core surrounded by many layers of protection and control. The leader and the system become "shock-proof," according to Arendt. The surrounding layers include "the front organizations, the various professional societies, the party membership, the party bureaucracy, the elite formations and police groups." These layers give the appearance of a normal world. At the same time, they exert total control and watchfulness over the lives of the people. Ideology still exists but largely as a tool of propaganda and education. Ideology often becomes a justification for oppression.[15]

Arendt used the image of a pyramid to distinguish authoritarianism from totalitarianism. As Arendt explained, authoritarian rulers seek to create a hierarchy composed of levels of power that closely resembles a pyramid. In this pyramid, the ruler occupies the top level. Other government and party officials occupy the middle levels, and the people are at the base. The resulting system is a command-and-control model—commands flow down from

The Shaping of Hannah Arendt's Intellectual Work

Hannah Arendt was born into a prominent Jewish family in Hanover, Germany, in 1906. Her father died when she was seven years old, and she was raised by her mother in dangerous times. Within a year, Europe cascaded into World War I and Russian and German armies began fighting one another not far from her home. Several years after the war, Arendt finished high school and entered university. In the 1920s, she studied philosophy with two highly influential German philosophers—Martin Heidegger and Karl Jaspers. She wrote her dissertation on love in the philosophy of St. Augustine, but politics and danger again intervened.

In 1933, as Hitler and his Nazi Party came to power, Arendt acted. She joined the German Zionist Organization—hardly a safe choice. She had begun researching evidence of anti-Semitism in Germany when she was arrested by the Gestapo, interrogated, and released by her jailer. She immediately escaped to Paris, France, where she worked to rescue Jewish children and help them get to Palestine. When the Germans invaded France in 1940, she was interned with her husband in a detention camp for enemy aliens. She escaped, was reunited with her husband, and fled to the United States in 1941. Arendt settled in New York City, where she was reunited

Hannah Arendt, c. 1930.

with her mother. Continuing to work for the cause of European Jewry, she began doing research for her first major book, *The Origins of Totalitarianism,* which was published in 1951, the same year she became a United States citizen. Throughout her adult life, Arendt strove to balance her commitments to political activism, political science, and political philosophy.

the leaders and obedience flows up. The commands are backed up by intimidation. They are enforced by coercion and, where necessary, repression. Obedience is based on fear not freedom.

But, unlike totalitarian regimes, authoritarian rulers are typically disinterested in changing the world. Their goals are limited to power for its own sake and for the personal protection and gain they derive from it. Therefore, they tend to focus on changing what those goals require and leaving everything else intact.[16]

Authoritarian rule can be "hard" or "soft." Under hard authoritarian rule, the government uses physical and often brute force to repress all forms of dissent by violent means. The repression is not kept secret because one of its goals is to instill fear in the general population. Soft authoritarian rule often creeps into existence gradually. The leader promises a restoration of security, order, and national pride. Elections are held, but the political opposition is intimidated. People enjoy nonpolitical rights (freedom to travel, to work, and to own property), but the government assumes control of the major media outlets. Government policy is always carried out in strict accord with the letter of the law, but it is based on rule by the laws that the regime writes to suit its purposes.

One source of authoritarian rule is military power. In this variation, a military commander or group of officers seizes control of the civilian government. Often, the military assumes power under conditions of anarchy—real or fabricated. People who fear disorder usually welcome the military because it promises to restore order. The commander swears he will obey the law and step down as soon as normal conditions are restored. He often does not keep his promises. Historical examples include Julius Caesar, Napoleon Bonaparte, and Simón Bolívar.[17] Far rarer is the model of leadership followed by George Washington, who led his country in war and then, like the Roman hero Cincinnatus, traded his sword for a plow and returned to the life of a citizen and farmer.[18]

WHAT FORMS CAN CORRUPTION TAKE?

Corruption in government is the abuse of power in ways that subvert justice. This temptation exists in every government, but each form of government has its own particular temptations. A tyrant who seeks absolute power can subvert a monarchy, an aristocracy can become greedy for more wealth and seek to manipulate the people, and a majority can run roughshod over the rights of the minority. These, for Aristotle, were the principal dangers posed by government and the allure of its power.

Centuries later, the British historian Lord John Acton (1834–1902) coined a phrase to describe this phenomenon: "Power tends to corrupt; absolute power corrupts absolutely. Great men are almost always bad men."[19] Aristotle would have agreed with Lord Acton's first sentence but not with his second sentence. He believed that great people could also be great rulers. Nevertheless, he was a pragmatist. He understood that most men are inclined to pursue their own self-interests; that is why he supported the idea of a free citizenry governed by the rule of law. Like James Madison centuries later, Aristotle also foresaw the need for auxiliary precautions. Balancing rival interests was chief among those precautions.

Corruption can take different forms. Aristotle was concerned primarily with systemic corruption. This is the form of corruption where an entire system of government is subverted by the interests of successive rulers. At this level, the corruption spreads like dry rot and drags the entire political system from good government to bad or from bad government to worse.

In 1989, for example, university students assembled throughout China to protest against this level of corruption. In the spring of that year, students went on hunger strikes and rallied on several occasions to demand an end to government corruption and the abuse of power. The most well-known and tragic of those demonstrations took place at Tiananmen Square in Beijing on June 4, 1989. The world watched on television while armed forces repressed the protests, killing four hundred to eight hundred students and jailing hundreds or perhaps thousands more.

Another form of political corruption is the abuse of power by one leader. This form of corruption is serious, but it does not usually bring down the system. One of the most notorious examples of corruption at this level is known by one word—Watergate. In June 1972, a team of burglars broke into the Democratic Party national headquarters located in the Watergate apartment complex in Washington, D.C. The burglars were apprehended and tried. During their trial, it became clear that they were linked to President Richard Nixon's reelection committee, and subsequently, it also became clear that President Nixon himself was involved in the cover-up of the Watergate incident. Investigations into the Watergate break-in and attempted cover-up revealed numerous examples of two basic forms of corruption by a leader: obstruction of justice, including presidential involvement in the cover-up of the Watergate break-in, and abuse of power, including the use of government agencies such as the Federal Bureau of Investigation for political gain. In late July 1974, the Judiciary Committee of the U.S. House of Representatives adopted articles of impeachment against President Nixon. At the same time, the U.S. Supreme Court ruled by a vote of 8 to 0 that President Nixon had to turn over tape-recorded conversations he had with his key aides about the Watergate crisis. With impeachment likely, President Nixon resigned from office on August 9, 1974.

A third form of corruption is the abuse of power by a single yet widespread practice. Bribery is the most typical example of this. Bribery occurs when someone pays a government official (with money or a favor) to do something dishonest. Bribery can occur on the street when someone pays a traffic officer to avoid a ticket. Bribery can also occur in the corporate corridors of power when a company pays government officials to award the company (and not its competitors) a large contract or to look the other way when the company breaks the law.

When governments become corrupt, they exact a heavy price on every citizen. Resources for the common good are diverted to the personal gain of a few. Corrupt governments create a climate of uncertainty that endangers commerce. That uncertainty discourages investment in businesses and the creation of new jobs. When a government breaks the law, it thereby invites every other citizen to break the law. This destroys the government's legitimacy and the people's trust in it.

A recent United Nations meeting concluded, "Corruption in government is pervasive and is apparently expanding. . . . It has become systematic and a way of life in many countries."[20] Transparency International has developed a corruption index ranking the level of corruption in most countries of the world. The organization defines *corruption* as "the abuse of public office for private gain." Scores range from 0 (completely corrupt) to

10 (not corrupt), with 5 being a borderline score. Its 2008 index gave a passing grade of 5.1 or higher to only 52 of 180 countries.[21]

Awareness of the problem of corruption is growing, and people throughout the world are searching for ways to combat it. As one scholar puts it:

> *Corruption is an embarrassing subject. . . . Around the globe, corruption is increasingly a central issue in election campaigns, popular uprisings, and military coups. . . . Our focus should go beyond individuals to corrupt institutions—corrupt systems of incentives, information and power. Solutions must go beyond "throw the rascals out. . . ." Campaigns against corruption must go beyond words and beyond party politics. Big fish must be fried, prevention must be stressed, and both bureaucrats and ordinary citizens must participate.*[22]

REVIEWING AND USING THE CHAPTER

1. Review the criteria of good government. Which principles would you add to the list? Which, if any, would you modify or delete?

2. What are the characteristics of bad government? Provide a historical or contemporary example of bad government.

3. How do the norms of good citizenship vary across political cultures?

4. Why do you think that corruption has proved to be a difficult problem for all societies, through time and across the globe?

5. Identify a current example of each of the three forms of corruption: systemic, abuse of power by one leader, and abuse of power by a widespread practice like bribery. Then compare your examples. Use current newspapers, other periodicals, and the Internet as sources of information.

EXTENSION ACTIVITIES

How do you think ordinary citizens can participate effectively in campaigns against corruption? Describe three ways that you as an individual or as a member of a group can help reduce or end corruption in your own community or country.

WEB RESOURCES

Comparing Types of Government
www.nationmaster.com/graph/gov_gov_typ-government-type

This Web site, created by Luke Metcalfe, uses data from the CIA "World Factbook" to allow its users to easily explore and compare governments that exist in the world today. The database is searchable and allows its users to construct their own graphs and create their own comparisons on a variety of government-related issues.

Descriptions of Types of Government
http://news.bbc.co.uk/cbbcnews/hi/find_out/guides/world/united_nations/types_of_government/newsid_2151000/2151570.stm

Created and maintained by the British Broadcasting Corporation (BBC) for K–12 students and teachers, this Web site contains brief descriptions of the types of government frequently mentioned in the news, such as anarchy, capitalist, communist, democracy, dictatorship, federal government, monarchy, regional or local, republic, revolutionary government, totalitarian state, and transitional.

Political Corruption
www.u4.no/themes/political-corruption/main.cfm

Hosted and maintained by the Anti-Corruption Resources Center, this Web site provides a clear definition of political corruption, discusses current and historic cases of corruption, provides possible responses to various forms of political corruption, and contains links to a variety of other corruption-related resources.

Transparency International: Political Corruption
www.transparency.org

Transparency International (TI) is a global coalition formed to combat corruption. Each year since 1995 TI has published "A Corruption Perceptions Index" that ranks the level of corruption in most countries of the world. This index can be found on its Web site, along with regional analyses, policy research, and tools for getting involved in the fight against corruption.

NOTES

1 Jared Diamond, *Collapse: How Societies Choose to Fail or Succeed* (New York: Penguin Books, 2005).

2 Fernando Henrique Cardoso, "Scholarship and Statesmanship," *Journal of Democracy* 16, no. 2 (April 2005), 11.

3 Isaiah Berlin, "Political Judgement," in *The Sense of Reality: Studies in Ideas and Their History,* ed. Henry Hardy (New York: Farrar, Straus and Giroux, 1996), 40.

4 Ibid., 47.

5 James Madison, *"The Federalist No. 55,"* in *The Federalist Papers,* by Alexander Hamilton, James Madison, and John Jay, ed. Clinton Rossiter (New York: New American Library, 1961), 346.

6 Leo Strauss, "What Is Political Philosophy?" in *Princeton Readings in Political Thought: Essential Texts since Plato,* ed. Mitchell Cohen and Nicole Ferman (Princeton, N.J.: Princeton University Press, 1996), 642–643.

7 Donald S. Lutz, *Principles of Constitutional Design* (Cambridge, UK: Cambridge University Press, 2006), 23.

8 The starting point for the study of representative government remains Hannah Pitkin, *The Concept of Representation* (Berkeley, Calif.: University of California Press, 1967).

9 Quoted in Sara Robbins, ed., *Law: A Treasury of Art and Literature* (New York: Beaux Arts Editions, 1990), 51.

10 Quoted in ibid., 52.

11 President John Fitzgerald Kennedy, "Inaugural Address, January 20, 1961," in *Ask Not: The Inauguration of John F. Kennedy and the Speech That Changed America,* ed. Thurston Clarke (New York: Henry Holt and Company, 2004), xvi.

12 The following discussion summarizes Russell Dalton, "Citizenship Norms and Political Participation in America: The Good News is . . . the Bad News Is Wrong," Occasional Paper Series, Center for Democracy and Civil Society, Washington, D.C., October 2006.

13 George Orwell, *1984* (New York: Signet, 1961), 220.

14 Hannah Arendt, "On the Nature of Totalitarianism: An Essay in Understanding," in *Essays in Understanding: 1930–1954,* ed. Jerome Kohn (New York: Schocken Books, 1994), 328–360. The most powerful prisoner's memoir of the terror of camp life remains Aleksandr I. Solzhenitsyn, *The Gulag Archipelago, 1918–1956,* 3 vols. (New York: Harper & Row, 1973); the authorized abridged edition of this book is also available in paperback in one volume (New York: HarperCollins, 2002). The most eye-opening analysis of what motivated one of the officials in the Nazi concentration camp system is Hannah Arendt, "Eichmann in Jerusalem: A Report on the Banality of Evil," excerpted in *The Portable Hannah Arendt,* ed. Peter Baehr (London: Penguin, 2000), 313–388.

15 Hannah Arendt, "What Is Authority," excerpted in *The Portable Hannah Arendt,* ed. Peter Baehr (London: Penguin, 2000), 468.

16 Ibid.

17 For more on military leaders as political leaders, see S. E. Finer's *The Man on Horseback: The Role of the Military in Politics* (New York: Praeger, 1962). Also see Samuel P. Huntington, *The Soldier and the State: The Theory and*

Politics of Civil-Military Relations (Cambridge, Mass.: Harvard University Press, 1957).

18 Daniel J. Elazar and Ellis Katz, eds., *American Models of Revolutionary Leadership: George Washington and Other Founders* (Lanham, Md.: University Press of America, 1992).

19 Letter from John Emerich Edward Dalberg-Acton (Lord Acton) to Bishop Mandell Creighton, 1887, available at www.phrases.org.uk/meanings/288200.html.

20 United Nations Department of Technical Cooperation for Development, "Corruption in Government," JCD/SEM, 90/2 INT-89-R56, United Nations, New York, 1990, 4, 6, 12.

21 Transparency International, www.infoplease.com/world/statistics/2008-transparency-international-corruption-perceptions.html.

22 Robert Klitgaard, "Strategies for Reform," in *The Global Resurgence of Democracy,* ed. Larry Diamond and Marc F. Plattner (Baltimore, Md.: Johns Hopkins University Press, 1993), 230–231, 243.

CLASSICAL MODELS OF REPUBLICAN GOVERNMENT

Athens, Rome, and Jerusalem are three great cities of the ancient world that offer different models of classical republicanism. As you will learn in the first chapter of this unit, Athens moved away from aristocratic control toward democracy perhaps as early as 500 BCE. The Roman Republic, founded shortly after Athens embraced democracy, lasted much longer than republican governments in Greece. For nearly 2,000 years after its collapse, the Roman Republic remained the model of good government in the Western world. Many important and contemporary ideas about government—such as the rule of law, citizenship, political equality, and democracy—trace their beginnings to these two cities.

In this unit's second chapter, you will learn that Athens and Rome were not the only ancient models of republican government. Biblical Israel

CHAPTER 11:

HOW DID THE GREEKS AND ROMANS DESIGN THEIR REPUBLICS?

CHAPTER 12:

HOW DID BIBLICAL ISRAEL BECOME A REPUBLICAN STATE?

offers one of the most important non-European examples of republicanism. Under the Israelite model, the polity was formed and reformed by covenants in which God was a party to some and a witness to others. As you will learn, this form of government—covenantal republicanism—shaped Israeli society for many centuries. Biblical Israel offers insights into republicanism that cannot be gleaned from the study of Athens and Rome alone.

BIG IDEAS

- Comparing the histories of ancient Athens and Rome provides important insights into the origins and workings of early republican and democratic governments.

- The origins of many important and contemporary ideas about government—such as the rule of law, citizenship, political equality, and democracy—trace their beginnings to ancient Greece and Rome.

- Republican government in ancient Greece and Rome depended on (1) effective leadership, (2) competent citizens, (3) institutional balance, and (4) freedom.

- The Roman Empire retained elements of republicanism until the Diocletian period, when the empire became an autocratic and bureaucratic state.

Purpose of This Chapter

Our history of republics begins with the story of ancient Athens and Rome. The Roman Republic was founded within three years of the founding of Athenian democracy. Yet the Roman Republic lasted much longer, grew much larger in population and territory, and had a more immediate and lasting impact on the history of government than Athens's democracy. Even the Roman Empire kept a republican veneer for the first three centuries of the common era. For nearly 2,000 years after its collapse, the Roman Republic remained the model of good government in the Western world. During most of that time, Athenian democracy was viewed as an example of mob rule. Why did Athens adopt a mixed republican model and then convert it to a democracy? How did the Roman Republic expand and remain a republic? What enduring lessons and ideas can be discovered from the study of ancient Athens and the Roman Republic? The answers to these and other important questions about the origins of republican government are explored in the histories of Athenian democracy and the Roman Republic.

Terms to Know

archons	*demes*	philosopher-king
Christianity	draconian	plebeians
Code of Solon	Germanic republicanism	republic
conciliar republics	Justinian Code	*res publica*
Council of 400	ostracism	Stoicism
demagogue	patricians	

HOW DID ATHENS BECOME A MIXED REPUBLIC?

Athens had been a mixed republic long before it turned to democracy around 500 BCE.[1] Homer, the great Greek poet, left the impression that Athens, like many other Greek cities, had a popular assembly for centuries before it became a democracy. But the Athenian assembly, like all of the others, did not meet regularly and was little more than a rubberstamp for some form of council that possessed much more political power. The power trail in predemocratic Athens begins with the Athenian Council.

In the centuries before Athenian democracy, Athens, like most Greek polities, was mostly a *closed aristocracy,* an aristocracy in which membership was inherited. Most Greek councils were controlled by the aristocracy, and the council was the supreme legislative and judicial body. Its members were former archons who served on the council for life.

Archons (rulers) were the chief executive officers. Separate archons presided over religious, military, and council affairs. They were elected for one-year terms by the popular assembly. When the Athenian code needed reform, a supreme archon would be selected as its reformer. He was known as the lawgiver. To be an archon or a significant leader, you had to be a member of the aristocracy.

In this frieze from the Parthenon in Athens, Greece, a child assists an archon (a ruler) in the folding of his ceremonial robe.

By the early 600s BCE, the aristocracy had a stranglehold on Athens. The aristocracy owned or controlled most of the land and the money in circulation. As a result, most of the farmers did not own the land they farmed. They were like tenant farmers, perhaps even serfs, who were bound to the soil by their indebtedness. The aristocracy held on to political power by refusing to open council membership to the emerging middle class or the low-born wealthy.

Sometime in the seventh century BCE, the Athenian Council appointed a fellow aristocrat named Draco as archon to write a code of laws. The goal of the Code of Draco was to legitimize an even tighter aristocratic grip on the economy. Little is known about Draco. He might be a mythical figure. But his code was harsh—so harsh that even today the word **draconian** is used to describe severe laws that are brutally enforced. Draco's code hit the poor and indebted farmers especially hard. The most notorious measures included a sentence of death for stealing fruit, other petty theft, and idleness. The enslavement of debtors (or their children!) was the punishment for failing to make payments on loans.

During this time, agriculture fell on hard times and the economy suffered. Few were satisfied with the situation; many indebted farmers wanted to rebel. This alarmed the aristocracy because those farmers made up the bulk of the *hopolites,* the heavily armed soldiers and muscle power of the Athenian army. The middle class seemed ready to lend its financial support to the hopolites. Fearing the possible alliance of the middle class and tenant farmers, many aristocrats realized that they had gone too far in repressing the rights and interests of others and decided something needed to change.

In 594 BCE, the aristocracy turned to Solon for help. The council appointed him chief archon for the standard one-year term to achieve an extraordinary feat. Solon's challenge was to correct the imbalance in Athens by constitutional means and to do it before the hopolites revolted. To do that, Solon had to reform not only the city's legal constitution but its moral and social constitutions as well. The council gave Solon the authority to recodify Athenian law, redesign Athenian government, and reform the economy. (See Bold Thinkers: Solon.)

In the annals of history, there is no greater act of statesmanship than correcting the imbalance of a polity's constitution. That is what the Glorious Revolution accomplished in England when it corrected the imbalance caused by an absolutist monarch. It is what the leaders of the American Revolution meant when they demanded "no taxation without representation." And it is what Abraham Lincoln meant when he declared that the American union "cannot endure, permanently half slave and half free."

Solon of Athens was not the first such statesman, but he set the bar for those who followed. He proposed constitutional reforms in which there was something for everyone and a better balance between the interests of the aristocracy and the citizenry. His reforms involved all aspects of Athenian life and the Athenian constitution.

Solon's reforms of the law became known as the **Code of Solon**, and it replaced the Code of Draco. Solon insisted that the new code be written down and made public so that it could be read by all. The code eliminated unfair punishments; provided equal access to the courts for rich and poor alike; and required all citizens to use the law, not violence, to resolve their disputes. Any citizen could file a lawsuit against any other citizen, regardless of their respective stations in life.

Solon persuaded landowners that the soil quality of Athens favored the manufacture of clay pottery and the production of olives, not grain. The export of Athenian pottery and olive oil brought lucrative profits that refueled the economy. The Code of Solon canceled all debts and freed debtors from enslavement, which satisfied the poor. (See More About . . . Slaves and Citizens in Athens.) But Solon did not redistribute the ownership of the land, and this inaction satisfied the rich. Solon's economic development plan provided future reformers with an important lesson—people of all classes are more receptive to political reforms when the economy prospers and lifts all boats.

Solon also laid the foundations for Athenian democracy, which came along a century later, by creating a mixed republican government. He established the **Council of 400**, a deliberative body with broad membership that included the new middle class. He also widened eligibility for holding archonships or chief magistrate positions beyond the aristocrats to include low-born men of wealth. He empowered the assembly, regularized its meetings, and opened those meetings to all.

Solon believed a mixed republican government that balanced the interests and influence of rich and poor

BOLD THINKERS
Solon

Solon (c. 639–c. 559 BCE) was entrusted with the daunting task of lawgiver because he was widely regarded as one of the wisest and most fair-minded leaders of his day. In part, he earned this reputation by writing

Solon, depicted in a Roman sculpture after a Greek original.

political poetry. His poems sharply criticized the rich for enslaving the poor and bringing the city to ruin. He criticized the poor for their excessive and outrageous behavior. He criticized all citizens—rich, poor, and middling—for filling the city with acts of wrongdoing. Solon then exhorted all citizens to right their own wrongs and work together to restore good government. The path he urged was constitutional reform and moderation in all things. "Nothing to excess" became his creed. He called for *eunomia*—a balanced and harmonious constitution that "makes crooked judgments straight." The aristocracy trusted Solon because of his wisdom and patriotism. They preferred moderate reform by a fellow aristocrat to popular revolt. His poetry called on Athens to treat everyone fairly, to open the government to all, and to ease the burdens on the poor. Solon's criticisms propelled him to popular lawgiver, but two centuries later another critic, Socrates, was put to death for his impious and antidemocratic criticism.

alike was the best form of government. "Envied for their wealth though they were," Solon pointed out, "I sought to preserve the powerful from the hatred of the oppressed. Taking my

Slaves and Citizens in Athens

Slavery existed in aristocratic Athens side by side with serfdom. But when Solon freed the farmers of their indebtedness, he also ended the institution of serfdom. Sadly, the large landowners, deprived of their serfs, turned to slavery to fill the labor vacuum. When Athens became a democracy, the number of citizens increased, as did their civic duties. To make time for their political activities, citizens purchased slaves. Citizens whose ancestors had been serfs became slave owners. This is one of the great paradoxes of Athenian democracy. At its height, democratic Athens had a population of approximately 300,000. Only 30,000, or 10 percent, were adult male citizens with the right to participate in government. However, roughly 150,000, or one-half of the total population, were slaves.

stand, I used my strong shield to protect both sides of the class divide, allowing neither to gain an advantage over the other that would be unjust." Solon, like Aristotle, was a pragmatist and a centrist. He envisioned a natural and just order in which all interests would have their place—as he put it, a place in which "rough edges would be smoothed out, appetites tamed, and presumption curbed."[2]

Solon did not establish a democracy, but his reforms are credited with laying the foundation for democracy a century later. His achievements in only one year earned him the title of the Lawgiver of Athens and he became one of the ancient Greeks' Seven Sages, a title reserved for the most renowned and revered lawgivers and philosophers. In the history of bold thinkers, he deserves a place of honor for restoring good government through reform and the law rather than through revolution and violence.

HOW DID ATHENS BECOME A DEMOCRACY?

When Solon finished his archonship, he went into self-imposed exile for ten years in the hope that Athenians would take that time to adjust to their new constitution. Although he had reformed Athenian law, government, and the economy, he could not change human nature. Almost immediately, the aristocrats began to squabble over power among themselves and their democratic rivals.

Solon's reforms did not end class conflict. Over the next sixty years, there were periods of popular unrest and periods when an aristocrat took command to restore law and order. Pisistratus, an aristocrat who happened to be Solon's second cousin, briefly seized control twice. In 546 BCE, Pisistratus seized power a third time with the help of foreign mercenaries (professional soldiers for hire). This time he ruled as a tyrant for nearly twenty years until his death in 527 BCE.

Pisistratus was no ordinary tyrant. He was a **demagogue**, a popular leader of the common people who remained in power by pandering to the people. He forced many aristocrats to flee, held their sons hostage, and confiscated their lands. With this new public wealth, he was able to reduce taxes, lower the interest on farmers' loans, undertake massive public works projects that employed many workers, conquer rich foreign lands, and endow the arts.

Pisistratus was neither the first nor the last tyrant to seize power out of chaos or to hold on to it by appeasing the people. But he did provide the populist model for the successful tyrant—keep the streets safe, improve the economy, avoid being unnecessarily harsh, and the people will accept your authority.

Pisistratus's son Hippias inherited his father's throne but not his cleverness and restraint. His father had maintained a balance between presentation and performance, between what he promised and what he delivered. When Hippias's brother was assassinated for abusing power, Hippias turned to open repression and that bred conspiracy against him.[3]

In 510 BCE, an aristocrat named Cleisthenes overthrew Hippias with the aid of a Spartan army led by their king, Cleomenes. The Spartans promptly installed an oligarchy in Athens. Civil war ensued.

Cleisthenes turned against Cleomenes and led the pro-democratic faction that pushed back the Spartans in 508 BCE. Like Solon and Pisistratus, Cleisthenes was a clever aristocrat who identified with the plight of the people and won them over to his side. Like Pisistratus, he was guided by a mix of principled motives based on democratic ideals and practical motives based on self-interest.

History has been both too kind and too unkind to Cleisthenes. Some historians record Cleisthenes as the father of Athenian democracy; others see him as a self-serving opportunist who courted the people for his own benefit and that of his family. Both views are true. Cleisthenes was a principled democrat and a practical opportunist.[4]

Cleisthenes was rewarded for his heroics with the chief archonship in 508 BCE. He promptly introduced a reform package that transformed Athens from a mixed republic to the world's first democracy. (See Figure 11.1.)

Cleisthenes wanted to reform, not abolish, Solon's constitutional framework. He proposed that Athens become a democracy in which the people were sovereign and their assembly was supreme. He also wanted to create a Council of 500 to propose laws to the

Figure 11.1 The Rise and Fall of Athenian Democracy

TIMELINE

Early 600s BCE	The aristocracy has a stranglehold over Athens.
594 BCE	Solon is appointed to reform the constitutions of Athens.
546 BCE	The demagogue Pisistratus begins his twenty-year rule as tyrant.
508 BCE	Sparta's rule over Athens ends; Cleisthenes calls for a series of democratic reforms.
506 BCE	Athens becomes the world's first democracy.
461 BCE	Pericles begins his leadership of Athens.
431 BCE	At the height of Athenian democracy, the Peloponnesian War breaks out between Athens and Sparta.
404 BCE	Sparta defeats Athens.
399 BCE	An Athenian jury sentences Socrates to death.

assembly and implement the laws passed by the assembly. He invented the institution of **demes,** or geographical districts, to organize people by neighborhoods instead of clans. He came up with the novel idea that *demes* should be organized into ten tribes. Each tribe would be entitled to fifty representatives to the Council of 500, thereby providing for equal representation of all tribes. In both the assembly and council, citizens would have the right to gather, speak, and vote as equals. Outside these government institutions, all citizens would have equal rights that included freedom of speech. Later, it was proposed that each tribe should have the power to elect a *strategos* (general). When this office was adopted, it quickly became the most powerful office in Athens—much like a local boss with political and military favors to dispense.

In the history of government, these reforms were of singular importance. They distinguished democracy as a new and unique form of republican government. This was accomplished in two ways. First, these reforms preserved the framework of republican government, including the rule of law that Solon had put in place a century earlier. Second, Cleisthenes's reforms infused that framework with the idea of political equality.

From that point onward, political equality became the distinguishing principle of constitutional democracy. The result was a new republican form of constitutional democracy composed of the rule of law, political freedom, and political equality.

Political equality pervaded the new democracy. Here is a list of the most important features of equality in the new democracy.

- The population was divided into political units (Athenian tribes or modern-day districts) of approximately equal size.
- Political units of equal size were equally represented, in the sense that each unit was entitled to the same number of representatives. For example, each of the ten Athenian tribes had fifty representatives.
- All eligible citizens had an equal vote for their representatives or an equal chance of being selected as a representative by lottery.
- All citizens had an equal right to express their political beliefs, and they were equally free to do so.
- All citizens were guaranteed equal treatment under the law.

These features encapsulate how people still think of democratic equality: equal representation, equal voting rights, equal freedom of expression, and equal justice. There is a significant difference between the ancient and modern conceptions—even in democratic Athens, equality was not for everyone.

Political equality was reserved to male citizens with full political rights—about 10 percent of the total population. Since the early nineteenth century, the idea of political equality has spread both globally and within individual countries. Where constitutional democracy is a political reality, universal suffrage and human rights soon follow. Universal suffrage means that all citizens have the right to vote. Human rights include the belief that every human being can become a fully empowered citizen.

POLITICS IN ACTION

Civic Duties of an Athenian Citizen

In the fifth century BCE, when Athenian democracy was at its height, roughly 30,000 of the total population were eligible to participate in government. If you were one of the 30,000 fully empowered citizens, here is what would be required of you.

- You would be conscripted at age eighteen into universal military service for two years, and you would be on active duty for forty years (until the age of sixty). When you became a member of the entering class, forty-two years after reaching eighteen, you would be required to arbitrate legal disputes.
- You would be a member of the popular assembly that met regularly to consider and vote on legislation prepared by magistrates and committees. Up to 6,000 citizens served at a time. The meetings began at dawn, and slaves would come to collect you if it was your turn to serve. You would have to hold on to a long rope dipped in red paint so your stains would prove your attendance. You would be fined if you were caught without paint stains.
- At least once in your life you would serve on the council. It met for an entire year, and you would be required to attend its meetings. You would be selected for this honor by lottery.
- You also would be subject to a year's service on any of a variety of executive committees having to do with public contracts, weights and measures, port administration, or grain policing.
- You would be required to serve on a jury. All citizens were jurors and subject to jury duty. The average jury consisted of 501 members. As many as ten juries served simultaneously, so you would not be able to avoid your judicial duties.
- Each year you would turn out with the other citizens to elect the chief magistrates (that is, chief executives), who served a one-year term of office. You would also be expected to elect a general to lead your tribe.
- You might also draw the winning lot for service as one of the lower magistrates or administrators, numbering 1,100 per year.
- Each spring you would gather with other citizens to consider ostracizing those who threatened the polity.
- Before assuming each new position, you would have to swear an oath of allegiance at the oath stone.

Mabel Lang, *The Athenian Citizen: Democracy in the Athenian Agora,* rev. ed., ed. John McK. Camp II (Athens: American School of Classical Studies at Athens, 2004).

Before Cleisthenes's reforms could be fully implemented, he received word in 507 BCE that King Cleomenes of Sparta was leading a small expeditionary force to reoccupy Athens. Cleisthenes fled. Cleomenes and the Spartans marched into Athens and occupied the Acropolis with the help of Isagoras, a powerful aristocrat and leader of the antidemocratic opposition. But the citizenry, to their credit, rose up against their occupiers and the treacherous Isagoras. Cleomenes and the Spartans were pushed out of Athens.

Hearing that the Spartans had fled the city, Cleisthenes scurried back to town and resumed his leadership of the democratic forces. Both the aristocrats and democrats concluded that Cleisthenes and his reforms were better than Cleomenes and occupation.

In 506 BCE, Athens officially adopted Cleisthenes's reforms and became the world's first democracy. For the first time, a people chose to combine the rule of law with equality—that was the major effect of Cleisthenes's reforms. The city then set about the task of implementing the new reforms. (See Politics in Action: Civic Duties of an Athenian Citizen.)

A new political language came into being. According to one account, the struggle for democracy added over two hundred new words that used the root *isos* (meaning "equal"). Among the most important were *isotes* (equality), *isonomia* (equal treatment under the law), *isegoria* (free speech), and *isologia* (free speech in the assembly now open to all citizens).[5]

HOW DID DEMOCRACY FARE IN FIFTH-CENTURY ATHENS?

The adoption of democracy in Athens did not end opposition to it. Democrats and aristocrats were now equally free to criticize, argue, and compete with one another. And they did not hesitate to do so. According to Aristotle, every democratic leader of significance had an antidemocratic foe. Solon, for example, was opposed by Pisistratus, who later became a tyrant. Pro-democratic Cleisthenes was opposed by Isagoras, and Pericles by Cimon.

Nor did democracy bring an end to Athens's tensions with Sparta. Those tensions became a cold war lasting about seventy years. In 431 BCE, at the height of Athenian democracy, that cold war became a hot war known as the Peloponnesian War, which embroiled the Greek world for nearly thirty years.

Athens's foreign conflict was closely related to her ongoing internal division between aristocrats and democrats. This convergence of foreign and domestic affairs played a central role in the rising and falling fortunes of Athens in the fifth century. For the Greeks, Sparta was the center of the aristocratic world as much as Athens represented the democratic world. Each power did its best to expand its world and undercut its rival. Eventually, internal divisions polarized Athens, but that happened only after Athens suffered the humiliation of defeat in its war with Sparta.

The rising and falling fortunes of Athens and its democracy during this exciting century look something like a bell-shaped curve (see Figure 11.2). The curve represents three phases of roughly equal duration. Phase 1 (506–460 BCE) marks the rise of Athenian democracy by the defeat of the Persians in 480 BCE and then the exile of Cimon, a prominent leader of the

Figure 11.2 The Fortunes of Athenian Democracy, 506–399 BCE

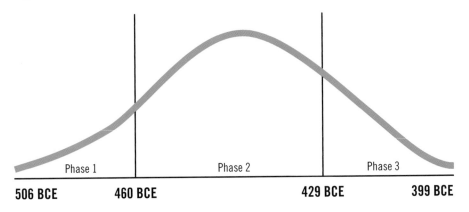

| Phase 1 | Phase 2 | Phase 3 |

| 506 BCE | 460 BCE | 429 BCE | 399 BCE |

pro-Spartan and antidemocratic faction, in 460 BCE. Phase 2 (461–429 BCE) is remembered as the Age of Pericles. During this period, Pericles, Athenian democracy's greatest statesman, led Athens in its golden age and the opening battles of the Peloponnesian War. Phase 3 (429–399 BCE) begins with the death of Pericles and includes the city's steady decline in leadership and the fortunes of war. It ends with the famous trial of Socrates.

THE AGE OF PERICLES

Pericles was a wealthy aristocrat who invested his creative energies and wealth in the democratic cause. He first came to public attention in the decade after the Persian Wars by sponsoring great playwrights who dramatized the defeat of Persia and other great events. During that time, Pericles became more seriously involved in politics, and in 461 BCE, he became the chief statesman of Athens.

Pericles was a brilliant orator, democratic reformer, military strategist, and patron of the arts. He encouraged freedom of expression, even when comedic playwrights staged plays that made fun of him. He did not hesitate to invest his own money in the beautification of Athens. He also did not hesitate to outmaneuver his opponents.

In 460 BCE, democrats, undoubtedly with Pericles's support, amassed the votes needed to ostracize their leading opponent, Cimon. **Ostracism** was the practice of exiling an Athenian citizen for ten years. (See Politics in Action: Ostracism.) Political leaders

Pericles, in a Roman marble copy of a Greek bust.

POLITICS IN ACTION
Ostracism

Cleisthenes introduced the practice of ostracism. Every spring, citizens gathered and cast their votes for whoever was, in their opinion, the most dangerous man in the polity. The person with the most votes was ostracized—exiled for a period of ten years. Each citizen used a broken piece of pottery (called an *ostrakon*) as his ballot. This practice was introduced as a way of identifying and banishing the most ambitious members of the antidemocratic camp. However, it also became a way for one faction to neutralize the leader of an opposing faction.

Broken pieces of pottery used in Athens, Greece, to ostracize Aristides, Cimon, and Themistocles. At the bottom of the photo are Athenian weights.

found it quite handy when looking for ways to eliminate a rival. In 443 BCE, Pericles ostracized his last great opponent, Thucydides (not to be confused with the historian of the same name); the ostracism of Thucydides consolidated Pericles's control.

In 451 BCE, Pericles convinced the assembly to adopt another measure to control their opponents. This measure denied Athenian citizenship to the children of non-Athenian mothers. Since intermarriages between Athenian fathers and non-Athenian mothers were most common among the aristocracy, Pericles used a populist goal ("purifying Athenian citizenship") to achieve a partisan goal (reducing political opposition). In this rather underhanded way, he used antiforeign sentiment to reduce the future population of aristocratic citizens who might one day grow up to vote democracy down. This measure backfired on Pericles when he fell in love with and married a foreign woman; his children were denied citizenship by his own policy.

Under Pericles's leadership, Athens flourished. Pericles demanded high achievement, allowed more freedom, and found the money to pay for various public projects. He got aristocrats to compete with one another on who could invest more in ship building. In less than ten years, he rebuilt the Acropolis temples and replenished the artwork that had been destroyed by the Persians.

The age of Pericles is perhaps most remembered for its works of drama, history, and philosophy. Pericles created an air of freedom and excellence that stimulated some of the world's greatest writers. The world of drama was transformed by a who's who of tragic playwrights. The three great tragedians and some of their most famous works were Aeschylus (*Prometheus Bound*), Sophocles (*Antigone* and *Oedipus Rex*), and Euripides (*Medea*). Shortly after Pericles's death, Aristophanes wrote a series of political comedies that left few unscathed. He lampooned Athenian imperialism in *The Babylonians,* the current leader Cleon in *Knights,* Socrates in *The Clouds,* lawyers and litigiousness in *The Wasps,* fellow playwrights in *The Frogs,* women in the *Assemblywoman,* and the rich in *Wealth.*

History and philosophy came of age during this period. Herodotus (484–425 BCE), widely regarded as the father of history, was influenced by his brief four-year stay in Athens (447–443 BCE). Although his master work, *Histories,* was not completed at his death, Herodotus was the first to separate history from myth. Another significant Greek historian, Thucydides (460–396 BCE), most famous for his *History of the Peloponnesian War,* studied history as a science. His theories on the origins of war and the nature of politics are still widely used today.

Philosophical discourse and the exchange of ideas flourished during the age of Pericles as in no other time. For half a century Athens tolerated the biting attacks of its sharpest critic, the philosopher and teacher Socrates (470–399 BCE). Not only that, the city also tolerated his school for young aristocrats and some of its most dishonorable graduates and hangers-on, who would later strike out against the city.

THE PELOPONNESIAN WAR

Under Pericles's leadership, relations with Sparta worsened. Sparta and Athens had been rivals throughout the fifth century. Each had imperial ambitions, wanting to protect and expand their leagues or alliance systems. The Spartans led the Peloponnesian League; the Athenians led the Delian League, a fifth-century military alliance of approximately 150 polities and colonies. Pericles saw increased glory and fortunes for Athens in its foreign exploits. Under Pericles, Athens grew more, not less, ambitious. He worked to transform the Delian League into more of a loose empire than a league of equals. Pericles made this official when he moved the Delian treasury to Athens. He claimed that Athens was shouldering the costs of the league and therefore deserved control over its treasury.

Sparta and Athens were not only imperial rivals. The root of their conflict lay in the fact that Sparta and Athens symbolized rival ways of life. Sparta took pride in its oligarchy, martial culture, and army. Athens took pride in its democracy, freedom, literary accomplishments, and navy. Athens and Sparta fomented civil war wherever they could. Athenians supported democrats in the Spartan empire; Spartans supported oligarchs in the Athenian empire. Today, when one state foments discord in another's backyard this is called *state-sponsored acts of aggression.* When local insurgents ask for foreign support to strengthen their side, this is known as the *internationalization of internal conflict.* Whichever term is used, the results are the same—domestic and foreign sources of conflict converge and escalate the conflict.

In 431 BCE the cold war between Athens and Sparta turned into a hot war, known as the Peloponnesian War. According to Thucydides's history of that war, Sparta attacked Athens because it feared Athenian ascendancy. But recall that Pericles did not shy away from a glorious war.

The war quickly turned ugly, as all wars do. A horrible plague struck Athens, killing a large percentage of its people—including Pericles. He was succeeded by a succession of populist leaders, or demagogues, who rose to power by inflaming the citizenry.

Dark days followed, setting in motion the third and declining phase of Athens. During those dark days, Athens was beset by continued plague, Spartan attacks, and a devastating fire. Economic decline followed. In 404 BCE, Sparta defeated Athens after the war had been waged for nearly thirty years. Sparta promptly installed a dictatorship of oligarchs in Athens that became known as the Thirty Tyrants. Their rule was brief yet bloody. Its most notorious leader, Critias, waged a ruthless campaign of arrests, executions, and property seizures.

In time, the bloodbath disturbed even Sparta. They toppled the Thirty Tyrants and allowed Athenians to reinstate a modified version of democracy. As long as Athens thrived, its democracy survived. So too did its tolerance for dissent—even for its most vocal dissenter, Socrates. But in defeat and humiliation, Athenians looked for scapegoats, and Socrates was a most convenient target.

SOCRATES

Socrates was born around 470 BCE, just about the time that Pericles was beginning his political career. History has recorded Socrates as a champion of wisdom, truth, and virtue who stood up against "the establishment" and its conventions even when he knew he would be tried and sentenced to death for his convictions. He was a social gadfly—a critic who stung society for its half-truths, imperfections, and failings.

In that regard, Socrates's role has been compared with Jesus, who taught four centuries later.[6] However, unlike the teachings of Jesus, Socrates was decidedly antidemocratic in his philosophy. In the age of Pericles, Athenians tolerated Socrates, but in defeat, Athenians turned on him.

For half a century, during good times and bad, Socrates relentlessly attacked democratic Athens on three grounds.[7] First, Socrates argued that the best polity was not a free society of equal citizens but a herd that was best governed by a wise and powerful king. His star student Plato, also an ardent antidemocrat, used the term **philosopher-king** to describe such a ruler. In the long-standing conflict between aristocrats representing the interests of "the few" and democrats representing "the many," Socrates sided with the aristocrats.

Second, Socrates agreed with his compatriots that the cardinal Greek value was virtue. He argued, however, that virtue required true knowledge. In a democratic age, Socrates asserted, true knowledge was not for everyone; rather, it was for a privileged few. Third, Socrates taught that the pursuit of true knowledge was a solitary pursuit. This argument challenged the very foundations of the Greek polity as a human association of sociable creatures.

Socrates's teachings influenced not only loyal Athenians but also sympathizers to the Spartan cause. That list included Alcibedes, the most famous defector to the Spartan cause, and the infamous Critias, a leader of the Thirty Tyrants.

In 399 BCE, after war-torn Athens regained its democracy, an Athenian jury charged Socrates with impiety (that is, lacking respect for the gods) and corrupting the youth (that is, turning the youth against the city and its democracy). He was convicted by a jury of 501

The Death of Socrates, *by Jacques Louis David, 1787. This painting, created shortly before the French Revolution, was widely seen as a call to resist unjust authority. The painting inspired Thomas Jefferson (who attended the painting's unveiling) to write a friend, "The best thing is the* Death of Socrates *by David, and a superb one it is."*

jurors (a typical size) and, after considerable haggling, was sentenced to death. Socrates could have argued his way out of this sentence or escaped, but he chose to die a martyr. He committed suicide by drinking a poisonous mixture of hemlock surrounded by his friends and students, including Plato.

Athens convicted Socrates for his ideas; not his actions. In reaching their verdict, Athenians violated the essence of Athenian freedom. Socrates was a loner and gadfly, but he had served with great courage in battle, was a loyal Athenian, and had never committed a treasonous act. As a philosopher and teacher, he spoke out against democracy and favored aristocracy—that should not be a crime in a free society. There were aggravating circumstances—democracy and aristocracy had been at war, and a few of Socrates's associates had defected to the enemy. But Socrates himself never encouraged or condoned their actions. In the final analysis, the jury used Socrates as a convenient scapegoat for Athens's troubles. The political fact that he had goaded them into it is not an excuse for their actions; nor is the historical fact that other societies have reacted the same way under similar circumstances. (See More About . . . The Scapegoat in Political History.)

TYRANNY AND DEMOCRACY

The history of Athens is a tale of leadership and citizenship. It is a tale of statesmen with the vision of a better world and bold thinkers with the courage to dissent. But it is

In Leviticus 16 of the Hebrew Bible, God tells Moses to instruct his brother Aaron to select two he-goats for an offering. One is to be sacrificed; the other is to be sent into the wilderness. The goat sent into the wilderness is to be a form of atonement. This goat is to bear the sins of Aaron, his family, and his community.

Over time, the meaning of *scapegoat* broadened to include anyone who was—rightly or wrongly—blamed for people's troubles. Socrates, for example, was among the first in a long and tragic line of political scapegoats.

Scapegoating is a tool of *propaganda,* the systematic use of emotionally loaded messages carefully designed to persuade people to act in a particular way. Adolf Hitler used scapegoating in Nazi propaganda to blame the Jews and other supposed conspirators for Germany's economic troubles, political losses, and dishonor after World War I. He then turned on other groups, including Poles, gypsies, and homosexuals.

also a story of leadership by tyrants and demagogues who sought to advance their own interests.

Ordinary citizens are not named in this story, but that should not diminish their roles. Indebted hoplites demanded reform of draconian laws, ordinary citizens rose up against Spartan occupation, and newly empowered citizens rose to the level of responsibility that democracy demanded. And a defeated and humiliated citizenry found in Socrates a convenient scapegoat for their misfortune. In all these episodes, leaders and citizens alike learned how to effectively apply ideas, interests, and institutions to solve political issues. It is in this mix that partial successes and partial failures can be found.

The story of Athens is a powerful tale in the history of government, but it is not the only one that offers important insights. At about the same time, another history of a republican government was unfolding in Rome.

WHY WAS ROME A REPUBLIC AND NOT A DEMOCRACY?

Rome was a republic for centuries. What explains its endurance? In the first century BCE, the Greek historian Polybius (c. 203–120 BCE) wrote a detailed analysis of governance in the Roman Republic. Polybius was a Greek historian who lived in the Roman Republic for many years; in fact, he lived with one of Rome's most powerful families, the Scipios. During his life in Rome, Polybius wrote a massive forty-volume history in which he presented his analysis of the government of the Roman Republic.[8]

Polybius identified three basic sets of Roman institutions of government: two consuls and other magistrates, the Senate, and the popular assemblies. The Greeks had similar institutions in their executive magistrates, council, and assembly.

Polybius characterized the assemblies (there were several) as the democratic feature of Roman government because they consisted of all of the citizens. He considered the Senate to be the aristocratic feature because it was a much smaller body that added a deliberative quality to Roman government and because its membership was drawn from the patrician class. Last, he described the consuls as the monarchic feature of Roman government. Even though there were two consuls, each was supposed to have his own sphere. In that sphere, each served as the chief executive, overseeing dozens of elected magistrates. Together, they were the executive arm of the republic in civilian and, when necessary, military affairs.

Who ruled the Roman Republic? The word **republic** comes from the Latin phrase *res publica,* which literally means "those things that fall into the public realm." Over time, *res publica* has been shortened to the public realm, the commonwealth, or the republic. All of these references are understood to mean good government, not simply mere government.

The Senate and people of Rome were the official sources of authority for the Roman Republic. Military standards and banners bore the abbreviation SPQR for *Senātus Populusque Rōmānus* (the Senate and people of Rome).

On paper, it appeared to Polybius that the citizenry ultimately ruled. Their assemblies elected the consuls, some of whom became censors who selected the senators. The assemblies had the power to pass or reject legislation and to declare war. They also served as a huge jury-like court of last resort.

Who held real power and who benefited? Most scholars agree on the answer—in reality, the most powerful institution of Roman republican government was the Senate. On paper, the Senate was an advisory body; in fact, it had enormous influence. Senators were appointed for life, they were former magistrates, they came from the most powerful families of Rome, and they controlled the budget and the distribution of land. Generally, the citizenry heeded the Senate's advice. So, too, did the consuls, except for those with personal ambitions of their own. The question is, how did the Senate become so influential and powerful?

The Roman Republic was divided into two classes: the **patricians**, or aristocracy, and the **plebeians**, or citizenry. These are the types of interests that Aristotle had in mind when he wrote of "rule by the few" and "rule by the many." Aristotle advocated mixed government because it could balance these two sets of interests and thereby resist despotism and majority tyranny.

The justifications for the Roman Senate, like most political justifications, included principled reasons (based on ideas) and practical reasons (based on interests and effects). The principled reason for a small advisory body such as the Roman Senate (or the Greek government council of elders) is that it provided the opportunity for deliberation—the thoughtful and prudent process of decision making. The practical reason is that it gave the patrician class an important seat at the table. From this position, the patricians would come to see their own interests served by a stable, well-administered, and fair government. The patricians also were placed in a position where they could counsel and, where necessary, check the excesses of a chief executive with power over the army. From this position, they were also well placed to calm, moderate, and influence the decisions of the citizenry in their popular assembly.

The popular assembly represented the citizenry and gave them a major seat at the table. In principle, citizen participation can temper passions, inform virtue, and check the abuse of power. Empowering a popular assembly also made political sense. To exclude the most numerous political element of society is very risky. A genuine republican government must provide its citizenry with some measure of freedom and consent. Deny citizens participation, and they are likely to rebel. With meaningful participation, the citizenry can be a check on the power and corruption of the consuls and senators.

Aristotle, like his Greek and Roman contemporaries, most feared the return of a tyrant. The Athenian *polis* and the Roman Republic both began by overthrowing tyrannical monarchs, and neither society wanted to see their return. They made sure their constitutions put checks on their chief executives. They did this by setting up a senate (or council) and assemblies that represented the two most powerful interests of society: wealth and numbers. In 336 BCE, for example, fearful of conquest by the Macedonian king, Athens even passed a law against despotism that put a bounty on anyone who tried to overthrow democracy.

For centuries, Rome flourished under a mixed republican government. Its economy prospered, its polity was stable, its citizen armies proved invincible in combat, and its borders expanded. Patricians benefited and so too did the citizenry. Gradually, plebeians achieved political equality with patricians. Plebeians received equal treatment under the law, they gained the right to serve as consuls and other magistrates, and plebeians and patricians were allowed to intermarry. Just as important, the inevitable jockeying for power within and between classes was largely peaceful.[9]

REPUBLIC AND EMPIRE

As the polity grew, so did the offices of government. The system became increasingly complex and unwieldy. Patrician families, ambitious generals, and aspiring office-seekers found it more convenient to wield influence outside the system of government. They developed personal and family networks through which they bought the support of plebeians. Corruption spread, and personal followings based on money and family connections became more important than civic ties to *civitas,* the larger community of citizens that held Rome together as a republic. Civil war ensued, and the winner, Lucius Cornelius Sulla, declared himself dictator in 88 BCE. Under the unwritten Roman constitution, dictatorship was an office that granted the dictator unlimited power to save the republic. As dictator, Sulla murdered his foes and cut back the powers of the citizenry. He thus set a dangerous precedent for the civil war that erupted forty years later between Gaius Julius Caesar and Gnaeus Pompey that ended with the dictatorship of Julius Caesar. (See Bold Thinkers: Cicero—"Father of the Country.")

After the assassination of Julius Caesar, Rome could have returned to republican rule, but it did not. Nor did it instantly become an empire. Three men briefly shared rule for a time, but only one survived. He was the great-nephew and heir of Julius Caesar, Gaius Octavius Thurinus, known (after Caesar adopted him) as Gaius Julius Caesar Octavianus. Octavianus was granted the title of commander (today, translated as "emperor") and named Augustus by an admiring Senate. Augustus solidified power in his own hands. But

BOLD THINKERS

Cicero—"Father of the Country"

At the youngest eligible age—forty-three—the ambitious lawyer Marcus Tullius Cicero was elected Roman consul for the year 63 BCE. His success in a high-profile prosecution had already won him renown as Rome's greatest orator. Triumphing in his election as consul over the patrician candidate Catiline, he had risen far from his small-town, local-gentry origins.

During his year as consul, Cicero foiled a Catiline-led conspiracy to overthrow the Roman Republic. In four powerfully eloquent speeches,

In this 1889 fresco by Cesare Maccari, Cicero denounces Catiline in the Senate.

he attacked Catiline and his followers. The conspirators fled, were caught, and were executed. A grateful Senate gave Cicero the title *pater patriae,* or "father of the country," the first time this honor had been awarded. Cicero was less successful, however, at navigating through the Roman civil war that soon followed.

Cicero proclaimed that it was his destiny to stand or fall with the liberty of the state. He believed that many political leaders of his time had been corrupted by power and wealth. Cicero was passionately loyal to the idea of the republic based on the rule of law and the authority of the Senate. With the power of persuasion as his only weapon, he courageously opposed Julius Caesar and Mark Antony, who had military might on their side. Cicero relentlessly defended the republic against those who would abandon the rule of law. He was exiled twice, pardoned, and finally assassinated.

he also kept the form of a mixed republic in place. He repeatedly declined attempts by the people and the Senate to persuade him to assume the title of dictator. Nonetheless, his rule marked the beginning of the Roman Empire and paved the way for the succession of Roman emperors that followed. Yet for three hundred years the Roman Empire retained a republican form of government—at least on paper.[10]

WHAT WAS THE IMPACT OF THE ROMAN EMPIRE IN EUROPE?

The Roman Empire ruled much of Europe, North Africa, and the Near East for nearly five hundred years. The beginning and end of the empire is a subject of considerable debate. However, it is generally agreed that (1) in 27 BCE Augustus became the first in a long line of Roman emperors and (2) in 476 CE, roughly five hundred years later, the last Roman emperor was deposed.

Emperor Trajan (Marcus Ulpius Trajanus, c. 53–117 CE) expanded the empire to its furthest points. At his death in 117 CE, the empire nearly reached to the Caspian Sea and Persian Gulf in the southeast. Its southern territories included all of the North African coast and the Nile Valley of Egypt. To the northwest, the empire included Britannia. To the northeast the empire stretched to the Rhine and Danube rivers.

From Britannia to Babylon, from Mauretania to Armenia, the Roman Empire embraced the Mediterranean world, Asia Minor, and Western Europe (see Map 11.1). Its demographic and geographical scope was significant—it ruled almost 100 million people across nearly 2 million square miles. More impressive still was its political span of control over both population and territory.

Two great enemies bordered the empire to the east. To the southeast lay the powerful Persian (Parthian) Empire. To the northeast, beyond the Rhine and Danube rivers, lay Germania, the home of the formidable Germanic tribes.

Roman imperial history can be divided into two roughly equal periods of government and administration. The dividing line is the rule of Emperor Diocletian (284–305 CE) and the measures he began introducing in 285 CE.

In studying the Roman Empire, it is important to keep in mind that empire is technically not a form of government. An empire is a large, multiethnic political entity that is created by conquest or colonization. Empire comes from the Latin *imperare,* meaning to impose or command. Originally, it was a military term and the *imperator* was a military commander.

The military played a significant role in creating and maintaining the empire. The early Roman Empire was controlled by its armies. In the early years of the empire, Roman armies numbered approximately 250,000 soldiers. They were permanently encamped in strategic outposts around the empire. This policy was not solely for military defense and communications. By spreading their armies around the empire, emperors slept easier knowing that an ambitious general would find it more difficult to gather enough forces to march on Rome.

A single leader, an emperor, ruled the Roman Empire, which suggests a form of monarchic rule (rule by the one). But that is only part of the story. At first glance, nothing seems more antithetical to the republican ideal—of government based on the rule of law and the consent of the governed—than the monarchic rule of an imperialistic empire. Yet history provides various examples of republics with empires, from ancient Athens to modern Britain and France.

Map 11.1 The Roman Empire, 100 BCE–117 CE

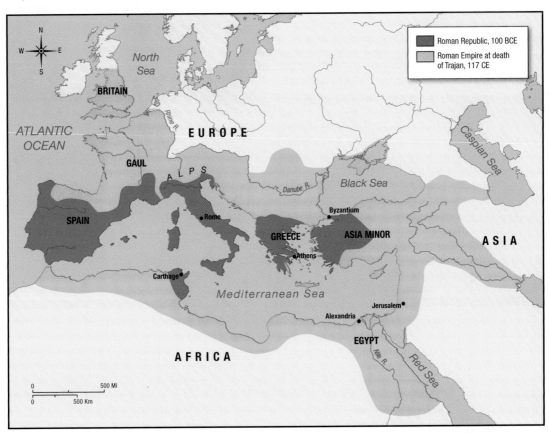

Rome's first emperor, Augustus, kept in place Rome's republican form of government. The Senate and people of Rome remained the sources of authority for Roman government; military standards and banners still bore the abbreviation SPQR. In theory, the Senate, the people, and the emperor shared constitutional power. The Senate remained a viable political institution.

Augustus liked to say that he was merely "first among equals" in his relations with the senators. In fact, the emperor had the final say. In the early years of the empire, senators would occasionally call for a restoration of republican rule, but this became increasingly risky and soon ceased.

The emperor's real power depended on his control of the armies. Imperial succession had no rule of heredity or divine right. Nor were emperors required to be Roman-born or of aristocratic origin. As a result, it was not unusual for generals of common background and occasionally of foreign birth to become emperors.

For three centuries, the imperial government lacked a large bureaucracy of civil servants. The empire was divided into provinces, and a governor was assigned to each one. The governor was an imperial officer sent to govern a province on the emperor's behalf. The

governor typically combined military and civilian authority. His civilian administrative staff was usually small. He often relied on provincial leaders, such as a council of elders, king, or chieftain, for local relations and administrative tasks. Such tasks included the collection of taxes. Local subjects could petition the governor for favors, or they could send an emissary to Rome. The governor became the local source of patronage, providing jobs and other political favors in exchange for loyalty. Through the governor, Roman law and culture, including coinage, were introduced throughout the empire. (See More About . . . Coinage in the Early Roman Empire.)

The political philosophy of the Roman Empire was a mix of Greek Hellenism and Roman imperialism. From the Greeks came the importance of reason, logic, and rhetoric. (Ironically, the empire also drew on republican ideas.) The Romans reorganized natural law—the idea that nature, not people, is the universal source of all law. The empire became famous for taking abstract Greek ideas and reapplying them to service the practical needs of imperial order and expansion. For example, the Roman emperors redefined natural law to suit their interests. Nature, they proclaimed, recognized the laws of the empire as the legitimate source of local law. On this basis, they sought to replace customary law (the local customs of conquered peoples) with imperial Roman law.

Their success varied. Generally, people who had lived under Roman rule the longest and who lived closest to Rome were the most likely to accept imperial law; this was true for the Italian and Spanish provinces. To the north, local leaders were more entrenched and had more autonomy. The Germanic people, such as the Saxons in Britannia, were more rebellious.

Many provincial leaders accepted, or appeared to accept, Roman law and customs because they wanted to advance in the imperial system. As important, they learned Latin or Greek—to not speak a "civilized" language was to be a "barbarian" (a Greek term meaning the speaker of a language that was not Greek).

But philosophical and political disagreements often lay just below the appearance of unity. These disagreements centered on several related issues: What was the ultimate source of law? What was good law? Who was the good citizen? There were three formidable challenges to imperial law and philosophy: Stoicism, Christianity, and Germanic republicanism.

Stoicism was the Hellenistic Greek philosophy that the individual had two sets of responsibility: (1) a patriotic duty to the polity and its laws, and (2) an ethical duty as a human being to be in accord with the universal laws of nature. Two Roman Stoics, Marcus Aurelius and Seneca, wrote in imperial times about these dual responsibilities. (See Bold Thinkers: Marcus Aurelius—Emperor and Stoic.) In their writing, they maintained that the conflict between patriotism and humanism could be reconciled.

Christianity posed another challenge. A principal value of Christianity is the idea that all human beings are equal in the sight of God. But does this also mean that every human polity on Earth should disavow imperialism and become a holy commonwealth of republican values? The gospel according to Matthew (22:21) carefully circumvents this issue: "Render unto Caesar the things which are Caesar's, and render unto God the things which are God's." The Roman philosopher and Christian theologian St. Augustine (354–430 CE) offered the foundational interpretation of this message. He concluded that there are two cities or kingdoms—one belonging to Caesar and the other to God—and the two may indeed be irreconcilable. (See Bold Thinkers: Saint Augustine and *The City of God.*)

Long after the fall of the Roman Empire, a long and illustrious line of thinkers sought to reconcile Aristotelian and Christian thinking on this very point. St. Thomas Aquinas (1225–1274), the Italian philosopher and theologian, sought to balance the teachings of Aristotle and the Church. Marsilius of Padua (c. 1275–1342), the Italian political philosopher, rejected Church hierarchy as a source of divine authority in favor of a more republican view of the role of the clergy in helping build a holy commonwealth. Martin Luther (1483–1546), the German leader of the Protestant Reformation, rejected the teachings of Aristotle in favor of the Church. Italian humanists such as Niccolò Machiavelli (1469–1527) repudiated both Aristotle and the Church in favor of a more modern republican view, while northern humanists such as Desiderius Erasmus (c. 1466–1536) sought to balance classical and Christian thinking in federal or covenantal theology.[11] We explore the ideas of these bold thinkers in later chapters.

Christian thinkers were not the only ones who tried to reconcile Greek teachings with revealed or spiritual teaching al-Farabi (?–950 CE) and Maimonides (Moses ben Maimon, 1135–1204) were engaged in similar pursuits in the worlds of Islamic and Judaic thought, respectively.

Germanic republicanism was a more immediate threat to the Roman Empire. Germania lay just outside the empire, but tribes from that region had migrated westward into the

BOLD THINKERS

Marcus Aurelius—Emperor and Stoic

Born into a prominent and wealthy family, Marcus Aurelius (121–180 CE) was adopted by future emperor Antoninus Pius and brought up as his heir. When he became Roman emperor in 161 CE, Marcus shared power as co-emperor with his adoptive brother Lucius Verus. Marcus himself remained the dominant partner during a reign marked by continual military crises on the imperial frontiers.

Although the long eastern campaign (162–166 CE) against the Parthians proved successful, the returning legions carried a deadly plague to Rome. Soon afterward, Marcus and Verus led the fight against a German invasion on the northern border. They beat back the Germans, but Verus died during the campaign. In 177, Marcus made his son Commodus co-emperor.

Known for his gentle character and broad learning, Marcus Aurelius wrote his *Meditations* during ten years of campaigning. A much-revered work of spiritual guidance

This statue of Marcus Aurelius, made during his reign, is the only complete bronze equestrian statue to survive from antiquity. Most such statues were melted down during the Middle Ages.

and moral self-improvement, *Meditations* embodies his understanding of Stoic philosophy. Through reason, the Stoics taught, mankind can accept the fate that governs the universe. Then, a person can regulate his or her life by emulating the fundamentally rational universe's calm and order. Thus, by learning to accept events with a strong and serene mind, an individual can acquire great moral virtue.

empire. These included the Saxons in Britannia and the Franks in what is now France. Other tribes such as the Vandals periodically invaded the Roman Empire.

The Romans never subdued the Germans. The Romans saw Rome as the center of civilization and Germania as the center of the uncivilized world. But the Germans were a free people, and they took pride in their freedom. Just as important, the Germans were a republican people who founded conciliar republics wherever they settled. **Conciliar republics** were an early type of republican government in which the political community was governed by a

BOLD THINKERS

Saint Augustine and *The City of God*

The Visigoths, a Germanic tribe, sacked Rome in 410 CE. This traumatic event led many Romans to believe that their gods were punishing Rome for abandoning them and adopting Christianity as the official imperial religion. Augustine, bishop of Hippo (a provincial Roman city in North Africa), wrote his treatise *The City of God* to comfort Roman Christians. In the book, he explained Christianity's relationship to the Roman government and to other philosophies and religions.

Augustine, later Saint Augustine, explained human history as the ongoing conflict between the City of God (people promoting Christian values and forgoing earthly pleasures) and the City of Man (those straying from the City of God). In the end, the City of God would triumph. Christianity's message, according to Augustine, was centered on the spiritual, not the political, world.

Augustine was born in what is now Algeria, of Berber ancestry (the Berbers were the largest ethnic group of North Africa). His mother, St. Monica, raised him in the Christian faith. As a young man, he lived in Carthage, where he abandoned Christianity, adopted a Gnostic religion, took a mistress, studied Greek philosophy, and taught rhetoric. He later moved to Milan, where he was influenced by St. Ambrose, who converted him to Christianity. Returning to Africa to study, he became bishop of Hippo (in what is now Algeria) in 396. He died in 430 while a Vandal army was besieging the city. A major figure of Western Christianity, Augustine wrote a vast number of influential letters, sermons, and theological works, including *Confessions,* an autobiographical meditation.

council of elders. (*Conciliar* is the adjective form of *council.*) This type of republic arose in small communities where a people (organized as a tribe) expected elders to govern based on unwritten customs. Over time, some of their customs became one source of a certain type of law known as customary law.

In 212 CE, Emperor Caracalla (188–217 CE) extended Roman citizenship to all free noncitizens throughout the empire. But like many imperial grants, appearances proved deceptive. Over the previous two hundred years, the differences between citizens and free noncitizens had largely eroded; most citizens had lost the right to vote and noncitizens had received some rights of citizens. A new distinction had emerged between upper- and lower-order citizens. The latter had fewer rights and received stiffer punishments for committing crimes. Caracalla's grant of citizenship merely confirmed this distinction. It also achieved another important purpose—it dramatically increased tax revenues because only citizens were obligated to pay certain taxes.

THE BUREAUCRATIC STATE

In the third century CE, the Roman Empire was weakened by invasion, civil war, and inflation. When Diocletian (Caius Aurelius Valerius Diocletianus, 245–313 CE) became emperor in 284, he promised to restore Roman power. He did so—but at a heavy price. Diocletian transformed the Augustinian system from an empire with a republican veneer to an authoritarian system with a strong bureaucracy. Diocletian divided the empire into eastern and western parts. The eastern part evolved into the Byzantine Empire, which survived 1,000 years after the Western Roman Empire collapsed. Diocletian also doubled the number of provinces and the size of the civil service or bureaucracy. He dramatically increased the size of the army and stationed troops outside cities and along the empire's borders. During his reign, the army reached 1 million strong.

The new Diocletian system included twice as many provincial governors. These governors ruled smaller provinces and saw their powers reduced to largely judicial functions. In each province, the governor shared power with a military commander and a financial officer who assessed property and collected taxes. As responsibilities became more specialized, the number and variety of offices increased. To pay for the increase in civilian and military personnel, taxes also increased. At the same time, tax rates were more equitable and tax collection occurred on a more regular basis. Thus, the bureaucratic state was born in the West.

ROMAN LAW

Law was the lifeblood of Rome, both as a republic and an empire. Everything of importance was governed by laws. Romans loved to systematically collect and classify things. Codifying the law was one of their greatest accomplishments. The process began when Roman sages collected and recorded Rome's early laws on the "Twelves Tables" (that is, tablets). The process dramatically increased in imperial times. As imperial administration became more complex, so did the law. The new Diocletian system generated more imperial edicts that reached more people more quickly in the smaller provinces. But the new system also prompted more petitions, court cases, and appeals.

Codifying the law became a full-time endeavor for a new class of professionals. The most extensive codification occurred some fifty years after the Western Roman Empire collapsed. In the 530s CE, Emperor Justinian I (483–565 CE) of the Eastern, or Byzantine, Empire issued the *Corpus Iuris Civilis* (the Code of Civil Law), known as the **Justinian Code**. This code is a systematic collection of the myriad Roman laws from ancient republican times.

But there is a reason why it is called the Justinian Code. The Justinian Code was the emperor's code—just like Hammurabi's Code over 2,000 years earlier and the Napoleonic Code nearly 1,300 years later. The Justinian Code made clear that the law comes from the emperor, not the other way around. It also established the supremacy of the emperor's rule over the law. In the process, it turned the rule of law into an instrument of imperial power.

Hammurabi's Code, the Justinian Code, and the Napoleonic Code are treated as milestones in the history of the law. But each of them rejected the supremacy of the rule of law over the rule of individuals with power.

Thus, the Justinian Code helped create the legal fiction that the emperor was above the law. For centuries, European kings, queens, and emperors looked to this document as an early source of legitimacy for absolute rule. Fiction became reality when they succeeded.

The Romans emancipated the idea of law from mere custom, on the one hand, and from mere caprice, on the other. They regarded law as something to be formed by enlightened intelligence, consistent with reason and the nature of things; and they associated it with the solemn action of official power. It must be added that Roman law favored the state, or the public interest as seen by the government, rather than the interests or liberties of individuals.[12]

REVIEWING AND USING THE CHAPTER

1. Compare and contrast the Code of Solon and the Code of Draco.

2. How did the reforms of Cleisthenes expand the idea of political equality? How do ancient Greek ideas about political equality differ from popular beliefs about equality today?

3. What are the similarities and differences between Athenian democracy and Roman republicanism?

4. How did the Roman Senate become so powerful?

5. How does the cold war between Sparta and Athens compare to the twentieth-century cold war between the United States and the Soviet Union?

6. Which features of the Roman Empire were most consistent with the idea of republicanism? Which features seem antithetical to the idea of republicanism? Provide specific examples to support your answer.

EXTENSION ACTIVITY

Since the mid-1970s there have been numerous national movements in which leaders and citizens have joined together peaceably to topple a corrupt regime and restore constitutional balance. These include the People Power Movement in the Philippines, the anti-apartheid movement in South Africa, and the Rose Revolution in the Republic of Georgia. Select one of these examples and research the role played by leaders and citizens in bringing about reform.

WEB RESOURCES

British Broadcasting System: Ancient History
www.bbc.co.uk/history/ancient

This Web site provides access to a variety of resources that focus on the study of ancient cultures, including Greece and Rome. It is student-friendly, featuring not only accessible readings about Greece and Rome but also interactive games, ancient works of art, and links to other resources.

Exploring Ancient World Cultures on the World Wide Web
http://eawc.evansville.edu/about.htm

Hosted by the University of Evansville and Anthony F. Beavers, this outstanding Web site is designed to assist students and teachers in their exploration of the ancient world. Its users will find primary and secondary sources, images, and annotated links to dozens of other sites that focus on ancient Greece and Rome.

Historical Novels: Ancient History
www.historicalnovels.info/Ancient.html

Maintained by Margaret Donsbach, this site contains an annotated list of hundreds of historical novels about ancient Greece and Rome.

Perseus Digital Library
www.perseus.tufts.edu/hopper

Hosted by Gregory R. Crane and Tufts University, this Web site provides full access to hundreds of primary and secondary sources on the history, culture, and politics of ancient Greece and Rome.

NOTES

1 This section and the next draw on the following works: John Dunn, *Democracy: A History* (New York: Atlantic Monthly Press, 2005), Chap. 1; Mogens H. Hansen, *The Athenian Democracy in the Age of Demosthenes* (Oxford: Blackwell, 1991); Tom Holland, *Persian Fire: The First World Empire and the Battle for the West* (New York: Anchor Books, 2005); Simon Hornblower, "Creation and Development of Democratic Institutions in Ancient Greece," in *Democracy: The Unfinished Journey, 508 BC to AD 1993*, ed. John Dunn (Oxford: Oxford University Press, 1992), 1–16; Carl J. Richard, *Twelve Greeks and Romans Who Changed the World* (Lanham, Md.: Rowman and Littlefield, 2003), 36–41.

2 The quotations in this paragraph are from Holland, *Persian Fire,* 107.

3 Ibid., 127.

4 Hornblower, "Creation and Development," 7.

5 I. F. Stone in *The Trial of Socrates* (New York: Anchor, 1989; originally 1988), 216.

6 For a succinct yet classic comparison, see Karl Jaspers, *Socrates, Buddha, Confucius, Jesus: The Paradigmatic Individuals,* ed. Hannah Arendt, trans. Ralph Manheim (San Diego, Calif.: Harcourt Brace, 1962; originally published in German in 1957).

7 See I. F. Stone's intriguing account of how a free society tolerated and then condemned its most ardent critic; ibid., esp. 9, 39, and 99.

8 Polybius's analysis appears in "Rome at the End of the Punic Wars," Book 6 of his *History.*

9 Two excellent histories of Rome, one spanning the full history of the city through the end of the western empire and the other focusing on the fall of the republic, are Christopher S. Mackay, *Ancient Rome: A Military and Political History* (Cambridge, UK: Cambridge University Press, 2005); Tom Holland, *Rubicon: The Last Years of the Roman Republic* (New York: Doubleday, 2004). For a classic depiction of the Roman Republic as an increasingly fragile and corrupt oligarchy, see Sir Ronald Syme, *The Roman Revolution* (Oxford: Oxford University Press, 1939, and later editions). See also the classic biography of Julius Caesar, Matthias Gelzer, *Caesar: Politician and Statesman,* trans. Peter Needham (Cambridge, Mass.: Harvard University Press, 1968). For a modern challenge, see Fergus Millar, *The Crowd in Rome in the Late Republic* (Ann Arbor: University of Michigan Press, 1998); Fergus Millar, *The Roman Republic and the Augustan Revolution,* ed. Hannah M. Cotton and Guy M. Rogers (Chapel Hill: University of North Carolina Press, 2002); Fergus Millar, *The Roman Republic in Political Thought* (Hanover, N.H.: University Press of New England, 2002).

10 See Sir Ronald Syme, *The Roman Revolution* (Oxford: Oxford University Press, 1939, and later editions); Pat Southern, *Augustus* (London: Routledge, 1998).

11 Ernest Fortin, "St. Thomas Aquinas," in *History of Political Philosophy,* 3rd ed., ed. Leo Strauss and Joseph Cropsey (Chicago: University of Chicago Press, 1987), 271.

12 R. R. Palmer, Joel Colton, and Lloyd Kramer, *A History of the Modern World,* 10th ed. (Boston: McGraw Hill, 2007), 15.

BIG IDEAS

- The model of republicanism in biblical Israel differs from those of ancient Greece or Rome.

- The biblical model of republicanism defines the republic as a holy commonwealth established by political covenant.

- Political covenants can be used to chart the major stages in the constitutional development of biblical Israel.

- The major stages of constitutional development in biblical Israel include the confederation of the twelve tribes established at Mount Sinai, the united constitutional monarchy established by King David, the Jewish communities formed in Babylonian exile, the Second Commonwealth established by the Succoth covenant, and the Hasmonean dynasty founded after the Maccabeen Revolt.

Purpose of This Chapter

The European experience with republican ideas occupies a central place in the history of government. Republican ideas, however, developed independently the world over. This chapter focuses on one of the most important non-European examples of republicanism—biblical Israel. Jerusalem, Athens, and Rome were three of the great cities of the ancient world that offered differing models of classical republicanism. Much less is known about the Jerusalem model of covenantal republicanism than about the Athenian *polis* or the Roman Republic. The history of republican ideas in biblical Israel, however, provides powerful political insights and perspectives not found in ancient Athens or Rome. This chapter takes a closer look at the constitutional development of biblical Israel from Moses to Nehemiah—a time span of nearly 1,000 years.

Terms to Know

charisma	*edah*	messiah
constitutionalism	federalism	monotheism
constitutional monarchy	fidelity	political covenant
covenant	Hellenization	separation of powers
diaspora	Judaism	

WHAT DISTINGUISHES BIBLICAL ISRAEL AS A MODEL OF REPUBLICANISM?

Biblical Israel holds a well-known place in history as the birthplace of **Judaism**—the first world religion based on **monotheism** (the belief in one God). Less known is Israel's political significance as the first republican state, in Asia if not the world. Rarely are these two sides of Israel's history studied together.

But neglecting Israel's political history is a mistake. According to biblical tradition, the Israelites formed a monotheistic and republican polity at the same moment—around 1300 BCE—at Mount Sinai. And those two strands of Israel's history and the history of the Jewish people have been intertwined ever since.

Biblical texts are among the oldest and most detailed written clues to the political organization of ancient republics outside Europe. For thousands of years, its simple stories have provided human beings with a source of inspiration and guidance in the conduct of their personal lives. At the same time, these stories are a rich source of political instruction and moral lessons about how societies should be governed and toward what end. All the reasons for the success and failure of republics are played out time and time again in this one small land. It is this quality that turns these stories into political parables of republican self-government. These stories offer valuable political insights, as does the political guidance offered by sacred texts of other peoples—from the Letters of Paul to the teachings of the Buddha.

WHAT ARE THE CORNERSTONES OF BIBLICAL ISRAEL AS A REPUBLIC?

Edah is the Hebrew equivalent of both the Greek *polis* (polity) and the Roman republic.[1] The three concepts are similar in that they refer to a republican society with a form of

MORE ABOUT . . .

Jewish Revolts

The Maccabean Revolt erupted in the 160s BCE when Antiochus IV, the Seleucid king, sought to Hellenize Judea and had the effrontery to turn the Jerusalem Temple into a pagan shrine where pork was offered as a sacrifice on the altar.

The Jewish War, or the Great Revolt, broke out under Roman rule one hundred years later in 66 BCE. Roman procurators (administrators of conquered provinces) had turned Judea (Latin for Judah) into a kleptocracy (literally "rule by thieves"; a corrupt government in which rulers use the powers of government for their own personal financial benefit). Procurator Florus carried this too far when he raided the Temple for its treasures, precipitating the Jewish War.

The Bar Kochba Uprising (132–135 CE), named after its leader, began when Roman Emperor Hadrian sought to assimilate the Jewish people by erasing Judaism. He

This silver coin created during the Bar Kochba Uprising (132–135 CE) has "For the Freedom of Jerusalem" inscribed on its reverse side.

prohibited circumcision. Under penalty of death, he also banned the ordination of rabbis, the observance of the Sabbath, the public reading of the Torah, and the teaching of law. The last straw for the Jewish people was his erecting a Roman shrine to the god Jupiter on the site of the Jerusalem Temple.

government based on the consent of the citizenry and the rule of law. There is, however, a world of difference between the Israelite model of republicanism and the Greek and Roman models of republicanism.

The Israelite model defines the republic as a holy commonwealth based on the monotheistic belief in divine revelation. Guidance comes from prophets who convey God's deep concern for the human plight, exhort the people, check the power of kings and priests, and uncloak false prophets.[2] The Greek model relies on the application of reason in a polytheistic world. Guidance is supplied by philosophers, who have sharpened their powers of reason. The Roman model builds on the pragmatic application of the rule of law to conflicts over freedom and order. Guidance is provided by statesmen such as Cicero, who are trained in the law. The difference among these three models is not simply theoretical. Conquerors often took violent measures to Hellenize and then Romanize Israel. And these efforts precipitated Jewish rebellions on at least three occasions.[3] (See More About . . . Jewish Revolts.)

The Israelite model of *edah*, then, is a holy commonwealth with a divinely inspired moral purpose. It is created as an association of people who form a covenant with one another and with God or with God's blessing. (See Bold Thinkers: Leo Strauss on Jerusalem and Athens.)

BOLD THINKERS

Leo Strauss on Jerusalem and Athens

Leo Strauss (1899–1973) was an influential professor of political philosophy who taught generations of students, primarily at the University of Chicago. According to his daughter, herself a professor of classics, Strauss "insistently confronted his students with the question of the 'good life.' For him, the choice boiled down to the life in accordance with Revelation or the life according to Reason—Jerusalem versus Athens. The vitality of Western tradition, he felt, lay in the invigorating tension between the two."[1]

In 1967, Strauss wrote a seminal article on Jerusalem and Athens in which he compared biblical faith and Greek thought. He focused his comparison on the Greek philosopher Socrates and biblical prophets such as Isaiah and Jeremiah. Strauss argued that both Socrates and the prophets shared a belief in the centrality of justice and righteousness, and in their connectivity. For both, individuals' doing the morally right thing and acting justly or fairly toward one another were one and the same. For Socrates and the prophets, the ideal society was one free of evil because of its perfectly just nature. They differed, according to Strauss, in their beliefs about the perfect society. The prophets believed that human nature and, hence, society can and will be perfected in a messianic age (see Isaiah 11). For the prophets, this belief was an act of faith in divine revelation. By contrast, Socrates believed that the perfect society is possible but unlikely because human nature is incorrigible. It cannot be improved, let alone perfected. For Socrates, this basic truth, like all true knowledge, came not from divine revelation but from science and reason. Socrates, like Plato, also believed that only the philosophers held such knowledge and that the best possible society could come only when these philosophers were kings. Aristotle rejected this view and looked instead to a balanced constitution that represented the major interests and ideals of society.

---

1. Jenny Strauss Clay, "The Real Leo Strauss," *New York Times,* June 7, 2003, Sec. A, 15, available at www.nytimes.com/2003/06/07/opinion/the-real-leo-strauss.html.

The *edah* has taken several forms. From biblical accounts, these included:

- the mobile polity organized by Moses at Mount Sinai
- the permanent polity led by Joshua in the land of Canaan
- the tribal republics governed by the judges
- the united constitutional monarchy of David and Solomon
- the divided kingdoms of Israel and Judah
- the small communities created in exile, first during the Babylonian Diaspora
- the reformed republic of Ezra and Nehemiah
- the vassal state ruled by the Greeks and Seleucids
- the commonwealth that fought for its independence under the leadership of the Hasmoneans (popularly known as the Maccabees)

In each form it has taken, the *edah* was established by a covenant (*brit* in Hebrew) or, more specifically, a political covenant.

A **covenant** is an agreement in which God is invoked as either a party or a witness. In the Near East, the earliest covenants were treaties. There were two types of commonly used treaties: 1) treaties between equal nations and 2) suzerainty (unequal treaties). An example of an equal treaty is one between the Egyptians and the Hittites. A suzerainty, on the other hand, involved a conquering nation as overlord. An example of suzerainty is between the Sumerian Empire and a conquered vassal people.

In the Book of Genesis, the early covenants between God and the patriarchs—Noah, Abraham, and Jacob—took the form of suzerainty treaties. God was the lord; the Hebrews were his subjects. God initiated these early covenants and dictated their terms. They did not take effect until the patriarch consented to the terms. Circumcision became the sign of the covenant with Abraham. By God's commandment, it is performed on every Jewish male when he is eight days old.

In the Book of Exodus, the Ten Commandments and other covenants adopted at Mount Sinai were very different from the existing models of equal and unequal treaties. The Mount Sinai experience was a transformative event. In this classical biblical tale, around 1300 BCE Moses led the Jewish people in a daring escape from Egyptian bondage into the Sinai desert, where they gathered themselves at Mount Sinai. There, God, Moses, the Jewish people, and their tribal leaders all formed a covenant with one another to transform the Jewish people, called Hebrews, into citizens of a new polity called Israel.

Biblical scholar Nahum Sarna put his finger on the two revolutionary differences between the Sinai model of covenants and the ancient Near Eastern treaty models. First, the Sinai covenants did not simply regulate foreign relations; they regulated every aspect of human life and society. Second, the parties making the covenant expanded from the leaders of two states to God and an entire people.[4] In those two respects, the Ten Commandments and the other Sinai covenants established the rule of law, thereby meeting one of the criteria of what it means to be a republic.

The rule of law begins with the idea that no person is above the law (see Chapter 9). At Sinai, the Israelites accepted God's law as the supreme law—all human laws must conform to that higher law. Other Near Eastern societies at the time were governed by kings who were considered to be gods or descended from gods. These kings made their own law. In the absence of separation of powers, they often also served as the high priests and judges who interpreted the law.

Republics also must be based on the consent of the citizenry. Beginning with the Sinai covenants, biblical covenants became more consent-based and egalitarian: (1) God negotiates with the Israelite leaders; (2) God urges those leaders to call an assembly of all the people; and (3) there are covenants between political leaders and an assembly of all the people in which all the people consent to obey God's commandments. Joshua succeeds Moses, and beginning with Joshua's covenant, leaders initiate covenants directly with the people and bring in God as a witness rather than a party. There is, in a word, an element of trust that begins to open up all of these covenantal relationships.

Over time, the Israelites became adept at forming covenants for political purposes. As the idea evolved, a **political covenant** came to mean an agreement in which people voluntarily come together as equal partners and bind themselves both to each other and to God, and God is a party or witness to the agreement. The goal of this type of covenant is to form or reform a republic that is dedicated to the common good in the form of a divinely inspired moral purpose.

Daniel J. Elazar, a political scientist and a biblical scholar, wrote an important book that lays out the constitutional history of biblical Israel. According to Elazar, the political covenant was an instrument of constitutional change.[5] The Hebrew Bible (the Torah, or five books of Moses) contains twenty-four such covenants—from the covenant with Noah to the covenants of Ezra and Nehemiah.[6] There are also postbiblical covenants, such as the Hasmonean covenant (see Table 12.1).

Table 12.1 Constitutional Development of Israel in Biblical and Postbiblical Times to the Roman Occupation (63 BCE)

Approximate dates (all dates BCE)	Constitutional covenants and forms of government
1300	The Sinai, or Mosaic, covenants mark the transition of the Israelites from a people to a polity founded on the Ten Commandments.
Date uncertain	The Deuteronomic Constitution expands on the Sinai covenants, establishing a framework of government, beliefs, and social relations.
Beginning 1260	Joshua's covenant establishes a sedentary polity in Canaan with a fixed territory for each of the twelve tribes. Ten tribes are established in the northern region called Israel. Two tribes are established in the southern region called Judah (later renamed Judea by the Romans).
Beginning 1200	Tribal covenants initiated by judges (such as Deborah and Samson) legitimize judges' rule for two centuries after Joshua's death.
Beginning 1020	Saul's covenant authorizes the transformation of Israel from a republican confederation to a united constitutional monarchy with Saul as its king.
Beginning 1000	The Davidic covenant authorizes the continuation of a united monarchy with David as king.
965–930	Solomon's covenant authorizes construction of the First Temple and establishment of the First Commonwealth.
930	The monarchy is permanently divided when Rehoboam of Judah, Solomon's son, insults the northern tribes. The northern tribes secede, form the Northern Kingdom of Israel, and elect Jeroboam as their king.
930–721	Nineteen kings rule the Northern Kingdom for more than two hundred years until it is conquered by the Assyrians in 721 BCE.
930–587	Nineteen kings rule the Southern Kingdom of Judah for roughly 350 years until it is conquered by the Babylonians in 587 BCE; the Davidic covenant is renewed four times in Judah. Asa, king of Judah (roughly 910–870), prohibits paganism and defends the land against two invasions. Jehoiada the Priest restores the Davidic monarchy in 837 BCE. Hezekiah, king of Judah (715–687), reunites the monarchy. Josiah, king of Judah (640–609), restores constitutional rule.

(Continued)

Table 12.1 (Continued)

Approximate dates (all dates BCE)	Constitutional covenants and forms of government
Beginning 587	Babylonians conquer Judah and deport the Jewish people to Babylonia, where they reinvent covenants to form congregational communities.
Beginning 539	Cyrus I, ruler of the Persian Empire, conquers the Babylonian Empire and allows the Israelites to return to Israel.
	Israel is confined to the Jerusalem city-state of Judah, which becomes a self-governing vassal state in the Persian Empire for more than two hundred years until it is conquered by Alexander the Great.
	The Succoth covenant (around 440 BCE), the last of the biblical covenants, renews the Sinai covenant and paves the way for the Second Commonwealth.
Beginning 331	Alexander the Great conquers Judah and the Persian Empire.
	Israel is occupied as a self-governing vassal state of Alexander's short-lived empire, and then as a vassal state to the Syrian-based Seleucid Empire and the Egyptian-based Ptolemaic Empire.
	Hellenism (Greek culture) is the dominant intellectual and cultural influence; some Jews are swayed by Hellenism, but others rebel.
Beginning 168	Antiochus IV, Seleucid king, imposes Hellenistic restrictions on Jewish practices and desecrates the Second Temple.
	A Jewish revolt is led by the priestly Hasmonean family.
Beginning 140	Simeon, Judah Maccabee's brother, initiates first major postbiblical covenant that alters the Succoth Constitution.
63	Rome annexes Israel.

Sources: Daniel J. Elazar, *Covenant & Polity in Biblical Israel: Biblical Foundations and Jewish Expressions, Vol. 1: The Covenant Tradition in Politics* (New Brunswick, N.J.: Transaction Publishers, 1995), 212–213. Dating relies primarily on Raymond P. Scheindlin, *A Short History of the Jewish People* (New York: Oxford University Press, 2000).

Political covenants have been put to various constitutional uses. They have created polities, established governments, significantly altered forms of government, reformed political and religious life, and renewed earlier covenants. Together, they represent the major turning points and stages in the constitutional development of biblical Israel. They also embody the idea that government should be limited.

HOW DID BIBLICAL ISRAEL EVOLVE AS A TRIBAL CONFEDERACY?

THE SINAI COVENANTS

The Sinai covenants established Israel as a polity. According to biblical accounts, the Sinai covenants were initiated by God with Moses and via Moses with the leaders of the tribes. Some of these covenants were made at Mount Sinai in the beginning of their desert wanderings; others were made in Moab toward the end of their wanderings. The most famous of the Sinai covenants relates to the Ten Commandments, also known by its Greek name, the Decalogue.

At Sinai, the Israelites became a full-fledged polity. They agreed to adopt the Ten Commandments, which became the new polity's first principles and the preamble to their constitution. The polity was designed as a mobile polity, suitable for a life of wandering in the desert. God even instructed the Jewish people how to pack the Ten Commandments, or covenant, for the journey. They were told to (1) build a wooden container for the Ten Commandments, known as the Ark of the Covenant; (2) attach strong poles to each corner of the Ark so it could be carried; and (3) fashion a collapsible tent, called the Tabernacle of the Covenant, which could be set up for special ceremonies along the way.

The new government was a theocracy in the sense that God ruled through Moses as his prime minister. (His successor Joshua was the only other leader to govern with this title.) In this position, Moses acted as a prophet who interpreted God's word. In a separate covenant, God appointed Moses' brother Aaron and his sons to be the priests. They acted as a court of last resort and organized religious rituals.

The Israelites also remained a confederation of tribes. The tribal elders became the judges. Executive responsibility for day-to-day administration was turned over to other tribal leaders who became magistrates of the new polity. Ultimately, the new government was a republic. The tribal elders gathered as a council to make decisions. The entire people (including women and children) acted as the body politic and came together in a general assembly to give their consent to important decisions.[7]

This was a mixed republican form of government based on the principle of separation of powers. Three *ketarim* (literally, "crowns" or domains) were created: (1) the civil leadership, represented by tribal elders and judges; (2) the religious leadership, represented by a high priest (Aaron) and a priestly class that began with his sons and their descendants; and (3) the prophetic leadership, represented by Moses and responsible for teaching the Torah and the word of God. Each major stage of Israel's constitutional development that followed reconstituted this tripartite division of powers (see Table 12.2).

Table 12.2 Separation of Powers in the Constitutional Development of Israel

	Tribal confederacy	Constitutional monarchy	Second Commonwealth	Hasmonean dynasty
Covenant	Sinai	Davidic	Succoth	Hasmonean
Civil leader	Tribal elders	King	Great Assembly	Priest-king
Religious leader	High priest	High priest	High priest	
Prophetic leadership	Prime minister	Prophet	Scribes	Sanhedrin

Source: Daniel J. Elazar, *Covenant & Polity in Biblical Israel: Biblical Foundations and Jewish Expressions, Vol. 1: The Covenant Tradition in Politics* (New Brunswick, N.J.: Transaction Publishers, 1995).

In 1947, a Bedouin shepherd looking for a stray goat entered a cave near the Dead Sea and found ancient jars filled with scrolls. Biblical scholars soon realized that the scrolls contained many portions of the Hebrew Bible, including Deuteronomy. With some scrolls dating to the third century BCE, they are older than any other biblical manuscripts. Scholars are still working to restore and publish the scrolls.

THE DEUTERONOMIC CONSTITUTION

After their Mount Sinai sojourn, Moses led his people into the Sinai Desert, where the Bible records their wanderings of forty years. In actuality, they were not a nomadic people who were constantly in motion; they were a semi-nomadic people who spent time at different oases. The Kadesh-barnea oasis served as a major gathering and resting point where the people, tribal elders, and appointed leaders had the time try out their new institutions and get used to them.[8]

Toward the end of their wanderings, the Israelites reached the Plains of Moab. Here, according to biblical accounts, Moses wrote out the entire constitution of the Israelites in the Book of Deuteronomy, one of the five books of the Torah. (Today, most scholars believe that Deuteronomy was written much later and that it codified provisions of the Mosaic constitution that had been revised and updated over the centuries.)

The provisions of this constitution include a restatement and expansion of first principles, provisions about the land, provisions about the authority and powers of governmental institutions, criminal laws and procedures, a bill of rights, and civil laws and obligations (including neighborliness and the regulation of lending, farming, safety and hygiene, sexual practices, marriage, divorce, and naturalization). As a covenant, this constitution also contained blessings and curses. Finally, the Deuteronomy Constitution recorded Moses' rewriting of the Torah, his transfer of leadership to Joshua, and his death.[9] The people gathered as an assembly to approve this constitution and renew earlier covenants.

By rewriting the Torah, Moses affirmed his legal station—not as lawgiver (that was God's role) but as the transmitter of the law. In that laborious act of rewriting, Moses also affirmed that he was bound by the law. The Book of Deuteronomy confirms these points when it provides that Israel may have a king but that he must be elected by the people and he must follow the law. To do that, the king must have read the Torah all his life. He must do this "to revere the Lord his God" and "to observe faithfully every word of this Teaching as well as these laws."[10] These instructions are an early expression of the idea of **constitutionalism**, the belief that governments receive their authority from and are limited by a higher law than their own.

JOSHUA'S COVENANT

As the Book of Joshua records, Joshua, Moses' heir, initiated this covenant, making it the first of the constitution-like covenants that was initiated by humans, not God. Joshua struck this covenant with tribal representatives before God at Shechem, the place where Abraham entered Canaan and built an altar. Joshua initiated this covenant only after he led the tribes into the Promised Land of Canaan and they had established their own territory by conquering their foes. Ten tribes settled in the northern lands, called Israel. Two tribes settled in the south, known as Judah.

Joshua's covenant marked the transition of the Israelite's polity from a semi-nomadic existence to a permanent state of settlement. This required various adjustments, including the location of the Torah in a permanent Ark. Joshua retained the position of prime minister previously held by Moses, a position that was more like a prophet than an executive.

After the death of Joshua, the central leadership position of prime minister was abolished. Political power floated back to the tribes and the elders of the confederation. According to the Book of Judges, the elders increasingly turned to tribal judges for assistance. Originally, the judges were primarily responsible for resolving legal disputes. But, as time went on, the tribal judges assumed the responsibilities of military leadership and executive administration. Eventually, those responsibilities took as much or more time as their legal responsibilities. Leadership remained diffuse and scattered among the tribes. The tribes bickered with one another. Judges such as Samson could raise troops to defeat minor foes but not the major threat—the Philistines.

This phase of history was assessed in the Book of Judges. The assessment was mixed. There was general agreement that the political system was out of balance—in the absence of unified leadership, the tribal forces of diversity and diffusion had become too strong.

Samuel was a judge who rose to national prominence as a prophet. Other leaders looked to him to unify the country and defeat the Philistines. Samuel was certainly a wise man, but he was not a military leader. The Israelites encountered defeat after defeat before the advancing Philistines, who finally captured the Ark of the Covenant around 1050 BCE.

HOW DID A REPUBLICAN STATE EMERGE IN ISRAEL?

SAUL'S COVENANTS

The capture of the Ark was the last straw. Tribal leaders pressured the aging and despondent prophet Samuel to find and anoint a king who could unite them and defeat the Philistines. "Appoint a king for us," they said, "to govern us like all other nations."[11] (The phrase *like other nations* indicates how commonplace monarchy had become.)

Samuel bemoaned the sorry state of affairs that had pushed the leaders of a republican people to beg for a king. He lectured the tribal leaders on what they could expect of life under a monarchy—even a constitutionally limited one. A king, said Samuel, will take your sons for his armies, your daughters for his court, and a tenth of all you own for his treasury. The leaders were not dissuaded.

At Samuel's behest, God found a suitable king—Saul of the southern tribe of Benjamin—and brought him to Samuel. Around 1020 BCE, Samuel anointed Saul king with the acclamation of the tribal elders. The shift to monarchy was so important that Samuel also called a full assembly of the people, who gave their consent.[12] (See More About . . . Anointing Kings.)

Saul's covenants were most unusual. They were initiated by the tribal leaders, who handed over many of their military and financial powers to a reluctant king in the hopes that he could unite them and defeat the Philistines. Usually, it is the king who must persuade reluctant tribes or noblemen to unite. Saul was Israel's first king. Together, he, the tribes, and Samuel reconstituted Israel as a united constitutional monarchy. If Saul had defeated the Philistines and restored peace, Israel might have transitioned from a tribal society into a state, but it was not meant to be.

Saul tried to unite the tribes of Israel and Judah, but tensions developed from the start. There were tensions between the republican culture of the Israelites and the centralizing demands of a confederation at war against a powerful enemy. There were also tensions between the tribes that felt some allegiance to Saul and those that did not. Historically, the levy or mobilization of troops had been a tribal matter. Saul had acquired this power, but only some of the tribes allowed him to exercise it.

For the next twenty years, Saul led his troops into one battle after another. At one point, he recruited mercenaries and rebuilt an army of paid professional soldiers. They demanded the right to take booty (that is, the plunder of vanquished enemies). Samuel the prophet had long forbidden the practice, but Saul decided to authorize it.

In that decision, Saul crossed the line that separates the legitimate use of power and its abuse. He violated long-established Israelite traditions of warfare by allowing the taking of booty. He also violated constitutional procedures by countermanding Samuel. From this time forward, the prophets became vigilant watchdogs of royal usurpation and an institutional check on the king's powers.

Employing mercenaries (and allowing them to take booty) did not help to win the war. Saul began to lose battles and fell into the depths of depression. At night, Saul's depression worsened. He flew into dangerous fits of rage and jealousy that impaired his judgment. The

MORE ABOUT . . .

Anointing Kings

To *anoint* means "to rub with oil." In the ancient Near East, it was common practice to cleanse and purify the body with oils such as olive oil. Those who could afford it added scented spices such as frankincense and myrrh. In Exodus, God instructs the priests in how to make holy oil from a blend of oils and spices to be used to consecrate (set apart) the Ark and Tabernacle of the Covenant. This holy oil was later used to anoint Saul as king. When applied to kings and others appointed to high office, anointment symbolizes the divine gift of authority (that is, the right to govern) and charisma (that is, the ability to govern by inspiring others). See especially the Septuagint and Vulgate version of I Samuel 10:1. The title *Christ* is from the Greek *kristos*, meaning "the anointed one."

Samuel is shown anointing Saul in this medieval French manuscript illumination.

Bible makes it clear that Saul suffered from a deep character flaw that made him unfit for rule. Around 1000 BCE, Saul saw his troops decimated and his sons killed at the battle of Mount Gilboa. Desperate and depressed, Saul threw himself on his sword. The Philistines beheaded Saul and hung his body on a fortress wall side by side with those of his sons.[13]

The story of Saul shows that declarations of unity and monarchy are not enough to win wars. Good leadership is essential—both by tribal leaders and by the king. God had endowed Saul with **charisma**, the gift to inspire others, that is, the ability to govern. But Saul had allowed that charismatic authority to slip through his fingers by indulging in self-pity and allowing his emotions to cloud his judgment.

THE DAVIDIC COVENANTS

The Davidic covenants are David's covenants with God, tribal representatives, and the people. Together, those covenants reunited the monarchy by establishing David as king and recognizing his progeny as a dynasty. His rise to power and reign are recorded in the Books of Samuel.

The biblical stories of David and Saul are closely intertwined. Saul was king from 1020 to 1000 BCE. Sometime in the second half of his reign, Saul's downward spiral became so apparent that God decided to find and anoint a new king in secret. He took Samuel the prophet on this secret mission to Bethlehem in Judah. They visited the house of Jesse, where Samuel interviewed each of Jesse's sons beginning with the eldest. God selected the youngest, David, and decided to transfer the gift of charisma, or divine inspiration, from Saul to David. Samuel secretly anointed David then and there. At the time, David's older brothers were soldiers in Saul's army, but the Bible describes David as a shepherd boy, old enough to bring food and water to his brothers in battle but not old enough to fight.

Biblical stories differ on the sequence of what happened next. In one version, David was first sent to soothe Saul. This episode reveals David's poetic side. He soothed Saul's depression and rage in the evenings by playing the lyre or harp and reciting psalms. Saul welcomed David into his home, where David and Saul's son Jonathan became instant friends. In a second version, before meeting Saul, David demonstrated his skill and courage as a warrior by killing Goliath, the Philistine's champion, with a stone from his shepherd's sling. (See More About . . . Three Faces of David.)

Whichever side of David was revealed first, Saul quickly recognized David's leadership qualities. Saul made David a commander of his armies and gave his daughter Michal to David in marriage. David's popularity soared—on the battlefield, among the people, and within Saul's own family. Clearly there was more than charisma at work. Young David had natural abilities to inspire those around him.

Saul soon became jealous of David for having the same qualities that he had first admired. In a fit of rage, Saul branded David an outcast, and David became a brigand forced to live outside the king's law. During this period, David discovered yet another facet of his leadership abilities as a resourceful outcast. He raised a small fighting force of 600 loyal troops and continued to fight the Philistines while eluding Saul's troops. In the process, David matured into a young man and a military commander toughened by life on the run. It is difficult to say how long David lived the life of a brigand. Perhaps it was several years. If that was the case, the period would have been sometime between 1005 and 1000 BCE, when Saul died by his own sword at Mount Gilboa. At the time of Saul's death, David commanded the last military force in Israel. That gave David a small power base from which to maneuver.

David was still in his twenties, but he had an instinct for politics. It was now time to translate his secret covenant with God and anointment by Samuel into a political reality. He chose not to demand what was his by divine gift. Instead, as a native of Judah, he first went to the southern tribal elders and persuaded them to anoint him king of Judah. In the north, Saul's trusted commander Abner waged a rebellion against David's forces, but it quickly ended when Abner was killed. David instantly opened negotiations with the northern leaders, and they made him king of Israel in another covenant.

Within a year of Saul's death, David had reunited the kingdom and proceeded to unite the country. Around 995 BCE, he captured the Canaanite city of Jerusalem, which sat between the northern and southern tribes, and made it his capital. He then defeated the Philistines.

MORE ABOUT . . .

Three Faces of David

David has been a popular subject of artists' renderings and of our own imagination. The David that most readily comes to mind is the young David: shepherd boy, writer of psalms, and giant slayer. In the 1430s, the Italian Renaissance artist Donatello captured this youthful image—artistic, sensitive, and saucy. Donatello's David seems forever young, but David was no Peter Pan. He was a determined young man, secretly anointed king, proven in battle, and ready for leadership. This is the complex image of David captured by Michelangelo in his 1504 sculpture. Viewed from the front, the way most people do, Michelangelo's David is a powerful, well-sculpted figure of a man, ready for his next battle and confident about winning. But viewed from a different angle, where you can study David's face and look deeply into his soul, you can see another David—determined, focused, calculating his foe's next move.

David, by Michelangelo.

David, by Donatello.

DAVID AND THE FORMATION OF THE REPUBLICAN STATE

David helped transform Israel into a republican state. He centralized power but not completely. He created a united kingdom but not a unitary state. He built a powerful state, but he did so without destroying the republican, confederal, and covenantal pillars of the Israelite polity.

Israel became a united **constitutional monarchy**. The constitutional element placed real limits on the powers of the king by forcing the king to share power with other political institutions that were sufficiently powerful to make sure the king complied. These power-sharing institutions were of two types: (1) the priests and prophets, as a biblical precursor of the modern principle of **separation of powers,** in which national power is divided among three branches (see Table 12.2), and (2) the tribal leaders backed up by their militias, as a biblical precursor of the modern principle of **federalism,** in which national power is checked by the power of regional governments.

Separation of powers in ancient times was a logical consequence of the specialization of political institutions. In centralized chiefdoms, the king might have been a god, a priest, a warrior, and a lawmaker all rolled into one. As society became more complex, government institutions became more specialized. Eventually, there were separate people who were kings, priests, and generals. This was part of the larger transition from tribally based societies to state-based societies.

But there was more at work here than natural political evolution. There was also the monotheistic belief that a king could not be a god. While "elsewhere the king was a god, in Israel it was God who was king."[14] In addition, there was the republican belief that the king should not interfere in the duties of the priesthood to officiate at ceremonies or the duties of the prophets to interpret the word of God.

King David moved the constitutional offices of priests and prophets to Jerusalem and folded them into his court, but he was willing to observe their constitutional independence. Certainly, Nathan the prophet retained his independence even when he told David what he did not want to hear. The problem, as we have observed elsewhere, is that kings are too often unwilling to share power or uphold the independence of other power holders.

Some of David's successors lacked his faith in the constitutional separation of powers. They appointed false prophets who did their bidding, and these rulers also took on priestlier roles in religious ceremonies (such as burning incense in the Temple). The prophets, in turn, maintained that theirs was "the voice of supreme authority." The prophet "not only rivaled the decisions of the king and the counsel of the priest, he defied and even condemned their words and deeds"; the prophets did not condemn the monarchy as an institution, but they "insisted that human pretension to sovereignty was dangerous, a fake and a caricature."[15]

Federalism underwent a significant change when the united constitutional monarchy was created. For centuries, the twelve tribes had been the central authority in the tribal confederacy established at Sinai. In the new constitutional monarchy, they became member parts of a national federal system. That transition was comparable in one way to the transition 2,800 years later from the Articles of Confederation to the U.S. Constitution of 1787; that is, the tribal leaders and the king had to learn how to share power in a brand new kind of federal system.

Balance was maintained by the constant tension between the centralizing forces of David's court and the noncentralizing forces of the twelve tribes and their leaders. Neither side vanquished the other or surrendered to it. But there was ongoing tribal unrest and occasional tribal rebellion.

There were various sources of tension and balance.[16] David embarked on national programs of economic development and national defense. He undertook major public construction projects from roads to public buildings. He also built a national standing army of mercenaries that defeated and obliterated many foreign armies. On one hand, these projects brought considerable prosperity and protection to the commonwealth. On the other hand, he increased taxes to pay for these projects, and he increased the conscription of young men to work on them. He also built a national bureaucracy to oversee these projects as well as tax collection and conscription. As we have seen, these are all natural developments in the transition from tribally based to state-based societies (see Chapter 4).

Understandably, many of these developments angered tribal leaders. They accused David of favoring one region over another in his building program. They also understood that David relied on mercenaries rather than tribal militias so that he would not have to worry about the conflicting tribal loyalties of his men. On various occasions, tribes rebelled. David's army defeated all rebellions, but he ordered his army to show restraint. No tribes or militias were obliterated, which showed a great measure of restraint in ancient times.

Jerusalem was another source of tension. David conquered Jerusalem and then rebuilt the city as the geographical and political center of Israel. This was a major drain on the national treasury, and the tribes saw no direct benefit from it. David dreamed of building a central temple in Jerusalem, bringing the Ark of the Covenant to it, and making that city the religious center of Israel. But the prophet Nathan told him that his wish would be denied. Moreover, the tribal priests made it clear that they were unwilling to give up their regional shrines, so David relented.

Within twenty years, David succeeded where Saul had failed. David not only defeated the Philistines but also every other foe and potential foe in the region. In the process, he transformed Israel into the largest and mightiest state in the Near East. Israel was prosperous and at peace. But this did little to quiet the resentment of tribal leaders, many of whom did everything they could to check David's power.

Despite the constitutional limits of David's monarchy, there was a striking difference between the Davidic and Mosaic covenants with God. As Chaim Potok explained, "The Mosaic covenant required of each family that it establish a certain relationship with YHWH [Yahweh]; the Davidic covenant was a move in the direction of making the king and the state intermediate between the people and YHWH."[17]

HOW DID SOLOMON AND REHOBOAM CORRUPT THE REPUBLICAN STATE?

THE REIGN OF SOLOMON

Around 965 BCE, David died and his son Solomon became king. Like his father, Solomon presided over a united monarchy for nearly forty years, and like his father, Solomon is credited with many achievements that strengthened the kingdom. Yet, as in his father's reign, there was discord and dissension beneath the surface. David was the warrior-king who united the tribes, formed a republican state, and expanded and secured its borders. Solomon was the statesman-king who used his renowned wisdom and negotiating skills to bring peace and prosperity to the Israelites—at least for awhile.

Solomon's accomplishments are indeed impressive. Early in his reign, he focused on the economic development of the country. He established commercial treaties and safe trade routes with neighboring powers. He developed the copper mining industry as a source of trade and state revenue. Israel became a powerful trading empire. The country increased in population and prosperity, new cities were founded, literature and the arts flourished.

The population also became more diverse during Solomon's reign. Solomon sealed his agreements by marriage alliances. Although this practice was not uncommon, Solomon took it to excess. According to the I Book of Kings, Solomon's harem numbered seven hundred wives and three hundred concubines. Exaggeration made the obvious point—Solomon had many foreign wives. Less obvious is that commerce brings foreign influences and cultural diversity. Solomon knew that, and he fostered it in his personal life and in the public life of the nation. But he went too far, and that was his undoing.

Prosperity and increased revenue allowed Solomon to embark on a massive building program. His crowning achievement was the building of the First Temple in Jerusalem to house the Ark of the Covenant. The Temple was more than a symbol of national power. It consolidated the religious power of priests, shrines, rituals, and ceremonies in Jerusalem. Solomon recognized that this would drain the tribes of their religious power, so before beginning the project he persuaded tribal elders to agree and to seal the bargain with a covenant.

As wise as Solomon was, he allowed his desire for greatness to exceed the limits of his constitutional office. The costs of maintaining a large bureaucracy and his many building projects, including an elaborate palace, exceeded his revenues. He increased the tax burden on the people and conscripted able-bodied men as common laborers. To pay off a mounting trade deficit with the Phoenician city-state of Tyre, he gave that city a number of Israel's northern towns. That act angered the northern tribes.

Moreover, Solomon played favorites. He directed state revenues to his tribal lands of Judah and Jerusalem in the south, and he rewarded members of his court aristocracy with large gifts and contracts. Massive spending programs in Jerusalem and on its Temple incurred the wrath of the tribal priests and other tribal interests. Finally, toward the end of his reign, he supported the foreign gods of his foreign wives by building shrines to those gods. That angered God, who, according to biblical accounts, told Solomon that he would tear away Solomon's kingdom from his son, who would be left with only one tribe to rule.[18]

By the end of his reign, the united constitutional monarchy was unraveling at the seams. Royal excess, aristocratic greed, and policies of tribal favoritism had eroded much of Israel's republican base, and its constitutional framework crumbled. The situation was especially precarious in the north, where resentment was highest.

REHOBOAM DIVIDES THE STATE

When Solomon died in 930 BCE, his son Rehoboam became king. Rehoboam immediately traveled north to regain the support of the people of the northern tribes. What happened next is told in I Kings 12 and interpreted by the American historian Barbara Tuchman in her history of misgovernment by folly.[19]

Rehoboam was intercepted by a delegation of tribal leaders including Jeroboam, one of David's rebellious generals. They told him to lighten his father's yoke (that is, the taxes and conscriptions), and they would serve him. Rehoboam consulted with his council of elders who advised him to listen to the northern delegation. Be gracious and conciliatory, they advised, and he would win back the northern tribes forever. But Rehoboam turned next to his young friends and asked their advice. Tell them this, his cocky friends counseled: "My father imposed a heavy yoke on you, and I will add to your yoke; my father flogged you with whips, but I will flog you with scorpions."[20]

Swollen with the arrogance of power, Rehoboam took the advice of his rash friends. Disaster resulted. The Israelites of the north issued their now-famous response: "To your tents, O Israel! Now look to your own House, O David."[21] The northern tribes seceded, and the monarchy remained permanently divided and badly weakened.

By his actions, Rehoboam had broken David's covenants with God and the twelve tribes. The Davidic covenants were not fully renewed until the reign of Josiah three hundred years later. Rehoboam would go down in history as the king who was "ample in folly."[22]

WHO IS THE GOOD KING?

The Bible lavishes great attention on the leadership of David. According to Nahum Sarna's calculations, the Bible devotes 150 chapters to the forty-one kings of Israel—40 percent of those chapters focus on David.[23] Why is such attention lavished on David? What clue does this offer about the biblical view of good leadership?

According to Sarna, the Bible measures political leadership by one central standard—fidelity, not simply to God but to "centralized worship" and "its exclusive concentration" in Jerusalem.[24] Solomon earned the highest of praise when he built the Temple, and that was the basis of his covenant. He lost approval when he built shrines to foreign gods.

Fidelity is faithfulness to your obligations. In the biblical sense, this means faithfulness to covenantal obligations, beginning with the Ten Commandments. At its core, the covenant is an exchange of obligations; rights flow from those obligations, not the reverse.

Fidelity is not the only standard by which the Bible judges good leadership. Other standards—political judgment, wisdom, moderation, and valor—are also of value. But they gain in value only when the leader carries out covenantal obligations. Great reformers such as Nehemiah and Ezra were constitutional architects of the first order. They reformed government, the law, and the economy. Yet biblical accounts treat these achievements as secondary to and in service of their efforts to renew the Sinai covenants.

During the divided monarchy, fidelity to centralized worship came into conflict with republicanism. The northern tribes wanted to preserve their religious shrines, which were no less Jewish than the Temple in Jerusalem. Biblical accounts accuse their leaders of idolatry, yet historical accounts show that the republican idea of a limited constitutional monarchy was far stronger in the north than in the south. Historical evidence suggests that the tribes and prophets were stronger in the north as political checks on royal power and that the northern kings were more willing to heed the prophets and remain at peace with tribal leaders.[25]

By contrast, Judah became a centralized state with a powerful army. Over time, the tribal identities of Judah's people were submerged in the identity of the state. As a centralized state, Judah withstood conquest for nearly twice as long as the northern kingdom of Israel. Yet it also withstood the efforts of reformers who sought to restore the faithfulness of Judah's citizenry and the republicanism of its polity.

HOW DID HEZEKIAH AND JOSIAH REFORM JUDAH?

Thus far, we have seen political covenants used to establish and reconstitute the polity. Political covenants also have served a second major function—to right political wrongs. This function has been carried out by palace revolt, constitutional reform, covenantal renewal, and revolutions for national independence.

The northern tribes were conquered around 720 BCE by Assyria, the most powerful empire in the region. The Assyrians then deported most of the northern Israelites to upper Mesopotamia and imported captives from Syria and Babylonia into the north.[26] The northern tribes never regained their political footing as the prevailing polity in their own homeland.

In 715 BCE, only a few years after the Assyrians conquered the northern kingdom and deported its population, Hezekiah became the king of Judah. He ruled until his death in 687 BCE. He was a pious man, a great unifier, and a brilliant strategist. Judah became a vassal state in the Assyrian Empire and paid a handsome tribute to avoid invasion. Hezekiah realized that the Assyrians would not be satisfied with half a loaf. He expected a major Assyrian attack against Judah. He also saw a decline in the righteousness of Judeans, and he saw the remnant population of Israelites isolated in the north.

Hezekiah invited the Israelites remaining in the north and his fellow Judeans to a huge Passover celebration in Jerusalem. The celebration had powerful political significance. Passover was the remembering of the Hebrews' escape from bondage in Egypt. It also symbolized their transformation from Hebrews to Israelites and their entry into citizenship, a status legitimized by the Sinai covenants when the people became a citizenry. Observing Passover became an obligation of every citizen.[27] (See More About . . . Passover.)

A great number of Israelites participated in Hezekiah's Passover celebration. Hezekiah engaged the participants—northerners and southerners alike—in cleaning and purifying the streets of Jerusalem. In these civic and religious deeds, Hezekiah also gained the support of Isaiah the prophet. While civic spirits were high, the king persuaded northerners and southerners to reunite against the impending Assyrian invasion. Hezekiah's coalition building did not stop there; he helped forge an international coalition with neighboring states against the Assyrians.

MORE ABOUT . . .

Passover

Passover (*Pesach* in Hebrew) is the celebration of the Israelites' escape, or exodus, and liberation from slavery in Egypt around 1300 BCE. Since that time, Jewish people all over the world have assembled with family and friends to celebrate Passover on the fifteenth night of Nisan, the first month of the Hebrew calendar.

This important holiday lasts a week. During that time it is forbidden to eat or own any foods containing a leavening agent such as yeast. This commemorates the Jewish people's being forced to flee Egypt so quickly that they did not have time to wait for their bread dough to rise. Preparations for this holiday begin days in advance because the Jewish home must be thoroughly cleaned of all forbidden foods. In the process, excitement builds.

Jewish families begin Passover with a seder (the word *seder* means "order") as part of a special dinner. The specific order of the steps of a seder are detailed in a book, the *Haggadah*. Also detailed are ceremonial foods that symbolize the bitter and sweet aspects of freedom from slavery. Symbolic foods include matzah (unleavened

Jewish family praying before Seder dinner during Passover festival.

bread). Throughout the seder, certain questions are asked and answered, and children are encouraged to participate. In fact, certain questions are reserved for the youngest child present. The point of a seder is for celebrants to renew their citizenship and gain a deeper understanding of the importance of the Exodus. It is also an occasion to reach out and invite friends, out-of-towners who have no place to go, and others in need to celebrate.

Around 700 BCE, the fatal moment came when the Assyrians entered Judah with a mighty army. There was much devastation, and the Assyrians advanced on Jerusalem. Hezekiah had fortified the city for a long siege. He had strengthened the city's walls, built the Siloam tunnel as a source of water for the city, and dried up the surface water supplies that would have been available to the Assyrians. Then, according to 2 Chronicles, Hezekiah the king and Isaiah the prophet "cried out to the heavens" and God "sent an angel who annihilated" the Assyrian army.[28] The unification and fortification undoubtedly also helped. Whatever the reasons, the Assyrians turned back from their advance on Jerusalem, and the city was saved.

Josiah became king of Judah in 638 BCE at the age of eight. As Josiah grew to manhood, he observed the declining righteousness of his own people. Josiah began his reforms in the eighteenth year of his reign, around 620 BCE. He decided first to clean and repair the Temple. According to biblical accounts, the high priest discovered a scroll named "the book of the law," believed to be the lost Book of Deuteronomy. The book contained the Sinai covenant together with the Deuteronomic Constitution.[29]

Josiah then called a great assembly of the people and leaders of Judah and Jerusalem to gather at the Temple. Before this public assembly, Josiah read the entire scroll, drawing particular attention to the Sinai covenant, the laws of the constitution, and their obligations. He then persuaded the people and their leaders to make a covenant with him before God to obey all the covenants and laws in the book. The covenant was made, thereby renewing the Sinai covenants and adopting the Deuteronomic Constitution as the constitution of the land. This was a major constitutional reformation. Like Hezekiah's reforms, Josiah's did not last long after his time, but both left an enduring legacy for subsequent reformers.

By this time, Babylonia had replaced Assyria as the most powerful empire in the region. Less than twenty years after Josiah's constitutional reforms, the Babylonian army led by Nebuchadnezzar advanced on Judah and made it a vassal state. There were two rebellions, but both failed. In 587 BCE, the Babylonian army overran Jerusalem and destroyed it. The people were deported to Babylonia, where they remained in forced exile for nearly fifty years.

HOW WAS THE POLITY TRANSFORMED IN DIASPORA?

The Babylonian exile ended the Israelites' monarchy but not their sense of citizenship. The last Judean monarch was also exiled to Babylonia, where he lived along with the surviving Judean nobility and other exiled Jews. But how were they to survive as a polity, an *edah*, divided into small communities without a common territory or government? The Jewish people were not enslaved as they had been in Egypt a thousand years before, but they were a vassal people in a foreign land. Nonetheless, they still shared in common a collective memory of their political past, especially the recent reforms of Hezekiah and Josiah. The celebration of Passover and the discovery of the book of laws also gave them a common sense of citizenship.

Over time, the Jewish citizenry and their Judean elders in exile redefined the meaning of polity and citizenship around the Torah instead of around a unified form of government or the kings and priests who had led them in the past. The Torah became the means of instruction and socialization, both religious and political. Prevented from forming a unified polity, the Jewish people formed small civil communities. Within those communities they formed covenants in small groups to create religious congregations or assemblies (*knessot;* singular, *knesset*). Each congregation was housed in a *bet knesset,* commonly known as a synagogue (a Greek word that means "to bring together"). And within these congregations they looked to new leaders, called *rabbis,* who became their teachers of the Torah. The rabbinate was a more democratic institution than the priesthood. Priests had to be Levis (descendants of Aaron), and they formed an exclusive elite class.

This new form of *edah* was transformative. The idea of republicanism remained, but it was stronger and more democratic than before. The older republican forms and identities (tribe and state) were replaced by new forms and identities associated with the Jewish community. These new forms could be transported anywhere and reestablished everywhere. (To create a congregation required only ten male Jews.) This was the new political reality, and it was well suited to a dispersed people living in foreign lands.

Diaspora is the term used to refer to this new reality (derived from a Greek word meaning "to be dispersed or scattered"). Accompanying this new reality was a new hope for a **messiah**, a liberator who would lead them back to Jerusalem. Since then, this experiment has become the model of *edah* put into practice by millions of diaspora Jews around the world.

HOW DID THE SUCCOTH COVENANT RESTORE ISRAEL AS A REPUBLICAN POLITY?

Cyrus I of the Persian Empire was no messiah, but in 539 BCE he conquered the Babylonian Empire and allowed the Jewish people to return to Judah. Shortly thereafter, Cyrus recognized Judah (including Jerusalem) as a self-governing vassal state within the Persian Empire. For centuries, this was the last remaining nucleus of the once-mighty republican state of the Israelites.

Nehemiah was a Jewish administrator who served as the Persian Empire's provincial governor of Judah for a dozen or so years beginning around 445 BCE. At that time, Judah was a poor province, and Jerusalem was a city in disrepair. Nehemiah was sent to Jerusalem to oversee the physical restoration of the city. He began by rebuilding the walls that surrounded and protected the city. At the time, all self-respecting cities were walled cities—the walls defined the city, protected it from attack, and gave its residents a pride of place. Nehemiah's ultimate goal was to reestablish Judah as a constitutional republic. This was no small task, but he had a persuasive partner who shared his vision.

Ezra was an official Jewish scribe and a leader of the Jewish community in Babylon. (See Politics in Action: The Biblical Scribe.) Somehow he persuaded the king of Persia to authorize his return to Jerusalem to make the Torah the law of the land. One theory is that he convinced the court that the Torah would reestablish the rule of law in Judah and thereby make Judah a stronger and more unified buffer state between Persia and Egypt. Whatever the reason, Ezra was granted authorization, an official entourage, and the title Royal Secretary for the Law of the God of Heaven.[30]

Ezra appeared in Jerusalem about the time that Nehemiah was laying plans for the covenant renewal, sometime around the mid-400s BCE. After some years, between 445 and 440 BCE, the Bible makes special note of a general assembly of the people gathered in Jerusalem. It was not an unexpected gathering because it was Succoth, a seven-day holiday in autumn when the Jewish people were expected to make a pilgrimage to the Temple in Jerusalem. The Jewish people were also expected to camp out in booths (*succoth*) or huts symbolizing the shelters built by the Israelites during their wanderings in the Sinai Desert. But this Succoth gathering was to serve an additional purpose.

Ezra appeared at the public gathering and began to read the Torah. He continued reading the Torah on each of the remaining days of Succoth. At some point in the public reading, the people were persuaded to renew the covenant. There is no mention of politicking behind the

POLITICS IN ACTION
The Biblical Scribe

The biblical scribe (*sofer* in Hebrew) was a copyist and calligrapher whose main responsibility was to copy the Torah by hand—letter by letter according to detailed rules of transcription. When the Torah became the center of life in the Babylonian exile, the scribe gained in importance. The scribe, like the rabbi, became a democratizing influence in the Jewish community by making the Torah available to both large and small congregations. The biblical scribe was also a democratic development

A modern Jewish scribe demonstrates for high school students the art of writing a Torah.

in the evolution of scribes, who formerly had served as royal scribes in the courts of kings. The scribe was seen as a learned man in the community. He also transcribed other religious works. In addition, he issued official records, eventually becoming responsible for keeping and maintaining them. In this regard, the scribe was similar to the secretary of state of a modern-day U.S. state. In the Succoth Constitution, scribes were given authority over the third branch of government, which previously had been held by the prophets.

Daniel J. Elazar, *Covenant & Polity in Biblical Israel: Biblical Foundations and Jewish Expressions, Vol. 1: The Covenant Tradition in Politics* (New Brunswick, N.J.: Transaction Publishers, 1995), 409.

scenes, but public acts of approval are rarely entirely spontaneous. In any event, the people affirmed their approval by covenanting directly with God to renew the Sinai covenant and the laws of Moses. This is the Succoth covenant—the last and perhaps the most republican of the biblical covenants.

A more detailed document followed. This was a constitution that laid out the offices and powers of the new government of the Second Commonwealth. The Succoth Constitution set out a republican government composed of three branches: the Great Assembly, the high priest, and the scribes (see Table 12.2).

The Great Assembly consisted of 120 members who were organized as twelve congregations of ten members each. The twelve congregations symbolically represented the original twelve tribes—but only symbolically. Realistically, this new assembly recognized the fact that the Jewish people were now scattered across the Near East and that the tribes no longer had a place in the national system of government. The Great Assembly was important for another reason—for the first time, the Jewish people created a national polity in which civil leadership rested with a national legislature, not a king or tribal leaders. In this sense, the Succoth constitutional system was more in line with today's conception of republican government. Nehemiah became the first head of the Great Assembly.

The second branch of government, responsible for religious leadership, was filled by the high priest. This was a continuation of the same position that had existed since the covenant with Aaron at Mount Sinai (see Table 12.2).

The third branch was responsible for prophetic leadership, but the days of the prophets had come to an end. In their place, the constitution placed the scribes, and Ezra became the first leader of this branch. According to Elazar, the scribes were the most powerful branch at first. Later, the priests supplanted the scribes as the most powerful branch.[31]

POSTSCRIPT ON REVOLUTION BY COVENANT

The Succoth Constitution and the Second Commonwealth remained in effect for a century until Judah was overrun by the forces of Alexander the Great in 331 BCE. Then for nearly two hundred years, Judah was occupied as a vassal state of the Greeks and then their Syrian and Egyptian surrogates—the Seleucid and Ptolemaic dynasties, respectively.

During these centuries of occupation, the greatest challenge that Judah faced was not the tyranny of kings but the influence of Greek culture and thought—a process known as **Hellenization**. It was a classic battle between religious traditionalists and secular modernists. And the battle divided the Jewish community until the Seleucid King Antiochus IV united the Jewish community against him by desecrating the Jerusalem Temple in his Hellenistic zeal.

As a result, a little-known family of priests, the Hasmoneans, began a revolt that lasted roughly twenty-five years. In 142 BCE, the Hasmoneans, led by Judah Maccabee (Judah the Hammer), won, and the Seleucid Empire of Syria granted the province of Judah its independence. Two years later, Simeon, Judah's brother, initiated the first major postbiblical covenant.

Simeon's covenant authorized a constitution that significantly altered the government established by the Succoth Constitution. The new constitution was certainly the first in Israel and the Near East that established a new government by constitutional means in the wake of a successful revolutionary war for national independence.

Simeon's constitution centralized power to a dangerous level by verging on absolute monarchy. He did this by consolidating two of the three branches of government into one person—a priest-king who was both the single civic leader and the single high priest or religious leader of the polity (see Table 12.2). Prophetic leadership was held by a council of elder sages, but it became more of a council to the king than a council of the polity as a whole. Later, it was renamed the Sanhedrin (the Greek term for such councils).

Simeon made sure that he became the first priest-king. He also made sure that the position was filled by hereditary succession, thereby establishing the Hasmonean dynasty. The throne passed to his son and his son's sons and then to one of their wives, who became Queen Salome of Alexandra around 76 BCE. The Hasmonean kings built a mighty army that expanded Judah's borders nearly to what they were in the time of King Solomon. As kings, the high priests promptly ordered the forced conversion of all their new subjects.

Commerce expanded, prosperity returned, and the king's treasury grew. But the center of politics had shifted from the community to the royal court. For nearly eighty years, it seemed that peace and prosperity were the handmaidens of centralized and near-absolute power. But then the great Roman war machine rumbled east. In 67 BCE, Rome annexed Syria. That same year, Queen Salome died, leaving a power vacuum in the dynasty. Two of her sons were rivals for the throne, and civil war ensued. The Romans supported the weaker of the two, who gratefully opened the gates of Jerusalem to the Roman army.[32]

Rome annexed Israel in 63 BCE, but it did not tighten the screws at first. Nonetheless, occupation was occupation. Israel had lost its hard-fought political sovereignty. In addition, Rome, then enthralled with Hellenistic culture, resumed the process of Hellenization with imperial sanctions. There was constant unrest and two unsuccessful rebellions; the Romans crushed both and destroyed the city of Jerusalem. There also were many quiet yet heroic acts of nonviolent civil disobedience. Jewish rabbis, including the revered Rabbi Akiva (also spelled Akiba), continued to observe their faith despite Roman Emperor Hadrian's banning of Jewish practices. The Romans executed Rabbi Akiva and other rabbis—the executions were public and painful.

Judea (the Roman name for Judah) became a tightly controlled Roman province. The center of Jewish political life shifted from Israel to Jewish communities living in the diaspora around the world.

Biblical Israel provides an important example of republicanism for comparison with other early and prominent attempts at republican government—particularly those in ancient Greece and Rome. But were republican ideas used anywhere else in the ancient world? If so, how do these other early examples compare with Greece, Rome, and Israel? And what lessons can we learn from examining and comparing these early attempts at republican government? The next chapter answers these questions by examining other non-European examples of republican government.

REVIEWING AND USING THE CHAPTER

1. What is a covenant, and how was this idea used to advance republican ideas in ancient Israel?

2. Compare the covenants of Moses and David. How were they alike, and how did they differ?

3. "David helped transform Israel into a republican state." What specific examples can you cite to support this assertion?

4. In what way did the Succoth covenant restore Israel's republicanism?

5. What insights does the Bible provide about political leadership?

6. How did the Jewish people retain republicanism in conquest and exile?

EXTENSION ACTIVITY

Compare the republics of ancient Rome, Greece, and Israel. What big ideas did these republics share that helped to make each a success, and what common factors led to their demise?

WEB RESOURCES

Ancient History Sourcebook: Israel
www.fordham.edu/halsall/ancient/asbook06.html

A part of the History Sourcebook Project of Fordham University, this Web site provides an abundance of information about ancient Israel, including original essays and links to other electronic resources and documents.

Jerusalem Center for Public Affairs: The Polity in Biblical Israel
www.jcpa.org/dje/articles3/apl-ch1.htm

This Web site offers an excellent discussion of authority, power, and leadership in biblical Israel by one of the foremost scholars in the field, Daniel J. Elazar.

Jewish Virtual Library: Ancient Jewish History
www.jewishvirtuallibrary.org/jsource/Judaism/ jewhist.html

This section of the Jewish Virtual Library contains over three hundred entries that focus on important ideas, individuals, and institutions of ancient Jewish history.

NOTES

1 The following discussion of *edah* draws on the work of Daniel J. Elazar, especially *Kinship and Consent: The Jewish Political Tradition and Its Contemporary Uses,* 2nd ed. (New Brunswick, N.J.: Transaction Publishers, 1997), 3–4; *Covenant & Polity in Biblical Israel: Biblical Foundations and Jewish Expressions, Vol. 1: The Covenant Tradition in Politics* (New Brunswick, N.J.: Transaction Publishers, 1995).

2 Abraham J. Heschel, *The Prophets* (New York: Harper & Row, 1962), 6, 14–15, 310, 611–615.

3 See Martin Goodman, *Rome and Jerusalem: The Clash of Ancient Civilizations* (New York: Alfred A. Knopf, 2007); John J. Collins, *Between Athens and Jerusalem: Jewish Identity in the Hellenistic Diaspora,* 2nd ed. (Grand Rapids, Mich.: Wm. B. Eerdmans, 1999).

4 Nahum Sarna, "The Decalogue," *Studies in Biblical Interpretation* (Philadelphia: Jewish Publication Society, 2000), 233.

5 Elazar, *Covenant & Polity in Biblical Israel.*

6 Ibid., 212–213. Chaim Potok has written eloquently about the covenant idea and its biblical applications in *Wanderings: History of the Jews* (New York: Fawcett, 1987), esp. "Canaan: The Rival Covenants," 90–196. Also see the pioneering scholarly treatment of the covenant idea by Delbert Hiller, *Covenant: The History of a Biblical Idea* (Baltimore: Johns Hopkins University Press, 1969). See also Elazar, *Kinship and Consent.* For a more recent and readable history along these lines, see Raymond P. Scheindlin, *A Short History of the Jewish People* (New York: Oxford University Press, 2000), Chaps. 1–3.

7 This breakdown of Israel's mixed government and the following analysis of separation of powers come from Elazar, *Covenant & Polity in Biblical Israel,* 186–189.

8 Potok, *Wanderings,* 105.

9 Ibid., 214–222.

10 Deuteronomy 17:19–20.

11 I Samuel 8:5.

12 I Samuel 8:12.

13 Potok, *Wanderings,* 131.

14 Edmond Jacob, *Theology of the Old Testament* (New York: Harper & Row, 1958), quoted in Abraham J. Heschel, "The Separation of Powers," *Prophets,* 609.

15 Heschel, *Prophets,* 614.

16 See Elazar, *Covenant & Polity in Biblical Israel,* 306–313.

17 Potok, *Wanderings,* 142.

18 I Kings 11:11–13; Scheindlin, *Short History of the Jewish People,* 14.

19 Barbara W. Tuchman, *The March of Folly: From Troy to Vietnam* (New York: Ballantine Books, 1984), 8–10.

20 I Kings 12:9–11.

21 I Kings 12:16.

22 Tuchman, *March of Folly,* 10.

23 Nahum Sarna, "The Biblical Sources for the History of the Monarchy," *Studies in Biblical Interpretation,* 37.

24 Ibid., 44.

25 Elazar, *Covenant & Polity in Biblical Israel,* 333.

26 Scheindlin, *Short History of the Jewish People,* 19.

27 Exodus 12:43–51.

28 2 Chronicles 32:20–21.

29 But it also contained later additions and revisions, leaving future scholars to ponder whether the original Book of Deuteronomy had been written long after the Sinai experience or whether the newly discovered book was a later version of the original.

30 Potok, *Wanderings,* 233; Scheindlin, *Short History of the Jewish People,* 31.

31 The discussion of the three branches draws on Elazar, *Covenant & Polity in Biblical Israel,* 359–360.

32 The discussion of Hasmonean rule draws on Potok, *Wanderings,* 243–251.

EARLY EUROPEAN AND NON-EUROPEAN REPUBLICS

Republican traditions are not unique to Europe. From ancient times to the early modern period, republics existed in Asia, Africa, and the Americas. The study of these republics is sometimes challenging because few left written records. But scholars are nonetheless succeeding in piecing together their history. This is important because comparing premodern republics around the world provides an opportunity to identify and interpret their similarities and differences. In the first chapter of this unit, you will read about the republican experience outside of Europe.

A republic's success, in Asia, Africa, or any other part of the world, depends on many factors. Two factors are key: balance and moderation. The power of one set of various interests must be balanced by that of other interests in society. The absence of balance leads to excess, that is, the absence of moderation. As you will learn in the second chapter of this unit, balancing the competing forces in a republic has been and will always

CHAPTER 13:

HOW DO EARLY EUROPEAN AND NON-EUROPEAN REPUBLICS COMPARE?

CHAPTER 14:

WHY DID SO MANY NON-EUROPEAN REPUBLICS FAIL?

be tricky. Successful republics tend to share certain characteristics. Similarly, a review of why some republics fail reveals that these republics share several flaws. As you will learn in the second chapter of this unit, comparing non-European republics with one another and with European republics sheds light on why some republics have thrived while others have failed.

BIG IDEAS

- Republicanism is not limited to Europe. Prior to 1600, republican ideas developed on every inhabited continent.

- Republicanism is not new. For thousands of years, diverse peoples and cultures shared a belief in republican ideas such as freedom, equality, the rule of law, and the consent of the governed.

- To trace the history of non-European republics, historians and political scientists must rely on a variety of sources, such as sacred texts, observations of foreigners, autobiographies, ethnographies, and material culture.

- Early non-European republics developed a variety of social institutions to support republican ideas. These institutions include kinship networks, age-graded networks, customary law, spiritual societies, and mutual aid societies.

- Comparing European and non-European republics provides important clues about why some succeeded and others failed.

Purpose of This Chapter

What Was the Significance of Republicanism outside Europe before 1600?

How Do Scholars Study the History of Non-European Republics?

How Did Republican Values Shape the Social Institutions of Non-European Republics?
> Kinship and Republican Values
> Age Grading and Republican Values
> Religion and Republican Values

Why Is the Mutual Aid Society a Uniquely Republican Institution?

Purpose of This Chapter

Republicanism is not unique to Europe. It is the human expression of people who believe it is possible to have both a love of freedom and a healthy respect for the law. From ancient times to the early modern period, republics existed in Asia, Africa, and the Americas. Most of these republics left few written records, making it difficult to piece together their history. Nonetheless, it is an important history. Comparing premodern republics around the world provides an opportunity to identify and interpret their similarities and differences. These comparisons also hold important clues about why some republics failed while others succeeded.

Terms to Know

age-graded networks	lineage networks	mutual aid societies
kinship	matrilineal society	republicanism

WHAT WAS THE SIGNIFICANCE OF REPUBLICANISM OUTSIDE EUROPE BEFORE 1600?

In 1600, most people lived in empires and kingdoms, not republics. This was true throughout the world. Most people, European and non-European alike, were ruled as subjects by a distant king, sultan, or emperor. "Man should first select a King," according to an ancient Indian text, "and only after that should he select a wife, and earn wealth. For if he has no King to protect them, what would become of his wife and wealth?"[1] This was the view of a people accustomed to being ruled by a king.

But "most people" is not all people. Some people—a minority worldwide to be sure—lived in republics. These republics were not confined to any one region or race. In fact, evidence of early republics has been found on every inhabited continent. The most famous examples include the Iroquois Nations of North America, the Igbo of West Africa, biblical Israel in the Near East, the North Indian republics in Vedic and Buddhist times, and the Melanesian islanders of the Pacific.[2]

These examples vary widely in time and space. The republics of ancient India and Israel were contemporaries and relatively well-documented. Records suggest that they existed between 1500 and 500 BCE. After that period, they were conquered by larger empires and recaptured their independence for only small periods of time.

Iroquois and Igbo societies flourished much later than did the Indian and Israelite republics. They also existed in different time periods from one another. The Igbo established a constitutional monarchy sometime between 1000 and 1100 CE, and the Iroquois founded their confederation around 500 years later.

Unearthing the story of early non-European republics is different from, and more difficult than, researching their European counterparts. In Europe, it makes more sense to look for republican life in different regions during the same time intervals. The histories of medieval Venice and Novgorod, Russia, for example, share more in common with one another than either share with Israel or India during that time. Outside Europe, by contrast, we must look at different time periods for evidence of republican life.

Using the best available evidence, exemplar republics can be found on every inhabited continent prior to 1600 CE. In each of these republics, there is evidence of an organized set of republican beliefs that shaped their ideals, identity, and politics. In other words, these were self-conscious republics, not accidental ones.

Consider the Igbo (also spelled Ibo). They lived east of the Niger River Delta in what is today southeastern Nigeria. Freedom was part of their culture. They defined themselves as free and equal citizens, not the subjects of an overlord. There is a traditional Igbo saying: "the Igbo have no kings."[3] But the Igbo were not anarchists. They used rules to govern their lives, and they relied on the elders to interpret those rules. The elders drew on custom and tradition in making their decisions, and their decisions were subject to popular consent.

Republicanism is not unique to Europeans. Diverse peoples around the world who had little or no contact independently discovered republican principles long before 1600.

Table 13.1 Two Key Characteristics of a Republic

> 1. Freedom through the law
>   - Independence from external control
>   - Freedom from rule by kings and tyrants
>   - Freedom to participate in government
>
> 2. Political equality

Although they organized and applied those principles in different ways, the principles were essentially the same worldwide. And that is the essential point: republican ideas seemed to have developed independently and similarly throughout the world. This appearance of similar political principles across diverse societies suggests that republicanism is a *human* idea, not simply an idea of particular cultures or groups of people. This does not mean that republicanism is a *universal* idea. We know from world history and current events that it has not taken root everywhere.

Republicanism is a human idea that cuts across cultures and time periods: it is the belief that freedom is balanced by (or secured through) a healthy respect for the law (Table 13.1). That is, ancient republican peoples prized their freedom, but they also recognized the need for the rule of law. Republican societies were more egalitarian than monarchies. They also provided for the consent of the governed.

The goal of this chapter and the next is to explore why republicanism took root in some places and not others. More research is needed to fully understand this, and that research requires a comparative approach. "The study of the past," remarked the historian Frederick Teggart (1870–1946), "can become effective only when it is fully realized that all peoples have histories, that these histories run concurrently and in the same world, and that the act of comparing them is the beginning of knowledge."[4] (See Whatever Happened to . . . The Historical Republics.)

HOW DO SCHOLARS STUDY THE HISTORY OF NON-EUROPEAN REPUBLICS?

In Europe ancient and medieval republics left behind a rich legacy of written material. Scholars may bemoan what has been lost, but what remains fills many libraries—so much remains that European history is largely the study of the written past. When scholars study ancient and medieval European republics, they can draw on the writings of a variety of philosophers and historians, statesmen and their advisors, merchants, and nobility. Church records, court records, tax rolls, town records, and other official documents provide an even deeper view of political life.

Outside Europe, it is a different matter. Empires such as Persia and China have an accessible written past. But most non-European republics do not. In some cases, republics were

THE HISTORICAL REPUBLICS

- The Melanesian Islands survived colonialism and secured their freedom as sovereign and independent states. Today, these islands include the states of Papua New Guinea, Solomon Islands, Fiji, and Vanuatu.
- The Iroquois Confederacy has survived unconquered for centuries. Today, it includes six self-governing nations whose status is formalized in treaties guaranteed by the Supremacy Clause of the U.S. Constitution.
- The Igbo became one of the largest ethnic groups in sub-Saharan Africa. They are concentrated primarily in southeastern Nigeria in an area formerly known as Biafra. Many Igbo are Christians. Conflict between northern Muslims and southern Christians has been a persistent theme of modern Nigerian history.
- Biblical Israel provided the Jewish people with a republican model that was replicated over the centuries in their diaspora communities and later in the modern state of Israel.
- The republics of early India became an important source of political ideas and institutions in the national independence movement of modern India. Republican institutions such as the *panchayat* system of autonomous village councils still exist. (See Chapter 14, Politics in Action: The Panchayat.)

conquered by empires when they were still oral societies; in others, republics had a written past that was destroyed by their conquerors or the passage of time.

How do you explore the political past of a society where politics and the law were unwritten custom? What primary sources should be used? Where should you look? The answers vary by time and place, but there are some general patterns in the types of sources available, their uses, and their limits.

The sacred texts of ancient India and Israel provide the oldest and most detailed written clues about the political organization of ancient republics outside Europe. For thousands of years, these sacred texts have provided people with a source of inspiration and guidance in the conduct of their personal lives. At the same time, these texts are a rich source of political wisdom and insight about how societies should be governed and toward what ends. Three sets of texts are of particular importance to the study of republican government: the *Vedas,* the Buddhist writings, and the *Tanakh.*

The *Vedas* (which means "revealed knowledge") are sacred Hindu texts. The oldest were composed orally as early as 1500 BCE. Over the centuries, they set forth the key beliefs and practices of Hinduism. The Vedic period of civilization takes its name from those texts. Vedic texts also include two great epics—the *Mahabharata* and *Ramayana*—that still inform Hindu philosophy and Indian culture today. Although Vedic sacred texts and mythologies

MORE ABOUT . . .

Comparing Hinduism and Buddhism

The Vedas speak of a trinity of Brahma (the creator), Vishnu (the preserver), and Shiva (the destroyer). Hindus believe in the transmigration of the soul after death and its continual rebirth until some reach salvation. Rebirth takes different forms, depending on the rightness of your past actions (*karma*). The rightness of your actions depends on your duties (*dharma*) in this lifetime. Those duties depend, in turn, on the caste, or social class, into which you are born.

Each caste is assigned duties; rules and rituals formalize caste differences. The caste system became a rigid hierarchy or social pyramid. At the top of the pyramid sat the king.

Buddhism arose partly as a republican response to the hierarchical tendencies of Hinduism. According to the teachings of the Buddha, even the lowest born could seek the Four Noble Truths by following the Noble Eightfold path to *nirvana,* or spiritual bliss. The Four Truths are that dissatisfaction and suffering are (1) universal, (2) caused by desire and attachment, (3) can be ended, and (4) are ended by following the Eightfold Path. That Path consists of right understanding, right thinking, right speech, right action, right living, right effort, right mindfulness, and right concentration through meditation. (The word *right* here means "righteous.")

The three pillars of Buddhism are the Buddha, *dharma* (his teachings), and *sangha* ("association or community"). *Sangha* in Buddhism refers primarily to the Buddhist

Figure of Brahma carved into an Indian temple. He has four faces, one facing each direction (only three are visible) and is holding the Rig Veda, one of the ancient Hindu scriptures.

monastic orders that were formed and to the larger community of Buddhists. Buddhist writings used the term *gana-sangha* ("clan-based community") to refer to the republics that existed in the late Vedic period and the Buddha's lifetime.

endorsed monarchy and castes, they also shed historical light on the existence of early republics and their institutions.

Buddhist writings contain the teachings of the Buddha ("the Enlightened One") written down by his disciples and followers. The Buddha, born Siddhartha Gautama (563–483 BCE), like Jesus, modeled a democratic spirit in which everyone—rich and poor, male and female—could seek truth and attain salvation by following the right path. Buddhist texts also provide valuable histories of republics and monarchies in the late Vedic period. (See More About . . . Comparing Hinduism and Buddhism.)

The *Tanakh* (Hebrew Bible) consists of three parts: the Torah (which means "teaching") comprises the five books of Moses (from Genesis to Deuteronomy); the *Nevi'im* (Prophets) contains the books of Joshua, Judges, Samuel, and Kings; and *Kethuvim* (Writings) contains Psalms, Proverbs, and the heroic tales of Ruth, Esther, Daniel, Ezra, and Nehemiah. The word *tanakh* is an abbreviation made up of the first Hebrew letter of the name of each of the three parts with vowels added to make it pronounceable ($T[a]N[a]Kh$). When these books were written remains a subject of considerable debate. Some scholars tie the writing of the Torah back to Moses, while others view the Hebrew Bible as a work in progress written over the centuries after Moses. When they were written detracts little from their value as divine revelation and continuing inspiration for members of various faiths, including Judaism, Christianity, and Islam. As you learned in the last chapter, the Hebrew Bible provides a unique record of all the major stages and turning points in the political development of a single people and their polity over many centuries.

Contemporary foreign observers provide a second written source of political clues. Arab and European travelers—explorers, conquerors, missionaries, merchants, and slave traders—recorded their observations of the non-European world. Their views were colored by the cultures from which they came and whatever they were seeking. As such, their accounts contain biases and inaccuracies, some more than others. As long as that is taken into account, foreign observations can provide comparative perspectives, political insights, and important political clues that might otherwise never be uncovered. Some foreign accounts also are valuable because they recorded oral traditions and preserved fragile records that would otherwise be lost.

In West Africa, for example, before the arrival of Europeans, coastal trading cities governed themselves as local republics under a council of elders, an elected king, or both. When European trade became important, some of these trading cities converted to oligarchies. Canoe Houses (trading companies) were established, each run by a strong man who could bargain with European traders on a more equal footing. That is all that most foreigners saw; few traveled elsewhere. Yet a description of the Canoe House, considered in proper perspective, offers valuable lessons about the political responses of one people to the economic opportunities offered by another.

Few Arab or European travelers looked for republican ways of life in their travels. There were various reasons: they were looking for other things, they were attracted to wealthy empires, they had little interest in studying forms of government, or they had preconceived notions of non-European rule as primitive or imperial but not republican. (See More About . . . The World that Ibn Battuta Saw.) Fortunately, some travelers recognized clues of republican life and were interested in what they saw. In some cases, the interest was ethnographic: they were interested in observing and recording the oral traditions of a people.

Cadwallader Colden (1688–1776), a British imperial representative to the Iroquois Confederacy, is an example of this kind of traveler. Colden was a man of the Enlightenment—a physician, British imperial officer, farmer, scientist, philosopher, and anthropologist. In the

MORE ABOUT . . .

The World That Ibn Battuta Saw

Ibn Battuta (1304–1368 or 1377) was the most famous of medieval Muslim travelers. In his memoir, *Rihla* (or *Journey*), he recounted his travels in the first half of the fourteenth century throughout the Islamic world, from North Africa to North India and then on to China. His memoir is rich in insights about the lands he visited. But, like other Muslim historians of his day, Ibn Battuta wrote about Muslim rulers for Muslim readers. For example, his recollections of North India take up 20 percent of the *Rihla*, but they focus largely on the past and present Muslim rulers of India as a sultanate. There is no attention given to indigenous Indian sources of republicanism.

1760s, he served as provincial governor of New York. As a British imperial representative to the Iroquois Confederacy, he spent time with the Iroquois. From this experience, he wrote *The History of the Five Indian Nations* [of the Iroquois Confederacy], *Depending on the Province of New-York in America,* published in two parts (in 1727 and 1747). In his book, Colden effectively combined history and ethnography (a precursor of cultural anthropology). His study recounts the history of the Iroquois and their relations with the English and French colonies from the early 1600s to the mid-1700s. He also included important first-person accounts of the government and politics of the Iroquois and the relations among their five nations.

Autobiographies and histories by native observers are a third source of information and ideas. Such accounts are rare in largely oral societies, but they are all the more valuable when they are found. They provide a firsthand or recollected account of a republican society by a member of that society. Of course, these accounts have their biases too. Some native writers were boosters, who wrote in glowing terms of their country and their own contributions to it. Others were detractors, writing largely in negative terms of their country, especially if they were on the losing side of a political battle.

An early example of such a writer is Flavius Josephus (37–c. 100 CE), who was a Jerusalem-born Jew who wrote two histories and an autobiography during the Roman occupation of Jerusalem. His first history, *The Jewish Revolt,* is the only surviving detailed account of the Jewish Revolt of 66–70 CE against the Romans. His second, *Antiquities of the Jews,* is a history of the Jews from their beginnings to the Jewish Revolt. Josephus was a Pharisee, a member of one of three Jewish factions at the time, and hence an active participant in Jerusalem religious affairs and politics. He also was the commander of Jewish forces in Galilee during the Jewish Revolt. After his troops were almost entirely destroyed, he was the only survivor of the fighting who did not commit suicide. (In those days, a valorous commander on the losing side of a war might throw himself on his sword as an act of honor.) Instead, Josephus gave himself up to the Romans and lived under their protection for many years. He even became a Roman citizen. As a participant, eyewitness, and inside player, his detailed accounts fill a large void in the history of the Jews in the first century CE. At the same time, according to historian Martin Goodman, "Josephus' narrative is permeated by the ambivalence that inevitably arose from this complex political career, first as a defender of Jerusalem, then as an apologist for the regime that destroyed it."[5]

BOLD THINKERS

Olaudah Equiano

Olaudah Equiano (1749–1797) led a fascinating life. He was Igbo by birth, became a slave in the Carolinas, bought his freedom, and then migrated to England. In England, he became an influential member of the movement to abolish the slave trade in the British Empire. To raise awareness and money for the movement, Equiano wrote his autobiography in 1789 titled *The Interesting Narrative of the Life of Olaudah Equiano, or Gustavus Vassa the African*. Gustavus Vassa was Equiano's slave name.

The book became a best-seller and gave English readers a firsthand account of life in an African village, the middle passage, slavery, and the meaning of freedom to a former slave. Some scholars suggest that Equiano was really born in America and invented his African childhood. Nonetheless, his descriptions of Igbo government square with other accounts and may have come from conversations with fellow slaves.

Title page from Olaudah Equiano's 1789 autobiography.

For more on Equiano and the controversy over his birthplace, see Vincent Carretta, *Equiano, the African: Biography of a Self-Made Man* (London: Penguin Books, 2005); Adam Hochschild, *Bury the Chains: Prophets and Rebels in the Fight to Free an Empire's Slaves* (Boston: Houghton Mifflin, 2005).

A related genre of historical writing is the slave narrative and the freedman's autobiography. One example is the best-selling autobiography of Olaudah Equiano, an Igbo and former slave. (See Bold Thinkers: Olaudah Equiano.) Part of his autobiography is a detailed account of life in an Igbo village. In this description, Equiano likened Igbo government to the pastoral phase of the Israelites in the age of Hebrew patriarchs (Abraham, Isaac, and Jacob); Equiano explained that he was struck "very forcibly" by this analogy. Some of the similarities he identified include government by a mix of chiefs, judges, wise men, and elders; the authority of the head of the household; the law of retaliation (an eye for an eye); circumcision; sacrifices and burnt offerings; and washings and purifications.[6] He, too, wrote from a bias—the abolitionist view that Africans were the descendants of Noah's son Ham. That bias, however, does not call into question the accuracy of his comparison, only the intent.

Beginning in the nineteenth century, ethnographers and historians began to systematically record earlier oral traditions. Although most early ethnographers were Europeans, some were not. Jomo Kenyatta (1889–1978), for example, a leader of the Gikuyu (also spelled Kikuyu) and the founding father of modern Kenya, studied anthropology at the University of London. In 1938, Kenyatta wrote a fascinating study of the Gikuyu, titled *Facing Mount Kenya.*

New generations of historians, anthropologists, and archaeologists also learned how to find, decipher, and interpret various kinds of evidence that had been previously ignored for centuries. Some of this evidence can be applied to the study of political organizations. Such evidence includes genealogies, which are useful in reconstructing political chronologies; radiocarbon dating and other methods of dating artifacts; and language patterns, which can be used to trace immigration and settlement patterns. Other evidence includes emblem glyphs (royal symbols), used to piece together facts about political organization; material culture (artifacts) used in political rituals and ceremonies; and archaeological evidence on how settlements and buildings were laid out and used for political purposes. These sources have provided scholars with important clues about the values, social institutions, laws, and governing arrangements of early non-European republics and how they compare with European republics.

HOW DID REPUBLICAN VALUES SHAPE THE SOCIAL INSTITUTIONS OF NON-EUROPEAN REPUBLICS?

Freedom through the law was an essential value common to European and non-European republics. In most republics, *freedom* had three meanings (see Table 13.1). First, it meant freedom from external control. Republics fiercely defended themselves against foreign conquest. Nevertheless, many lost this struggle because they refused to form confederations with others for fear of losing their independence. Second, it meant freedom from the unchecked rule by kings. A republic, in any meaningful sense, required a form of government in which the executive (a king or chief), legislature (council or assembly), and judiciary (arbiters or priests) shared power. Third, it meant freedom, as citizens, to participate in the government. Republican citizenship was a badge of distinction proudly worn. That badge proclaimed, "We are not subjects of a monarch. We are free."

In all three of these meanings, freedom had its limits; and those limits were set by the law. *Law* here meant more than just the laws adopted by the government; it meant the rule of law—that no one is above the law. Non-European republics held fast to this ideal no less than their European counterparts. Some republics relied on unwritten law in the form of customs and traditions passed down through the generations by oral history; other republics moved to a system of written and codified law. Regardless of the form, the people of most republics believed that some laws were so important that they originated in a higher spiritual or natural source. The Ten Commandments is perhaps the most famous example.

Another core republican value was political equality—that all citizens shared the same rights and responsibilities. But, in practice, full citizenship was rarely available to everyone. Some republican societies, such as the Iroquois, were relatively egalitarian—women participated in governing councils, and slavery was uncommon. Other republican societies, such as ancient Athens and Rome, had more slaves than citizens and barred female citizens from full participation.

Slavery existed in non-European as well as European republics. Generally speaking, however, slavery and other forms of bondage, such as serfdom, were less prevalent in non-European republics. Practically speaking, the premodern economies of non-European republics did not support extensive slavery. These economies were not known for having large plantations, feudal estates, wide gaps between rich and poor, or large aristocratic classes of leisure. The international slave trade did not reach a point before 1600 where it threatened the nature of such economies.

There were exceptions. Igbo men used accumulated wealth to buy more slaves and wives. By contrast, the Iroquois turned war captives over to the matriarchs, who decided whom to adopt and whom to execute. With adoption and execution as the two main choices, slavery was rare. Nevertheless, adopted captives were often subjected to hard labor.

The scale and density of non-European republican communities indicate that many of these settlements were more compact, smaller in population, and less densely populated than the Greek and Roman polities. One exception was ancient Israel when it united the twelve tribes and the city of Jerusalem. A second exception occurred in North India, where some republics were comparable in size to the larger Greek polities such as Athens.

The republics that survived the longest were located in the safety of woodlands, rain forests, mountains, or islands. Republics were least likely to survive on the open savannahs, steppes, or desert regions, where they were exposed to conquest by more powerful opponents.

Typically, settlements in the same tribe joined together to form an alliance or confederation. In this regard, they were similar in appearance and scale to the republics of the Germanic, Celtic, and Scandinavian peoples in northern Europe. In some instances, one or more settlements would break away and become a micro republic.

By and large, non-European republics were concentrated in strings of small towns and villages that took days to traverse, not in large cities or extensive territorial republics that took weeks to traverse. In West Africa and Northeast America, republican settlements were situated like islands in an archipelago or stars in a galaxy. Some geographers use the term *galactic* to describe this pattern of settlement. Most non-European settlements were part of a larger republic. They valued their trade or kinship connections with neighboring communities, but they also valued their independence.

There is evidence that some non-European republics were larger and more diverse in population than their more authoritarian neighbors. Scholars have found evidence of different language groups living in the same clusters of free Igbo communities. The Igbo were free to move. Intermarriage was acceptable, and Igbo men often married outside their village and brought their in-laws home with them. Igbo villages also offered refuge for escaped slaves, war captives, and others seeking a free life. A similar pattern existed in free German cities, where those who sought refuge became free after a year and a day. Another example is Venice, which was founded by war refugees who fled to its misty islands and lagoons to escape Lombard invaders.

KINSHIP AND REPUBLICAN VALUES

Kinship, a system of social organization based on family ties, was the most important institution of social organization and control within most early societies, republican or otherwise. Kinship, to be clear, is not a republican institution; it exists in all polities (see Chapter 4). But in republican societies, kinship and other social institutions are influenced by republican principles. There is more equality among members, more freedom for members, and more consent by members.

Kinship ties began within the extended family. Depending on custom, the extended family might have included the father, his wife or wives, unmarried children, grandparents and other elder relatives, as well as married sons with their wife/wives and children. As discussed in Chapter 4, the extended family was the social unit of the clan, a larger social unit of extended families that traced their bloodline back to a common ancestor. The clan was the social unit of the tribe, and the tribe considered itself "a people" or "nation." Some early tribes joined with other tribes to form confederations, such as the twelve tribes of Israel and the Five (later Six) Nations of the Iroquois.

Lineage networks are relationships that bind people together in a common bloodline. In this network, the clan was the essential link between the family and the larger world. Clans organized and governed themselves along matrilineal or patrilineal lines, depending on custom.

The role of women varied considerably from one non-European culture to another. The Iroquois were a **matrilineal society** in which each clan traced its lineage through the female line. Elder matrons presided over their clan, and women organized the village economy. Matrons selected the village leaders, and they designated the nobility. Matrons also held council meetings to advise the male elders. In Vedic India, women were allowed to attend meetings of the *sabhas* (councils of elders). In West Africa, Arab visitors were shocked by the relative freedom of women and their presence in public.

In a small village, there might be only one clan, but immigration and population growth created large villages, towns, and cities composed of several clans. Growth also created large clans that grew beyond one village into clusters of villages.

The Germanic peoples in Europe were also organized by lineage networks and clans. And Athenians lived in clan-based communities until their city-state became a democracy. Cleisthenes, the founder of Athenian democracy, introduced a system of *demes* (political neighborhoods) that brought together a mix of residents from different clans. His goal was to redirect identity and loyalty from clans to the polity as a whole.

Secret societies, cult societies that claimed a strong link to the spiritual world, were important social institutions that cut across clans and age grades. These secret societies presented a fearsome force when they entered a village at night claiming supernatural powers and wearing masks. As a result, they often became a powerful institution of social control, sometimes more powerful than the government itself. When government officials needed to raise revenues or collect debt payments, they might call on these societies to serve as collection agencies. One of the most powerful masked cults in West Africa was the Ekpe (meaning "leopard") of the Cross River area of western Nigeria and eastern Cameroon.

Cult societies and religious guilds were also important institutions of medieval European life. Before the European Renaissance, spirituality was a core value in European as well as non-European societies. In premodern societies, where life was often precarious, spirituality defined people's place in the cosmos, guided their way, and protected them from evil. In turn, it required acknowledgment of an all-powerful spiritual force.

AGE GRADING AND REPUBLICAN VALUES

Age-graded networks, a system of social organization based on age, were another important social institution that could be tailored to republican principles. In societies organized in this way, each age grade had particular responsibilities in the community. There were networks of junior warriors, senior warriors, and elders. In republics with more than one clan, age grades brought people together from different clans, providing an important source of political socialization into the larger community. Age-graded networks also provided a way to break down social barriers between clans.

RELIGION AND REPUBLICAN VALUES

Religious belief systems were an important source of political values. Judaism and Buddhism, for example, supported republican values, including the equality of all human beings, nonhierarchical forms of human association, the belief that rulers are subject to a higher authority, and government by consent. By comparison, Hinduism, Confucianism, and Islam have been used by rulers to justify imperial values, including stratified societies based on social inequality, rigid hierarchies of power, and omnipotent secular rulers of a unified state. The dominant political orientation of Christianity have historically floated between the republicanism envisioned by Paul and the hierarchical structure organized by Peter.

The distinguishing feature of European society was not its level of spirituality, but the unifying role of the Church.[7] There was no counterpart institution elsewhere. Judaism was consolidated around a single Temple in Jerusalem that King Solomon built, but its followers were primarily Israelites; it was not a widespread faith. Buddhism became a widespread faith, but it had no unifying Church. Islam, too, became a widespread religion without a single Church. (See More About . . . Spiritual Societies.)

WHY IS THE MUTUAL AID SOCIETY A UNIQUELY REPUBLICAN INSTITUTION?

Mutual aid societies are a type of self-governing association in which members pledge to come to the aid of other members or the community as a whole. Members work together or contribute financially to meet needs that they cannot solve alone. Historically, mutual aid societies were a natural outgrowth of kinship ties. Large clans had mutual aid societies for their social, economic, and spiritual needs. Over time, some mutual aid societies expanded in scope to serve an entire village. In some instances, they were, in effect, the local government of a village.

Mutual aid societies met a wide range of needs. Among the Iroquois, for example, clan-based societies organized community harvests, the storage of surplus grain, and its distribution to the poor. Most ancient cultures organized mutual aid societies to care for the poor and others in need (such as orphans, widows, the elderly, priests, and even runaway slaves). In later centuries, South American slaves from West Africa formed mutual aid societies (*cabildo*) to raise money for the manumission (freeing) of slaves.

For pious Jews of ancient Israel, philanthropy was a form of religious observance. Most praiseworthy were those who gave anonymously within organized mutual aid networks.

In ancient Greece, by contrast, wealthy family networks publicly sponsored civic amenities, such as temple construction, festivals, and theatrical plays.

Specialized mutual aid societies performed ceremonial duties, such as burying the dead and honoring deities. In ancient Israel, for example, these responsibilities were performed by the Levis, one of the twelve tribes. Mutual aid societies also supplied the labor for community economic projects. They dug irrigation ditches, maintained roads, cleared the forest, and harvested crops.

In theory, the mutual aid society is the classic republican institution. It certainly fits the republican expectations of seventeenth-century English philosopher John Locke, who saw human beings coming together voluntarily as equals to deal with common social needs that none could serve alone. In practice, however, not all mutual aid societies retained their republican character. Some fell under the

POLITICS IN ACTION
Village Autonomy in Imperial China

Chinese emperors ruled a vast territory through a large bureaucracy. Some emperors tried to exert firm control over their domain; others did not. Usually the Chinese villages endured these cycles. Typically, village temples and the ancestral halls of clans did much of the work of local government. The temples served the entire community; they helped police the community and maintain its roads. The halls served their clans; they collected revenues to honor clan ancestors, fed poorer clan members, and educated clan children. Many villages also had active cooperative associations of unmarried women and sacred-text readers, to name two examples. The governing bodies of these various organizations often consisted of councils of elders and a headman.

control of a dictatorial patriarch, an oligarchy of wealthy members, or the local representative of a distant emperor.

Conversely, many mutual aid societies flourished in empires, where a benevolent or distant emperor allowed them to retain their republican character or turned a blind eye to them. This was the case in the Persian Empire, which granted local autonomy to Jewish and other ethnoreligious communities. In ancient China, mutual aid societies were widespread at the village level while, at the imperial level, China was governed by the emperor and a mandarin class of scholar-bureaucrats. (See Politics in Action: Village Autonomy in Imperial China.) The Chinese polity was (and still is) a delicate balance of hierarchical and republican forces.[8]

At the community level, then, people often joined together—in empires or republics—to improve their lives, develop their communities, and aid those in need. And they routinely created republican associations to accomplish these goals.

Did it make a difference whether those local communities existed in republics or empires? The answer is this: in an empire, the emperor granted villagers their autonomy, and what he granted he could withdraw or ignore. But in a republic, local autonomy was part of the birthright of freedom. The history of imperial China, for example, is punctuated by episodes of peasant rebellions against harsh imperial laws, excessive taxation without representation, and centralization of power. (See Politics in Action: The Yellow Turban Revolt.) Before 1600, the combined death toll of these rebellions numbered in the tens of millions.

POLITICS IN ACTION
The Yellow Turban Revolt

In the waning years of China's Han Dynasty, widespread crop failures forced many families to leave their farms and seek work with large landowners. The glut of available labor led to low wages for many of these peasant families. In addition, flooding along the Yellow River and a heavy tax burden increased the pressures on the peasantry.

The poor economic conditions, combined with an increasingly corrupt and out-of-touch ruling dynasty, created a fertile environment for rebellion. In the latter part of the second century CE, a Taoist healer named Zhang Jiao began to call for the overthrow of the Han Dynasty. He declared that all peoples should have equal rights and that land should be distributed fairly among the people.

By 184 CE, Zhang Jiao had developed a huge following. That year, his forces took up arms against Emperor Ling's armies. For several months, the rebels, wearing yellow scarves around their heads to show their loyalty to Zhang Jiao, enjoyed considerable success. The rebels captured several cities and gained control of widespread areas. By the next year, however, Emperor Ling's armies had defeated most of the rebels.

Despite this setback, rebellion erupted again in 185 CE, and fighting raged until 205 CE. The rebellion was put down, but meanwhile military and local officials had increased their own authority at the expense of the Han Dynasty. The dynasty collapsed two decades after crushing the rebellion.

REVIEWING AND USING THE CHAPTER

1. What clues do ancient and sacred texts such as the *Vedas,* the teachings of Buddha, and the *Tanakh* reveal about the development of republican ideas in non-European societies?

2. How did early non-European republics define *freedom, the rule of law,* and *equality?* How does that differ from your own understanding of those ideas?

3. What social institutions supported the development of non-European republics?

EXTENSION ACTIVITY

Kinship networks, mutual aid societies, age-graded networks, and secret societies are ancient institutions that still exist throughout the world. Identify and describe one contemporary example of each, and explain its role in society.

WEB RESOURCES

The Constitution of the Iroquois Nations
www.kahonwes.com/constitution.html

This Web site provides the complete text of the Constitution of the Iroquois Nations.

History of India
http://historyindia.org

A well-organized Web resource, this site provides links to timelines, primary documents, essays, and biographies of important topics and individuals in the history of India. Of particular note is the link to "politics."

New World Encyclopedia: Igbo People
www.newworldencyclopedia.org/entry/Igbo_People

This encyclopedia entry traces the history of the Igbo people from its origins to the present day and discusses various aspects of Igbo culture, including religion and politics.

NOTES

[1] Quoted in Stanley Wolpert, *India,* 3rd ed. (Berkeley, Calif.: University of California Press, 2005), 201.

[2] Cadwallader Colden, *The History of the Five Indian Nations* (Ithaca, N.Y.: Cornell University Press, 1958; originally published in two volumes in 1727 and 1747); Daniel K. Richter, *The Ordeal of the Long-House* (Chapel Hill, N.C.: University of North Carolina Press, 1992); Elizabeth Isichei, *The History of the Igbo People* (New York: St. Martin's Press, 1976); J. P. Sharma, *Republics in Ancient India* (Leiden: E. J. Brill, 1968); Ram Sharan Sharma, *Aspects of Political Ideas and Institutions in Ancient India,* 5th ed. (Delhi: Motilal Banarsidass, 2005). See also John Phillip Reid, *A Law of Blood: The Primitive Law of the Cherokee Nation* (De Kalb, Ill.: Northern Illinois University Press, 2006; originally published by New York University Press,

1970); Jomo Kenyatta, *Facing Mount Kenya: The Tribal Life of the Gikuyu* (London: Secker and Warburg, 1938); Michael Taylor, *Community, Anarchy, and Liberty* (Cambridge, UK: Cambridge University Press, 1982).

3 Elizabeth Isichei, *A History of African Societies to 1870* (Cambridge, UK: Cambridge University Press, 1997), 242–243.

4 Frederick Teggart, *Rome and China* (1939), quoted in John Darwin, *After Tamerlane: The Global History of Empire since 1405* (New York: Bloomsbury Press, Macmillan, 2008), xi.

5 Martin Goodman, *Rome and Jerusalem: The Clash of Ancient Civilizations* (New York: Alfred A. Knopf, 2007), 5.

6 Quoted in Vincent Carretta, *Equiano, the African: Biography of a Self-Made Man* (London: Penguin Books, 2005), 317.

7 See Theodore K. Rabb, *The Last Days of the Renaissance and the March to Modernity* (New York: Basic Books, Perseus Books, 2006), Chap. 1.

8 Lucian W. Pye, *The Mandarin and the Cadre: China's Political Cultures* (Ann Arbor, Mich.: University of Michigan Press, 1988).

CHAPTER 14
WHY DID SO MANY NON-EUROPEAN REPUBLICS FAIL?

BIG IDEAS

- As early societies grew in population and diversity, they required more specialized institutions of government to meet basic needs.

- Two stages typically characterize the development of early republican societies: tribal republics and republican states.

- Most tribal republics in Europe and elsewhere organized themselves as conciliar (council-based) republics and many formed tribal confederacies with a mixed form of government.

- As tribal confederacies grew, some formed republican states with specialized and structured governments while others were conquered by more powerful empires.

- Comparing European and non-European republics provides important clues about why some succeed and others fail.

Purpose of This Chapter

No successful society is static or frozen in time. All successful societies must evolve and adapt to new circumstances and changing needs. Early human societies were no exception. Typically, they evolved over stages of development. Two important stages in that development were tribes and states. The transition from tribe-based to state-based societies was marked by increases in population and ethnic diversity as well as the specialization of social, economic, and political institutions. Republican principles helped to organize many tribes and states in Europe as well as in non-European regions of the world. How did republican governments change in the transition from tribe to state? What new institutions and functions did these governments develop to adapt to new circumstances? What principles did they apply to the organization of government? And why did some succeed while others failed? Comparing non-European republics with one another and with European republics helps answer these questions.

Terms to Know

arrogance	fusion	tribal confederation
conciliar republic	gerontocracies	tribe
excessive centralization	Jainism	wooden-headedness
factionalism	selfishness	
fission	state	

HOW DID THE EVOLUTION OF EARLY SOCIETIES AFFECT THE FORMS AND FUNCTIONS OF THEIR GOVERNMENT?

Early human societies in Europe and throughout the world were not frozen in time.[1] New circumstances produced new needs that often required political, social, and economic change. The success or failure of these early societies depended on their ability to adapt in the face of these new challenges. Early societies responded to new circumstances in different ways. Some, such as the Assyrians, were inventive and innovative, while others, such as the Egyptians, adapted to change by borrowing the innovations of others. Some sought political unification, while others responded with political fragmentation and still others looked to the republican remedies of mixed government. Some successfully adapted, while others failed to adapt.

Jared Diamond, the award-winning geographer, physiologist, and evolutionary biologist, has traveled the globe in search of the reasons why some societies succeed and others fail. According to Diamond, China exemplifies the unified approach to language and government, while New Guinea typifies the fragmented approach. Despite persistent ethnic and environmental differences, China was unified politically by 221 BCE. Most of its population speaks Mandarin, and it has always had one system of writing. By contrast, New Guinea, with a tiny fraction of China's population and only one-tenth of China's land area, consists of micro-populations scattered over many islands and ecosystems speaking 1,000 of the world's 6,000 languages.[2]

Notwithstanding these differences, anthropologists have found several common patterns of change and adaptation in early societies. As early societies evolved, for example, their populations tended to increase in size and diversity. Their populations also became less mobile, more settled, and more urbanized. At the same time, their economies became more specialized. Food production gradually replaced subsistence farming, labor became more specialized, and economic systems developed for the exchange of goods and services.

As their demographic and economic circumstances changed, the social organization of these societies tended to become more complex and stratified. Kinship ties remained important, but those ties were supplemented by other connections that brought some people together and kept others apart. The division of labor is a good example. Occupations became more specialized; people became apothecaries (the forerunners of today's pharmacists), blacksmiths (some of whom made armor for soldiers), bakers and candlestick-makers, carpenters, farmers, merchants, and scribes (who wrote and copied documents by hand). In medieval Europe, the members of the same occupations often formed guilds and often lived in the same neighborhoods. These associations became an additional source of identity, loyalty, and organization.

These social and economic changes influenced the evolution of law and government in two ways. First, population growth, diversity, and density placed new demands on all governing institutions. More people had to be fed, a permanent territory had to be defended from foreign attack, and more property had to be protected against theft. Second, to meet these demands, the institutions of law and government evolved in much the same way as social and economic institutions. They became more specialized, more structured, and more formal.

These social, economic, and political processes converged at various stages of development. Two stages are of particular importance: the transition to tribal societies and the transition from tribes to states. There is no uniform line separating these two stages. A society's political development might have jumped ahead of other changes as a result of strong and far-sighted leadership. Or the political development might have lagged behind social and economic changes because of weak, divided, or unimaginative leadership. Nonetheless, the differences between tribes and states are substantial, and they provide one way of comparing governments over time. Table 14.1 highlights the more important differences between tribes and states.

Table 14.1 Differences between Early Tribes and States

	Tribes	States
Population size	Hundreds to thousands	Hundreds of thousands
Level of diversity	Homogeneous	Heterogeneous
Social organization and identity	Kinship ties to clan and tribe	Political and territorial ties to the state Economic ties to occupation and class
Economy	Pastoral to agricultural and reciprocal	Diversified, including commercial and redistributive
Settlement pattern	Seminomadic to sedentary	Sedentary with urbanization
Governance	Council and chief	More specialized and structured institutions
Decision making	By custom and kinship	By written and codified laws
Republican examples	Conciliar republic to tribal confederation	Republican city-state to urban confederation or unified federation
Centralized examples	Chiefdom to tribute system	Kingdom to empire

HOW DID EARLY TRIBES DEVELOP?

A **tribe** is a society composed of multiple clans that share a common ancestry. The tribe is not the earliest stage of social evolution (see Chapter 4), but it is the first stage that requires formal institutions of government. In earlier stages, humans formed families that grew naturally into extended families that developed into clans that formed bands for their protection. The population of a productive band might have grown from the dozens to the low hundreds. Everyone knew one another and all were direct blood relatives.

The formation of a tribe represented a self-conscious and political decision to bring together clans of common ancestry that were not directly related to one another. This decision instantly increased the population of the primary governing unit from hundreds to thousands. Over time, some tribes increased in population to the tens of thousands. It may be an exaggeration, perhaps, but the Book of Genesis numbers the twelve tribes of Israel at around 600,000 people when they gathered at Mount Sinai.

The tribal stage brought the transition of society from a seminomadic pastoral people to a sedentary people with permanent settlements of farmers and herders. Society was organized primarily by clans, but people were beginning to identify not only with their clan but also with the tribe. The exchange of goods and services was largely reciprocal, meaning that people traded with one another in groups or as small collectives for what they needed.

The new demands of tribal settlements required a more structured government with more specialized institutions. Most pretribal societies had relied on elders for their governance. As tribes evolved in size and complexity, many established a more formalized council of elders. The council was assigned a special meeting place and met at regular intervals. Members instituted more specific qualifications for council members and agreed on their powers and limits.

As tribes grew, they faced various challenges: environmental disaster, lost herds, burned crops, famine, dried water wells, invasion, civil war, and power grabs by strong men. At each crisis point, societies made different choices or had different choices thrust upon them. This created divergent paths of development. Some tribes turned toward unification and centralization, while others fiercely guarded their isolation and independence. Tribal republics tended toward mixed models of internal government and a foreign policy of confederation.

HOW DID EARLY STATES DEVELOP?

A **state**, as a stage of societal evolution, is a society that is organized on the basis of political and territorial ties, not kinship. The transition from tribe to state was occasioned by the rapid acceleration of population growth (surpassing 50,000 people) and increased diversity. Some states grew by peacefully unifying tribes that did not share common ancestry; others grew by conquest.

The formation of the state also accelerated the development of societies in other ways:

- The diversification of economic activity, markets, and labor
- The transition to a redistributive economy, in which the state collected taxes partly to build and maintain roads, bridges, ports, grain warehouses, and other public works
- The urbanization of the population; that is, the growth in the number and size of cities[3]

State formation expanded governments in terms of the size of their budgets and bureaucracies, the scope of their responsibilities, and the number and specialization of their institutions. The state often established a state religion, funded the construction of religious shrines and temples, and underwrote a priestly class. The state was a primary consumer of the new technology of writing. Written laws replaced unwritten customs. States trained scribes to codify the law and professional judges to decide cases in new formal courts. The state established a professional army, a police force, tax collectors, and other bureaucrats.

There were principled and political reasons for these developments. Somewhere in the transition from tribe to state, a society changed from a land of kith and kin to a land of strangers.[4] The basis of trust also had to quickly change. Government, the law, order, and justice could no longer rely on an informal system in which everyone knew whom to trust, what to expect, and who was in charge. This was one of the practical reasons why law and government became more formalized. Written law, enforced by paid police and applied by professional judges, was now essential in a large and complex society where most people no longer knew one another.

Much of these political developments also centered on the fact that the new states were in conflict with their tribal base for the identity and loyalty of the people. Many states—republican and monarchic alike—formed professional armies of mercenary soldiers because they did not trust either the fighting power or the loyalty of tribal militias.

Governments instituted other measures to redirect people's identity and loyalty from their tribe to the state. One example was formalizing citizenship as membership in the state. Another was the census to track people for purposes of taxation and military service. In ancient Athens, Cleisthenes reassigned people from their tribal territories to districts, which became the basis for military service. But tribal identities were not so easily erased. Some tribal identities persist today, while many evolved into ethnic identities within larger multinational or multicultural states.

Two conclusions can be drawn about the place of republicanism in this early history. First, republican governments existed in both the tribe-based and state-based stages of development. This finding challenges the widely accepted view that political development was characterized by the increased centralization as well as specialization of institutions. Not all tribal decisions were based on consent; some leaders relied on force and intimidation. Nor did all early states become centralized; some were republican. Political centralization, in other words, was not the only pathway to political development. There was also a well-traveled and successful republican path in which states sought to balance the centralizing and noncentralizing forces of society. Most societies did indeed evolve into more centralized states, or they were conquered by them. Some, however, chose a republican path that successfully protected them from foreign invasion.

Second, republican governments existed in Europe and in non-European regions at both stages of development. Early Europe experienced a long and strong history of tribal republicanism, as did other regions of the world. Outside Europe, however, most tribal republics perished, became kingdoms, or were absorbed by empires before they had a chance to become full-fledged republican states. That is, the survival rate of republican states was higher for European than non-European republics. This, in fact, is the most important difference between the trajectories (paths) of political development for European and non-European republics.

The reasons for this distinction are complex and controversial. The next section takes a closer look at those non-European republics that successfully made the transition from isolated tribal republics to tribal confederacies. We then explore two non-European republican societies: North India during Buddhist times and Israel in biblical times. These societies that made the second transition to republican states left behind sufficient written and archeological records for us to study that transition.

HOW WERE TRIBAL REPUBLICS GOVERNED?

Most non-European tribe-based republics were modified conciliar republics.[5] A **conciliar republic** is a republic that is governed by a council of elders. As society grew and developed, tribal republics often developed a modified conciliar government or a mixed government in which a council of elders ruled in concert with a chieftain or king as the military leader, with both subject to the approval of a general assembly on important decisions.

Mixed government was commonplace among European and non-European republics. Aristotle anticipated three uses of mixed republican government: as a check against tyranny by the one, as a way to balance society's dominant interests, and as a separation of government powers or functions in the name of efficiency. Unfortunately, there is little comparative research on exactly why particular polities adopted a mixed form.

Non-European conciliar republics were also **gerontocracies**, relying on rule by elders. Like Venice, a European gerontocracy, they respected the leadership values of practical wisdom, maturity, patience, and tolerance that often came with age and experience. Qualifications for membership varied, but generally council membership was not open to all elders; councils of elders often included men of wealth, status, wisdom, or a combination of all three.

Councils were the most important governing institution in non-European tribal republics. A council of elders governed the community as a whole. In addition, social organizations (clans, age-graded organizations, and secret societies) were often governed internally by their own councils. As a governing institution, the council was well suited for allowing deliberation by a few respected leaders.

Non-European republics differed in the role of the people in the deliberative and decision-making process. In many non-European republics, the council of elders deliberated and then brought its important decisions before all the people or before an assembly of citizens for discussion and decision. Typically, this process had three stages: closed council deliberation, open discussion with community members, and community decision making by consensus (sometimes requiring unanimous approval).

In Amerindian cultures, spirituality was an important part of the decision-making process. Council members asked the spiritual leader of the polity to invoke spiritual assent for their deliberations and their decisions. Occasionally, secret societies would take on this task without being asked.

Some republics bordered on anarchy: consensus was difficult, obedience to decisions was not required, and chiefs did not last long. In other republics, an ambitious chief might win the loyalty of the warriors, seize power, and establish a chiefdom in place of the republic. Most non-European republics fluctuated somewhere between complete anarchy and absolute monarchy. In the eyes of many visitors, this middle ground looked like mild chaos—unruly and uncertain. Nevertheless, this was a form of mixed republican governance. And, of course, no two republics were exactly the same and no republic remained unchanged. Like European republics, non-European republics adapted to new circumstances and new challenges.

Tribal republics valued their independence, but few grew and developed in complete isolation. Interaction among tribes took various forms: some tribes shared a common ethnic origin and gathered for common ceremonies; some tribes traded with one another and learned about new tools, inventions, and ideas in the process; some tribes formed alliances with one another to better provide for their common defense; and many tribes used intermarriage to confirm or bless treaties and alliances.

In some instances, tribal republics with long and deep contact with one another formed tribal confederations. This was usually the result of a conscious political decision, often in response to common challenges. A **tribal confederation** is a formal association of tribes that voluntarily agree to come together for limited purposes, usually some combination of trade, defense, and foreign policy. In Europe, the Athenian-led Delian League is an example of a confederation; another example is the Hanseatic League of imperial European cities. Outside Europe, Indian republics in early Buddhist times relied heavily on confederations for trade and protection. So, too, did the twelve tribes of Israel and Judah.

A famous Amerindian confederation was the Iroquois Confederacy of Five (later Six) Nations. The Iroquois referred to themselves and their confederacy as *Haudenosaunnee* (meaning "people of the longhouse"). The Iroquois were a communal people who valued kinship and their clans. For community solidarity and individual identity, they lived in longhouses, rectangular houses that might each accommodate as many as twenty extended families of a particular clan.

The longhouse also had symbolic value. The lands of the Iroquois Confederacy were viewed as its collective longhouse. Each of the Five Nations maintained a national fire that symbolically represented a hearth in the longhouse of the confederacy. The Seneca in the west were the "Keepers of the Western Door." The Mohawk to the east were the "Keepers of

An Iroquois man dances and chants in the snow outside a reconstructed traditional longhouse. Longhouses provided the Iroquois with a sense of community solidarity and individual identity.

the Eastern Door," and the Onondaga were the "Keepers of the Central Council Fire and Wampum." The longhouse symbolized peace under one law, but it also stood for the united power of warriors who could be quickly mobilized from five nations.[6]

The same challenges that required confederation among tribes often required the modification of the government within tribes. At this stage of development, tribal republics often developed a more formal and specialized government in which a council of elders shared power with one or more chieftains and spiritual leaders.

The power of chieftains and their mode of selection varied considerably. In some instances, republics relied strictly on war chiefs, while in others the chieftains had broader powers in peace as well as war. In many of these mixed republics, the chief was elected by the council of elders or by an assembly of the citizenry. In some republics, royal edicts or council law had to be ratified by some form of popular consent or council approval. As Cadwallader Colden recorded, based on his eighteenth-century observations about such a system among the Iroquois:

> *Each Nation is an absolute Republick by itself, govern'd in all Publick Affairs of War and Peace by the Sachems [chiefs] or Old Men [council of elders], whose Authority and Power is gain'd by and consists wholly in the Opinion the rest of the Nation have of their Wisdom and Integrity. They never execute their Resolutions by Compulsion or Force upon any of their People.[7]*

These bronze castings were excavated at Igbo-Ukwo, Nigeria. Ritual scarring can be seen in the figure at right. After a limited monarchy developed in Igbo society, the king gathered a staff of ritual leaders recognizable by their unique pattern of facial scarring.

The Igbo of West Africa created a limited monarchy. Sometime in the late 900s CE, a branch of the Igbo founded the holy center of Nri, and it grew into a city. In the next century, a monarchy was founded at that site and became known as the Kingdom of Nri. At its peak, roughly between 1100 and 1400, it was said to include as much as half of Igboland. Nri may have eventually evolved into a republican state, but there is not enough evidence to be certain. However, it is clear that it became a limited monarchy with an intricate system for controlling monarchic tendencies and balancing power. Three developments support this assertion.

First, the chief executive, called the *Eze Nri* ("King of Nri"), was more like a ritual figure or high priest than a king. Around him, he gathered other ritual specialists recognizable by a particular pattern of facial scars and a peace staff. According to legend, they traveled the kingdom like missionaries with a message of peace. That is, the Nri were governed more like a theocracy, relying on spiritual powers, than a monarchy based on military prowess.

Second, Nri nobility, as in many African societies, was composed of different levels called "titles." These titles were acquired, not inherited. Acquiring a title involved an elaborate process of "lavish expenditure and a state of ritual purity."[8] Among the Nri, the title *eze* was the highest title. According to tradition, the Nri were governed by one *eze,* but as time went on the number of *eze* titleholders increased into the hundreds to form an upper nobility comparable to the barons of England or the magnates of Poland. It is believed that the number of *eze* titles increased as a check against a "grasping and avaricious" ruler.[9]

Third, when the ruling *eze* died, there was an interregnum (a hiatus period between rulers) that might last as long as seven years. As in all things political, there was probably a mix of reasons for this system. One reason was that time was needed to find the right spiritual leader with sufficient supernatural powers to rule; also, there was a need to balance and check the two sets of political interests—the overly ambitious *eze* and the overly ambitious nobles (the titled *ezes*)—either of which might seek to upset the system and grab power.[10]

HOW DID SOME POLITIES IN INDIA BECOME STATES?

The India historian John Keay began one of his works by comparing the political geography of Europe and India. Both subcontinents, he observed, have about the same area (4 million square kilometers). And both nourished republics, kingdoms, and empires. But their topography is very different.

Europe is a land of natural barriers—mountains, peninsulas (for example, Scandinavia, Iberia, and Italy), and islands (for example, Great Britain and Ireland)—that have fostered isolation and diversity by providing a variety of peoples with natural defenses against conquest. By contrast, India's topography includes a corridor of river valleys in the north (from what is today Pakistan east to Bihar) and the massive Deccan Plains in the south. These lands posed few natural barriers to conquest and unification. As Keay put it, "for Europe geography decreed fragmentation," while "for India it intended integrity."[11]

In northern India, politics initially defied geography. On one hand, as Keay explained, the broad river valleys in the north opened a human corridor to "commercial exchange" and "cultural uniformity." On the other hand, this corridor was home to a variety of independent monarchies and republics that fostered political diversity for centuries until eventually they were conquered by one of their number—the Mauryan Empire.[12]

Sometime around 700 BCE, sixteen of these independent monarchies and republics were established as *Mahajanapada*. The standard translation of the term is "Great Polity" or "State"; the term is used historically to refer to the epic period in the middle of the first millennium BCE (roughly 700–300 BCE) when these sixteen *Mahajanapadas* were formed as states, flourished, and were eventually conquered. This period is contemporaneous with the Classical Age of ancient Greece and Rome.

State formation was a gradual process. The process began during the Late Vedic period, perhaps as early as 900 BCE. (The name of this period takes its name from the sacred writings of this period, the *Vedas*.) Vedic societies were tribal, clan-based, nomadic, pastoral, and known for their powerful armies and militaristic culture. Vedic polities ranged widely from conciliar republics governed by a council of elders to chiefdoms governed by a *raja* (chief or king). Those in the middle of the spectrum were mixed republics or limited chiefdoms in which a chief shared power with a council and an assembly.

The *sabha* was a council of notable elders (including women) who assisted and checked the chief in administrative matters. Typically, the *raja* was elected by the *sabha* or the upper nobility. (Today, both houses of the Indian parliament are called *sabhas*.) The *samiti* was a popular assembly of all eligible males. Some Vedic polities also had a third institution, called the *vidhata*. This was a religious council that took care of religious ceremonies.[13]

The gradual transition from the Vedic polities to the Great Polities had all the familiar earmarks of state formation. These included the formation of permanent settlements, the development of irrigated agriculture, increased food production, increased population size, increased size and number of settlements, the building of large cities, economic specialization, and the growth of trade and commerce (social and political earmarks) and formal institutions of government, the government monopoly of military force, taxation as a source of state revenue, the rise of government bureaucracy, and a large class of nobility that provided a pool of leadership (political earmarks). Northern India developed a flourishing urban civilization that boasted parks, palaces, academies of learning, and temples.

The sixteen Great Polities existed along a diagonal corridor that included the present-day Indian states of Uttar Pradesh and Bihar and parts of Nepal, Afghanistan, and Pakistan. Six of

Jain Temple, Jaipur, Rajasthan, India.

the sixteen Great Polities (nearly 40 percent) were republican states: Kamboja, Kuru, Panchala, Shurasena, Malla, and Vrijji. The other ten were kingdoms.

Each state republic was typically a confederation of clan-based tribal republics joined by diplomacy and intermarriage. Vrijji, for example, was a confederation of eight smaller republics. (To give some sense of scale, Vaishali, the capital city of one of those smaller republics, was said to have 7,707 parks, each with a palace where a different aristocratic family resided.) The confederations were typically governed by a council composed of members from districts in each of the member republics. The chairman of the council, sometimes referred to as the *raja*, was the chief executive of the confederation government. Each confederation also had a judicial system for settling disputes among its members. That is, for the most part, they each had a mixed form of government that included a constitutional monarch with limited powers and a council of elders. They also had similar patterns of foreign relations and historical development.

Historians do not know why some of the Great Polities became republics while others remained kingdoms. There is ample evidence that the formation of these republics occurred at a time of considerable unrest. This unrest was manifest in religious movements against the ritual, hierarchy, exclusivity, and power created by the dominant caste of Brahmin priests. Only members of the Brahmin caste could be priests, and membership was hereditary. Signs of growing dissatisfaction with this monopoly of religious power appeared in the eighth century writings of Upanishad mystics.

Similar unrest appeared two to three centuries later in the teachings of two great ascetics. The older of the two, known as the Mahavira (Great Hero) founded **Jainism**, a set of spiritual principles that includes self-denial, nonviolence, and truthfulness. The younger ascetic, known as the Buddha (Enlightened One), developed a set of spiritual principles that included Four Noble Truths (see Chapter 13). The political significance of Buddhism was the republican idea that even the lowest born could seek the Four Noble Truths by following the Noble Eightfold Path to *nirvana* ("spiritual bliss").

POLITICS IN ACTION
The *Panchayat*

What is the oldest continuously operating council in the world? Most of the Indian republics had a *panchayat* system at the village level. *Panchayat* means "rule by a council of five." Its members were elected and carried out administrative and judicial tasks. The village *panchayat* system still exists today, making this the oldest continuously operating council form of government in the world. (See Chapter 13, Whatever Happened To . . . The Historical Republics.)

Both the Mahavira and the Buddha were born into republics that were members of the Vrijji Confederation. Both were born into a princely life of wealth, and both left that life and walked barefoot as ascetics in search of truth. In their travels, both gained large followings in a relatively short time. During the time of the Buddha, some of the six great republics became more democratic and turned to a form of government known as *gana-rajyas* ("rule of the assembly").

It is possible that the republics of the Great Polities were formed as a political expression of anti-Brahman, anticaste sentiments. Nevertheless, within several centuries of their formation, Mahavira and Buddha left them in shame and disgust. Perhaps these republics were losing their sense of republicanism as they became more stratified, centralized, and competitive. (See Politics in Action: The *Panchayat*.)

By the middle of the sixth century BCE, the kingdom of Magadha developed imperial ambitions. Its rulers pushed westward, conquering and annexing most republics and kingdoms along the way, and forming the Magadha Empire. This was the precursor of the famous Mauryan Empire (321–124 BCE) founded by Chandragupta. (See Bold Thinkers: Kautilya.)

The Mauryan Empire pushed further westward, annexing Kamboja. After fighting a successful yet bloody campaign, the legendary Mauryan emperor Ashoka (273–232 BCE) rejected violence and converted to Buddhism. He restored some republican institutions, but his reforms were not maintained by the emperors who followed him.

After Ashoka, republicanism survived in village governments, Buddhist monasteries, and some republics such as Kamboja that were allowed to retain a measure of self-government under imperial rule. Indian republicanism was rediscovered 2,000 years later by the Indian National Congress Party, which was founded in 1885 to lead the movement for Indian independence from British rule.

BOLD THINKERS

Kautilya

Kautilya was the key advisor to Chandragupta, founder of the Mauryan Empire. Kautilya's policies were crucial in consolidating most of the Indian subcontinent under Mauryan rule. The empire passed down intact to Chandragutpa's son and then to his grandson, Ashoka, who is considered one of the greatest kings in world history.

Kautilya's political philosophy and policies were eventually captured in written form in *Arthashastra* ("Science of the Polity"), based on a text by Kautilya and added to by many thinkers over many years. Kautilya offered science as a means of power to conquer the world. The book was an influential practical analysis of his political world.

Kautilya believed that a ruler should use any method necessary to attain his goals without any moral or ethical considerations. Some of his measures were harsh; for instance, he endorsed the use of secret agents to kill enemy leaders and sow discord among them. According to Max Weber, compared to *Arthashastra* "Machiavelli's *The Prince* is harmless."[1] On the other hand, Kautilya believed in the humane treatment of subjects and of conquered soldiers. In domestic politics, he suggested an elaborate welfare state, or a socialized monarchy.

The extreme measures upheld by Kautilya brought order out of chaos, allowing for the great moral transformations of Ashoka's rule. *Arthashastra* remains an important source of the history of republicanism in India.

1. Quoted in Roger Boesche, *The First Great Political Realist: Kautilya and His* Arthashastra (Lanham, Md.: Lexington Books, 2002), 7.

HOW DID THE REPUBLICAN POLITY OF BIBLICAL ISRAEL EVOLVE?

Of all ancient sources of non-European republics, the Hebrew Bible provides the longest and most detailed account of the constitutional development of a republican people. Chapter 12 assesses the uses and dangers of using the Hebrew Bible not as history but as a source of political insight; it takes a close and careful look at the lessons to be learned from the constitutional development of the Israelites. Our review here focuses on two major stages in the constitutional evolution of biblical Israel: the transition from tribes to tribal confederation and the transition from tribal confederation to republican state.

The Israelites legitimized each stage of constitutional development by a political covenant (see Chapter 12). To do this, they first had to adapt the covenantal idea from its ancient Near Eastern use as a foreign treaty between nations to its new use as an instrument of constitutional change within one nation.

There were two preconditions to the Israelites' reinvention of the covenantal idea. The Israelites were a republican people and a monotheistic people who believed in one God who they called YAWEH. Therefore, their political covenants had to embody those two principles. As the biblical idea evolved, a political covenant came to mean an agreement by which people voluntarily come together and bind themselves as equal partners with one another and to God as a party or witness to form a holy commonwealth that is dedicated to a divinely inspired moral purpose.

As recounted in the Book of Exodus, the Israelites struck their first political covenants at Mount Sinai shortly after they escaped slavery in Egypt. In the Sinai covenants, the Israelites agreed with God, Moses, and one another to (1) create a polity based on the Ten Commandments, (2) obey those commandments as citizens of that new polity, (3) form that polity as a confederation of the twelve tribes, and (4) establish a confederation government based on the separation of powers between three institutions of leadership: a council of tribal elders, who were responsible for civil leadership; a high priest, who was responsible for organizing religious ceremonies and maintaining religious shrines; and a prime minister (Moses and then Joshua), who carried out the prophetic responsibility of interpreting the word of God.

According to biblical historians, the date of the Sinai covenants was sometime around 1300 BCE. As told in the Book of Exodus, the Israelites then wandered in the desert for forty years. They were a tribal people and a seminomadic people, much as they had been before they were enslaved in Egypt.

When Moses died, his heir Joshua led the Israelites into the land of Canaan. Here they fought the local inhabitants to carve out a territory for each of the twelve tribes. The Israelites became a sedentary people—two tribes settled in the southern region of the country, which they called Judah (later renamed Judea by the Romans) and ten tribes occupied the northern region, which they called Israel (creating no small amount of confusion in the years to come). Joshua then initiated covenants with God and the people that contained two elements: the recognition of the change from a mobile polity to a permanent polity and the authorization of the continuation of the tribal confederation with the same form of government established at Sinai.

Tribes turned inward to their new homelands, and tribal leadership became stronger and more entrenched. Centuries passed. In roughly 1020 BCE, the Philistines invaded Israel and the divided tribes were no match for them. Tribal leaders urged Samuel the prophet to help them find a king to lead them. They were willing to give up a significant portion of their power and independence to unite around one king. But, with Samuel's coaching, they insisted on a constitutional or limited monarchy. They decided that they needed to unite, but they did not want a unitary state.

Tribal leaders agreed to the establishment of a federal republican state, first through a covenant with King Saul, who failed them (and himself), and then with King David, who was a brilliant success. The government was a constitutional monarchy, with the king's powers checked and balanced by the powers of a high priest, a prophet, and the tribal elders.

David's covenants (known as the Davidic covenants) transformed Israel into a republican state with a united constitutional monarchy. But becoming a state required more than a covenant. David's civil, military, and foreign achievements enabled Israel to gain acceptance as a state among its neighboring states. Israel's population, markets, foreign trade, number of occupations, and number of roads and public buildings all grew under David's leadership. David helped establish a formal government with armies, bureaucracies, taxes, and other specialized institutions. Under David's leadership, Israel conquered its enemies, expanded its territory, and secured its borders.

WHY DID SOME REPUBLICS FAIL?

Polities usually fail because of a run of bad luck, bad decisions, dangerous neighbors, or some combination of these factors. Of the three, avoiding bad decisions is especially important. Human beings have more control over their own decisions than over fate or hostile neighbors. Moreover, human beings can use their decision-making abilities to control some of the worst effects of human nature, fate, and hostile neighbors. Many factors influence a good decision, but wise judgment is key. Because there is no guarantee that all future decisions will be wise ones, statesmen try to design forms of government that will reduce the effects of bad decisions in the future. Good judgment can minimize the effects of bad luck. Polities cannot choose their neighbors, but they can unite against foreign aggression.

To argue, for example, that most republics failed because they were overwhelmed by more powerful empires misses an important point—some republics fought back and won. The tribes of Israel defeated the Philistines. The Greeks pushed back the Persians. Even the mighty Roman armies were contained and eventually destroyed by the Germanic tribes.

The Israelites succeeded by uniting under effective leadership. The twelve tribes of Israel formed a republican state with a united constitutional monarchy led by David. The Greeks also succeeded by uniting. Athens and Sparta put aside their differences, joined forces, and persuaded their allies to join with them.

The right choice was not always the first choice. The Israelites first chose Saul to lead them and only later united around David. And the circumstances favoring the right choice did not last forever. Athens and Sparta did not reunite centuries later when Athens was threatened by Philip II of Macedonia.

Why did Athens and Sparta eventually fail? Was it inevitable that sooner or later each would meet a foe too mighty to withstand? We think not. In both instances, the evidence of political failure points first to the failure to unite in time against a common foe.

Demosthenes (c. 384–322 BCE), the greatest of Greek orators, was convinced that Philip II had global ambitions and that sooner rather than later he would invade Athens. He tried in vain to convince Athenians of the impending danger. But most Athenians were duped by Philip's promises of peace. In the *Philippics* ("orations against Philip"), Demosthenes laid out a strategy of republican unity. He urged his fellow Athenians to wake up from their lethargy, ignore Philip's reassurances of peaceful coexistence, set their disagreements aside, restore republican government at home, unite for their common defense, confederate with former allies abroad, and prepare for war without delay. Unity eventually came, but it was too late—Athens was defeated.

Two twentieth-century scholars, Barbara Tuchman and Jared Diamond, have analyzed the history of political failure in republics and nonrepublics. They approached this subject in different ways and from different directions, but they both came to a similar conclusion—bad decisions are a major source of political failure. Barbara Tuchman, the renowned American historian, presented her interpretations in *The March of Folly*. Tuchman focused on misgovernment by folly, which she defined as the continued pursuit of policy contrary to a people's self-interest and contrary to the mounting evidence available at the time.[14] Jared

Diamond focused at the macro level on the causes of societal failure in *Collapse: How Societies Choose to Succeed or Fail.*[15] As the subtitle indicates, Diamond also attributed societal failure to human beings who make disastrous decisions.

Tuchman's and Diamond's interpretations vary in many respects, but their area of overlap includes three human failings in the decision-making process: wooden-headedness, arrogance, and selfishness. **Wooden-headedness**, or stubbornness, according to Tuchman, is the primary cause of foolish decisions. Tuchman defined wooden-headedness as the assessment of a situation based on "preconceived fixed notions while ignoring or rejecting any contrary signs."[16] Diamond focused on a related source of failure, "the failure to attempt to solve [a problem] after it has been perceived."[17] **Arrogance**, or an attitude of superiority, is a human source of reckless decisions. "Folly," Tuchman wrote, "is the child of power." Excessive power, Tuchman explained, "frequently causes failure to think."[18] The classic biblical example is the arrogance of Rehoboam, David's grandson, who insulted the northern tribal leaders of Israel and thereby divided the monarchy that David had spent his life unifying.

Selfishness, or self-interest, is a third source of failure. Self-interest can be a positive force when it brings people together to advance their own interests and contribute to the common good. This is what Alexis de Tocqueville referred to as self-interest properly understood. But self-interest carried to excess can breed what Diamond termed a "clash of interests" in which political suspicion, mistrust, and jealousy make cooperation unlikely if not impossible. Diamond pointed to a related source of societal failure, a "clash of values," in which leaders and citizens alike become locked in a war of competing belief systems that make cooperation impossible.[19] The civil war between oligarchs and democrats in Athens resulted from a clash of both interests and values.

These three human flaws are not the only sources of political failure, but they are important sources in all polities, both republican and nonrepublican. What specifically are the types of republican failure? And how are they triggered by bad decisions?

According to Aristotle, the key to republican success is balance and moderation. He argued persuasively that the reverse also applied—imbalance and excess are the causes of republican failure. Achieving republican balance is no simple task. Republics are constantly pulled in opposite directions by two forces. Centripetal forces pull the republic toward the center, while centrifugal forces push the republic away from the center. Republican politics is the result of the constant tension between these two forces; centrists demand unity in the name of order; noncentrists demand diversity in the name of freedom.

This constant tension can be a good thing. "Ambition," wrote James Madison "must be made to counter ambition." He continued, "This policy of supplying, by opposite and rival interests, the defect of better motives, might be traced through the whole system of human affairs, private as well as public."[20] Like Aristotle, Madison believed that a well-designed constitution could allow rival interests to balance one another and help control the effects of bad decisions. But even the best constitution cannot eliminate bad decisions. Republics, after all, are human associations, not machines. Hence, balance and moderation must also be values that inspire the way people conduct themselves in the political arena.

Figure 14.1 shows four republican pathways to failure. Each results from the excesses of centrifugal or centripetal forces in domestic or foreign policy. Let us take them one by one.

Figure 14.1 Why Republics Fail

	Centrifugal forces	Centripetal forces
Internal imbalance	Factionalism ($\to$ anarchy)	Centralization ($\to$ tyranny)
External imbalance	Fission ($\to$ isolated states)	Fusion ($\to$ empire)

FACTIONALISM

Factionalism—the excessive divisiveness of factions—occurs when a society is divided by opposing political factions that are unable to find consensus or compromise solutions to the conflicts that divide them. As defined by James Madison, a *faction* is "a number of citizens, whether amounting to a majority or minority of the whole, who are united and actuated by some common impulse of passion, or of interest, adverse to the rights of other citizens, or to the permanent and aggregate interests of the community."[21]

Madison saw factionalism as the most serious danger facing republics. He believed that factionalism was caused by the confluence of several factors: human nature, which fosters differences in opinions; the unequal distribution of property, which is the primary source of divergent interests; inflammatory politicians who seek to fan those differences into animosities; and republican liberty, which allows diversity and dissent in the name of the freedom of expression.[22] Eliminating any of these factors, reasoned Madison, was not the answer because that would destroy the very reasons for wanting republicanism in the first place. Instead, Madison advocated a policy of controlling the effects of these four factors by allowing rival interests to cancel one another out.

The causes of factionalism would be incomplete without selfishness. People pursue their own self-interests; lose sight of the common good; mistrust one another; and divide into opposing factions, which makes cooperation difficult if not impossible. Factionalism can take various forms, but Madison was correct in pointing to the unequal distribution of property and the political ambitions of powerful opponents. Historical European examples include the divisions between aristocrats and democrats in Athens, patricians and plebeians in Rome, the king and Parliament in England, and the king and knights in the Polish-Lithuanian Commonwealth. Outside Europe, the Bible records the constant battling between kings and tribal leaders over taxation and the military draft.

James Madison (1751–1836) believed that factions could lead to excessive divisiveness. For this reason, he argued, factions posed the gravest danger to republics.

Some non-European republics, such as the Iroquois and Igbo, set very high standards of freedom and consensus. Individuals were often free to withhold their approval of council decisions. This was the case even in societies where council decisions were not binding without a consensus achieved by unanimous consent.

In such instances, the decision-making process might stretch out for a long time, even on critical issues. Europeans who observed the process were amazed at the patience—and stubbornness—of the parties involved. Anarchy and chaos might result. Failure to reach consensus might also result in conquest and subjugation. An important European example is the Polish-Lithuanian Commonwealth. The commonwealth became easy prey for neighboring empires, partly because of the deadlocks created during the period when any commonwealth knight could veto a royal decision.

EXCESSIVE CENTRALIZATION

Excessive centralization occurs when an ambitious leader of a powerful faction overturns the delicate balance of power by seizing absolute control of the reins of government. Historically, this was the fate of many failed republics; they remained intact but under the thumb of a single tyrant or a faction of oligarchs.

Aristotle designed his mixed republic to avoid this threat of tyranny. He wrote with admiration of Solon, the Athenian lawmaker who had designed such a republic 250 years earlier.

The founders of the Roman Republic designed their government in much the same way. Whether the Roman Republic was a success because it lasted nearly five hundred years or a failure because it ultimately fell prey to the imperial designs of Julius Caesar is a matter of interpretation. But there is no doubt that factionalism in the last century of the Roman Republic created the ideal opportunity for ambitious men to seize power.

FISSION

Fission occurs when foreign relations break down and confederated republics split apart or when republics fail to confederate in the first place. The isolation resulting from fission was devastating for many republics.

Confederation was the ideal foreign policy for ancient republics. On one hand, they avoided the dangers of fission and complete isolation. They had trading partners to obtain the resources they did not have, allies for common protection, and a continuous source of new ideas and inventions. On the other hand, they avoided the dangers of fusion and complete consolidation.

Many growing tribal republics and young republican states reached a stage of development that called for some form of confederation. In Europe, the Greek democracies joined the Delian League, the northern Italian city-republics allied in the Lombard League to repel imperial and papal armies, and the free imperial cities in the Holy Roman Empire formed the Hanseatic League. All the non-European republics discussed in this and earlier chapters formed confederations at one time in their premodern histories. Confederations united the twelve tribes of Israel, the five Iroquois nations, and many of the Igbo communities of West Africa. In northern India, the six republics of the Great Polities stood apart from one another, but internally most of them were confederations of smaller republics or they confederated with neighboring small republics.

FUSION

Fusion occurs when republics are fused together or consolidated into a single centralized state and lose their republican nature. Before the Americans created a federal republican state in 1787, most republics either rejected political unification or never had the opportunity to try it. It was commonly believed that republics had to be small and homogeneous in population. If a republic grew too large, it was believed, only a strong central government could hold the society together. Many people feared that such a centralized government would tend to gather power to itself (and away from the people) to ensure its continued survival. In the process, citizens would lose their sense of community, their freedom, and their control over the government.

Rome was a rare example of a republic that became an empire and yet retained its republican character for centuries. It did this by creating an empire governed by laws, guaranteeing the equal application of those laws to all peoples, and eventually extending citizenship to its conquered peoples.

However, as we have seen, there were other European republics, and some non-European republics, that reached a total population numbering in the hundreds of thousands and a citizenry numbering in the tens of thousands. Certainly, this was a scale that made it impossible for individuals to know everyone. This was also a scale that set real limits both on individual freedom and on popular control over the government. The formation of a republican state presented a reasonable solution to this problem. It offered a new basis of civic identity, a new conception of limited freedom, and a form of unity for common needs that avoided complete consolidation. Most republican states were city-states like Athens, with a city and surrounding countryside. Some were territorial states like biblical Israel, consisting of united tribes, each with its own extended territory.

LEARNING FROM THE PAST

In the next unit, we turn to the history of republicanism in the medieval and early modern era and in the age of Enlightenment. Five great revolutions are considered: the Renaissance, the Reformation, the Glorious Revolution of 1689, the American constitutional revolution of 1787, and the French Revolution of 1789. The bold thinkers that inspired these revolutions and the statesmen who led them were well aware of the republican history that preceded them. How did these modern revolutionaries seek to avoid the republican failures of the past? How successful were they? Did they see the ancient experiences of Athens, Rome, and Jerusalem as models to follow or as flawed thinking to avoid?

REVIEWING AND USING THE CHAPTER

1. Identify and describe the typical stages in the development of republican states. Provide specific examples to illustrate each stage.

2. Compare the origins and development of republics in Africa and India. How were they alike, and how did they differ?

3. What ideas made the Iroquois Confederacy a successful model of tribal confederation?

4. Of the four common pathways to republican failure (factionalism, centralization, fission, and fusion), which is most dangerous in today's political environment? Why?

EXTENSION ACTIVITIES

1. The exercise of wise judgment is critical to the success of any republic. What principles or ideas should guide the exercise of wise judgment? Use specific examples to support your answer.

2. Select two non-European republics that existed before 1600. Using Figure 14.1 as a guide, research them and explain why they succeeded or failed.

WEB RESOURCES

The British Museum: Ancient India
www.ancientindia.co.uk/staff/hinduism/resources.html

This entry gives students and teachers a variety of resources useful in the study of ancient India, including brief background essays, discussion questions, worksheets, and other classroom activities.

Manus: India and Its Neighbors
www.sscnet.ucla.edu/southasia/History/mainhist.html

Created and maintained by Vinay Lal, associate professor of history at UCLA, this Web site contains a series of original and concise essays about the political history of India. Here you will also find original essays about the culture, landscape, religions, and social issues of India.

The New York State Museum Project: Iroquois Web Resources
www.history.com/encyclopedia.do?vendorId=FWNE.fw..ir042600.a#FWNE.fw.ir042600.a

This Web site provides links to dozens of Web-based resources to aid in the study of Iroquois culture and history.

NOTES

[1] This section draws on the following general works: Morton H. Fried, *The Evolution of Political Society: An Essay in Anthropology* (New York: Random House, 1967); Elman Rogers Service, *Origins of the State and Civilization: The Process of Cultural Evolution;* (New York: Norton, 1975); S. E. Finer, *The History of Government, Vol. 1: Ancient Monarchies and Empires* (New York: Oxford University Press, 1997); Jared Diamond, *Guns, Germs, and Steel: The Fates of Human Societies* (New York: W. W. Norton, 1997).

[2] Diamond, *Guns, Germs, and Steel,* 306, 324.

[3] Ibid., 278–281.

[4] Ibid., 273.

[5] This section draws on Cadwallader Colden, *The History of the Five Indian Nations* (Ithaca, N.Y.: Cornell University Press, 1958; originally published in two volumes in 1727 and 1747); Daniel K. Richter, *The Ordeal of the Long-House* (Chapel Hill: University of North Carolina Press, 1992); Elizabeth Isichei, *The History of the Igbo People* (New York: St. Martin's Press, 1976); John Keay, *India: A History* (New York: Grove Press, 2000); Stanley Wolpert, *India: A New History,* 7th ed. (New York: Oxford University, 2004). See also John Phillip Reid, *A Law of Blood: The Primitive Law of the Cherokee Nation* (De Kalb, Ill.: Northern Illinois University Press, 2006; originally published by New York University Press, 1970); Jomo Kenyatta, *Facing Mount Kenya: The Tribal Life of the Gikuyu* (London: Secker and Warburg, 1938); Michael Taylor, *Community, Anarchy, and Liberty* (Cambridge, UK: Cambridge University Press, 1982).

[6] New York State Museum, "Iroquois Longhouse," available at www.nysm.nysed.gov/IroquoisVillage/constructionone.html; Richter, *Ordeal of the Long-House,* Chap. 2.

[7] Colden, *History of the Five Indian Nations,* xx.

[8] Elizabeth Isichei, *A History of African Societies to 1870* (Cambridge, UK: Cambridge University Press, 1997), 248.

[9] This observation was made by Reverend Julius Spencer of the Niger Mission, Asaba, 1901, quoted in ibid.

[10] On the Nri kingdom see ibid., 246–249.

[11] Keay, *India,* xxiii.

[12] Ibid., xxv.

[13] R. C. Bhardwaj, "India," in *World Encyclopedia of Parliaments and Legislatures,* ed. George Thomas Kurian, Vol. 1 (Washington, D.C.: Congressional Quarterly, 1998), 318–319.

[14] Barbara W. Tuchman, *The March of Folly: From Troy to Vietnam* (New York: Ballantine Books, 1984).

[15] Jared Diamond, *Collapse: How Societies Choose to Fail or Succeed* (New York: Penguin Books, 2005).

[16] Tuchman, *March of Folly,* 5, 7.

[17] Diamond, *Collapse,* 438.

[18] Tuchman, *March of Folly,* 32.

[19] Diamond, *Collapse,* 427–428, 431.

[20] James Madison, "The Federalist No. 51," in *The Federalist Papers,* by Alexander Hamilton, James Madison, and John Jay, ed. Clinton Rossiter (New York: New American Library, 1961), 322.

[21] James Madison, "The Federalist No. 10," in *The Federalist Papers,* by Alexander Hamilton, James Madison, and John Jay, ed. Clinton Rossiter (New York: New American Library, 1961), 78.

[22] Ibid., 79.

REPUBLICS IN MEDIEVAL AND EARLY MODERN TIMES

For centuries, much of Europe was governed as part of the Roman Empire. This ended in the fifth century after Rome was sacked repeatedly by Germanic tribes. The political void created by the loss of centralized Roman government left many regions without government—or, at least, without competent government. Europeans suddenly faced a difficult question: What kind of government would replace Roman control?

As you will learn in chapter 15, this question was answered by three political ideas: feudalism, monarchism, and republicanism. Republicanism during the Middle Ages was perhaps most apparent in the role it played in securing the rule of law. Republicanism was reflected in the use of the law as a basis for protecting freedoms and creating governments. Parliaments arose as a form of virtual representation and as a check on the monarchy. In addition, communes and confederations provided self-government, protection, and trade among the free medieval cities.

Republicanism was a common thread running from the Middle Ages through the Renaissance. Chapter 16 follows this thread. Republicans in the fifteenth century had begun to question the medieval

CHAPTER 15:

WHAT WERE THE KEY DEVELOPMENTS OF REPUBLICANISM DURING THE MIDDLE AGES?

CHAPTER 16:

WHY DID THE RENAISSANCE AND REFORMATION REVIVE CLASSICAL REPUBLICANISM?

order that locked individuals in their places in the group into which they were born and in the hierarchy by which they were governed. A new way of thinking evolved, with a more humanistic interest in the centrality of the individual. This way of thinking was strongly influenced by the rediscovery of the texts of ancient Greek and Roman philosophers. Humanist and republican movements soon arose across Europe. As you will learn in the second chapter of this unit, the classical Roman republicanism of the virtuous citizen and the good republic was especially important in Italian, German, Dutch, and English political thought.

CHAPTER 15

WHAT WERE THE KEY DEVELOPMENTS OF REPUBLICANISM DURING THE MIDDLE AGES?

BIG IDEAS

- Medieval Europe was influenced by republicanism as well as feudalism and monarchism.

- Republicanism developed in different ways in the three different estates of the nobility, Church, and commoners.

- The Middle Ages contributed to the development of important republican institutions, including the rule of law, parliaments, constitutional monarchy, and the city as a republic.

Purpose of This Chapter

Republicanism was as important to the Middle Ages as was feudalism and monarchism. Together, these three great ideas exerted tremendous influence on the political mosaic of the Middle Ages. Perhaps the most important republican idea of the Middle Ages was freedom through the rule of law. The nobility, Church reformers, and cities used four instruments to realize that idea: (1) the law as a basis for protecting freedoms and creating governments (including charters such as the Magna Carta), (2) the parliament as a form of virtual representation and as a check on the king in most European monarchies, (3) the commune (for example, the Italian city-republics and free imperial cities) as a form of self-government, and (4) the confederation (for example, the Hanseatic League) as a form of protection and trade among free cities.

Terms to Know

charter	commune	Medieval Renaissance
charters of incorporation	customary law	monarchism
city charter of incorporation	Dark Ages	parliament
city-states	feudalism	
	free imperial cities	

WHAT WAS THE SIGNIFICANCE OF FEUDALISM AND MONARCHISM IN THE MIDDLE AGES?

At the peak of its power, the Roman Empire maintained a strict and often brutally enforced system of law and order across Western

Europe. In that system, roads connected people, cities prospered, trade and commerce grew, and art and architecture flourished. The empire kept the peace, maintained the roads, and supported the economy.

In the fifth century, the Roman Empire lost its grip over its western lands. Rome itself was sacked twice in that century. Then, in 476 CE, Odoacer deposed Romulus Augustulus, the last Western Roman emperor, and became the first Germanic king of Italy.

The decline of the empire created a power vacuum across Europe. Armies of Huns, Goths, and Vandals swept across the continent. Order gradually evaporated into chaos, travel and trade became risky, commercial cities declined, and hard economic times set in. These were bleak times for Europe.

Some historians use the term **Dark Ages** to refer to the five hundred years of European history following the collapse of the Roman Empire (roughly 500–1000 CE). The Dark Ages is not only descriptive of economic hardships, it also describes lost history. Writings from earlier periods disappeared or went untranslated in these chaotic times. Only Arabic and Jewish thinkers knew about Aristotle's and Plato's major works. In many ways, Europeans in this period had to start from scratch. Moreover, few records survived from this period, so we know little about how Europe recovered.

The Dark Ages was largely confined to Europe and Russia. Other parts of the world continued to develop, even flourish, during the period. East of Rome, the Byzantine Empire (also known as the Eastern Roman Empire) flourished during the Dark Ages. In addition, Islam was born and Muslim Arabs carved out an empire that stretched from Persia to Spain. Farther east, Bengal became the first independent Buddhist and republican kingdom of northern India, and the Sui and Tang dynasties reunified and strengthened the Chinese Empire.

The great political challenge of the Dark Ages was the transformation of peoples into polities. As Europe slowly recovered, the continent became a mosaic of diverse political interests. The first cultural influence on the scene was the Catholic Church. In the countryside, clergy established churches, organized parishes, and created monasteries of learning across Europe. The Church controlled numerous cities (called ecclesiastical cities) that were governed by bishops. The Church also had a presence in other towns and cities. Popes sought an even wider domain. Their goal was to see that the Church became the soul of Europe, not from any one cathedral or citadel but through the clergy in every community.

Popes also sought to extend their control over kings by insisting that all royal investitures be sanctified by an oath administered by the Church. If a king refused, he could be excommunicated and his nobles put under *interdict,* a Church order that excluded them from participation in most sacraments. This meant that priests were forbidden from performing their baptisms, marriages, and burials. Kings chafed under the popes' power and often challenged their authority. Rivalry between popes and kings was rife. (See Politics in Action: Henry IV versus Pope Gregory VII.)

The nobility in the countryside converted their lands into manors and fought to protect and expand their lands. The stronger and richer nobles acquired ever larger domains and entered into alliances with *magnates*—high nobility called barons, dukes, and counts. The most powerful often became kings.

POLITICS IN ACTION
Henry IV versus Pope Gregory VII

Pope Gregory VII (c.1020–1085) and Holy Roman Emperor Henry IV (1050–1106) vied dramatically for power in late eleventh-century Europe. Before Gregory became pope, simony (selling church offices), clerical marriage, and political and economic abuses within the Church had become widespread. Many of these problems, in Gregory's view, stemmed from lay investiture (the appointment of Church bishops by lay rulers). When Pope Gregory tried to end this practice, he quickly came into conflict with Henry. As holy Roman emperor, Henry jealously guarded his authority to appoint German bishops.

Henry had good reason to distrust the motives of church leaders. Because he had come to the throne as a child, others had ruled in his stead until he became an adult. During his regency, Church leaders had moved aggressively to take imperial wealth and power.

When Pope Gregory forbade lay investiture in 1075, the brutal struggle began. Following Henry's excommunication by Gregory, warfare erupted in Germany when many nobles rebelled against Henry's authority to rule.

This contemporary 11th-century manuscript illumination shows Henry IV asking Matilda of Tuscany and the Abbot of Cluny to intercede for him with Pope Gregory.

After Henry did penance in January 1077, Gregory lifted his excommunication. Nevertheless, the struggle continued. Henry later attacked Rome, deposed Pope Gregory, and even chose a rival antipope.

Gradually, the cities and commerce began to recover. Among the first cities to recover were those in Germanic lands and in the city republics in northern Italy. Merchants controlled the commercial cities. They formed powerful guilds or associations to represent their interests. Guild and city leaders negotiated with their overlord (a nobleman or the king) for a charter that granted their city self-government and some limited freedoms.

Out of this diversity, three political systems emerged: feudalism, monarchism, and republicanism. All three systems developed simultaneously and influenced one another. Republicanism is often ignored in this history, but republican principles and institutions played an important role in the development of free cities, Italian city republics, limited monarchies, and Church organization.

There were tensions within and among feudalism, monarchism, and republicanism. But the prolonged coexistence of these three systems is one of the distinguishing features of the European Middle Ages. Mixed republican government was at the center of these attempts to balance power and interests within and among these systems. The results strengthened the legal and political foundations of the modern world.

Feudalism is a hierarchical system of mutual obligations between lords and vassals. As a hierarchy, feudal society was arranged into levels like a pyramid. Each person was assigned to a specific level of society where he or she held a particular rank. In this system, the lord granted an interest in land (called a *fief*) and protection to his vassal in exchange for the vassal's pledge of *fealty* (loyalty or homage) and service to the lord.

As a hierarchical system, feudalism could be centralized or decentralized. Power can float up or down a hierarchy. At first, power was dispersed among the various levels of noblemen as lords. But, over time, the kings managed to centralize power. Their ability to do so, however, was frequently checked by the collective resistance of noblemen.

Feudalism dominated much of the European countryside from the ninth century to the fourteenth century. Its existence was most apparent in England, where the Normans imposed a feudal system after they conquered England in 1066. William the Conqueror claimed all lands. He kept one-fifth as crown lands, he gave one-quarter to the Church, and he distributed the rest among 170 barons. They held their lands on condition of allegiance to the king. The barons provided troops for the king's wars and taxes for his courts. The king, in turn, controlled the barons' inheritance and family marriages. He also had at his disposal enormous patronage in the form of jobs (such as sheriffs and constables) that he could dole out as rewards to loyal subjects.[1]

According to some scholars, feudalism is the great medieval idea. That idea is often pictured as an elaborate "chain of being"—a divinely inspired hierarchy in which everyone's rank is fixed and unchangeable.[2]

At the top of the feudal pyramid, there was the relationship between the king as lord and the high nobility (called magnates) who were in his service as vassals. The magnates, in turn, had lower nobility (called knights) in their service as vassals. (Some kings grew so strong that they could claim the knights as vassals too.) Many knights became lords of manors and engaged free farmers, indebted farmers, and bonded serfs as vassals. When called to service, noblemen of all ranks were expected to gather their vassals and follow their king into battle. If the noblemen's land produced resources of value, the king also expected a share of those resources.

This exchange of obligations had elements of equality and inequality. The obligations were unequal: land for service, and protection for troops. So too were the parties involved: lord and vassal. But the agreement had an element of equality. In theory, the feudal exchange required the mutual agreement of reciprocal obligations freely entered into by both sides. The two parties each agreed to carry out his obligations despite their unequal status. In fact, an oath was sworn before God to bind both parties to the agreement.

In practice, the lord was typically freer than the vassal. "Is there any more elusive notion," writes the social historian Marc Bloch, "than the free will of a small man."[3] Nonetheless, as Europe prospered, so too did many vassals. Prosperous vassals increasingly had little desire to take on the more onerous conditions of military service. They particularly disliked long periods of service far from home. Many began to buy their way out of longer tours.

Feudalism also had a republican element. The feudal agreement and oath-taking became an important source of the rule of law, especially the idea that no one (not even the king) was above the law. Every agreement had to be confirmed by an oath administered by the Church and sworn before God. Once sworn, the oath had the effect of law. To break an oath was unthinkable, even if the parties were of unequal status.

Monarchism is the theory that one ruler (such as the king) should hold supreme political power (or sovereignty). But *supreme* power did not entitle the king to absolute or complete power. That idea did not gain currency until centuries later.

Economic competition developed in feudal systems between the monarch at the top of the hierarchy and the middle levels of nobility (from the magnates down to the knights). They all sought to control land, collect revenues derived from the land, and control the soldiers that such revenue could equip. Prosperity increased the available resources, which often helped to reduce the conflicts over them. As Europe prospered, so did the kings, magnates, and other nobility.

In a monarchy, the king tended to centralize power. In a feudal system, the nobility attempted to decentralize power. The Aristotelian answer to these tendencies was, of course, balance, so that neither pulls the system to its extreme. Because of these two overlapping systems, power floated, and the results differed from kingdom to kingdom. In England, for example, the barons sought to limit the king's powers. In Poland, magnates (the equivalent of barons) sided with the king against the knights. In the Germanic lands of the Holy Roman Empire, princes were loyal to the emperor, yet they were autonomous in their own principalities. In northern Italy, the landed nobility eventually settled in the cities where they kept the peace among rival merchant families.

However, the long-term trend in Europe was toward monarchism, not feudalism. Over the centuries, monarchs became stronger, loyalties flowed upward to the king at the top of the pyramid, and the feudal networks between nobility and vassals eroded. By the seventeenth century, the issue was not whether monarchism would outpace feudalism but whether monarchism should be absolute.

WHAT WAS THE SIGNIFICANCE OF REPUBLICANISM IN THE MIDDLE AGES?

Republicanism in medieval Europe centered on the idea of freedom through the law. The medieval understanding of freedom was different from today's understanding of freedom as an individual right. Medieval freedoms were granted as collective liberties and privileges,

MORE ABOUT . . .
A World of Guilds

A guild was a mutual aid society. In the Middle Ages, guilds arose throughout Europe. Guilds were associations of people who contributed to a common purpose. The word *guild* comes from the Anglo-Saxon *geld,* which has two meanings: "to pay, contribute" and "to sacrifice, worship." Both meanings are built into the idea of guilds. A guild's purpose might be religious or secular. But, like all organizations of medieval life, even secular guilds were expected to advance their members' penitence and salvation.

The composition and activities of guilds varied widely over centuries, geographical regions, and industries. Members often lived in the same neighborhood, where shop signs and street names proudly announced their presence. Religious guilds organized devout prayers, masses, and alms distribution. Rural guilds functioned as burial or benefit societies. In many cities, the charter required the government's city council to consist of members from specified guilds. Merchant guilds were long-distance traders' organizations, enforcing contracts and protecting members and merchandise against interference by rulers.

Craft guilds (such as those for bakers and brewers) established and maintained product quality, acted for market advantage, and supervised vocational education. Master craftsmen employed journeymen, short-term laborers hoping to advance to master level. Masters also

Instructions to the Bakers Guild of York, England, shown in a 16th-century manuscript.

taught apprentices—often teenage boys working for room, board, and possibly a small stipend. Apprenticeships typically lasted five to nine years.

usually to a particular corporate body such as a city. The granted freedoms would then be assigned or trickle down to the individual members of that body or rank. Freedom was not an end in itself but the means by which cities and other corporate bodies were expected to pursue the common good.

The law was also understood differently than it is today. In medieval times, and in fact throughout much of history, the law was seen as an end in itself. "Law was the right ordering of society binding on all."[4] Law was a common good. In contrast, today the law is often seen as an instrument used by individuals and groups to secure their own interests.

Consent of the governed and political representation existed, but they too were different from today's understanding of those concepts. Consent and representation were virtual, not actual. There was no generally accepted understanding as yet of a polity in which the people as a whole elected representatives who acted on their behalf in a permanent legislative body. Typically, a council of elders or other important individuals was trusted to make decisions for the realm as a whole. When they lost the public's trust, they ran the risk of losing their position—or their heads.

People were defined by their rank or status and then, within their rank, by the group into which they were born or to which they were assigned. Within that group, they might be politically equal, but there was no conception of equality across groups, except for their unity in faith. Group solidarity and cohesion were the most important social values in the medieval world. People identified themselves by the larger group to which they belonged. Some of these groups became institutionalized as guilds. (See More About . . . A World of Guilds.)

The collective impulse in medieval Europe was also reflected in the way political interests were structured. The nobility, the Church, and commoners made up three large orders or estates. Sometimes referred to informally as the fighters, the prayers, and the workers, these three orders defined political life in medieval Europe. Only the kings were outside their domain.

The third estate, the commoners, was the most diverse. The leaders of this third estate began with the wealthiest burghers (burgesses in English and *bourgeoisie* in French) who lived in towns (*burgh* in German, *bourg* in French, and borough or bury in English). This estate also included city officials, village freemen (who owned land free of debt), and knights of the low nobility.

Each estate had interests and freedoms to protect. To do so, each estate drew on a mix of instruments that evolved into important republican institutions. These included:

- The law, especially the charter, as a basis for protecting freedoms and creating governments
- Parliament as a form of virtual representation and a check on the king
- The commune as a form of self-governing city coming from customary law
- Confederation among cities (for example, the Hanseatic League) as a form of protection and trade

Medieval cities, for example, sought charters that would give them the status of free self-governing cities. They also formed confederations to expand and protect their trading networks. Noblemen formed alliances with cities and bishops to strengthen their negotiating position with the king. Over time, these alliances evolved into permanent republican institutions such as councils, assemblies, and parliaments. Estates used instruments such as these to protect their freedoms, check the powers of the king, and establish a representative place for their estate in the new kingdoms and empires of the Middle Ages. In some kingdoms, councils elected kings and assemblies had the power to veto the king's law.

Estates also drew on a variety of legal traditions. The Church fashioned its own legal system from Roman law and early Church law. Italian cities also relied in part on Roman law.

POLITICS IN ACTION
Justice in Medieval England

Monarchs and the three medieval estates administered justice by means of different duties and powers. Overlapping and occasionally conflicting jurisdictions were a hallmark of medieval justice. King Henry II (1133–1189), following Anglo-Saxon tradition, served as protector of the realm in London's royal courts. He also reformed the traditional legal system—one of sworn oaths, trial by ordeal, and trial by combat—by instituting traveling royal courts and promoting trials by a judge and twelve jurors.

English nobles granted justice through their own system of manor courts. These regularly convened courts applied to the residents and landholders within a lord's manor. The nobility jealously protected their judicial powers (as opposed to the royal justice system) because of the power, prestige, and revenue that the manor courts provided.

The Church reserved its own courts for priests, monks, and other clergy. An elaborate body of canon law (church law) arose to deal with the specific issues of justice within the Church. In addition, members of the clergy could avoid being tried in a secular court by claiming "benefit of clergy." The Church courts' inability to pronounce death sentences greatly increased the appeal of benefit of clergy. Over time, anyone who could recite specific Bible verses became eligible for benefit of clergy. Psalm 51 became a popular verse for the illiterate to memorize to avoid death by hanging in a secular court—hence its nickname, "the neck verse."

The Court of King's Bench in the 15th century. In the foreground prisoners chained to the bar await their sentence.

Medieval commoners also participated in administering justice. In those days of few local police officials, villagers were bound by law to help search for a criminal fugitive once the hue and cry had been raised. People failing to rally to a hue and cry faced fines if caught. In addition, varying commercial customs and laws of towns and fairs governed English merchants. And guilds, even though they were voluntary organizations, could punish errant members, although not too severely because members could always quit. Those who left, however, might still have to contend with powerful guild members, who often ran their towns.

In 410 CE, the Visigoths, a main branch of the East Germanic Goth tribe, sacked Rome. They then settled in the southern part of the Roman province of Gaul, creating their own Visigothic kingdom in Toulouse. They later gained control of the Iberian Peninsula (including present-day Portugal and Spain) and southern France.

Visigothic laws, originally based solely on oral tradition, were first compiled in writing by King Euric during the late fifth century. The earliest Visigothic laws followed the "personality of the law" principle; that is, different legal rulings were applied to different ethnic groups.

King Leovgild's major revision, the *Book of Judges* (in Latin, the *Forum Iudicum*), formed the basis of the twelve books now known as the *Visigothic Code,* proclaimed by King Recceswinth in 654. Significantly, Recceswinth imposed his *Forum Iudicum* territorially—a single body of nearly six hundred rules applied to all the king's subjects, both Romans and Visigoths. The *Visigothic Code*'s impressive scope and unique theoretical discussions of the law's role in the social and political order have proven influential for hundreds of years.

Elsewhere in Western Europe and the Holy Roman Empire, Germanic and local laws also were customary important sources of law.[5] (See Features on Justice in Medieval England and More About . . . The *Visigothic Code.*)

In the early twelfth century, Europe began to climb its way out of the Dark Ages. No one estate, institution, or individual was in complete control. Quite the contrary, all three estates seemed relatively well-positioned politically. Historians refer to the period that followed as the Medieval Renaissance.

The **Medieval Renaissance** was an important period of European history that lasted for two centuries, roughly from the 1120s to the 1340s, before Europe was decimated by the Black Death. In the history of republics, the Medieval Renaissance is the great bridge between the achievements of classical Athens and Rome as republics and the modern Renaissance that began with the Italian and northern humanist movements of the late 1400s.

During the Medieval Renaissance, the Church supported the construction of wondrous cathedrals such as Chartres. Universities flourished. Greek and Roman texts were rediscovered, and bold thinkers penned pioneering works of philosophy, theology, and law. Great kings—such as Henry II of England, Frederick Barbarossa of Germany, and Philip Augustus of France—grew powerful. Feudal rules of chivalry were codified. Noblemen fought for royal charters guaranteeing their freedom and privileges, and cities became more prosperous and won new charters that provided corporate self-government and freedoms.[6]

HOW REPUBLICAN WERE THE MEDIEVAL ESTATES?

THE CHURCH

In every period of history, Church organization has been a product of the tensions between two political philosophies: monarchism and republicanism. The Middle Ages was no exception.

Vatican II: Pauline Philosophy Meets the Twentieth Century

In October 1962, Pope John XXIII called the Second Vatican Council, perhaps the Roman Catholic Church's most significant twentieth-century event. In every respect, Vatican II looked to restore Pauline philosophy and create a more active participant role for congregants.

Meeting in four sessions in St. Peter's Basilica through December 1965, the council sought to move beyond the Church's previously defensive and condemnatory stance toward modern life. Vatican II was a truly ecumenical, or worldwide, event set amid social change in the 1960s. A total of 2,860 bishops attended, including bishops from developing nations in South and Central America, Asia, and elsewhere.

For Roman Catholic believers, Vatican II became a watershed event. A new liturgy—with the priest facing the congregation and conducting the Mass, which was no longer in Latin but in the congregation's vernacular language—replaced the traditional Catholic liturgy. Encouraged now to participate in the liturgy,

Vatican II—the meeting of Pope John XXIII's ecumenical council in St. Peter's Basilica, Vatican City.

congregants also were given responsibility to pursue justice by engaging the world politically. Departing from visions of the Church as the kingdom of God on Earth, the council described the Church as a sacrament to the world and a pilgrim Church looking forward to full realization.

Monarchism in the Church began with St. Peter, who favored a centralized hierarchy headed by the pope. The pope was the bishop of Rome and the whole Church. This doctrine is known as the Petrine (Peter's) Primacy. It guided many of the Church's early popes. Pope Leo I (440–461), for example, believed that the New Testament established the supremacy of Peter as the leader of the Church and that the pope and bishop of Rome was Peter's successor.[7] Within the Church, power flowed along hierarchical lines—from pope to bishops (who were the Church's nobility), and from bishops to clergy and their flock. Some popes sought absolute control over bishops and kings. Other popes allowed power to slip through their fingers or genuinely sought to share power with the bishops.

But this is not the complete story. Although the Church has been organized hierarchically throughout much of its history, it has not always been centralized. Several republican elements have kept the Church from complete centralization and autocracy.

Republicanism in the Catholic Church can trace its roots to antiquity. St. Paul favored a more noncentralized and community-based organization of church congregants. The Pauline

Letters (written by Paul) provide guidance on how to design Christian communities. His influence can be seen in various republican practices and institutions.

First, Paul's philosophy called for the active participation of congregants. In the early days of the Church, this was accomplished in several ways: (1) adult baptism in which the adult was aware of and participated in the baptism; (2) liturgy, including readings and prayers, conducted by congregants not priests; and (3) public confessions in which people confessed their sins before their neighbors against whom they had sinned. In all these ways, congregants were active participants, using a language they understood. In contrast, in the medieval Catholic Church, the liturgy was delivered by the clergy in Latin, and the congregants became passive onlookers listening to a language they did not understand.[8] The changes made to Church doctrine in 1962 can be seen as a shift to the Pauline position. (See More About . . . Vatican II: Pauline Philosophy Meets the Twentieth Century.)

Second, Paul's republican philosophy took the form of Church decision making by synods (councils). The term *synod* comes from the Greek word for meeting (this is also the root of the word *synagogue*). In the first centuries of the Church, before Christianity became the imperial religion of Rome synods met to make Church doctrine and resolve disputes among churches. Later, in the fifteenth century, this republican tradition was revived in the Conciliar Movement (discussed in Chapter 16).[9]

Third, some popes were more republican in their philosophy than others. For example, Gregory the Great (590–604) was certainly more republican than Pope Leo, who centralized the Church in the last decades of the Roman Empire. "Rule from the highest place," said Gregory, "is good if the one who is in charge is more in control of his vices than of his brothers."[10]

Fourth, since medieval times, the role of the cardinals has kept the Church from becoming an autocracy under one ruler. The word *cardinal* comes from the Latin *cardo,* meaning "hinge." In the Middle Ages, the office of cardinal did indeed function like a hinge that helped regulate the flow of power up and down the hierarchy. The College of Cardinals also functioned much like a senate—as a check on the monarchic powers of the pope. For example, the cardinals elected the pope. In this way, the cardinals could help set the direction of papal policy. This electoral practice also prevented papal succession based on divine right or heredity. In all these ways, the cardinals represented the interests of the few and, thus, the aristocratic element of the Church.[11]

Fifth, over time, power floated in the Church hierarchy. The Church emerged from the Dark Ages as the most widespread institution in Europe. Priests were present in most cities and in many towns and villages. Those priests who controlled large and powerful churches were given the title bishop, and the term *diocese* was applied to their domain. Priests and bishops became powerful forces in the Church hierarchy. As a result, in medieval times, the Church hierarchy was a pyramid that became wider moving from the top to the base (see Figure 15.1).

Sixth, monastic orders have had a republicanizing influence since medieval times. Monasteries were organized as fraternal associations and attracted clergy who sought

Figure 15.1 Catholic Church Structure

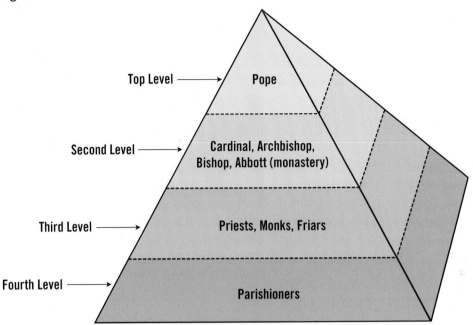

an egalitarian life of contemplation and reflection. Some monastic orders developed a hierarchical structure, but many remained nonhierarchical and noncentralized. Religious guilds developed along similar lines, as fraternities committed to good works.

Seventh, the Byzantine Church was organized with a stronger element of republicanism than was the Roman Church. While it was more structured than the Christian community of Paul, the organizational creed of the Byzantine Church was still community and communion. It aspired to be a fellowship of believers and a federation of churches. (See More About . . . Churches, East and West.)

Eighth and finally, the Church's legal system had a strong commitment to the rule of law—another republican influence. As medieval scholar Walter Ullmann explained, the Church believed that society should be regulated by the rule of law, not by monarchs who stood above the law. The Church also believed that law must be just and that justice was a Christian ideal. Law, in other words, should be based on faith, not the other way around.[12]

In its administration, Church law developed a decidedly bureaucratic tendency. In the early Church, there was the belief that Church decisions should follow Roman law when canon law (the body of law developed by the Church) was silent. Canon law was applied not only within the Church but also within the ecclesiastical cities controlled by the Church. It also was used elsewhere when a member of the clergy was accused of a crime or when Church property was contested.

MORE ABOUT . . .

Churches, East and West

Long before the east-west schism split them into two separate religious institutions in 1054, the Eastern (Byzantine or Eastern Orthodox) and Western (Roman Catholic) halves of the Church often found themselves in disagreement.

The outlooks of the two churches differed for several reasons. First, they had developed in strikingly different circumstances. When the unified civil government collapsed in the Western Roman Empire, the Church found itself as the sole source of authority in many cities and regions. Bishops undertook secular administrative responsibilities. Over time, as royal rule began to reemerge, it had to face the Church's independent power. Eastern bishops, by contrast, were dominated by Byzantine imperial and Islamic authority.

Also, cultural and linguistic differences between Latins (west) and Greeks (east) heightened controversies about scriptural interpretation and the use of religious images. In addition, the churches claimed authority over overlapping territories throughout the Mediterranean region.

Viewed from Constantinople, Church tradition did not support the pope's monarchical style. Although the

Now a museum, Hagia Sophia served as the seat of the Orthodox Patriarch of Constantinople for centuries before being turned into a mosque after the Ottoman Turks conquered Constantinople. The four minarets were added by the Turks.

patriarch of Constantinople was viewed as first among equals of the four patriarchs, he lacked direct authority over them. Furthermore, the celibacy of Catholic priests and Western use of unleavened bread for the Eucharist seemed unwarranted or offensive. Seen from Rome, Constantinople's patriarch was constantly generating trouble: aspiring to become the Eastern pope; dominating the other three patriarchs; and plotting with his chief ally, the Byzantine emperor.

By the thirteenth century, it seemed to republican thinkers that the Church had lost its way in a bureaucratic sea of rules, decrees, and orders. Within the Church, there arose advocates of republicanism, such as Marsilius of Padua, who called for the fundamental reform of Church governance. (See Bold Thinkers: Marsilius of Padua—Medieval Republican.)

THE NOBILITY

The different levels of nobility, from magnates to knights, made up the broad aristocratic class of the Middle Ages. Included in their number were noblemen who also served as Church bishops and abbots of monasteries.

BOLD THINKERS

Marsilius of Padua—Medieval Republican

"The first real and effective source of law is the people or the body of citizens . . . ," declared Italian political philosopher Marsilius of Padua (c.1275–c.1342) in the tract *Defensor Pacis* ("the defender of peace"). Marsilius, a university teacher and rector (head of the teaching body) in Paris, probably collaborated to write and publish this revolutionary idea in 1324.

Backing its arguments with citations from Aristotle, *Defensor Pacis* held that rulers serve only as delegates of the people, who hold all power. Popular will, as expressed in the ruler, is the only law. Moreover, without the people's support, the Church lacked all authority. The tract declared that the Church's power should be subordinate to secular rulers—a scandalous notion in the fourteenth century.

Defensor Pacis provided Holy Roman Emperor Louis IV with timely assistance in his power struggle with Pope John XXII. Condemned by the pope but protected by the emperor, Marcilius attended the imperial court and accompanied the emperor to his coronation in Rome. Two centuries later in England, royal minister Thomas Cromwell had *Defensor Pacis* translated into English to buttress Henry VIII's battles with the Church. Republican leaders also later referred to this work.

In the feudal system, noblemen occupied a middle or hinge position in which they were likely to serve four secular functions at the same time. A nobleman could be (1) a vassal to a king or emperor, (2) the lord of his own manor, (3) the commander of his own troops, and (4) a seigneur (or protective overlord) over a local community (for example, a village or even a city).

Noblemen had multiple roles and tasks in medieval society. This is one reason why noblemen came to make such an important contribution to the history of republican government. In that history, they are remembered most for standing up to kings and thereby checking the absolutism of monarchs.

The collective strength of the nobility was itself an important republican factor. In all likelihood, noblemen were motivated by a mixture of republican principles and political interests. Together, they had the military muscle to force kings to recognize the freedoms of others and the limits on royal power. By the thirteenth century, the nobility had also accumulated significant wealth from the cities they protected, the various revenues of their lands and tenants, and the spoils of war.

King John signed the Magna Carta partly because he needed the loyal support of his barons and the armies and revenues they could supply. The barons also had the good

POLITICS IN ACTION
Ancient Customary Law and Common Law

What is the difference between ancient customary law and modern common law? Ancient Germanic customary law was a distant ancestor of Anglo-American common law. Ancient laws relied mainly on unwritten custom, while modern common law relies primarily on court precedent, prior court decisions that bear directly on the case at hand. If you were charged with a crime in ancient times you would face trial, which meant a trial by ordeal to be decided before the gods. For example, you might be bound and thrown into a cold river; if you floated you were guilty because it was believed that water accepts only the innocent. In the Middle Ages, councils and assemblies served both legislative and judicial functions. Common law was born out of the collection of their laws and cases.

judgment to enlist the support of the bishops and city merchants. And they drew on long-established legal traditions, including Germanic customary law from Saxon times.

Customary law is unwritten law based on custom. Germanic customary law dated from ancient times, and Germanic invaders relied on these customs wherever they settled. As the medieval historian Fritz Kern put it, Germanic law was "the law of one's fathers." It was based on the idea that the law protected liberty and the state protected the law. The ruler and the ruled were bound to the law by the feudal oaths they swore. Rulers who failed to uphold the law could lose the loyalty of their subjects. Those subjects could then invoke the right to resistance and rebellion. For example, in England, the barons relied partly on this right of resistance in their claim for the Magna Carta, a charter of liberties from the king.[13] (See Politics in Action: Ancient Customary Law and Common Law.)

Customary law helped establish the rule of law, the idea that no one is above the law. It also gave the nobility the political legitimacy they needed in their constitutional struggles with the king. Although customary legal systems varied from one kingdom to another, they shared several features that distinguished them from Roman imperial law, as listed in Table 15.1.

The Alsatian priest Manegold of Lautenbach invoked Germanic customary law in defense of the pope in the Investiture Controversy that began in the late eleventh century. Manegold wrote, "Since no one can create himself emperor or king, the people elevates a certain one person over itself to this end, that he govern and rule it according to the principle of righteous government; but if in any wise he transgress the contract by virtue of which he is chosen, he absolves the people from the obligation of submission, because he has first broken faith with it."[14]

Manegold's three main points are the essence of republican thinking: the people should elect their rulers; rulers should govern righteously; and if the ruler violates his contract with the people, the people are no longer obliged to obey him. Manegold wrote these words seven hundred years before the U.S. Declaration of Independence was written, yet the similarities are striking. The second paragraph of the Declaration of Independence states, "Governments are instituted among Men, deriving their just powers from the consent of the governed,—That

Table 15.1 German Customary Law versus Roman Imperial Law

German customary law	Roman imperial law
Based on unwritten customs	Based on written and codified law
Precursor of common law, based on court precedent and general principles that leave wide room for judicial discretion	Precursor of civil law based on detailed laws that leave little room for judicial discretion
Favors a political system that may be either noncentralized with local self-government and a council or centralized with a king who is elected and checked by noblemen	Favors a political system that is centralized with a strong king
The law is supreme over the king, and electors (noblemen) retain the right of resistance	The king is supreme over the law

whenever any Form of Government becomes destructive of these ends, it is the Right of the People to alter or to abolish it, and to institute new Government."

In England, the barons and bishops drew partly on this legal authority when they forced King John to sign the Magna Carta in 1215. Seven years later, Hungarian noblemen used similar legal authority to force King Andras II to sign the Golden Bull of 1222. Named for the seal affixed to it, this document limited the powers of both the king and Church in Hungary.[15]

The Magna Carta and the Golden Bull were charters. A **charter** is a legally binding grant or gift from a sovereign authority such as the king or parliament. Typically, charters confer freedoms or create institutions. Medieval charters were often long and wide-ranging. The Magna Carta has a preamble followed by sixty-three provisions.

Charters of incorporation are a type of charter used to create governmental and nongovernmental corporations. They also guarantee freedoms and privileges to the corporation and to its members, enumerate the corporation's powers and limits, and frame its government organization and offices. This list of charter purposes might sound familiar. Charters of incorporation are the precursors of modern republican constitutions. But there is one big difference. A royal charter is a grant by the king, but a republican constitution is fundamental law that rests on the rule of law and the consent of the governed—principles that stand above the king.

Centuries later, of course, the leaders of the American Revolution rejected the charter as the source of freedom. One of those leaders, John Dickinson (1732–1808) of Pennsylvania and Delaware, wrote, "Our liberties do not come from charters; for these are only the declaration of pre-existing rights. [Our liberties] do not depend on parchments or seals; but come from the King of Kings and Lord of all the earth."[16]

In theory, a royal charter such as the Magna Carta was irrevocable—it could not be recalled or taken back. In practice, a powerful king could find ways to revoke his grant. Shortly after King John signed the Magna Carta at Runnymede, he went to his feudal lord, Pope Innocent III, and asked to be absolved from his vows to the barons. Innocent, not a republican enthusiast, gladly agreed. He then suspended one of the Runnymede leaders, Stephen Langton, the archbishop of Canterbury. Only King John's death shortly thereafter allowed for a peaceful resolution of the matter.[17]

The process of entrenching the Magna Carta (that is, making sure that no king could revoke it) was long and arduous. Before the close of the thirteenth century, three men— Henry of Bracton, Simon de Montfort, and King Edward I—made lasting contributions to that process. Henry of Bracton strengthened Article 39 of the Magna Carta, which guaranteed accused freemen the protection of a jury and "the law of the land." Simon de Montfort and King Edward I began the process of transforming the king's council into a parliament.[18]

FROM CHARTER TO RULE OF LAW. Article 39 of the Magna Carta provided that no freeman shall be taken, arrested, dispossessed, or exiled, "except by the lawful judgment of his peers or by the law of the land." But what was a "lawful judgment" and what were the "laws of the land"? The answer was essential to a freeman, whose life might depend on it.

In the 1250s, the English judge and clergyman Henry of Bracton (c.1210–1268) set about the task of systematically compiling the laws of the land. Bracton was no ordinary scribe writing a king's code. Quite the contrary, his goal was to bind the king more tightly to the rule of law. The king, wrote Bracton, must "temper his power by law, which is the bridle of power." "Nothing," continued Bracton, "is more fitting for a sovereign than to live by the laws."[19] Bracton never completed his work, but what he did accomplish was published. Bracton believed that the laws of the land must be published—printed, circulated widely, and made public—for two reasons. First, publishing the laws served as a check against kings and royal agents who might violate existing laws or claim they were enforcing a law that did not exist. Second, the people needed to know the laws that could be used in their prosecution and defense. In this way, Bracton helped put pressure on future kings who might try to wriggle out of their legal commitments.

FROM ROYAL COUNCIL TO PARLIAMENT. Articles 12 and 14 of the Magna Carta confirmed the conciliar rights of the barons. Article 12 provided that no scutage (tax) could be imposed without "the common counsel of the kingdom." This meant that the king could not impose a tax without the consultation and approval ("counsel") of the barons meeting as a "council" (the body giving their counsel) of the realm. Article 14 set forth the members of the council as barons, bishops, and other high nobility. It also provided that the king was responsible for calling the meeting. But it allowed the king to limit his summons to the barons.

Before the Magna Carta, the council of barons was a royal council (known by its Latin name, Curia Regis). The king saw the royal council as his personal advisor. For the barons, it represented their right to be consulted. The Magna Carta made this council a check on the king. Like a senate, it had the power to approve or reject royal taxes. But the council was not a legislature—it could not pass laws. Nor was the council a representative body in the modern sense of the term. The barons serving on the council were free agents and represented no one but themselves. But, in the long history of constitutional representative government, the establishment of the council of barons was an important step. The Magna Carta transformed the royal council into a common council. A royal council served the king; a common council served the realm.

About the time Bracton's work was published, the English barons won another concession from the Crown. King John's son King Henry III (1207–1272) agreed to strengthen the council of barons. Several years later, the king reneged, and the barons rebelled. They were led by the king's brother-in-law, Simon de Montfort (1208–1265), the sixth Earl of Leicester. Montfort won the first baronial war (1263–1264) and established a representative body without royal authorization known as Montfort's Parliament. His victory, however, was short-lived. He was killed in battle in 1265 by his nephew, the son of Henry III, who later became King Edward I.

Thirty years later, in 1295, Edward I established the Model Parliament. It was so named because it became the model that others followed, even though Edward modeled it after his uncle's parliament. The Model Parliament is the origin of the House of Commons of the British parliament.[20]

Parliament, from the French *parler* ("to talk"), originally meant a meeting or conference to discuss and debate. It was not yet a legislature because it had no lawmaking powers. Nor was it a representative body because its members still acted on their own. But it was more than a mere assembly or gathering of people, and it was more than a royal council. Edward's parliament was a formal institution. It had wider powers than the royal council and a wider membership. In addition to the barons and bishops, it now included two knights from every shire and two burgesses from every borough.[21]

Today, a parliament is generally understood to be a legislature with the power to make laws. But preconceived notions about the past can be misleading. Nelson Polsby, one of the world's experts on parliaments and legislatures, once remarked, "There occasionally arises a natural confusion among scholars because sometimes lawmaking is done outside legislatures, and sometimes legislatures do things other than lawmaking."[22] The parliaments of the thirteenth century are just such an example.

The king was still sovereign. It would take another three hundred years before England became a constitutional monarchy with a mixed republican government. But English government was now more than a monarchy. In parliament, there were both an aristocratic element (the barons and bishops) and a democratic element (the commoners—the knights and burgesses). Viewed another way, each of the three estates and the king now had a place at the table. Virtual representation was the norm. So too was virtual consent; the people gave their consent through passive acceptance, not through voting. Long before John Locke wrote about the right to revolution, the right to resistance had been invoked with some success in England.

The creation of the Model Parliament was not an isolated event. The oldest parliament still in existence is believed to be the Icelandic Althing, which first met in 930 CE. (See More About . . . The World's Oldest Parliament.) In Spain, six separate kingdoms each created its own parliament (Corte), beginning with Leone in 1118 and ending with Navarre in 1300. In 1182, the Polish parliament (Sejm) first appeared as an extension of the popular assembly (*wiec*). In 1235, the Parliament of Scotland was created from the royal council of bishops and earls. In 1307, the Parlement of Paris evolved as a judicial and legislative body from the French royal council. The Holy Roman Empire lagged behind this trend. (See More About . . . The Holy Roman Empire.)

Note that these parliaments originated in two ways. Some, such as the English parliament, were the product of the power struggles between noblemen and the king; the noblemen fought for parliaments as a way of protecting their collective powers and checking the powers of the king. Others, such as the Icelandic Althing and the Polish Sejm, were created from below. In Poland, for example, the local councils in each province elected members to serve on a provincial assembly; then, all the provincial assemblies elected members to serve on the national parliament.

THE FREE CITY

Cities developed outside the feudal system, which is where they preferred to remain. To ensure its freedom, a city acquired a charter and became a **commune**, the designation for all free self-governing cities.

During the latter part of the Dark Ages, merchant cities began to resurface under the control of powerful merchant families. Merchants understood that economic prosperity required freedom from onerous royal and feudal regulations. They sought free trade, reduced taxes, and other freedoms. At the same time, the merchant cities needed protection against attacks by marauding armies led by noblemen and brigands.

Beginning in the twelfth century, city leaders began to strike bargains with their neighboring prince and eventually with the king. It was a natural bargain—kings and princes needed gold to fight their wars; cities needed a guarantee of protection and a grant of self-government. Each bargain took the form of a **city charter of incorporation**, a legally binding grant by the city's sovereign (a nobleman or the king) to the city's governing officials. These were often the same noblemen who fought for their charter liberties from the king they served.

The sovereign granted the city its self-government in exchange for financial payments and a pledge of military service. Typically, the charter authorized self-government and released the city from certain onerous taxes and conditions of military service. The charter might also prescribe or recognize the city's form of government, list its powers and limits, and lay out its offices. In exchange, the city agreed to make regular payments of a certain amount. The charter either became the city's constitution or it allowed the city to write its own constitution.

Typically, a city charter also granted liberties to the city's residents. For example, it was common to grant freedom to a serf or slave who sought refuge in a free city and escaped capture for "a year and a day." But these were not individual freedoms in the modern sense of the term. They were corporate liberties assigned to the city and accruing to the individual only as a member of the community. They were group, not individual, freedoms.

Free cities sprang up across Europe but were strongest and most numerous in two regions: (1) the region along the North Sea and Baltic coast, including Bruges, Hamburg, Lübeck, Danzig, and Riga; and (2) northern Italy, including Bologna, Florence, Genoa, Milan, and Venice.

Free imperial cities in the region were part of the Holy Roman Empire. They negotiated their charters directly with the emperor. Internally, they were governed by strong guilds of two types: merchant guilds and craft guilds. The cities had clear and well-defined mixed republican governments. The monarchic element was supplied by the emperor from afar, the merchant guilds constituted the aristocratic element, and the craft guilds constituted the democratic element.

MORE ABOUT . . .
The Holy Roman Empire

The Holy Roman Empire lagged behind other kingdoms in institutionalizing checks on the emperor. The major reason is that the holy Roman emperor was already checked by political forces. The empire was, in actuality, a loose assemblage of approximately four hundred principalities, free cities, and other local and regional entities. Noblemen, bishops, and city leaders fiercely guarded their local autonomy. From the earliest days of the empire, the emperor was elected by the leaders of the largest tribes in the empire. Diets (or pre-parliamentary assemblies) of estate leaders met infrequently to select a new emperor, prepare for war, or resolve issues such as investiture or inheritance. In 1356, the Diet of Nuremberg issued a Golden Bull that began to formalize traditional practices. For example, it created an electoral college, identified its seven electors, and prescribed specific procedures for the election process. The Golden Bull also formalized a long-developing power play by noblemen to undercut the strength of cities, barring cities from creating confederations or leagues. Included in the ban was the powerful Swabian League formed by more than twenty cities in 1331.

In the middle of the twelfth century, the city of Lübeck rose to economic prominence. Over the next century, the merchant guilds (called *hansa*) of Lübeck and other coastline cities of the Baltic and Northern seas joined forces to expand their trade network. The result was the Hanseatic League, which flourished for centuries. At its height, the league dominated international trading routes and markets from London and Bruges in the west to Riga and distant Novgorod in the east.

Italian **city-states** secured their independence and formed their governments by treaty. Around 1175, most of the cities in northern Italy joined the Lombard League. Their purpose was to secure their self-government from Holy Roman Emperor Frederick Barbarossa.

They defeated the empire in battle, and their self-government was guaranteed by the Peace of Constance of 1183. The Constance treaty thus served as a charter of freedoms for the Lombard cities.

Italian cities also differed from Germanic cities in their internal governance. The guilds were not as strong in some Lombard cities, such as Venice, as they were in the Hanseatic cities. In some Italian cities, merchant aristocratic families remained so strong that merchant guilds were unnecessary. By contrast, in many English and Germanic cities merchant guilds were so strong that they were the city government. The Roman Republic remained the model of government and law for the Italian city-states, while the Germanic conciliar model influenced the governance of Hanseatic cities. (In Chapter 16, we take a closer look at the Venetian Republic, the most durable, peaceful, and prosperous republic from the Middle Ages to the Enlightenment.)

HOW DID THE MEDIEVAL RENAISSANCE END?

The Medieval Renaissance came to a sudden and tragic end in the 1340s. The Black Death was a major cause, but even before then bad harvests, famine, disease, and hard economic times had become a vicious cycle with no end in sight. People became unnerved and turned to conflict and violence. Self-flagellation, witch hunts, violent crime, peasant uprisings, urban worker revolts, wars between nations (for example, the Hundred Years War between France and England), and wars between rival noble factions within nations (for example, the English War of the Roses) spread across the continent.

The loss of human life during the 1300s was staggering. According to one generally accepted estimate, European population fell from "roughly 70 million in 1300 to 45 million in 1400."[23] That means 35 percent, or one of every three people, died during this century of devastation.

No estate survived unscathed. All suffered the loss of human life and property. The next chapter examines how these estates emerged from the fourteenth century and what role republicanism played in the Renaissance of the fifteenth century.

REVIEWING AND USING THE CHAPTER

1. How did England develop as a constitutional monarchy?

2. In what ways was the medieval Church republican?

3. The ideas of monarchism, feudalism, and republicanism "exerted tremendous influence on the political mosaic of the Middle Ages." Identify and explain the major influences of each.

EXTENSION ACTIVITY

Reexamine the three estates presented in this chapter. In which one would you prefer to live? And at what station or position? Why?

WEB RESOURCES

Euro Docs: Medieval and Renaissance Europe
http://eudocs.lib.byu.edu/index.php/History_of_Medieval_%26_Renaissance_Europe:_Primary_Documents

Hosted by Brigham Young University, this Web site provides an extensive and annotated list of links to important primary source documents in the history of Medieval and Renaissance Europe.

Internet Medieval Sourcebook
www.fordham.edu/halsall/sbook.html

Part of the History Sourcebook Project of Fordham University, this Web site includes excellent original essays as well as links to other electronic resources and documents that focus on the history of Medieval Europe.

Stanford Encyclopedia of Philosophy: Medieval Political Philosophy
http://plato.stanford.edu/entries/medieval-political

This encyclopedia entry supplies an excellent and well-organized discussion of medieval political philosophy, a large bibliography, and links to other Internet sources.

Stanford University Libraries and Academic Information Resources: Medieval Studies
www.sul.stanford.edu/depts/ssrg/medieval/medieval.html

This Web site includes a vast array of high quality medieval studies resources, such as guides, bibliographies, encyclopedias, indexes, images, and manuscripts.

NOTES

1 Danny Donziger and John Gillingham, *1215: The Year of Magna Carta* (New York: Simon & Schuster, 2003), 167.

2 The classic treatment of this medieval view remains Arthur O. Lovejoy, *The Great Chain of Being: A Study of the History of an Idea* (Cambridge, Mass: Harvard University Press, 1936; and many later editions). Note, however, that many scholars have found much more turbulence and diversity in medieval thought. For a modern treatment, see Marcia L. Colish, *Medieval Foundations of the Western Intellectual Tradition, 400–1400* (New Haven, Conn.: Yale University Press, 1997).

3 Marc Bloch, *The Cambridge Economic History of Europe, Vol. I: The Agrarian Life of the Middle Ages*, ed. M. M. Postan (Cambridge, UK: Cambridge University Press, 1966), 61.

4 Brian Z. Tamanaha, *Law as a Means to an End: Threat to the Rule of Law* (Cambridge, UK: Cambridge University Press, 2006), 1.

5 For a brief historical survey of these sources of medieval law, see Brian Z. Tamanaha, *On the Rule of Law: History, Politics, Theory* (Cambridge, UK: Cambridge University Press, 2004), Chap. 2.

6 David Hackett Fischer, *The Great Wave: Price Revolutions and the Rhythm of History* (New York: Oxford University, 1996), 13. And, of course, Norman F. Cantor, *The Civilization of the Middle Ages*, rev. ed. (New York: Harper Perennial, 1993).

7 Hans Küng, *The Catholic Church: A Short History* (New York: The Modern Library, 2003), 57–58.

8 Ibid., 64.

9 Daniel J. Elazar, *Covenant & Commonwealth: From Christian Separation through the Protestant Reformation, Vol. 2: The Covenant Tradition in Politics* (New Brunswick, N.J.: Transaction Publishers, 1996), 42.

10 *Pastoral Rule* (II, VI, 22), quoted in ibid., 66.

11 Ibid.

12 Walter Ullmann, *A History of Political Thought: The Middle Ages* (Middlesex, UK: Penguin Books, 1965).

13 Fritz Kern, *Kingship and Law in the Middle Ages* (New York: Harper Torchbook, 1956).

14 Quoted in Reinhold Laakmann, *Manegold of Lautenbach* (Hamburg: Hamburg University Press, 1969) and reprinted in Elazar, *Covenant & Commonwealth*, 75.

15 Robert Bideleux and Ian Jeffries, *A History of Eastern Europe: Crisis and Change* (London and New York: Routledge, 1998), 193.

16 Quoted in Charles Edward Merriam, *A History of American Political Theories* (New York: Augustus M. Kelly, 1969), 48.

17 Cantor, *Civilization of the Middle Ages*, 454–455.

18 For an analysis of each provision of Magna Carta, see William Sharp McKechnie, *Magna Carta: A Commentary of the Great Charter of King John, with an Historical Introduction* (Glasgow, UK: Maclehose, 1914), available at the Online Library of Liberty, a project of the Liberty Fund, http://oll.libertyfund.org.

19 Henry Bracton, *On the Laws and Customs of England*, Vol. 3 (Cambridge, Mass.: Harvard University Press, 1968), 305–306.

20 The classic study is Edward Porritt assisted by Annie Porrit, *The Unreformed House of Commons: Parliamentary Representation before 1832*, 2 vols. (Cambridge, UK: Cambridge University Press, 1903; reprint ed., New York: Augustus M. Kelley, 1963).

21 For more on these distinctions, see Gary W. Copeland and Samuel C. Patterson, "Parliaments and Legislatures," in *World Encyclopedia of Parliaments and Legislatures*, ed. George Thomas Kurian (Washington, D.C.: Congressional Quarterly, 1998), Vol. 1, xix–xxxi.

22 Nelson W. Polsby, "Legislatures," in *Handbook of Political Science*, ed. Fred Greenstein and Nelson W. Polsby (Reading, Mass.: Addison-Wesley, 1975), 258.

23 R. R. Palmer, Joel Colton, and Lloyd Kramer, *A History of the Modern World*, 10th ed. (Boston: McGraw Hill, 2007), 50.

CHAPTER 16

WHY DID THE RENAISSANCE AND REFORMATION REVIVE CLASSICAL REPUBLICANISM?

BIG IDEAS

- Republicanism was an essential idea in modern Renaissance political thought.

- Civic humanism led to the revival and modernization of classical republicanism.

- Christian humanism and Reformed Protestantism inspired the development of covenantal republicanism.

Purpose of This Chapter

Republicans in the fifteenth century were alarmed by the rise of territorial monarchs. They were disillusioned by the political bickering within free cities and by corruption in the Church. They began to question the medieval order and chain of being that locked people in the group into which they were born and in the hierarchy by which they were governed. A new way of thinking evolved with a more humanistic interest in the centrality of the individual. Humanism, as it was called, developed two strands: civic humanism in Italy, which is associated with Machiavelli, and Christian humanism in northern Europe, which is associated with Erasmus. Each strand contributed to the intellectual development of republicanism. The Christian humanist movement paved the way for Reformed Protestantism early in the sixteenth century.

Terms to Know

Christian humanism	classical republicanism	gerontocracy
civic humanism	Conciliar Movement	humanism
civic virtue	covenantal republicanism	

WHAT WERE THE SOURCES OF POLITICAL CONFLICT IN THE FOURTEENTH CENTURY?

Throughout the fourteenth century, Europeans were struck by a series of devastating events. Bad harvests, food shortages, the Black Death, and other diseases took a terrible toll in human life and suffering. Declining wages and increases in the cost of living compounded the human misery. This period also saw an increase in war, crime, and other forms of social disorder.

Around 1400, economic conditions began to improve. Prices stabilized, wages slowly increased, rents dropped, interest rates declined, standards of living improved, and peace returned. The political equilibrium lagged behind this economic recovery. For much of the 1400s, the political world remained as divisive as it had been in the 1300s—perhaps more so. Polarizing political conflicts often turned violent; corruption in government was widespread.

One source of conflict came from the clash of royal ambitions. In the fourteenth and fifteenth centuries, kings sought wider national domains and became increasingly embroiled in warfare, both with one another and in dynastic conflicts within their realms. French and English kings, for example, clashed over French territory in what became known as the Hundred Years War. Some kings were weakened by these difficulties, while others saw an opportunity to consolidate their power. In either case, they needed more revenue to fight their wars and that meant increases in taxes.

A second source of conflict was the clash between papal and royal ambitions. Popes sought wider secular control over kings and their realms. In France, the power struggle between the pope and king was particularly severe. Finally, in 1309 King Philip IV of France kidnapped the pope. For the next seventy years, the papacy resided in Avignon in what became known as the Babylonian captivity. Not to be outdone, the anti-French wing in the College of Cardinals elected a second pope who resided in Rome. The secular rulers of England and most parts of Germany pooled their resources to pay for the new Roman papacy. In what became known as the Great Schism, two and sometimes three popes reigned simultaneously until the late 1440s.

By the 1400s, corruption had permeated the papacy and the Church hierarchy. Priests and parishioners grew disillusioned with the Church and began to look elsewhere—to mysticism, religious guilds, and commerce—for salvation. Church leaders devised a republican response known as the Conciliar Movement.

The **Conciliar Movement** relied on a series of councils in the first half of the fifteenth century to resolve some of the problems facing the Church. The two major Church councils of this period were the Council of Constance (1414–1418) and the Council of Basle (1439–1448). As emergency institutions, these councils were a success. They succeeded in reunifying the papacy, and the Basle Council elected the new pope. These councils also introduced reforms that would have transformed the Church into a republican organization. However, the new pope rejected those reforms, and the council system fell into disuse.

During this period, parliaments worked overtime to forestall royal abuses of power. Many noblemen formed their own armies and contributed to the general disorder of the times.

The cities were not immune from these larger conflicts. In northern Italian cities, for example, long-standing factional rivalries existed between those who supported the pope (the Guelphs) and those who supported the imperial power of the holy Roman emperor (the Ghibellines). Most northern Italian cities were divided by these factions. When a city became ungovernable, the city fathers or the dominant faction would call on the services of an outside nobleman to restore order. This practice had begun as early as the 1150s when Bologna hired a prince to assume dictatorial powers as the *podestà*, or powerholder. Many powerful Italian families, such as the Borgias and Medicis, were tapped for this role.

Only Venice succeeded in remaining neutral in these conflicts. Venice looked neither north to the emperor nor south to the pope. Located on Italy's eastern coast, on the Adriatic Sea, Venice made the strategic decision to look to the sea and to the east for her future—to Constantinople and eventually to China.[1]

WHY DID THE VENETIAN REPUBLIC REMAIN SO STABLE?

The Venetian Republic (1297–1797)[2] was the most durable, peaceful, and prosperous republic of the Middle Ages and early modern period. Long before Venice became a republic, it was a province in the Roman Empire. In the late fifth century, Lombard invaders swept south toward Venice, pushing thousands of refugees ahead of them. Many of these refugees found safe haven in the desolate lagoons and islands off the Venetian shoreline. In 697, Venice organized itself as a commune composed of the city, its island settlements, and the surrounding countryside.

This eighteenth-century painting depicts a busy scene of Venice during the Republic years. The Republic's relative peace and stability, along with the natural defenses offered by its seaside location, allowed Venice to thrive for hundreds of years.

Map 16.1 Trade Routes of Venice and Genoa

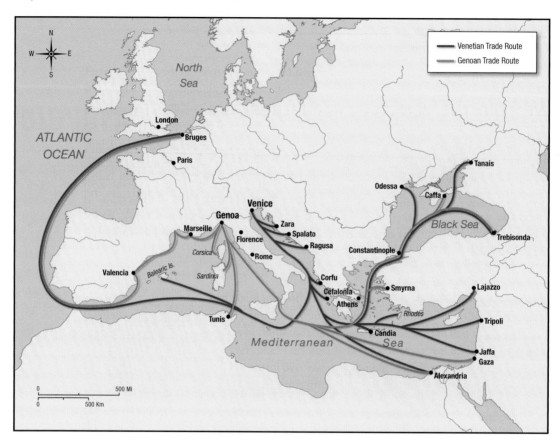

Over the next six hundred years, Venice developed a rich and powerful trading network throughout the Byzantine Empire (see Map 16.1). In the process, it was influenced in its art and architecture by Byzantium. During this period, one of its strongest trading rivals for western markets was the northern Italian city of Genoa. The two great cities fought one another off and on for centuries. During one of these wars, the great Venetian trader and explorer Marco Polo was captured in 1296 and imprisoned in Genoa, where he wrote of his travels in China. (See More About . . . Marco Polo.)

In 1297, Venetians adopted a republican constitution. Venice retained its republican government for five centuries. During this period, neighboring cities such as Florence swung wildly between democratic upheavals, bitter factionalism, and autocratic order. Venice preferred a steady middle course that relied for its politics on aristocratic leaders and democratic policies. During its last century, however, the Venetian Republic became too self-confident. It became a symbol of aristocratic decadence and economic stagnation. In 1797, Napoleon ceded the impotent Venetian Republic to Austria without a fight.

MORE ABOUT . . .
Marco Polo

In 1271, Marco Polo (1254–1324), a seventeen-year-old born into a Venetian trading family, journeyed along the Silk Road to China with his merchant father Niccolò and uncle Maffeo. The Polo family conducted a highly profitable trading business with the East. Around 1274, the travelers reached the court of the Mongol emperor Kublai Khan, who ruled the unified empire of Mongolia and China.

During the next seventeen years, the Polos remained in China. The emperor appreciated Marco's storytelling ability, dispatched him to distant lands on exploratory missions, and may have appointed him governor of the city of Yangzhou. The Polos began their return journey to Venice in 1295, sailing from eastern China to Persia and then traveling overland through Turkey to Constantinople. The long and difficult return trip took two years.

Soon after his return, Polo was captured and imprisoned while commanding a warship in a battle against the rival Genoese. Polo and a fellow prisoner, the writer Rustichello da Pisa, together wrote out the story of Polo's

Marco Polo setting out from Venice in 1271.

travels. The book, Il Milione, known in English as *The Travels of Marco Polo,* turned out to be an instant sensation. Medieval readers enjoyed it as an imaginative tale rather than as the true story of one of the earliest European journeys to the East.

Venice's constitution of 1297 was patterned after the Roman Republic and provided for a mixed republican form of government. Its governing institutions included an assembly (the Great Council), a smaller and more deliberative legislative body (the Senate), a cabinet (the Collegio), a chief executive (called the *doge,* pronounced dohj) elected by the Great Council, a small group of advisers to the doge (Signoria), and a grand chancellor who appointed the city's civil servants. Venice also boasted a separate court system with judges and juries.

In the Roman Republic, mixed government meant not only mixed institutions; it also meant that those institutions represented a mix of aristocratic and democratic interests. All of Venice's government officials were elected, usually for terms of one year or less. However, only members of the aristocracy could vote for or hold elected offices.

Beginning in 1297, the membership in the Great Council of Venice became hereditary. As a new constitutional rule, membership was forever limited to the adult male descendents of the families that sat in the Council in 1297. In 1296, there were only 210 members. Eventually, there were 3,000 members. Allowing for population growth, there were still exceptions granted to the 1297 rule.

The Great Council elected most of the other government officials. As the republic developed, the number of elected offices increased. Eventually, the Great Council became a full-time election board. It had little time to make laws, and the Senate became the primary body responsible for passing or rejecting legislation. The Collegio and its members became responsible for proposing legislation. Only the aristocracy could serve in the Senate or the Collegio and hold other elected offices. In its form of government, Venice was a mixed republic dominated by a closed aristocracy. All policymaking institutions and their elective offices were controlled by the city's old aristocratic families.

The civil service system was controlled by the city's second and broader class—the *cittadini,* or citizens. The grand chancellor was the head of the city's civil service system. This position could be held only by a member of the citizen class, not the aristocratic class. The grand chancellor appointed all the city's civil servants; many, if not most, of these appointments went to members of the citizen class.

This feature supplied the democratic element of the city's mixed republican government. During the Renaissance, approximately 7,000 citizens worked as civil servants for the city. This number represented about 5 percent of the total population; however, most city workers had families. If the average family of city workers was only four people, that means that 20 percent of the population was fed, clothed, and housed by city wages.[3]

There were both principled and practical reasons for engaging the citizenry in the civil service; it provided citizens with a role and stake in their government, but it also coopted them with patronage jobs. Either way, it worked. Indications are that the citizenry generally took pride in their civic role and supported their government. For a variety of factors, Venice did not experience the level of civic unrest common in other Italian cities; perhaps the citizen-based civil service was one of them.

There were no serfs and no broad class of slaves. Except for a relatively small number of household slaves, the people of Venice, citizens and noncitizens alike, were free. They possessed freedom of movement and occupation as well as free speech and assembly. This level of freedom was unparalleled in Europe. There also was a high level of tolerance for differing views and religions.

Venice did not maintain a large standing army or police force. Instead, the city preserved order by relying on a shadowy institution known as the Council of Ten. Created after an unsuccessful conspiracy in 1310, this council was only supposed to last for a few months. Instead, it lasted more than four centuries!

The council had the power to investigate leaders suspected of corruption and citizens suspected of treason. It had a renowned spy network, and its emergency police powers were virtually unlimited. For this very reason, its powers were held in check by stringent legal measures to prevent any one or a combination of the Council of Ten from abusing their powers or being corrupted.

The checks on the council's power included a one-year term for each member; no reelection before one year out of office had passed; only one family member allowed to serve at a time; three chairmen to watch one another, with the chairmanship rotating every month; the chairmen being sequestered so they could not be influenced; and the doge and signoria being members as a check on the Council of Ten.[4]

The Venetian judicial system was the envy of Europe. All inhabitants, citizens and noncitizens alike, were equal under the law and possessed the same rights when accused of a crime. Moreover, the level of justice was high for its day; investigations were conducted with scrupulous detail and impartiality, and the government provided legal counsel to those too poor to afford one.

Whereas other city republics were wracked by violent political conflicts of every description, Venice had a five-hundred-year political history of relative peace and stability. There was no popular uprising or other visible sign of popular discontent with the system. Nor were there murderous feuds among aristocratic families or civil war. The watchful eye of the Council of Ten undoubtedly helped keep potential uprisings, coups, and feuds in check. But no single institution could be so effective for so many centuries unless the leaders and people alike prized stability and held some affinity for their constitutional system.

What else explains Venice's stability? The geography had a stabilizing influence, especially in lowland maritime republics such as Venice. Italians who sought freedom were attracted to the safety of Venice's lagoons and islands and the benefits of an impregnable natural port. Those natural defenses kept Venice free from imperial conquest. It was well positioned for sea trade with the east and for land trade with the west. The need for canals, dikes, and other hydraulic projects demanded a high level of civic cooperation and an efficient administration.[5] (See Politics in Action: The Constitution of Venice.)

The commercial success of the republic undoubtedly promoted its political stability and harmony. By 1400, the Venetian Republic had a far-flung trading empire with over 3,000 merchant ships. At that time, the republic was one of the richest polities in Europe. Its public treasury had a large surplus, and the republic maintained an efficient commission for the distribution of grain. As a result, its people did not suffer from the levels of famine and poverty elsewhere in Europe.[6]

POLITICS IN ACTION
The Constitution of Venice

Venice's form of government was an urban aristocratic republic in a world of urban aristocratic republics. All policymaking offices were reserved for the aristocracy. At the same time, the city's constitution provided for some forms of peace, justice, and democracy.

- *Peace* was maintained by the Council of Ten. The council was an instrument of social control; it had spies everywhere. But it was carefully checked and balanced by internal and external measures. Its watchful eye fell equally on the rich, the poor, and those in between. It did not seem to have a suffocating influence on freedom of speech.
- *Justice* was maintained by a criminal justice system, including courts that were widely known for their adherence to the principle of equal treatment of the law.
- *Democracy* was accommodated in the context of the times by a civil service system headed and staffed by the common citizenry.

MORE ABOUT . . .
Venetian Virtue

A dramatic example of Venetian virtue is told in the story of Doge Francesco Foscari (1373–1457). Francesco Foscari was elected doge of Venice in 1423 and served in that capacity until shortly before his death. During his reign, he led Venice in a series of protracted wars against Milan. Venice won notable victories; however, led by the mercenary Francesco Sforza, Milan eventually conquered Venice. During the resulting peace, Sforza released Venice from his control, and Foscari was left to stabilize and rebuild war-torn Venice. In 1445, his son Jacopo was found guilty of treason and sentenced to exile on the island of Crete. Jacopo appealed to his father the doge for a pardon. Heartbroken, his father could not sanction treason and approved his own son's exile for the well-being of Venice. This true story was immortalized in Lord Byron's play *The Two Foscari* and in Giuseppe Verdi's opera *I Due Foscari*.

Political instability was also bad for business. A merchant aristocracy with international commercial interests had little time to fight, and they probably saw fighting as unprofitable. In a rich republic, where the wealth is spread around, people have less cause to be disgruntled.

Jacob Burckhardt (1818–1897), the great Swiss historian, offered a cultural interpretation in his book, *The Civilization of the Renaissance in Italy* (1860). According to Burckhardt, Venice and Florence had two different cultures. Venetians had a merchant culture that valued social stability and an orderly society; these values were good for business, even if the stability seemed stagnant to artists and intellectuals. By contrast, the Florentines had a more individualistic culture that valued a competitive and creative spirit. Florence attracted the world's finest artists and intellectuals, but the environment was volatile and divisive.

Other political thinkers and historians emphasize the Venetians' genuine commitment to **civic virtue** as a key factor in Venice's success. (See More About . . . Venetian Virtue.) Florentines spoke eloquently of republican civic virtue, but it was the Venetians who practiced what the Florentines preached. Most Florentine leaders were oligarchs, not republicans. They had a history of bitterly fighting one another and repressing rebellion with an iron fist. In 1378, for example, an alliance of conservative forces put down the revolt of the *ciompi* (lower-class wool-carders) seeking guild status. The revolt became a convenient excuse for stronger oligarchic control in the name of stability.

S. E. Finer (1915–1993), the eminent comparative government specialist, points to one unusual feature of Venice's government that may well be associated with the civic virtue of its officials and the stability of its constitutional history. Venice, according to Finer, was governed by a **gerontocracy**, literally, rule by elders. The doge had to be over seventy years of age with a long career in public service; all other senior officials were seventy to eighty years old; the minimum age for a senator was thirty, and an individual had to be twenty-five to enter the Great Council (in Florence, the age was fourteen).[7]

Venetians were a prudent people—perhaps even stodgy. In their merchant culture, they prized the values of prudence, caution, and patience in their life and in their leaders. They regarded leaders of ambition and vision with suspicion. A young person, of course, could be as mature and responsible as an older person, but Venetians preferred elders as their leaders, and their constitution reflected that choice. As you may recall, the Germanic conciliar republics relied on a similar principle; so, too, did the non-European republics.

HOW DID THE MODERN RENAISSANCE REDEFINE REPUBLICANISM?

Venice managed to avoid the worst of the economic and political instability of the fourteenth and fifteenth centuries. Economic equilibrium finally came to the rest of Europe in the mid- to late 1400s. The economies of the other northern Italian cities were the first to recover. And gradually economic equilibrium spread to other parts of Europe before the end of the 1400s.

In his economic history, David Hackett Fischer had this to say about the importance of economic equilibriums: "Each period of equilibrium had a distinct cultural character. All were marked in their later stages by the emergence of ideas of order and harmony such as appeared in the Renaissance of the twelfth century, the Italian Renaissance of the *quattrocentro* [1400s], the Enlightenment of the early eighteenth century, and the Victorian era."[8]

Historically, the modern Renaissance in Italy was born out of two forces: economic equilibrium and political disequilibrium. People were disillusioned by the corruption, bickering, and folly of their political world. Bold thinkers looked more deeply for root causes. They grew skeptical of the great medieval idea of order and harmony, in which everyone was locked into a fixed position by birth. Skepticism raised questions, and questions brought scientific and philosophical inquiry about the nature of man in the universe, about the universe itself, and about God's plan for it. At the same time, skepticism prompted ethical and political questions: What is the good society? What is the role of the citizen and government in it? What then does it mean to be a good citizen and a good leader?

Around 1487, the Italian philosopher Giovanni Pico della Mirandola (1463–1494) put his finger on the great idea of the modern Renaissance and the modern era to follow. That idea is human dignity. Pico's *Oration on the Dignity of Man* became the creed of Renaissance humanism. In the following excerpt from Pico's book, God explains this to Adam.

> *We have given you, O Adam, no visage proper to yourself, nor endowment properly your own, in order that whatever place, whatever form, whatever gifts you may, with premeditation, select, these same you may have and possess through your own judgement and decision. The nature of all other creatures is defined and restricted within laws which We have laid down; you, by contrast, impeded by no such restrictions, may, by your own free will, to whose custody We have assigned you, trace for yourself the lineaments of your own nature. I have placed you at the very center of the world, so that from that vantage point you may with greater ease glance round about you on all that the world contains.*

We have made you a creature neither of heaven nor of earth, neither mortal nor immortal, in order that you may, as the free and proud shaper of your own being, fashion yourself in the form you may prefer. It will be in your power to descend to the lower, brutish forms of life; you will be able, through your own decision, to rise again to the superior orders whose life is divine.[9]

Pico's *Oration* is a testament to the unbounded potential of man. (Notice that Pico addresses Adam, not Eve too.) Man begins at the center of the universe and ascends or descends depending on the choices he is now free to make. (See Bold Thinkers: Pico della Mirandola—Renaissance Man.)

Humanism is a philosophical movement of the Renaissance that rested on the centrality of the human being as a free agent, capable of folly and wisdom. Humanists questioned the medieval order in which human beings have a fixed position in the group into which they were born and in the hierarchy by which they were governed. Humanists also questioned the folly and corruption of their political world. They questioned the Church as an institution but not the importance of religion in society. Few were secularists; fewer still were atheists. They were disappointed by the intolerance and constant squabbling they saw around them.

Humanists looked back to antiquity for role models and teachings. They strongly advocated a classical, scriptural, and humanistic education. Such an education required a knowledge of the Greek and Latin languages. How else could someone read the classical and scriptural texts, let alone translate them into a vernacular language? Humanistic education also required the study of classical logic, rhetoric, and virtues. In their politics, most humanists were republicans. In fact, humanism set republicanism on its modern trajectory.

Humanists did not agree on everything. Two schools of humanistic thought were prominent in Medieval Europe: (1) the Florentine school of civic humanism, associated with the political philosopher Niccolò Machiavelli (1469–1527) and his theory of classical republicanism, and (2) the northern school of Christian humanism associated with the Dutch philosopher and theologian Desiderius Erasmus (c. 1466–1536) and the theory of covenantal republicanism.

Civic humanism is the Italian Renaissance movement that flourished in Florence in the late fifteenth and early sixteenth centuries. As the terms *civic* and *classical* suggest, this school of thought was primarily secular in its views; it broke with medievalism and much preferred the classical models of the Greek and Roman republics.

Machiavelli revitalized the classical republican ideas in his *Discourses on the First Ten Books of Titus Livius* (known as the *Discourses on Livy*).[10] Livy (c. 59 BCE–17 CE) was a Roman philosopher and historian in the time of Emperor Augustus; he devoted his life to writing a history of the Roman Republic in 142 chapters.

Machiavelli wrote *Discourses* for three time periods: past, present, and future. As a historian of Rome's past, Machiavelli sought answers to the question, what made the Roman Republic great? As a commentator on his present world, Machiavelli reflected on the sorry state of Florentine politics, plagued as he saw it by political infighting among oligarchs, Church corruption, and the rigidity of Church doctrines. How, he asked, could Florence

BOLD THINKERS

Pico della Mirandola—Renaissance Man

Giovanni Pico della Mirandola (1463–1494) fulfills our image of a Renaissance man. He studied everything (including law, philosophy, mathematics, and mysticism) everywhere (including Florence, Paris, and Rome) and was highly regarded by his fellow humanists.

When Pico settled in Florence in 1484, the city's patron, Lorenzo de' Medici himself, invited Pico to join the Medici Platonic Academy. There he studied Greek philosophy and wrote poetry and a number of philosophical works. He was also the first Christian scholar to employ Kabbalistic doctrine (Jewish mystical teachings) to support Christian theology.

While in Arezzo, Pico abducted Margherita, the young wife of another Medici. Despite Lorenzo's support during the ensuing scandal, Pico had to keep on the move. In Rome in 1486, as part of his ambitious attempt to unify all schools of thought, Pico posted nine hundred theses from various authorities on logic, mathematics, physics, and other topics, offering to defend them against all opponents. His celebrated *Oration on the Dignity of Man* accompanied the posting.

Accused of heresy by the pope, Pico was eventually cleared. Later, Girolamo Savonarola, a fiery preacher hostile to Renaissance humanism (and the Medici family), reconverted Pico to orthodoxy. Pico died by arsenic poisoning at the age of thirty-one, probably at the order of one of Lorenzo de' Medici's sons.

regain her greatness? As a philosopher, perhaps the world's first modern political philosopher, Machiavelli anticipated the future challenge of individualism in the modern world. He recognized that individual freedom would create excesses of individualism in which citizens ignored the common good and repeatedly clashed over competing self-interests. What, he asked, would redirect citizens to seek the common good when they were now completely free to follow their own self-interests?

Classical republicanism is the term most frequently used to describe Machiavelli's answers to the challenges facing the Roman and Florentine republics. But his answer also was a forerunner of modern republicanism, especially in the way he dealt with individualism, diversity, and conflict. In his theory, Machiavelli offered six main points and a practical reason for each.

1. The Roman Republic was great because it was free. Liberty is the key to greatness because it provides people with the best incentive to make money and defend their country.

2. A republic with a mixed republican government and a balanced constitution is the best way to acquire liberty and maintain a free way of life. In this way, both the few (the wealthy) and the many (the people) have a share of political power in the polity. Therefore, both sides will have a principled and self-interested incentive to advance the common good of the polity.

3. The people are better safeguards of liberty than their leaders, but both are of optimum value if they possess civic virtue. **Civic virtue** for Machiavelli meant that the citizen and the leader each must be prepared to "advance not his own interests but the general good, not his own posterity but the common fatherland."[11]

4. Machiavelli believed that citizens and their leaders must be prepared to use any means necessary to advance and protect the common good of their country at all costs. Machiavelli is emphatic on this point; even evil acts are justifiable in the interest of the common good. In *The Prince,* Machiavelli urged this morality of expediency ("the ends justify the means") for leaders. In *Discourses,* he urged this morality for the citizenry as well. For Machiavelli, the citizen's highest civic virtue is the courageous defense of the polity. The word virtue comes from the Latin word *vir,* meaning "man." For Machiavelli, as for the ancient Greeks and Romans, virtue had two meanings: manly courage and moral excellence or civic goodness.

5. But how does the republic instill civic virtue in the people? Machiavelli examined several answers: good leaders, the rule of law, civic education, and a spirit of patriotism.

6. Machiavelli believed that tension and conflict could be healthy in a polity of diverse interests. This is in contrast to the position of most republicans, who believed that good citizens should work together in harmony.

As a forerunner of modern republicanism, Machiavelli's philosophy influenced the Italian Renaissance of the sixteenth century, the English Revolution of the seventeenth century, and the American and French revolutions of the eighteenth century.

Christian humanism was an intellectual movement that flourished in northern Europe (especially in the Netherlands) at the same time as civic humanism in Florence and that is associated with Desiderius Erasmus. Machiavelli and Erasmus were contemporaries. Erasmus wrote *Education of a Christian Prince* in 1516, three years after Machiavelli finished *The Prince.* (See Points of View: Erasmus and Machiavelli—Advising Princes.)

Unlike Machiavelli, Erasmus was a theologian, not a political philosopher. He devoted his life to understanding and translating Scripture. He sought to humanize the Church, not reform it. His biographer, Johan Huizinga, described him as the rarest of men—a calm and moderate idealist in an age of passionate zealots.[12]

POINTS OF VIEW

Erasmus and Machiavelli—Advising Princes

In 1516, the Dutch humanist Desiderius Erasmus (1466–1536) published his *Institutio Principis Christiani* (*The Education of a Christian Prince*). The famous independent scholar wrote this work to advise his young patron, King Charles of Spain, who later became the powerful Holy Roman Emperor Charles V. Erasmus insisted that the principles of sincerity and honor must guide a prince's actions. He even portrayed the prince as a servant of the people. Erasmus encouraged the ruler to attract his people's love, suggesting that a broad education best serves a prince by providing knowledge he can apply to governing his people justly rather than oppressing them.

Three years earlier, the involuntarily retired Florentine statesman Niccolò Machiavelli (1469–1527) wrote his *Il Principe* (*The Prince*) for Lorenzo II de' Medici, who at that time ruled Florence. Focusing on how a prince can most practically employ political force and practical wisdom to maintain control, he argued that a ruler is safer when feared than loved but safest when he has power and prudence on his side. Machiavelli, a veteran party politician, brilliantly described the ways a successful prince can make this happen. Young Lorenzo, who briefly ruled Florence from 1513 to 1519, was Machiavelli's hope for a prince capable of expelling foreign occupiers, uniting Italy, and giving Machiavelli a government position. Lorenzo never hired Machiavelli, who dedicated himself to political, historical, and literary writing during the remainder of his life.

Desiderius Erasmus (left) and Niccolò Machiavelli.

Like Machiavelli, Erasmus was ahead of his time but in a different way. Erasmus sought to strengthen the Church by reconciling medieval and Renaissance interpretations of doctrine. Yet his efforts angered important conservatives and reformers alike. Erasmus believed that "Christ dwells everywhere; piety is practiced under every garment, if only a kindly disposition is not wanting."[13]

Erasmus, like Machiavelli, believed that the mixed republic was the ideal form of government. However, he rejected the Machiavellian notion that human beings could be good citizens by committing evil acts. For Erasmus, the good citizen and the good person were synonymous. Erasmus looked to biblical as well as classical models of good government and citizenship. To the Christian prince, he urged three values: moderation, adaptability, and duty. Above all, the prince must be wise, and the citizen must be tolerant and of goodwill.

What was Erasmus's greatest contribution to republican ideas? Huizinga put it this way: "in so far as people still believe in the ideal that moral education and general tolerance may make humanity happier, humanity owes much to Erasmus."[14] How different are the legacies of Erasmus and Machiavelli!

Covenantal republicanism developed among the second generation of Christian humanists who followed Erasmus. This generation included reformers who broke with the medieval Church and established Reformed churches in what became known as the Age of Reformation. The reformers differed over what they sought to reform and how. Our concern here is with their political (not theological) reforms and their implications for republicanism.

According to the modern European historian R. R. Palmer, there were three types of Reformed sects in terms of their political orientations: Anabaptists, Lutherans (and Anglicans), and Reformed Protestants (of whom the most numerous were Calvinists). Anabaptist sects came out of the radical movement of the working poor who protested the corruption of the Church. Lutherans recognized the authority of the state and found ready alliances with established states and their monarchs. (Anglicanism was a product of the state and the ambitions of King Henry VIII of England.) Calvinists and other Reformed Protestants were more likely to represent the middle class of the free cities. They believed it was the obligation of God's chosen few to Christianize the state.

POLITICS IN ACTION
Republicanism Spurs First National Independence Movement

Dutch Calvinists and republicans waged the first successful war of national independence against a foreign monarch in modern times. In the process, the Dutch created a mixed federal republic representing nobles and towns—the United Provinces—that adopted a federal system that was similar to Poland's. At its center were provincial assemblies (called states in the Dutch system). Each assembly represented the nobles and towns in its province and was, in turn, represented in the union assembly (called the States-General). Representatives were required to follow the instructions of their constituents.

Jonathan I. Israel, *The Dutch Republic: Its Rise, Greatness, and Fall, 1477–1806* (Oxford: Oxford University Press, 1995).

Reformed Protestant churches included Swiss Calvinists, French Huguenots, Dutch Protestants, Scottish Presbyterians, and English separatists and Puritan congregationalists. (The Pilgrims who settled Plymouth believed in the radical idea that they were coming to the New World as pilgrims to found a city on a hill to await the second coming of Christ. The Puritans who later settled Massachusetts Bay sought to purify the Church of England.)[15]

Calvinists were antistatists and antimonarchists. They were republicans who believed in a special form of self-government in which people come together by political covenant to build a holy commonwealth or republic on Earth. (See Politics in Action: Republicanism Spurs First National Independence Movement.)

A political covenant is a voluntary and mutual agreement among equals who come together with God as a witness to form a political association that has a divinely inspired moral purpose. The sixteenth-century idea of political covenant was adapted from two sources: the biblical covenants in the Hebrew Bible and the church covenants creating the Reformed churches.

The sixteenth-century political covenant was a forerunner of Locke's seventeenth-century idea of a compact and Rousseau's eighteenth-century idea of a social contract. There is one obvious difference. Social contracts and compacts are secular agreements; they do not invoke God as a witness, and they do not claim a divinely inspired purpose.

The Mount Sinai covenant is among the first recorded political covenants. It is described in the Hebrew Bible (Exodus 19 and 20). In that description, God first presents Moses with a set of commandments (known as the Ten Commandments). God also instructs Moses that, if the Israelites consent to obey those commandments, they will become a holy nation. But they must consent. Moses then meets with the elders of the twelve tribes of Israel, who agree to obey God's laws.[16]

The Mayflower Compact is a covenant, even though late-eighteenth-century historians labeled it a compact. It is reproduced here.

The Mayflower Compact, 1620

In the name of God, Amen [1]. We whose names are underwritten, the loyal subjects of our dread [awesome] sovereign Lord, King James, by the grace of God, of Great Britain, France, and Ireland king, defender of the faith, etc., Having undertaken, for the glory of God [2], and advancement of the Christian

The signing of the Mayflower Compact, 1620.

faith [3], and honour of our king and country, a voyage to plant the first colony in the Northern parts of Virginia, do by these presents [words] solemnly and mutually in the presence of God [4], and one another, covenant [5] and combine ourselves together into a civil body politick [6], for our better ordering and preservation and furtherance of the ends aforesaid [7]; and by virtue hereof [8] to enact, constitute, and frame such just and equal laws, ordinances, acts, constitutions, and offices, from time to time, as shall be thought most meet [necessary] and convenient for the general good of the Colony, unto which we promise all due submission and obedience. In witness whereof we have hereunder subscribed our names at Cape-Cod the 11 of November, in the year of the reign of our sovereign lord, King James, of England, France, and Ireland the eighteenth, and of Scotland the fiftie fourth. Anno Dom. 1620.[17]

Notice that the covenantal elements of the compact have been numbered and that the numbers correspond to the following explanation.

- God is invoked as a witness in the opening statement (1) and again in (4). Signing this document is taking an oath.
- The first two purposes of the new colony are religious in (2) and (3).
- The signers use the verb *covenant* (5) to describe their action.
- The signers make clear that the document is a political covenant by referring to the association they form as a "civil body politick" (6).
- The signers make clear that the purpose of the political covenant in (7) and (8) includes the religious purposes of the colony in (2) and (3).[18]

In the early modern period, Calvinists and other Reformed Protestants wielded power in Geneva, the Dutch Republic, Scotland, and New England. But how important was classical republicanism and covenantal republicanism in the English Revolution of the seventeenth century and in the American and French revolutions of the eighteenth century? Consider this question as you read the next chapter.

REVIEWING AND USING THE CHAPTER

1. What made the Venetian Republic so successful? How did it become an example of a "durable, stable, and peaceful" mixed government?

2. Compare the political ideas of Machiavelli with those of Erasmus. How were they alike, and how were they different?

3. Do you agree with Machiavelli's or Erasmus's view of leadership? Should the good leader commit evil acts in the name of the polity? If you answered no, are there exceptions? If you answered yes, are there limits?

EXTENSION ACTIVITY

Carefully analyze the last paragraph of the U.S. Declaration of Independence. Is the Declaration a political covenant, compact, or a combination of the two? Choose and defend your position.

WEB RESOURCES

Internet Medieval Sourcebook: Renaissance
www.fordham.edu/halsall/sbook1x.html

A part of the History Sourcebook Project of Fordham University, this Web site includes excellent original essays and links to other electronic resources and documents that focus on the history of Renaissance Europe.

Stanford Encyclopedia of Philosophy: Erasmus and Machiavelli
http://plato.stanford.edu/entries/erasmus (Erasmus)

http://plato.stanford.edu/entries/machiavelli (Machiavelli)

These encyclopedia entries provide excellent and well-organized discussions of the ideas of two of the most influential Renaissance philosophers, Desiderius Erasmus and Niccolò Machiavelli. The entries include well-organized essays as well as large bibliographies and links to other Internet sources.

World Civilizations: An Internet Classroom and Anthology
www.wsu.edu/~dee/REN

Maintained by Washington State University, this Web site will take its users to a variety of excellent resources on the Italian Renaissance including original essays, images, a glossary, a bibliography, and links to other resources.

NOTES

1 John Julius Norwich, *A History of Venice* (New York: Vintage Books, 1989), 181–183.

2 For more on Venice, see William J. Bouwsma, *Venice and the Defense of Republican Liberty: Renaissance Values in the Age of the Counter-Reformation* (Berkeley, Calif.: University of California Press, 1968); William H. McNeill, *Venice: The Hinge of Europe, 1081–1797* (Chicago: University of Chicago Press, 1974); Alvise Zorzi, *Venice, 697–1797: A City, a Republic, an Empire,* rev. ed. (Woodstock, N.Y.: Overlook Press, 2001).

3 Bouwsma, *Venice and the Defense of Republican Liberty,* 60.

4 Norwich, *History of Venice,* 499.

5 Bouwsma, *Venice and the Defense of Republican Liberty,* 57–58.

6 S. E. Finer, *The History of Government* (Oxford: Oxford University Press, 1997), Vol. 2, 991–992.

7 Ibid., Vol. 2, 1011.

8 David Hackett Fischer, *The Great Wave: Price Revolutions and Rhythm of History* (New York: Oxford University Press, 1996), 239.

9 Pico della Mirandola, *Oration on the Dignity of Man,* available at www.cscs.umich.edu/~crshalizi/Mirandola.

10 The standard translation of the *Discourses on Livy* is in Niccolò Machiavelli, *Machiavelli: The Chief Works and Others,* trans. Allan Gilbert (Durham, N.C.: Duke University Press, 1965), Vol. 1. A translation is also available electronically at the Online Library of Liberty. Important interpretations include J. G. A. Pocock, *The Machiavellian Moment: Florentine Political Thought and the Atlantic Republican Tradition* (Princeton, N.J.: Princeton University Press, 2003); Quentin Skinner, *Machiavelli: A Very Short Introduction* (New York: Oxford University Press, 1981, 2001); Harvey C. Mansfield, *Machiavelli's New Modes and Orders: A Study of the Discourses on Livy* (Chicago: University of Chicago Press, 2001).

11 Machiavelli, *Machiavelli,* 218, quoted in Skinner, *Machiavelli,* 62.

12 Johan Huizinga, *Erasmus and the Age of Reformation* (New York: Harper & Row, 1957; originally translated from Dutch in 1924), 190.

13 Quoted in ibid., 192.

14 Ibid.

15 R. R. Palmer, Joel Colton, and Lloyd Kramer, *A History of the Modern World,* 10th ed. (Boston: McGraw-Hill, 2007), 76–79, 86–87.

16 For more on this and other biblical covenants, see Daniel J. Elazar, *The Covenant Tradition in Politics, Vol. 1: Covenant & Polity in Biblical Israel: Biblical Foundations and Jewish Expressions* (New Brunswick, N.J.: Transaction Publishers, 1995).

17 Donald S. Lutz, "The Mayflower Compact," in *Roots of the Republic: American Founding Documents Interpreted,* ed. Stephen L. Schechter (Madison, Wisc.: Madison House, 1990), 22–23.

18 For more on how to interpret the Mayflower Compact and other documents, such as the Declaration of Independence, see Stephen L. Schechter, ed., *Roots of the Republic: American Founding Documents Interpreted* (Madison, Wisc.: Madison House, 1990).

REPUBLICANISM AND DEMOCRACY IN THE MODERN AGE

Republics arise in many ways. In the seventeenth and eighteenth centuries, three revolutions redefined both how republics arise and what form they take. As you will learn in the first chapter of this unit, it is no exaggeration to say that the English, American, and French revolutions reinvented republican government. These revolutions demonstrated that a people willing to engage in politics and fight for their beliefs can alter or abolish a government that has forfeited its right to govern. This crucial first step toward self-government taken by the people of England, America, and France would also strongly influence the development of republicanism around the world.

The American and French revolutions paved the way for the great political theme of the next two hundred years—the rise of democracy. In the centuries that followed

CHAPTER 17:

HOW DID THE ENGLISH, AMERICAN, AND FRENCH REVOLUTIONS REINVENT REPUBLICAN GOVERNMENT?

CHAPTER 18:

HOW DID DEMOCRACY TRANSFORM REPUBLICAN GOVERNMENT AFTER 1800?

Athenian democracy, people regarded democracy as majority tyranny. This view began to change in the 1800s, and by the end of the twentieth century, most of the world's polities had embraced democracy. The appeal of democracy had become so strong that many nations that had not embraced democracy *claimed* to have done so. The second chapter of this unit explores the paths that democracy has taken on its way to becoming a valued political ideal in the world.

CHAPTER 17

HOW DID THE ENGLISH, AMERICAN, AND FRENCH REVOLUTIONS REINVENT REPUBLICAN GOVERNMENT?

BIG IDEAS

- The English, American, and French revolutions helped to reinvent and define modern republican government.

- The Glorious Revolution in England ensured that the unwritten British constitution conformed to republican principles such as a government limited by checks and balances and the separation of powers.

- The American and French revolutions redefined such republican principles as consent of the governed, the rule of law, representation, and the common good and altered the ways people thought about the kind of government that would best support these principles.

- The English, American, and French revolutions were shaped by different pasts and inspired by different visions of the future.

Purpose of This Chapter

Political change is no easy task. Throughout the history of the political world, significant changes to forms of government are relatively infrequent and often violent. Examining the English, American, and French revolutions provides insights into the process of political change. This chapter examines how these three revolutions were conceived and what they accomplished. You will analyze how these watershed moments in history are similar, how they are different, and how each reinvented republican government.

Terms to Know

abdication	enclosure	Napoleonic Code
absolute monarchy	English Bill of Rights	parliamentarians
Act of Settlement	Estates-General	parliamentary supremacy
constitutional monarchy	federalism	royalists
country gentry	fundamental law	supreme law
Court of Star Chamber	general will	
divine right	judicial review	

REINVENTING REPUBLICAN GOVERNMENT

The English, American, and French Revolutions reinvented republican government. They neither copied the republican past, nor did they ignore or destroy it. In certain ways, every people with a republican form of government must reinvent government for themselves. The very act of doing so is the first step in making a government "of the people, by the people, for the people." When taking that first step toward self-government, there is no guarantee of success; but without it, there is every chance of failure. Republics, by definition, require self-government, which in turn requires a citizenry willing to engage in politics. Republics do not usually work if they are imposed on a people unwilling to govern themselves.

These three revolutions also reinvented republican government in a second way—as international models of enlightened republican government in the modern age. The leaders of each vigorously promoted their example on the world stage.

In addition to reinventing republican government, these revolutions share other similarities. Perhaps the most important similarity is their historical context. These were not isolated events. Although a century separated England's Glorious Revolution from her French and American counterparts and an ocean separated the American Revolution from its European cousins, these revolutions were related. In fact, the Glorious Revolution can be viewed as the political and intellectual parent of both the American and French revolutions.

England's Glorious Revolution of 1688–1689 marks a unique milestone in the history of republican government. It is the first revolution that established a mixed republican government. The Glorious Revolution also established the framework of government that, with some important changes, still operates in the United Kingdom today. In 1689, that government was a mix of monarchy and aristocracy; today, it is predominantly a democracy with ceremonial remnants of its aristocratic and monarchic past. The English Bill of Rights of 1689 codified the results of the Glorious Revolution. It remains for the British people what the Declaration of Independence and the U.S. Bill of Rights became for Americans—a treasured symbol of English constitutional liberty. The Act of Settlement of 1701 (explored later in this chapter) is another product of the Glorious Revolution. It still provides the basic constitutional outline of the British system of government. In this sense, the Glorious Revolution is the parent of the present government.

The historical legacy of the American Revolution of 1776 is even stronger. The American Declaration of Independence is an enduring statement of principles on which America is based. It is the core of what has come to be known as the American creed. The U.S. Constitution of 1787 gave that declaration and the American people a constitutional framework of government that, with some important changes, remains in place today. President Abraham Lincoln's Gettysburg Address (1863) captured the legacy of the Declaration of Independence: "Four score and seven years ago our fathers brought forth on this continent, a new nation, conceived in Liberty, and dedicated to the proposition that all men are created equal."[1]

Like the American Revolution, the French Revolution of 1789 was a political and intellectual child of the Glorious Revolution. French commitment to the ideas of equal liberty under law and republican government extended the principles of the Glorious Revolution. Both revolutions were inspired by powerful ideas—ideas that continue to inspire leaders, citizens, and constitution makers the world over.

The idea of liberty was not new in these three republics; a free citizenry equal in its right to liberty is one of the defining criteria of republican government. However, these may be the first republics since ancient Rome that were conceived in liberty by constitutional revolution. The Glorious Revolution helped to lay the political and intellectual foundation for the American and French revolutions that followed.

WHAT WERE THE SOURCES AND EFFECTS OF ENGLAND'S GLORIOUS REVOLUTION?

Elizabeth I ruled England for 45 years (1558–1603) with a firm, steady hand. Literature and the arts flourished in what became known as the Elizabethan age. The empire and economy grew during her reign. During much of this period, the royal court grew rich and powerful, and so too did the landed country gentry.

The **country gentry**, a broad class of country gentlemen just below the nobility class, benefited from the overseas trade, the woolen industry, and the ancient practice of enclosure. **Enclosure** allowed the gentry to expand the pastures where their sheep grazed. This practice deprived the common people of land that they believed was traditionally held in common for the benefit of all. Inflation and enclosure injured the lower classes. (See More About . . . The Enclosure Movement.) The country gentry grew stronger, and so did their influence in Parliament.

The country gentry were the largest part of the *political population* (that is, the fully empowered citizenry) of England. With the wealthier aristocracy, they controlled the countryside. The country gentry were the tax collectors, the army officers, the justices of the peace, and the lawyers who controlled the day-to-day aspects of public administration throughout England. They also dominated the House of Commons. The wealthier aristocracy dominated the House of Lords.

When Elizabeth died without an heir, the House of Tudor died with her. (See More About . . . The Tudors.) Her successor, James I, was the first of four Stuart kings to rule

Beginning in the last half of the Middle Ages, English landowners began enclosing tracts of common land with fences, ditches, and other barriers. Prior to enclosure, fields, pastureland, and wasteland were held in common and free tenants were given rights to small strips of land. Twenty years after the signing of the Magna Carta, the English parliament passed the Statute of Merton (1235), allowing lords of the manor to legally enclose tracts of land as long as land remained for their tenants. Therefore, the Statute of Merton further limited the king's power and increased the power of the landlords. As the wool trade grew in the fourteenth century, so too did demand for more pastureland. Landlords found ways to expel tenants and fence off large areas for their growing flocks. Increased enclosures during the reign of the Tudors spiked social unrest, and the enclosure movement slowed. As the technology of the Industrial Revolution began to make wool even more profitable, enclosure began to grow again in the last half of the eighteenth century.

England in the seventeenth century. James I (1603–1625) and his oldest son Charles I (1625–1649) ruled England for forty-five years. Bitter divisions wracked English politics during the seventeenth century. Royal interests and those of the gentry (in the country and in Parliament) increasingly came into conflict. So too did their policies over religion, taxation, finance, and war.

Equally important, the two sides clashed over the authority to rule. James I was convinced that, as king, he ruled by **divine right**, that is, that his authority to rule came directly from God. He pushed this point indirectly and cautiously. His son, Charles I, was blunt where his father had been shrewd, and soon Charles pushed Parliament into opposition. Parliament claimed ultimately that the Crown's authority came from the consent of the governed. Although at first stymied in many of his policies, Charles I decided to rule without Parliament. He proved surprisingly successful in raising his own money. He also succeeded at administering his own brand of justice in royal courts such as the infamous **Court of Star Chamber**. On paper, the Court of Star Chamber's primary function was to decide political libel and treason cases; in practice, its primary purpose became upholding the power of the king.[2]

After Charles I was forced to call a new Parliament in 1638, the conflict resumed and worsened. Then in 1642 civil war broke out between the **royalists**, who supported the king, and the **parliamentarians**, who supported republican principles and government. Led by Oliver Cromwell, the parliamentarians were victorious. In 1649, under Cromwell's leadership, they beheaded Charles I, abolished the monarchy, and established the Commonwealth and Protectorate. The leaders of the revolution experimented briefly with republican government. This included the attempt to draft a new republican constitution known as the Instrument of Government in 1653. But the next year they gave up and established a Protectorate with Cromwell as Lord Protector. The Protectorate ruled almost as autocratically as had the Stuarts.[3]

Before Oliver Cromwell died in 1658, he designated his son Richard to succeed him as Lord Protector. Richard ruled briefly and ineffectively. The members of a newly elected Parliament recognized that Richard could not sustain the Protectorate and that the people of

The Tudors were one of the most influential royal families in English history. The Tudor dynasty (also known as the House of Tudor) ruled from 1485 to 1603. Perhaps the most influential Tudor monarch was Henry VIII, who oversaw the rise of the Protestant Reformation in England. The Tudor dynasty, although relatively brief, led to (1) the reorganization of English power and culture, (2) the strengthening of the monarch, (3) England's rise as a naval power, (4) increased nationalism, (5) an outburst of literature and scholarship, and (6) fundamental changes in the English church.

Elizabeth I ruled England from 1558 to 1603.

England yearned for a more stable and legitimate government. They therefore restored the Stuart monarchy in 1660. The reign of Charles II (1660–1685) lasted for twenty-five years and proved relatively stable, especially given the continuing tensions between the Crown and Parliament. During this period, two emerging groups that we have come to recognize as early political parties gathered strength in Parliament. The Whigs made up the country party of the gentry. They stood up for the rights of Parliament as representing the British nation. The Tories composed the court party that supported the Crown.

England was not the only European country wracked by economic and political crisis during the first two-thirds of the seventeenth century. Across Europe, this was a time of crisis. Economically, prices rose, wages and other income declined, agriculture and commerce slowed, and food shortages and famine spread. Demographically, the population declined for the first time since the Black Death. Wars, sectarian violence, urban unrest, peasant revolts, and ethnic uprisings were commonplace.[4]

The Thirty Years War (1618–1648) is perhaps the most famous example of seventeenth-century violence in Europe, but it wasn't the only one. The west saw the Portuguese revolt (1640–1668), the Catalan War in Spain (1640–1653), and the Irish rebellion (1641–1649). The east witnessed the Cossack revolts (1638 and 1647–1653), the Ukrainian peasant revolts (1647–1653), the Moscow revolts (1633, 1637, 1645, and 1648), and the Janissary (mercenary soldiers) revolts north of Istanbul (1622, 1625, and 1648).[5]

By 1650, armies were larger than at any time since the Roman Empire.[6] Governments tried desperately to raise revenues. Most failed, and deficit spending increased. In France, for example, the government levied a tax on court officers of the Paris High Court (known as the Parlement). The court refused to pay and its leaders, after calling for constitutional reforms, were arrested. In protest, Parisians rioted with slingshots (called *frondes*), breaking the

A 1652 battle during the Fronde rebellion. The two Fronde rebellions failed to curb royal authority; instead, they paved the way for the absolutism of Louis XIV.

windows of government supporters' homes. Known as the first Fronde rebellion, it was followed by a second and much longer Fronde rebellion by the nobility, who also rebelled across France against high taxes.

The nobility who led the second Fronde rebellion failed to push for constitutional reforms, as had the English. Instead, marauding bands of veteran soldiers and their princes ransacked the country, fought one another, and even brought Spain into the conflict. Peace was not restored until 1660. France was still a patchwork of local laws and rulers linked by allegiance to the king. As R. R. Palmer, the noted historian of European history, explains, "There were some local 'customs' or regional systems of law; it was observed that travelers sometimes changed laws more often than they changed horses. . . . Tolls were levied by manorial lords. . . . Neither coinage nor weights and measures were uniform throughout the country."[7]

In 1661, at the age of twenty-three, young Louis XIV announced he was ready to assume French rule. He had carefully analyzed the disorder that plagued his country. He concluded that the people, from the lowliest commoner to the highest prince, were ready for peace and order. He gambled that they were ready to pay the political price. The price he imposed was **absolute monarchy**, a form of royal rule in which the king had absolute control over judicial administration and the military based on his divine right to rule as God's representative on earth. In exchange, the king agreed to rule fairly, not arbitrarily, and to bring order and uniformity to a divided kingdom.[8] The people of France accepted Louis XIV's offer.

In England, the Stuart monarchy had been restored one year earlier in 1660. Its first king, Charles II, ruled with moderation from 1660 to 1685. Tensions between the Crown and Parliament erupted again during the brief reign of Charles's brother and successor, James II (1685–1688). Whereas Charles II had managed to keep his Catholic leanings and his royal ambitions in check, James II was different. His arrogance was unrestrained by prudence or shrewdness. He quickly made public his allegiance to the Catholic faith and his absolutist ambitions. In a short amount of time, he raised revenues and an army as large as 30,000 men.[9]

James II came close to establishing a Catholic absolute monarchy in which he as king wielded unlimited power. But resistance to his rule began to build. Unlike France, the country was at peace, political opposition was united, Parliament had become a powerful institution, and the English had developed a healthy respect for the rule of law. Opposition Whig leaders looked for foreign support and found it in the Dutch Protestant William, Prince of Orange. Accepting the invitation of James's opponents, William led his troops to England, officers in James's army defected, many Tories joined the Whig opposition, and James fled the country. In fleeing, James threw the Great Seal of England into the Thames River. By this desperate and contemptuous act, James hoped to stymie the processes of government because no legislation could take effect without being certified by application of the Great Seal.

Nature hates a political vacuum, and Parliament stepped in to fill the void. It defined James's flight as an **abdication**, a renunciation of the throne and its power. Operating without the Great Seal, Parliament declared William and his wife Mary to be the lawful king and queen of England. Parliament then passed the English Bill of Rights in 1689.

The **English Bill of Rights** established **parliamentary supremacy** over the Crown in two ways: (1) by holding royal acts subject to the consent of the governed as expressed by Parliament and (2) by ensuring the independence of Parliament from the Crown.

The Bill of Rights also included a list of grievances against James II, which set an important precedent for the list of grievances drawn up eighty-seven years later against King George III in the U.S. Declaration of Independence. Another part of the English Bill of Rights enumerated the rights of the accused and freedoms of expression. Like the U.S. Bill of Rights a century later, the English Bill of Rights of 1689 made those rights and freedoms legally enforceable. In this way, the English Bill became a list of what government *shall not* do, not a moral declaration of what it *should not* do.

Virtually overnight, England confirmed its government as a **constitutional monarchy**. On paper, England was a constitutional monarchy because the powers of the Crown were limited by the Bill of Rights and other constitutional documents. These documents legitimized the powers of Parliament and the rights of the people as limits on the Crown. In reality, England was more like a mixed republican government that recognized and balanced the interests of the aristocracy, the country gentry, the Crown, and the rights of the people.

In the **Act of Settlement** of 1701, Parliament more explicitly assembled key pieces of the new republic into constitutional form. The Act of Settlement shifted the royal succession from the Stuarts to the heirs of William and Mary, strengthened the House of Commons, separated the Parliament and the Crown as institutions, and placed the government and its ministers between the Parliament and the Crown. This statute also removed the courts from royal control and created an independent judiciary.

Under other legislation, from 1670 to 1720, "the citizen himself—under the protection of those courts—enjoyed freedoms in respect of domicile, property, free speech and expression, and to a degree of religious tolerance."[10] In 1707, Parliament passed the Act of Union that united England and Scotland under a single Parliament. Thereafter the nation was called Great Britain. The following fifty years saw the emergence of three additional institutions of contemporary British government: the prime minister, the cabinet, and party government. (See Figure 17.1.)

The Glorious Revolution transformed the form of government in Great Britain. And it did so without bloodshed. The name of the 1701 act states candidly how the transformation was to occur—by "settlement."

Settlement is an interesting choice of words. The *Oxford English Dictionary* cites the jurist and legal commentator Sir William Blackstone (1723–1780) and others on this 1701 use of the term. The 1701 act "settled," or resolved, the long-standing conflicts between Parliament and the Crown. It also looked "to settle," or put in a fixed and permanent position, relations between the Crown, Parliament, and courts in a new constitutional framework.

This was the republic that John Locke had hoped for when he returned to England after the Glorious Revolution and that Voltaire celebrated in his 1728 *Letters Concerning the English Nation.* The revolution's most influential advocate was the French jurist and political philosopher Charles Louis Secondat, Baron de Montesquieu.[11] Born in 1689, the year of the Glorious Revolution, Montesquieu published his masterwork, *The Spirit of the Laws,* in 1748. By that year, the outlines of England's constitutional monarchy or monarchic republic were clear. (See Bold Thinkers: Montesquieu.)

Figure 17.1 Timeline of Revolutionary Events

TIMELINE

1642	English Civil War begins
1648	The first Fronde rebellion erupts in France
1689	Glorious Revolution ends in England
1689	Parliament adopts Bill of Rights
1701	Parliament enacts Act of Settlement
1707	Parliament enacts the Act of Union
1776	Continental Congress signs American Declaration of Independence
1787	Federal Convention drafts United States Constitution in Philadelphia
1789	French Revolution begins
1803	*Marbury v. Madison* establishes judicial review in the United States

BOLD THINKERS

Montesquieu

Born during the reign of Louis XIV into the French aristocracy, Charles Louis de Secondat baron de La Brede Montesquieu (1689–1755) was a legal scholar, satirist, and political philosopher. Montesquieu's most influential work, *The Spirit of the Laws*, took him twenty years to write and explored the relationships between law and society. In it, Montesquieu argued for constitutional government limited by, among other things, the rule of law and the separation of powers. His ideas continue to influence constitution makers to this day.

In *The Spirit of the Laws,* Montesquieu surveyed the vast spectrum of nations, peoples, and forms of government from ancient times to his own. He was particularly fascinated with England—a fascination that was shared throughout the European world. He wanted to find out why England had succeeded, whereas other monarchies and republics had failed to preserve the liberty of the people. He looked at the constitution, character, climate, and culture of the English, factors that he examined and compared to other countries. He praised England's balanced constitution, the separation of powers in its government, and the checks of each branch of government on one another. He wrote extensively on these points, and the American founders studied his analysis carefully a generation later.[12]

Montesquieu also analyzed the importance of the ruler's character. Spurred by his mastery of classical political thought, he believed that in monarchies the character of the ruler must be honorable. In republics whose guiding principle was virtue, the character of its leaders and people had to be virtuous. He also found climate important, especially the cold and damp English weather. Montesquieu believed that the English climate was a cause of the stubbornness of the English people, and he saw their stubbornness as a way of protecting their liberties: "Other nations have made the interests of commerce yield to those of politics; the English, on the contrary, have ever made their political interests give way to those of commerce. They know better than any other people how to value, at the same time, these three great advantages—religion, commerce, and liberty."[13]

HOW DID THE ENGLISH, AMERICAN, AND FRENCH VIEWS OF REVOLUTION DIFFER?

Two important differences separate the English, American, and French revolutions. Each was inspired by a different past and by a different vision of the future.

The English revolutionaries looked to restore a balanced form of government. The imbalances they observed in the preceding century had produced turmoil and divisiveness. Those imbalances upset the realm and its political system. The English revolutionaries saw this situation as a direct consequence of the corruption and arbitrariness of the Crown and its supporters.

Those taking part in the Glorious Revolution understood the idea of a political revolution differently than the French revolutionaries a century later. For the English of the seventeenth century, the word *revolution* was used in the astronomical sense—a body rotating until it returned to its original position. That was the primary meaning of the term in those days, not just in England but throughout Europe and the Americas. *Political revolution* thus meant restoration to the original position of balance and consensus from which the Stuarts' tyrannical government had taken England off course.

This restoration view survived throughout the next century. Writing in his great 1790 polemic against the French Revolution, the conservative thinker and statesman Edmund Burke (1729–1797) gave memorable expression to this interpretation of the Glorious Revolution: "If ever there was a time favourable for establishing the principle, that a king of popular choice was the only legal king . . . it was at the Revolution."[14]

By "popular choice," Burke did not mean a monarchy elected by the entire citizenry. Instead, he operated from a conception of virtual representation, in which the authority of republican monarchy came from the implied consent of a much smaller segment of the governed. That consent remained passive until it was threatened. Then, the governed had the right to revolt. This was not by any means a democratic revolution of all the people. It was, both in theory and practice, a republican revolution. The authority of the monarch was based on consent, not divine right. And the basis of that consent expanded beyond a few high-ranking aristocrats to include all of the nobility and all of the country gentry.

The British colonists in North America faced a different past and present in 1776. They were further removed from England's medieval past, national monarchy, and feudal laws of loyalty and inheritance. Between 1607 (the date of the first permanent English settlement at Jamestown, Virginia) and 1776, the American colonies had experienced nearly 150 years of virtual self-government. By the mid-eighteenth century, the colonists saw themselves as Englishmen enjoying English rights and English law. For some time, they had enjoyed a relatively high level of political freedom, economic opportunity, social movement, and affordable land. In his 1776 testimony on the Stamp Act, Benjamin Franklin was justified when he assured Parliament that no subjects of George III were more loyal to him or to the mother country than those residing in the thirteen American colonies.

The·TIMES are Dreadful, Dismal Doleful Dolorous, and DOLLAR-LESS.

In this 1765 engraving, a Tory stamp agent is strung up on a Liberty Pole while another is about to be tarred and feathered in an anti-Stamp Act demonstration. The image below the engraving is a comment from the Pennsylvania Journal on the colonists' plight, 1765.

Still, the American revolutionaries shared a conception of political revolution similar to their counterparts in England. Indeed, at first, Americans regarded their opposition to British colonial policy as virtually identical in principle to the Glorious Revolution against Stuart tyranny. The difference was that, at first, a hostile and indifferent Parliament (rather than a usurping monarch) was the Americans' target. Americans objected to the Stamp Act of 1765 and subsequent parliamentary tax acts as "taxation without representation." In their view, the acts of Parliament violated the very principles of republican government that British subjects everywhere in the empire were supposed to enjoy. In particular, those acts violated an important principle of virtual representation—one part of the empire should not be taxed without taxing the rest.[15] As Americans saw it, those acts also violated the rule of law because Parliament overstepped its bounds in passing the Stamp Act and subsequent tax acts. In sum, what they objected to in British colonial policy in the 1760s and 1770s was precisely its radical innovations that seemed to set aside nearly two centuries of what they deemed to be constitutional government.

Most historians agree that the American Revolution was not a revolution to destroy its own republican past. Some historians, going even further, assert that the American Revolution was not a modern revolution at all but rather an attempt to recover the civic humanism and republican past of the Renaissance. J. G. A. Pocock, the leading exponent of this view, maintains that the American Revolution looks "less as the first political act of revolutionary enlightenment than as the last great act of the Renaissance."[16] The disputes among American historians about whether the revolution was truly revolutionary are disputes of degree and not of kind. The revolution was Janus-faced. Like the ancient Roman god Janus, it looked backward and forward at the same time. It looked backward to preserve the Americans' heritage of English constitutionalism and republican political thought; and it looked forward to integrate and synthesize that heritage within a new challenging American context.

By contrast, the French in 1789 were subjects, not free citizens. Many French farmers were still tenant farmers or serfs. The French lived under a system that was at one and the same time an oppressive feudal society and an absolutist monarchy. Taxation was a major political issue in France, as in America. However, in France the issue was tax inequality, not political representation. Taxes in France were oppressive and highly selective, bringing most of their weight to bear on the peasantry and the emerging middle class while leaving most of the nobility and the Church untouched. The economic system included the *corvée*, a system of forced labor that tormented the peasantry. Yet, even with such harsh measures, the economy was bankrupt. In some provinces, representative assemblies (known as *estates-general*) and courts (known as *parlements*) provided fairer taxation policies and more political rights than elsewhere. The French **Estates-General**, a national representative assembly of three estates (nobility, clergy, and commoners), was the closest institution to the British parliament—but it had not been convened since 1614.[17]

As a result, observed the French philosopher and liberal thinker the Marquis de Condorcet (1743–1794), the French Revolution was—and had to be—"more far-reaching" and "violent" than the American Revolution. The French Revolution sent shock waves throughout Europe. As it began to cut down everything in its path, wrote Condorcet, it "attacked at once the despotism of kings, the political inequality of many constitutions only partly free, the pride of the nobility, the domination, intolerance, and wealth of the priesthood, and the abuses of the feudal system."[18] Sadly, it eventually cut down Condorcet himself and a legion of liberal thinkers like him.

This is an essential difference between the English and American revolutions, on one hand, and the French Revolution, on the other. The French Revolution helped to establish the modern understanding of revolution—a tumultuous upheaval intended to sweep away most or all vestiges of the existing legal and political order. The French Revolution overthrew, violently and completely, the existing system of French government. By contrast, the Americans already had a republic, and a popular one at that. Before the American Revolution, eligible voters numbered between 50 and 60 percent of the adult white male population; by 1790 that percentage had swelled to 60 to 70 percent.[19]

In most colonies-turned-states, Americans moved quickly and peacefully to adopt state constitutional frameworks that reflected the majority sentiment of balanced and moderate government.[20] There were exceptions. Pennsylvania was the first state, soon followed by Georgia and the "independent republic of Vermont" (which did not become a state until 1791), to adopt a far more radically republican government than had previously existed.

Between 1776 and 1780, all of the states adopted republican governments framed by constitutions that provided for the direct popular election of legislative representatives. They were not ready to do the same for the new nation. Instead, Americans adopted the Articles of Confederation, which provided for a hybrid structure that was in some ways a confederation of republics and in other ways a union. The delegates to the Confederation Congress were named by the states, whether by vote of state governments or (as in Connecticut) by popular election. There was no president of the United States but, rather, a president of the United States in Congress Assembled, more like the chairman of the board of a large business corporation; he was elected by the delegates. There were only a few executive departments in the new Confederation government: War, Foreign Affairs, and Treasury. But the Articles did not sanction those departments; nor did it sanction the only judicial body of the new Confederation—the Court of Appeals in Cases of Capture.[21]

In 1787–1788, slightly more than a decade after the Declaration of Independence, conventions elected by the voters in eleven states had ratified a new constitution creating an innovative federal republic. That document, named the Constitution of the United States, guaranteed a republican form of government to each state and created a new general government with a republican form. Its Preamble proclaimed, "We the People of the United States . . . do ordain and establish this Constitution for the United States of America." The new nation now had a federal government based on the principle of popular sovereignty. The new Constitution provided for a House of Representatives elected directly by the people, a president elected indirectly by the people through their electors, and a Senate appointed by state legislatures that were in turn elected by the people (or, in Connecticut, elected directly by the people).[22]

The French did not achieve lasting consensus over their constitutional form of government until the 1870s. Only then, after the disastrous Franco-Prussian War and the fall of Emperor Napoleon III, were the French able to adopt a republic (their third) in which monarchists and monarchism were permanently vanquished.[23] Between 1789 and 1804, the French had gone through six national constitutions. Before 1871, the governments of France included a reign of Jacobin terror, the Napoleonic Empire, various Bonaparte and Bourbon monarchies, and two republics.

Yet, amid all those crosscurrents, the French held fast to the promise of their first national constitution-like document, the Declaration of the Rights of Man and the Citizen. Adopted in the opening months of the French Revolution of 1789, that document, like the American Declaration of Independence, declared the natural rights of individuals and dedicated government to the preservation of those rights. The French Declaration went further. It was the first to recognize the people as "a Nation." It then declared the Nation as the "basis of all sovereignty."

In their Declaration, the French revolutionaries created what looked like the first national democracy, different from the smaller democracies of ancient Greek city-states. But that would prove to be an illusion. One might assume that the Nation was really another way of referring to the People who composed it, but that point was never made entirely clear.

The French Declaration established a unitary central government as the embodiment of the Nation. To do that, it provided three essential points that it borrowed from the Swiss-born political philosopher, Jean-Jacques Rousseau (1712–1788). The Declaration provided that (1) the nation has a "general will," (2) "all citizens have a right to participate in shaping it," and (3) "legislation is the expression of the general will."

In one bold stroke, the French Declaration let the genie of democracy out of the bottle and reestablished the state as its sole champion. The people came to believe in the promises of the French Declaration. They demanded that every French government fulfill those promises, whether Jacobin, Bonapartist, or Bourbon. All of those governments swore to those promises as if they were a biblical covenant.

There was, however, a gap between rhetoric and practice. Few of those governments delivered on their promise. Most of the earliest governments were empires or monarchies in which the size of the eligible electorate was relatively small and legislative elections were indirect, through electors.

How then did these very two different republican revolutions contribute to the reinvention of republican government? What did the American and French revolutions change?

To answer this question systematically, the following sections of this chapter compare these two revolutions in terms of our criteria of good republican government. Those criteria (introduced in Chapter 10) are (1) free government based on the consent of the governed; (2) balanced government in representing society's most important interests; (3) limited government based on the rule of law; (4) just government based on equal justice under the law; and (5) enlightened government guided by the common good, not by the self-interest of the ruler.

HOW DID THE AMERICAN AND FRENCH REVOLUTIONS REDEFINE CONSENT AND REPRESENTATION?

Republican government requires consent of the governed and the freedoms that consent demands. Chapter 10 distinguishes three models of consent and representation: consent by direct participation in ancient republics, virtual consent in medieval republics, and consent by elective representation in modern republics.

The Americans were the first people to adopt the third model. They began that process in the colonies and then in the states. As noted earlier, eligible voters numbered between 50 and 60 percent of the adult white male population before the revolution; by 1790, the percentage had risen to 60–70 percent.

The French were the second people to embrace the model of elective representation. The French Declaration states in Article 6: "All citizens have a right to participate in [legislation] either in person, or through their representatives." The French revolutionary leaders proved more cautious. Their first national constitution (of 1791) provided for the *indirect* election of representatives to the national legislature through electors; this was similar to the American model of presidential election. There was also a steep property qualification for voting that disqualified most adult males. The 1791 Constitution extended the franchise to only 17 percent of the total population.[24]

Napoleon Bonaparte (1769–1821) did not think much of the citizen's right to participate, yet he found it expedient to hold a national plebiscite (an all-or-nothing national election) to legitimize many of his decisions. Of course, his brother rigged the outcomes to make sure Napoleon won by huge margins.[25] "The appeal to the people," Napoleon confided, "has the double advantage of legalizing the prolongation of my power and of purifying its origins." With even more bluntness, he remarked, "I did in no way usurp the Crown. I picked it up from the gutter. The people set it upon my head."[26]

Aristotle's model of republican government called for a balanced representation of three social classes: the monarch (the one), the aristocracy (the few), and the people (the many). Most republics followed Aristotle's model. One of the most important changes in the American state and federal constitutions was a shift in the basis of representation from social class to geographical constituency.

The U.S. Constitution of 1787 distinguished three geographical constituencies: local, state, and national. It then created a balanced system representing those constituencies. The House of Representatives represented the local constituencies; the Senate represented the state constituencies; and the president represented the nation as a whole. The new Constitution also enumerated national legislative powers in Article I, Section 8. Although the new Constitution strengthened the national government, it left many powers in the hands of the states. These features forced classes and groups to sort out their differences on a geographical basis. In this way, geography was used to dilute or diffuse these interests and the potential divisiveness they might cause. This innovation found greater force in the American system because of the difficulties of travel and communication in the early American republic. However, as the means of travel and communication improved during the nineteenth century, these innovations sharpened the sectional divisions that ultimately led in 1861 to civil war.[27] Generally, the American founders were more fearful of economic conflicts between classes than territorial differences among states.

The French revolutionaries did not attempt to balance geographical differences. Their first government actually retained the classic idea of balancing monarchic and democratic elements. Even after they sent Louis XVI to the guillotine, the French periodically restored the monarchy. More to the point, however, the French did not support the idea of balancing geographical constituencies. In fact, they preferred that there be no intermediate bodies between the people and one central government to represent them as a collective nation.

HOW DID THE AMERICAN AND FRENCH REVOLUTIONS PROVIDE FOR THE RULE OF LAW?

Republican government must be based on the rule of law. Rule of law is the idea that no government, and certainly no ruler, is above the law. All individuals, no matter how high or how low in the social or political order, are bound to obey the law and are entitled to claim its protections. All previous republican governments had a constitution, that is, a body of rules that prescribed the form and purposes of that government and its relationship to society. These rules were not always written down in a single document or ratified by the people. At times, they were the pronouncements of one man, as in the case of Solon (the founder of Athenian law), Cleisthenes (who established Athenian democracy), and Lycurgus (the law-giver of Sparta).

The Americans were masters of constitution-making. They had gained much constitutional experience over the previous 170 years. Sometime along the way, constitution writing had become an expectation and a habit in creating new governments. In 1787, they invented a two-step process of constitution-making in which a specially empowered convention prepares a written constitution for a second phase of public debate and approval, or ratification. They established a template for modern constitutions in the form of a single written document with a preamble of principles, a framework of government, and a bill or declaration of rights.

Over time, Americans elevated their constitutions to the status of both **supreme law** and **fundamental law**. As supreme law, constitutions became the highest form of law; as fundamental law, constitutions became the foundation for the rule of law. As both, constitutions became the standard for determining the validity of ordinary laws and the actions of the government. Equally important, the constitution-making process and the constitution itself both gave rise to a written public record that citizens could use as a standard to evaluate the actions of their governments.

Constitution-making proved more arduous in France. Nevertheless, the French Declaration of the Rights of Man and the Citizen is a work of political genius. It declares the rights of all people everywhere, and hence it has gained universal appeal over the centuries. But it is a declaration—a statement of principles—like the U.S. Declaration of Independence; it is not a law. To become legally enforceable it must be recognized as law by the French constitution. By contrast, the U.S. Bill of Rights was adopted as part of the U.S. Constitution. It is therefore a legally binding and enforceable instrument. As a result, it does not protect everyone in the world, but it does protect all people (not just citizens) who are subject to U.S. law.

As a result, the French Declaration of Rights has had wide appeal around the world not only to those who love freedom but also to those who love power. The latter group includes dictators who have rushed to embrace the language of the French Declaration knowing they will never have to enforce it. As Alexis de Tocqueville observed, "In the French Revolution there were two opposite tendencies which must not be confused; one favored freedom, the other despotism."[28]

HOW DID THE AMERICAN AND FRENCH REVOLUTIONS REDESIGN THE SYSTEM OF JUSTICE?

Republican governments must apply the rule of law not only as a limit on government powers but also as a standard of justice. The Americans developed a new federal system of justice comprising three features that had never before been combined.

First, state legislatures, like their colonial predecessors, and state constitutional conventions remained the engines of social justice. In the early years of the republic, for example, they liberalized inheritance laws, abolished slavery in the northern states, provided debtor relief, shifted criminal justice from retribution to deterrence and rehabilitation, and established prisons as institutions of deterrence and rehabilitation.

Second, state courts continued to use English common law (English court precedents and principles), relying initially on the valuable synthesis that they found in William Blackstone's

MORE ABOUT . . .

Sir William Blackstone and *Commentaries on the Laws of England*

Sir William Blackstone (1723–1780) was an English lawyer, legal scholar, and member of Parliament. His *Commentaries on the Laws of England* was the first comprehensive treatment of English common law. The book was not a critical analysis of the law; Blackstone's purpose was to provide educated individuals with an understanding of how the legal system worked. The influence of the *Commentaries* on American history was great. It not only served as the backbone of the colonial legal system, but it made the legal system accessible to the educated in the colonies. In particular, the clarification of common-law restrictions on freedom of speech and the press led to further resentment against English rule and helped provide a legal foundation for colonial grievances.

Sir William Blackstone. Abraham Lincoln studied Blackstone's Commentaries *extensively in preparing to become a lawyer.*

Commentaries. (See More About . . . Sir William Blackstone and *Commentaries on the Laws of England.*) State courts quickly began to Americanize the common law, however, heeding the teachings of such jurists as James Kent and Joseph Story, who wrote influential *Commentaries* on American law.[29]

Third, the U.S. Constitution of 1787 adapted the English innovation of an independent judiciary. The Constitution created an independent federal judiciary with a Supreme Court and other courts to be created by the Congress. The Supreme Court eventually became an important umpire of the controversies in the federal system. **Judicial review** enabled the courts to review and overturn state and federal laws on the basis of their constitutional validity. In 1803, *Marbury v. Madison* established the power of judicial review over federal legislation. This is particularly important because it gave the Supreme Court an important check on the power of the other branches of the national government.[30]

In contrast, the French revolutionaries preferred a more uniform and centralized system of justice. In 1804, one year after *Marbury*, Napoleon promulgated his most lasting legacy—the Code Napoléon. Like earlier codes, from Hammurabi's to Rome's, the **Napoleonic Code** brought together in a systematic fashion all the old and new laws that the new regime had decided to keep. "Thus, for all Frenchmen," the eminent French historian François Furet

(1927–1997) concluded, "there was but one Act governing the civil relations which bound them together, one single law for the new nation."[31]

At the same time, there was something new about the Napoleonic Code. No other enterprise of the French Revolution better captured the French Enlightenment belief in rational decision making. No other enterprise of the revolution better captured its commitment to "liberty, equality, and fraternity." As Furet explained, "The new social world comprised only equal individuals, subject to the same laws which fixed their rights and obligations, and which—in case of litigation—the judge had to apply rather than interpret."[32]

HOW DID THE AMERICAN AND FRENCH REVOLUTIONS ALTER THE BLUEPRINT OF MIXED GOVERNMENT?

Most republican governments had some form of mixed government. Many followed Aristotle's blueprint calling for government with a deliberative element, an administrative element, and a judicial element. Those elements usually took the form of separate institutions: a deliberative senate or cabinet, administrative magistrates, and a supreme assembly that could be reconstituted as a court. But each of those institutions had a combination of executive, legislative, and judicial powers. In other words, governments had separate institutions, but these institutions did not have neatly separated powers—two or more institutions simultaneously held similar powers. Earlier republics with separate institutions did not necessarily restrict members of one branch from serving simultaneously in another branch.

The U.S. Constitution of 1787 was the first national constitution to shift from separation of institutions to separation of powers. This model, borrowing from Montesquieu, began by separating the powers of government into three functions: lawmaking, law implementation, and law adjudication or judging. It then assigned each function to a separate institution and gave each institution an independent base in the Constitution. A bicameral Congress would make the laws, the president would head an executive branch responsible for implementing the law, and an independent judiciary would adjudicate and interpret the law. Visually, this principle might look like the 0s in Table 17.1.

The American model also separated the personnel of each branch. No one could serve simultaneously in two branches of government (or in two houses of the Congress). Unlike the British parliamentary model, the American chief executive was separately elected and was not a sitting member of Parliament.

The American model provided an elaborate system of checks in which each branch had something that the other two branches needed to complete their assigned function. The president, for example, had the power to veto legislative bills, but Congress had the power to override those vetoes and to approve the budget that the president needed to administer the law. Those checks might look like the Xs in Table 17.1.

The idea of balance was another key feature of the American model. The framers of the U.S. Constitution did not see balance as the result of checks, as tempting as the imagery of

Table 17.1 The American Model of Mixed Government

	Lawmaking	Law implementation	Law adjudication
Legislative branch	0	X	X
Executive branch	X	0	X
Judicial branch	X	X	0

balancing a checkbook might be. Instead, they saw balance in a different way—as balancing constituencies. Each institution would represent a different constituency (for example, local, state, or national), and they carefully balanced duration of office so that each institution served a different term of office (that is, two, four, six years, and life).

The French would have none of this. The institutional model of the French Revolution rejected the English and American models of a mixed and balanced constitution. It rejected Montesquieu in favor of Rousseau.[33] In his *Social Contract,* Rousseau distinguished "the will" that determines an act from "the force" that executes it. The former became the legislature and the latter the executive.

The **general will** resides in the body politic and describes the collective will or interests of the people as a whole, which subordinates individual self-interest. There were to be no real checks of one on the other and no balance whatsoever. Instead, there would be a clear chain of command from the national populace to its national legislature and executive. One of those two institutions would be supreme, depending on the constitution. The direction might well change now and again. In the French Revolution's first government, the legislature held ultimate power, not the king. In the Empire, Napoleon held ultimate power, not the legislature.

Whatever the chain of command, the French model held that nothing should obstruct, check, limit, or cloud the relationship between one unified people and one central government authority—even if the price was a dictatorial government. What John Adams found most revealing—and alarming—about this principle of unity was that even the legislature could not be divided in two. It must remain unicameral.

The U.S. Constitution also reinvented the principle of **federalism**, the idea that political power can be divided between a general government and its member governments. Until that time, *federation* and *confederation* were synonyms, both referring to a limited union among equal states, much like the American Articles of Confederation, the Swiss Confederacy, or the Dutch Republic. The framers of 1787 turned federalism into an element that could be joined in various ways with a national element to form a compound republic. In the way that water is a compound of hydrogen and oxygen (H_2O), the new American republic can be seen as a compound of federal and national elements (F_2N_2). "In strictness," wrote Publius in *The Federalist* No. 39, the result was "neither a national nor a federal Constitution, but a composition of both."[34]

The French would have none of this either. Again, there were to be no intermediate institutions between the general will of the people and the national legislature. That principle applied to territorial institutions as well. The French revolutionary government abolished all local and regional governments from the Old Regime.[35] In 1800, the new government created a hierarchical system of geographical *departments* to replace the old provinces. The central government appointed a *prefect* to head each department. The prefect was utterly and completely responsible to the central government for his salary, fringe benefits, promotions, and orders. If the prefect became too close to the community in which he served he was transferred to another department.

By 1802, the French government had established a special educational system for *prefects* and other civil servants. (See Politics in Action: The French *Prefect* System.) That system included special high schools known as *lycées* and culminated in

POLITICS IN ACTION
The French *Prefect* System

Created in 1790 by the Constituent Assembly, the French prefecture system was an attempt to break up the historical regions of France and create a uniform system of local administration under the tight control of the national government. Regions were divided into local units called *departments* (currently numbering one hundred in France proper). The national Ministry of Interior assigned a *prefect*, or representative, of the state to each department. The prefect represented the state and implemented national policy. The prefect system continues to this day in France.

membership in the Legion of Honor. It provided a good way to attract, indoctrinate, unify, and politically neutralize new civil servants, creating an impressive corps of loyal and efficient civil servants. They were drawn from all ranks: 22 percent from the sons of old nobility, 20 percent from the popular classes, and 58 percent from the middle class.[36]

This system, known as the prefectural system, has remained in place ever since. (See Map 17.1.) According to Tocqueville, centralization did not begin with the French Revolution. Centralization had been a part of French history for centuries. "The Revolution perfected it but did not create it."[37]

HOW DID THE AMERICAN AND FRENCH REVOLUTIONS REDEFINE THE COMMON GOOD?

Aristotle believed that republican government must aim at serving the common good, not the self-interests of the rulers or the interests of a particular stratum of society. For Aristotle, this was a creed. How did the English, American, and French revolutionaries conceive the common good and the role of government in its advancement? What were their similarities, and how did they differ?

Well into the nineteenth century, all three republics maintained a traditional republican conception of the common good. They had their differences, to be sure, within their countries as well as among them. Thomas Paine and John Adams, two great American revolutionaries, for example, disagreed vigorously over which form of government was best. They also

Map 17.1 The Current System of Departments in France

DEPARTMENTS OF FRANCE:

01 Ain
02 Aisne
03 Allier
04 Alpes-de-Haute-Provence
05 Hautes-Alpes
06 Alpes-Maritimes
07 Ardèche
08 Ardennes
09 Ariège
10 Aube
11 Aude
12 Aveyron
13 Bouches-du-Rhône
14 Calvados
15 Cantal
16 Charente
17 Charente-Maritime
18 Cher
19 Corrèze
2A Corse-du-Sud (Ajaccio)
2B Haute-Corse (Bastia)

21 Côte d'Or
22 Côtes d'Armor
23 Creuse
24 Dordogne
25 Doubs
26 Drôme
27 Eure
28 Eure-et-Loir
29 Finistère
30 Gard
31 Haute-Garonne
32 Gers
33 Gironde
34 Hérault
35 Ille-et-Vilaine
36 Indre
37 Indre-et-Loire
38 Isère
39 Jura
40 Landes
41 Loir-et-Cher

42 Loire
43 Haute-Loire
44 Loire-Atlantique
45 Loiret
46 Lot
47 Lot-et-Garonne
48 Lozère
49 Maine-et-Loire
50 Manche
51 Marne
52 Haute-Marne
53 Mayenne
54 Moselle
55 Meuse
56 Morbihan
57 Meurthe-et-Moselle
58 Nièvre
59 Nord
60 Oise
61 Orne
62 Pas-de-Calais

63 Puy-de-Dôme
64 Pyrénées-Atlantiques
65 Hautes-Pyrénées
66 Pyrénées Orientales
67 Bas-Rhin
68 Haut-Rhin
69 Rhône
70 Haute-Saône
71 Saône-et-Loire
72 Sarthe
73 Savoie
74 Haute-Savoie
75 Paris
76 Seine-Maritime
77 Seine-et-Marne
78 Yvelines
79 Deux-Sèvres
80 Somme
81 Tarn
82 Tarn-et-Garonne
83 Var

84 Vaucluse
85 Vendée
86 Vienne
87 Haute-Vienne
88 Vosges
89 Yonne
90 Territoire de Belfort
91 Essonne
92 Hauts-de-Seine
93 Seine-Saint-Denis
94 Val-de-Marne
95 Val-d'Oise

OVERSEAS DEPARTMENTS:
Guadeloupe
Martinique
French Guiana
Réunion

disagreed over the principles on which those forms should rest. Paine emphasized the republican principles of popular consent, majority rule, and liberty. Adams focused on the rule of law, protection of minority rights, and civic virtue. Paine wrote a vigorous defense of the French Revolution entitled *The Rights of Man*. Adams's series of newspaper essays, *The Discourses on Davila,* maintained that the revolution was doomed to failure because the revolutionaries were dismissing the lessons of history about how to build good republican governments.

These differences were important, but so too were the common bonds of republicanism. Even the most ardent American and French revolutionaries were more comfortable talking about the common good of the general community than they were speaking publicly about the interests of the individual in society. Individualism was viewed as a danger, if it was discussed at all. Few would have subscribed to the pluralistic view of today that the common good is based on the sum total of individual interests. Democracy was still widely regarded in negative terms. The American and French revolutionaries fought for popular republican government. Many still saw democracy as a slippery slope leading to majority tyranny.

At the same time, Americans in the era of the American Revolution and the early republic were beginning to recognize that the pursuit of individual interests might not be a threat to republican government. Instead, it appeared that a diversity of interests might well be the guardian of republican stability. Moreover, the idea that individuals could seek to fulfill their own destiny by their own abilities was beginning to take hold as one of the central tenets of the young republic. Within a few decades, these ideas were comfortably, if inconsistently, enshrined side by side with the equally treasured quest for the common good.[38]

The French *philosophes* saw the common good as something that could be discovered through reason and "the general will." Private interest was a cancer to be removed. In contrast, the English and Scottish moral philosophers looked at the importance of good works, philanthropy, and benevolent social policy as a pathway to the common good. The American founders were looking for constitutional avenues to the common good. Like the British, they saw private interests and factions as inherent in human nature but as capable of being enlightened. Despite these differences, most political thinkers of the day believed that the common good was definable and that defining the common good was the obligation of an educated citizenry.

Among the challenges of the next century, none for Americans would cut deeper into the meaning of democracy than the extension of slavery into the territories. Was it democracy's obligation to allow citizens to vote slavery in or out with a majority decision? That was Stephen Douglas's position. Or was modern democracy obligated to end slavery to create a more just and moral society? That was Abraham Lincoln's position. The debates between Lincoln and Douglas are among the great defining moments of democracy and government in the nineteenth century.

REVIEWING AND USING THE CHAPTER

1. Why are revolutions important? What insights do they provide about a government and its people?

2. On what principles was England's Glorious Revolution based? Provide examples to support your answer.

3. What were the most significant differences among the English, French, and American revolutions?

4. What is the rule of law, and what made it a key element of the American and French revolutions?

EXTENSION ACTIVITY

The English, American, and French revolutions, and the ideas on which they were based, continue to influence dozens of countries and millions of people. Select a constitution from a country other than Great Britain, France, and the United States. What effects, if any, did the English, American, and French revolutions have on the country's constitution?

WEB RESOURCES

The American Revolution Homepage
http://americanrevwar.homestead.com/files/INDEX2.HTM#contents

Created by Ron McGranahan, this award-winning Web site contains an encyclopedia of important events, individuals, and ideas associated with the American Revolution as well as timelines, images, and links to other resources.

The Glorious Revolution of 1688
http://www.thegloriousrevolution.org/default.asp

This Web site provides a series of excellent resources associated with in-depth study of the Glorious Revolution. Created by professors Donald E. Wilkes Jr. and Matthew

Kramer of the University of Georgia Law School, it includes a detailed chronology of events, an extensive bibliography, a list of important quotations, and links to other resources.

Liberty, Equality, and Fraternity: Exploring the French Revolution
http://chnm.gmu.edu/revolution/about.html

A collaboration of George Mason University and the City University of New York, this Web site offers a lively introduction to the French Revolution as well as an extraordinary archive of important documents, maps, and songs from the French Revolution.

NOTES

1 Abraham Lincoln, Gettysburg Address, available at www.loc.gov/exhibits/gadd/images/Gettysburg-2.jpg.

2 For an interesting revisionist view, see G. R. Elton, *Star Chamber Stories* (London: Methuen, 1958).

3 The standard biography of Cromwell, even after more than a century, remains Sir Charles Firth, *Oliver Cromwell and the Rule of the Puritans in England* (London and New York: Oxford University Press, 1953; originally 1900).

4 David Hackett Fischer, *The Great Wave: Price Revolutions and the Rhythm of History* (Oxford: Oxford University Press, 1996), 91–97.

5 Ibid., 98–99.

6 Ibid., 97.

7 R. R. Palmer, Joel Colton, and Lloyd Kramer, *A History of the Modern World*, 10th ed. (Boston: McGraw Hill, 2007), 172.

8 Ibid., 174–175.

9 S. E. Finer, *The History of Government* (Oxford: Oxford University Press, 1999), Vol. 3, 1343.

10 Ibid., Vol. 3, 1356.

11 For an excellent brief treatment that should be reprinted, see Judith N. Shklar, *Montesquieu* (Oxford and New York: Oxford University Press, 1987).

12 On this point, see Anne M. Cohler, *Montesquieu's Comparative Politics and the Spirit of American Constitutionalism* (Lawrence: University Press of Kansas, 1988); Paul M. Spurlin, *Montesquieu in America, 1760–1801* (Baton Rouge: Louisiana State University Press, 1940; reprinted New York: Octagon Books, 1969).

13 Baron de Montesquieu, *The Spirit of the Laws,* trans. Thomas Nugent (New York: Hafner Press, 1975), Vol. 1, 321. This is the translation familiar to Americans in the late eighteenth century.

14 E. J. Payne, ed., *Selected Works of Edmund Burke, Vol. II: Reflections on the Revolution in France* (Indianapolis, Ind.: Liberty Fund Press, 1999; reprint), 20.

15 John Phillip Reid, *Constitutional History of the American Revolution,* abridged ed. (Madison: University of Wisconsin Press, 1995), 47.

16 J. G. A. Pocock, "Virtue and Commerce in the Eighteenth Century," *Journal of Interdisciplinary History* (Summer 1972): 120.

17 William Doyle, *The French Revolution: A Very Short Introduction* (Oxford: Oxford University Press, 2001), 33.

18 Marie-Jean-Antoine-Nicholas de Caritat, Marquis de Condorcet, *Sketch for a Historical Picture of the Progress of the Human Mind,* quoted in Finer, *History of Government,* Vol. 3, 1518.

19 Alexander Keyssar, *The Right to Vote: The Contested History of Democracy in the United States* (New York: Basic Books, 2000), 7, 24.

20 See generally Donald S. Lutz, *Popular Consent and Popular Control: Whig Political Theory in the First State Constitutions* (Baton Rouge: Louisiana State University Press, 1980); Donald S. Lutz, *The Origins of American Constitutionalism* (Baton Rouge: Louisiana State University Press, 1988).

21 See generally Richard B. Bernstein with Kym S. Rice, *Are We to Be a Nation? The Making of the Constitution* (Cambridge, Mass.: Harvard University Press, 1987), Chaps. 2, 4.

22 Ibid., Chaps. 6–8.

23 This is the central theme of François Furet in his *Revolutionary France: 1770–1880,* trans. Antonia Nevill (Oxford: Blackwell, 1992).

24 Finer, *History of Government,* Vol. 3, 1535.

25 Doyle, *French Revolution,* 82.

26 Quoted in Finer, *History of Government,* Vol. 3, 1560.

27 Daniel Walker Howe, *What Hath God Wrought: The United States, 1815–1848* (New York: Oxford University Press, 2007).

28 Alexis de Tocqueville, *Democracy in America,* trans. George Lawrence, ed. J. P. Mayer (Garden City, N.Y.: Anchor Books, 1969), 97.

29 On Blackstone, see generally Daniel J. Boorstin, *The Mysterious Science of the Law: An Essay on Blackstone's Commentaries* (Cambridge, Mass.: Harvard University Press, 1941; new ed., Chicago: University of Chicago Press, 1996). On the Americanization of English common law, see

William E. Nelson, *Americanization of the Common Law: The Impact of Legal Change on Massachusetts Society, 1760–1830* (Cambridge, Mass.: Harvard University Press, 1975; new ed., Athens, Ga.: University of Georgia Press, 1994). On Joseph Story, see R. Kent Newmyer, *Supreme Court Justice Joseph Story: Statesman of the Old Republic* (Chapel Hill, N.C.: University of North Carolina Press, 1985); on James Kent, see John Theodore Horton, *James Kent: A Study in Conservatism, 1763–1847* (New York: Appleton-Century, 1939).

30 See generally William E. Nelson, Marbury v. Madison: *The Origins and Legacy of Judicial Review* (Lawrence: University Press of Kansas, 2000).

31 Furet, *Revolutionary France,* 230.

32 Ibid.

33 Norman Hampson, *Will and Circumstance: Montesquieu, Rousseau, and the French Revolution* (Norman: University of Oklahoma Press, 1983).

34 Alexander Hamilton, James Madison, and John Jay, *The Federalist Papers,* ed. Clinton Rossiter (New York: New American Library, 1961), 246. For counterpoised discussions, see Forrest McDonald, *States Rights and the Union: Imperium in Imperio, 1776–1876* (Lawrence: University Press of Kansas, 2000); Rogan Kersh, *Dreams of a More Perfect Union* (Ithaca, N.Y.: Cornell University Press, 2001). See also the review of these two books by R. B. Bernstein, in *Journal of American History* 89, no. 2 (September 2002): 617–618.

35 For two valuable treatments, see Louis Bergeron, *France under Napoleon,* trans. R. R. Palmer (Princeton, N.J.: Princeton University Press, 1981); Isser Woloch, *The New Regime: Transformations of the French Civic Order, 1789–1820s* (New York: W. W. Norton, 1994).

36 Roger Price, *A Concise History of France,* updated ed. (Cambridge, UK: Cambridge University Press, 2001), 132.

37 Tocqueville, *Democracy in America,* App. 1, 723, 97n.

38 The path-breaking study on this is Gordon S. Wood, *The Radicalism of the American Revolution* (New York: Alfred A. Knopf, 1991).

CHAPTER 18

HOW DID DEMOCRACY TRANSFORM REPUBLICAN GOVERNMENT AFTER 1800?

BIG IDEAS

- Representative democracy arose in the nineteenth century as a new form of republic, not as an alternative to republican government.

- Representative democracy is distinguished from other republics by its commitment to political equality for all.

- Democratization is the political process by which the world and the countries within it have become more democratic.

- Democratization coincides with other processes, including liberalization, constitutionalization, the rise of nationalism, the rise of ideology, and the technological revolution.

- Three models of representative democracy were developed in the twentieth century: liberal majoritarian, liberal coalition, and tutelary.

- A variety of factors account for the successful maintenance of representative democracies.

Purpose of This Chapter

Democracy is one of the great political themes of the nineteenth and twentieth centuries. In 1800, democracy was a suspect idea; no polity defined itself as democratic. By 2000, democracy was a widely cherished political ideal in the world. More than half of the world's countries were genuine democracies. Why did democracy gain this political traction? How did it evolve over the past two centuries? What are democracy's forms today? What factors account for a people's success in keeping it?

Terms to Know

balanced polity	liberal majoritarian democracy	political equality
democracy	majority factionalism	popular sovereignty
democratization	nonliberal tutelary democracy	representative democracy
liberal coalition democracy	the people	

WHY WAS DEMOCRACY REINVENTED AS A REPUBLIC?

Democracy—its ebb and flow—is one of the great political themes of the nineteenth and twentieth centuries. In 1800, democracy was roundly condemned as majority tyranny; no polity defined itself as democratic. By 2000, democracy was a widely cherished political ideal in the world. By that time, approximately 60 percent of the countries in the world were genuine democracies, and most of the rest claimed they were democratic.

A **democracy** is a polity based on rule by the people. Its first principle, **popular sovereignty**, recognizes the people as the legitimate source of government's authority. Within a polity, democracy is more than a form of government. It also is a political idea and a social condition.

Scholars use the term **democratization** to refer to the process by which the world and the individual countries within it became more democratic over the course of the nineteenth and twentieth centuries. This process began in the nineteenth century with the reformulation of democracy as a type of republic, not as an alternative to republican government. Without that first step, democracy would not have gained the traction it has. Here is how that happened.

THE IDEA OF REPRESENTATIVE DEMOCRACY

For centuries following the collapse of Athenian democracy, republicans and monarchists alike condemned democracy. In 1787, the American statesman James Madison offered the standard distinction. He defined pure democracy as "a society in which a small group of citizens assemble and administer the government in person."[1] He cited as the leading example Athens in the fifth century BCE. Madison then contrasted this form of government with a republic, which he defined as "a government in which the scheme of representation takes place."[2]

Madison considered democracy to be permanently flawed. He believed it was inherently turbulent and contentious, a threat to personal security and private property, short-lived, and violent in its demise.[3] A democracy, concluded Madison, was a breeding ground for **majority**

factionalism, that is, majorities guided not by reason but by passion and self-interest in ways that endangered individual and minority rights.[4]

The distinction between direct democracy and representative republics began to unravel in American politics by the 1820s. At the time, people began to openly use the term *democracy* to refer to a reform movement aimed at making government more, not less, representative of the people. The movement's leaders proposed doing this by eliminating the property requirement that

was a condition for voting and holding office. In this way, they sought to increase the number of elected offices and expand suffrage to all adult white males.

Adopted in state after state, these reforms helped to elect Andrew Jackson and other Democratic Party candidates. Not only did more people become eligible to vote, but the new electorate, mobilized by an exciting campaign and a well-organized political party, turned out in record numbers totaling 57 percent of eligible voters—twice as high as in previous elections.

In the 1850s, liberal thinkers such as English philosopher John Stuart Mill developed a theory of representative democracy after it had become a political reality in the United States. According to this theory, widely accepted today, **representative democracy** is a type of republican government that is representative of *all* the people, and is based on the principle of universal suffrage. (See More About . . . Universal Suffrage.) A synonym of *representative democracy* is *democratic republic*.

In the mid-nineteenth century, the theory of representative democracy was a compromise among three political views. It satisfied many radicals, who sought more power for the people. It appealed to liberals and other moderates, who wanted to tame democracy's excesses by refining public opinion. And it became more palatable to conservatives, who saw the opportunity to preserve monarchies by writing constitutions that provided for increased political rights and a representative assembly with some powers. As Charles Maier, a historian of nineteenth-century Europe, put it, democracy had to be made safe for the world in the nineteenth century. But by the next century, Woodrow Wilson proclaimed that the world must be made safe for democracy as a justification for America's entry into World War I.[5]

Representative democracy made it possible to gradually expand the political meaning of *the people* to include *all* the people. As a political term, *the people* appears in phrases such as "We the People"—the first three words of the U.S. Constitution. In this use, **the people** refers to the political population of a polity and especially to those who are fully empowered citizens with the right to vote and represent others. (See Political Ideas in Action: Inspired by Revolution.)

POLITICAL IDEAS IN ACTION

Inspired by Revolution

At the beginning of the 1800s, as in centuries past, much of the political world consisted of empires governed by monarchs who ruled absolutely. The American and French Revolutions awakened national and republican sentiments around the world. In Europe and the Americas, those awakenings were immediate. Quite a few Latin Americans and Europeans had fought in the American and French Revolutions. Many more were taking sides as Napoleon marched across Europe. In 1799, the Latin American revolutionary leader Francisco de Miranda observed, "We have before our eyes two great examples, the American and the French Revolutions. Let us prudently imitate the first and cautiously shun the second."[1]

---

1. Quoted in Marshall G. Eakin, *The History of Latin America: Collision of Cultures* (New York: Palgrave Macmillan, 2007), 170.

In republics before 1800, as Chapters 11–17 demonstrate, citizenship was a small and exclusive political class. In most republics, the number of citizens with full political rights rarely exceeded 10–20 percent of a republic's total population. This was also true in ancient democracies. In Athens, for example, fully empowered citizens numbered roughly 30,000 people in a city-state of 300,000. Excluded were women, foreigners (those not born of an Athenian citizen-mother), and common laborers. The same exclusions were commonplace in other republics, including the early American republic.

THE IDEA OF POLITICAL EQUALITY

Beginning in the early nineteenth century, the idea of political equality began to take on an increasingly universalistic and egalitarian meaning. As a result, **political equality** came to mean that all citizens are politically equal. This was a revolutionary formulation of the republican principle of consent of the governed. It meant not only that most people were entitled to certain inalienable rights (for example, life, liberty, and property) but that everyone was entitled to citizenship and that every citizen held the right to vote and to participate in his government.

Practically speaking, this reformulation of political equality became the essential difference between the modern democratic republic and all other previous republics. To be clear, this does not mean that equality became more important than freedom or any of the other long-established criteria of republican government. (See More About . . . Republican Criteria Reviewed.) Those criteria remained in effect. Political equality expanded the pool of political participants.

The liberal French philosopher Alexis de Tocqueville (1805–1859) was the first political thinker to draw the conclusion that equality is what distinguishes modern democratic republics from earlier types of republics. He believed every society would be gripped by the egalitarian imperative—members of a group without the right to vote would see others with it, wonder why they were different, and demand it for themselves. Eventually, this imperative would go beyond the right to vote and place demands on all public policies.

Like other liberals of his day, de Tocqueville maintained that democracy could be joined with republicanism by creating democratic republics, or representative democracies, that used the republican principle of representation to balance liberty and the democratic impulse of equality. De Tocqueville saw the democratic revolution as an extension of (not a departure from) the republican revolutions of the late seventeenth and eighteenth centuries in England, America, and France. In his comparative observations of Europe and America in the 1830s, de Tocqueville found more evidence of democracy as a social revolu-

MORE ABOUT . . .
Republican Criteria Reviewed

1. Representative government that balances and moderates the dominant interests in society

2. Free government based on the consent of the governed

3. Limited government based on the rule of law

4. Just government based on the principle of equal justice

5. A citizenry and leaders guided by the common good

As the availability of affordable mail spread in the early nineteenth century, some governments worked to blunt its effectiveness as a tool for civic awareness. In the decades before the American Civil War many southern states banned the mailing of abolitionist literature. This image portrays the 1835 nighttime raid on the Charleston, South Carolina, post office by a mob. Abolitionist literature such as The Liberator, *the* Boston Atlas, *and* Commercial Gazette *have been removed and strewn about.*

MORE ABOUT . . .
Technology and Politics

Modern technological advances have revolutionized not only the way that people live and work but also the way they practice politics. In the nineteenth century, the steam-powered engine, the railroad, and the telegraph helped transform many countries from rural agricultural societies to urban industrial societies. Millions of people migrated to the new industrial cities in search of jobs and a better life. Improvements in transportation, communications, and industrial production transformed all human activities, from agriculture to medicine and warfare.

By the end of the nineteenth century, people, material, and information traveled with greater speed, volume, and distance than ever before in world history. Between 1800 and 1900, hundreds of millions of people migrated across national borders and oceans and from the countryside to cities and new frontier regions within countries.

Faster movement of larger numbers of people, material, and information transformed commerce, politics, and war. The rise of national postal services in the nineteenth century played an important role in this transformation process. By mid-century, national postal services were delivering everyone's post or mail, regardless of the sender's class or creed, faster, cheaper, and at the same rate from anywhere to everywhere.

The result was a boon for national unification movements in countries as diverse as the United States, Germany, and British India. The postal services, along with the railroad, the telegraph, the telephone, and the rise of newspapers increased civic awareness and the equality of conditions, both of which Alexis de Tocqueville found so important to the spread of democracy as a social process.

tion than as a revolution in government. Long before the industrial revolution, changes in law and technology were creating a growing equality of conditions and rights. De Tocqueville cited firearms as the great equalizer on the battlefield; any peasant with a gun could bring down the highest nobleman on a horse. He also saw the equalizing influence of the printing press and the mail, which afforded rich and poor alike the opportunity to read or learn how to read. In addition, he pointed to legal changes that made it possible for peasants to own their own land and for a new middle class to trade, create financial capital from their profits, and invest those profits in expanding businesses.[6] (See More About . . . Technology and Politics.)

De Tocqueville believed that democracy was dangerous in excess. He worried that the egalitarian impulse would create a "me too" attitude that would fuel individualism and materialism. People would then lose interest in the common good and simply seek personal gain, and democratic leaders might become demagogues who wooed the people with false promises of national prosperity.

De Tocqueville believed that these dangers could be checked by an educated and engaged citizenry. He was convinced that the civic spirit of the people was the best protection against the democratic dangers of individualism. The people, he insisted, must learn how to cooperate with others to achieve common interests. The people must develop a habit of cooperation in the political arena and in their communities.

Modern scholars, many of whom agree with de Tocqueville's position, have identified the following criteria of democracy.

- Citizens must have the right to vote in free, fair, and competitive elections.
- Citizens must have the freedom to express their political views and to form parties and other political associations—even if they oppose the government in power.
- Citizens must have free access to all points of view.
- The government must be responsive to the common good of the people.[7]

The first three conditions relate to a democratic citizenry; the fourth focuses on democratic government. Both are essential to democracy.

DIMENSIONS OF THE DEMOCRATIC REPUBLIC

Democratic republics are complete polities. In comparing democratic republics with one another and with other forms of government, it is helpful to draw on Aristotle's theory of constitutions and its alternatives.

According to Aristotle, every polity has a broad constitution (or makeup) consisting of three dimensions: (1) a moral dimension, which includes the polity's ethical standards and political ideals; (2) a social and economic dimension, which includes the various classes and communities in society; and (3) a legal dimension, which includes all a society's laws and governmental institutions. Recall that Aristotle advocated a **balanced polity**, in which all three constitutional dimensions were kept in balance. In particular, he expected the polity's legal and governmental constitution to represent the major interests in society and to uphold society's core cultural norms.

The modern democratic republic is no exception. The moral dimension of the modern democratic republic centers on the idea that all people are equally endowed with the political right to govern themselves. This idea rests, in turn, on the belief that the people can be trusted to do so. The socioeconomic dimension relies on an increasing equality of social conditions and the increasing capacity of more and more people to govern themselves. The legal dimension embodies the principles, form, and purposes of democratic government. Nowhere is the legal constitution laid out more succinctly than in Abraham Lincoln's Gettysburg Address (1863). In that address, Lincoln expressed the hope that "government of the people, by the people, for the people, shall not perish from the earth."[8]

- "Government of the people" refers to the *principle* of popular sovereignty, by which government derives its authority from the consent of the governed, and the principle of political equality, which includes all the people.

- "Government by the people" refers to the *form* of a democratic government in which an expanded citizenry has the power to elect its representatives and hold them accountable.

- "Government for the people" refers to the *purposes* of democratic government. Lincoln's political philosophy centered on two legitimate purposes: (1) promoting the common

THE REPUBLICAN PARTY GOING TO THE RIGHT HOUSE.

Abraham Lincoln's support for abolition and the right to vote for African Americans and women led to vocal opposition. In this political cartoon (circa 1860), Lincoln's supporters are portrayed as radicals and eccentrics. For example, a free African American declares that white people have no rights that he is bound to respect. Behind him a suffragette demands, "I want woman's rights enforced, and man reduced in subjection to her authority."

welfare by meeting those needs that the people could not (his examples included roads, schools, and assistance to the helpless) and (2) righting moral wrongs, the chief one of these wrongs being the abomination of slavery.[9]

When Lincoln referred to "the people," it is clear from his other speeches and writings that he meant all the people. His sympathies for the abolition of slavery, black suffrage, and women's rights were well known and occasionally lampooned by his political opponents.

WHAT ARE THE CHARACTERISTICS OF DEMOCRATIZATION?

Democratization is the process by which the world and individual countries became more democratic over the course of the nineteenth and twentieth centuries. Implied in this definition is the idea that democratic polities are not created in a single day. They evolve, and that evolution is not necessarily linear—it can include setbacks as well as advances. Also implied is the comparative idea that democracies have evolved differently in different world regions over time.

A good example of this is the adoption of universal suffrage. In 1765, English jurist William Blackstone spoke for most traditional republicans, when he wrote that suffrage should be limited to people with "a will of their own."[10] On this basis, a lengthy list of individuals were often excluded:

- Women because they were dependent on their fathers, husbands, or some other male guardian
- People without real property (that is, land) in the belief that they could be influenced by their landlords
- Common laborers because they were believed to be subject to the policies of their employers
- Foreigners, people of color, and certain religious groups because they may have foreign allegiances or simply because they were considered inferior
- Slaves, serfs, and others held in bondage by their masters

The worldwide movement toward universal suffrage began in 1755 when Corsica briefly allowed suffrage for both men and women. In the 1820s, many American states adopted universal white male suffrage. The United States and Europe began adopting universal male suffrage in 1870 (see Table 18.1). In 1870, the United States adopted a federal constitutional

Table 18.1 Adoption of Universal Male Suffrage in Europe

Country	Year
France	1870
Germany	1870
Switzerland	1874
Italy	1882
Belgium	1894
Netherlands	1894
Norway	1898
Spain	1900
Austria	1907
Sweden	1909
United Kingdom	1918

Source: S. E. Finer, *The History of Government* (Oxford: Oxford University Press, 1999), Vol. 3, 1638.

amendment prohibiting the denial of voting rights on the basis of race. That amendment, however, proved difficult to enforce in most southern states until the federal government began to enforce it in 1965 with passage of the Voting Rights Act. Women's suffrage trailed further behind. New Zealand was the only nation-state to adopt women's suffrage before 1900. There are still countries in the Arab world that deny women's suffrage (for example, Saudi Arabia) or limit it in some way (for example, Lebanon).

Democratization is preeminently a political process. Hence, it also is a human process subject to the strengths and frailties of the people and their political leaders. Over the past two centuries, democratization has generated a host of political issues from the abolition of slavery to the adoption of universal suffrage. On some occasions, those issues have been resolved peacefully by coalition-building, compromise, and nonviolent resistance. On other occasions, they have sparked international wars, civil wars, and revolutions on a scale never before seen in world history.

Some democratization issues tend to cluster together in a particular political generation and world region, such as the abolition of feudalism in Napoleonic Europe or decolonization in post–World War II Asia. This clustering can create what political scientist Samuel P. Huntington calls a "snowball effect."[11] But these effects are infrequent and not powerful enough to sustain a linear one-way democratic path in which the world steadily becomes increasingly democratic. Although there was some hope of democracy sweeping the world in the euphoria of the 1990s following the collapse of the Soviet Union, that hope became guarded in the first decade of the twenty-first century when democracy saw setbacks in Eastern Europe and broke down in Russia, Venezuela, Nigeria, and more than a dozen other countries.[12]

The political interests for or against democracy have been fairly evenly balanced over the past two centuries. As a result, there has been an ebb and flow of democratization. Huntington has charted three waves and counterwaves of democratization in the nineteenth and twentieth centuries. But Huntington recognized that history is messy. The democratic transitions and reversals in each wave are irregular and rarely return to the status quo ante (the way things were before). Each wave has crosscurrents and exceptions that make for murky outcomes (see Table 18.2).

Democratization did not develop in isolation. The spread of democracy in the nineteenth and twentieth centuries coincided with other social and political processes. Among the most important are liberalization, constitutionalization, the spread of nationalism, and the technological revolution. *Coincided* is a carefully chosen word here. Care must be taken not to confuse these processes or their characteristics. Liberalization and democratization coincided in the West, for example, but their historical relationship elsewhere is still unclear. Hence, it is more accurate to speak of liberal democracy as a type of democracy rather than an inherent trait of all democracies. To cite another example, constitutionalization and democratization may seem natural allies; it is difficult to imagine a legitimate form of democracy that is not a constitutional democracy. Yet, in the nineteenth century, one European monarchy after another converted from absolutism to a constitutional monarchy as a way of preserving the monarchy by appeasing its democratic opponents. (See Politics in Action: Democracy's Potential Allies.)

Table 18.2 Waves of Democracy in the Nineteenth and Twentieth Centuries

Waves	Examples
First wave (1828–1926)	Democratization of the U.S. polity beginning in the 1820s and the election of Andrew Jackson in 1828
	Establishment of the French Republic in 1870, followed by the constitutionalization of European monarchies
	Short-lived democracy in Argentina and a few other Latin American countries
	Between World Wars I and II in Europe, where nearly ten countries tried and failed to sustain constitutional democratic governments
First reverse wave (1922–1942)	Brought on by the rise of communist, fascist, and militarist regimes in Europe, Japan, and Latin America
Second wave (1943–1962)	Allied occupation and democratization of West Germany, Italy, and Japan
	First postwar wave of national independence for British colonies, including India, Ghana, and Malaysia
Second reverse wave (1958–1975)	One-party dictatorships and military takeovers in Latin America and many newly independent countries in Africa and Asia
Third wave (1974–1999)	Restoration of democracy in many Latin American countries
	Breakup of the Soviet Union and its satellite communist regimes in Eastern Europe
	Move from one-party dictatorship to democracy in various sub-Saharan African countries
Third reverse wave (1999–)	Breakdown of democracy in Pakistan, Russia, Nigeria, and Venezuela
	Erosion of democracy in central and Eastern Europe

Sources: Samuel P. Huntington, *The Third Wave: Democratization in the Late Twentieth Century* (Norman: University of Oklahoma Press, 1991), 16–26; for the third reverse wave, Larry Diamond, *The Spirit of Democracy* (New York: Times Books, 2008), Chap. 3.

Democratization is a global process. It has circumnavigated the globe leaving no country or culture untouched. This was not accidental. Democracy became an international ideal that nations have fought to defend in World War I, World War II, and the cold war. Today, democracy is widely promoted by nongovernmental organizations such as Freedom House and through democracy assistance programs sponsored by various Western nations.

Democratization has drawn on new forms of political organization to mobilize people and public opinion on a national and international scale. These include the mass political party to mobilize voters; trade unions to organize labor; and international citizen movements to advance a particular cause, the first of which was created in 1787 to abolish the slave trade in the British Empire. (See Politics in Action: The First Citizens' Movement.) Democratization

POLITICS IN ACTION
Democracy's Potential Allies

Liberalization as a political process and movement centers on the passage of laws that recognize and protect the rights of the individual in society. Identification of specific rights and provisions for their protection have varied widely in world history. Liberal measures have included abolishing feudalism by confiscating church lands, abolishing privileges reserved to a few noblemen, and freeing the serfs; abolishing slavery and the slave trade; guaranteeing the economic rights to own property, engage in free trade, and make contracts; and recognizing and enforcing human rights in international law.

Constitutionalization is a related process by which individual rights are guaranteed by a constitutional system (often including a written constitution) that enumerates protected rights, provides for their enforcement, restricts arbitrary and absolute government rule, establishes a representative legislature, and provides for its popular election. In European history, constitutionalization helped bring about the transition from absolute monarchies to constitutional monarchies and then to parliamentary monarchies and republics.

Nationalism is the belief that "a people" bound by a common culture, language, and history have the right to independent and sovereign statehood. How this has occurred has varied, depending on the circumstances of the people seeking statehood. Consider three nineteenth-century examples. For the Germans and Italians, nationalism meant national unification. In the Americas, nationalism centered on national independence from colonial rule. And in Eastern Europe, nationalism was the century-long struggle for national separation and self-determination from multinational empires.

The technological revolution is the invention, application, and spread of technological advances in transportation, communications, finance, and economic production. In communications, for example, new technologies included the telegraph, telephone, television, cell phones, and the Internet. As these technologies became cheaper to produce, sell, and purchase, they became more readily available and more widely used by more and more people. This process increased the equality of social conditions in much the same way that firearms equalized battle conditions.

is also responsible for the development of ideology as a set of ideas designed for broad popular appeal *and* action. Most words ending in *-ism* (such as liberalism, conservatism, socialism, and feminism) trace their origins back to the early stages of democratization in the 1830s, 1840s, and 1850s. None of these would have been possible without the technological revolution in transportation and communication that began in the early nineteenth century. "Organize, organize, organize" became the new democratic mantra.

Democratization is ongoing and incomplete. New democracies face the challenge of consolidating their democratic advances. Mature democracies in the United States, Canada,

The Khmer Rouge, the communist regime that took control of Cambodia in 1975, rejected modern technology as part of the process of stripping away individuals' rights. In this 1978 photograph, workers are processing crops by hand. Khmer Rouge leaders attempted to create a completely agrarian society in which modern technology was banned. The return to the land was intended to purify the people as a whole, erase all urban and foreign influences, brutally control those who objected, and create a basis for a new communist society.

Western Europe, Australia, and New Zealand face the challenge of reinvigorating democracy at a time of declining public trust in government and other political institutions. Both are likely to remain twenty-first century challenges.

WHAT FORMS DOES REPRESENTATIVE DEMOCRACY TAKE?

The idea of representative democracy was conceived in the middle of the nineteenth century, but its widespread adoption is a twentieth-century phenomenon—and especially a post–World War II phenomenon. In the intervening period (roughly 1850–1950), the purpose of representative democracy has evolved.

In the nineteenth century, representative democracy was intended to refine public opinion and enlarge the electorate. The role of the elected representative was to stand *for* the people. In the twentieth century, governments grew dramatically in their scope and purpose. Along the way, they have centralized their powers and become more bureaucratic in their

POLITICS IN ACTION

The First Citizens' Movement

In 1800, according to one estimate, more than three-quarters of all people alive (and not in prison) were in some form of bondage. Slavery was still practiced throughout much of the world. In addition, millions of human beings were bound as serfs around the world. Forced labor was also commonplace, in some places as a form of taxation. Britain ruled the high seas partly due to the practice of naval impressment. During the Napoleonic Wars the British navy included 140,000 men, of whom an estimated one-third to half had been "pressed" (kidnapped) into service.[1]

The abolitionist movement began in London on May 22, 1787 (a date that happened to coincide with the assembling of delegates thousands of miles away at the Federal Convention in Philadelphia). In London on that date, a dozen men gathered in a print shop to discuss the abolition of slavery in the British Empire.

The British abolitionists who met in 1787 organized a citizens' movement that became a blueprint for future citizen-based movements around the world. They crisscrossed the country in all seasons and conditions. They spoke at local gatherings, debated opponents (debating societies were very popular in those days), distributed pamphlets, organized local abolitionist groups, led demonstrations, spoke with seamen on slave ships, and gathered petition signatures to present to Parliament. Their movement used the first successful consumer boycott (of sugar); thousands of British children grew up without ever having tasted sugar as their way of protesting slavery. (Life for slaves on sugar plantations was particularly dangerous.) After twenty years of citizens' dedicated politicking, a bill emerged from Parliament to abolish the slave trade in 1807. But it was not until 1833 that a bill passed Parliament that abolished slavery altogether, and that did not take full effect until 1838—over fifty years after the movement was founded.

---

1. Adam Hochschild, *Bury the Chains: Prophets and Rebels in the Fight to Free an Empire's Slaves* (Boston: Houghton Mifflin, 2005), 2, 222–223.

organization. In this environment, the role of elected representatives has expanded. Today, they are expected both to stand *for* the people and to stand *between* the people and government bureaucracy. By filtering out imprudent and impulsive public opinion, representatives provide a check on the excesses of majority rule. By exercising legislative oversight, they monitor the government bureaucracy and hold it accountable to public scrutiny. Today, "representative government must not only represent, it must also govern."[13]

Three forms of representative democracy evolved over the course of the twentieth century to meet these challenges. All are constitutional democracies. The first type is liberal majoritarian democracy; this favors majority rule but not at the expense of minority rights. The second type is liberal coalition (sometimes called consensus or consociational) democracy; this brings minorities into the governing process. The third type of democracy is nonliberal tutelary; this guides the people toward democracy without denying basic human rights.

The Dutch-born political scientist Arend Lijphart has carefully compared the first two models: liberal majoritarian and liberal coalition. Lijphart first distinguished majoritarian and coalition democracies in his path-breaking study of democracy in 1984.[14] Asian specialist Lucian Pye developed the model for the third type of democracy, tutelary or guided democracy. Pye makes a convincing case that tutelary democracy is neither illiberal democracy nor "soft" authoritarianism; rather, Pye argues, it is a particularly appropriate description of various Asian democracies.[15]

These three types of democracies are ideal types. In other words, they are theoretical models that are useful in locating, classifying, and comparing real-world polities; however, political systems rarely exemplify all of the attributes of one type. The United Kingdom is the oldest majoritarian democracy, yet it is under pressure today to adopt coalition features. Belgium is a good example of coalition democracy. The United States is partly majoritarian (primarily in its political party–electoral systems) and partly coalition-based (primarily in its governmental power-sharing arrangements of federalism, separation of powers, and checks and balances). Indonesia is primarily tutelary, while Japan has moved from tutelary to a middle position among tutelary, liberal majoritarian, and liberal coalition types. Thus, polities can be a mix of types, and they can change from one type to another.

Each type of representative democracy is a modern answer to the classic question: How can republican government constitutionally balance the interests of the majority ("the many") and the minority ("the few")? How can republican government moderate the potential democratic excesses of majoritarianism and individualism? In this respect, these types are not a break with the republican past—they are modern variations of it and of the ideas of mixed republican government and a balanced constitution. In this way, representative democracies become democratic republics.

These three types do not exist in a vacuum. Each works best with the right supports—a particular type of political culture, civil society, political party system, electoral system, and system of government. And each can fail without these supports. Chapters 6 and 7 of this book explore those cultural and institutional supports.

LIBERAL MAJORITARIAN DEMOCRACY

Liberal majoritarian democracy is based on the principle of majority rule and minority rights. In this model, the purpose of democracy is to empower majorities and protect minorities. The birthplace of this model is Westminster—the historic seat of British parliament. (See More About . . . The Palace of Westminster.) Hence, this model is also known as the Westminster model.

Historically, this type of democracy originated in a relatively homogenous British society. The British people shared a strong national identity that included a strong commitment to liberal values. They took pride in a common heritage of laws and rights united by Parliament and the Crown. Out of this shared culture emerged three strong political traditions: radical

MORE ABOUT . . .

The Palace of Westminster

The Palace of Westminster sits on the banks of the River Thames in London. King Edward the Confessor built his palace there in the eleventh century. Nearby he also constructed Westminster Abbey, where all England's kings and queens have been crowned. The palace served as the principal London residence of English monarchs until 1512, when Henry VIII moved his family out following a fire.

Known today as the Houses of Parliament, the Palace of Westminster contains more than 1,100 rooms and 3 miles of corridors. The current building was constructed during the nineteenth century after a fire destroyed almost all of the existing structure. The opulently decorated Chamber of the House of Lords occupies the southern portion of the palace. Here many important ceremonies take place, including the State Opening of Parliament, attended by the English monarch.

The much less lavishly appointed Chamber of the House of Commons is situated at the palace's northern

Houses of Parliament, London.

end. Members of the government party occupy benches to the right of the speaker's chair; the opposition party members sit to the left, facing the government members. Within these close quarters, the members of Parliament vigorously debate legislation in the United Kingdom.

republicans, who supported a democracy that represented and responded to working-class interests (first, the Chartists; later, the Labour Party); Whigs (later, Liberals), who supported a republic united by the Crown; and Tories (later, Conservatives) who supported the monarchy.

Over the centuries, each of those three traditions has formed a strong political party—much stronger than political parties in the United States, for example. Usually, two of these parties have prevailed at any time, and the third has been a minor party. In the nineteenth and early twentieth centuries, the two major parties were the Liberal Party and Conservative Party. Today, they are the Conservative Party and Labour Party (a party that has moderated its radical past). As long as British culture and society remained relatively homogenous, most people could channel their interests and values into one of the two major parties.

The belief in majority rule is an essential ingredient of the liberal majoritarian, or Westminster, model. Majority rule is supported by the governmental system (the parliamentary model) and electoral system (winner-take-all, or first-past-the-post). The Parliament is the legislative body. It is either unicameral or bicameral with a weak upper house. Members of the lower house are popularly elected (sometimes the upper house is also). Unlike the American presidential system, the executive or head of government (called a prime minister) is not separately elected by the people. Constitutionally, there is unification, not separation, of the executive and legislative bodies. The prime minister (PM) is the leader of the majority party, elected as a member of Parliament (MP) along with other MPs, and selected by Parliament to form a government. To do this, the PM forms a cabinet from members of his or her party. In this way, there is little possibility of a divided government in which one party controls one branch and another party controls another. The majority party is given a full chance to govern.

Historically, English courts had no power of judicial review (the power to review and declare an act of Parliament void). Judicial review would have violated the principle of parliamentary supremacy. As a check on the abuse of power, Parliament has the power to issue a vote of no confidence in its government, in which case the government must resign. Alternatively, the PM or the cabinet can dissolve the Parliament. And, of course, voters can switch their allegiance to another party.

The winner-take-all electoral system is designed to achieve a strong majority government without abridging minority rights. In the British system, the country is divided into parliamentary districts, usually called constituencies. Each constituency is allocated one parliamentary seat, and one candidate from each party competes for that seat. Usually, the candidate with the most votes wins, even if it is only a plurality (that is, the most but not a majority) of the votes cast. Some countries with this system require a majority for a candidate to win, so that if a candidate wins only a plurality of the votes a run-off election is held to determine the winner.

Strong party discipline holds this system together. Voters cannot split their vote because they have only one vote. Candidates campaign with their party; independents are not tolerated. In Parliament, members vote with their party; if they do not, they can be expelled from their party. Members of the cabinet show "collective responsibility"; that is, in public the ministers stick together and support their party and PM.

LIBERAL COALITION DEMOCRACY

Liberal coalition democracy is based on the idea that minorities form coalitions to achieve majority status. The principle is that "all who are affected by a decision should have the chance to participate in making that decision either directly or indirectly through chosen representatives."[16] The reality is that many countries with a coalition-based democracy have heterogeneous societies in which there is no clear majority.

There are various ways of sharing power. The American model relies on federalism, separation of powers, and checks and balances. Together, these principles force political parties to form geographical and ideological coalitions of minority interests if they plan to win elections and pass legislation. However, the U.S. model also has two majoritarian features: two major parties and winner-take-all elections. In this system, the states maintain a historic role in the system by having their own governments and a seat at the federal table. In addition, each party can win control of three governing institutions (the chief executive and two strong legislative houses).

The continental European model of liberal coalition democracy relies on a multiparty system and proportional representation. In this system, a variety of parties compete for multiple seats in each legislative district. The more votes a party wins in a district, the more seats its candidates win in that district. The number of seats a party receives is in proportion to the percentage of votes it wins, hence the term *proportional representation.* For example, in a district with nine seats, a party winning one-third of the votes in the election should receive three seats. While all but the weakest parties win something, minority parties must learn how to form majority coalitions in the legislature to govern effectively. Belgium, the Netherlands, and Switzerland are examples of this coalition or consensus model.

NONLIBERAL TUTELARY DEMOCRACY

Nonliberal tutelary democracy (from the Latin *tutelarius,* meaning "guardianship") is commonly known as *guided democracy.* It is most prevalent in Asian cultures that place a high value on harmony, hierarchy, and group solidarity. Self-assertiveness, open competitiveness, public disagreement, and individualism are viewed as negative social qualities.[17] As a result, Western liberalism is viewed with suspicion but not categorically rejected.

In this type of democracy, there is one dominant political party. Examples include the original Chinese Nationalist Party led by Sun Yat-sen, the Indian Congress Party, and the Japanese Liberal Democratic Party. Outside Asia, the primary example today is South Africa's African National Congress (ANC) Party. The role of the dominant party is to bring people together and guide them on a path toward economic and democratic development. Often, economic development precedes democratic development.

This type of democracy must meet several criteria; otherwise, it is simply a dressed-up illiberal democracy or "soft" authoritarian system. The government must allow minor parties to operate and must protect their freedoms of speech and association. Regular elections must be held, they must be free and fair, and minor parties must be allowed to compete. Minor-party candidates must win no less than 30 percent of votes cast. Also, these minor parties must be allowed to join together to form an opposition coalition in the legislature, and members of the legislative opposition must be free to criticize government policy. As with other republican forms of government, guided democracy must benefit the country as a whole, not a corrupt few in power. Government policies must not discriminate against minorities (such as the Chinese and Indian minorities in Southeast Asia).

The leaders of most guided democracies today say that one-party dominance and strong leadership are temporary measures. When the people and minor parties are ready to acquire more power, they must be allowed to do so. In other words, guided democracies must be willing to share power. This has occurred in Japan, South Korea, and the Philippines, for example. Japan now has elements of majoritarian and coalition models along with remnants of the tutelary model. Malaysia has evolved from its tutelary past along a different path. (See Politics in Action: Westminster in Kuala Lumpur.)

POLITICS IN ACTION
Westminster in Kuala Lumpur

Much of what is today known as Malaysia won its independence from Great Britain in 1957. Six years later, the Federation of Malaysia was created, combining a constitutional monarchy with federalism. Modeled on the Westminster parliamentary system, its government is headed by the *yang di-pertuan agong* (or king), one of the nine hereditary rulers of Malaysia's peninsular states. He is elected to a five-year term by the Conference of Rulers. He also leads Malaysia's Islamic community.

The Malaysian parliament's two houses meet at the capital in Kuala Lumpur. The Dewan Negara (Senate) has sixty-nine members serving three-year terms: twenty-six are elected by the thirteen state assemblies and forty-three are appointed by the king on the prime minister's advice. The Dewan Rakyat (House of Representatives) consists of 222 members serving five-year terms, directly elected by voters. Historically, the Barisian Nasional (BN) multiracial coalition party, led by the United Malays National Organization (UNMO), has controlled the two-thirds parliamentary majority required to amend Malaysia's constitution.

From 1981 to 2003, Prime Minister Mahathir bin Mohamad, Asia's longest-serving elected leader, dominated an increasingly authoritarian regime in Malaysia. Although he promoted the nation's rapid industrial progress, he strictly controlled the media and severely limited the judiciary's power. He also supported preferential treatment for Malays and supported Malay claims to ethnic superiority, which greatly offended the minority Chinese and Indian communities.

After October 2003, however, Malaysia's BN prime minister, Abdullah Ahmad Badawi, proved far more open to political compromise. But the initial high expectations for progress on human rights and democratization were disappointed. After major agitation for toleration of dissent and fairer elections, opposition parties broke the BN's stranglehold in the March 2008 general election. These parties won 36.9 percent of the parliament and gained control of five of the thirteen state legislatures. Reform efforts have continued since the 2009 election of Mohamed Najib bin Abdul Razak as prime minister.

WHAT FACTORS SUPPORT SUSTAINABLE DEMOCRACY?

The type of democracy is an important factor in both the founding and maintenance of constitutional democracies. But institutions must be judged against the functions they serve. The importance of institutional forms depends on how well they represent a society's political interests, embody a society's best political ideals, balance the powers and limits of government, and enhance government's performance. (See Chapter 4.)

Each type has its particular strengths and weaknesses in carrying out those functions. Consider the party-electoral systems of liberal majoritarian and coalition democracies. Majoritarian systems tend to unify electorates while providing some party competition, but in so doing they tend to undercut minority candidates, parties, and platforms. Majoritarian systems work best in countries in which the people are relatively homogeneous or seek to lay minority differences aside and become more homogeneous. Coalition-based systems reinforce existing divisions and strengthen minority parties, but the policy outcomes depend on how well a diversity of parties can form coalitions and compromise. Coalitional systems work best in countries in which there are deeply entrenched minority cultures that show little interest in unification yet are willing to share power.

Even the best-designed institutions are no guarantee that a people will be able to keep it. What else accounts for a people's success in creating and keeping a republic? Here are some additional factors that previous chapters and outside scholarship have linked to successful republican and democratic government.[18]

- Self-image. A people must be ready to think of themselves as a republican people and a constitutional people, as free citizens subject to the law, and not as obedient subjects of another master.

- Mutual trust and legitimacy. Citizens must have a sufficient level of mutual trust in one another and in their leaders to take the initial risk of adopting a republic that relies on the consent of the governed. To sustain a republic, the initial level of trust must be reinforced by a just constitution in which all people have a stake, wise electoral choices by citizens, and a government limited by a constitution.[19] As Chapter 8 explains, good government cannot govern without legitimacy—that is, the people's belief that government has the authority to govern. This is especially true for democracies because they rely so heavily on the consent of the governed. (See More About . . . The Tragedy of the Commons.)

- Republican efficacy. Democratic types of republican government are more likely to last in a polity where the people can draw on some shared experience and success at collective self-government. It might be a voluntary civic association, a kinship network, or a village irrigation system. Republican history and cultural values are important, but they are not prerequisites to republicanism. The Peruvian economist Hernando de Soto makes this point forcefully and persuasively when he urges the West not to discount the democratic chances of long repressed peoples who want democracy and have the will to hold on to it.[20]

- Economics. Prosperity is helpful, but not essential, to the founding of a republic. Ancient Athens, medieval Venice, and modern America were not prosperous when they first became republics. In fact, studies show that democratic and republican revolutions are most likely to occur when there are economic downturns or inequalities.[21] Nevertheless, republics and democracies that last often have sufficient resources for growth and a market mentality to prosper as free republics. Based on research from various studies, Larry Diamond reports that economic development increases the likelihood that a country will (1) turn from authoritarian to democratic rule and (2) sustain the democracy it has established.[22]

The Tragedy of the Commons

The "tragedy of the commons" dramatically illustrates the importance of shared trust. Oxford economist William Forster Lloyd introduced this parable in 1833 during his lectures about medieval pastureland. When pastureland (the "commons") is available to all, cattle owners want to increase their herd size. But if the herds grow unchecked, the interests of all the cattle owners will suffer as the land becomes damaged by overgrazing.

In 1968, biologist Garrett Hardin returned to this idea in a controversial essay. Hardin applied the idea of the commons to modern-day resources such as the atmosphere, rivers, oceans, and even Earth itself. Hardin argued that virtually all such commons are in danger of overexploitation: "Ruin is the destination toward which all men rush, each pursuing his own best interest in a society that believes in the freedom of the commons. Freedom in a commons brings ruin to all."[1]

Technology, Hardin asserted, could not save the commons. People have to work together to manage the resources properly, much as citizens of a republic must mutually trust one another for the polity to flourish, trusting other individuals to make and obey laws for the good of all. Without that trust, who will take the first step toward the good of the commons?

---

1. Garrett Hardin, "The Tragedy of the Commons," *Science* 162, no. 3859 (1968), 1244.

- Leadership. Good leadership is essential to the challenge of founding and sustaining republics. Leaders of strong republican character and practical wisdom must step forward when needed and depart when their time has past. As a result, there must be an ongoing if not constant supply of them. This requires a political culture and civil society that cultivates constitutional leadership and vigilant citizenship. Nowhere is this more tragically evident than in Africa where so many postcolonial leaders consolidated their own personal power at the expense of the public good. And nowhere has the positive value of good leadership been more apparent than in Africa since 1990 when a new generation of leaders rose up to restore their people's hope for democracy and development.[23]

- Balance and moderation. As explained in Chapter 10, the citizenry and their leaders must be able to maintain a balance of interests. Favoring the few over the many or the many over the few is not a recipe for republican or democratic success. Also essential is another balancing act explored in Chapter 14—leaders and citizens must be able to balance the forces of complete centralization in the name of order and the forces of complete decentralization in the name of freedom.

REVIEWING AND USING THE CHAPTER

1. How did the idea of representative democracy develop in the nineteenth and twentieth centuries?

2. According to Alexis de Tocqueville, an enlightened and engaged citizenry is the best way to check the excesses of democracy. Describe and explain three ways an enlightened and engaged citizenry can check these excesses.

3. What additional social and political processes coincided with democratization in the nineteenth and twentieth centuries? How did these processes fuel the spread of democracy?

4. This chapter identifies three types of democracy: liberal majoritarian, liberal coalition, and nonliberal tutelary. Identify and clearly describe one country that emphasizes each type of democracy.

EXTENSION ACTIVITY

You are part of a delegation to consider amending the U.S. Constitution. As chair of the Committee on Form, you must analyze and evaluate the form of government created by the Constitution. What are the strengths of that form? What changes or amendments would you suggest to modify that form?

WEB RESOURCES

The Alexis de Tocqueville Tour Exploring Democracy in America
www.tocqueville.org

Users of this Web site will find an exhaustive and well-organized list of links detailing de Tocqueville's trip to the United States in the 1830s. Students and teachers will find Webcasts; full-text electronic books, de Tocqueville's notes and journal entries describing his impressions of America; a list of modern references to his writings; and maps, photos, and links to other resources.

International Institute for Democracy and Electoral Assistance (IDEA)
www.idea.int/vt

The International IDEA Voter Turnout Web site contains a comprehensive collection of global political participation statistics. Regularly updated voter turnout figures for national presidential and parliamentary elections since 1945 (including European elections) are presented country by country.

World History of Democracy
www.nipissingu.ca/department/history/ muhlberger/histdem/index.htm

Created, organized, and maintained by Professor Steven Muhlberger at Nipissing University, this Web site provides analytical original essays, links to additional resources, and an annotated bibliography of additional print materials that will aid students and teachers who study the history of democracy.

NOTES

1 James Madison, "*The Federalist,* No. 10," in *The Federalist Papers,* by Alexander Hamilton, James Madison, and John Jay, ed. Clinton Rossiter (New York: New American Library, 1961), 81.

2 Ibid.

3 Ibid.

4 Ibid.

5 Charles S. Maier, "Democracy since the French Revolution," in *Democracy: The Unfinished Journey, 508 BC to AD 1993,* ed. John Dunn (Oxford: Oxford University Press, 1992), 126.

6 Alexis de Tocqueville, *Democracy in America,* ed. and trans. Harvey C. Mansfield and Delba Winthrop (Chicago: University of Chicago Press, 2000), 4–5.

7 Larry Diamond, "Thinking about Hybrid Regimes," *Journal of Democracy* 13, no. 2 (2002), 21. This list condenses a list of eight criteria developed by Robert Dahl, *Polyarchy: Participation and Opposition* (New Haven, Conn.: Yale University Press, 1971).

8 Abraham Lincoln, "'Gettysburg Address,' Final Text, November 19, 1863," in *The Collected Works of Abraham Lincoln,* ed. Roy Basler (New Brunswick, N.J.: Rutgers University Press, 1953), Vol. 7, 23.

9 Abraham Lincoln, "Fragments on Government and Slavery" (July 1, 1854?) in *The Collected Works of Abraham Lincoln,* ed. Roy Basler (New Brunswick, N.J.: Rutgers University Press, 1953), Vol. 2, 221.

10 William Blackstone, *Commentaries on the Laws of England* (Chicago and London, 1765), Vol. 1, 165.

11 Samuel P. Huntington, *The Third Wave: Democratization in the Late Twentieth Century* (Norman: University of Oklahoma Press, 1991), 33.

12 On twenty-first-century reversals, see Larry Diamond, *The Spirit of Democracy* (New York: Times Books, 2008), Chap. 3.

13 Samuel H. Beer, "The Roots of New Labour: Liberalism Rediscovered," *Economist,* February 7, 1998, 25.

14 Arend Lijphart, *Democracies: Patterns of Majoritarian and Consensus Government in Twenty-One Countries* (New Haven, Conn.: Yale University Press, 1984). Updated in Arend Lijphart, *Patterns of Democracy: Government Forms and Performance in Thirty-Six Countries* (New Haven, Conn.: Yale University Press, 1999).

15 Lucian W. Pye, "Dominant Party Democracies in Asia," in *Encyclopedia of Democracy,* ed. Seymour Martin Lipset (Washington, D.C.: Congressional Quarterly, 1995), Vol. 2, 372–376.

16 Attributed to Sir Arthur Lewis, the Nobel prize–winning economist; quoted in Lijphart, *Democracies,* 31.

17 Pye, "Dominant Party Democracies in Asia," 374.

18 For recent analyses of the relevant literature, see Barbara Geddes, "What Do We Know about Democratization after Twenty Years?" *Annual Review of Political Science* 2 (1999): 115–144; Axel Hadenius and Jan Teorell, "Pathways from Authoritarianism," *Journal of Democracy* 18, no. 1 (January 2007): 143–156.

19 Francis Fukuyama, *Trust: The Social Virtues and the Creation of Prosperity* (New York: Free Press, 1995).

20 Hernando de Soto, *The Other Path: The Invisible Revolution in the Third World,* trans. J. Abbott (New York: Basic Books, 1989).

21 See Geddes, "What Do We Know about Democratization?"

22 Diamond, *Spirit of Democracy,* 97.

23 See Nobel Peace Prize laureate Wangari Maathai, *The Challenge for Africa* (New York: Pantheon Books, 2009), Chap. 2.

INDEX

Figures and tables are indicated by f and t following the page number. Italic page numbers indicate illustrations.

on balance, 59, 141, 211, 215, 323, 390, 407
on centralization of power, 325
on citizen participation in politics, 26–28
comparative politics study by, 47–48, 48*t*
as constitutionalist, 88
on constitution of polities, 56–57, 189, 206
on corruption, 226
on demagogues, 160
on foes of democracy, 242
on forms of government, 140, 147–148, 147*t*
on human nature, 30, 85
mixed republics and, 159
on moderation, 323
on monarchy, 148
on political culture, 112
political philosophy of, 57
on polity, 55
as republican philosopher, 99
Arlington National Cemetery, 130
Armenia, unicameral legislature in, 197
Arrogance, 323
Arthashastra, 320
Arthur, Chester, 24
Articles of Confederation (U.S.), 142, 144, 387
Ashoka (emperor), 319, 320
Aspirational ideas, 6, 8, 9–10, 9*f*
Assyrian Empire, 153, 280, 309
Athens. *See* Greece (ancient)
Atkins v. Virginia (2002), 40
Augustine (saint), 255, 257
Augustus, 250–251, 252, 253
Australia, constitution of, 201
Authoritarianism
    as governance condition, 64, 64*t*
    as political end, 31, 32*f*
    power relationships and, 167
    procedural legitimacy and, 178
    totalitarianism distinguished from, 221–226
Authority
    defined, 61, 170, 170*f*
    of government, 168–171
    sources of, 171–175, 172*t*
Autonomy
    as citizenship norm, 220, 221*t*
    liberalism and, 99
    rights and, 203

B

Babylonian Empire, 282, 283
Badawi, Abdullah Ahmad, 419
Bader Meinhof Gang, 91
Balance of powers, 198

Balance principle
    democracy and, 421
    governance and, 211–216
    polities and, 59, 215, 407
    republican government and, 215–216
Barisian Nasional (BN, Malaysia), 419
Bar Kochba Uprising (132–135 CE), 264
Battuta, Ibn, 298
Beer, Samuel Hutchinson, 45, 46, *46*
Benevolent despots, 152
Benin, Freedom House ranking for, 161
Berlin, Isaiah, *13*, 13–14, 213
Biblical scribes, 284
Bicameral legislature, 142, 144, 145, 196, 199
Billington, James H., 91
Bill of Rights (U.S.)
    constitutionalism and, 176
    individualistic culture and, 134
    individual vs. collective rights in, 201
    as instrumental idea, 7
    intermediate institutions in, 203
    as law, 391
    negative rights in, 99, 202
bin Laden, Osama, 224
Birth
    as authority source, 173
    as citizenship criteria, 114–115
Bismarck, Otto von, 149
Blackstone, William, 383, 391–392, *392*, 409
Bloch, Marc, 336
Bold thinkers
    Aristotle, 25, 57
    Augustine (saint), 257
    Beer, Samuel Hutchinson, 46, *46*
    Berlin, Isaiah, *13*, 13–14
    Cicero, 251
    Equiano, Olaudah, 299
    Herodotus, 154
    Kautilya, 320
    King, Martin Luther, Jr., 77
    Kirk, Russell, 97
    Marcus Aurelius, 256, *256*
    Marsilius of Padua, 345
    Montesquieu, 384
    Pico della Mirandola, Giovanni, 365
    Solon, 237, *237*
    Strauss, Leo, 265
    Urukagina, 59
Bolívar, Simón, 226
Botswana, Freedom House ranking for, 161
Boussuet, Jacques-Bénigne, 92
Boycotts. *See* Protests

Bracton, Henry of, 149, 348
Brahmin caste, 318
Brazil
    governmental authority established in constitution
      of, 195, 196
    youth gangs in, 72
Breyer, Stephen G., 40
Brezhnev, Leonid, 128
Bribery, 205, 227
Bronowski, Jacob, 7
Buchan, John, 25
Buckley, William F., 97
Buddhism, 132, 296, 319
Bulgaria, unicameral legislature in, 197
Burckhardt, Jacob, 362
Bureaucracy, 123, 156
Burke, Edmund, 22–23, 24, 96, 385
Burr, Aaron, 144
Butts, R. Freeman, 39
Byzantine Empire, 258, 333, 343

C
Cadre culture, 132
Calvinists, 368–369, 370
Canadian constitution, 201
Candelaria Massacre (1993), 72
Caracalla (emperor), 257
Cardoso, Fernando Henrique, 14, 212–213
Carey, Henry, 21–22
Caribbean, personal dictatorships in, 151
Caste, 296, 318
Catalan War (1640–1653), 380
Catholicism, 341–343, 343*f*, 344, 382
Center for Democracy and Civil Society, Georgetown
      University, 220
Center for the Study of Democracy, University of
      California at Irvine, 45
Central America, personal dictatorships in, 151
Centralized states, 94, 177, 280, 312–313, 325
Charisma, 174, 178
Charles I (king of England), 86, 379
Charles II (king of England), 380, 381–382
Charter of Freedom (Persia), *152*, 153
Charter of Rights and Freedoms of 1982 (Canada), 201
Charters of incorporation, 347
Check of powers, 197–198
Chiefdoms, 66
China
    authority sources in, 172, 173
    political culture in, 131–135
    political protests in, 73, *73*, 74
    Tiananmen Square demonstrations (1989), 227

    totalitarianism in, 224
    unified approach to language and government, 309
    village autonomy in, 304, 305
Christian humanism, 366–367
Christian societies
    church-state separation in, 75
    in Middle Ages, 340–344
    republicanism and, 303
    Roman Empire and, 255
Cicero, Marcus Tullius, 99, 219, 251
Citizen movements, 411, 414
Citizenship
    criteria, 114–115, 404
    defined, 114
    norms of good citizenship, 219–220
    political culture and, 114–117, 119–123, 120*t*
    republicanism and, 97
    in Roman Empire, 257
City charter of incorporation, 350
The City of God (Augustine), 257
City-states, 42, 351
The Civic Cultures (Almond & Verba), 117
Civic duties, 241
Civic efficacy, 117
Civic humanism, 364–365
Civic identity, 114, 312
Civic political cultures, 118
Civic resistance, 170
Civic virtue, 30, 97, 98, 145
Civil disobedience, 168–169
The Civilization of the Renaissance in Italy (Burckhardt), 362
Civil laws, 71
Civil rights movement, 77, 169
Civil service system, 360
Civil society arena, 20*f*, 21, 56–57, 56*t*
Clans, 65
Classical liberalism, 100–101
Classical republicanism, 98–99, 101, 365–366
Cleisthenes, 239–240, 242, 244, 312, 390
Cleomenes, 239, 242
Code of Draco, 236
Code of Solon, 236
Colden, Cadwallader, 297–298, 315
Collapse: How Societies Choose to Fail or Succeed
      (Diamond), 63, 212, 323
Collective responsibility, 150
Collective rights, 201
Collectivism, 129
College of Cardinals, 342
Colombia, civil disorder in, 72
Commensurateness principle, 77
Commentaries on the Laws of England (Blackstone), 392

Common defense, 71
Common good
    community-oriented communities and, 75
    English, American, and French Revolutions impact
        on, 395–397
    republican government and, 219
    republicanism and, 98
Common law, 391–392
Common Sense (Paine), 144, *145*
Communes, 350
Communism and constitutionalism, 200
Communist Party (Russia), 128
Community apartments, 129
Community-oriented societies, 75
Comparative method
    country selection, 44
    defined, 37–38
    for political ideas, 37–50
    research methods, 45–48
    research questions, 44
    study subjects for, 41–43
    topic selection, 44
    unit of analysis and unit of observation, 43
    uses and dangers of, 38–41
Comparative politics, 38
Comparing Governments (Finer), 206
Conciliar Movement, 356
Conciliar republics, 66, 256–257, 313
Condorcet, Marquis de, 387
Confucius and Confucianism
    on balance and moderation, 211
    as constitutionalist, 88
    on human nature, 84
    imperialism and, 303
    on justice, 76
    political culture and, 96
    Zhou dynasty and, 173–174
Congress Party (India), 418
Consent of governed
    by actual representation, 217
    as authority source, 174–175
    by direct participation, 216
    English, American, and French Revolutions impact
        on, 389–390
    republican government and, 216–218
    by virtual representation, 216
Conservatism, 96–97
The Conservative Mind (Kirk), 97
Constituency, 22
Constitution (U.S.). *See also* Bill of Rights (U.S.)
    American polity defined in, 195
    Bill of Rights added to, 7

debates on, 143–144
drafting of, 388
emergency powers, 64
governmental authority established, 196
length of, 189
natural rights theory and, 100
Preamble, 23, 70, 75
representative constituencies in, 390
separation of powers, 393
supremacy clause, 62
Constitutional Convention (1787, U.S.), 193
Constitutionalism, 94–102. *See also specific philosophies
    of government*
    as authority source, 175, 184
    defined, 188–189
    differences, 95–102
    need for government view of, 88–89, 88*t*
    as philosophy of government, 94–102
    power and, 187–209
    power harnessed by, 187–209
    republicanism and, 97–99
    rule of law and, 203–205
    similarities, 94–95
Constitutionalization, 149
Constitutional monarchy, 149, 275–277, 382
Constitutional supremacy, 199
Constitutions. *See also specific countries*
    as code, 192
    defined, 189
    design principles for, 191–194
    differences in, 189–191
    as framework document, 191–192
    importance of, 206–207
    Israel (biblical), 267–268, 267–268*t*,
        270–271
    as political ideal, 192
    of polities, 56–57, 56*t*
    purposes of, 194–203
        delineating government–people relationship,
            200–203
        establishing government, 194–196
        framing government and assign powers and limits,
            196–199
    as revolutionary manifesto, 192
    as series of traditions, 192
Contract laws, 71–72
Cooperative associations, 71, 133
Corruption
    forms of, 226–228
    as governance indicator, 181
    rule of law and, 205
    in Russia, 131

Finland, unicameral legislature in, 197
Fischer, David Hackett, 363
Fission, republic failures due to, 325–326
Florence, Italy, 362
A Force More Powerful (Ackerman & Duvall), 169
Forever wild public parks, 191, 192
Forms of government, 139–163
    anarchy, 48*t*, 87–88, 128
    aristocracy, 48*t*, 147*t*, 148, 155–158
    as blueprint of government performance,
        142–143
    democracy, 147*t*, 148, 158–161
    despotism, 48*t*, 147*t*, 148, 150–151
    as expression of dominant political values, 141
    hybrid democracy, 160
    hybrid monarchy, 151–153
    imperial rule, 153–155
    importance of choosing, 140–147
    majority tyranny, 48*t*, 147*t*, 148, 159–160
    as map of power relationships, 142
    monarchy, 48*t*, 147, 147*t*, 148–155
    oligarchy, 48*t*, 147*t*, 148, 155–158
    of polities, 56*t*, 57
    as representation of dominant political interests,
        141–142
    typology of, 48, 48*t*, 147–148, 147*t*
Foscari, Francesco, 362
Foscari, Jacopo, 362
France. *See also* French Revolution
    citizenship criteria, 115
    constitution of, 189
    form of government changes in, 142
    Fronde rebellions, 380–381, *381*
    monarchy in, 142
    polity defined in, 195
    power relationships in, 356
    prefect system, 395, 396*f*
    protests in, 124, *124*
    secularism in, 125–126
    statism in, 123
Franklin, Benjamin, 58, 60, 385
Frederick Barbarossa (emperor), 340, 351
Free cities, 350–352
Freedom, protection of, 69*t*, 73–74
Freedom House Annual Survey on Freedom,
    45, 160–161, 161*t*, 170
Freedom of assembly, 201
Freedom of association, 99, 203
Freedom of press, 21, 203
Freedom of religion, 125, 203. *See also* Religion
Freedom of speech, 99
Free imperial cities, 351

Free markets, 100, 102
French Revolution
    common good redefined, 395–397
    consent of governed and representation redefined by,
        389–390
    English and American revolutions compared to,
        385–389
    justice system redesigned, 391–393
    Latin Americans and Europeans
        participating in, 404
    mixed government blueprint and, 393–395
    natural rights theory and, 100
    republicanism and, 125
    rule of law and, 390–391
    timeline, 383*f*
Freymann, Eyck, 27
Friedman, Milton, 102
Fronde rebellions, 380–381, *381*
Fundamentality of constitutions, 189
Fundamental law, 391
Furet, François, 392–393
Fusion, republic failures due to, 326

G
Gandhi, Mohandas, *168*, 169
Gao Mingxuan, 150
Gapon, Georgii, 169
Generalization process, 39
General will, 394, 397
George III (king of England), 385
George, David Lloyd, 101
Georgetown University Center for Democracy and Civil
    Society, 220
Germanic republicanism, 255–256
Germany
    centralized government in, 199
    citizenship criteria, 115
    constitution (1949), 70, 196
    customary law of, 346, 347*t*
    polity defined in, 195
    totalitarianism in, 224
German Zionist Organization, 225
Gerontocracies, 313, 362
Gettysburg Address, 378, 407–408
Global Corruption Barometer Report (Transparency
    International), 205
Glorious Revolution (England), 236, 378–389, 383*f*
Godwin, William, 89
Golden Bull of 1222, 347
Golden Bull of 1356, 351
Golden Rule, 84
Goodman, Martin, 298

history of, 294–300
significance of, 293–294
social institutions, 300–303
Nongovernmental organizations
constitutionalism and, 200
power relationships and, 58, 142
Nonliberal tutelary democracy, 418
Nonviolent resistance, 168–169
Normative ideas, 5, 58–59
North Korea, dictatorship in, 188
Novgorod, Russia, 126–127, 128
Novodevichy, 130
Nozick, Robert, 102
Nyalali, Francis, 141

O

October Revolution of 1917 (Russia), 128
Odoacer (emperor), 333
The Old Regime and the French Revolution
(Tocqueville), 176
Oligarchy
in ancient Greece, 245
defined, 148
as form of government, 48*t*, 147*t*, 148, 155–158
Oliver, Frederick Scott, 25
One-party states, 151
On the Laws and Customs of England (Bracton), 149
Oration on the Dignity of Man (Pico), 363, 365
The Origins of Totalitarianism (Arendt), 225
Orthodox religious affiliations, 135
Orwell, George, 224
Ostracism, 243, 244
Ottoman Turks, 126
Outcome level of legitimacy, 176

P

Paine, Thomas, 144, 145, 395, 397
Palace of Westminster, 416
Palmer, R. R., 368, 381
Panchayat, 319
Parliamentary development in Middle Ages, 348–350
Parliamentary supremacy, 199, 379, 382
Participation, 220, 221*t*
Passover, 280, 281
Patricians, 249–250
Patriotism, 55
Patronage, 254
Pauline Letters, 341–342
Paxton, Robert, 179, 188
Peace of Constance (1183), 352
Pennsylvania, form of government choices by,
144–147

People's Freedom (anarchist group), 90
Performance level of legitimacy, 176
forms of government and, 142–143
Pericles, 155, *243*
Persian Empire, 152, 153–154, 252, 305
Personal dictatorships, 151
Personality, 110, 110*t*
Pessimists, 87
Peter and Paul Cathedral (St. Petersburg, Russia), 130
Peter the Great (tsar), 128
Petrine Primacy, 341
Philip Augustus (king of France), 340
Philip II of Macedonia, 322
Philip IV (king of France), 356
Philippics (Demosthenes), 322
Philippines, non-violent resistance in, 169
Philosopher-kings, 246, 265
Philosophies of government, 82–104
absolutism, 92–93
anarchy, 89–91
constitutionalist philosophies, 94–102
democratic statism, 93–94
human nature and, 83–87
necessity of government, 87–89
statism, 91–94
Physics, Rhetoric, Ethics (Aristotle), 25
Pico della Mirandola, Giovanni, 363, 365
Pindar (Greek poet), 218
Pisa, Rustichello da, 359
Pisistratus, 238–239
Plato
on authority sources, 174
on human nature, 85
on ideal state, 224
on political culture, 112
Plebeians, 249–250
Plural executives, 146, 147
Plutocracy, 156
Pocock, J. G. A., 386
Poland
hybrid monarchy in, 152
monarchy in, 336
non-violent resistance in, 169
parliament in, 349, 350
Policy arena, 20–21, 20*f*
Polish-Lithuanian Commonwealth, 152, 325
Political covenants, 266
Political crimes, 127
Political culture, 108–138
citizen roles informed by, 119–123, 120*t*
citizenship and, 114–117
defined, 111–117

Redistributive systems, 75
Reflections on the Revolution in France
    (Burke), 96
Reformation Age, 368, 380
Reformed Protestants, 368
Regulatory quality as governance indicator, 181
Rehoboam (biblical), 278–279, 323
Religion. *See also* Israel (biblical); *specific religions*
    guilds and, 337
    in India, 318–319
    justice and, 339
    in Middle Ages, 333, 334, 340–344
    political culture and, 120
    republican values and, 303
    Roman Empire and, 255
    secularism and, 125
    statism and, 126–128
    system legitimacy and, 177
    traditionalist cultures and, 122
    in U.S., 135
Renaissance, 360
Representative democracy
    classical liberalism and, 101
    development of, 402–404
    English, American, and French Revolutions impact on,
        389–390
    forms of, 413–419
Repressive power, 221
The Republic (Plato), 112, 174
Republican government
    characteristics of, 294, 294*t*
    in constitutionalist spectrum, 97–99
    culture of, 118
    democracy and, 401–423
    England's Glorious Revolution and, 378–384
    good government criteria, 214–219
        common good as guide for citizens and
            leaders, 219
        free government based on consent of governed,
            216–218
        just government based on equal justice principle,
            218–219
        limited government based on rule of law, 218
        representative government based on principle of
            balance, 215–216
    Greek designs for, 235–248
    of Israel (biblical), 262–288, 320–321
    in Middle Ages, 332–354
        Church organization and, 340–344
        feudalism and monarchies, 332–336
        free cities, 350–352
        nobility and, 344–350

parliamentary development, 348–350
    rule of law and, 348
    mutual aid societies and, 304–305
    non-European
        failure of, 322–326
        governance of, 313–316
        history of, 294–300
        significance of, 293–294
        social institutions, 300–303
    political culture of, 119–120*t*, 121–122
    Renaissance redefinition of, 363–370
    Roman designs for, 248–259
Republican Party (U.S.), 58
Research methods, 45–48
Research questions, 44
Res publica, 249
Retributive justice, 67
Rights
    constitutional, 202
    government role in, 202–203
    individualistic culture and, 134
    individual vs. collective, 201
    intermediate institutions and, 203
    majority tyranny and, 148
    minority, 144, 145, 201
    negative, 99, 202
    self-determination, 42
    positive, 99, 202
Rights-holders, 201
The Rights of Man (Paine), 397
Roman Catholicism, 341–343, 343*f*, 344
Roman Empire
    bureaucratic state of, 258
    citizenship valued by, 216, 257
    ethnicity in political culture of, 114
    fission in, 325
    fusion in, 326
    impact on Europe, 252–259
    imperial rule of, 250–251, 253*f*
    Israel and, 286
    legal framework of, 258–259, 346, 347*t*
    mixed republic of, 215
    political culture and, 120
    power relationships in, 351
    republican government of, 98, 248–259
Romanov, Mikhail, 172
Romanov dynasty, 172–173
Romulus Augustulus, 333
Roosevelt, Eleanor, 6
Roosevelt, Franklin D., 101
Roper v. Simmons (2005), 40
Rosas, Juan Manuel de, 56, 151

Rosetta Stone, 68
Rousseau, Jean-Jacques, *93*
    democratic statism, 93
    French Declaration and, 388
    on governmental powers, 168
    as republican philosopher, 99
    on statism and individualism, 125
Royalists, 379
Rule of law
    American Revolution and, 390–391
    constitutionalism and, 203–205
    criteria of, 204–205
    form of government and, 145
    as governance indicator, 181
    in Middle Ages, 337, 348
    republican government and, 218
    in Roman Empire, 258–259
Rural guilds, 337
Russell, Bertrand, 167
Russia
    anarchist movement in, 90–91, 128
    criminal code, 127
    oligarchy in, 156, 158
    statist political culture in, 126–131
    totalitarianism in, 224
Russian Orthodox Church, 126–127, 128

S
Sabha, 317
Sallust, 8
Salome of Alexandra, 286
Samizdat, 128
Samuel (biblical), 271–272
Sanhedrin, 285
Santayana, George, 97
Sarkozy, Nicolas, 124
Sarmiento, Domingo, 55–56
Sarna, Nahum, 266, 279
Saudi Arabia as theocratic society, 76
Saul (king of Israel), 272–273
Savonarola, Girolamo, 365
Scalia, Antonin, 40
Scapegoats, 248
Second Vatican Council, 341
Secularism, 125–126. *See also* Separation of church
    and state
Self-determination rights, 42
Selfishness, 323
Self-preservation instinct, 86
Semya (Russian oligarchy), 157
Senegal, Freedom House ranking for, 161

Separation of church and state, 75, 125–126
Separation of powers
    in ancient Israel, 269, 269*t*, 276
    constitutionalism and, 197–198, 197*t*
    in U.S., 144–145, 197, 197*t*, 393–394, 394*t*
Sforza, Francesco, 362
Shang, Lord, 91
Shang Yang (emperor of China), 150
Shantytowns, 133, *133*
Shared interests, 57–58
Shared trust, 420, 421
Siena, Italy, 222–223
Simeon, 285–286
Sinai covenants, 266, 268–270, 369
Sit-ins. *See* Protests
Slavery, 238, 301, 411, 414
Smiley, Prentis, Jr., *40*
Smith, Adam, 74, 100, 102
Social capital, 111
The Social Contract (Rousseau), 168
Social contract theory, 92, 182
Social instinct, 69
Social institutions, 300–303
Social order, 220, 221*t*
Socioeconomic constitution, 56–57, 56*t*, 140
Socrates, 85, 245, 246–247, *247*, 265
Soft authoritarianism, 129, 178, 226
Solidarity as citizenship norm, 220, 221*t*
Solomon (biblical), 277–278
Solon, 236, 237, 237–238, 390
Somalia, civil disorder in, 72
Sophocles, 245
South Africa
    constitution (1997), 196, 201
    Freedom House ranking for, 161
    as nonliberal tutelary democracy, 418
    non-violent resistance in, 169
South Korea, Freedom House ranking for, 161
Sovereignty
    of monarch, 92
    popular, 402
Soviet Union. *See also* Russia
    statism in, 128–129
    totalitarianism in, 224
Spain, parliaments in, 349
The Spirit of the Laws (Montesquieu), 116, 383, 384
Spiritual societies, 303
Stalin, Joseph, 30, 130
Stamp Act of 1765, 386
Star Chamber Court, 379
State-controlled dictatorships, 151

Statecraft, 12–15
State of nature, 83
States
    defined, 41, 66
    development of, 310t, 311–313, 316–319
State-sponsored acts of aggression, 245
Statism
    in China, 131–132
    as philosophy of government, 87, 88t, 91–94
    political culture of, 118, 119–120t, 121,
        123–135
Statute of Merton (1235, England), 379
Stelae, 68, 68
Stimson, Henry L., 202
Stoicism, 85, 255, 256
Storage redistributive system, 75
Story, Joseph, 392
Strauss, Leo, 83, 214, 265
Strikes. *See* Protests
Substantive justice, 78
Succoth covenant, 283–285
Sui dynasty, 333
Sun Yat-sen, 418
Supremacy clause, 62
Supreme being as authority source, 171–173. *See also*
        Divine authority
Supreme Court (U.S.). *See also specific cases*
    foreign law consideration by, 40
    on gun control laws, 61
    judicial review and, 392
Supreme law, 391
Survival instinct, 69
Sustainable democracy, 419–421
Suzerainty treaties, 266
Swabian League, 351
Sweden, unicameral legislature in, 197
Switzerland
    constitution of, 200
    decentralized government in, 199
    gun control laws in, 61
System level of legitimacy, 176

T

Taft, William Howard, 130
Taiping Rebellion (China), 132
Taiwan, Freedom House ranking for, 161
Tanakh. See Hebrew Bible
Tang dynasty, 333
Taoism, 84, 132
Taxation
    American Revolution and, 386

French Revolution and, 387
    material improvement via, 75
Technical knowledge, 12
Technology and politics, 73, 406, 412
Teggart, Frederick, 294
Ten Commandments, 269
Thailand, military juntas in, 157
Theocratic societies, 76, 269
Theoretical knowledge, 12
Thirty Years War (1618–1648), 380
Thomas, Clarence, 40
Thomas Aquinas, 255
Thoughts on Government (Adams), 144
Thucydides, 244, 245
Tiananmen Square demonstrations (1989), 227
Timocracy, 155
Tocqueville, Alexis de
    on centralization, 395
    on democracy in America, 44
    on French Revolution, 391
    on political culture, 116–117
    on political equality, 404–405, 406
    on representative democracy, 159
    on self-interest, 121, 323
    on statism and individualism, 125
    on system legitimacy, 176–177
Tontons Macoutes, 151
Tories, 380, 382, 416
Totalitarianism
    authoritarianism distinguished from, 221–226
    as political end, 32, 32f
Traditionalism
    in China, 131–132
    political culture of, 118–119, 119–120t, 122–123, 123t,
        131–135
    in Russia, 128, 130
    in U.S., 135
"Tragedy of the commons," 421
Trajan, 252
Transparency International, 227–228
The Travels of Marco Polo (Pisa), 359
Treason, 127
Treaty of Westphalia (1648), 42
Trial by ordeal, 346
Tribal states
    comparative studies and, 43
    development of, 65, 310t, 311, 314
    fission and, 325
    Israel (biblical) as, 268–271, 311
Truman, Harry, 25
Tuchman, Barbara, 279, 322